Payment Tables for Auto Loans

Michael Sherman, Ph.D.

CONTEMPORARY
BOOKS, INC.
CHICAGO • NEW YORK

CONTENTS

Thomas Locke, Computer Analyst

Copyright © 1987 by Michael Sherman
All rights reserved
Published by Contemporary Books, Inc.
180 North Michigan Avenue, Chicago, Illinois 60601
Manufactured in the United States of America
International Standard Book Number: 0-8092-4735-6

Published simultaneously in Canada by Beaverbooks, Ltd.
195 Allstate Parkway, Valleywood Business Park
Markham, Ontario L3R 4T8 Canada

INTRODUCTION

The purpose of these tables is to show lenders, auto dealers, and consumers how various auto financing plans compare. In a competitive financing market, a promotional, low-interest rate financing plan can save hundreds or even thousands of dollars in interest over the life of the loan. Or, a special financing plan can provide the consumer with greater purchasing power. You need no advanced mathematical skills to understand the tables. Just read the instructions and follow the directions as described in the examples.

Each interest rate within these tables appears on two facing pages. The left-facing page has loan terms from 12 to 36 months, the right-facing page has loan terms from 42 to 72 months. Each loan term has two entries, one for the monthly payment and one for the total interest paid through the life of the loan. Each page contains loan amount entries from $1,000 to $50,000 plus adjusting entries in $1 increments from $1 to $9, in $10 increments from $10 to $90, and in $100 increments from $100 to $900. All monthly payment entries are rounded up to the next penny amount. Remember that when your loan amount is not exactly equal to the entries displayed in the left-hand column of each page, simply combine entries to achieve the desired loan amount and the corresponding monthly payments and total interest. To obtain a high degree of accuracy, combine as few entries as possible when you solve a problem.

EXAMPLE

How much is saved on a $9,200 auto loan over a 48-month term with a 7.9% promotional rate versus a 14% market rate? What is the difference in the monthly payment?

First, find the 7.9% rate on pages 82 and 83. The 48-month term is on page 83. Move down the loan amount column until you find a row entry for $9,200. Since there is no row entry for exactly this loan amount, you must combine row entries from $200 and $9,000 to get the total interest and the monthly payment. The total-interest entries are $34 and $1,526; and their sum is $1,560. The corresponding monthly payment entries are $4.88 and $219.30; and their sum is $224.18.

Next, find the 14% rate on pages 136 and 137. The 48-month term is on page 137. Once again, combine the two row entries for $200 and $9,000 to get the total interest and the monthly payment. The total-interest entries are $63 and $2,805; and their sum is $2,868. The corresponding payment entries are $5.47 and $245.94; and their sum is $251.41. The total interest saved with the promotional rate is $2,868 minus $1,560; or $1,308. The difference in the monthly payment is $251.41 less $224.18; or $27.23.

EXAMPLE

How much larger a loan can be financed by a $300 monthly payment over 36 months with an 8.9% promotional rate versus a 13.5% market rate?

First, find the 8.9% rate on pages 92 and 93. The 36-month column is on page 92. Move up the monthly payment column until you find a row entry for $300. Since there is no row entry for exactly this monthly payment, find the next lower payment entry of $285.78. Read across to the corresponding loan amount entry of $9,000. You are $14.22 short of the desired $300 monthly payment.

Continue reading up the monthly payment column until you find $14.22. Since there is no row entry for $14.22, find the next lower payment entry of $12.71. Read across to the corresponding loan amount entry of $400. The sum of $285.78 and $12.71 leaves you $1.51 short of the desired $300 monthly payment.

Continue reading up the monthly payment column until you find $1.51. Since there is no row entry for $1.51, find the next lower payment entry of $1.28. Read across to the corresponding loan amount entry of $40. The sum of the three monthly payment entries ($285.78, $12.71, and $1.28) leaves you $0.23 short of the desired $300 monthly payment.

Continue reading up the monthly payment column until you find $0.23. Read across to the corresponding loan amount entry of $7. The sum of your four monthly payment entries equals the desired $300 monthly payment. You can finance the sum of the corresponding loan amount entries, $9,000, $400, $40, and $7; or $9,447 at 8.9% for 36 months.

Next, find the 13.5% rate on pages 132 and 133. The 36-month term is on page 132. Move up the monthly payment column until you find a row entry for $300. Since there is no row entry for exactly this monthly payment, find the next lower payment entry of $271.49. Read across to the corresponding loan amount entry of $8,000. You are $28.51 short of the desired $300 monthly payment.

Continue reading up the monthly payment column until you find $28.51. Since there is no row entry for $28.51, find the next lower payment entry of $27.15. Read across to the corresponding loan amount entry of $800. The sum of $271.49 and $27.15 leaves you $1.36 short of the desired $300 monthly payment.

Continue reading up the monthly payment column until you find $1.36. Read across to the corresponding loan amount entry of $40. The sum of your three payment entries equals the desired $300 monthly payment. You can finance the sum of the corresponding loan amount entries, $8,000, $800, and $40; or $8,840 at 13.5% for 36 months. The rate difference in the two plans allows you to borrow an additional $607 ($9,447 minus $8,840) for the same monthly payment.

The above examples compared financing arrangements where the loan terms were identical. Keep in mind that the same principles work with financing at different rates and different terms. Clearly, interest savings can be increased by combining both lower promotional rates and shorter loan terms. Or, purchasing power can be enhanced by combining lower promotional rates with longer loan terms.

0.25%   AUTO LOAN PAYMENTS

AMOUNT OF LOAN	12 MOS		24 MOS		30 MOS		36 MOS	
	MONTHLY PAYMENT	TOTAL INTRST	MONTHLY PAYMENT	TOTAL INTRST	MONTHLY PAYMENT	TOTAL INTRST	MONTHLY PAYMENT	TOTAL INTRST
$ 1	0.09	0	0.05	0	0.04	0	0.03	0
2	0.17	0	0.09	0	0.07	0	0.06	0
3	0.26	0	0.13	0	0.11	0	0.09	0
4	0.34	0	0.17	0	0.14	0	0.12	0
5	0.42	0	0.21	0	0.17	0	0.14	0
6	0.51	0	0.26	0	0.21	0	0.17	0
7	0.59	0	0.30	0	0.24	0	0.20	0
8	0.67	0	0.34	0	0.27	0	0.23	0
9	0.76	0	0.38	0	0.31	0	0.26	0
10	0.84	0	0.42	0	0.34	0	0.28	0
20	1.67	0	0.84	0	0.67	0	0.56	0
30	2.51	0	1.26	0	1.01	0	0.84	0
40	3.34	0	1.68	0	1.34	0	1.12	0
50	4.18	0	2.09	0	1.68	0	1.40	0
60	5.01	0	2.51	0	2.01	0	1.68	0
70	5.85	0	2.93	0	2.35	1	1.96	1
80	6.68	0	3.35	0	2.68	1	2.24	1
90	7.52	0	3.76	0	3.01	0	2.51	0
100	8.35	0	4.18	0	3.35	1	2.79	0
200	16.69	0	8.36	1	6.69	1	5.58	1
300	25.04	0	12.54	1	10.04	1	8.37	1
400	33.38	1	16.72	1	13.38	1	11.16	2
500	41.73	1	20.89	1	16.73	1	13.95	2
600	50.07	1	25.07	2	20.07	2	16.74	3
700	58.42	1	29.25	2	23.41	2	19.52	3
800	66.76	1	33.43	2	26.76	3	22.31	3
900	75.11	1	37.60	2	30.10	3	25.10	4
1,000	83.45	1	41.78	3	33.45	4	27.89	4
2,000	166.90	3	83.56	5	66.89	7	55.77	8
3,000	250.34	4	125.33	8	100.33	10	83.66	12
4,000	333.79	5	167.11	11	133.77	13	111.54	15
5,000	417.24	7	208.88	13	167.21	16	139.43	19
6,000	500.68	8	250.66	16	200.65	20	167.31	23
7,000	584.13	10	292.43	18	234.09	23	195.20	27
8,000	667.57	11	334.21	21	267.53	26	223.08	31
9,000	751.02	12	375.98	24	300.97	29	250.97	35
10,000	834.47	14	417.76	26	334.42	33	278.85	39
11,000	917.91	15	459.53	29	367.86	36	306.74	43
12,000	1,001.36	16	501.31	31	401.30	39	334.62	46
13,000	1,084.81	18	543.08	34	434.74	42	362.51	50
14,000	1,168.25	19	584.86	37	468.18	45	390.39	54
15,000	1,251.70	20	626.63	39	501.62	49	418.28	58
16,000	1,335.14	22	668.41	42	535.06	52	446.16	62
17,000	1,418.59	23	710.18	44	568.50	55	474.05	66
18,000	1,502.04	24	751.96	47	601.94	58	501.93	69
19,000	1,585.48	26	793.73	50	635.39	62	529.82	74
20,000	1,668.93	27	835.51	52	668.83	65	557.70	77
21,000	1,752.38	29	877.29	55	702.27	68	585.59	81
22,000	1,835.82	30	919.06	57	735.71	71	613.47	85
23,000	1,919.27	31	960.84	60	769.15	75	641.36	89
24,000	2,002.71	33	1,002.61	63	802.59	78	669.24	93
25,000	2,086.16	34	1,044.39	65	836.03	81	697.13	97
26,000	2,169.61	35	1,086.16	68	869.47	84	725.01	100
27,000	2,253.05	37	1,127.94	71	902.91	87	752.90	104
28,000	2,336.50	38	1,169.71	73	936.36	91	780.78	108
29,000	2,419.95	39	1,211.49	76	969.80	94	808.67	112
30,000	2,503.39	41	1,253.26	78	1,003.24	97	836.55	116
31,000	2,586.84	42	1,295.04	81	1,036.68	100	864.44	120
32,000	2,670.28	43	1,336.81	83	1,070.12	104	892.32	124
33,000	2,753.73	45	1,378.59	86	1,103.56	107	920.21	128
34,000	2,837.18	46	1,420.36	89	1,137.00	110	948.09	131
35,000	2,920.62	47	1,462.14	91	1,170.44	113	975.98	135
36,000	3,004.07	49	1,503.91	94	1,203.88	116	1,003.86	139
37,000	3,087.52	50	1,545.69	97	1,237.32	120	1,031.75	143
38,000	3,170.96	52	1,587.46	99	1,270.77	123	1,059.63	147
39,000	3,254.41	53	1,629.24	102	1,304.21	126	1,087.52	151
40,000	3,337.85	54	1,671.02	104	1,337.65	130	1,115.40	154
42,000	3,504.75	57	1,754.57	110	1,404.53	136	1,171.17	162
44,000	3,671.64	60	1,838.12	115	1,471.41	142	1,226.94	170
46,000	3,838.53	62	1,921.67	120	1,538.29	149	1,282.71	178
48,000	4,005.42	65	2,005.22	125	1,605.18	155	1,338.48	185
50,000	4,172.32	68	2,088.77	130	1,672.06	162	1,394.25	193

AMOUNT OF LOAN	42 MOS MONTHLY PAYMENT	42 MOS TOTAL INTRST	48 MOS MONTHLY PAYMENT	48 MOS TOTAL INTRST	60 MOS MONTHLY PAYMENT	60 MOS TOTAL INTRST	72 MOS MONTHLY PAYMENT	72 MOS TOTAL INTRST
$ 1	0.03	0	0.03	0	0.02	0	0.02	0
2	0.05	0	0.05	0	0.04	0	0.03	0
3	0.08	0	0.07	0	0.06	1	0.05	1
4	0.10	0	0.09	0	0.07	0	0.06	0
5	0.12	0	0.11	0	0.09	0	0.07	0
6	0.15	0	0.13	0	0.11	0	0.09	0
7	0.17	0	0.15	0	0.12	1	0.10	0
8	0.20	0	0.17	0	0.14	0	0.12	1
9	0.22	0	0.19	0	0.16	1	0.13	0
10	0.24	0	0.21	0	0.17	0	0.14	0
20	0.48	0	0.42	0	0.34	0	0.28	0
30	0.72	0	0.63	0	0.51	1	0.42	0
40	0.96	0	0.84	0	0.68	1	0.56	0
50	1.20	0	1.05	0	0.84	0	0.70	0
60	1.44	1	1.26	0	1.01	1	0.84	0
70	1.68	1	1.47	1	1.18	1	0.98	1
80	1.92	1	1.68	1	1.35	1	1.12	1
90	2.16	1	1.89	1	1.51	1	1.26	1
100	2.40	1	2.10	1	1.68	1	1.40	1
200	4.79	1	4.19	1	3.36	2	2.80	2
300	7.18	2	6.29	2	5.04	2	4.20	3
400	9.57	2	8.38	2	6.71	3	5.60	3
500	11.96	2	10.47	3	8.39	3	7.00	4
600	14.35	3	12.57	3	10.07	4	8.40	5
700	16.75	4	14.66	4	11.75	5	9.80	6
800	19.14	4	16.76	4	13.42	5	11.20	6
900	21.53	4	18.85	5	15.10	6	12.60	7
1,000	23.92	5	20.94	5	16.78	7	14.00	8
2,000	47.84	9	41.88	10	33.55	13	27.99	15
3,000	71.75	14	62.82	15	50.32	19	41.99	23
4,000	95.67	18	83.76	20	67.10	26	55.98	31
5,000	119.59	23	104.70	26	83.87	32	69.98	39
6,000	143.50	27	125.64	31	100.64	38	83.97	46
7,000	167.42	32	146.58	36	117.41	45	97.97	54
8,000	191.34	36	167.52	41	134.19	51	111.96	61
9,000	215.25	41	188.46	46	150.96	58	125.96	69
10,000	239.17	45	209.40	51	167.73	64	139.95	76
11,000	263.08	49	230.34	56	184.51	71	153.95	84
12,000	287.00	54	251.28	61	201.28	77	167.94	92
13,000	310.92	59	272.22	67	218.05	83	181.94	100
14,000	334.83	63	293.16	72	234.82	89	195.93	107
15,000	358.75	68	314.10	77	251.60	96	209.93	115
16,000	382.67	72	335.04	82	268.37	102	223.92	122
17,000	406.58	76	355.98	87	285.14	108	237.92	130
18,000	430.50	81	376.92	92	301.92	115	251.91	138
19,000	454.42	86	397.86	97	318.69	121	265.91	146
20,000	478.33	90	418.80	102	335.46	128	279.90	153
21,000	502.25	95	439.74	108	352.23	134	293.90	161
22,000	526.16	99	460.68	113	369.01	141	307.89	168
23,000	550.08	103	481.62	118	385.78	147	321.88	175
24,000	574.00	108	502.56	123	402.55	153	335.88	183
25,000	597.91	112	523.50	128	419.32	159	349.87	191
26,000	621.83	117	544.44	133	436.10	166	363.87	199
27,000	645.75	122	565.38	138	452.87	172	377.86	206
28,000	669.66	126	586.32	143	469.64	178	391.86	214
29,000	693.58	130	607.26	148	486.42	185	405.85	221
30,000	717.49	135	628.20	154	503.19	191	419.85	229
31,000	741.41	139	649.14	159	519.96	198	433.84	236
32,000	765.33	144	670.08	164	536.73	204	447.84	244
33,000	789.24	148	691.02	169	553.51	211	461.83	252
34,000	813.16	153	711.96	174	570.28	217	475.83	260
35,000	837.08	157	732.90	179	587.05	223	489.82	267
36,000	860.99	162	753.84	184	603.83	230	503.82	275
37,000	884.91	166	774.78	189	620.60	236	517.81	282
38,000	908.83	171	795.72	195	637.37	242	531.81	290
39,000	932.74	175	816.66	200	654.14	248	545.80	298
40,000	956.66	180	837.60	205	670.92	255	559.80	306
42,000	1,004.49	189	879.48	215	704.46	268	587.79	321
44,000	1,052.32	197	921.36	225	738.01	281	615.77	335
46,000	1,100.16	207	963.24	236	771.55	293	643.76	351
48,000	1,147.99	216	1,005.12	246	805.10	306	671.75	366
50,000	1,195.82	224	1,047.00	256	838.64	318	699.74	381

0.50%   AUTO LOAN PAYMENTS

AMOUNT OF LOAN	12 MOS MONTHLY PAYMENT	12 MOS TOTAL INTRST	24 MOS MONTHLY PAYMENT	24 MOS TOTAL INTRST	30 MOS MONTHLY PAYMENT	30 MOS TOTAL INTRST	36 MOS MONTHLY PAYMENT	36 MOS TOTAL INTRST
$ 1	0.09	0	0.05	0	0.04	0	0.03	0
2	0.17	0	0.09	0	0.07	0	0.06	0
3	0.26	0	0.13	0	0.11	0	0.09	0
4	0.34	0	0.17	0	0.14	0	0.12	0
5	0.42	0	0.21	0	0.17	0	0.14	0
6	0.51	0	0.26	0	0.21	0	0.17	0
7	0.59	0	0.30	0	0.24	0	0.20	0
8	0.67	0	0.34	0	0.27	0	0.23	0
9	0.76	0	0.38	0	0.31	0	0.26	0
10	0.84	0	0.42	0	0.34	0	0.28	0
20	1.68	0	0.84	0	0.68	0	0.56	0
30	2.51	0	1.26	0	1.01	0	0.84	0
40	3.35	0	1.68	0	1.35	1	1.12	0
50	4.18	0	2.10	0	1.68	0	1.40	0
60	5.02	0	2.52	0	2.02	1	1.68	0
70	5.85	0	2.94	0	2.35	1	1.96	1
80	6.69	0	3.36	1	2.69	1	2.24	1
90	7.53	0	3.77	1	3.02	1	2.52	1
100	8.36	0	4.19	1	3.36	1	2.80	1
200	16.72	1	8.38	1	6.71	1	5.60	2
300	25.07	1	12.57	2	10.07	2	8.40	2
400	33.43	1	16.76	2	13.42	2	11.20	3
500	41.78	1	20.95	3	16.78	3	14.00	4
600	50.14	2	25.14	3	20.13	4	16.80	5
700	58.50	2	29.32	4	23.49	5	19.60	6
800	66.85	2	33.51	4	26.84	5	22.40	6
900	75.21	3	37.70	5	30.20	6	25.20	7
1,000	83.56	3	41.89	5	33.55	7	28.00	8
2,000	167.12	5	83.77	10	67.10	13	55.99	16
3,000	250.68	8	125.66	16	100.65	20	83.98	23
4,000	334.24	11	167.54	21	134.20	26	111.97	31
5,000	417.80	14	209.43	26	167.75	33	139.97	39
6,000	501.36	16	251.31	31	201.30	39	167.96	47
7,000	584.92	19	293.19	37	234.85	46	195.95	54
8,000	668.48	22	335.08	42	268.40	52	223.94	62
9,000	752.04	24	376.96	47	301.95	59	251.94	70
10,000	835.60	27	418.85	52	335.50	65	279.93	77
11,000	919.16	30	460.73	58	369.04	71	307.92	85
12,000	1,002.72	33	502.61	63	402.59	78	335.91	93
13,000	1,086.27	35	544.50	68	436.14	84	363.91	101
14,000	1,169.83	38	586.38	73	469.69	91	391.90	108
15,000	1,253.39	41	628.27	78	503.24	97	419.89	116
16,000	1,336.95	43	670.15	84	536.79	104	447.88	124
17,000	1,420.51	46	712.03	89	570.34	110	475.88	132
18,000	1,504.07	49	753.92	94	603.89	117	503.87	139
19,000	1,587.63	52	795.80	99	637.44	123	531.86	147
20,000	1,671.19	54	837.69	105	670.99	130	559.85	155
21,000	1,754.75	57	879.57	110	704.53	136	587.85	163
22,000	1,838.31	60	921.45	115	738.08	142	615.84	170
23,000	1,921.87	62	963.34	120	771.63	149	643.83	178
24,000	2,005.43	65	1,005.22	125	805.18	155	671.82	186
25,000	2,088.99	68	1,047.11	131	838.73	162	699.82	194
26,000	2,172.54	70	1,088.99	136	872.28	168	727.81	201
27,000	2,256.10	73	1,130.87	141	905.83	175	755.80	209
28,000	2,339.66	76	1,172.76	146	939.38	181	783.79	216
29,000	2,423.22	79	1,214.64	151	972.93	188	811.79	224
30,000	2,506.78	81	1,256.53	157	1,006.48	194	839.78	232
31,000	2,590.34	84	1,298.41	162	1,040.03	201	867.77	240
32,000	2,673.90	87	1,340.29	167	1,073.57	207	895.76	247
33,000	2,757.46	90	1,382.18	172	1,107.12	214	923.75	255
34,000	2,841.02	92	1,424.06	177	1,140.67	220	951.75	263
35,000	2,924.58	95	1,465.95	183	1,174.22	227	979.74	271
36,000	3,008.14	98	1,507.83	188	1,207.77	233	1,007.73	278
37,000	3,091.70	100	1,549.71	193	1,241.32	240	1,035.72	286
38,000	3,175.25	103	1,591.60	198	1,274.87	246	1,063.72	294
39,000	3,258.81	106	1,633.48	204	1,308.42	253	1,091.71	302
40,000	3,342.37	108	1,675.37	209	1,341.97	259	1,119.70	309
42,000	3,509.49	114	1,759.13	219	1,409.06	272	1,175.69	325
44,000	3,676.61	119	1,842.90	230	1,476.16	285	1,231.67	340
46,000	3,843.73	125	1,926.67	240	1,543.26	298	1,287.66	356
48,000	4,010.85	130	2,010.44	251	1,610.36	311	1,343.64	371
50,000	4,177.97	136	2,094.21	261	1,677.46	324	1,399.63	387

AUTO LOAN PAYMENTS 0.50%

AMOUNT OF LOAN	42 MOS		48 MOS		60 MOS		72 MOS	
	MONTHLY PAYMENT	TOTAL INTRST	MONTHLY PAYMENT	TOTAL INTRST	MONTHLY PAYMENT	TOTAL INTRST	MONTHLY PAYMENT	TOTAL INTRST
$ 1	0.03	0	0.03	0	0.02	0	0.02	0
2	0.05	0	0.05	0	0.04	0	0.03	0
3	0.08	0	0.07	0	0.06	1	0.05	1
4	0.10	0	0.09	0	0.07	0	0.06	0
5	0.13	0	0.11	0	0.09	1	0.08	1
6	0.15	0	0.13	0	0.11	1	0.09	0
7	0.17	0	0.15	0	0.12	0	0.10	1
8	0.20	0	0.17	0	0.14	0	0.12	1
9	0.22	0	0.19	0	0.16	1	0.13	0
10	0.25	1	0.22	1	0.17	0	0.15	1
20	0.49	1	0.43	1	0.34	1	0.29	1
30	0.73	1	0.64	1	0.51	1	0.43	1
40	0.97	1	0.85	1	0.68	1	0.57	1
50	1.21	1	1.06	1	0.85	1	0.71	1
60	1.45	1	1.27	1	1.02	1	0.85	1
70	1.69	1	1.48	1	1.19	1	0.99	1
80	1.93	1	1.69	1	1.36	2	1.13	1
90	2.17	1	1.90	1	1.52	1	1.27	1
100	2.41	1	2.11	1	1.69	1	1.42	2
200	4.81	2	4.21	2	3.38	3	2.83	4
300	7.21	3	6.32	3	5.07	4	4.24	5
400	9.61	4	8.42	4	6.76	6	5.65	7
500	12.02	5	10.53	5	8.44	6	7.06	8
600	14.42	6	12.63	6	10.13	8	8.47	10
700	16.82	6	14.74	8	11.82	9	9.88	11
800	19.22	7	16.84	8	13.51	11	11.29	13
900	21.63	8	18.95	10	15.20	12	12.70	14
1,000	24.03	9	21.05	10	16.88	13	14.11	16
2,000	48.05	18	42.10	21	33.76	26	28.21	31
3,000	72.08	27	63.15	31	50.64	38	42.31	46
4,000	96.10	36	84.19	41	67.52	51	56.41	62
5,000	120.12	45	105.24	52	84.40	64	70.51	77
6,000	144.15	54	126.29	62	101.28	77	84.61	92
7,000	168.17	63	147.33	72	118.16	90	98.71	107
8,000	192.19	72	168.38	82	135.04	102	112.81	122
9,000	216.22	81	189.43	93	151.92	115	126.92	138
10,000	240.24	90	210.47	103	168.80	128	141.02	153
11,000	264.26	99	231.52	113	185.68	141	155.12	169
12,000	288.29	108	252.57	123	202.56	154	169.22	184
13,000	312.31	117	273.61	133	219.44	166	183.32	199
14,000	336.33	126	294.66	144	236.32	179	197.42	214
15,000	360.36	135	315.71	154	253.20	192	211.52	229
16,000	384.38	144	336.75	164	270.07	204	225.62	245
17,000	408.40	153	357.80	174	286.95	217	239.72	260
18,000	432.43	162	378.85	185	303.83	230	253.83	276
19,000	456.45	171	399.89	195	320.71	243	267.93	291
20,000	480.47	180	420.94	205	337.59	255	282.03	306
21,000	504.50	189	441.99	216	354.47	268	296.13	321
22,000	528.52	198	463.03	225	371.35	281	310.23	337
23,000	552.54	207	484.08	236	388.23	294	324.33	352
24,000	576.57	216	505.13	246	405.11	307	338.43	367
25,000	600.59	225	526.17	256	421.99	319	352.53	382
26,000	624.61	234	547.22	267	438.87	332	366.64	398
27,000	648.64	243	568.27	277	455.75	345	380.74	413
28,000	672.66	252	589.31	287	472.63	358	394.84	428
29,000	696.68	261	610.36	297	489.51	371	408.94	444
30,000	720.71	270	631.41	308	506.39	383	423.04	459
31,000	744.73	279	652.45	318	523.26	396	437.14	474
32,000	768.75	288	673.50	328	540.14	408	451.24	489
33,000	792.78	297	694.55	338	557.02	421	465.34	504
34,000	816.80	306	715.59	348	573.90	434	479.44	520
35,000	840.82	314	736.64	359	590.78	447	493.55	536
36,000	864.85	324	757.69	369	607.66	460	507.65	551
37,000	888.87	333	778.73	379	624.54	472	521.75	566
38,000	912.90	342	799.78	389	641.42	485	535.85	581
39,000	936.92	351	820.83	400	658.30	498	549.95	596
40,000	960.94	359	841.87	410	675.18	511	564.05	612
42,000	1,008.99	378	883.97	431	708.94	536	592.25	642
44,000	1,057.04	396	926.06	451	742.70	562	620.46	673
46,000	1,105.08	413	968.15	471	776.45	587	648.66	704
48,000	1,153.13	431	1,010.25	492	810.21	613	676.86	734
50,000	1,201.18	450	1,052.34	512	843.97	638	705.06	764

9

AUTO LOAN PAYMENTS

AMOUNT OF LOAN	12 MOS MONTHLY PAYMENT	12 MOS TOTAL INTRST	24 MOS MONTHLY PAYMENT	24 MOS TOTAL INTRST	30 MOS MONTHLY PAYMENT	30 MOS TOTAL INTRST	36 MOS MONTHLY PAYMENT	36 MOS TOTAL INTRST
$ 1	0.09	0	0.05	0	0.04	0	0.03	0
2	0.17	0	0.09	0	0.07	0	0.06	0
3	0.26	0	0.13	0	0.11	0	0.09	0
4	0.34	0	0.17	0	0.14	0	0.12	0
5	0.42	0	0.21	0	0.17	0	0.15	0
6	0.51	0	0.26	0	0.21	0	0.17	0
7	0.59	0	0.30	0	0.24	0	0.20	0
8	0.67	0	0.34	0	0.27	0	0.23	0
9	0.76	0	0.38	0	0.31	0	0.26	0
10	0.84	0	0.42	0	0.34	0	0.29	0
20	1.68	0	0.84	0	0.68	0	0.57	1
30	2.52	0	1.26	0	1.01	0	0.85	1
40	3.35	0	1.68	0	1.35	1	1.13	1
50	4.19	0	2.10	0	1.69	1	1.41	1
60	5.03	0	2.52	0	2.02	1	1.69	1
70	5.86	0	2.94	1	2.36	1	1.97	1
80	6.70	0	3.36	1	2.70	1	2.25	1
90	7.54	0	3.78	1	3.03	1	2.53	1
100	8.37	0	4.20	1	3.37	1	2.82	2
200	16.74	0	8.40	1	6.74	2	5.63	3
300	25.11	1	12.60	2	10.10	3	8.44	4
400	33.47	1	16.80	3	13.47	4	11.25	5
500	41.84	2	21.00	4	16.83	5	14.06	6
600	50.21	2	25.20	5	20.20	6	16.87	7
700	58.58	3	29.40	6	23.57	7	19.68	8
800	66.94	3	33.60	6	26.93	8	22.49	10
900	75.31	4	37.80	7	30.30	9	25.30	11
1,000	83.68	4	42.00	8	33.66	10	28.11	12
2,000	167.35	8	83.99	16	67.32	20	56.21	24
3,000	251.02	12	125.98	24	100.98	29	84.31	35
4,000	334.69	16	167.98	32	134.63	39	112.41	47
5,000	418.37	20	209.97	39	168.29	49	140.51	58
6,000	502.04	24	251.96	47	201.95	59	168.61	70
7,000	585.71	29	293.96	55	235.61	68	196.71	82
8,000	669.38	33	335.95	63	269.26	78	224.81	93
9,000	753.06	37	377.94	71	302.92	88	252.91	105
10,000	836.73	41	419.93	78	336.58	97	281.01	116
11,000	920.40	45	461.93	86	370.23	107	309.11	128
12,000	1,004.07	49	503.92	94	403.89	117	337.21	140
13,000	1,087.74	53	545.91	102	437.55	127	365.31	151
14,000	1,171.42	57	587.91	110	471.21	136	393.41	163
15,000	1,255.09	61	629.90	118	504.86	146	421.51	174
16,000	1,338.76	65	671.89	125	538.52	156	449.61	186
17,000	1,422.43	69	713.89	133	572.18	165	477.71	198
18,000	1,506.11	73	755.88	141	605.84	175	505.81	209
19,000	1,589.78	77	797.87	149	639.49	185	533.91	221
20,000	1,673.45	81	839.86	157	673.15	195	562.01	232
21,000	1,757.12	85	881.86	165	706.81	204	590.11	244
22,000	1,840.79	89	923.85	172	740.46	214	618.21	256
23,000	1,924.47	94	965.84	180	774.12	224	646.31	267
24,000	2,008.14	98	1,007.84	188	807.78	233	674.41	279
25,000	2,091.81	102	1,049.83	196	841.44	243	702.51	290
26,000	2,175.48	106	1,091.82	204	875.09	253	730.61	302
27,000	2,259.16	110	1,133.82	212	908.75	263	758.71	314
28,000	2,342.83	114	1,175.81	219	942.41	272	786.81	325
29,000	2,426.50	118	1,217.80	227	976.06	282	814.91	337
30,000	2,510.17	122	1,259.79	235	1,009.72	292	843.01	348
31,000	2,593.85	126	1,301.79	243	1,043.38	301	871.11	360
32,000	2,677.52	130	1,343.78	251	1,077.04	311	899.21	372
33,000	2,761.19	134	1,385.77	258	1,110.69	321	927.31	383
34,000	2,844.86	138	1,427.77	266	1,144.35	331	955.41	395
35,000	2,928.53	142	1,469.76	274	1,178.01	340	983.51	406
36,000	3,012.21	147	1,511.75	282	1,211.67	350	1,011.61	418
37,000	3,095.88	151	1,553.74	290	1,245.32	360	1,039.71	430
38,000	3,179.55	155	1,595.74	298	1,278.98	369	1,067.81	441
39,000	3,263.22	159	1,637.73	306	1,312.64	379	1,095.91	453
40,000	3,346.90	163	1,679.72	313	1,346.29	389	1,124.01	464
42,000	3,514.24	171	1,763.71	329	1,413.61	408	1,180.21	488
44,000	3,681.58	179	1,847.70	345	1,480.92	428	1,236.41	511
46,000	3,848.93	187	1,931.68	360	1,548.24	447	1,292.61	534
48,000	4,016.27	195	2,015.67	376	1,615.55	467	1,348.81	557
50,000	4,183.62	203	2,099.65	392	1,682.87	486	1,405.01	580

AUTO LOAN PAYMENTS 0.75%

AMOUNT OF LOAN	42 MOS MONTHLY PAYMENT	42 MOS TOTAL INTRST	48 MOS MONTHLY PAYMENT	48 MOS TOTAL INTRST	60 MOS MONTHLY PAYMENT	60 MOS TOTAL INTRST	72 MOS MONTHLY PAYMENT	72 MOS TOTAL INTRST
$ 1	0.03	0	0.03	0	0.02	0	0.02	0
2	0.05	0	0.05	0	0.04	0	0.03	0
3	0.08	0	0.07	0	0.06	1	0.05	1
4	0.10	0	0.09	0	0.07	0	0.06	0
5	0.13	0	0.11	0	0.09	0	0.08	1
6	0.15	0	0.13	0	0.11	0	0.09	0
7	0.17	0	0.15	0	0.12	0	0.10	0
8	0.20	0	0.17	0	0.14	0	0.12	1
9	0.22	0	0.20	1	0.16	1	0.13	0
10	0.25	1	0.22	1	0.17	0	0.15	1
20	0.49	1	0.43	1	0.34	0	0.29	1
30	0.73	1	0.64	1	0.51	1	0.43	1
40	0.97	1	0.85	1	0.68	1	0.57	1
50	1.21	1	1.06	1	0.85	1	0.72	2
60	1.45	1	1.27	1	1.02	1	0.86	2
70	1.69	1	1.49	2	1.19	1	1.00	2
80	1.94	1	1.70	2	1.36	2	1.14	2
90	2.18	1	1.91	2	1.53	2	1.28	2
100	2.42	2	2.12	2	1.70	2	1.43	3
200	4.83	3	4.24	4	3.40	4	2.85	5
300	7.24	4	6.35	5	5.10	6	4.27	7
400	9.66	6	8.47	7	6.80	8	5.69	10
500	12.07	7	10.58	8	8.50	10	7.11	12
600	14.48	8	12.70	10	10.20	12	8.53	14
700	16.90	10	14.81	11	11.90	14	9.95	16
800	19.31	11	16.93	13	13.59	15	11.37	19
900	21.72	12	19.04	14	15.29	17	12.79	21
1,000	24.14	14	21.16	16	16.99	19	14.21	23
2,000	48.27	27	42.31	31	33.98	39	28.42	46
3,000	72.40	41	63.47	47	50.96	58	42.63	69
4,000	96.53	54	84.62	62	67.95	77	56.84	92
5,000	120.66	68	105.77	77	84.94	96	71.05	116
6,000	144.79	81	126.93	93	101.92	115	85.25	138
7,000	168.92	95	148.08	108	118.91	135	99.46	161
8,000	193.05	108	169.24	124	135.90	154	113.67	184
9,000	217.18	122	190.39	139	152.88	173	127.88	207
10,000	241.31	135	211.54	154	169.87	192	142.09	230
11,000	265.44	148	232.70	170	186.85	211	156.29	253
12,000	289.57	162	253.85	185	203.84	230	170.50	276
13,000	313.71	176	275.00	200	220.83	250	184.71	299
14,000	337.84	189	296.16	216	237.81	269	198.92	322
15,000	361.97	203	317.31	231	254.80	288	213.13	345
16,000	386.10	216	338.47	247	271.79	307	227.33	368
17,000	410.23	230	359.62	262	288.77	326	241.54	391
18,000	434.36	243	380.78	277	305.76	346	255.75	414
19,000	458.49	257	401.93	293	322.75	365	269.96	437
20,000	482.62	270	423.08	308	339.73	384	284.17	460
21,000	506.75	284	444.24	324	356.72	403	298.37	483
22,000	530.88	297	465.39	339	373.70	422	312.58	506
23,000	555.01	310	486.54	354	390.69	441	326.79	529
24,000	579.14	324	507.70	370	407.68	461	341.00	552
25,000	603.28	338	528.85	385	424.66	480	355.21	575
26,000	627.41	351	550.01	400	441.65	499	369.41	598
27,000	651.54	365	571.16	416	458.64	518	383.62	621
28,000	675.67	378	592.31	431	475.62	537	397.83	644
29,000	699.80	392	613.47	447	492.61	557	412.04	667
30,000	723.93	405	634.62	462	509.59	575	426.25	690
31,000	748.06	419	655.78	477	526.58	595	440.46	713
32,000	772.19	432	676.93	493	543.57	614	454.66	736
33,000	796.32	445	698.08	508	560.55	633	468.87	759
34,000	820.45	459	719.24	524	577.54	652	483.08	782
35,000	844.58	472	740.39	539	594.53	672	497.29	805
36,000	868.71	486	761.55	554	611.51	691	511.50	828
37,000	892.85	500	782.70	570	628.50	710	525.70	850
38,000	916.98	513	803.85	585	645.49	729	539.91	874
39,000	941.11	527	825.01	600	662.47	748	554.12	897
40,000	965.24	540	846.16	616	679.46	768	568.33	920
42,000	1,013.50	567	888.47	647	713.43	806	596.74	965
44,000	1,061.76	594	930.78	677	747.40	844	625.16	1,012
46,000	1,110.02	621	973.08	708	781.38	883	653.58	1,058
48,000	1,158.28	648	1,015.39	739	815.35	921	681.99	1,103
50,000	1,206.55	675	1,057.70	770	849.32	959	710.41	1,150

11

0.90% AUTO LOAN PAYMENTS

AMOUNT OF LOAN	12 MOS MONTHLY PAYMENT	12 MOS TOTAL INTRST	24 MOS MONTHLY PAYMENT	24 MOS TOTAL INTRST	30 MOS MONTHLY PAYMENT	30 MOS TOTAL INTRST	36 MOS MONTHLY PAYMENT	36 MOS TOTAL INTRST
$ 1	0.09	0	0.05	0	0.04	0	0.03	0
2	0.17	0	0.09	0	0.07	0	0.06	0
3	0.26	0	0.13	0	0.11	0	0.09	0
4	0.34	0	0.17	0	0.14	0	0.12	0
5	0.42	0	0.22	0	0.17	0	0.15	0
6	0.51	0	0.26	0	0.21	0	0.17	0
7	0.59	0	0.30	0	0.24	0	0.20	0
8	0.67	0	0.34	0	0.27	0	0.23	0
9	0.76	0	0.38	0	0.31	0	0.26	0
10	0.84	0	0.43	0	0.34	0	0.29	0
20	1.68	0	0.85	0	0.68	0	0.57	1
30	2.52	0	1.27	0	1.02	0	0.85	1
40	3.35	0	1.69	1	1.35	1	1.13	1
50	4.19	0	2.11	1	1.69	1	1.41	1
60	5.03	0	2.53	1	2.03	1	1.69	1
70	5.87	0	2.95	1	2.37	1	1.98	1
80	6.70	0	3.37	1	2.70	1	2.26	1
90	7.54	0	3.79	1	3.04	1	2.54	1
100	8.38	1	4.21	1	3.38	1	2.82	2
200	16.75	1	8.42	2	6.75	3	5.64	3
300	25.13	2	12.62	3	10.12	4	8.45	4
400	33.50	2	16.83	4	13.49	5	11.27	6
500	41.88	3	21.03	5	16.87	6	14.09	7
600	50.25	3	25.24	6	20.24	7	16.90	8
700	58.62	3	29.45	7	23.61	8	19.72	10
800	67.00	4	33.65	8	26.98	9	22.54	11
900	75.37	4	37.86	9	30.36	11	25.35	13
1,000	83.75	5	42.06	9	33.73	12	28.17	14
2,000	167.49	10	84.12	19	67.45	24	56.33	28
3,000	251.23	15	126.18	28	101.17	35	84.50	42
4,000	334.97	20	168.24	38	134.89	47	112.66	56
5,000	418.71	25	210.30	47	168.62	59	140.83	70
6,000	502.45	29	252.36	57	202.34	70	168.99	84
7,000	586.19	34	294.41	66	236.06	82	197.16	98
8,000	669.93	39	336.47	75	269.78	93	225.32	112
9,000	753.67	44	378.53	85	303.51	105	253.49	126
10,000	837.41	49	420.59	94	337.23	116	281.65	139
11,000	921.15	54	462.65	104	370.95	129	309.82	154
12,000	1,004.89	59	504.71	113	404.67	140	337.98	167
13,000	1,088.63	64	546.76	122	438.39	152	366.15	181
14,000	1,172.37	68	588.82	132	472.12	164	394.31	195
15,000	1,256.11	73	630.88	141	505.84	175	422.48	209
16,000	1,339.85	78	672.94	151	539.56	187	450.64	223
17,000	1,423.59	83	715.00	160	573.28	198	478.81	237
18,000	1,507.33	88	757.06	169	607.01	210	506.97	251
19,000	1,591.07	93	799.11	179	640.73	222	535.14	265
20,000	1,674.81	98	841.17	188	674.45	234	563.30	279
21,000	1,758.55	103	883.23	198	708.17	245	591.47	293
22,000	1,842.29	107	925.29	207	741.89	257	619.63	307
23,000	1,926.03	112	967.35	216	775.62	269	647.80	321
24,000	2,009.77	117	1,009.41	226	809.34	280	675.96	335
25,000	2,093.51	122	1,051.47	235	843.06	292	704.13	349
26,000	2,177.25	127	1,093.52	244	876.78	303	732.29	362
27,000	2,260.99	132	1,135.58	254	910.51	315	760.46	377
28,000	2,344.73	137	1,177.64	263	944.23	327	788.62	390
29,000	2,428.47	142	1,219.70	273	977.95	339	816.79	404
30,000	2,512.21	147	1,261.76	282	1,011.67	350	844.95	418
31,000	2,595.95	151	1,303.82	292	1,045.39	362	873.12	432
32,000	2,679.69	156	1,345.87	301	1,079.12	374	901.28	446
33,000	2,763.43	161	1,387.93	310	1,112.84	385	929.45	460
34,000	2,847.17	166	1,429.99	320	1,146.56	397	957.61	474
35,000	2,930.91	171	1,472.05	329	1,180.28	408	985.78	488
36,000	3,014.65	176	1,514.11	339	1,214.01	420	1,013.94	502
37,000	3,098.39	181	1,556.17	348	1,247.73	432	1,042.11	516
38,000	3,182.13	186	1,598.22	357	1,281.45	443	1,070.27	530
39,000	3,265.87	190	1,640.28	367	1,315.17	455	1,098.44	544
40,000	3,349.61	195	1,682.34	376	1,348.89	467	1,126.60	558
42,000	3,517.09	205	1,766.46	395	1,416.34	490	1,182.93	585
44,000	3,684.57	215	1,850.58	414	1,483.78	513	1,239.26	613
46,000	3,852.05	225	1,934.69	433	1,551.23	537	1,295.59	641
48,000	4,019.53	234	2,018.81	451	1,618.67	560	1,351.92	669
50,000	4,187.01	244	2,102.93	470	1,686.12	584	1,408.25	697

AUTO LOAN PAYMENTS 0.90%

AMOUNT OF LOAN	42 MOS		48 MOS		60 MOS		72 MOS	
	MONTHLY PAYMENT	TOTAL INTRST	MONTHLY PAYMENT	TOTAL INTRST	MONTHLY PAYMENT	TOTAL INTRST	MONTHLY PAYMENT	TOTAL INTRST
$ 1	0.03	0	0.03	0	0.02	0	0.02	0
2	0.05	0	0.05	0	0.04	0	0.03	0
3	0.08	0	0.07	0	0.06	1	0.05	1
4	0.10	0	0.09	0	0.07	0	0.06	0
5	0.13	0	0.11	0	0.09	1	0.08	1
6	0.15	0	0.13	0	0.11	0	0.09	0
7	0.17	0	0.15	0	0.12	0	0.10	0
8	0.20	0	0.17	0	0.14	0	0.12	1
9	0.22	0	0.20	1	0.16	1	0.13	0
10	0.25	1	0.22	1	0.18	1	0.15	1
20	0.49	1	0.43	1	0.35	1	0.29	1
30	0.73	1	0.64	1	0.52	1	0.43	1
40	0.97	1	0.85	1	0.69	1	0.58	2
50	1.21	1	1.07	1	0.86	2	0.72	2
60	1.46	1	1.28	1	1.03	2	0.86	2
70	1.70	1	1.49	2	1.20	2	1.00	2
80	1.94	1	1.70	2	1.37	2	1.15	3
90	2.18	2	1.91	2	1.54	2	1.29	3
100	2.42	2	2.13	2	1.71	3	1.43	3
200	4.84	3	4.25	4	3.42	5	2.86	6
300	7.26	5	6.37	6	5.12	7	4.29	9
400	9.68	7	8.49	8	6.83	10	5.71	11
500	12.10	8	10.61	9	8.53	12	7.14	14
600	14.52	10	12.74	12	10.24	14	8.57	17
700	16.94	11	14.86	13	11.94	16	10.00	20
800	19.36	13	16.98	15	13.65	19	11.42	22
900	21.78	15	19.10	17	15.35	21	12.85	25
1,000	24.20	16	21.22	19	17.06	24	14.28	28
2,000	48.40	33	42.44	37	34.11	47	28.55	56
3,000	72.59	49	63.66	56	51.16	70	42.82	83
4,000	96.79	65	84.88	74	68.21	93	57.09	110
5,000	120.98	81	106.10	93	85.26	116	71.37	139
6,000	145.18	98	127.32	111	102.31	139	85.64	166
7,000	169.37	114	148.53	129	119.36	162	99.91	194
8,000	193.57	130	169.75	148	136.41	185	114.18	221
9,000	217.76	146	190.97	167	153.46	208	128.46	249
10,000	241.96	162	212.19	185	170.51	231	142.73	277
11,000	266.15	178	233.41	204	187.56	254	157.00	304
12,000	290.35	195	254.63	222	204.61	277	171.27	331
13,000	314.55	211	275.84	240	221.66	300	185.55	360
14,000	338.74	227	297.06	259	238.72	323	199.82	387
15,000	362.94	243	318.28	277	255.77	346	214.09	414
16,000	387.13	259	339.50	296	272.82	369	228.36	442
17,000	411.33	276	360.72	315	289.87	392	242.64	470
18,000	435.52	292	381.94	333	306.92	415	256.91	498
19,000	459.72	308	403.15	351	323.97	438	271.18	525
20,000	483.91	324	424.37	370	341.02	461	285.45	552
21,000	508.11	341	445.59	388	358.07	484	299.73	581
22,000	532.30	357	466.81	407	375.12	507	314.00	608
23,000	556.50	373	488.03	425	392.17	530	328.27	635
24,000	580.70	389	509.25	444	409.22	553	342.54	663
25,000	604.89	405	530.46	462	426.27	576	356.82	691
26,000	629.09	422	551.68	599	443.32	599	371.09	718
27,000	653.28	438	572.90	499	460.37	622	385.36	746
28,000	677.48	454	594.12	518	477.43	646	399.63	773
29,000	701.67	470	615.34	536	494.48	669	413.91	802
30,000	725.87	487	636.56	555	511.53	692	428.18	829
31,000	750.06	503	657.78	715	528.58	715	442.45	856
32,000	774.26	519	678.99	592	545.63	738	456.72	884
33,000	798.45	535	700.21	610	562.68	761	471.00	912
34,000	822.65	551	721.43	629	579.73	784	485.27	939
35,000	846.84	567	742.65	647	596.78	807	499.54	967
36,000	871.04	584	763.87	666	613.83	830	513.81	994
37,000	895.24	600	785.09	684	630.88	853	528.09	1,022
38,000	919.43	616	806.30	702	647.93	876	542.36	1,050
39,000	943.63	632	827.52	721	664.98	899	556.63	1,077
40,000	967.82	648	848.74	740	682.03	922	570.90	1,105
42,000	1,016.21	681	891.18	777	716.14	968	599.45	1,160
44,000	1,064.60	713	933.61	813	750.24	1,014	627.99	1,215
46,000	1,112.99	746	976.05	850	784.34	1,060	656.54	1,271
48,000	1,161.39	778	1,018.49	888	818.44	1,106	685.08	1,326
50,000	1,209.78	811	1,060.92	924	852.54	1,152	713.63	1,381

1.00% AUTO LOAN PAYMENTS

AMOUNT OF LOAN	12 MOS MONTHLY PAYMENT	12 MOS TOTAL INTRST	24 MOS MONTHLY PAYMENT	24 MOS TOTAL INTRST	30 MOS MONTHLY PAYMENT	30 MOS TOTAL INTRST	36 MOS MONTHLY PAYMENT	36 MOS TOTAL INTRST
$ 1	0.09	0	0.05	0	0.04	0	0.03	0
2	0.17	0	0.09	0	0.07	0	0.06	0
3	0.26	0	0.13	0	0.11	0	0.09	0
4	0.34	0	0.17	0	0.14	0	0.12	0
5	0.42	0	0.22	0	0.17	0	0.15	0
6	0.51	0	0.26	0	0.21	0	0.17	0
7	0.59	0	0.30	0	0.24	0	0.20	0
8	0.68	0	0.34	0	0.28	0	0.23	0
9	0.76	0	0.38	0	0.31	0	0.26	0
10	0.84	0	0.43	0	0.34	0	0.29	0
20	1.68	0	0.85	0	0.68	0	0.57	0
30	2.52	0	1.27	0	1.02	0	0.85	1
40	3.36	0	1.69	1	1.36	1	1.13	1
50	4.19	0	2.11	1	1.69	1	1.42	1
60	5.03	0	2.53	1	2.03	1	1.70	1
70	5.87	0	2.95	1	2.37	1	1.98	1
80	6.71	1	3.37	1	2.71	1	2.26	1
90	7.55	1	3.79	1	3.04	1	2.54	1
100	8.38	1	4.22	1	3.38	1	2.83	2
200	16.76	1	8.43	2	6.76	3	5.65	3
300	25.14	2	12.64	3	10.13	4	8.47	5
400	33.52	2	16.85	4	13.51	5	11.29	6
500	41.90	3	21.06	5	16.89	7	14.11	8
600	50.28	3	25.27	6	20.26	8	16.93	9
700	58.65	4	29.48	8	23.64	9	19.75	11
800	67.03	4	33.69	9	27.02	11	22.57	13
900	75.41	5	37.90	10	30.39	12	25.39	14
1,000	83.79	5	42.11	11	33.77	13	28.21	16
2,000	167.58	11	84.21	21	67.54	26	56.42	31
3,000	251.36	16	126.31	31	101.30	39	84.63	47
4,000	335.15	22	168.41	42	135.07	52	112.84	62
5,000	418.93	27	210.52	52	168.83	65	141.05	78
6,000	502.72	33	252.62	63	202.60	78	169.25	93
7,000	586.50	38	294.72	73	236.36	91	197.46	109
8,000	670.29	43	336.82	84	270.13	104	225.67	124
9,000	754.07	49	378.92	94	303.90	117	253.88	140
10,000	837.86	54	421.03	105	337.66	130	282.09	155
11,000	921.64	60	463.13	115	371.43	143	310.29	170
12,000	1,005.43	65	505.23	126	405.19	156	338.50	186
13,000	1,089.22	71	547.33	136	438.96	169	366.71	202
14,000	1,173.00	76	589.43	146	472.72	182	394.92	217
15,000	1,256.79	81	631.54	157	506.49	195	423.13	233
16,000	1,340.57	87	673.64	167	540.25	208	451.33	248
17,000	1,424.36	92	715.74	178	574.02	221	479.54	263
18,000	1,508.14	98	757.84	188	607.79	234	507.75	279
19,000	1,591.93	103	799.94	199	641.55	247	535.96	295
20,000	1,675.71	109	842.05	209	675.32	260	564.17	310
21,000	1,759.50	114	884.15	220	709.08	272	592.38	326
22,000	1,843.28	119	926.25	230	742.85	286	620.58	341
23,000	1,927.07	125	968.35	240	776.61	298	648.79	356
24,000	2,010.85	130	1,010.45	251	810.38	311	677.00	372
25,000	2,094.64	136	1,052.56	261	844.15	325	705.21	388
26,000	2,178.43	141	1,094.66	272	877.91	337	733.42	403
27,000	2,262.21	147	1,136.76	282	911.68	350	761.62	418
28,000	2,346.00	152	1,178.86	293	945.44	363	789.83	434
29,000	2,429.78	157	1,220.97	303	979.21	376	818.04	449
30,000	2,513.57	163	1,263.07	314	1,012.97	389	846.25	465
31,000	2,597.35	168	1,305.17	324	1,046.74	402	874.46	481
32,000	2,681.14	174	1,347.27	334	1,080.50	415	902.66	496
33,000	2,764.92	179	1,389.37	345	1,114.27	428	930.87	511
34,000	2,848.71	185	1,431.48	356	1,148.04	441	959.08	527
35,000	2,932.49	190	1,473.58	366	1,181.80	454	987.29	542
36,000	3,016.28	195	1,515.68	376	1,215.57	467	1,015.50	558
37,000	3,100.07	201	1,557.78	387	1,249.33	480	1,043.70	573
38,000	3,183.85	206	1,599.88	397	1,283.10	493	1,071.91	589
39,000	3,267.64	212	1,641.99	408	1,316.86	506	1,100.12	604
40,000	3,351.42	217	1,684.09	418	1,350.63	519	1,128.33	620
42,000	3,518.99	228	1,768.29	439	1,418.16	545	1,184.75	651
44,000	3,686.56	239	1,852.50	460	1,485.69	571	1,241.16	682
46,000	3,854.13	250	1,936.70	481	1,553.22	597	1,297.58	713
48,000	4,021.70	260	2,020.90	502	1,620.75	623	1,353.99	744
50,000	4,189.28	271	2,105.11	523	1,688.29	649	1,410.41	775

AMOUNT OF LOAN	42 MOS		48 MOS		60 MOS		72 MOS	
	MONTHLY PAYMENT	TOTAL INTRST	MONTHLY PAYMENT	TOTAL INTRST	MONTHLY PAYMENT	TOTAL INTRST	MONTHLY PAYMENT	TOTAL INTRST
$ 1	0.03	0	0.03	0	0.02	0	0.02	0
2	0.05	0	0.05	0	0.04	0	0.03	0
3	0.08	0	0.07	0	0.06	1	0.05	1
4	0.10	0	0.09	0	0.07	0	0.06	0
5	0.13	0	0.11	0	0.09	1	0.08	1
6	0.15	0	0.13	0	0.11	0	0.09	0
7	0.17	0	0.15	0	0.12	1	0.11	1
8	0.20	0	0.18	1	0.14	0	0.12	1
9	0.22	0	0.20	1	0.16	1	0.13	0
10	0.25	1	0.22	1	0.18	1	0.15	1
20	0.49	1	0.43	1	0.35	1	0.29	1
30	0.73	1	0.64	1	0.52	1	0.43	1
40	0.97	1	0.86	1	0.69	1	0.58	2
50	1.22	1	1.07	1	0.86	2	0.72	2
60	1.46	1	1.28	1	1.03	2	0.86	2
70	1.70	1	1.49	2	1.20	2	1.01	3
80	1.94	1	1.71	2	1.37	2	1.15	3
90	2.19	2	1.92	2	1.54	2	1.29	3
100	2.43	2	2.13	2	1.71	3	1.44	4
200	4.85	4	4.26	4	3.42	5	2.87	7
300	7.28	6	6.38	6	5.13	8	4.30	10
400	9.70	7	8.51	8	6.84	10	5.73	13
500	12.12	9	10.64	11	8.55	13	7.16	16
600	14.55	11	12.76	12	10.26	16	8.59	18
700	16.97	13	14.89	15	11.97	18	10.03	22
800	19.40	15	17.01	16	13.68	21	11.46	25
900	21.82	16	19.14	19	15.39	23	12.89	28
1,000	24.24	18	21.27	21	17.10	26	14.32	31
2,000	48.48	36	42.53	41	34.19	51	28.64	62
3,000	72.72	54	63.79	62	51.29	77	42.95	92
4,000	96.96	72	85.05	82	68.38	103	57.27	123
5,000	121.20	90	106.31	103	85.47	128	71.58	154
6,000	145.44	108	127.57	123	102.57	154	85.90	185
7,000	169.67	126	148.84	144	119.66	180	100.21	215
8,000	193.91	144	170.10	165	136.75	205	114.53	246
9,000	218.15	162	191.36	185	153.85	231	128.84	276
10,000	242.39	180	212.62	206	170.94	256	143.16	308
11,000	266.63	198	233.88	226	188.04	282	157.48	339
12,000	290.87	217	255.14	247	205.13	308	171.79	369
13,000	315.11	235	276.40	267	222.22	333	186.11	400
14,000	339.34	252	297.67	288	239.32	359	200.42	430
15,000	363.58	270	318.93	309	256.41	385	214.74	461
16,000	387.82	288	340.19	329	273.50	410	229.05	492
17,000	412.06	307	361.45	350	290.60	436	243.37	523
18,000	436.30	325	382.71	370	307.69	461	257.68	553
19,000	460.54	343	403.97	391	324.79	487	272.00	584
20,000	484.78	361	425.23	411	341.88	513	286.32	615
21,000	509.01	378	446.50	432	358.97	538	300.63	645
22,000	533.25	397	467.76	452	376.07	564	314.95	676
23,000	557.49	415	489.02	473	393.16	590	329.26	707
24,000	581.73	433	510.28	493	410.25	615	343.58	738
25,000	605.97	451	531.54	514	427.35	641	357.89	768
26,000	630.21	469	552.80	534	444.44	666	372.21	799
27,000	654.45	487	574.06	555	461.54	692	386.52	829
28,000	678.68	505	595.33	576	478.63	718	400.84	860
29,000	702.92	523	616.59	596	495.72	743	415.15	891
30,000	727.16	541	637.85	617	512.82	769	429.47	922
31,000	751.40	559	659.11	637	529.91	795	443.79	953
32,000	775.64	577	680.37	658	547.00	820	458.10	983
33,000	799.88	595	701.63	678	564.10	846	472.42	1,014
34,000	824.12	613	722.89	699	581.19	871	486.73	1,045
35,000	848.35	631	744.16	720	598.29	897	501.05	1,076
36,000	872.59	649	765.42	740	615.38	923	515.36	1,106
37,000	896.83	667	786.68	761	632.47	948	529.68	1,137
38,000	921.07	685	807.94	781	649.57	974	543.99	1,167
39,000	945.31	703	829.20	802	666.66	1,000	558.31	1,198
40,000	969.55	721	850.46	822	683.75	1,025	572.63	1,229
42,000	1,018.02	757	892.99	864	717.94	1,076	601.26	1,291
44,000	1,066.50	793	935.51	904	752.13	1,128	629.89	1,352
46,000	1,114.98	829	978.03	945	786.32	1,179	658.52	1,413
48,000	1,163.45	865	1,020.55	986	820.50	1,230	687.15	1,475
50,000	1,211.93	901	1,063.08	1,028	854.69	1,281	715.78	1,536

1.25% AUTO LOAN PAYMENTS

AMOUNT OF LOAN	12 MOS		24 MOS		30 MOS		36 MOS	
	MONTHLY PAYMENT	TOTAL INTRST	MONTHLY PAYMENT	TOTAL INTRST	MONTHLY PAYMENT	TOTAL INTRST	MONTHLY PAYMENT	TOTAL INTRST
$ 1	0.09	0	0.05	0	0.04	0	0.03	0
2	0.17	0	0.09	0	0.07	0	0.06	0
3	0.26	0	0.13	0	0.11	0	0.09	0
4	0.34	0	0.17	0	0.14	0	0.12	0
5	0.42	0	0.22	0	0.17	0	0.15	0
6	0.51	0	0.26	0	0.21	0	0.17	0
7	0.59	0	0.30	0	0.24	0	0.20	0
8	0.68	0	0.34	0	0.28	0	0.23	0
9	0.76	0	0.38	0	0.31	0	0.26	0
10	0.84	0	0.43	0	0.34	0	0.29	0
20	1.68	0	0.85	0	0.68	0	0.57	1
30	2.52	0	1.27	0	1.02	0	0.85	1
40	3.36	0	1.69	1	1.36	1	1.14	1
50	4.20	0	2.12	1	1.70	1	1.42	1
60	5.04	0	2.54	1	2.04	1	1.70	1
70	5.88	1	2.96	1	2.38	1	1.99	2
80	6.72	1	3.38	1	2.71	1	2.27	2
90	7.56	1	3.80	1	3.05	2	2.55	2
100	8.39	1	4.23	2	3.39	2	2.84	2
200	16.78	1	8.45	3	6.78	3	5.67	4
300	25.17	2	12.67	4	10.17	5	8.50	6
400	33.56	3	16.89	5	13.55	7	11.33	8
500	41.95	3	21.11	7	16.94	8	14.16	10
600	50.34	4	25.33	8	20.33	10	16.99	12
700	58.73	5	29.55	9	23.72	12	19.83	14
800	67.12	5	33.77	10	27.10	13	22.66	16
900	75.51	6	38.00	12	30.49	15	25.49	18
1,000	83.90	7	42.22	13	33.88	16	28.32	20
2,000	167.80	14	84.43	26	67.75	33	56.64	39
3,000	251.70	20	126.64	39	101.63	49	84.95	58
4,000	335.60	27	168.85	52	135.50	65	113.27	78
5,000	419.50	34	211.06	65	169.38	81	141.59	97
6,000	503.40	41	253.27	78	203.25	98	169.90	116
7,000	587.30	48	295.48	92	237.12	114	198.22	136
8,000	671.19	54	337.70	105	271.00	130	226.54	155
9,000	755.09	61	379.91	118	304.87	146	254.85	175
10,000	838.99	68	422.12	131	338.75	163	283.17	194
11,000	922.89	75	464.33	144	372.62	179	311.48	213
12,000	1,006.79	81	506.54	157	406.50	195	339.80	233
13,000	1,090.69	88	548.75	170	440.37	211	368.12	252
14,000	1,174.59	95	590.96	183	474.24	227	396.43	271
15,000	1,258.48	102	633.18	196	508.12	244	424.75	291
16,000	1,342.38	109	675.39	209	541.99	260	453.07	311
17,000	1,426.28	115	717.60	222	575.87	276	481.38	330
18,000	1,510.18	122	759.81	235	609.74	292	509.70	349
19,000	1,594.08	129	802.02	248	643.62	309	538.02	369
20,000	1,677.98	136	844.23	262	677.49	325	566.33	388
21,000	1,761.88	143	886.44	275	711.36	341	594.65	407
22,000	1,845.78	149	928.66	288	745.24	357	622.96	427
23,000	1,929.67	156	970.87	301	779.11	373	651.28	446
24,000	2,013.57	163	1,013.08	314	812.99	390	679.60	466
25,000	2,097.47	170	1,055.29	327	846.86	406	707.91	485
26,000	2,181.37	176	1,097.50	340	880.74	422	736.23	504
27,000	2,265.27	183	1,139.71	353	914.61	438	764.55	524
28,000	2,349.17	190	1,181.92	366	948.48	454	792.86	543
29,000	2,433.07	197	1,224.13	379	982.36	471	821.18	562
30,000	2,516.96	204	1,266.35	392	1,016.23	487	849.49	582
31,000	2,600.86	210	1,308.56	405	1,050.11	503	877.81	601
32,000	2,684.76	217	1,350.77	418	1,083.98	519	906.13	621
33,000	2,768.66	224	1,392.98	432	1,117.85	536	934.44	640
34,000	2,852.56	231	1,435.19	445	1,151.73	552	962.76	659
35,000	2,936.46	238	1,477.40	458	1,185.60	568	991.08	679
36,000	3,020.36	244	1,519.61	471	1,219.48	584	1,019.39	698
37,000	3,104.25	251	1,561.83	484	1,253.35	601	1,047.71	718
38,000	3,188.15	258	1,604.04	497	1,287.23	617	1,076.03	737
39,000	3,272.05	265	1,646.25	510	1,321.10	633	1,104.34	756
40,000	3,355.95	271	1,688.46	523	1,354.97	649	1,132.66	776
42,000	3,523.75	285	1,772.88	549	1,422.72	682	1,189.29	814
44,000	3,691.55	299	1,857.31	575	1,490.47	714	1,245.92	853
46,000	3,859.34	312	1,941.73	602	1,558.22	747	1,302.56	892
48,000	4,027.14	326	2,026.15	628	1,625.97	779	1,359.19	931
50,000	4,194.94	339	2,110.57	654	1,693.72	812	1,415.82	970

AMOUNT OF LOAN	42 MOS MONTHLY PAYMENT	42 MOS TOTAL INTRST	48 MOS MONTHLY PAYMENT	48 MOS TOTAL INTRST	60 MOS MONTHLY PAYMENT	60 MOS TOTAL INTRST	72 MOS MONTHLY PAYMENT	72 MOS TOTAL INTRST
$ 1	0.03	0	0.03	0	0.02	0	0.02	0
2	0.05	0	0.05	0	0.04	0	0.03	0
3	0.08	0	0.07	0	0.06	1	0.05	1
4	0.10	0	0.09	0	0.07	0	0.06	0
5	0.13	0	0.11	0	0.09	0	0.08	1
6	0.15	0	0.13	0	0.11	0	0.09	0
7	0.18	1	0.15	0	0.13	1	0.11	1
8	0.20	0	0.18	1	0.14	0	0.12	1
9	0.22	0	0.20	1	0.16	1	0.13	0
10	0.25	1	0.22	1	0.18	1	0.15	1
20	0.49	1	0.43	1	0.35	1	0.29	1
30	0.74	1	0.65	1	0.52	1	0.44	2
40	0.98	1	0.86	1	0.69	1	0.58	2
50	1.22	1	1.07	1	0.87	2	0.73	3
60	1.47	2	1.29	2	1.04	2	0.87	3
70	1.71	2	1.50	2	1.21	3	1.01	3
80	1.95	2	1.71	2	1.38	3	1.16	4
90	2.20	2	1.93	3	1.55	3	1.30	4
100	2.44	2	2.14	3	1.73	4	1.45	4
200	4.87	5	4.28	5	3.45	7	2.89	8
300	7.31	7	6.42	8	5.17	10	4.33	12
400	9.74	9	8.55	10	6.89	13	5.77	15
500	12.18	12	10.69	13	8.61	17	7.22	20
600	14.61	14	12.83	16	10.33	20	8.66	24
700	17.05	16	14.96	18	12.05	23	10.10	27
800	19.48	18	17.10	21	13.77	26	11.54	31
900	21.92	21	19.24	24	15.49	29	12.99	35
1,000	24.35	23	21.37	26	17.21	33	14.43	39
2,000	48.70	45	42.74	52	34.41	65	28.85	77
3,000	73.04	68	64.11	77	51.61	97	43.28	116
4,000	97.39	90	85.48	103	68.81	129	57.70	154
5,000	121.74	113	106.85	129	86.01	161	72.12	193
6,000	146.08	135	128.22	155	103.21	193	86.55	232
7,000	170.43	158	149.59	180	120.42	225	100.97	270
8,000	194.78	181	170.96	206	137.62	257	115.39	308
9,000	219.12	203	192.33	232	154.82	289	129.82	347
10,000	243.47	226	213.70	258	172.02	321	144.24	385
11,000	267.82	248	235.07	283	189.22	353	158.66	424
12,000	292.16	271	256.44	309	206.42	385	173.09	462
13,000	316.51	293	277.81	335	223.63	418	187.51	501
14,000	340.86	316	299.18	361	240.83	450	201.93	539
15,000	365.20	338	320.55	386	258.03	482	216.36	578
16,000	389.55	361	341.92	412	275.23	514	230.78	616
17,000	413.90	384	363.28	437	292.43	546	245.20	654
18,000	438.24	406	384.65	463	309.63	578	259.63	693
19,000	462.59	429	406.02	489	326.84	610	274.05	732
20,000	486.94	451	427.39	515	344.04	642	288.47	770
21,000	511.28	474	448.76	540	361.24	674	302.90	809
22,000	535.63	496	470.13	566	378.44	706	317.32	847
23,000	559.98	519	491.50	592	395.64	738	331.74	885
24,000	584.32	541	512.87	618	412.84	770	346.17	924
25,000	608.67	564	534.24	644	430.05	803	360.59	962
26,000	633.02	587	555.61	669	447.25	835	375.01	1,001
27,000	657.36	609	576.98	695	464.45	867	389.44	1,040
28,000	681.71	632	598.35	721	481.65	899	403.86	1,078
29,000	706.05	654	619.72	747	498.85	931	418.29	1,117
30,000	730.40	677	641.09	772	516.05	963	432.71	1,155
31,000	754.75	700	662.45	798	533.25	995	447.13	1,193
32,000	779.09	722	683.82	823	550.46	1,028	461.56	1,232
33,000	803.44	744	705.19	849	567.66	1,060	475.98	1,271
34,000	827.79	767	726.56	875	584.86	1,092	490.40	1,309
35,000	852.13	789	747.93	901	602.06	1,124	504.83	1,348
36,000	876.48	812	769.30	926	619.26	1,156	519.25	1,386
37,000	900.83	835	790.67	952	636.46	1,188	533.67	1,424
38,000	925.17	857	812.04	978	653.67	1,220	548.10	1,463
39,000	949.52	879	833.41	1,004	670.87	1,252	562.52	1,501
40,000	973.87	903	854.78	1,029	688.07	1,284	576.94	1,540
42,000	1,022.56	948	897.52	1,081	722.47	1,348	605.79	1,617
44,000	1,071.25	993	940.26	1,132	756.88	1,413	634.64	1,694
46,000	1,119.95	1,038	983.00	1,184	791.28	1,477	663.48	1,771
48,000	1,168.64	1,083	1,025.73	1,235	825.68	1,541	692.33	1,848
50,000	1,217.33	1,128	1,068.47	1,287	860.09	1,605	721.18	1,925

1.50% AUTO LOAN PAYMENTS

AMOUNT OF LOAN	12 MOS MONTHLY PAYMENT	12 MOS TOTAL INTRST	24 MOS MONTHLY PAYMENT	24 MOS TOTAL INTRST	30 MOS MONTHLY PAYMENT	30 MOS TOTAL INTRST	36 MOS MONTHLY PAYMENT	36 MOS TOTAL INTRST
$ 1	0.09	0	0.05	0	0.04	0	0.03	0
2	0.17	0	0.09	0	0.07	0	0.06	0
3	0.26	0	0.13	0	0.11	0	0.09	0
4	0.34	0	0.17	0	0.14	0	0.12	0
5	0.43	0	0.22	0	0.17	0	0.15	0
6	0.51	0	0.26	0	0.21	0	0.18	0
7	0.59	0	0.30	0	0.24	0	0.20	0
8	0.68	0	0.34	0	0.28	0	0.23	0
9	0.76	0	0.39	0	0.31	0	0.26	0
10	0.85	0	0.43	0	0.34	0	0.29	0
20	1.69	0	0.85	0	0.68	0	0.57	1
30	2.53	0	1.27	0	1.02	1	0.86	1
40	3.37	0	1.70	1	1.36	1	1.14	1
50	4.21	1	2.12	1	1.70	1	1.43	1
60	5.05	1	2.54	1	2.04	1	1.71	2
70	5.89	1	2.97	1	2.38	1	1.99	2
80	6.73	1	3.39	1	2.72	2	2.28	2
90	7.57	1	3.81	1	3.06	2	2.56	2
100	8.41	1	4.24	2	3.40	2	2.85	3
200	16.81	2	8.47	3	6.80	4	5.69	5
300	25.21	3	12.70	5	10.20	6	8.53	7
400	33.61	3	16.93	6	13.60	8	11.37	9
500	42.01	4	21.17	8	17.00	10	14.22	12
600	50.41	5	25.40	10	20.39	12	17.06	14
700	58.81	6	29.63	11	23.79	14	19.90	16
800	67.21	7	33.86	13	27.19	16	22.74	19
900	75.62	7	38.09	14	30.59	18	25.59	21
1,000	84.02	8	42.33	16	33.99	20	28.43	23
2,000	168.03	16	84.65	32	67.97	39	56.85	47
3,000	252.04	24	126.97	47	101.95	59	85.28	70
4,000	336.05	33	169.29	63	135.94	78	113.70	93
5,000	420.06	41	211.61	79	169.92	98	142.13	117
6,000	504.08	49	253.93	94	203.90	117	170.55	140
7,000	588.09	57	296.25	110	237.89	137	198.98	163
8,000	672.10	65	338.57	126	271.87	156	227.40	186
9,000	756.11	73	380.89	141	305.85	176	255.83	210
10,000	840.12	81	423.21	157	339.84	195	284.25	233
11,000	924.14	90	465.53	173	373.82	215	312.68	256
12,000	1,008.15	98	507.85	188	407.80	234	341.10	280
13,000	1,092.16	106	550.18	204	441.78	253	369.53	303
14,000	1,176.17	114	592.50	220	475.77	273	397.95	326
15,000	1,260.18	122	634.82	236	509.75	293	426.38	350
16,000	1,344.20	130	677.14	251	543.73	312	454.80	373
17,000	1,428.21	139	719.46	267	577.72	332	483.23	396
18,000	1,512.22	147	761.78	283	611.70	351	511.65	419
19,000	1,596.23	155	804.10	298	645.68	370	540.08	443
20,000	1,680.25	163	846.42	314	679.67	390	568.50	466
21,000	1,764.26	171	888.74	330	713.65	410	596.93	489
22,000	1,848.27	179	931.06	345	747.63	429	625.35	513
23,000	1,932.28	187	973.38	361	781.62	449	653.78	536
24,000	2,016.29	195	1,015.70	377	815.60	468	682.20	559
25,000	2,100.30	204	1,058.03	393	849.58	487	710.63	583
26,000	2,184.32	212	1,100.35	408	883.56	507	739.05	606
27,000	2,268.33	220	1,142.67	424	917.55	527	767.48	629
28,000	2,352.34	228	1,184.99	440	951.53	546	795.90	652
29,000	2,436.35	236	1,227.31	455	985.51	565	824.33	676
30,000	2,520.36	244	1,269.63	471	1,019.50	585	852.75	699
31,000	2,604.38	253	1,311.95	487	1,053.48	604	881.17	722
32,000	2,688.39	261	1,354.27	502	1,087.46	624	909.60	746
33,000	2,772.40	269	1,396.59	518	1,121.45	644	938.02	769
34,000	2,856.41	277	1,438.91	534	1,155.43	663	966.45	792
35,000	2,940.42	285	1,481.23	550	1,189.41	682	994.87	815
36,000	3,024.44	293	1,523.55	565	1,223.40	702	1,023.30	839
37,000	3,108.45	301	1,565.88	581	1,257.38	721	1,051.72	862
38,000	3,192.46	310	1,608.20	597	1,291.36	741	1,080.15	885
39,000	3,276.47	318	1,650.52	612	1,325.34	760	1,108.57	909
40,000	3,360.48	326	1,692.84	628	1,359.33	780	1,137.00	932
42,000	3,528.51	342	1,777.48	660	1,427.29	819	1,193.85	979
44,000	3,696.53	358	1,862.12	691	1,495.26	858	1,250.70	1,025
46,000	3,864.56	375	1,946.76	722	1,563.23	897	1,307.55	1,072
48,000	4,032.58	391	2,031.40	754	1,631.19	936	1,364.40	1,118
50,000	4,200.60	407	2,116.05	785	1,699.16	975	1,421.25	1,165

AUTO LOAN PAYMENTS   1.50%

AMOUNT OF LOAN	42 MOS		48 MOS		60 MOS		72 MOS	
	MONTHLY PAYMENT	TOTAL INTRST	MONTHLY PAYMENT	TOTAL INTRST	MONTHLY PAYMENT	TOTAL INTRST	MONTHLY PAYMENT	TOTAL INTRST
$ 1	0.03	0	0.03	0	0.02	0	0.02	0
2	0.05	0	0.05	0	0.04	0	0.03	0
3	0.08	0	0.07	0	0.06	1	0.05	1
4	0.10	0	0.09	0	0.07	0	0.06	1
5	0.13	0	0.11	0	0.09	0	0.08	1
6	0.15	0	0.13	0	0.11	1	0.09	0
7	0.18	1	0.16	1	0.13	1	0.11	1
8	0.20	0	0.18	1	0.14	0	0.12	1
9	0.23	1	0.20	1	0.16	1	0.14	1
10	0.25	1	0.22	1	0.18	1	0.15	1
20	0.49	1	0.43	1	0.35	1	0.30	2
30	0.74	1	0.65	1	0.52	1	0.44	2
40	0.98	1	0.86	1	0.70	2	0.59	2
50	1.23	2	1.08	2	0.87	2	0.73	3
60	1.47	2	1.29	2	1.04	2	0.88	3
70	1.72	2	1.51	2	1.22	3	1.02	3
80	1.96	2	1.72	3	1.39	3	1.17	4
90	2.21	3	1.94	3	1.56	4	1.31	4
100	2.45	3	2.15	3	1.74	4	1.46	5
200	4.90	6	4.30	6	3.47	8	2.91	10
300	7.34	8	6.45	10	5.20	12	4.36	14
400	9.79	11	8.60	13	6.93	16	5.82	19
500	12.23	14	10.74	16	8.66	20	7.27	23
600	14.68	17	12.89	19	10.39	23	8.72	28
700	17.12	19	15.04	22	12.12	27	10.18	33
800	19.57	22	17.19	25	13.85	31	11.63	37
900	22.01	24	19.33	28	15.58	35	13.08	42
1,000	24.46	27	21.48	31	17.31	39	14.54	47
2,000	48.91	54	42.96	62	34.62	77	29.07	93
3,000	73.37	82	64.44	93	51.93	116	43.60	139
4,000	97.82	108	85.92	124	69.24	154	58.13	185
5,000	122.28	136	107.39	155	86.55	193	72.66	232
6,000	146.73	163	128.87	186	103.86	232	87.20	278
7,000	171.19	190	150.35	217	121.17	270	101.73	325
8,000	195.64	217	171.83	248	138.48	309	116.26	371
9,000	220.10	244	193.30	278	155.79	347	130.79	417
10,000	244.55	271	214.78	309	173.10	386	145.32	463
11,000	269.01	298	236.26	340	190.41	425	159.86	510
12,000	293.46	325	257.74	372	207.72	463	174.39	556
13,000	317.92	353	279.21	402	225.03	502	188.92	602
14,000	342.37	380	300.69	433	242.34	540	203.45	648
15,000	366.83	407	322.17	464	259.65	579	217.98	695
16,000	391.28	434	343.65	495	276.96	618	232.52	741
17,000	415.74	461	365.12	526	294.27	656	247.05	788
18,000	440.19	488	386.60	557	311.58	695	261.58	834
19,000	464.65	515	408.08	588	328.89	733	276.11	880
20,000	489.10	542	429.56	619	346.20	771	290.64	926
21,000	513.56	570	451.03	649	363.51	811	305.18	973
22,000	538.01	596	472.51	680	380.82	849	319.71	1,019
23,000	562.47	622	493.99	712	398.13	888	334.24	1,065
24,000	586.92	651	515.47	743	415.44	926	348.77	1,111
25,000	611.38	677	536.94	773	432.75	965	363.30	1,158
26,000	635.83	705	558.42	804	450.06	1,004	377.84	1,204
27,000	660.29	732	579.90	835	467.37	1,042	392.37	1,251
28,000	684.74	759	601.38	866	484.68	1,081	406.90	1,297
29,000	709.20	786	622.86	897	501.99	1,119	421.43	1,343
30,000	733.65	813	644.33	928	519.30	1,158	435.96	1,389
31,000	758.11	841	665.81	959	536.61	1,197	450.50	1,436
32,000	782.56	868	687.29	990	553.92	1,235	465.03	1,482
33,000	807.02	895	708.77	1,021	571.23	1,274	479.56	1,528
34,000	831.47	922	730.24	1,052	588.54	1,312	494.09	1,574
35,000	855.93	949	751.72	1,083	605.85	1,351	508.62	1,621
36,000	880.38	976	773.20	1,114	623.16	1,390	523.15	1,667
37,000	904.84	1,003	794.68	1,145	640.47	1,428	537.69	1,714
38,000	929.29	1,030	816.15	1,175	657.78	1,467	552.22	1,760
39,000	953.74	1,057	837.63	1,206	675.09	1,505	566.75	1,806
40,000	978.20	1,084	859.11	1,237	692.40	1,544	581.28	1,852
42,000	1,027.11	1,139	902.06	1,299	727.02	1,621	610.35	1,945
44,000	1,076.02	1,193	945.02	1,361	761.64	1,698	639.41	2,038
46,000	1,124.93	1,247	987.97	1,423	796.26	1,776	668.47	2,130
48,000	1,173.84	1,301	1,030.93	1,485	830.88	1,853	697.54	2,223
50,000	1,222.75	1,356	1,073.88	1,546	865.50	1,930	726.60	2,315

AMOUNT OF LOAN	12 MOS		24 MOS		30 MOS		36 MOS	
	MONTHLY PAYMENT	TOTAL INTRST	MONTHLY PAYMENT	TOTAL INTRST	MONTHLY PAYMENT	TOTAL INTRST	MONTHLY PAYMENT	TOTAL INTRST
$ 1	0.09	0	0.05	0	0.04	0	0.03	0
2	0.17	0	0.09	0	0.07	0	0.06	0
3	0.26	0	0.13	0	0.11	0	0.09	0
4	0.34	0	0.17	0	0.14	0	0.12	0
5	0.43	0	0.22	0	0.18	0	0.15	0
6	0.51	0	0.26	0	0.21	0	0.18	0
7	0.59	0	0.30	0	0.24	0	0.20	0
8	0.68	0	0.34	0	0.28	0	0.23	0
9	0.76	0	0.39	0	0.31	0	0.26	0
10	0.85	0	0.43	0	0.35	1	0.29	0
20	1.69	0	0.85	0	0.69	1	0.58	1
30	2.53	0	1.28	1	1.03	1	0.86	1
40	3.37	0	1.70	1	1.37	1	1.15	1
50	4.21	1	2.13	1	1.71	1	1.43	2
60	5.05	1	2.55	1	2.05	2	1.72	2
70	5.89	1	2.98	2	2.39	2	2.00	2
80	6.74	1	3.40	2	2.73	2	2.29	2
90	7.58	1	3.82	2	3.07	2	2.57	3
100	8.42	1	4.25	2	3.41	2	2.86	3
200	16.83	2	8.49	4	6.82	5	5.71	6
300	25.24	3	12.73	6	10.23	7	8.57	9
400	33.66	4	16.98	8	13.64	9	11.42	11
500	42.07	5	21.22	9	17.05	12	14.27	14
600	50.48	6	25.46	11	20.46	14	17.13	17
700	58.89	7	29.71	13	23.87	16	19.98	19
800	67.31	8	33.95	15	27.28	18	22.83	22
900	75.72	9	38.19	17	30.69	21	25.69	25
1,000	84.13	10	42.44	19	34.10	23	28.54	27
2,000	168.26	19	84.87	37	68.19	46	57.07	55
3,000	252.38	29	127.30	55	102.28	68	85.61	82
4,000	336.51	38	169.73	74	136.37	91	114.14	109
5,000	420.63	48	212.16	92	170.47	114	142.67	136
6,000	504.76	57	254.59	110	204.56	137	171.21	164
7,000	588.88	67	297.02	128	238.65	160	199.74	191
8,000	673.01	76	339.45	147	272.74	182	228.27	218
9,000	757.13	86	381.88	165	306.83	205	256.81	245
10,000	841.26	95	424.31	183	340.93	228	285.34	272
11,000	925.38	105	466.74	202	375.02	251	313.87	299
12,000	1,009.51	114	509.17	220	409.11	273	342.41	327
13,000	1,093.63	124	551.60	238	443.20	296	370.94	354
14,000	1,177.76	133	594.03	257	477.29	319	399.47	381
15,000	1,261.89	143	636.46	275	511.39	342	428.01	408
16,000	1,346.01	152	678.89	293	545.48	364	456.54	435
17,000	1,430.14	162	721.32	312	579.57	387	485.08	463
18,000	1,514.26	171	763.75	330	613.66	410	513.61	490
19,000	1,598.39	181	806.18	348	647.76	433	542.14	517
20,000	1,682.51	190	848.61	367	681.85	456	570.68	544
21,000	1,766.64	200	891.04	385	715.94	478	599.21	572
22,000	1,850.76	209	933.48	404	750.03	501	627.74	599
23,000	1,934.89	219	975.91	422	784.12	524	656.28	626
24,000	2,019.01	228	1,018.34	440	818.22	547	684.81	653
25,000	2,103.14	238	1,060.77	458	852.31	569	713.34	680
26,000	2,187.26	247	1,103.20	477	886.40	592	741.88	708
27,000	2,271.39	257	1,145.63	495	920.49	615	770.41	735
28,000	2,355.52	266	1,188.06	513	954.58	637	798.94	762
29,000	2,439.64	276	1,230.49	532	988.68	660	827.48	789
30,000	2,523.77	285	1,272.92	550	1,022.77	683	856.01	816
31,000	2,607.89	295	1,315.35	568	1,056.86	706	884.55	844
32,000	2,692.02	304	1,357.78	587	1,090.95	729	913.08	871
33,000	2,776.14	314	1,400.21	605	1,125.04	751	941.61	898
34,000	2,860.27	323	1,442.64	623	1,159.14	774	970.15	925
35,000	2,944.39	333	1,485.07	642	1,193.23	797	998.68	952
36,000	3,028.52	342	1,527.50	660	1,227.32	820	1,027.21	980
37,000	3,112.64	352	1,569.93	678	1,261.41	842	1,055.75	1,007
38,000	3,196.77	361	1,612.36	697	1,295.51	865	1,084.28	1,034
39,000	3,280.89	371	1,654.79	715	1,329.60	888	1,112.81	1,061
40,000	3,365.02	380	1,697.22	733	1,363.69	911	1,141.35	1,089
42,000	3,533.27	399	1,782.08	770	1,431.87	956	1,198.41	1,143
44,000	3,701.52	418	1,866.95	807	1,500.06	1,002	1,255.48	1,197
46,000	3,869.77	437	1,951.81	843	1,568.24	1,047	1,312.55	1,252
48,000	4,038.02	456	2,036.67	880	1,636.43	1,093	1,369.62	1,306
50,000	4,206.27	475	2,121.53	917	1,704.61	1,138	1,426.68	1,360

AUTO LOAN PAYMENTS 1.75%

AMOUNT OF LOAN	42 MOS		48 MOS		60 MOS		72 MOS	
	MONTHLY PAYMENT	TOTAL INTRST	MONTHLY PAYMENT	TOTAL INTRST	MONTHLY PAYMENT	TOTAL INTRST	MONTHLY PAYMENT	TOTAL INTRST
$ 1	0.03	0	0.03	0	0.02	0	0.02	0
2	0.05	0	0.05	0	0.04	0	0.03	0
3	0.08	0	0.07	0	0.06	1	0.05	1
4	0.10	0	0.09	0	0.07	0	0.06	0
5	0.13	0	0.11	0	0.09	0	0.08	1
6	0.15	0	0.13	0	0.11	1	0.09	0
7	0.18	1	0.16	1	0.13	1	0.11	1
8	0.20	0	0.18	1	0.14	0	0.12	1
9	0.23	1	0.20	1	0.16	1	0.14	1
10	0.25	1	0.22	1	0.18	1	0.15	1
20	0.50	1	0.44	1	0.35	1	0.30	2
30	0.74	1	0.65	1	0.53	2	0.44	2
40	0.99	2	0.87	2	0.70	2	0.59	2
50	1.23	2	1.08	2	0.88	3	0.74	3
60	1.48	2	1.30	2	1.05	3	0.88	3
70	1.72	2	1.52	3	1.22	3	1.03	4
80	1.97	3	1.73	3	1.40	4	1.18	5
90	2.22	3	1.95	4	1.57	4	1.32	5
100	2.46	3	2.16	4	1.75	5	1.47	6
200	4.92	7	4.32	7	3.49	9	2.93	11
300	7.37	10	6.48	11	5.23	14	4.40	17
400	9.83	13	8.64	15	6.97	18	5.86	22
500	12.29	16	10.80	18	8.71	23	7.33	28
600	14.74	19	12.96	22	10.46	28	8.79	33
700	17.20	22	15.12	26	12.20	32	10.25	38
800	19.66	26	17.27	29	13.94	36	11.72	44
900	22.11	29	19.43	33	15.68	41	13.18	49
1,000	24.57	32	21.59	36	17.42	45	14.65	55
2,000	49.13	63	43.18	73	34.84	90	29.29	109
3,000	73.70	95	64.76	108	52.26	136	43.93	163
4,000	98.26	127	86.35	145	69.68	181	58.57	217
5,000	122.82	158	107.94	181	87.10	226	73.21	271
6,000	147.39	190	129.52	217	104.52	271	87.85	325
7,000	171.95	222	151.11	253	121.94	316	102.49	379
8,000	196.51	253	172.69	289	139.35	361	117.13	433
9,000	221.08	285	194.28	325	156.77	406	131.77	487
10,000	245.64	317	215.87	362	174.19	451	146.41	542
11,000	270.20	348	237.45	398	191.61	497	161.06	596
12,000	294.77	380	259.04	434	209.03	542	175.70	650
13,000	319.33	412	280.63	470	226.45	587	190.34	704
14,000	343.89	443	302.21	506	243.87	632	204.98	759
15,000	368.46	475	323.80	542	261.28	677	219.62	813
16,000	393.02	507	345.38	578	278.70	722	234.26	867
17,000	417.58	538	366.97	615	296.12	767	248.90	921
18,000	442.15	570	388.56	651	313.54	812	263.54	975
19,000	466.71	602	410.14	687	330.96	857	278.18	1,029
20,000	491.27	633	431.73	723	348.38	903	292.82	1,083
21,000	515.84	665	453.31	759	365.80	948	307.46	1,137
22,000	540.40	697	474.90	795	383.21	993	322.11	1,192
23,000	564.97	729	496.49	832	400.63	1,038	336.75	1,246
24,000	589.53	760	518.07	867	418.05	1,083	351.39	1,300
25,000	614.09	792	539.66	904	435.47	1,128	366.03	1,354
26,000	638.66	824	561.25	940	452.89	1,173	380.67	1,408
27,000	663.22	855	582.83	976	470.31	1,219	395.31	1,462
28,000	687.78	887	604.42	1,012	487.73	1,264	409.95	1,516
29,000	712.35	919	626.00	1,048	505.14	1,308	424.59	1,570
30,000	736.91	950	647.59	1,084	522.56	1,354	439.23	1,625
31,000	761.47	982	669.18	1,121	539.98	1,399	453.87	1,679
32,000	786.04	1,014	690.76	1,156	557.40	1,444	468.51	1,733
33,000	810.60	1,045	712.35	1,193	574.82	1,489	483.16	1,788
34,000	835.16	1,077	733.94	1,229	592.24	1,534	497.80	1,842
35,000	859.73	1,109	755.52	1,265	609.66	1,580	512.44	1,896
36,000	884.29	1,140	777.11	1,301	627.07	1,624	527.08	1,950
37,000	908.85	1,172	798.69	1,337	644.49	1,669	541.72	2,004
38,000	933.42	1,204	820.28	1,373	661.91	1,715	556.36	2,058
39,000	957.98	1,235	841.87	1,410	679.33	1,760	571.00	2,112
40,000	982.54	1,267	863.45	1,446	696.75	1,805	585.64	2,166
42,000	1,031.67	1,330	906.62	1,518	731.59	1,895	614.92	2,274
44,000	1,080.80	1,394	949.80	1,590	766.42	1,985	644.21	2,383
46,000	1,129.93	1,457	992.97	1,663	801.26	2,076	673.49	2,491
48,000	1,179.05	1,520	1,036.14	1,735	836.10	2,166	702.77	2,599
50,000	1,228.18	1,584	1,079.31	1,807	870.94	2,256	732.05	2,708

1.90% AUTO LOAN PAYMENTS

AMOUNT OF LOAN	12 MOS		24 MOS		30 MOS		36 MOS	
	MONTHLY PAYMENT	TOTAL INTRST	MONTHLY PAYMENT	TOTAL INTRST	MONTHLY PAYMENT	TOTAL INTRST	MONTHLY PAYMENT	TOTAL INTRST
$ 1	0.09	0	0.05	0	0.04	0	0.03	0
2	0.17	0	0.09	0	0.07	0	0.06	0
3	0.26	0	0.13	0	0.11	0	0.09	0
4	0.34	0	0.17	0	0.14	0	0.12	0
5	0.43	0	0.22	0	0.18	0	0.15	0
6	0.51	0	0.26	0	0.21	0	0.18	0
7	0.59	0	0.30	0	0.24	0	0.21	1
8	0.68	0	0.34	0	0.28	0	0.23	0
9	0.76	0	0.39	0	0.31	0	0.26	0
10	0.85	0	0.43	0	0.35	1	0.29	1
20	1.69	0	0.85	0	0.69	1	0.58	1
30	2.53	0	1.28	1	1.03	1	0.86	1
40	3.37	0	1.70	1	1.37	1	1.15	1
50	4.21	1	2.13	1	1.71	1	1.43	2
60	5.06	1	2.55	1	2.05	2	1.72	2
70	5.90	1	2.98	2	2.40	2	2.01	2
80	6.74	1	3.40	2	2.74	2	2.29	2
90	7.58	1	3.83	2	3.08	2	2.58	3
100	8.42	1	4.25	2	3.42	3	2.86	3
200	16.84	2	8.50	4	6.84	5	5.72	6
300	25.26	3	12.75	6	10.25	8	8.58	9
400	33.68	4	17.00	8	13.67	10	11.44	12
500	42.10	5	21.25	10	17.08	12	14.30	15
600	50.52	6	25.50	12	20.50	15	17.16	18
700	58.94	7	29.75	14	23.92	18	20.02	21
800	67.36	8	34.00	16	27.33	20	22.88	24
900	75.78	9	38.25	18	30.75	23	25.74	27
1,000	84.20	10	42.50	20	34.16	25	28.60	30
2,000	168.39	21	85.00	40	68.32	50	57.20	59
3,000	252.59	31	127.49	60	102.48	74	85.80	89
4,000	336.78	41	169.99	80	136.64	99	114.40	118
5,000	420.97	52	212.49	100	170.79	124	143.00	148
6,000	505.17	62	254.98	120	204.95	149	171.60	178
7,000	589.36	72	297.48	140	239.11	173	200.20	207
8,000	673.55	83	339.98	160	273.27	198	228.80	237
9,000	757.75	93	382.47	179	307.42	223	257.40	266
10,000	841.94	103	424.97	199	341.58	247	285.99	296
11,000	926.13	114	467.46	219	375.74	272	314.59	325
12,000	1,010.33	124	509.96	239	409.90	297	343.19	355
13,000	1,094.52	134	552.46	259	444.05	322	371.79	384
14,000	1,178.71	145	594.95	279	478.21	346	400.39	414
15,000	1,262.91	155	637.45	299	512.37	371	428.99	444
16,000	1,347.10	165	679.95	319	546.53	396	457.59	473
17,000	1,431.29	175	722.44	339	580.68	420	486.19	503
18,000	1,515.49	186	764.94	359	614.84	445	514.79	532
19,000	1,599.68	196	807.44	379	649.00	470	543.38	562
20,000	1,683.87	206	849.93	398	683.16	495	571.98	591
21,000	1,768.07	217	892.43	418	717.32	520	600.58	621
22,000	1,852.26	227	934.92	438	751.47	544	629.18	650
23,000	1,936.45	237	977.42	458	785.63	569	657.78	680
24,000	2,020.65	248	1,019.92	478	819.79	594	686.38	710
25,000	2,104.84	258	1,062.41	498	853.95	619	714.98	739
26,000	2,189.03	268	1,104.91	518	888.10	643	743.58	769
27,000	2,273.23	279	1,147.41	538	922.26	668	772.18	798
28,000	2,357.42	289	1,189.90	558	956.42	693	800.78	828
29,000	2,441.62	299	1,232.40	578	990.58	717	829.37	857
30,000	2,525.81	310	1,274.89	597	1,024.73	742	857.97	887
31,000	2,610.00	320	1,317.39	617	1,058.89	767	886.57	917
32,000	2,694.20	330	1,359.89	637	1,093.05	792	915.17	946
33,000	2,778.39	341	1,402.38	657	1,127.21	816	943.77	976
34,000	2,862.58	351	1,444.88	677	1,161.36	841	972.37	1,005
35,000	2,946.78	361	1,487.38	697	1,195.52	866	1,000.97	1,035
36,000	3,030.97	372	1,529.87	717	1,229.68	890	1,029.57	1,065
37,000	3,115.16	382	1,572.37	737	1,263.84	915	1,058.17	1,094
38,000	3,199.36	392	1,614.87	757	1,298.00	940	1,086.76	1,123
39,000	3,283.55	403	1,657.36	777	1,332.15	965	1,115.36	1,153
40,000	3,367.74	413	1,699.86	797	1,366.31	989	1,143.96	1,183
42,000	3,536.13	434	1,784.85	836	1,434.63	1,039	1,201.16	1,242
44,000	3,704.52	454	1,869.84	876	1,502.94	1,088	1,258.36	1,301
46,000	3,872.90	475	1,954.84	916	1,571.26	1,138	1,315.56	1,360
48,000	4,041.29	495	2,039.83	956	1,639.57	1,187	1,372.75	1,419
50,000	4,209.68	516	2,124.82	996	1,707.89	1,237	1,429.95	1,478

AUTO LOAN PAYMENTS 1.90%

AMOUNT OF LOAN	42 MOS		48 MOS		60 MOS		72 MOS	
	MONTHLY PAYMENT	TOTAL INTRST	MONTHLY PAYMENT	TOTAL INTRST	MONTHLY PAYMENT	TOTAL INTRST	MONTHLY PAYMENT	TOTAL INTRST
$ 1	0.03	0	0.03	0	0.02	0	0.02	0
2	0.05	0	0.05	0	0.04	0	0.03	0
3	0.08	0	0.07	0	0.06	1	0.05	1
4	0.10	0	0.09	0	0.07	0	0.06	0
5	0.13	0	0.11	0	0.09	0	0.08	1
6	0.15	0	0.13	0	0.11	1	0.09	0
7	0.18	1	0.16	1	0.13	1	0.11	1
8	0.20	1	0.18	1	0.14	0	0.12	1
9	0.23	1	0.20	1	0.16	1	0.14	1
10	0.25	1	0.22	1	0.18	1	0.15	1
20	0.50	1	0.44	1	0.35	1	0.30	2
30	0.74	1	0.65	1	0.53	2	0.45	2
40	0.99	2	0.87	2	0.70	2	0.59	2
50	1.24	2	1.09	2	0.88	3	0.74	3
60	1.48	2	1.30	2	1.05	3	0.89	4
70	1.73	3	1.52	3	1.23	4	1.03	4
80	1.98	3	1.74	4	1.40	4	1.18	5
90	2.22	3	1.95	4	1.58	5	1.33	6
100	2.47	4	2.17	4	1.75	5	1.48	7
200	4.93	7	4.34	8	3.50	10	2.95	12
300	7.39	10	6.50	12	5.25	15	4.42	18
400	9.86	14	8.67	16	7.00	20	5.89	24
500	12.32	17	10.83	20	8.75	25	7.36	30
600	14.78	21	13.00	24	10.50	30	8.83	36
700	17.25	25	15.16	28	12.24	34	10.30	42
800	19.71	28	17.33	32	13.99	39	11.77	47
900	22.17	31	19.49	36	15.74	44	13.24	53
1,000	24.63	34	21.66	40	17.49	49	14.71	59
2,000	49.26	69	43.31	79	34.97	98	29.42	118
3,000	73.89	103	64.96	118	52.46	148	44.12	177
4,000	98.52	138	86.61	157	69.94	196	58.83	236
5,000	123.15	172	108.26	196	87.43	246	73.54	295
6,000	147.78	207	129.91	236	104.91	295	88.24	353
7,000	172.41	241	151.57	275	122.39	343	102.95	412
8,000	197.04	276	173.22	315	139.88	393	117.66	472
9,000	221.66	310	194.87	354	157.36	442	132.36	530
10,000	246.29	344	216.52	393	174.85	491	147.07	589
11,000	270.92	379	238.17	432	192.33	540	161.78	648
12,000	295.55	413	259.82	471	209.81	589	176.48	707
13,000	320.18	448	281.47	511	227.30	638	191.19	766
14,000	344.81	482	303.13	550	244.78	687	205.90	825
15,000	369.44	516	324.78	589	262.27	736	220.60	883
16,000	394.07	551	346.43	629	279.75	785	235.31	942
17,000	418.69	585	368.08	668	297.23	834	250.02	1,001
18,000	443.32	619	389.73	707	314.72	883	264.72	1,060
19,000	467.95	654	411.38	746	332.20	932	279.43	1,119
20,000	492.58	688	433.04	786	349.69	981	294.14	1,178
21,000	517.21	723	454.69	825	367.17	1,030	308.84	1,236
22,000	541.84	757	476.34	864	384.65	1,079	323.55	1,296
23,000	566.47	792	497.99	904	402.14	1,128	338.26	1,355
24,000	591.10	826	519.64	943	419.62	1,177	352.96	1,413
25,000	615.73	861	541.29	982	437.11	1,227	367.67	1,472
26,000	640.35	895	562.94	1,021	454.59	1,275	382.38	1,531
27,000	664.98	929	584.60	1,061	472.07	1,324	397.08	1,590
28,000	689.61	964	606.25	1,100	489.56	1,374	411.79	1,649
29,000	714.24	998	627.90	1,139	507.04	1,422	426.50	1,708
30,000	738.87	1,033	649.55	1,178	524.53	1,472	441.20	1,766
31,000	763.50	1,067	671.20	1,218	542.01	1,521	455.91	1,826
32,000	788.13	1,101	692.85	1,257	559.49	1,569	470.62	1,885
33,000	812.76	1,136	714.50	1,296	576.98	1,619	485.32	1,943
34,000	837.38	1,170	736.16	1,336	594.46	1,668	500.03	2,002
35,000	862.01	1,204	757.81	1,375	611.95	1,717	514.74	2,061
36,000	886.64	1,239	779.46	1,414	629.43	1,766	529.44	2,120
37,000	911.27	1,273	801.11	1,453	646.91	1,815	544.15	2,179
38,000	935.90	1,308	822.76	1,492	664.40	1,864	558.85	2,237
39,000	960.53	1,342	844.41	1,532	681.88	1,913	573.56	2,296
40,000	985.16	1,377	866.07	1,571	699.37	1,962	588.27	2,355
42,000	1,034.41	1,445	909.37	1,650	734.33	2,060	617.68	2,473
44,000	1,083.67	1,514	952.67	1,728	769.30	2,158	647.09	2,590
46,000	1,132.93	1,583	995.97	1,807	804.27	2,256	676.51	2,709
48,000	1,182.19	1,652	1,039.28	1,885	839.24	2,354	705.92	2,826
50,000	1,231.45	1,721	1,082.58	1,964	874.21	2,453	735.33	2,944

AUTO LOAN PAYMENTS

AMOUNT OF LOAN	12 MOS MONTHLY PAYMENT	12 MOS TOTAL INTRST	24 MOS MONTHLY PAYMENT	24 MOS TOTAL INTRST	30 MOS MONTHLY PAYMENT	30 MOS TOTAL INTRST	36 MOS MONTHLY PAYMENT	36 MOS TOTAL INTRST
$ 1	0.09	0	0.05	0	0.04	0	0.03	0
2	0.17	0	0.09	0	0.07	0	0.06	0
3	0.26	0	0.13	0	0.11	0	0.09	0
4	0.34	0	0.18	0	0.14	0	0.12	0
5	0.43	0	0.22	0	0.18	0	0.15	0
6	0.51	0	0.26	0	0.21	0	0.18	0
7	0.59	0	0.30	0	0.24	0	0.21	1
8	0.68	0	0.35	0	0.28	0	0.23	0
9	0.76	0	0.39	0	0.31	0	0.26	0
10	0.85	0	0.43	0	0.35	1	0.29	0
20	1.69	0	0.86	1	0.69	1	0.58	1
30	2.53	0	1.28	1	1.03	1	0.86	1
40	3.37	0	1.71	1	1.37	1	1.15	1
50	4.22	1	2.13	1	1.72	1	1.44	2
60	5.06	1	2.56	1	2.06	2	1.72	2
70	5.90	1	2.98	2	2.40	2	2.01	2
80	6.74	1	3.41	2	2.74	2	2.30	2
90	7.59	1	3.83	2	3.08	2	2.58	3
100	8.43	1	4.26	2	3.43	3	2.87	3
200	16.85	2	8.51	4	6.85	6	5.73	6
300	25.28	3	12.77	6	10.27	8	8.60	10
400	33.70	4	17.02	8	13.69	11	11.46	13
500	42.12	5	21.28	11	17.11	13	14.33	16
600	50.55	7	25.53	13	20.53	16	17.19	19
700	58.97	8	29.78	15	23.95	19	20.05	22
800	67.40	9	34.04	17	27.37	21	22.92	25
900	75.82	10	38.29	19	30.79	24	25.78	28
1,000	84.24	11	42.55	21	34.21	26	28.65	31
2,000	168.48	22	85.09	42	68.41	52	57.29	62
3,000	252.72	33	127.63	63	102.61	78	85.93	93
4,000	336.96	44	170.17	84	136.81	104	114.58	125
5,000	421.20	54	212.71	105	171.01	130	143.22	156
6,000	505.44	65	255.25	126	205.21	156	171.86	187
7,000	589.68	76	297.79	147	239.41	182	200.50	218
8,000	673.92	87	340.33	168	273.62	209	229.15	249
9,000	758.15	98	382.87	189	307.82	235	257.79	280
10,000	842.39	109	425.41	210	342.02	261	286.43	311
11,000	926.63	120	467.95	231	376.22	287	315.07	343
12,000	1,010.87	130	510.49	252	410.42	313	343.72	374
13,000	1,095.11	141	553.03	273	444.62	339	372.36	405
14,000	1,179.35	152	595.57	294	478.82	365	401.00	436
15,000	1,263.59	163	638.11	315	513.03	391	429.64	467
16,000	1,347.83	174	680.65	336	547.23	417	458.29	498
17,000	1,432.07	185	723.19	357	581.43	443	486.93	529
18,000	1,516.30	196	765.73	378	615.63	469	515.57	561
19,000	1,600.54	206	808.27	398	649.83	495	544.21	592
20,000	1,684.78	217	850.81	419	684.03	521	572.86	623
21,000	1,769.02	228	893.35	440	718.23	547	601.50	654
22,000	1,853.26	239	935.89	461	752.44	573	630.14	685
23,000	1,937.50	250	978.43	482	786.64	599	658.78	716
24,000	2,021.74	261	1,020.97	503	820.84	625	687.43	747
25,000	2,105.98	272	1,063.51	524	855.04	651	716.07	779
26,000	2,190.22	283	1,106.05	545	889.24	677	744.71	810
27,000	2,274.45	293	1,148.59	566	923.44	703	773.35	841
28,000	2,358.69	304	1,191.13	587	957.64	729	802.00	872
29,000	2,442.93	315	1,233.67	608	991.84	755	830.64	903
30,000	2,527.17	326	1,276.21	629	1,026.05	782	859.28	934
31,000	2,611.41	337	1,318.75	650	1,060.25	808	887.92	965
32,000	2,695.65	348	1,361.29	671	1,094.45	834	916.57	997
33,000	2,779.89	359	1,403.83	692	1,128.65	860	945.21	1,028
34,000	2,864.13	370	1,446.37	713	1,162.85	886	973.85	1,059
35,000	2,948.37	380	1,488.91	734	1,197.05	912	1,002.50	1,090
36,000	3,032.60	391	1,531.45	755	1,231.25	938	1,031.14	1,121
37,000	3,116.84	402	1,573.99	776	1,265.46	964	1,059.78	1,152
38,000	3,201.08	413	1,616.54	797	1,299.66	990	1,088.42	1,183
39,000	3,285.32	424	1,659.08	818	1,333.86	1,016	1,117.07	1,215
40,000	3,369.56	435	1,701.62	839	1,368.06	1,042	1,145.71	1,246
42,000	3,538.04	456	1,786.70	881	1,436.46	1,094	1,202.99	1,308
44,000	3,706.52	478	1,871.78	923	1,504.87	1,146	1,260.28	1,370
46,000	3,874.99	500	1,956.86	965	1,573.27	1,198	1,317.56	1,432
48,000	4,043.47	522	2,041.94	1,007	1,641.67	1,250	1,374.85	1,495
50,000	4,211.95	543	2,127.02	1,048	1,710.07	1,302	1,432.13	1,557

AUTO LOAN PAYMENTS 2.00%

AMOUNT OF LOAN	42 MOS		48 MOS		60 MOS		72 MOS	
	MONTHLY PAYMENT	TOTAL INTRST	MONTHLY PAYMENT	TOTAL INTRST	MONTHLY PAYMENT	TOTAL INTRST	MONTHLY PAYMENT	TOTAL INTRST
$ 1	0.03	0	0.03	0	0.02	0	0.02	0
2	0.05	0	0.05	0	0.04	0	0.03	0
3	0.08	0	0.07	0	0.06	1	0.05	1
4	0.10	0	0.09	0	0.08	1	0.06	1
5	0.13	0	0.11	0	0.09	0	0.08	1
6	0.15	0	0.14	1	0.11	1	0.09	0
7	0.18	1	0.16	1	0.13	1	0.11	1
8	0.20	0	0.18	1	0.15	1	0.12	1
9	0.23	1	0.20	1	0.16	1	0.14	1
10	0.25	1	0.22	1	0.18	1	0.15	1
20	0.50	1	0.44	1	0.36	2	0.30	2
30	0.75	2	0.66	2	0.53	2	0.45	2
40	0.99	2	0.87	2	0.71	3	0.60	3
50	1.24	2	1.09	2	0.88	3	0.74	4
60	1.49	3	1.31	3	1.06	4	0.89	4
70	1.73	3	1.52	3	1.23	4	1.04	5
80	1.98	3	1.74	4	1.41	5	1.19	6
90	2.23	4	1.96	4	1.58	5	1.33	6
100	2.47	4	2.17	4	1.76	6	1.48	7
200	4.94	7	4.34	8	3.51	11	2.96	13
300	7.41	11	6.51	12	5.26	16	4.43	19
400	9.87	15	8.68	17	7.02	21	5.91	26
500	12.34	18	10.85	21	8.77	26	7.38	31
600	14.81	22	13.02	25	10.52	31	8.86	38
700	17.28	26	15.19	29	12.27	36	10.33	44
800	19.74	29	17.36	33	14.03	42	11.81	50
900	22.21	33	19.53	37	15.78	47	13.28	56
1,000	24.68	37	21.70	42	17.53	52	14.76	63
2,000	49.35	73	43.40	83	35.06	104	29.51	125
3,000	74.02	109	65.09	124	52.59	155	44.26	187
4,000	98.69	145	86.79	166	70.12	207	59.01	249
5,000	123.37	182	108.48	207	87.64	258	73.76	311
6,000	148.04	218	130.18	249	105.17	310	88.51	373
7,000	172.71	254	151.87	290	122.70	362	103.26	435
8,000	197.38	290	173.57	331	140.23	414	118.01	497
9,000	222.06	327	195.26	372	157.79	465	132.76	559
10,000	246.73	363	216.96	414	175.28	517	147.51	621
11,000	271.40	399	238.65	455	192.81	569	162.26	683
12,000	296.07	435	260.35	497	210.34	620	177.01	745
13,000	320.75	472	282.04	538	227.87	672	191.76	807
14,000	345.42	508	303.74	580	245.39	723	206.51	869
15,000	370.09	544	325.43	621	262.92	775	221.26	931
16,000	394.76	580	347.13	662	280.45	827	236.01	993
17,000	419.44	616	368.82	703	297.98	879	250.76	1,055
18,000	444.11	653	390.52	745	315.50	930	265.51	1,117
19,000	468.78	689	412.21	786	333.03	982	280.26	1,179
20,000	493.45	725	433.91	828	350.56	1,034	295.01	1,241
21,000	518.13	761	455.60	869	368.09	1,085	309.76	1,303
22,000	542.80	798	477.30	910	385.62	1,137	324.51	1,365
23,000	567.47	834	498.99	952	403.14	1,188	339.27	1,427
24,000	592.14	870	520.69	993	420.67	1,240	354.02	1,489
25,000	616.82	906	542.38	1,034	438.20	1,292	368.77	1,551
26,000	641.49	943	564.08	1,076	455.73	1,344	383.52	1,613
27,000	666.16	979	585.77	1,117	473.25	1,395	398.27	1,675
28,000	690.83	1,015	607.47	1,159	490.78	1,447	413.02	1,737
29,000	715.50	1,051	629.16	1,200	508.31	1,499	427.77	1,799
30,000	740.18	1,088	650.86	1,241	525.84	1,550	442.52	1,861
31,000	764.85	1,124	672.55	1,282	543.37	1,602	457.27	1,923
32,000	789.52	1,160	694.25	1,324	560.89	1,653	472.02	1,985
33,000	814.19	1,196	715.94	1,365	578.42	1,705	486.77	2,047
34,000	838.87	1,233	737.64	1,407	595.95	1,757	501.52	2,109
35,000	863.54	1,269	759.33	1,448	613.48	1,809	516.27	2,171
36,000	888.21	1,305	781.03	1,489	631.00	1,860	531.02	2,233
37,000	912.88	1,341	802.72	1,531	648.53	1,912	545.77	2,295
38,000	937.56	1,378	824.42	1,572	666.06	1,964	560.52	2,357
39,000	962.23	1,414	846.11	1,613	683.59	2,015	575.27	2,419
40,000	986.90	1,450	867.81	1,655	701.12	2,067	590.02	2,481
42,000	1,036.25	1,523	911.20	1,738	736.17	2,170	619.52	2,605
44,000	1,085.59	1,595	954.59	1,820	771.23	2,274	649.02	2,729
46,000	1,134.94	1,667	997.98	1,903	806.28	2,377	678.53	2,854
48,000	1,184.28	1,740	1,041.37	1,986	841.34	2,480	708.03	2,978
50,000	1,233.63	1,812	1,084.76	2,068	876.39	2,583	737.53	3,102

25

2.25%   AUTO LOAN PAYMENTS

AMOUNT OF LOAN	12 MOS MONTHLY PAYMENT	12 MOS TOTAL INTRST	24 MOS MONTHLY PAYMENT	24 MOS TOTAL INTRST	30 MOS MONTHLY PAYMENT	30 MOS TOTAL INTRST	36 MOS MONTHLY PAYMENT	36 MOS TOTAL INTRST
$ 1	0.09	0	0.05	0	0.04	0	0.03	0
2	0.17	0	0.09	0	0.07	0	0.06	0
3	0.26	0	0.13	0	0.11	0	0.09	0
4	0.34	0	0.18	0	0.14	0	0.12	0
5	0.43	0	0.22	0	0.18	0	0.15	0
6	0.51	0	0.26	0	0.21	0	0.18	0
7	0.60	0	0.30	0	0.25	1	0.21	1
8	0.68	0	0.35	0	0.28	1	0.24	1
9	0.76	0	0.39	0	0.31	0	0.26	0
10	0.85	0	0.43	0	0.35	1	0.29	1
20	1.69	0	0.86	1	0.69	1	0.58	1
30	2.54	1	1.28	1	1.03	1	0.87	1
40	3.38	1	1.71	1	1.38	1	1.16	2
50	4.22	1	2.14	1	1.72	2	1.44	2
60	5.07	1	2.56	1	2.06	2	1.73	2
70	5.91	1	2.99	2	2.41	2	2.02	3
80	6.75	1	3.42	2	2.75	3	2.31	3
90	7.60	1	3.84	2	3.09	3	2.59	3
100	8.44	1	4.27	2	3.44	3	2.88	4
200	16.88	3	8.54	5	6.87	6	5.76	7
300	25.31	4	12.80	7	10.30	9	8.63	11
400	33.75	5	17.07	10	13.73	12	11.51	14
500	42.18	6	21.33	12	17.16	15	14.38	18
600	50.62	7	25.60	14	20.59	18	17.26	21
700	59.05	9	29.86	17	24.02	21	20.13	25
800	67.49	10	34.13	19	27.45	24	23.01	28
900	75.92	11	38.39	21	30.88	26	25.88	32
1,000	84.36	12	42.66	24	34.32	30	28.76	35
2,000	168.71	25	85.31	47	68.63	59	57.51	70
3,000	253.06	37	127.96	71	102.94	88	86.26	105
4,000	337.41	49	170.61	95	137.25	118	115.01	140
5,000	421.77	61	213.26	118	171.56	147	143.76	175
6,000	506.12	73	255.91	142	205.87	176	172.52	211
7,000	590.47	86	298.56	165	240.18	205	201.27	246
8,000	674.82	98	341.21	189	274.49	235	230.02	281
9,000	759.18	110	383.86	213	308.80	264	258.77	316
10,000	843.53	122	426.51	236	343.11	293	287.52	351
11,000	927.88	135	469.16	260	377.42	323	316.28	386
12,000	1,012.23	147	511.81	283	411.74	352	345.03	421
13,000	1,096.59	159	554.46	307	446.05	382	373.78	456
14,000	1,180.94	171	597.11	331	480.36	411	402.53	491
15,000	1,265.29	183	639.76	354	514.67	440	431.28	526
16,000	1,349.64	196	682.41	378	548.98	469	460.03	561
17,000	1,434.00	208	725.06	401	583.29	499	488.79	596
18,000	1,518.35	220	767.71	425	617.60	528	517.54	631
19,000	1,602.70	232	810.36	449	651.91	557	546.29	666
20,000	1,687.05	245	853.01	472	686.22	587	575.04	701
21,000	1,771.41	257	895.66	496	720.53	616	603.79	736
22,000	1,855.76	269	938.31	519	754.84	645	632.55	772
23,000	1,940.11	281	980.96	543	789.15	675	661.30	807
24,000	2,024.46	294	1,023.61	567	823.47	704	690.05	842
25,000	2,108.82	306	1,066.26	590	857.78	733	718.80	877
26,000	2,193.17	318	1,108.91	614	892.09	763	747.55	912
27,000	2,277.52	330	1,151.56	637	926.40	792	776.30	947
28,000	2,361.87	342	1,194.21	661	960.71	821	805.06	982
29,000	2,446.23	355	1,236.86	685	995.02	851	833.81	1,017
30,000	2,530.58	367	1,279.51	708	1,029.33	880	862.56	1,052
31,000	2,614.93	379	1,322.16	732	1,063.64	909	891.31	1,087
32,000	2,699.28	391	1,364.81	755	1,097.95	939	920.06	1,122
33,000	2,783.64	404	1,407.46	779	1,132.26	968	948.82	1,158
34,000	2,867.99	416	1,450.11	803	1,166.57	997	977.57	1,193
35,000	2,952.34	428	1,492.76	826	1,200.88	1,026	1,006.32	1,228
36,000	3,036.69	440	1,535.41	850	1,235.20	1,056	1,035.07	1,263
37,000	3,121.05	453	1,578.06	873	1,269.51	1,085	1,063.82	1,298
38,000	3,205.40	465	1,620.71	897	1,303.82	1,115	1,092.58	1,333
39,000	3,289.75	477	1,663.36	921	1,338.13	1,144	1,121.33	1,368
40,000	3,374.10	489	1,706.01	944	1,372.44	1,173	1,150.08	1,403
42,000	3,542.81	514	1,791.32	992	1,441.06	1,232	1,207.58	1,473
44,000	3,711.51	538	1,876.62	1,039	1,509.68	1,290	1,265.09	1,543
46,000	3,880.22	563	1,961.92	1,086	1,578.30	1,349	1,322.59	1,613
48,000	4,048.92	587	2,047.22	1,133	1,646.93	1,408	1,380.09	1,683
50,000	4,217.63	612	2,132.52	1,180	1,715.55	1,467	1,437.60	1,754

26

AUTO LOAN PAYMENTS 2.25%

AMOUNT OF LOAN	42 MOS MONTHLY PAYMENT	42 MOS TOTAL INTRST	48 MOS MONTHLY PAYMENT	48 MOS TOTAL INTRST	60 MOS MONTHLY PAYMENT	60 MOS TOTAL INTRST	72 MOS MONTHLY PAYMENT	72 MOS TOTAL INTRST
$ 1	0.03	0	0.03	0	0.02	0	0.02	0
2	0.05	0	0.05	0	0.04	0	0.03	0
3	0.08	0	0.07	0	0.06	0	0.05	1
4	0.10	0	0.09	0	0.08	1	0.06	0
5	0.13	0	0.11	0	0.09	0	0.08	1
6	0.15	0	0.14	1	0.11	1	0.09	1
7	0.18	1	0.16	1	0.13	1	0.11	1
8	0.20	1	0.18	1	0.15	1	0.12	1
9	0.23	1	0.20	1	0.16	1	0.14	1
10	0.25	1	0.22	1	0.18	1	0.15	1
20	0.50	1	0.44	1	0.36	2	0.30	2
30	0.75	2	0.66	2	0.53	2	0.45	2
40	1.00	2	0.88	2	0.71	3	0.60	3
50	1.24	2	1.10	3	0.89	3	0.75	4
60	1.49	3	1.31	3	1.06	4	0.90	5
70	1.74	3	1.53	3	1.24	4	1.05	6
80	1.99	4	1.75	4	1.42	5	1.19	6
90	2.24	4	1.97	5	1.59	5	1.34	6
100	2.48	4	2.19	5	1.77	6	1.49	7
200	4.96	8	4.37	10	3.53	12	2.98	15
300	7.44	12	6.55	14	5.30	18	4.46	21
400	9.92	17	8.73	19	7.06	24	5.95	28
500	12.40	21	10.91	24	8.82	29	7.44	36
600	14.87	25	13.09	28	10.59	35	8.92	42
700	17.35	29	15.27	33	12.35	41	10.41	50
800	19.83	33	17.45	38	14.11	47	11.89	56
900	22.31	37	19.63	42	15.88	53	13.38	63
1,000	24.79	41	21.81	47	17.64	58	14.87	71
2,000	49.57	82	43.61	93	35.28	117	29.73	141
3,000	74.35	123	65.42	140	52.92	175	44.59	210
4,000	99.13	163	87.22	187	70.55	233	59.45	280
5,000	123.91	204	109.03	233	88.19	291	74.31	350
6,000	148.69	245	130.83	280	105.83	350	89.17	420
7,000	173.48	286	152.64	327	123.47	408	104.03	490
8,000	198.26	327	174.44	373	141.10	466	118.89	560
9,000	223.04	368	196.24	420	158.74	524	133.75	630
10,000	247.82	408	218.05	466	176.38	583	148.61	700
11,000	272.60	449	239.85	513	194.02	641	163.47	770
12,000	297.38	490	261.66	560	211.65	699	178.33	840
13,000	322.17	531	283.46	606	229.29	757	193.19	910
14,000	346.95	572	305.27	653	246.93	816	208.05	980
15,000	371.73	613	327.07	699	264.57	874	222.91	1,050
16,000	396.51	653	348.88	746	282.20	932	237.77	1,119
17,000	421.29	694	370.68	793	299.84	990	252.63	1,189
18,000	446.07	735	392.48	839	317.48	1,049	267.49	1,259
19,000	470.86	776	414.29	886	335.11	1,107	282.35	1,329
20,000	495.64	817	436.09	932	352.75	1,165	297.21	1,399
21,000	520.42	858	457.90	979	370.39	1,223	312.07	1,469
22,000	545.20	898	479.70	1,026	388.03	1,282	326.94	1,540
23,000	569.98	939	501.51	1,072	405.66	1,340	341.80	1,610
24,000	594.76	980	523.31	1,119	423.30	1,398	356.66	1,680
25,000	619.55	1,021	545.12	1,166	440.94	1,456	371.52	1,749
26,000	644.33	1,062	566.92	1,212	458.58	1,515	386.38	1,819
27,000	669.11	1,103	588.72	1,259	476.21	1,573	401.24	1,889
28,000	693.89	1,143	610.53	1,305	493.85	1,631	416.10	1,959
29,000	718.67	1,184	632.33	1,352	511.49	1,689	430.96	2,029
30,000	743.45	1,225	654.14	1,399	529.13	1,748	445.82	2,099
31,000	768.24	1,266	675.94	1,445	546.76	1,806	460.68	2,169
32,000	793.02	1,307	697.75	1,492	564.40	1,864	475.54	2,239
33,000	817.80	1,348	719.55	1,538	582.04	1,922	490.40	2,309
34,000	842.58	1,388	741.35	1,585	599.67	1,980	505.26	2,379
35,000	867.36	1,429	763.16	1,632	617.31	2,039	520.12	2,449
36,000	892.14	1,470	784.96	1,678	634.95	2,097	534.98	2,519
37,000	916.93	1,511	806.77	1,725	652.59	2,155	549.84	2,588
38,000	941.71	1,552	828.57	1,771	670.22	2,213	564.70	2,658
39,000	966.49	1,593	850.38	1,818	687.86	2,272	579.56	2,728
40,000	991.27	1,633	872.18	1,865	705.50	2,330	594.42	2,798
42,000	1,040.83	1,715	915.79	1,958	740.77	2,446	624.14	2,938
44,000	1,090.40	1,797	959.40	2,051	776.05	2,563	653.87	3,079
46,000	1,139.96	1,878	1,003.01	2,144	811.32	2,679	683.59	3,218
48,000	1,189.52	1,960	1,046.62	2,238	846.60	2,796	713.31	3,358
50,000	1,239.09	2,042	1,090.23	2,331	881.87	2,912	743.03	3,498

AUTO LOAN PAYMENTS

AMOUNT OF LOAN	12 MOS		24 MOS		30 MOS		36 MOS	
	MONTHLY PAYMENT	TOTAL INTRST	MONTHLY PAYMENT	TOTAL INTRST	MONTHLY PAYMENT	TOTAL INTRST	MONTHLY PAYMENT	TOTAL INTRST
$ 1	0.09	0	0.05	0	0.04	0	0.03	0
2	0.17	0	0.09	0	0.07	0	0.06	0
3	0.26	0	0.13	0	0.11	0	0.09	0
4	0.34	0	0.18	0	0.14	0	0.12	0
5	0.43	0	0.22	0	0.18	0	0.15	0
6	0.51	0	0.26	0	0.21	0	0.18	0
7	0.60	0	0.30	0	0.25	1	0.21	1
8	0.68	0	0.35	0	0.28	0	0.24	1
9	0.77	0	0.39	0	0.31	0	0.26	0
10	0.85	0	0.43	0	0.35	1	0.29	0
20	1.69	0	0.86	1	0.69	1	0.58	1
30	2.54	0	1.29	1	1.04	1	0.87	1
40	3.38	1	1.72	1	1.38	1	1.16	2
50	4.23	1	2.14	1	1.73	2	1.45	2
60	5.07	1	2.57	2	2.07	2	1.74	3
70	5.92	1	3.00	2	2.41	2	2.03	3
80	6.76	1	3.43	2	2.76	3	2.31	3
90	7.61	1	3.85	2	3.10	3	2.60	4
100	8.45	1	4.28	3	3.45	4	2.89	4
200	16.90	3	8.56	5	6.89	7	5.78	8
300	25.34	4	12.83	8	10.33	10	8.66	12
400	33.79	5	17.11	11	13.77	13	11.55	16
500	42.24	7	21.39	13	17.22	17	14.44	20
600	50.68	8	25.66	16	20.66	20	17.32	24
700	59.13	10	29.94	19	24.10	23	20.21	28
800	67.58	11	34.21	21	27.54	26	23.09	31
900	76.02	12	38.49	24	30.98	29	25.98	35
1,000	84.47	14	42.77	26	34.43	33	28.87	39
2,000	168.94	27	85.53	53	68.85	66	57.73	78
3,000	253.40	41	128.29	79	103.27	98	86.59	117
4,000	337.87	54	171.05	105	137.69	131	115.45	156
5,000	422.34	68	213.81	131	172.11	163	144.31	195
6,000	506.80	82	256.57	158	206.53	196	173.17	234
7,000	591.27	95	299.33	184	240.95	229	202.03	273
8,000	675.73	109	342.09	210	275.37	261	230.90	312
9,000	760.20	122	384.85	236	309.79	294	259.76	351
10,000	844.67	136	427.61	263	344.21	326	288.62	390
11,000	929.13	150	470.37	289	378.63	359	317.48	429
12,000	1,013.60	163	513.13	315	413.05	392	346.34	468
13,000	1,098.06	177	555.89	341	447.47	424	375.20	507
14,000	1,182.53	190	598.65	368	481.89	457	404.06	546
15,000	1,267.00	204	641.41	394	516.31	489	432.93	585
16,000	1,351.46	218	684.17	420	550.73	522	461.79	624
17,000	1,435.93	231	726.93	446	585.15	555	490.65	663
18,000	1,520.40	245	769.69	473	619.57	587	519.51	702
19,000	1,604.86	258	812.45	499	654.00	620	548.37	741
20,000	1,689.33	272	855.21	525	688.42	653	577.23	780
21,000	1,773.79	285	897.97	551	722.84	685	606.09	819
22,000	1,858.26	299	940.73	578	757.26	718	634.96	859
23,000	1,942.73	313	983.49	604	791.68	750	663.82	898
24,000	2,027.19	326	1,026.25	630	826.10	783	692.68	936
25,000	2,111.66	340	1,069.01	656	860.52	816	721.54	975
26,000	2,196.12	353	1,111.78	683	894.94	848	750.40	1,014
27,000	2,280.59	367	1,154.54	709	929.36	881	779.26	1,053
28,000	2,365.06	381	1,197.30	735	963.78	913	808.12	1,092
29,000	2,449.52	394	1,240.06	761	998.20	946	836.98	1,131
30,000	2,533.99	408	1,282.82	788	1,032.62	979	865.85	1,171
31,000	2,618.45	421	1,325.58	814	1,067.04	1,011	894.71	1,210
32,000	2,702.92	435	1,368.34	840	1,101.46	1,044	923.57	1,249
33,000	2,787.39	449	1,411.10	866	1,135.88	1,076	952.43	1,287
34,000	2,871.85	462	1,453.86	893	1,170.30	1,109	981.29	1,326
35,000	2,956.32	476	1,496.62	919	1,204.72	1,142	1,010.15	1,365
36,000	3,040.78	489	1,539.38	945	1,239.14	1,174	1,039.01	1,404
37,000	3,125.25	503	1,582.14	971	1,273.57	1,207	1,067.88	1,444
38,000	3,209.72	517	1,624.90	998	1,307.99	1,240	1,096.74	1,483
39,000	3,294.18	530	1,667.66	1,024	1,342.41	1,272	1,125.60	1,522
40,000	3,378.65	544	1,710.42	1,050	1,376.83	1,305	1,154.46	1,561
42,000	3,547.58	571	1,795.94	1,103	1,445.67	1,370	1,212.18	1,638
44,000	3,716.51	598	1,881.46	1,155	1,514.51	1,435	1,269.91	1,717
46,000	3,885.45	625	1,966.98	1,208	1,583.35	1,501	1,327.63	1,795
48,000	4,054.38	653	2,052.50	1,260	1,652.19	1,566	1,385.35	1,873
50,000	4,223.31	680	2,138.02	1,312	1,721.03	1,631	1,443.07	1,951

AUTO LOAN PAYMENTS   2.50%

AMOUNT OF LOAN	42 MOS		48 MOS		60 MOS		72 MOS	
	MONTHLY PAYMENT	TOTAL INTRST	MONTHLY PAYMENT	TOTAL INTRST	MONTHLY PAYMENT	TOTAL INTRST	MONTHLY PAYMENT	TOTAL INTRST
$ 1	0.03	0	0.03	0	0.02	0	0.02	0
2	0.05	0	0.05	0	0.04	0	0.03	0
3	0.08	0	0.07	0	0.06	0	0.05	1
4	0.10	0	0.09	0	0.08	1	0.06	0
5	0.13	0	0.11	0	0.09	0	0.08	1
6	0.15	0	0.14	1	0.11	1	0.09	0
7	0.18	1	0.16	1	0.13	1	0.11	1
8	0.20	0	0.18	1	0.15	1	0.12	1
9	0.23	1	0.20	1	0.16	1	0.14	1
10	0.25	1	0.22	1	0.18	1	0.15	1
20	0.50	1	0.44	1	0.36	1	0.30	1
30	0.75	2	0.66	2	0.54	2	0.45	2
40	1.00	2	0.88	2	0.71	3	0.60	3
50	1.25	3	1.10	3	0.89	3	0.75	4
60	1.50	3	1.32	3	1.07	4	0.90	5
70	1.75	4	1.54	4	1.25	5	1.05	6
80	2.00	4	1.76	4	1.42	5	1.20	6
90	2.25	5	1.98	5	1.60	6	1.35	7
100	2.49	5	2.20	6	1.78	7	1.50	8
200	4.98	9	4.39	11	3.55	13	3.00	16
300	7.47	14	6.58	16	5.33	20	4.50	24
400	9.96	18	8.77	21	7.10	26	5.99	31
500	12.45	23	10.96	26	8.88	33	7.49	39
600	14.94	27	13.15	31	10.65	39	8.99	47
700	17.43	32	15.34	36	12.43	46	10.48	55
800	19.92	37	17.54	42	14.20	52	11.98	63
900	22.41	41	19.73	47	15.98	59	13.48	71
1,000	24.90	46	21.92	52	17.75	65	14.98	79
2,000	49.79	91	43.83	104	35.50	130	29.95	156
3,000	74.68	137	65.75	156	53.25	195	44.92	234
4,000	99.57	182	87.66	208	70.99	259	59.89	312
5,000	124.46	227	109.58	260	88.74	324	74.86	390
6,000	149.35	273	131.49	312	106.49	389	89.83	468
7,000	174.24	318	153.40	363	124.24	454	104.80	546
8,000	199.13	363	175.32	415	141.98	519	119.77	623
9,000	224.03	409	197.23	467	159.73	584	134.74	701
10,000	248.92	455	219.15	519	177.48	649	149.72	780
11,000	273.81	500	241.06	571	195.23	714	164.69	858
12,000	298.70	545	262.97	623	212.97	778	179.66	936
13,000	323.59	591	284.89	675	230.72	843	194.63	1,013
14,000	348.48	636	306.80	726	248.47	908	209.60	1,091
15,000	373.37	682	328.72	779	266.22	973	224.57	1,169
16,000	398.26	727	350.63	830	283.96	1,038	239.54	1,247
17,000	423.15	772	372.54	882	301.71	1,103	254.51	1,325
18,000	448.05	818	394.46	934	319.46	1,168	269.48	1,403
19,000	472.94	863	416.37	986	337.20	1,232	284.45	1,480
20,000	497.83	909	438.29	1,038	354.95	1,297	299.43	1,559
21,000	522.72	954	460.20	1,090	372.70	1,362	314.40	1,637
22,000	547.61	1,000	482.11	1,141	390.45	1,427	329.37	1,715
23,000	572.50	1,045	504.03	1,193	408.19	1,491	344.34	1,792
24,000	597.39	1,090	525.94	1,245	425.94	1,556	359.31	1,870
25,000	622.28	1,136	547.86	1,297	443.69	1,621	374.28	1,948
26,000	647.18	1,182	569.77	1,349	461.44	1,686	389.25	2,026
27,000	672.07	1,227	591.68	1,401	479.18	1,751	404.22	2,104
28,000	696.96	1,272	613.60	1,453	496.93	1,816	419.19	2,182
29,000	721.85	1,318	635.51	1,504	514.68	1,881	434.16	2,260
30,000	746.74	1,363	657.43	1,557	532.43	1,946	449.14	2,338
31,000	771.63	1,408	679.34	1,608	550.17	2,010	464.11	2,416
32,000	796.52	1,454	701.25	1,660	567.92	2,075	479.08	2,494
33,000	821.41	1,499	723.17	1,712	585.67	2,140	494.05	2,572
34,000	846.30	1,545	745.08	1,764	603.42	2,205	509.02	2,649
35,000	871.20	1,590	767.00	1,816	621.16	2,270	523.99	2,727
36,000	896.09	1,636	788.91	1,868	638.91	2,335	538.96	2,805
37,000	920.98	1,681	810.82	1,919	656.66	2,400	553.93	2,883
38,000	945.87	1,727	832.74	1,972	674.40	2,464	568.90	2,961
39,000	970.76	1,772	854.65	2,023	692.15	2,529	583.87	3,039
40,000	995.65	1,817	876.57	2,075	709.90	2,594	598.85	3,117
42,000	1,045.43	1,908	920.39	2,179	745.39	2,723	628.79	3,273
44,000	1,095.21	1,999	964.22	2,283	780.89	2,853	658.73	3,429
46,000	1,145.00	2,090	1,008.05	2,386	816.38	2,983	688.67	3,584
48,000	1,194.78	2,181	1,051.88	2,490	851.88	3,113	718.61	3,740
50,000	1,244.56	2,272	1,095.71	2,594	887.37	3,242	748.56	3,896

AMOUNT OF LOAN	12 MOS MONTHLY PAYMENT	12 MOS TOTAL INTRST	24 MOS MONTHLY PAYMENT	24 MOS TOTAL INTRST	30 MOS MONTHLY PAYMENT	30 MOS TOTAL INTRST	36 MOS MONTHLY PAYMENT	36 MOS TOTAL INTRST
$ 1	0.09	0	0.05	0	0.04	0	0.03	0
2	0.17	0	0.09	0	0.07	0	0.06	0
3	0.26	0	0.13	0	0.11	0	0.09	0
4	0.34	0	0.18	0	0.14	0	0.12	0
5	0.43	0	0.22	0	0.18	0	0.15	0
6	0.51	0	0.26	0	0.21	0	0.18	0
7	0.60	0	0.31	0	0.25	0	0.21	1
8	0.68	0	0.35	0	0.28	1	0.24	1
9	0.77	0	0.39	0	0.32	1	0.27	1
10	0.85	0	0.43	0	0.35	1	0.29	0
20	1.70	0	0.86	1	0.70	1	0.58	1
30	2.54	0	1.29	1	1.04	1	0.87	1
40	3.39	1	1.72	1	1.39	2	1.16	2
50	4.23	1	2.15	2	1.73	2	1.45	2
60	5.08	1	2.58	2	2.08	2	1.74	3
70	5.93	1	3.01	2	2.42	3	2.03	3
80	6.77	1	3.43	2	2.77	3	2.32	4
90	7.62	1	3.86	3	3.11	3	2.61	4
100	8.46	2	4.29	3	3.46	4	2.90	4
200	16.92	3	8.58	6	6.91	7	5.80	9
300	25.38	5	12.87	9	10.36	11	8.70	13
400	33.84	6	17.15	12	13.82	15	11.59	17
500	42.29	7	21.44	15	17.27	18	14.49	22
600	50.75	9	25.73	18	20.72	22	17.39	26
700	59.21	11	30.01	20	24.18	25	20.28	30
800	67.67	12	34.30	23	27.63	29	23.18	34
900	76.13	14	38.59	26	31.08	32	26.08	39
1,000	84.58	15	42.88	29	34.54	36	28.98	43
2,000	169.16	30	85.75	58	69.07	72	57.95	86
3,000	253.74	45	128.62	87	103.60	108	86.92	129
4,000	338.32	60	171.49	116	138.13	144	115.89	172
5,000	422.90	75	214.36	145	172.66	180	144.86	215
6,000	507.48	90	257.23	174	207.19	216	173.83	258
7,000	592.06	105	300.10	202	241.72	252	202.80	301
8,000	676.64	120	342.97	231	276.25	288	231.77	344
9,000	761.22	135	385.84	260	310.78	323	260.75	387
10,000	845.80	150	428.71	289	345.31	359	289.72	430
11,000	930.38	165	471.58	318	379.84	395	318.69	473
12,000	1,014.96	180	514.45	347	414.37	431	347.66	516
13,000	1,099.54	194	557.32	376	448.90	467	376.63	559
14,000	1,184.12	209	600.20	405	483.43	503	405.60	602
15,000	1,268.70	224	643.07	434	517.96	539	434.57	645
16,000	1,353.28	239	685.94	463	552.49	575	463.54	687
17,000	1,437.86	254	728.81	491	587.02	611	492.51	730
18,000	1,522.44	269	771.68	520	621.55	647	521.49	774
19,000	1,607.02	284	814.55	549	656.08	682	550.46	817
20,000	1,691.60	299	857.42	578	690.61	718	579.43	859
21,000	1,776.18	314	900.29	607	725.14	754	608.40	902
22,000	1,860.76	329	943.16	636	759.68	790	637.37	945
23,000	1,945.34	344	986.03	665	794.21	826	666.34	988
24,000	2,029.92	359	1,028.90	694	828.74	862	695.31	1,031
25,000	2,114.50	374	1,071.77	722	863.27	898	724.28	1,074
26,000	2,199.08	389	1,114.64	751	897.80	934	753.26	1,117
27,000	2,283.66	404	1,157.51	780	932.33	970	782.23	1,160
28,000	2,368.24	419	1,200.39	809	966.86	1,006	811.20	1,203
29,000	2,452.82	434	1,243.26	838	1,001.39	1,042	840.17	1,246
30,000	2,537.40	449	1,286.13	867	1,035.92	1,078	869.14	1,289
31,000	2,621.98	464	1,329.00	896	1,070.45	1,114	898.11	1,332
32,000	2,706.56	479	1,371.87	925	1,104.98	1,149	927.08	1,375
33,000	2,791.14	494	1,414.74	954	1,139.51	1,185	956.05	1,418
34,000	2,875.72	509	1,457.61	983	1,174.04	1,221	985.02	1,461
35,000	2,960.30	524	1,500.48	1,012	1,208.57	1,257	1,014.00	1,504
36,000	3,044.88	539	1,543.35	1,040	1,243.10	1,293	1,042.97	1,547
37,000	3,129.46	554	1,586.22	1,069	1,277.63	1,329	1,071.94	1,590
38,000	3,214.04	568	1,629.09	1,098	1,312.16	1,365	1,100.91	1,633
39,000	3,298.62	583	1,671.96	1,127	1,346.69	1,401	1,129.88	1,676
40,000	3,383.20	598	1,714.83	1,156	1,381.22	1,437	1,158.85	1,719
42,000	3,552.36	628	1,800.58	1,214	1,450.28	1,508	1,216.79	1,804
44,000	3,721.52	658	1,886.32	1,272	1,519.35	1,581	1,274.74	1,891
46,000	3,890.68	688	1,972.06	1,329	1,588.41	1,652	1,332.68	1,976
48,000	4,059.84	718	2,057.80	1,387	1,657.47	1,724	1,390.62	2,062
50,000	4,229.00	748	2,143.54	1,445	1,726.53	1,796	1,448.56	2,148

AUTO LOAN PAYMENTS 2.75%

AMOUNT OF LOAN	42 MOS		48 MOS		60 MOS		72 MOS	
	MONTHLY PAYMENT	TOTAL INTRST	MONTHLY PAYMENT	TOTAL INTRST	MONTHLY PAYMENT	TOTAL INTRST	MONTHLY PAYMENT	TOTAL INTRST
$ 1	0.03	0	0.03	0	0.02	0	0.02	0
2	0.06	0	0.05	0	0.04	0	0.04	0
3	0.08	0	0.07	0	0.06	0	0.05	0
4	0.11	0	0.09	0	0.08	0	0.07	1
5	0.13	0	0.12	0	0.09	0	0.08	1
6	0.16	0	0.14	1	0.11	1	0.10	1
7	0.18	1	0.16	1	0.13	1	0.11	1
8	0.21	1	0.18	1	0.15	1	0.13	1
9	0.23	1	0.20	1	0.17	1	0.14	1
10	0.26	1	0.23	1	0.18	1	0.16	2
20	0.51	1	0.45	2	0.36	2	0.31	2
30	0.76	2	0.67	2	0.54	2	0.46	3
40	1.01	2	0.89	3	0.72	3	0.61	4
50	1.26	3	1.11	3	0.90	4	0.76	5
60	1.51	3	1.33	4	1.08	5	0.91	6
70	1.76	4	1.55	4	1.26	6	1.06	7
80	2.01	4	1.77	5	1.43	6	1.21	7
90	2.26	5	1.99	6	1.61	7	1.36	8
100	2.51	5	2.21	6	1.79	7	1.51	9
200	5.01	10	4.41	12	3.58	15	3.02	17
300	7.51	15	6.61	17	5.36	22	4.53	26
400	10.01	20	8.81	23	7.15	29	6.04	35
500	12.51	25	11.02	29	8.93	36	7.55	44
600	15.01	30	13.22	35	10.72	43	9.05	52
700	17.51	35	15.42	40	12.51	51	10.56	60
800	20.01	40	17.62	46	14.29	57	12.07	69
900	22.51	45	19.83	52	16.08	65	13.58	78
1,000	25.01	50	22.03	57	17.86	72	15.09	86
2,000	50.01	100	44.05	114	35.72	143	30.17	172
3,000	75.01	150	66.08	172	53.58	215	45.25	258
4,000	100.01	200	88.10	229	71.44	286	60.33	344
5,000	125.01	250	110.13	286	89.29	357	75.42	430
6,000	150.01	300	132.15	343	107.15	429	90.50	516
7,000	175.01	350	154.17	400	125.01	501	105.58	602
8,000	200.01	400	176.20	458	142.87	572	120.66	688
9,000	225.01	450	198.22	515	160.73	644	135.74	773
10,000	250.01	500	220.25	572	178.58	715	150.83	860
11,000	275.02	551	242.27	629	196.44	786	165.91	946
12,000	300.02	601	264.29	686	214.30	858	180.99	1,031
13,000	325.02	651	286.32	743	232.16	930	196.07	1,117
14,000	350.02	701	308.34	800	250.01	1,001	211.15	1,203
15,000	375.02	751	330.37	858	267.87	1,072	226.24	1,289
16,000	400.02	801	352.39	915	285.73	1,144	241.32	1,375
17,000	425.02	851	374.41	972	303.59	1,215	256.40	1,461
18,000	450.02	901	396.44	1,029	321.45	1,287	271.48	1,547
19,000	475.02	951	418.46	1,086	339.30	1,358	286.56	1,632
20,000	500.02	1,001	440.49	1,144	357.16	1,430	301.65	1,719
21,000	525.02	1,051	462.51	1,200	375.02	1,501	316.73	1,805
22,000	550.03	1,101	484.53	1,257	392.88	1,573	331.81	1,890
23,000	575.03	1,151	506.56	1,315	410.73	1,644	346.89	1,976
24,000	600.03	1,201	528.58	1,372	428.59	1,715	361.98	2,063
25,000	625.03	1,251	550.61	1,429	446.45	1,787	377.06	2,148
26,000	650.03	1,301	572.63	1,486	464.31	1,859	392.14	2,234
27,000	675.03	1,351	594.65	1,543	482.17	1,930	407.22	2,320
28,000	700.03	1,401	616.68	1,601	500.02	2,001	422.30	2,406
29,000	725.03	1,451	638.70	1,658	517.88	2,073	437.39	2,492
30,000	750.03	1,501	660.73	1,715	535.74	2,144	452.47	2,578
31,000	775.04	1,552	682.75	1,772	553.60	2,216	467.55	2,664
32,000	800.04	1,602	704.77	1,829	571.45	2,287	482.63	2,749
33,000	825.04	1,652	726.80	1,886	589.31	2,359	497.71	2,835
34,000	850.04	1,702	748.82	1,943	607.17	2,430	512.80	2,922
35,000	875.04	1,752	770.85	2,001	625.03	2,502	527.88	3,007
36,000	900.04	1,802	792.87	2,058	642.89	2,573	542.96	3,093
37,000	925.04	1,852	814.89	2,115	660.74	2,644	558.04	3,179
38,000	950.04	1,902	836.92	2,172	678.60	2,716	573.12	3,265
39,000	975.04	1,952	858.94	2,229	696.46	2,788	588.21	3,351
40,000	1,000.04	2,002	880.97	2,287	714.32	2,859	603.29	3,437
42,000	1,050.05	2,102	925.01	2,400	750.03	3,002	633.45	3,608
44,000	1,100.05	2,202	969.06	2,515	785.75	3,145	663.62	3,781
46,000	1,150.05	2,302	1,013.11	2,629	821.46	3,288	693.78	3,952
48,000	1,200.05	2,402	1,057.16	2,744	857.18	3,431	723.95	4,124
50,000	1,250.05	2,502	1,101.21	2,858	892.90	3,574	754.11	4,296

AUTO LOAN PAYMENTS

AMOUNT OF LOAN	12 MOS MONTHLY PAYMENT	12 MOS TOTAL INTRST	24 MOS MONTHLY PAYMENT	24 MOS TOTAL INTRST	30 MOS MONTHLY PAYMENT	30 MOS TOTAL INTRST	36 MOS MONTHLY PAYMENT	36 MOS TOTAL INTRST
$ 1	0.09	0	0.05	0	0.04	0	0.03	0
2	0.17	0	0.09	0	0.07	0	0.06	0
3	0.26	0	0.13	0	0.11	0	0.09	0
4	0.34	0	0.18	0	0.14	0	0.12	0
5	0.43	0	0.22	0	0.18	0	0.15	0
6	0.51	0	0.26	0	0.21	0	0.18	0
7	0.60	0	0.31	0	0.25	1	0.21	1
8	0.68	0	0.35	0	0.28	0	0.24	1
9	0.77	0	0.39	0	0.32	1	0.27	1
10	0.85	0	0.43	0	0.35	1	0.30	1
20	1.70	0	0.86	1	0.70	1	0.59	1
30	2.54	0	1.29	1	1.04	1	0.88	2
40	3.39	1	1.72	1	1.39	2	1.17	2
50	4.24	1	2.15	2	1.73	2	1.46	3
60	5.08	1	2.58	2	2.08	2	1.75	3
70	5.93	1	3.01	2	2.43	3	2.04	3
80	6.78	1	3.44	3	2.77	3	2.33	4
90	7.62	1	3.87	3	3.12	4	2.62	4
100	8.47	2	4.30	3	3.46	4	2.91	5
200	16.93	3	8.59	6	6.92	8	5.81	9
300	25.40	5	12.89	9	10.38	11	8.72	14
400	33.86	6	17.18	12	13.84	15	11.62	18
500	42.33	8	21.47	15	17.30	19	14.52	23
600	50.79	9	25.77	18	20.76	23	17.43	27
700	59.26	11	30.06	21	24.22	27	20.33	32
800	67.72	13	34.35	24	27.68	30	23.23	36
900	76.19	14	38.65	28	31.14	34	26.14	41
1,000	84.65	16	42.94	31	34.60	38	29.04	45
2,000	169.30	32	85.88	61	69.20	76	58.08	91
3,000	253.95	47	128.82	92	103.79	114	87.12	136
4,000	338.60	63	171.75	122	138.39	152	116.15	181
5,000	423.25	79	214.69	153	172.99	190	145.19	227
6,000	507.89	95	257.63	183	207.58	227	174.23	272
7,000	592.54	110	300.56	213	242.18	265	203.27	318
8,000	677.19	126	343.50	244	276.78	303	232.30	363
9,000	761.84	142	386.44	275	311.37	341	261.34	408
10,000	846.49	158	429.37	305	345.97	379	290.38	454
11,000	931.13	174	472.31	335	380.57	417	319.41	499
12,000	1,015.78	189	515.25	366	415.16	455	348.45	544
13,000	1,100.43	205	558.19	397	449.76	493	377.49	590
14,000	1,185.08	221	601.12	427	484.36	531	406.53	635
15,000	1,269.73	237	644.06	457	518.95	569	435.56	680
16,000	1,354.38	253	687.00	488	553.55	607	464.60	726
17,000	1,439.02	268	729.93	518	588.15	645	493.64	771
18,000	1,523.67	284	772.87	549	622.74	682	522.67	816
19,000	1,608.32	300	815.81	579	657.34	720	551.71	862
20,000	1,692.97	316	858.74	610	691.94	758	580.75	907
21,000	1,777.62	331	901.68	640	726.53	796	609.79	952
22,000	1,862.26	347	944.62	671	761.13	834	638.82	998
23,000	1,946.91	363	987.56	701	795.72	872	667.86	1,043
24,000	2,031.56	379	1,030.49	732	830.32	910	696.90	1,088
25,000	2,116.21	395	1,073.43	762	864.92	948	725.93	1,133
26,000	2,200.86	410	1,116.37	793	899.51	985	754.97	1,179
27,000	2,285.51	426	1,159.30	823	934.11	1,023	784.01	1,224
28,000	2,370.15	442	1,202.24	854	968.71	1,061	813.05	1,270
29,000	2,454.80	458	1,245.18	884	1,003.30	1,099	842.08	1,315
30,000	2,539.45	473	1,288.11	915	1,037.90	1,137	871.12	1,360
31,000	2,624.10	489	1,331.05	945	1,072.50	1,175	900.16	1,406
32,000	2,708.75	505	1,373.99	976	1,107.09	1,213	929.19	1,451
33,000	2,793.39	521	1,416.93	1,006	1,141.69	1,251	958.23	1,496
34,000	2,878.04	536	1,459.86	1,037	1,176.29	1,289	987.27	1,542
35,000	2,962.69	552	1,502.80	1,067	1,210.88	1,326	1,016.31	1,587
36,000	3,047.34	568	1,545.74	1,098	1,245.48	1,364	1,045.34	1,632
37,000	3,131.99	584	1,588.67	1,128	1,280.08	1,402	1,074.38	1,678
38,000	3,216.63	600	1,631.61	1,159	1,314.67	1,440	1,103.42	1,723
39,000	3,301.28	615	1,674.55	1,189	1,349.27	1,478	1,132.45	1,768
40,000	3,385.93	631	1,717.48	1,220	1,383.87	1,516	1,161.49	1,814
42,000	3,555.23	663	1,803.36	1,281	1,453.06	1,592	1,219.57	1,905
44,000	3,724.52	694	1,889.23	1,342	1,522.25	1,668	1,277.64	1,995
46,000	3,893.82	726	1,975.11	1,403	1,591.44	1,743	1,335.71	2,086
48,000	4,063.12	757	2,060.98	1,464	1,660.64	1,819	1,393.79	2,176
50,000	4,232.41	789	2,146.85	1,524	1,729.83	1,895	1,451.86	2,267

AUTO LOAN PAYMENTS 2.90%

AMOUNT OF LOAN	42 MOS MONTHLY PAYMENT	42 MOS TOTAL INTRST	48 MOS MONTHLY PAYMENT	48 MOS TOTAL INTRST	60 MOS MONTHLY PAYMENT	60 MOS TOTAL INTRST	72 MOS MONTHLY PAYMENT	72 MOS TOTAL INTRST
$ 1	0.03	0	0.03	0	0.02	0	0.02	0
2	0.06	0	0.05	0	0.04	0	0.04	0
3	0.08	0	0.07	0	0.06	1	0.05	1
4	0.11	1	0.09	0	0.08	1	0.07	1
5	0.13	0	0.12	1	0.09	0	0.08	1
6	0.16	1	0.14	1	0.11	1	0.10	1
7	0.18	1	0.16	1	0.13	1	0.11	1
8	0.21	1	0.18	1	0.15	1	0.13	1
9	0.23	1	0.20	1	0.17	1	0.14	1
10	0.26	1	0.23	1	0.18	1	0.16	2
20	0.51	1	0.45	2	0.36	2	0.31	2
30	0.76	2	0.67	2	0.54	2	0.46	3
40	1.01	2	0.89	3	0.72	3	0.61	4
50	1.26	3	1.11	3	0.90	4	0.76	5
60	1.51	3	1.33	4	1.08	5	0.91	6
70	1.76	4	1.55	4	1.26	5	1.07	7
80	2.01	4	1.77	5	1.44	6	1.22	8
90	2.26	5	1.99	6	1.62	7	1.37	9
100	2.51	5	2.21	6	1.80	8	1.52	9
200	5.02	11	4.42	12	3.59	15	3.03	18
300	7.53	16	6.63	18	5.38	23	4.55	28
400	10.03	21	8.84	24	7.17	30	6.06	36
500	12.54	27	11.05	30	8.97	38	7.58	46
600	15.05	32	13.26	36	10.76	46	9.09	54
700	17.55	37	15.47	43	12.55	53	10.61	64
800	20.06	43	17.68	49	14.34	60	12.12	73
900	22.57	48	19.89	55	16.14	68	13.64	82
1,000	25.07	53	22.10	61	17.93	76	15.15	91
2,000	50.14	106	44.19	121	35.85	151	30.30	182
3,000	75.21	159	66.28	181	53.78	227	45.45	272
4,000	100.27	211	88.37	242	71.70	302	60.60	363
5,000	125.34	264	110.46	302	89.63	378	75.75	454
6,000	150.41	317	132.55	362	107.55	453	90.90	545
7,000	175.47	370	154.64	423	125.48	529	106.05	636
8,000	200.54	423	176.73	483	143.40	604	121.20	726
9,000	225.61	476	198.82	543	161.32	679	136.35	817
10,000	250.68	529	220.91	604	179.25	755	151.49	907
11,000	275.74	581	243.00	664	197.17	830	166.64	998
12,000	300.81	634	265.09	724	215.10	906	181.79	1,089
13,000	325.88	687	287.18	785	233.02	981	196.94	1,180
14,000	350.94	739	309.27	845	250.95	1,057	212.09	1,270
15,000	376.01	792	331.36	905	268.87	1,132	227.24	1,361
16,000	401.08	845	353.45	966	286.79	1,207	242.39	1,452
17,000	426.14	898	375.54	1,026	304.72	1,283	257.54	1,543
18,000	451.21	951	397.63	1,086	322.64	1,358	272.69	1,634
19,000	476.28	1,004	419.72	1,147	340.57	1,434	287.84	1,724
20,000	501.35	1,057	441.81	1,207	358.49	1,509	302.98	1,815
21,000	526.41	1,109	463.90	1,267	376.42	1,585	318.13	1,905
22,000	551.48	1,162	485.99	1,328	394.34	1,660	333.28	1,996
23,000	576.55	1,215	508.08	1,388	412.26	1,736	348.43	2,087
24,000	601.61	1,268	530.17	1,448	430.19	1,811	363.58	2,178
25,000	626.68	1,321	552.26	1,508	448.11	1,887	378.73	2,269
26,000	651.75	1,374	574.35	1,569	466.04	1,962	393.88	2,359
27,000	676.81	1,426	596.44	1,629	483.96	2,038	409.03	2,450
28,000	701.88	1,479	618.53	1,689	501.89	2,113	424.18	2,541
29,000	726.95	1,532	640.62	1,750	519.81	2,189	439.33	2,632
30,000	752.02	1,585	662.71	1,810	537.73	2,264	454.47	2,722
31,000	777.08	1,637	684.80	1,870	555.66	2,340	469.62	2,813
32,000	802.15	1,690	706.89	1,931	573.58	2,415	484.77	2,903
33,000	827.22	1,743	728.98	1,991	591.51	2,491	499.92	2,994
34,000	852.28	1,796	751.07	2,051	609.43	2,566	515.07	3,085
35,000	877.35	1,849	773.16	2,112	627.36	2,642	530.22	3,176
36,000	902.42	1,902	795.25	2,172	645.28	2,717	545.37	3,267
37,000	927.49	1,955	817.34	2,232	663.20	2,792	560.52	3,357
38,000	952.55	2,007	839.43	2,293	681.13	2,868	575.67	3,448
39,000	977.62	2,060	861.52	2,353	699.05	2,943	590.82	3,539
40,000	1,002.69	2,113	883.61	2,413	716.98	3,019	605.96	3,629
42,000	1,052.82	2,218	927.79	2,534	752.83	3,170	636.26	3,811
44,000	1,102.95	2,324	971.97	2,655	788.67	3,320	666.56	3,992
46,000	1,153.09	2,430	1,016.15	2,775	824.52	3,471	696.86	4,174
48,000	1,203.22	2,535	1,060.33	2,896	860.37	3,622	727.16	4,356
50,000	1,253.36	2,641	1,104.51	3,016	896.22	3,773	757.45	4,536

AMOUNT OF LOAN	12 MOS		24 MOS		30 MOS		36 MOS	
	MONTHLY PAYMENT	TOTAL INTRST	MONTHLY PAYMENT	TOTAL INTRST	MONTHLY PAYMENT	TOTAL INTRST	MONTHLY PAYMENT	TOTAL INTRST
$ 1	0.09	0	0.05	0	0.04	0	0.03	0
2	0.17	0	0.09	0	0.07	0	0.06	0
3	0.26	0	0.13	0	0.11	0	0.09	0
4	0.34	0	0.18	0	0.14	0	0.12	0
5	0.43	0	0.22	0	0.18	0	0.15	0
6	0.51	0	0.26	0	0.21	0	0.18	0
7	0.60	0	0.31	0	0.25	1	0.21	1
8	0.68	0	0.35	0	0.28	0	0.24	1
9	0.77	0	0.39	0	0.32	1	0.27	1
10	0.85	0	0.43	0	0.35	1	0.30	1
20	1.70	0	0.86	1	0.70	1	0.59	1
30	2.55	1	1.29	1	1.04	1	0.88	2
40	3.39	1	1.72	1	1.39	2	1.17	2
50	4.24	1	2.15	2	1.74	2	1.46	3
60	5.09	1	2.58	2	2.08	2	1.75	3
70	5.93	1	3.01	2	2.43	3	2.04	3
80	6.78	1	3.44	3	2.78	3	2.33	4
90	7.63	2	3.87	3	3.12	4	2.62	4
100	8.47	2	4.30	3	3.47	4	2.91	5
200	16.94	3	8.60	6	6.93	8	5.82	10
300	25.41	5	12.90	10	10.40	12	8.73	14
400	33.88	7	17.20	13	13.86	16	11.64	19
500	42.35	8	21.50	16	17.33	20	14.55	24
600	50.82	10	25.79	19	20.79	24	17.45	28
700	59.29	11	30.09	22	24.25	28	20.36	33
800	67.76	13	34.39	25	27.72	32	23.27	38
900	76.23	15	38.69	29	31.18	35	26.18	42
1,000	84.70	16	42.99	32	34.65	40	29.09	47
2,000	169.39	33	85.97	63	69.29	79	58.17	94
3,000	254.09	49	128.95	95	103.93	118	87.26	141
4,000	338.78	65	171.93	126	138.57	157	116.33	188
5,000	423.47	82	214.91	158	173.21	196	145.41	235
6,000	508.17	98	257.89	189	207.85	236	174.49	282
7,000	592.86	114	300.87	221	242.49	275	203.57	329
8,000	677.55	131	343.85	252	277.13	314	232.65	375
9,000	762.25	147	386.84	284	311.77	353	261.74	423
10,000	846.94	163	429.82	316	346.41	392	290.82	470
11,000	931.64	180	472.80	347	381.05	432	319.90	516
12,000	1,016.33	196	515.78	379	415.69	471	348.98	563
13,000	1,101.03	212	558.76	410	450.33	510	378.06	610
14,000	1,185.72	229	601.74	442	484.97	549	407.14	657
15,000	1,270.41	245	644.72	473	519.61	588	436.22	704
16,000	1,355.10	261	687.70	505	554.25	628	465.30	751
17,000	1,439.80	278	730.69	537	588.89	667	494.39	798
18,000	1,524.49	294	773.67	568	623.54	706	523.47	845
19,000	1,609.19	310	816.65	600	658.18	745	552.55	892
20,000	1,693.88	327	859.63	631	692.82	785	581.63	939
21,000	1,778.57	343	902.61	663	727.46	824	610.71	986
22,000	1,863.27	359	945.59	694	762.10	863	639.79	1,032
23,000	1,947.96	376	988.57	726	796.74	902	668.87	1,079
24,000	2,032.65	392	1,031.55	757	831.38	941	697.95	1,126
25,000	2,117.35	408	1,074.54	789	866.02	981	727.04	1,173
26,000	2,202.04	424	1,117.52	820	900.66	1,020	756.12	1,220
27,000	2,286.73	441	1,160.50	852	935.30	1,059	785.20	1,267
28,000	2,371.43	457	1,203.48	884	969.94	1,098	814.28	1,314
29,000	2,456.12	473	1,246.46	915	1,004.58	1,137	843.36	1,361
30,000	2,540.82	490	1,289.46	947	1,039.22	1,177	872.44	1,408
31,000	2,625.51	506	1,332.42	978	1,073.86	1,216	901.52	1,455
32,000	2,710.20	522	1,375.40	1,010	1,108.50	1,255	930.60	1,502
33,000	2,794.90	539	1,418.38	1,041	1,143.14	1,294	959.68	1,548
34,000	2,879.59	551	1,461.37	1,073	1,177.78	1,333	988.77	1,596
35,000	2,964.28	571	1,504.35	1,104	1,212.43	1,373	1,017.85	1,643
36,000	3,048.98	588	1,547.33	1,136	1,247.07	1,412	1,046.93	1,689
37,000	3,133.67	604	1,590.31	1,167	1,281.71	1,451	1,076.01	1,736
38,000	3,218.37	620	1,633.29	1,199	1,316.35	1,491	1,105.09	1,783
39,000	3,303.06	637	1,676.27	1,230	1,350.99	1,530	1,134.17	1,830
40,000	3,387.75	653	1,719.25	1,262	1,385.63	1,569	1,163.25	1,877
42,000	3,557.14	686	1,805.22	1,325	1,454.91	1,647	1,221.42	1,971
44,000	3,726.53	718	1,891.18	1,388	1,524.19	1,726	1,279.58	2,065
46,000	3,895.92	751	1,977.14	1,451	1,593.47	1,804	1,337.74	2,159
48,000	4,065.30	784	2,063.10	1,514	1,662.75	1,883	1,395.90	2,252
50,000	4,234.69	816	2,149.07	1,578	1,732.03	1,961	1,454.07	2,347

AUTO LOAN PAYMENTS 3.00%

AMOUNT OF LOAN	42 MOS		48 MOS		60 MOS		72 MOS	
	MONTHLY PAYMENT	TOTAL INTRST	MONTHLY PAYMENT	TOTAL INTRST	MONTHLY PAYMENT	TOTAL INTRST	MONTHLY PAYMENT	TOTAL INTRST
$ 1	0.03	0	0.03	0	0.02	0	0.02	0
2	0.06	1	0.05	0	0.04	0	0.04	1
3	0.08	0	0.07	0	0.06	0	0.05	1
4	0.11	1	0.09	0	0.08	1	0.07	1
5	0.13	0	0.12	1	0.09	0	0.08	1
6	0.16	1	0.14	1	0.11	1	0.10	1
7	0.18	1	0.16	1	0.13	1	0.11	1
8	0.21	1	0.18	1	0.15	1	0.13	1
9	0.23	1	0.20	1	0.17	1	0.14	1
10	0.26	1	0.23	1	0.18	1	0.16	2
20	0.51	1	0.45	2	0.36	2	0.31	2
30	0.76	2	0.67	2	0.54	2	0.46	3
40	1.01	2	0.89	3	0.72	3	0.61	4
50	1.26	3	1.11	3	0.90	4	0.76	5
60	1.51	3	1.33	4	1.08	5	0.92	6
70	1.76	4	1.55	4	1.26	5	1.07	7
80	2.01	4	1.78	5	1.44	6	1.22	8
90	2.27	5	2.00	6	1.62	7	1.37	9
100	2.52	6	2.22	7	1.80	8	1.52	9
200	5.03	11	4.43	13	3.60	16	3.04	19
300	7.54	17	6.65	19	5.40	24	4.56	28
400	10.05	22	8.86	25	7.19	31	6.08	38
500	12.56	28	11.07	31	8.99	39	7.60	47
600	15.07	33	13.29	38	10.79	47	9.12	57
700	17.58	38	15.50	44	12.58	55	10.64	66
800	20.09	44	17.71	50	14.38	63	12.16	76
900	22.61	50	19.93	57	16.18	71	13.68	85
1,000	25.12	55	22.14	63	17.97	78	15.20	94
2,000	50.23	110	44.27	125	35.94	156	30.39	188
3,000	75.34	164	66.41	188	53.91	235	45.59	282
4,000	100.45	219	88.54	250	71.88	313	60.78	376
5,000	125.56	274	110.68	313	89.85	391	75.97	470
6,000	150.67	328	132.81	375	107.82	469	91.17	564
7,000	175.78	383	154.95	438	125.79	547	106.36	658
8,000	200.89	437	177.08	500	143.75	625	121.55	752
9,000	226.01	492	199.21	562	161.72	703	136.75	846
10,000	251.12	547	221.35	625	179.69	781	151.94	940
11,000	276.23	602	243.48	687	197.66	860	167.14	1,034
12,000	301.34	656	265.62	750	215.63	938	182.33	1,128
13,000	326.45	711	287.75	812	233.60	1,016	197.52	1,221
14,000	351.56	766	309.89	875	251.57	1,094	212.72	1,316
15,000	376.67	820	332.02	937	269.54	1,172	227.91	1,410
16,000	401.78	875	354.15	999	287.50	1,250	243.10	1,503
17,000	426.89	929	376.29	1,062	305.47	1,328	258.30	1,598
18,000	452.01	984	398.42	1,124	323.44	1,406	273.49	1,691
19,000	477.12	1,039	420.56	1,187	341.41	1,485	288.68	1,785
20,000	502.23	1,094	442.69	1,249	359.38	1,563	303.88	1,879
21,000	527.34	1,148	464.83	1,312	377.35	1,641	319.07	1,973
22,000	552.45	1,203	486.96	1,374	395.32	1,719	334.27	2,067
23,000	577.56	1,258	509.09	1,436	413.28	1,797	349.46	2,161
24,000	602.67	1,312	531.23	1,499	431.25	1,875	364.65	2,255
25,000	627.78	1,367	553.36	1,561	449.22	1,953	379.85	2,349
26,000	652.89	1,421	575.50	1,624	467.19	2,031	395.04	2,443
27,000	678.01	1,476	597.63	1,686	485.16	2,110	410.23	2,537
28,000	703.12	1,531	619.77	1,749	503.13	2,188	425.43	2,631
29,000	728.23	1,586	641.90	1,811	521.10	2,266	440.62	2,725
30,000	753.34	1,640	664.03	1,873	539.07	2,344	455.82	2,819
31,000	778.45	1,695	686.17	1,936	557.03	2,422	471.01	2,913
32,000	803.56	1,750	708.30	1,998	575.00	2,500	486.20	3,006
33,000	828.67	1,804	730.44	2,061	592.97	2,578	501.40	3,101
34,000	853.78	1,859	752.57	2,123	610.94	2,656	516.59	3,194
35,000	878.89	1,913	774.71	2,186	628.91	2,735	531.78	3,288
36,000	904.01	1,968	796.84	2,248	646.88	2,813	546.98	3,383
37,000	929.12	2,023	818.98	2,311	664.85	2,891	562.17	3,476
38,000	954.23	2,078	841.11	2,373	682.82	2,969	577.36	3,570
39,000	979.34	2,132	863.24	2,436	700.78	3,047	592.56	3,664
40,000	1,004.45	2,187	885.38	2,498	718.75	3,125	607.75	3,758
42,000	1,054.67	2,296	929.65	2,623	754.69	3,281	638.14	3,946
44,000	1,104.89	2,405	973.92	2,748	790.63	3,438	668.53	4,134
46,000	1,155.12	2,515	1,018.18	2,873	826.56	3,594	698.91	4,322
48,000	1,205.34	2,624	1,062.45	2,998	862.50	3,750	729.30	4,510
50,000	1,255.56	2,734	1,106.72	3,123	898.44	3,906	759.69	4,698

AMOUNT OF LOAN	12 MOS MONTHLY PAYMENT	12 MOS TOTAL INTRST	24 MOS MONTHLY PAYMENT	24 MOS TOTAL INTRST	30 MOS MONTHLY PAYMENT	30 MOS TOTAL INTRST	36 MOS MONTHLY PAYMENT	36 MOS TOTAL INTRST
$ 1	0.09	0	0.05	0	0.04	0	0.03	0
2	0.17	0	0.09	0	0.07	0	0.06	0
3	0.26	0	0.13	0	0.11	0	0.09	0
4	0.34	0	0.18	0	0.14	0	0.12	0
5	0.43	0	0.22	0	0.18	0	0.15	0
6	0.51	0	0.26	0	0.21	0	0.18	0
7	0.60	0	0.31	0	0.25	1	0.21	1
8	0.68	0	0.35	0	0.28	0	0.24	1
9	0.77	0	0.39	0	0.32	1	0.27	1
10	0.85	0	0.44	1	0.35	1	0.30	1
20	1.70	0	0.87	1	0.70	1	0.59	1
30	2.55	1	1.30	1	1.05	2	0.88	2
40	3.40	1	1.73	2	1.40	2	1.17	2
50	4.25	1	2.16	2	1.74	2	1.46	3
60	5.09	1	2.59	2	2.09	3	1.76	3
70	5.94	1	3.02	2	2.44	3	2.05	4
80	6.79	1	3.45	3	2.79	4	2.34	4
90	7.64	2	3.88	3	3.13	4	2.63	5
100	8.49	2	4.31	3	3.48	4	2.92	5
200	16.97	4	8.62	7	6.96	9	5.84	10
300	25.45	5	12.93	10	10.43	13	8.76	15
400	33.93	7	17.24	14	13.91	17	11.68	20
500	42.41	9	21.55	17	17.38	21	14.60	26
600	50.89	11	25.86	21	20.86	26	17.52	31
700	59.37	12	30.17	24	24.33	30	20.44	36
800	67.85	14	34.48	28	27.81	34	23.36	41
900	76.33	16	38.79	31	31.28	38	26.28	46
1,000	84.81	18	43.10	34	34.76	43	29.20	51
2,000	169.62	35	86.19	69	69.51	85	58.39	102
3,000	254.43	53	129.28	103	104.26	128	87.58	153
4,000	339.24	71	172.37	137	139.01	170	116.77	204
5,000	424.04	88	215.46	171	173.76	213	145.96	255
6,000	508.85	106	258.56	205	208.51	255	175.15	305
7,000	593.66	124	301.65	240	243.26	298	204.35	357
8,000	678.47	142	344.74	274	278.01	340	233.54	407
9,000	763.27	159	387.83	308	312.76	383	262.73	458
10,000	848.08	177	430.92	342	347.51	425	291.92	509
11,000	932.89	195	474.02	376	382.27	468	321.11	560
12,000	1,017.70	212	517.11	411	417.02	511	350.30	611
13,000	1,102.50	230	560.20	445	451.77	553	379.49	662
14,000	1,187.31	248	603.29	479	486.52	596	408.69	713
15,000	1,272.12	265	646.38	513	521.27	638	437.88	764
16,000	1,356.93	283	689.48	548	556.02	681	467.07	815
17,000	1,441.73	301	732.57	582	590.77	723	496.26	865
18,000	1,526.54	318	775.66	616	625.52	766	525.45	916
19,000	1,611.35	336	818.75	650	660.27	808	554.64	967
20,000	1,696.16	354	861.84	684	695.02	851	583.84	1,018
21,000	1,780.97	372	904.93	718	729.77	893	613.03	1,069
22,000	1,865.77	389	948.03	753	764.53	936	642.22	1,120
23,000	1,950.58	407	991.12	787	799.28	978	671.41	1,171
24,000	2,035.39	425	1,034.21	821	834.03	1,021	700.60	1,222
25,000	2,120.20	442	1,077.30	855	868.78	1,063	729.79	1,272
26,000	2,205.00	460	1,120.39	889	903.53	1,106	758.98	1,323
27,000	2,289.81	478	1,163.49	924	938.28	1,148	788.18	1,374
28,000	2,374.62	495	1,206.58	958	973.03	1,191	817.37	1,425
29,000	2,459.43	513	1,249.67	992	1,007.78	1,233	846.56	1,476
30,000	2,544.23	531	1,292.76	1,026	1,042.53	1,276	875.75	1,527
31,000	2,629.04	548	1,335.85	1,060	1,077.28	1,318	904.94	1,578
32,000	2,713.85	566	1,378.95	1,095	1,112.03	1,361	934.13	1,629
33,000	2,798.66	584	1,422.04	1,129	1,146.79	1,404	963.33	1,680
34,000	2,883.46	602	1,465.13	1,163	1,181.54	1,446	992.52	1,731
35,000	2,968.27	619	1,508.22	1,197	1,216.29	1,489	1,021.71	1,782
36,000	3,053.08	637	1,551.31	1,231	1,251.04	1,531	1,050.90	1,832
37,000	3,137.89	655	1,594.40	1,266	1,285.79	1,574	1,080.09	1,883
38,000	3,222.69	672	1,637.50	1,300	1,320.54	1,616	1,109.28	1,934
39,000	3,307.50	690	1,680.59	1,334	1,355.29	1,659	1,138.47	1,985
40,000	3,392.31	708	1,723.68	1,368	1,390.04	1,701	1,167.67	2,036
42,000	3,561.93	743	1,809.86	1,437	1,459.54	1,786	1,226.05	2,138
44,000	3,731.54	778	1,896.05	1,505	1,529.05	1,872	1,284.43	2,239
46,000	3,901.16	814	1,982.23	1,574	1,598.55	1,957	1,342.81	2,341
48,000	4,070.77	849	2,068.42	1,642	1,668.05	2,042	1,401.20	2,443
50,000	4,240.39	885	2,154.60	1,710	1,737.55	2,127	1,459.58	2,545

AUTO LOAN PAYMENTS 3.50%

AMOUNT OF LOAN	42 MOS MONTHLY PAYMENT	42 MOS TOTAL INTRST	48 MOS MONTHLY PAYMENT	48 MOS TOTAL INTRST	60 MOS MONTHLY PAYMENT	60 MOS TOTAL INTRST	72 MOS MONTHLY PAYMENT	72 MOS TOTAL INTRST
$ 1	0.03	0	0.03	0	0.02	0	0.02	0
2	0.06	1	0.05	0	0.04	0	0.04	1
3	0.08	0	0.07	0	0.06	1	0.05	1
4	0.11	1	0.09	0	0.08	1	0.07	1
5	0.13	0	0.12	1	0.10	1	0.08	1
6	0.16	1	0.14	1	0.11	1	0.10	1
7	0.18	1	0.16	1	0.13	1	0.11	1
8	0.21	1	0.18	1	0.15	1	0.13	1
9	0.23	1	0.21	1	0.17	1	0.14	1
10	0.26	1	0.23	1	0.19	1	0.16	2
20	0.51	1	0.45	2	0.37	2	0.31	3
30	0.76	2	0.68	3	0.55	3	0.47	4
40	1.02	2	0.90	3	0.73	4	0.62	5
50	1.27	3	1.12	4	0.91	5	0.78	6
60	1.52	4	1.35	5	1.10	6	0.93	7
70	1.78	5	1.57	5	1.28	7	1.08	8
80	2.03	5	1.79	6	1.46	8	1.24	9
90	2.28	6	2.02	7	1.64	8	1.39	10
100	2.54	7	2.24	8	1.82	9	1.55	12
200	5.07	13	4.48	15	3.64	18	3.09	22
300	7.60	19	6.71	22	5.46	28	4.63	33
400	10.14	26	8.95	30	7.28	37	6.17	44
500	12.67	32	11.18	37	9.10	46	7.71	55
600	15.20	38	13.42	44	10.92	55	9.26	67
700	17.74	45	15.65	51	12.74	64	10.80	78
800	20.27	51	17.89	59	14.56	74	12.34	88
900	22.80	58	20.13	66	16.38	83	13.88	99
1,000	25.34	64	22.36	73	18.20	92	15.42	110
2,000	50.67	128	44.72	147	36.39	183	30.84	220
3,000	76.00	192	67.07	219	54.58	275	46.26	331
4,000	101.33	256	89.43	293	72.77	366	61.68	441
5,000	126.67	320	111.79	366	90.96	458	77.10	551
6,000	152.00	384	134.14	439	109.16	550	92.52	661
7,000	177.33	448	156.50	512	127.35	641	107.93	771
8,000	202.66	512	178.85	585	145.54	732	123.35	881
9,000	228.00	576	201.21	658	163.73	824	138.77	991
10,000	253.33	640	223.57	731	181.92	915	154.19	1,102
11,000	278.66	704	245.92	804	200.11	1,007	169.61	1,212
12,000	303.99	768	268.28	877	218.31	1,099	185.03	1,322
13,000	329.32	831	290.63	950	236.50	1,190	200.44	1,432
14,000	354.66	896	312.99	1,024	254.69	1,281	215.86	1,542
15,000	379.99	960	335.35	1,097	272.88	1,373	231.28	1,652
16,000	405.32	1,023	357.70	1,170	291.07	1,464	246.70	1,762
17,000	430.65	1,087	380.06	1,243	309.26	1,556	262.12	1,873
18,000	455.99	1,152	402.41	1,316	327.46	1,648	277.54	1,983
19,000	481.32	1,215	424.77	1,389	345.65	1,739	292.95	2,092
20,000	506.65	1,279	447.13	1,462	363.84	1,830	308.37	2,203
21,000	531.98	1,343	469.48	1,535	382.03	1,922	323.79	2,313
22,000	557.32	1,407	491.84	1,608	400.22	2,013	339.21	2,423
23,000	582.65	1,471	514.19	1,681	418.42	2,105	354.63	2,533
24,000	607.98	1,535	536.55	1,754	436.61	2,197	370.05	2,644
25,000	633.31	1,599	558.91	1,828	454.80	2,288	385.46	2,753
26,000	658.64	1,663	581.26	1,900	472.99	2,379	400.88	2,863
27,000	683.98	1,727	603.62	1,974	491.18	2,471	416.30	2,974
28,000	709.31	1,791	625.97	2,047	509.37	2,562	431.72	3,084
29,000	734.64	1,855	648.33	2,120	527.57	2,654	447.14	3,194
30,000	759.97	1,919	670.69	2,193	545.76	2,746	462.56	3,304
31,000	785.31	1,983	693.04	2,266	563.95	2,837	477.98	3,415
32,000	810.64	2,047	715.40	2,339	582.14	2,928	493.39	3,524
33,000	835.97	2,111	737.75	2,412	600.33	3,020	508.81	3,634
34,000	861.30	2,175	760.11	2,485	618.52	3,111	524.23	3,745
35,000	886.64	2,239	782.47	2,559	636.72	3,203	539.65	3,855
36,000	911.97	2,303	804.82	2,631	654.91	3,295	555.07	3,965
37,000	937.30	2,367	827.18	2,705	673.10	3,386	570.49	4,075
38,000	962.63	2,430	849.53	2,777	691.29	3,477	585.90	4,185
39,000	987.96	2,494	871.89	2,851	709.48	3,569	601.32	4,295
40,000	1,013.30	2,559	894.25	2,924	727.67	3,660	616.74	4,405
42,000	1,063.96	2,686	938.96	3,070	764.06	3,844	647.58	4,626
44,000	1,114.63	2,814	983.67	3,216	800.44	4,026	678.41	4,846
46,000	1,165.29	2,942	1,028.38	3,362	836.83	4,210	709.25	5,066
48,000	1,215.95	3,070	1,073.09	3,508	873.21	4,393	740.09	5,286
50,000	1,266.62	3,198	1,117.81	3,655	909.59	4,575	770.92	5,506

39

AUTO LOAN PAYMENTS

AMOUNT OF LOAN	12 MOS		24 MOS		30 MOS		36 MOS	
	MONTHLY PAYMENT	TOTAL INTRST	MONTHLY PAYMENT	TOTAL INTRST	MONTHLY PAYMENT	TOTAL INTRST	MONTHLY PAYMENT	TOTAL INTRST
$ 1	0.09	0	0.05	0	0.04	0	0.03	0
2	0.18	0	0.09	0	0.07	0	0.06	0
3	0.26	0	0.13	0	0.11	0	0.09	0
4	0.35	0	0.18	0	0.14	0	0.12	0
5	0.43	0	0.22	0	0.18	0	0.15	0
6	0.52	0	0.26	0	0.21	0	0.18	0
7	0.60	0	0.31	0	0.25	1	0.21	1
8	0.69	0	0.35	0	0.28	0	0.24	1
9	0.77	0	0.39	0	0.32	1	0.27	1
10	0.86	0	0.44	1	0.35	1	0.30	1
20	1.71	1	0.87	1	0.70	1	0.59	1
30	2.56	1	1.30	1	1.05	2	0.89	2
40	3.41	1	1.74	2	1.40	2	1.18	2
50	4.26	1	2.17	2	1.75	3	1.48	3
60	5.11	1	2.60	2	2.10	3	1.77	4
70	5.96	2	3.04	3	2.45	4	2.06	4
80	6.81	2	3.47	3	2.80	4	2.36	5
90	7.66	2	3.90	4	3.15	5	2.65	5
100	8.51	2	4.34	4	3.50	5	2.95	6
200	17.01	4	8.67	8	7.00	10	5.89	12
300	25.52	6	13.00	12	10.50	15	8.83	18
400	34.02	8	17.33	16	13.99	20	11.77	24
500	42.52	10	21.66	20	17.49	25	14.71	30
600	51.03	12	25.99	24	20.99	30	17.65	35
700	59.53	14	30.32	28	24.49	35	20.59	41
800	68.03	16	34.66	32	27.98	39	23.54	47
900	76.54	18	38.99	36	31.48	44	26.48	53
1,000	85.04	20	43.32	40	34.98	49	29.42	59
2,000	170.08	41	86.63	79	69.95	99	58.83	118
3,000	255.11	61	129.95	119	104.92	148	88.24	177
4,000	340.15	82	173.26	158	139.89	197	117.66	236
5,000	425.18	102	216.57	197	174.87	246	147.07	295
6,000	510.22	123	259.89	237	209.84	295	176.48	353
7,000	595.26	143	303.20	277	244.81	344	205.90	412
8,000	680.29	163	346.51	316	279.78	393	235.31	471
9,000	765.33	184	389.83	356	314.76	443	264.72	530
10,000	850.36	204	433.14	395	349.73	492	294.13	589
11,000	935.40	225	476.46	435	384.70	541	323.55	648
12,000	1,020.43	245	519.77	474	419.67	590	352.96	707
13,000	1,105.47	266	563.08	514	454.64	639	382.37	765
14,000	1,190.51	286	606.40	554	489.62	689	411.79	824
15,000	1,275.54	306	649.71	593	524.59	738	441.20	883
16,000	1,360.58	327	693.02	632	559.56	787	470.61	942
17,000	1,445.61	347	736.34	672	594.53	836	500.02	1,001
18,000	1,530.65	368	779.65	712	629.51	886	529.44	1,060
19,000	1,615.68	388	822.97	751	664.48	934	558.85	1,119
20,000	1,700.72	409	866.28	791	699.45	984	588.26	1,177
21,000	1,785.76	429	909.59	830	734.42	1,033	617.68	1,236
22,000	1,870.79	449	952.91	870	769.39	1,082	647.09	1,295
23,000	1,955.83	470	996.22	909	804.37	1,131	676.50	1,354
24,000	2,040.86	490	1,039.53	949	839.34	1,180	705.91	1,413
25,000	2,125.90	511	1,082.85	988	874.31	1,229	735.33	1,472
26,000	2,210.93	531	1,126.16	1,028	909.28	1,278	764.74	1,531
27,000	2,295.97	552	1,169.48	1,068	944.26	1,328	794.15	1,589
28,000	2,381.01	572	1,212.79	1,107	979.23	1,377	823.57	1,649
29,000	2,466.04	592	1,256.10	1,146	1,014.20	1,426	852.98	1,707
30,000	2,551.08	613	1,299.42	1,186	1,049.17	1,475	882.39	1,766
31,000	2,636.11	633	1,342.73	1,226	1,084.15	1,525	911.80	1,825
32,000	2,721.15	654	1,386.04	1,265	1,119.12	1,574	941.22	1,884
33,000	2,806.18	674	1,429.36	1,305	1,154.09	1,623	970.63	1,943
34,000	2,891.22	695	1,472.67	1,344	1,189.06	1,672	1,000.04	2,001
35,000	2,976.26	715	1,515.99	1,384	1,224.03	1,721	1,029.46	2,061
36,000	3,061.29	735	1,559.30	1,423	1,259.01	1,770	1,058.87	2,119
37,000	3,146.33	756	1,602.61	1,463	1,293.98	1,819	1,088.28	2,178
38,000	3,231.36	776	1,645.93	1,502	1,328.95	1,869	1,117.70	2,237
39,000	3,316.40	797	1,689.24	1,542	1,363.92	1,918	1,147.11	2,296
40,000	3,401.43	817	1,732.56	1,581	1,398.90	1,967	1,176.52	2,355
42,000	3,571.51	858	1,819.18	1,660	1,468.84	2,065	1,235.35	2,473
44,000	3,741.58	899	1,905.81	1,739	1,538.78	2,163	1,294.17	2,590
46,000	3,911.65	940	1,992.44	1,819	1,608.73	2,262	1,353.00	2,708
48,000	4,081.72	981	2,079.06	1,897	1,678.67	2,360	1,411.82	2,826
50,000	4,251.79	1,021	2,165.69	1,977	1,748.62	2,459	1,470.65	2,943

AUTO LOAN PAYMENTS 3.75%

AMOUNT OF LOAN	42 MOS		48 MOS		60 MOS		72 MOS	
	MONTHLY PAYMENT	TOTAL INTRST	MONTHLY PAYMENT	TOTAL INTRST	MONTHLY PAYMENT	TOTAL INTRST	MONTHLY PAYMENT	TOTAL INTRST
$ 1	0.03	0	0.03	0	0.02	0	0.02	0
2	0.06	0	0.05	0	0.04	0	0.04	1
3	0.08	1	0.07	0	0.06	0	0.05	1
4	0.11	1	0.09	0	0.08	1	0.07	1
5	0.13	0	0.12	1	0.10	1	0.08	1
6	0.16	1	0.14	1	0.11	1	0.10	1
7	0.18	1	0.16	1	0.13	1	0.11	1
8	0.21	1	0.18	1	0.15	1	0.13	1
9	0.23	1	0.21	1	0.17	1	0.14	1
10	0.26	1	0.23	1	0.19	1	0.16	2
20	0.51	1	0.45	2	0.37	2	0.32	3
30	0.77	2	0.68	3	0.55	3	0.47	4
40	1.02	3	0.90	3	0.74	4	0.63	5
50	1.28	4	1.13	4	0.92	5	0.78	6
60	1.53	4	1.35	5	1.10	6	0.94	8
70	1.79	5	1.58	6	1.29	7	1.09	8
80	2.04	6	1.80	6	1.47	8	1.25	10
90	2.29	6	2.03	7	1.65	9	1.40	11
100	2.55	7	2.25	8	1.84	10	1.56	12
200	5.09	14	4.50	16	3.67	20	3.11	24
300	7.64	21	6.75	24	5.50	30	4.66	36
400	10.18	28	8.99	32	7.33	40	6.22	48
500	12.73	35	11.24	40	9.16	50	7.77	59
600	15.27	41	13.49	48	10.99	59	9.32	71
700	17.82	48	15.73	55	12.82	69	10.88	83
800	20.36	55	17.98	63	14.65	79	12.43	95
900	22.90	62	20.23	71	16.48	89	13.98	107
1,000	25.45	69	22.47	79	18.31	99	15.54	119
2,000	50.89	137	44.94	157	36.61	197	31.07	237
3,000	76.33	206	67.41	236	54.92	295	46.60	355
4,000	101.78	275	89.87	314	73.22	393	62.13	473
5,000	127.22	343	112.34	392	91.52	491	77.66	592
6,000	152.66	412	134.81	471	109.83	590	93.19	710
7,000	178.11	481	157.28	549	128.13	688	108.73	829
8,000	203.55	549	179.74	628	146.44	786	124.26	947
9,000	228.99	618	202.21	706	164.74	884	139.79	1,065
10,000	254.44	686	224.68	785	183.04	982	155.32	1,183
11,000	279.88	755	247.15	863	201.35	1,081	170.85	1,301
12,000	305.32	823	269.61	941	219.65	1,179	186.38	1,419
13,000	330.77	892	292.08	1,020	237.96	1,278	201.91	1,538
14,000	356.21	961	314.55	1,098	256.26	1,376	217.45	1,656
15,000	381.65	1,029	337.02	1,177	274.56	1,474	232.98	1,775
16,000	407.10	1,098	359.48	1,255	292.87	1,572	248.51	1,893
17,000	432.54	1,167	381.95	1,334	311.17	1,670	264.04	2,011
18,000	457.98	1,235	404.42	1,412	329.48	1,769	279.57	2,129
19,000	483.43	1,304	426.88	1,490	347.78	1,867	295.10	2,247
20,000	508.87	1,373	449.35	1,569	366.08	1,965	310.64	2,366
21,000	534.31	1,441	471.82	1,647	384.39	2,063	326.17	2,484
22,000	559.76	1,510	494.29	1,726	402.69	2,161	341.70	2,602
23,000	585.20	1,578	516.75	1,804	421.00	2,260	357.23	2,721
24,000	610.64	1,647	539.22	1,883	439.30	2,358	372.76	2,839
25,000	636.09	1,716	561.69	1,961	457.60	2,456	388.29	2,957
26,000	661.53	1,784	584.16	2,040	475.91	2,555	403.82	3,075
27,000	686.97	1,853	606.62	2,118	494.21	2,653	419.36	3,194
28,000	712.42	1,922	629.09	2,196	512.51	2,751	434.89	3,312
29,000	737.86	1,990	651.56	2,275	530.82	2,849	450.42	3,430
30,000	763.30	2,059	674.03	2,353	549.12	2,947	465.95	3,548
31,000	788.75	2,128	696.49	2,432	567.43	3,046	481.48	3,667
32,000	814.19	2,196	718.96	2,510	585.73	3,144	497.01	3,785
33,000	839.63	2,264	741.43	2,589	604.03	3,242	512.55	3,904
34,000	865.08	2,333	763.90	2,667	622.34	3,340	528.08	4,022
35,000	890.52	2,402	786.36	2,745	640.64	3,438	543.61	4,140
36,000	915.96	2,470	808.83	2,824	658.95	3,537	559.14	4,258
37,000	941.41	2,539	831.30	2,902	677.25	3,635	574.67	4,376
38,000	966.85	2,608	853.76	2,980	695.55	3,733	590.20	4,494
39,000	992.29	2,676	876.23	3,059	713.86	3,832	605.73	4,613
40,000	1,017.74	2,745	898.70	3,138	732.16	3,930	621.27	4,731
42,000	1,068.62	2,882	943.63	3,294	768.77	4,126	652.33	4,968
44,000	1,119.51	3,019	988.57	3,451	805.38	4,323	683.39	5,204
46,000	1,170.40	3,157	1,033.50	3,608	841.99	4,519	714.46	5,441
48,000	1,221.28	3,294	1,078.44	3,765	878.59	4,715	745.52	5,677
50,000	1,272.17	3,431	1,123.37	3,922	915.20	4,912	776.58	5,914

41

3.90% AUTO LOAN PAYMENTS

AMOUNT OF LOAN	12 MOS MONTHLY PAYMENT	12 MOS TOTAL INTRST	24 MOS MONTHLY PAYMENT	24 MOS TOTAL INTRST	30 MOS MONTHLY PAYMENT	30 MOS TOTAL INTRST	36 MOS MONTHLY PAYMENT	36 MOS TOTAL INTRST
$ 1	0.09	0	0.05	0	0.04	0	0.03	0
2	0.18	0	0.09	0	0.08	0	0.06	0
3	0.26	0	0.14	0	0.11	0	0.09	0
4	0.35	0	0.18	0	0.15	1	0.12	0
5	0.43	0	0.22	0	0.18	0	0.15	0
6	0.52	0	0.27	0	0.22	1	0.18	0
7	0.60	0	0.31	0	0.25	1	0.21	1
8	0.69	0	0.35	0	0.29	1	0.24	1
9	0.77	0	0.40	1	0.32	1	0.27	1
10	0.86	0	0.44	1	0.36	1	0.30	1
20	1.71	1	0.87	1	0.71	1	0.59	1
30	2.56	1	1.31	1	1.06	2	0.89	2
40	3.41	1	1.74	2	1.41	2	1.18	2
50	4.26	1	2.17	2	1.76	3	1.48	3
60	5.11	1	2.61	3	2.11	3	1.77	4
70	5.96	2	3.04	3	2.46	4	2.07	5
80	6.81	2	3.48	4	2.81	4	2.36	5
90	7.66	2	3.91	4	3.16	5	2.66	6
100	8.52	2	4.34	4	3.51	5	2.95	6
200	17.03	4	8.68	8	7.01	10	5.90	12
300	25.54	6	13.02	12	10.52	16	8.85	19
400	34.05	9	17.36	17	14.02	21	11.80	25
500	42.56	11	21.70	21	17.52	26	14.74	31
600	51.07	13	26.03	25	21.03	31	17.69	37
700	59.58	15	30.37	29	24.53	36	20.64	43
800	68.09	17	34.71	33	28.04	41	23.59	49
900	76.60	19	39.05	37	31.54	46	26.54	55
1,000	85.11	21	43.39	41	35.04	51	29.48	61
2,000	170.21	43	86.77	82	70.08	102	58.96	123
3,000	255.32	64	130.15	124	105.12	154	88.44	184
4,000	340.42	85	173.53	165	140.16	205	117.92	245
5,000	425.53	106	216.91	206	175.20	256	147.40	306
6,000	510.63	128	260.29	247	210.24	307	176.88	368
7,000	595.73	149	303.67	288	245.28	358	206.36	429
8,000	680.84	170	347.05	329	280.32	410	235.84	490
9,000	765.94	191	390.43	370	315.35	461	265.32	552
10,000	851.05	213	433.81	411	350.39	512	294.80	613
11,000	936.15	234	477.19	453	385.43	563	324.28	674
12,000	1,021.26	255	520.57	494	420.47	614	353.76	735
13,000	1,106.36	276	563.95	535	455.51	665	383.24	797
14,000	1,191.46	298	607.33	576	490.55	717	412.72	858
15,000	1,276.57	319	650.71	617	525.59	768	442.20	919
16,000	1,361.67	340	694.09	658	560.63	819	471.68	980
17,000	1,446.78	361	737.47	699	595.67	870	501.16	1,042
18,000	1,531.88	383	780.85	740	630.70	921	530.64	1,103
19,000	1,616.99	404	824.23	782	665.74	972	560.12	1,164
20,000	1,702.09	425	867.61	823	700.78	1,023	589.60	1,226
21,000	1,787.19	446	910.99	864	735.82	1,075	619.07	1,287
22,000	1,872.30	468	954.37	905	770.86	1,126	648.55	1,348
23,000	1,957.40	489	997.75	946	805.90	1,177	678.03	1,409
24,000	2,042.51	510	1,041.14	987	840.94	1,228	707.51	1,470
25,000	2,127.61	531	1,084.52	1,028	875.98	1,279	736.99	1,532
26,000	2,212.71	553	1,127.90	1,070	911.01	1,330	766.47	1,593
27,000	2,297.82	574	1,171.28	1,111	946.05	1,382	795.95	1,654
28,000	2,382.92	595	1,214.66	1,152	981.09	1,433	825.43	1,715
29,000	2,468.02	616	1,258.04	1,193	1,016.13	1,484	854.91	1,777
30,000	2,553.13	638	1,301.42	1,234	1,051.17	1,535	884.39	1,838
31,000	2,638.24	659	1,344.80	1,275	1,086.21	1,586	913.87	1,899
32,000	2,723.34	680	1,388.18	1,316	1,121.25	1,638	943.35	1,961
33,000	2,808.44	701	1,431.56	1,357	1,156.29	1,689	972.83	2,022
34,000	2,893.55	723	1,474.94	1,399	1,191.33	1,740	1,002.31	2,083
35,000	2,978.65	744	1,518.32	1,440	1,226.36	1,791	1,031.79	2,144
36,000	3,063.76	765	1,561.70	1,481	1,261.40	1,842	1,061.27	2,206
37,000	3,148.86	786	1,605.08	1,522	1,296.44	1,893	1,090.75	2,267
38,000	3,233.97	808	1,648.46	1,563	1,331.48	1,944	1,120.23	2,328
39,000	3,319.07	829	1,691.84	1,604	1,366.52	1,996	1,149.71	2,390
40,000	3,404.17	850	1,735.22	1,645	1,401.56	2,047	1,179.19	2,451
42,000	3,574.38	893	1,821.98	1,728	1,471.64	2,149	1,238.14	2,573
44,000	3,744.59	935	1,908.74	1,810	1,541.71	2,251	1,297.10	2,696
46,000	3,914.80	978	1,995.50	1,892	1,611.79	2,354	1,356.06	2,818
48,000	4,085.01	1,020	2,082.27	1,974	1,681.87	2,456	1,415.02	2,941
50,000	4,255.22	1,063	2,169.03	2,057	1,751.95	2,559	1,473.98	3,063

42

AUTO LOAN PAYMENTS   3.90%

AMOUNT OF LOAN	42 MOS MONTHLY PAYMENT	42 MOS TOTAL INTRST	48 MOS MONTHLY PAYMENT	48 MOS TOTAL INTRST	60 MOS MONTHLY PAYMENT	60 MOS TOTAL INTRST	72 MOS MONTHLY PAYMENT	72 MOS TOTAL INTRST
$ 1	0.03	0	0.03	0	0.02	0	0.02	0
2	0.06	0	0.05	0	0.04	0	0.04	0
3	0.08	0	0.07	0	0.06	1	0.05	1
4	0.11	1	0.10	1	0.08	1	0.07	1
5	0.13	0	0.12	1	0.10	1	0.08	1
6	0.16	1	0.14	1	0.12	1	0.10	1
7	0.18	1	0.16	1	0.13	1	0.11	1
8	0.21	1	0.19	1	0.15	1	0.13	1
9	0.23	1	0.21	1	0.17	1	0.15	2
10	0.26	1	0.23	1	0.19	1	0.16	2
20	0.52	2	0.46	2	0.37	2	0.32	3
30	0.77	3	0.68	3	0.56	4	0.47	4
40	1.03	3	0.91	4	0.74	4	0.63	5
50	1.28	4	1.13	4	0.92	5	0.78	6
60	1.54	5	1.36	5	1.11	7	0.94	8
70	1.79	5	1.58	6	1.29	7	1.10	9
80	2.05	6	1.81	7	1.47	8	1.25	10
90	2.30	7	2.03	7	1.66	10	1.41	12
100	2.56	8	2.26	8	1.84	10	1.56	12
200	5.11	15	4.51	16	3.68	21	3.12	25
300	7.66	22	6.77	25	5.52	31	4.68	37
400	10.21	29	9.02	33	7.35	41	6.24	49
500	12.76	36	11.27	41	9.19	51	7.80	62
600	15.31	43	13.53	49	11.03	62	9.36	74
700	17.86	50	15.78	57	12.87	72	10.92	86
800	20.41	57	18.03	65	14.70	82	12.48	99
900	22.96	64	20.29	74	16.54	92	14.04	111
1,000	25.52	72	22.54	82	18.38	103	15.60	123
2,000	51.03	143	45.07	163	36.75	205	31.20	246
3,000	76.54	215	67.61	245	55.12	307	46.80	370
4,000	102.05	286	90.14	327	73.49	409	62.40	493
5,000	127.56	358	112.68	409	91.86	512	78.00	616
6,000	153.07	429	135.21	490	110.23	614	93.60	739
7,000	178.58	500	157.75	572	128.61	717	109.20	862
8,000	204.09	572	180.28	653	146.98	819	124.80	986
9,000	229.60	643	202.81	735	165.35	921	140.40	1,109
10,000	255.11	715	225.35	817	183.72	1,023	156.00	1,232
11,000	280.62	786	247.88	898	202.09	1,125	171.60	1,355
12,000	306.13	857	270.42	980	220.46	1,228	187.20	1,478
13,000	331.64	929	292.95	1,062	238.83	1,330	202.80	1,602
14,000	357.15	1,000	315.49	1,144	257.21	1,433	218.40	1,725
15,000	382.66	1,072	338.02	1,225	275.58	1,535	234.00	1,848
16,000	408.17	1,143	360.55	1,306	293.95	1,637	249.60	1,971
17,000	433.68	1,215	383.09	1,388	312.32	1,739	265.20	2,094
18,000	459.19	1,286	405.62	1,470	330.69	1,841	280.80	2,218
19,000	484.70	1,357	428.16	1,552	349.06	1,944	296.40	2,341
20,000	510.21	1,429	450.69	1,633	367.43	2,046	312.00	2,464
21,000	535.72	1,500	473.23	1,715	385.81	2,149	327.60	2,587
22,000	561.23	1,572	495.76	1,796	404.18	2,251	343.20	2,710
23,000	586.74	1,643	518.29	1,878	422.55	2,353	358.80	2,834
24,000	612.25	1,715	540.83	1,960	440.92	2,455	374.40	2,957
25,000	637.76	1,786	563.36	2,041	459.29	2,557	390.00	3,080
26,000	663.27	1,857	585.90	2,123	477.66	2,660	405.60	3,203
27,000	688.78	1,929	608.43	2,205	496.03	2,762	421.20	3,326
28,000	714.29	2,000	630.97	2,287	514.41	2,865	436.80	3,450
29,000	739.80	2,072	653.50	2,368	532.78	2,967	452.40	3,573
30,000	765.31	2,143	676.04	2,450	551.15	3,069	467.99	3,695
31,000	790.82	2,214	698.57	2,531	569.52	3,171	483.59	3,818
32,000	816.33	2,286	721.10	2,613	587.89	3,273	499.19	3,942
33,000	841.84	2,357	743.64	2,695	606.26	3,376	514.79	4,065
34,000	867.35	2,429	766.17	2,776	624.63	3,478	530.39	4,188
35,000	892.86	2,500	788.71	2,858	643.01	3,581	545.99	4,311
36,000	918.37	2,572	811.24	2,940	661.38	3,683	561.59	4,434
37,000	943.88	2,643	833.78	3,021	679.75	3,785	577.19	4,558
38,000	969.39	2,714	856.31	3,103	698.12	3,887	592.79	4,681
39,000	994.90	2,786	878.84	3,184	716.49	3,989	608.39	4,804
40,000	1,020.41	2,857	901.38	3,266	734.86	4,092	623.99	4,927
42,000	1,071.43	3,000	946.45	3,430	771.61	4,297	655.19	5,174
44,000	1,122.45	3,143	991.52	3,593	808.35	4,501	686.39	5,420
46,000	1,173.47	3,286	1,036.58	3,756	845.09	4,705	717.59	5,666
48,000	1,224.49	3,429	1,081.65	3,919	881.83	4,910	748.79	5,913
50,000	1,275.51	3,571	1,126.72	4,083	918.58	5,115	779.99	6,159

AUTO LOAN PAYMENTS

AMOUNT OF LOAN	12 MOS		24 MOS		30 MOS		36 MOS	
	MONTHLY PAYMENT	TOTAL INTRST	MONTHLY PAYMENT	TOTAL INTRST	MONTHLY PAYMENT	TOTAL INTRST	MONTHLY PAYMENT	TOTAL INTRST
$ 1	0.09	0	0.05	0	0.04	0	0.03	0
2	0.18	0	0.09	0	0.08	0	0.06	0
3	0.26	0	0.14	0	0.11	0	0.09	0
4	0.35	0	0.18	0	0.15	1	0.12	0
5	0.43	0	0.22	0	0.18	0	0.15	0
6	0.52	0	0.27	0	0.22	0	0.18	0
7	0.60	0	0.31	0	0.25	1	0.21	1
8	0.69	0	0.35	0	0.29	0	0.24	1
9	0.77	0	0.40	1	0.32	1	0.27	1
10	0.86	0	0.44	1	0.36	1	0.30	1
20	1.71	1	0.87	1	0.71	1	0.60	2
30	2.56	1	1.31	1	1.06	2	0.89	2
40	3.41	1	1.74	2	1.41	2	1.19	3
50	4.26	1	2.18	2	1.76	3	1.48	3
60	5.11	1	2.61	3	2.11	3	1.78	4
70	5.97	2	3.04	3	2.46	4	2.07	5
80	6.82	2	3.48	4	2.81	4	2.37	5
90	7.67	2	3.91	4	3.16	5	2.66	6
100	8.52	2	4.35	4	3.51	5	2.96	7
200	17.03	4	8.69	9	7.02	11	5.91	13
300	25.55	7	13.03	13	10.53	16	8.86	19
400	34.06	9	17.37	17	14.04	21	11.81	25
500	42.58	11	21.72	21	17.55	27	14.77	32
600	51.09	13	26.06	25	21.05	32	17.72	38
700	59.61	15	30.40	30	24.56	37	20.67	44
800	68.12	17	34.74	34	28.07	42	23.62	50
900	76.64	20	39.09	38	31.58	47	26.58	57
1,000	85.15	22	43.43	42	35.09	53	29.53	63
2,000	170.30	44	86.85	84	70.17	105	59.05	126
3,000	255.45	65	130.28	127	105.25	158	88.58	189
4,000	340.60	87	173.70	169	140.34	210	118.10	252
5,000	425.75	109	217.13	211	175.42	263	147.62	314
6,000	510.90	131	260.55	253	210.50	315	177.15	377
7,000	596.05	153	303.98	296	245.59	368	206.67	440
8,000	681.20	174	347.40	338	280.67	420	236.20	503
9,000	766.35	196	390.83	380	315.75	473	265.72	566
10,000	851.50	218	434.25	422	350.84	525	295.24	629
11,000	936.65	240	477.68	464	385.92	578	324.77	692
12,000	1,021.80	262	521.10	506	421.00	630	354.29	754
13,000	1,106.95	283	564.53	549	456.09	683	383.82	818
14,000	1,192.10	305	607.95	591	491.17	735	413.34	880
15,000	1,277.25	327	651.38	633	526.25	788	442.86	943
16,000	1,362.40	349	694.80	675	561.34	840	472.39	1,006
17,000	1,447.55	371	738.23	718	596.42	893	501.91	1,069
18,000	1,532.70	392	781.65	760	631.50	945	531.44	1,132
19,000	1,617.85	414	825.08	802	666.59	998	560.96	1,195
20,000	1,703.00	436	868.50	844	701.67	1,050	590.48	1,257
21,000	1,788.15	458	911.93	886	736.75	1,103	620.01	1,320
22,000	1,873.30	480	955.35	928	771.84	1,155	649.53	1,383
23,000	1,958.45	501	998.78	971	806.92	1,208	679.06	1,446
24,000	2,043.60	523	1,042.20	1,013	842.00	1,260	708.58	1,509
25,000	2,128.75	545	1,085.63	1,055	877.09	1,313	738.10	1,572
26,000	2,213.90	567	1,129.05	1,097	912.17	1,365	767.63	1,635
27,000	2,299.05	589	1,172.48	1,140	947.25	1,418	797.15	1,697
28,000	2,384.20	610	1,215.90	1,182	982.34	1,470	826.68	1,760
29,000	2,469.35	632	1,259.33	1,224	1,017.42	1,523	856.20	1,823
30,000	2,554.50	654	1,302.75	1,266	1,052.50	1,575	885.72	1,886
31,000	2,639.65	676	1,346.18	1,308	1,087.59	1,628	915.25	1,949
32,000	2,724.80	698	1,389.60	1,350	1,122.67	1,680	944.77	2,012
33,000	2,809.95	719	1,433.03	1,393	1,157.75	1,733	974.30	2,075
34,000	2,895.10	741	1,476.45	1,435	1,192.84	1,785	1,003.82	2,138
35,000	2,980.25	763	1,519.88	1,477	1,227.92	1,838	1,033.34	2,200
36,000	3,065.40	785	1,563.30	1,519	1,263.00	1,890	1,062.87	2,263
37,000	3,150.55	807	1,606.73	1,562	1,298.09	1,943	1,092.39	2,326
38,000	3,235.00	828	1,650.15	1,604	1,333.17	1,995	1,121.92	2,389
39,000	3,320.85	850	1,693.58	1,646	1,368.25	2,048	1,151.44	2,452
40,000	3,406.00	872	1,737.00	1,688	1,403.34	2,100	1,180.96	2,515
42,000	3,576.30	916	1,823.85	1,772	1,473.50	2,205	1,240.01	2,640
44,000	3,746.60	959	1,910.70	1,857	1,543.67	2,310	1,299.06	2,766
46,000	3,916.90	1,003	1,997.55	1,941	1,613.83	2,415	1,358.11	2,892
48,000	4,087.20	1,046	2,084.40	2,026	1,684.00	2,520	1,417.16	3,018
50,000	4,257.50	1,090	2,171.25	2,110	1,754.17	2,625	1,476.20	3,143

AUTO LOAN PAYMENTS   4.00%

AMOUNT OF LOAN	42 MOS MONTHLY PAYMENT	42 MOS TOTAL INTRST	48 MOS MONTHLY PAYMENT	48 MOS TOTAL INTRST	60 MOS MONTHLY PAYMENT	60 MOS TOTAL INTRST	72 MOS MONTHLY PAYMENT	72 MOS TOTAL INTRST
$ 1	0.03	0	0.03	0	0.02	0	0.02	0
2	0.06	0	0.05	0	0.04	0	0.04	1
3	0.08	0	0.07	0	0.06	1	0.05	1
4	0.11	1	0.10	1	0.08	1	0.07	1
5	0.13	0	0.12	1	0.10	1	0.08	1
6	0.16	1	0.14	1	0.12	1	0.10	1
7	0.18	1	0.16	1	0.13	1	0.11	1
8	0.21	1	0.19	1	0.15	1	0.13	1
9	0.23	1	0.21	1	0.17	1	0.15	2
10	0.26	1	0.23	1	0.19	1	0.16	2
20	0.52	2	0.46	2	0.37	2	0.32	3
30	0.77	2	0.68	3	0.56	4	0.47	4
40	1.03	3	0.91	4	0.74	4	0.63	5
50	1.28	4	1.13	4	0.93	6	0.79	7
60	1.54	5	1.36	5	1.11	7	0.94	8
70	1.79	5	1.59	6	1.29	7	1.10	9
80	2.05	6	1.81	7	1.48	9	1.26	11
90	2.30	7	2.04	8	1.66	10	1.41	12
100	2.56	8	2.26	8	1.85	11	1.57	13
200	5.12	15	4.52	17	3.69	21	3.13	25
300	7.67	22	6.78	25	5.53	32	4.70	38
400	10.23	30	9.04	34	7.37	42	6.26	51
500	12.78	37	11.29	42	9.21	53	7.83	64
600	15.34	44	13.55	50	11.05	63	9.39	76
700	17.89	51	15.81	59	12.90	74	10.96	89
800	20.45	59	18.07	67	14.74	84	12.52	101
900	23.00	66	20.33	76	16.58	95	14.09	114
1,000	25.56	74	22.58	84	18.42	105	15.65	127
2,000	51.11	147	45.16	168	36.84	210	31.30	254
3,000	76.67	220	67.74	252	55.25	315	46.94	380
4,000	102.22	293	90.32	335	73.67	420	62.59	506
5,000	127.78	367	112.90	419	92.09	525	78.23	633
6,000	153.33	440	135.48	503	110.50	630	93.88	759
7,000	178.89	513	158.06	587	128.92	735	109.52	885
8,000	204.44	586	180.64	671	147.34	840	125.17	1,012
9,000	230.00	660	203.22	755	165.75	945	140.81	1,138
10,000	255.55	733	225.80	838	184.17	1,050	156.46	1,265
11,000	281.11	807	248.37	922	202.59	1,155	172.10	1,391
12,000	306.66	880	270.95	1,006	221.00	1,260	187.75	1,518
13,000	332.22	953	293.53	1,089	239.42	1,365	203.39	1,644
14,000	357.77	1,026	316.11	1,173	257.84	1,470	219.04	1,771
15,000	383.32	1,099	338.69	1,257	276.25	1,575	234.68	1,897
16,000	408.88	1,173	361.27	1,341	294.67	1,680	250.33	2,024
17,000	434.43	1,246	383.85	1,425	313.09	1,785	265.97	2,150
18,000	459.99	1,320	406.43	1,509	331.50	1,890	281.62	2,277
19,000	485.54	1,393	429.01	1,592	349.92	1,995	297.26	2,403
20,000	511.10	1,466	451.59	1,676	368.34	2,100	312.91	2,530
21,000	536.65	1,539	474.17	1,760	386.75	2,205	328.55	2,656
22,000	562.21	1,613	496.74	1,844	405.17	2,310	344.20	2,782
23,000	587.76	1,686	519.32	1,927	423.59	2,415	359.84	2,908
24,000	613.32	1,759	541.90	2,011	442.00	2,520	375.49	3,035
25,000	638.87	1,833	564.48	2,095	460.42	2,625	391.13	3,161
26,000	664.43	1,906	587.06	2,179	478.83	2,730	406.78	3,288
27,000	689.98	1,979	609.64	2,263	497.25	2,835	422.42	3,414
28,000	715.54	2,053	632.22	2,347	515.67	2,940	438.07	3,541
29,000	741.09	2,126	654.80	2,430	534.08	3,045	453.72	3,668
30,000	766.64	2,199	677.38	2,514	552.50	3,150	469.36	3,794
31,000	792.20	2,272	699.96	2,598	570.92	3,255	485.01	3,921
32,000	817.75	2,346	722.53	2,681	589.33	3,360	500.65	4,047
33,000	843.31	2,419	745.11	2,765	607.75	3,465	516.30	4,174
34,000	868.86	2,492	767.69	2,849	626.17	3,570	531.94	4,300
35,000	894.42	2,566	790.27	2,933	644.58	3,675	547.59	4,426
36,000	919.97	2,639	812.85	3,017	663.00	3,780	563.23	4,553
37,000	945.53	2,712	835.43	3,101	681.42	3,885	578.88	4,679
38,000	971.08	2,785	858.01	3,184	699.83	3,990	594.52	4,805
39,000	996.64	2,859	880.59	3,268	718.25	4,095	610.17	4,932
40,000	1,022.19	2,932	903.17	3,352	736.67	4,200	625.81	5,058
42,000	1,073.30	3,079	948.33	3,520	773.50	4,410	657.10	5,311
44,000	1,124.41	3,225	993.48	3,687	810.33	4,620	688.39	5,564
46,000	1,175.52	3,372	1,038.64	3,855	847.17	4,830	719.68	5,817
48,000	1,226.63	3,518	1,083.80	4,022	884.00	5,040	750.97	6,070
50,000	1,277.74	3,665	1,128.96	4,190	920.83	5,250	782.26	6,323

4.25%   AUTO LOAN PAYMENTS

AMOUNT OF LOAN	12 MOS		24 MOS		30 MOS		36 MOS	
	MONTHLY PAYMENT	TOTAL INTRST	MONTHLY PAYMENT	TOTAL INTRST	MONTHLY PAYMENT	TOTAL INTRST	MONTHLY PAYMENT	TOTAL INTRST
$ 1	0.09	0	0.05	0	0.04	0	0.03	0
2	0.18	0	0.09	0	0.08	0	0.06	0
3	0.26	0	0.14	0	0.11	0	0.09	0
4	0.35	0	0.18	0	0.15	1	0.12	0
5	0.43	0	0.22	0	0.18	0	0.15	0
6	0.52	0	0.27	0	0.22	1	0.18	0
7	0.60	0	0.31	0	0.25	1	0.21	1
8	0.69	0	0.35	0	0.29	1	0.24	1
9	0.77	0	0.40	1	0.32	1	0.27	1
10	0.86	0	0.44	1	0.36	1	0.30	1
20	1.71	1	0.88	1	0.71	1	0.60	2
30	2.56	1	1.31	1	1.06	2	0.89	2
40	3.42	1	1.75	2	1.41	2	1.19	3
50	4.27	1	2.18	2	1.76	3	1.49	4
60	5.12	1	2.62	3	2.12	4	1.78	4
70	5.97	2	3.05	3	2.47	4	2.08	5
80	6.83	2	3.49	4	2.82	5	2.38	6
90	7.68	2	3.92	4	3.17	5	2.67	6
100	8.53	2	4.36	5	3.52	6	2.97	7
200	17.06	5	8.71	9	7.04	11	5.93	13
300	25.58	7	13.07	14	10.56	17	8.90	20
400	34.11	9	17.42	18	14.08	22	11.86	27
500	42.64	12	21.77	22	17.60	28	14.82	34
600	51.16	14	26.13	27	21.12	34	17.79	40
700	59.69	16	30.48	32	24.64	39	20.75	47
800	68.22	19	34.83	36	28.16	45	23.71	54
900	76.74	21	39.19	41	31.68	50	26.68	60
1,000	85.27	23	43.54	45	35.20	56	29.64	67
2,000	170.53	46	87.08	90	70.39	112	59.28	134
3,000	255.80	70	130.61	135	105.59	168	88.91	201
4,000	341.06	93	174.15	180	140.78	223	118.55	268
5,000	426.33	116	217.69	225	175.98	279	148.18	334
6,000	511.59	139	261.22	269	211.17	335	177.82	402
7,000	596.85	162	304.76	314	246.37	391	207.45	468
8,000	682.12	185	348.30	359	281.56	447	237.09	535
9,000	767.38	209	391.83	404	316.76	503	266.72	602
10,000	852.65	232	435.37	449	351.95	559	296.36	669
11,000	937.91	255	478.90	494	387.14	614	325.99	736
12,000	1,023.18	278	522.44	539	422.34	670	355.63	803
13,000	1,108.44	301	565.98	584	457.53	726	385.26	869
14,000	1,193.70	324	609.51	628	492.73	782	414.90	936
15,000	1,278.97	348	653.05	673	527.92	838	444.53	1,003
16,000	1,364.23	371	696.59	718	563.12	894	474.17	1,070
17,000	1,449.50	394	740.12	763	598.31	949	503.81	1,137
18,000	1,534.76	417	783.66	808	633.51	1,005	533.44	1,204
19,000	1,620.02	440	827.19	853	668.70	1,061	563.08	1,271
20,000	1,705.29	463	870.73	898	703.89	1,117	592.71	1,338
21,000	1,790.55	487	914.27	942	739.09	1,173	622.35	1,405
22,000	1,875.82	510	957.80	987	774.28	1,228	651.98	1,471
23,000	1,961.08	533	1,001.34	1,032	809.48	1,284	681.62	1,538
24,000	2,046.35	556	1,044.88	1,077	844.67	1,340	711.25	1,605
25,000	2,131.61	579	1,088.41	1,122	879.87	1,396	740.89	1,672
26,000	2,216.87	602	1,131.95	1,167	915.06	1,452	770.52	1,739
27,000	2,302.14	626	1,175.48	1,212	950.26	1,508	800.16	1,806
28,000	2,387.40	649	1,219.02	1,256	985.45	1,564	829.79	1,872
29,000	2,472.67	672	1,262.56	1,301	1,020.64	1,619	859.43	1,939
30,000	2,557.93	695	1,306.09	1,346	1,055.84	1,675	889.06	2,006
31,000	2,643.19	718	1,349.63	1,391	1,091.03	1,731	918.70	2,073
32,000	2,728.46	742	1,393.17	1,436	1,126.23	1,787	948.34	2,140
33,000	2,813.72	765	1,436.70	1,481	1,161.42	1,843	977.97	2,207
34,000	2,898.99	788	1,480.24	1,526	1,196.62	1,899	1,007.61	2,274
35,000	2,984.25	811	1,523.77	1,570	1,231.81	1,954	1,037.24	2,341
36,000	3,069.52	834	1,567.31	1,615	1,267.01	2,010	1,066.88	2,408
37,000	3,154.78	857	1,610.85	1,660	1,302.20	2,066	1,096.51	2,474
38,000	3,240.04	880	1,654.38	1,705	1,337.39	2,122	1,126.15	2,541
39,000	3,325.31	904	1,697.92	1,750	1,372.59	2,178	1,155.78	2,608
40,000	3,410.57	927	1,741.46	1,795	1,407.78	2,233	1,185.42	2,675
42,000	3,581.10	973	1,828.53	1,885	1,478.17	2,345	1,244.69	2,809
44,000	3,751.63	1,020	1,915.60	1,974	1,548.56	2,457	1,303.96	2,943
46,000	3,922.16	1,066	2,002.67	2,064	1,618.95	2,569	1,363.23	3,076
48,000	4,092.69	1,112	2,089.75	2,154	1,689.34	2,680	1,422.50	3,210
50,000	4,263.21	1,159	2,176.82	2,244	1,759.73	2,792	1,481.77	3,344

46

AUTO LOAN PAYMENTS — 4.25%

AMOUNT OF LOAN	42 MOS Monthly Payment	42 MOS Total Intrst	48 MOS Monthly Payment	48 MOS Total Intrst	60 MOS Monthly Payment	60 MOS Total Intrst	72 MOS Monthly Payment	72 MOS Total Intrst
$ 1	0.03	0	0.03	0	0.02	0	0.02	0
2	0.06	0	0.05	0	0.04	0	0.04	1
3	0.08	0	0.07	0	0.06	1	0.05	1
4	0.11	1	0.10	1	0.08	1	0.07	1
5	0.13	0	0.12	1	0.10	1	0.08	1
6	0.16	1	0.14	1	0.12	1	0.10	1
7	0.18	1	0.16	1	0.13	1	0.12	2
8	0.21	1	0.19	1	0.15	1	0.13	1
9	0.24	1	0.21	1	0.17	1	0.15	2
10	0.26	1	0.23	1	0.19	1	0.16	2
20	0.52	1	0.46	2	0.38	3	0.32	3
30	0.77	2	0.69	3	0.56	4	0.48	5
40	1.03	3	0.91	4	0.75	5	0.64	6
50	1.29	4	1.14	5	0.93	6	0.79	7
60	1.54	4	1.37	6	1.12	7	0.95	8
70	1.80	6	1.59	6	1.30	8	1.11	10
80	2.06	7	1.82	7	1.49	9	1.27	11
90	2.31	7	2.05	8	1.67	10	1.42	12
100	2.57	8	2.27	9	1.86	12	1.58	14
200	5.14	16	4.54	18	3.71	23	3.16	28
300	7.70	23	6.81	27	5.56	34	4.73	41
400	10.27	31	9.08	36	7.42	45	6.31	54
500	12.84	39	11.35	45	9.27	56	7.88	67
600	15.40	47	13.62	54	11.12	67	9.46	81
700	17.97	55	15.89	63	12.98	79	11.04	95
800	20.54	63	18.16	72	14.83	90	12.61	108
900	23.10	70	20.43	81	16.68	101	14.19	122
1,000	25.67	78	22.70	90	18.53	112	15.76	135
2,000	51.34	156	45.39	179	37.06	224	31.52	269
3,000	77.00	234	68.08	268	55.59	335	47.28	404
4,000	102.67	312	90.77	357	74.12	447	63.04	539
5,000	128.34	390	113.46	446	92.65	559	78.80	674
6,000	154.00	468	136.15	535	111.18	671	94.56	808
7,000	179.67	546	158.84	624	129.71	783	110.32	943
8,000	205.34	624	181.53	713	148.24	894	126.08	1,078
9,000	231.00	702	204.22	803	166.77	1,006	141.84	1,212
10,000	256.67	780	226.92	892	185.30	1,118	157.60	1,347
11,000	282.33	858	249.61	981	203.83	1,230	173.36	1,482
12,000	308.00	936	272.30	1,070	222.36	1,342	189.12	1,617
13,000	333.67	1,014	294.99	1,160	240.89	1,453	204.88	1,751
14,000	359.33	1,092	317.68	1,249	259.42	1,565	220.64	1,886
15,000	385.00	1,170	340.37	1,338	277.95	1,677	236.40	2,021
16,000	410.67	1,248	363.06	1,427	296.48	1,789	252.15	2,155
17,000	436.33	1,326	385.75	1,516	315.01	1,901	267.91	2,290
18,000	462.00	1,404	408.44	1,605	333.54	2,012	283.67	2,424
19,000	487.66	1,482	431.14	1,695	352.07	2,124	299.43	2,559
20,000	513.33	1,560	453.83	1,784	370.60	2,236	315.19	2,694
21,000	539.00	1,638	476.52	1,873	389.13	2,348	330.95	2,828
22,000	564.66	1,716	499.21	1,962	407.66	2,460	346.71	2,963
23,000	590.33	1,794	521.90	2,051	426.18	2,571	362.47	3,098
24,000	616.00	1,872	544.59	2,140	444.71	2,683	378.23	3,233
25,000	641.66	1,950	567.28	2,229	463.24	2,794	393.99	3,367
26,000	667.33	2,028	589.97	2,319	481.77	2,906	409.75	3,502
27,000	693.00	2,106	612.66	2,408	500.30	3,018	425.51	3,637
28,000	718.66	2,184	635.36	2,497	518.83	3,130	441.27	3,771
29,000	744.33	2,262	658.05	2,586	537.36	3,242	457.03	3,906
30,000	769.99	2,340	680.74	2,676	555.89	3,353	472.79	4,041
31,000	795.66	2,418	703.43	2,765	574.42	3,465	488.54	4,175
32,000	821.33	2,496	726.12	2,854	592.95	3,577	504.30	4,310
33,000	846.99	2,574	748.81	2,943	611.48	3,689	520.06	4,444
34,000	872.66	2,652	771.50	3,032	630.01	3,801	535.82	4,579
35,000	898.33	2,730	794.19	3,121	648.54	3,912	551.58	4,714
36,000	923.99	2,808	816.88	3,210	667.07	4,024	567.34	4,848
37,000	949.66	2,886	839.58	3,300	685.60	4,136	583.10	4,983
38,000	975.32	2,963	862.27	3,389	704.13	4,248	598.86	5,118
39,000	1,000.99	3,042	884.96	3,478	722.66	4,360	614.62	5,253
40,000	1,026.66	3,120	907.65	3,567	741.19	4,471	630.38	5,387
42,000	1,077.99	3,276	953.03	3,745	778.25	4,695	661.90	5,657
44,000	1,129.32	3,431	998.41	3,924	815.31	4,919	693.42	5,926
46,000	1,180.65	3,587	1,043.80	4,102	852.36	5,142	724.94	6,196
48,000	1,231.99	3,744	1,089.18	4,281	889.42	5,365	756.45	6,464
50,000	1,283.32	3,899	1,134.56	4,459	926.48	5,589	787.97	6,734

4.50% AUTO LOAN PAYMENTS

AMOUNT OF LOAN	12 MOS		24 MOS		30 MOS		36 MOS	
	MONTHLY PAYMENT	TOTAL INTRST	MONTHLY PAYMENT	TOTAL INTRST	MONTHLY PAYMENT	TOTAL INTRST	MONTHLY PAYMENT	TOTAL INTRST
$ 1	0.09	0	0.05	0	0.04	0	0.03	0
2	0.18	0	0.09	0	0.08	0	0.06	0
3	0.26	0	0.14	0	0.11	0	0.09	0
4	0.35	0	0.18	0	0.15	1	0.12	0
5	0.43	0	0.22	0	0.18	0	0.15	0
6	0.52	0	0.27	0	0.22	1	0.18	0
7	0.60	0	0.31	0	0.25	1	0.21	1
8	0.69	0	0.35	0	0.29	1	0.24	1
9	0.77	0	0.40	1	0.32	1	0.27	1
10	0.86	0	0.44	1	0.36	1	0.30	1
20	1.71	1	0.88	1	0.71	1	0.60	2
30	2.57	1	1.31	1	1.06	2	0.90	2
40	3.42	1	1.75	2	1.42	2	1.19	3
50	4.27	1	2.19	3	1.77	3	1.49	4
60	5.13	2	2.62	3	2.12	4	1.79	4
70	5.98	2	3.06	3	2.48	4	2.09	5
80	6.84	2	3.50	3	2.83	5	2.38	6
90	7.69	2	3.93	4	3.18	5	2.68	7
100	8.54	2	4.37	5	3.54	6	2.98	7
200	17.08	5	8.73	10	7.07	12	5.95	14
300	25.62	7	13.10	14	10.60	18	8.93	21
400	34.16	10	17.46	19	14.13	24	11.90	28
500	42.69	12	21.83	24	17.66	30	14.88	36
600	51.23	15	26.19	29	21.19	36	17.85	43
700	59.77	17	30.56	33	24.72	42	20.83	50
800	68.31	20	34.92	38	28.25	48	23.80	57
900	76.85	22	39.29	43	31.78	53	26.78	64
1,000	85.38	25	43.65	48	35.31	59	29.75	71
2,000	170.76	49	87.30	95	70.62	119	59.50	142
3,000	256.14	74	130.95	143	105.92	178	89.25	213
4,000	341.52	98	174.60	190	141.23	237	118.99	284
5,000	426.90	123	218.24	238	176.53	296	148.74	355
6,000	512.28	147	261.89	285	211.84	355	178.49	426
7,000	597.65	172	305.54	333	247.15	414	208.23	496
8,000	683.03	196	349.19	381	282.45	474	237.98	567
9,000	768.41	221	392.84	428	317.76	533	267.73	638
10,000	853.79	245	436.48	476	353.06	592	297.47	709
11,000	939.17	270	480.13	523	388.37	651	327.22	780
12,000	1,024.55	295	523.78	571	423.68	710	356.97	851
13,000	1,109.93	319	567.43	618	458.98	769	386.72	922
14,000	1,195.30	344	611.07	666	494.29	829	416.46	993
15,000	1,280.68	368	654.72	713	529.59	888	446.21	1,064
16,000	1,366.06	393	698.37	761	564.90	947	475.96	1,135
17,000	1,451.44	417	742.02	808	600.20	1,006	505.70	1,205
18,000	1,536.82	442	785.67	856	635.51	1,065	535.45	1,276
19,000	1,622.20	466	829.31	903	670.82	1,125	565.20	1,347
20,000	1,707.58	491	872.96	951	706.12	1,184	594.94	1,418
21,000	1,792.95	515	916.61	999	741.43	1,243	624.69	1,489
22,000	1,878.33	540	960.26	1,046	776.73	1,302	654.44	1,560
23,000	1,963.71	565	1,003.90	1,094	812.04	1,361	684.18	1,630
24,000	2,049.09	589	1,047.55	1,141	847.35	1,421	713.93	1,701
25,000	2,134.47	614	1,091.20	1,189	882.65	1,480	743.68	1,772
26,000	2,219.85	638	1,134.85	1,236	917.96	1,539	773.43	1,843
27,000	2,305.23	663	1,178.50	1,284	953.26	1,598	803.17	1,914
28,000	2,390.60	687	1,222.14	1,331	988.57	1,657	832.92	1,985
29,000	2,475.98	712	1,265.79	1,379	1,023.88	1,716	862.67	2,056
30,000	2,561.36	736	1,309.44	1,427	1,059.18	1,775	892.41	2,127
31,000	2,646.74	761	1,353.09	1,474	1,094.49	1,835	922.16	2,198
32,000	2,732.12	785	1,396.73	1,522	1,129.79	1,894	951.91	2,269
33,000	2,817.50	810	1,440.38	1,569	1,165.10	1,953	981.65	2,339
34,000	2,902.87	834	1,484.03	1,617	1,200.40	2,012	1,011.40	2,410
35,000	2,988.25	859	1,527.68	1,664	1,235.71	2,071	1,041.15	2,481
36,000	3,073.63	884	1,571.33	1,712	1,271.02	2,131	1,070.89	2,552
37,000	3,159.01	908	1,614.97	1,759	1,306.32	2,190	1,100.64	2,623
38,000	3,244.39	933	1,658.62	1,807	1,341.63	2,249	1,130.39	2,694
39,000	3,329.77	957	1,702.27	1,854	1,376.93	2,308	1,160.14	2,765
40,000	3,415.15	982	1,745.92	1,902	1,412.24	2,367	1,189.88	2,836
42,000	3,585.90	1,031	1,833.21	1,997	1,482.85	2,486	1,249.38	2,978
44,000	3,756.66	1,080	1,920.51	2,092	1,553.46	2,604	1,308.87	3,119
46,000	3,927.42	1,129	2,007.80	2,187	1,624.08	2,722	1,368.36	3,261
48,000	4,098.17	1,178	2,095.10	2,282	1,694.69	2,841	1,427.86	3,403
50,000	4,268.93	1,227	2,182.40	2,378	1,765.30	2,959	1,487.35	3,545

48

AUTO LOAN PAYMENTS 4.50%

AMOUNT OF LOAN	42 MOS MONTHLY PAYMENT	42 MOS TOTAL INTRST	48 MOS MONTHLY PAYMENT	48 MOS TOTAL INTRST	60 MOS MONTHLY PAYMENT	60 MOS TOTAL INTRST	72 MOS MONTHLY PAYMENT	72 MOS TOTAL INTRST
$ 1	0.03	0	0.03	0	0.02	0	0.02	0
2	0.06	1	0.05	0	0.04	0	0.04	1
3	0.08	0	0.07	1	0.06	1	0.05	1
4	0.11	1	0.10	1	0.08	1	0.07	1
5	0.13	0	0.12	1	0.10	1	0.08	1
6	0.16	1	0.14	1	0.12	1	0.10	2
7	0.19	1	0.16	1	0.14	1	0.12	1
8	0.21	1	0.19	1	0.15	1	0.13	1
9	0.24	1	0.21	1	0.17	1	0.15	2
10	0.26	1	0.23	1	0.19	1	0.16	2
20	0.52	2	0.46	2	0.38	3	0.32	3
30	0.78	3	0.69	3	0.56	4	0.48	5
40	1.04	4	0.92	4	0.75	5	0.64	6
50	1.29	4	1.15	5	0.94	6	0.80	8
60	1.55	5	1.37	6	1.12	7	0.96	9
70	1.81	6	1.60	7	1.31	9	1.12	11
80	2.07	7	1.83	8	1.50	10	1.27	11
90	2.33	8	2.06	9	1.68	11	1.43	13
100	2.58	8	2.29	10	1.87	12	1.59	14
200	5.16	17	4.57	19	3.73	24	3.18	29
300	7.74	25	6.85	29	5.60	36	4.77	43
400	10.32	33	9.13	38	7.46	48	6.35	57
500	12.89	41	11.41	48	9.33	60	7.94	72
600	15.47	50	13.69	57	11.19	71	9.53	86
700	18.05	58	15.97	67	13.06	84	11.12	101
800	20.63	66	18.25	76	14.92	95	12.70	114
900	23.21	75	20.53	85	16.78	107	14.29	129
1,000	25.78	83	22.81	95	18.65	119	15.88	143
2,000	51.56	166	45.61	189	37.29	237	31.75	286
3,000	77.34	248	68.42	284	55.93	356	47.63	429
4,000	103.12	331	91.22	379	74.58	475	63.50	572
5,000	128.90	414	114.02	473	93.22	593	79.38	715
6,000	154.67	496	136.83	568	111.86	712	95.25	858
7,000	180.45	579	159.63	662	130.51	831	111.12	1,001
8,000	206.23	662	182.43	757	149.15	949	127.00	1,144
9,000	232.01	744	205.24	852	167.79	1,067	142.87	1,287
10,000	257.79	827	228.04	946	186.44	1,186	158.75	1,430
11,000	283.57	910	250.84	1,040	205.08	1,305	174.62	1,573
12,000	309.34	992	273.65	1,135	223.72	1,423	190.49	1,715
13,000	335.12	1,075	296.45	1,230	242.36	1,542	206.37	1,859
14,000	360.90	1,158	319.25	1,324	261.01	1,661	222.24	2,001
15,000	386.68	1,241	342.06	1,419	279.65	1,779	238.12	2,145
16,000	412.46	1,323	364.86	1,513	298.29	1,897	253.99	2,287
17,000	438.24	1,406	387.66	1,608	316.94	2,016	269.86	2,430
18,000	464.01	1,488	410.47	1,703	335.58	2,135	285.74	2,573
19,000	489.79	1,571	433.27	1,797	354.22	2,253	301.61	2,716
20,000	515.57	1,654	456.07	1,891	372.87	2,372	317.49	2,859
21,000	541.35	1,737	478.88	1,986	391.51	2,491	333.36	3,002
22,000	567.12	1,819	501.68	2,081	410.15	2,609	349.23	3,145
23,000	592.90	1,902	524.49	2,176	428.79	2,727	365.11	3,288
24,000	618.68	1,985	547.29	2,270	447.44	2,846	380.98	3,431
25,000	644.46	2,067	570.09	2,364	466.08	2,965	396.86	3,574
26,000	670.24	2,150	592.90	2,459	484.72	3,083	412.73	3,717
27,000	696.02	2,233	615.70	2,554	503.37	3,202	428.60	3,859
28,000	721.80	2,316	638.50	2,648	522.01	3,321	444.48	4,003
29,000	747.57	2,398	661.31	2,743	540.65	3,439	460.35	4,145
30,000	773.35	2,481	684.11	2,837	559.30	3,558	476.23	4,289
31,000	799.13	2,563	706.91	2,932	577.94	3,676	492.10	4,431
32,000	824.91	2,646	729.72	3,027	596.58	3,795	507.97	4,574
33,000	850.69	2,729	752.52	3,121	615.22	3,913	523.85	4,717
34,000	876.47	2,812	775.32	3,215	633.87	4,032	539.72	4,860
35,000	902.24	2,894	798.13	3,310	652.51	4,151	555.60	5,003
36,000	928.02	2,977	820.93	3,405	671.15	4,269	571.47	5,146
37,000	953.80	3,060	843.73	3,499	689.80	4,388	587.34	5,288
38,000	979.58	3,142	866.54	3,594	708.44	4,506	603.22	5,432
39,000	1,005.36	3,225	889.34	3,688	727.08	4,625	619.09	5,574
40,000	1,031.13	3,307	912.14	3,783	745.73	4,744	634.97	5,718
42,000	1,082.69	3,473	957.75	3,972	783.01	4,981	666.71	6,003
44,000	1,134.25	3,639	1,003.36	4,161	820.30	5,218	698.46	6,289
46,000	1,185.80	3,804	1,048.97	4,351	857.58	5,455	730.21	6,575
48,000	1,237.36	3,969	1,094.57	4,539	894.87	5,692	761.96	6,861
50,000	1,288.92	4,135	1,140.18	4,729	932.16	5,930	793.71	7,147

49

4.75% AUTO LOAN PAYMENTS

AMOUNT OF LOAN	12 MOS		24 MOS		30 MOS		36 MOS	
	MONTHLY PAYMENT	TOTAL INTRST	MONTHLY PAYMENT	TOTAL INTRST	MONTHLY PAYMENT	TOTAL INTRST	MONTHLY PAYMENT	TOTAL INTRST
$ 1	0.09	0	0.05	0	0.04	0	0.03	0
2	0.18	0	0.09	0	0.08	0	0.06	0
3	0.26	0	0.14	0	0.11	0	0.09	0
4	0.35	0	0.18	0	0.15	1	0.12	0
5	0.43	0	0.22	0	0.18	0	0.15	0
6	0.52	0	0.27	0	0.22	1	0.18	0
7	0.60	0	0.31	0	0.25	1	0.21	1
8	0.69	0	0.36	1	0.29	1	0.24	1
9	0.77	0	0.40	1	0.32	1	0.27	1
10	0.86	0	0.44	1	0.36	1	0.30	1
20	1.71	1	0.88	1	0.71	1	0.60	2
30	2.57	1	1.32	2	1.07	2	0.90	2
40	3.42	1	1.76	2	1.42	3	1.20	3
50	4.28	1	2.19	3	1.78	3	1.50	4
60	5.13	1	2.63	3	2.13	3	1.80	5
70	5.99	2	3.07	4	2.48	4	2.10	6
80	6.84	2	3.51	4	2.84	5	2.39	6
90	7.70	2	3.94	5	3.19	6	2.69	7
100	8.55	3	4.38	5	3.55	7	2.99	8
200	17.10	5	8.76	10	7.09	13	5.98	15
300	25.65	8	13.13	15	10.63	19	8.96	23
400	34.20	10	17.51	20	14.17	25	11.95	30
500	42.75	13	21.88	25	17.71	31	14.93	37
600	51.30	16	26.26	30	21.26	38	17.92	45
700	59.85	18	30.64	35	24.80	44	20.91	53
800	68.40	21	35.01	40	28.34	50	23.89	60
900	76.95	23	39.39	45	31.88	56	26.88	68
1,000	85.50	26	43.76	50	35.42	63	29.86	75
2,000	170.99	52	87.52	100	70.84	125	59.72	150
3,000	256.48	78	131.28	151	106.26	188	89.58	225
4,000	341.98	104	175.04	201	141.68	250	119.44	300
5,000	427.47	130	218.80	251	177.09	313	149.30	375
6,000	512.96	156	262.56	301	212.51	375	179.16	450
7,000	598.46	182	306.32	352	247.93	438	209.02	525
8,000	683.95	207	350.08	402	283.35	501	238.88	600
9,000	769.44	233	393.84	452	318.76	563	268.73	674
10,000	854.93	259	437.60	502	354.18	625	298.59	749
11,000	940.43	285	481.36	553	389.60	688	328.45	824
12,000	1,025.92	311	525.12	603	425.02	751	358.31	899
13,000	1,111.41	337	568.88	653	460.43	813	388.17	974
14,000	1,196.91	363	612.64	703	495.85	876	418.03	1,049
15,000	1,282.40	389	656.40	754	531.27	938	447.89	1,124
16,000	1,367.89	415	700.16	804	566.69	1,001	477.75	1,199
17,000	1,453.39	441	743.92	854	602.10	1,063	507.60	1,274
18,000	1,538.88	467	787.68	904	637.52	1,126	537.46	1,349
19,000	1,624.37	492	831.44	955	672.94	1,188	567.32	1,424
20,000	1,709.86	518	875.20	1,005	708.36	1,251	597.18	1,498
21,000	1,795.36	544	918.95	1,055	743.77	1,313	627.04	1,573
22,000	1,880.85	570	962.71	1,105	779.19	1,376	656.90	1,648
23,000	1,966.34	596	1,006.47	1,155	814.61	1,438	686.76	1,723
24,000	2,051.84	622	1,050.23	1,206	850.03	1,501	716.62	1,798
25,000	2,137.33	648	1,093.99	1,256	885.44	1,563	746.47	1,873
26,000	2,222.82	674	1,137.75	1,306	920.86	1,626	776.33	1,948
27,000	2,308.31	700	1,181.51	1,356	956.28	1,688	806.19	2,023
28,000	2,393.81	726	1,225.27	1,406	991.70	1,751	836.05	2,098
29,000	2,479.30	752	1,269.03	1,457	1,027.11	1,813	865.91	2,173
30,000	2,564.79	777	1,312.79	1,507	1,062.53	1,876	895.77	2,248
31,000	2,650.29	803	1,356.55	1,557	1,097.95	1,939	925.63	2,323
32,000	2,735.78	829	1,400.31	1,607	1,133.37	2,001	955.49	2,398
33,000	2,821.27	855	1,444.07	1,658	1,168.78	2,063	985.34	2,472
34,000	2,906.77	881	1,487.83	1,708	1,204.20	2,126	1,015.20	2,547
35,000	2,992.26	907	1,531.59	1,758	1,239.62	2,189	1,045.06	2,622
36,000	3,077.75	933	1,575.35	1,808	1,275.04	2,251	1,074.92	2,697
37,000	3,163.24	959	1,619.11	1,859	1,310.45	2,314	1,104.78	2,772
38,000	3,248.74	985	1,662.87	1,909	1,345.87	2,376	1,134.64	2,847
39,000	3,334.23	1,011	1,706.63	1,959	1,381.29	2,439	1,164.50	2,922
40,000	3,419.72	1,037	1,750.39	2,009	1,416.71	2,501	1,194.36	2,997
42,000	3,590.71	1,089	1,837.90	2,110	1,487.54	2,626	1,254.07	3,147
44,000	3,761.70	1,140	1,925.42	2,210	1,558.38	2,751	1,313.79	3,296
46,000	3,932.68	1,192	2,012.94	2,311	1,629.21	2,876	1,373.51	3,446
48,000	4,103.67	1,244	2,100.46	2,411	1,700.05	3,002	1,433.23	3,596
50,000	4,274.65	1,296	2,187.98	2,512	1,770.88	3,126	1,492.94	3,746

AUTO LOAN PAYMENTS 4.75%

AMOUNT OF LOAN	42 MOS		48 MOS		60 MOS		72 MOS	
	MONTHLY PAYMENT	TOTAL INTRST	MONTHLY PAYMENT	TOTAL INTRST	MONTHLY PAYMENT	TOTAL INTRST	MONTHLY PAYMENT	TOTAL INTRST
$ 1	0.03	0	0.03	0	0.02	0	0.02	0
2	0.06	1	0.05	0	0.04	0	0.04	1
3	0.08	0	0.07	0	0.06	1	0.05	1
4	0.11	1	0.10	1	0.08	1	0.07	1
5	0.13	0	0.12	1	0.10	1	0.08	1
6	0.16	1	0.14	1	0.12	1	0.10	1
7	0.19	1	0.17	1	0.14	1	0.12	2
8	0.21	1	0.19	1	0.16	2	0.13	1
9	0.24	1	0.21	1	0.17	1	0.15	2
10	0.26	1	0.23	1	0.19	1	0.16	2
20	0.52	2	0.46	2	0.38	3	0.32	3
30	0.78	3	0.69	3	0.57	4	0.48	5
40	1.04	4	0.92	4	0.76	6	0.64	6
50	1.30	5	1.15	5	0.94	6	0.80	8
60	1.56	6	1.38	6	1.13	8	0.96	9
70	1.82	6	1.61	7	1.32	9	1.12	11
80	2.08	7	1.84	8	1.51	11	1.28	12
90	2.34	8	2.07	9	1.69	11	1.44	14
100	2.59	9	2.30	10	1.88	13	1.60	15
200	5.18	18	4.59	20	3.76	26	3.20	30
300	7.77	26	6.88	30	5.63	38	4.80	46
400	10.36	35	9.17	40	7.51	51	6.40	61
500	12.95	44	11.46	50	9.38	63	8.00	76
600	15.54	53	13.75	60	11.26	76	9.60	91
700	18.13	61	16.05	70	13.13	88	11.20	106
800	20.72	70	18.34	80	15.01	101	12.80	122
900	23.31	79	20.63	90	16.89	113	14.40	137
1,000	25.90	88	22.92	100	18.76	126	15.99	151
2,000	51.79	175	45.84	200	37.52	251	31.98	303
3,000	77.68	263	68.75	300	56.28	377	47.97	454
4,000	103.57	350	91.67	400	75.03	502	63.96	605
5,000	129.46	437	114.59	500	93.79	627	79.95	756
6,000	155.35	525	137.50	600	112.55	753	95.94	908
7,000	181.24	612	160.42	700	131.30	878	111.93	1,059
8,000	207.13	699	183.33	800	150.06	1,004	127.92	1,210
9,000	233.02	787	206.25	900	168.82	1,129	143.91	1,362
10,000	258.91	874	229.17	1,000	187.57	1,254	159.90	1,513
11,000	284.80	962	252.08	1,100	206.33	1,380	175.89	1,664
12,000	310.69	1,049	275.00	1,200	225.09	1,505	191.88	1,815
13,000	336.58	1,136	297.92	1,300	243.84	1,630	207.86	1,966
14,000	362.47	1,224	320.83	1,400	262.60	1,756	223.85	2,117
15,000	388.36	1,311	343.75	1,500	281.36	1,882	239.84	2,268
16,000	414.25	1,399	366.66	1,600	300.12	2,007	255.83	2,420
17,000	440.14	1,486	389.58	1,700	318.87	2,132	271.82	2,571
18,000	466.03	1,573	412.50	1,800	337.63	2,258	287.81	2,722
19,000	491.92	1,661	435.41	1,900	356.39	2,383	303.80	2,874
20,000	517.81	1,748	458.33	2,100	375.14	2,508	319.79	3,025
21,000	543.71	1,836	481.25	2,100	393.90	2,634	335.78	3,176
22,000	569.60	1,923	504.16	2,200	412.66	2,760	351.77	3,327
23,000	595.49	2,011	527.08	2,300	431.41	2,885	367.76	3,479
24,000	621.38	2,098	549.99	2,400	450.17	3,010	383.75	3,630
25,000	647.27	2,185	572.91	2,500	468.93	3,136	399.74	3,781
26,000	673.16	2,273	595.83	2,600	487.68	3,261	415.72	3,932
27,000	699.05	2,360	618.74	2,700	506.44	3,386	431.71	4,083
28,000	724.94	2,447	641.66	2,800	525.20	3,512	447.70	4,234
29,000	750.83	2,535	664.58	2,900	543.96	3,638	463.69	4,386
30,000	776.72	2,622	687.49	3,000	562.71	3,763	479.68	4,537
31,000	802.61	2,710	710.41	3,100	581.47	3,888	495.67	4,688
32,000	828.50	2,797	733.32	3,199	600.23	4,014	511.66	4,840
33,000	854.39	2,884	756.24	3,300	618.98	4,139	527.65	4,991
34,000	880.28	2,972	779.16	3,400	637.74	4,264	543.64	5,142
35,000	906.17	3,059	802.07	3,499	656.50	4,390	559.63	5,293
36,000	932.06	3,147	824.99	3,600	675.25	4,515	575.62	5,445
37,000	957.95	3,234	847.91	3,700	694.01	4,641	591.61	5,596
38,000	983.84	3,321	870.82	3,799	712.77	4,766	607.60	5,747
39,000	1,009.73	3,409	893.74	3,900	731.52	4,891	623.58	5,898
40,000	1,035.62	3,496	916.65	3,999	750.28	5,017	639.57	6,049
42,000	1,087.41	3,671	962.49	4,200	787.80	5,268	671.55	6,352
44,000	1,139.19	3,846	1,008.32	4,399	825.31	5,519	703.53	6,654
46,000	1,190.97	4,021	1,054.15	4,599	862.82	5,769	735.51	6,957
48,000	1,242.75	4,196	1,099.98	4,799	900.34	6,020	767.49	7,259
50,000	1,294.53	4,370	1,145.82	4,999	937.85	6,271	799.47	7,562

AUTO LOAN PAYMENTS

AMOUNT OF LOAN	12 MOS		24 MOS		30 MOS		36 MOS	
	MONTHLY PAYMENT	TOTAL INTRST	MONTHLY PAYMENT	TOTAL INTRST	MONTHLY PAYMENT	TOTAL INTRST	MONTHLY PAYMENT	TOTAL INTRST
$ 1	0.09	0	0.05	0	0.04	0	0.03	0
2	0.18	0	0.09	0	0.08	0	0.06	0
3	0.26	0	0.14	0	0.11	0	0.09	0
4	0.35	0	0.18	0	0.15	1	0.12	0
5	0.43	0	0.22	0	0.18	0	0.15	0
6	0.52	0	0.27	0	0.22	1	0.18	0
7	0.60	0	0.31	0	0.25	1	0.21	1
8	0.69	0	0.36	1	0.29	1	0.24	1
9	0.78	0	0.40	1	0.32	1	0.27	1
10	0.86	0	0.44	1	0.36	1	0.30	1
20	1.72	1	0.88	1	0.71	1	0.60	2
30	2.57	1	1.32	2	1.07	2	0.90	3
40	3.43	1	1.76	2	1.42	3	1.20	3
50	4.28	1	2.20	3	1.78	3	1.50	4
60	5.14	2	2.63	3	2.13	4	1.80	5
70	5.99	2	3.07	4	2.49	4	2.10	6
80	6.85	2	3.51	4	2.84	5	2.40	6
90	7.71	2	3.95	5	3.20	6	2.70	7
100	8.56	3	4.39	5	3.55	7	3.00	8
200	17.12	5	8.77	10	7.10	13	5.99	16
300	25.67	8	13.15	16	10.65	20	8.98	23
400	34.23	11	17.54	21	14.20	26	11.98	31
500	42.79	13	21.92	26	17.75	33	14.97	39
600	51.34	16	26.30	31	21.30	39	17.96	47
700	59.90	19	30.68	36	24.84	45	20.95	54
800	68.45	21	35.07	42	28.39	52	23.95	62
900	77.01	24	39.45	47	31.94	58	26.94	70
1,000	85.57	27	43.83	52	35.49	65	29.93	77
2,000	171.13	54	87.66	104	70.97	129	59.86	155
3,000	256.69	80	131.48	156	106.46	194	89.78	232
4,000	342.25	107	175.31	207	141.94	258	119.71	310
5,000	427.81	134	219.14	259	177.43	323	149.64	387
6,000	513.37	160	262.96	311	212.91	387	179.56	464
7,000	598.94	187	306.79	363	248.40	452	209.49	542
8,000	684.50	214	350.62	415	283.88	516	239.41	619
9,000	770.06	241	394.44	467	319.37	581	269.34	696
10,000	855.62	267	438.27	518	354.85	646	299.27	774
11,000	941.18	294	482.10	570	390.34	710	329.19	851
12,000	1,026.74	321	525.92	622	425.82	775	359.12	928
13,000	1,112.31	348	569.75	674	461.30	839	389.04	1,005
14,000	1,197.87	374	613.58	726	496.79	904	418.97	1,083
15,000	1,283.43	401	657.40	778	532.27	968	448.90	1,160
16,000	1,368.99	428	701.23	830	567.76	1,033	478.82	1,238
17,000	1,454.55	455	745.06	881	603.24	1,097	508.75	1,315
18,000	1,540.11	481	788.88	933	638.73	1,162	538.67	1,392
19,000	1,625.68	508	832.71	985	674.21	1,226	568.60	1,470
20,000	1,711.24	535	876.54	1,037	709.70	1,291	598.53	1,547
21,000	1,796.80	562	920.36	1,089	745.18	1,355	628.45	1,624
22,000	1,882.36	588	964.19	1,141	780.67	1,420	658.38	1,702
23,000	1,967.92	615	1,008.02	1,192	816.15	1,485	688.30	1,779
24,000	2,053.48	642	1,051.84	1,244	851.64	1,549	718.23	1,856
25,000	2,139.05	669	1,095.67	1,296	887.12	1,614	748.16	1,934
26,000	2,224.61	695	1,139.50	1,348	922.60	1,678	778.08	2,011
27,000	2,310.17	722	1,183.32	1,400	958.09	1,743	808.01	2,088
28,000	2,395.73	749	1,227.15	1,452	993.57	1,807	837.93	2,165
29,000	2,481.29	775	1,270.98	1,504	1,029.06	1,872	867.86	2,243
30,000	2,566.85	802	1,314.80	1,555	1,064.54	1,936	897.79	2,320
31,000	2,652.42	829	1,358.63	1,607	1,100.03	2,001	927.71	2,398
32,000	2,737.98	856	1,402.46	1,659	1,135.51	2,065	957.64	2,475
33,000	2,823.54	882	1,446.28	1,711	1,171.00	2,130	987.56	2,552
34,000	2,909.10	909	1,490.11	1,763	1,206.48	2,194	1,017.49	2,630
35,000	2,994.66	936	1,533.94	1,815	1,241.97	2,259	1,047.42	2,707
36,000	3,080.22	963	1,577.76	1,866	1,277.45	2,324	1,077.34	2,784
37,000	3,165.79	989	1,621.59	1,918	1,312.94	2,388	1,107.27	2,862
38,000	3,251.35	1,016	1,665.42	1,970	1,348.42	2,453	1,137.19	2,939
39,000	3,336.91	1,043	1,709.24	2,022	1,383.90	2,517	1,167.12	3,016
40,000	3,422.47	1,070	1,753.07	2,074	1,419.39	2,582	1,197.05	3,094
42,000	3,593.59	1,123	1,840.72	2,177	1,490.36	2,711	1,256.90	3,248
44,000	3,764.72	1,177	1,928.38	2,281	1,561.33	2,840	1,316.75	3,403
46,000	3,935.84	1,230	2,016.03	2,385	1,632.30	2,969	1,376.60	3,558
48,000	4,106.96	1,284	2,103.68	2,488	1,703.27	3,098	1,436.45	3,712
50,000	4,278.09	1,337	2,191.34	2,592	1,774.23	3,227	1,496.31	3,867

AUTO LOAN PAYMENTS 4.90%

AMOUNT OF LOAN	42 MOS		48 MOS		60 MOS		72 MOS	
	MONTHLY PAYMENT	TOTAL INTRST	MONTHLY PAYMENT	TOTAL INTRST	MONTHLY PAYMENT	TOTAL INTRST	MONTHLY PAYMENT	TOTAL INTRST
$ 1	0.03	0	0.03	0	0.02	0	0.02	0
2	0.06	1	0.05	0	0.04	0	0.04	1
3	0.08	0	0.07	0	0.06	1	0.05	1
4	0.11	1	0.10	1	0.08	1	0.07	1
5	0.13	0	0.12	1	0.10	1	0.09	1
6	0.16	1	0.14	1	0.12	1	0.10	2
7	0.19	1	0.17	1	0.14	1	0.12	1
8	0.21	1	0.19	1	0.16	2	0.13	1
9	0.24	1	0.21	1	0.17	1	0.15	2
10	0.26	1	0.23	1	0.19	1	0.17	2
20	0.52	2	0.46	2	0.38	3	0.33	4
30	0.78	3	0.69	3	0.57	4	0.49	5
40	1.04	4	0.92	4	0.76	6	0.65	7
50	1.30	5	1.15	5	0.95	7	0.81	8
60	1.56	6	1.38	6	1.13	8	0.97	10
70	1.82	6	1.61	7	1.32	9	1.13	11
80	2.08	7	1.84	8	1.51	11	1.29	13
90	2.34	8	2.07	9	1.70	12	1.45	14
100	2.60	9	2.30	10	1.89	13	1.61	16
200	5.20	18	4.60	21	3.77	26	3.22	32
300	7.79	27	6.90	31	5.65	39	4.82	47
400	10.39	36	9.20	42	7.54	52	6.43	63
500	12.98	45	11.50	52	9.42	65	8.03	78
600	15.58	54	13.80	62	11.30	78	9.64	94
700	18.18	64	16.09	72	13.18	91	11.25	110
800	20.77	72	18.39	83	15.07	104	12.85	125
900	23.37	82	20.69	93	16.95	117	14.46	141
1,000	25.96	90	22.99	104	18.83	130	16.06	156
2,000	51.92	181	45.97	207	37.66	260	32.12	313
3,000	77.88	271	68.96	310	56.48	389	48.18	469
4,000	103.84	361	91.94	413	75.31	519	64.24	625
5,000	129.79	451	114.93	517	94.13	648	80.30	782
6,000	155.75	542	137.91	620	112.96	778	96.36	938
7,000	181.71	632	160.89	723	131.78	907	112.42	1,094
8,000	207.67	722	183.88	826	150.61	1,037	128.47	1,250
9,000	233.63	812	206.86	929	169.43	1,166	144.53	1,406
10,000	259.58	902	229.85	1,033	188.26	1,296	160.59	1,562
11,000	285.54	993	252.83	1,136	207.08	1,425	176.65	1,719
12,000	311.50	1,083	275.81	1,239	225.91	1,555	192.71	1,875
13,000	337.46	1,173	298.80	1,342	244.74	1,684	208.77	2,031
14,000	363.42	1,264	321.78	1,445	263.56	1,814	224.83	2,188
15,000	389.37	1,354	344.77	1,549	282.39	1,943	240.88	2,343
16,000	415.33	1,444	367.75	1,652	301.21	2,073	256.94	2,500
17,000	441.29	1,534	390.73	1,755	320.04	2,202	273.00	2,656
18,000	467.25	1,625	413.72	1,859	338.86	2,332	289.06	2,812
19,000	493.21	1,715	436.70	1,962	357.69	2,461	305.12	2,969
20,000	519.16	1,805	459.69	2,065	376.51	2,591	321.18	3,125
21,000	545.12	1,895	482.67	2,168	395.34	2,720	337.24	3,281
22,000	571.08	1,985	505.65	2,271	414.16	2,850	353.29	3,437
23,000	597.04	2,076	528.64	2,375	432.99	2,979	369.35	3,593
24,000	623.00	2,166	551.62	2,478	451.82	3,109	385.41	3,750
25,000	648.95	2,256	574.61	2,581	470.64	3,238	401.47	3,906
26,000	674.91	2,346	597.59	2,684	489.47	3,368	417.53	4,062
27,000	700.87	2,437	620.57	2,787	508.29	3,497	433.59	4,218
28,000	726.83	2,527	643.56	2,891	527.12	3,627	449.65	4,375
29,000	752.79	2,617	666.54	2,994	545.94	3,756	465.70	4,530
30,000	778.74	2,707	689.53	3,097	564.77	3,886	481.76	4,687
31,000	804.70	2,797	712.51	3,200	583.59	4,015	497.82	4,843
32,000	830.66	2,888	735.49	3,304	602.42	4,145	513.88	4,999
33,000	856.62	2,978	758.48	3,407	621.24	4,274	529.94	5,156
34,000	882.58	3,068	781.46	3,510	640.07	4,404	546.00	5,312
35,000	908.53	3,158	804.45	3,614	658.90	4,534	562.06	5,468
36,000	934.49	3,249	827.43	3,717	677.72	4,663	578.11	5,624
37,000	960.45	3,339	850.41	3,820	696.55	4,793	594.17	5,780
38,000	986.41	3,429	873.40	3,923	715.37	4,922	610.23	5,937
39,000	1,012.37	3,520	896.38	4,026	734.20	5,052	626.29	6,093
40,000	1,038.32	3,609	919.37	4,130	753.02	5,181	642.35	6,249
42,000	1,090.24	3,790	965.33	4,336	790.67	5,440	674.47	6,562
44,000	1,142.16	3,971	1,011.30	4,542	828.32	5,699	706.58	6,874
46,000	1,194.07	4,151	1,057.27	4,749	865.98	5,959	738.70	7,186
48,000	1,245.99	4,332	1,103.24	4,956	903.63	6,218	770.82	7,499
50,000	1,297.90	4,512	1,149.21	5,162	941.28	6,477	802.93	7,811

53

5.00%	AUTO LOAN PAYMENTS							
AMOUNT OF LOAN	**12 MOS**		**24 MOS**		**30 MOS**		**36 MOS**	
	MONTHLY PAYMENT	TOTAL INTRST	MONTHLY PAYMENT	TOTAL INTRST	MONTHLY PAYMENT	TOTAL INTRST	MONTHLY PAYMENT	TOTAL INTRST
$ 1	0.09	0	0.05	0	0.04	0	0.03	0
2	0.18	0	0.09	0	0.08	0	0.06	0
3	0.26	0	0.14	0	0.11	0	0.09	0
4	0.35	0	0.18	0	0.15	1	0.12	0
5	0.43	0	0.22	0	0.18	0	0.15	0
6	0.52	0	0.27	0	0.22	1	0.18	0
7	0.60	0	0.31	0	0.25	1	0.21	1
8	0.69	0	0.36	1	0.29	1	0.24	1
9	0.78	0	0.40	1	0.32	1	0.27	1
10	0.86	0	0.44	1	0.36	1	0.30	1
20	1.72	1	0.88	1	0.72	2	0.60	2
30	2.57	1	1.32	2	1.07	2	0.90	2
40	3.43	1	1.76	2	1.43	3	1.20	3
50	4.29	1	2.20	3	1.78	3	1.50	4
60	5.14	2	2.64	3	2.14	4	1.80	5
70	6.00	2	3.08	4	2.49	5	2.10	6
80	6.85	2	3.51	4	2.85	6	2.40	6
90	7.71	3	3.95	5	3.20	6	2.70	7
100	8.57	3	4.39	5	3.56	7	3.00	8
200	17.13	6	8.78	11	7.11	13	6.00	16
300	25.69	8	13.17	16	10.66	20	9.00	24
400	34.25	11	17.55	21	14.22	27	11.99	32
500	42.81	14	21.94	27	17.77	33	14.99	40
600	51.37	16	26.33	32	21.32	40	17.99	48
700	59.93	19	30.71	37	24.88	46	20.98	55
800	68.49	22	35.10	42	28.43	53	23.98	63
900	77.05	25	39.49	48	31.98	59	26.98	71
1,000	85.61	27	43.88	53	35.53	66	29.98	79
2,000	171.22	55	87.75	106	71.06	132	59.95	158
3,000	256.83	82	131.62	159	106.59	198	89.92	237
4,000	342.43	109	175.49	212	142.12	264	119.89	316
5,000	428.04	136	219.36	265	177.65	330	149.86	395
6,000	513.65	164	263.23	318	213.18	395	179.83	474
7,000	599.26	191	307.10	370	248.71	461	209.80	553
8,000	684.86	218	350.98	424	284.24	527	239.77	632
9,000	770.47	246	394.85	476	319.77	593	269.74	711
10,000	856.08	273	438.72	529	355.30	659	299.71	790
11,000	941.69	300	482.59	582	390.83	725	329.68	868
12,000	1,027.29	327	526.46	635	426.36	791	359.66	948
13,000	1,112.90	355	570.33	688	461.89	857	389.63	1,027
14,000	1,198.51	382	614.20	741	497.42	923	419.60	1,106
15,000	1,284.12	409	658.08	794	532.95	989	449.57	1,185
16,000	1,369.72	437	701.95	847	568.47	1,054	479.54	1,263
17,000	1,455.33	464	745.82	900	604.00	1,120	509.51	1,342
18,000	1,540.94	491	789.69	953	639.53	1,186	539.48	1,421
19,000	1,626.55	519	833.56	1,005	675.06	1,252	569.45	1,500
20,000	1,712.15	546	877.43	1,058	710.59	1,318	599.42	1,579
21,000	1,797.76	573	921.30	1,111	746.12	1,384	629.39	1,658
22,000	1,883.37	600	965.18	1,164	781.65	1,450	659.36	1,737
23,000	1,968.98	628	1,009.05	1,217	817.18	1,515	689.34	1,816
24,000	2,054.58	655	1,052.92	1,270	852.71	1,581	719.31	1,895
25,000	2,140.19	682	1,096.79	1,323	888.24	1,647	749.28	1,974
26,000	2,225.80	710	1,140.66	1,376	923.77	1,713	779.25	2,053
27,000	2,311.41	737	1,184.53	1,429	959.30	1,779	809.22	2,132
28,000	2,397.01	764	1,228.40	1,482	994.83	1,845	839.19	2,211
29,000	2,482.62	791	1,272.28	1,535	1,030.36	1,911	869.16	2,290
30,000	2,568.23	819	1,316.15	1,588	1,065.89	1,977	899.13	2,369
31,000	2,653.84	846	1,360.02	1,640	1,101.42	2,043	929.10	2,448
32,000	2,739.44	873	1,403.89	1,693	1,136.94	2,108	959.07	2,527
33,000	2,825.05	901	1,447.76	1,746	1,172.47	2,174	989.04	2,605
34,000	2,910.66	928	1,491.63	1,799	1,208.00	2,240	1,019.02	2,685
35,000	2,996.27	955	1,535.50	1,852	1,243.53	2,306	1,048.99	2,764
36,000	3,081.87	982	1,579.38	1,905	1,279.06	2,372	1,078.96	2,843
37,000	3,167.48	1,010	1,623.25	1,958	1,314.59	2,438	1,108.93	2,921
38,000	3,253.09	1,037	1,667.12	2,011	1,350.12	2,504	1,138.90	3,000
39,000	3,338.70	1,064	1,710.99	2,064	1,385.65	2,570	1,168.87	3,079
40,000	3,424.30	1,092	1,754.86	2,117	1,421.18	2,635	1,198.84	3,158
42,000	3,595.52	1,146	1,842.60	2,222	1,492.24	2,767	1,258.78	3,316
44,000	3,766.73	1,201	1,930.35	2,328	1,563.30	2,899	1,318.72	3,474
46,000	3,937.95	1,255	2,018.09	2,434	1,634.36	3,031	1,378.67	3,632
48,000	4,109.16	1,310	2,105.83	2,540	1,705.41	3,162	1,438.61	3,790
50,000	4,280.38	1,365	2,193.57	2,646	1,776.47	3,294	1,498.55	3,948

AUTO LOAN PAYMENTS 5.00%

AMOUNT OF LOAN	42 MOS MONTHLY PAYMENT	42 MOS TOTAL INTRST	48 MOS MONTHLY PAYMENT	48 MOS TOTAL INTRST	60 MOS MONTHLY PAYMENT	60 MOS TOTAL INTRST	72 MOS MONTHLY PAYMENT	72 MOS TOTAL INTRST
$ 1	0.03	0	0.03	0	0.02	0	0.02	0
2	0.06	1	0.05	0	0.04	0	0.04	1
3	0.08	0	0.07	0	0.06	1	0.05	1
4	0.11	1	0.10	1	0.08	1	0.07	1
5	0.14	1	0.12	1	0.10	1	0.09	1
6	0.16	1	0.14	1	0.12	1	0.10	1
7	0.19	1	0.17	1	0.14	1	0.12	2
8	0.21	1	0.19	1	0.16	2	0.13	1
9	0.24	1	0.21	1	0.17	1	0.15	2
10	0.27	1	0.24	2	0.19	2	0.17	2
20	0.53	2	0.47	3	0.38	3	0.33	4
30	0.79	2	0.70	4	0.57	4	0.49	5
40	1.05	4	0.93	5	0.76	6	0.65	7
50	1.31	5	1.16	6	0.95	7	0.81	8
60	1.57	6	1.39	7	1.14	8	0.97	10
70	1.83	7	1.62	8	1.33	10	1.13	11
80	2.09	8	1.85	9	1.51	11	1.29	13
90	2.35	9	2.08	10	1.70	12	1.45	14
100	2.61	10	2.31	11	1.89	13	1.62	17
200	5.21	19	4.61	21	3.78	27	3.23	33
300	7.81	28	6.91	32	5.67	40	4.84	48
400	10.41	37	9.22	43	7.55	53	6.45	64
500	13.01	46	11.52	53	9.44	66	8.06	80
600	15.61	56	13.82	63	11.33	80	9.67	96
700	18.21	65	16.13	74	13.21	93	11.28	112
800	20.81	74	18.43	85	15.10	106	12.89	128
900	23.41	83	20.73	95	16.99	119	14.50	144
1,000	26.01	92	23.03	105	18.88	133	16.11	160
2,000	52.01	184	46.06	211	37.75	265	32.21	319
3,000	78.01	276	69.09	316	56.62	397	48.32	479
4,000	104.02	369	92.12	422	75.49	529	64.42	638
5,000	130.02	461	115.15	527	94.36	662	80.53	798
6,000	156.02	553	138.18	633	113.23	794	96.63	957
7,000	182.03	645	161.21	738	132.10	926	112.74	1,117
8,000	208.03	737	184.24	844	150.97	1,058	128.84	1,276
9,000	234.03	829	207.27	949	169.85	1,191	144.95	1,436
10,000	260.04	922	230.30	1,054	188.72	1,323	161.05	1,596
11,000	286.04	1,014	253.33	1,160	207.59	1,455	177.16	1,756
12,000	312.04	1,106	276.36	1,265	226.46	1,588	193.26	1,915
13,000	338.04	1,198	299.39	1,371	245.33	1,720	209.37	2,075
14,000	364.05	1,290	322.42	1,476	264.20	1,852	225.47	2,234
15,000	390.05	1,382	345.44	1,581	283.05	1,984	241.58	2,394
16,000	416.05	1,474	368.47	1,687	301.94	2,116	257.68	2,553
17,000	442.06	1,567	391.50	1,792	320.82	2,249	273.79	2,713
18,000	468.06	1,659	414.53	1,897	339.69	2,381	289.89	2,872
19,000	494.06	1,751	437.56	2,003	358.56	2,514	306.00	3,032
20,000	520.07	1,843	460.59	2,108	377.43	2,646	322.10	3,191
21,000	546.07	1,935	483.62	2,214	396.30	2,778	338.21	3,351
22,000	572.07	2,027	506.65	2,319	415.17	2,910	354.31	3,510
23,000	598.07	2,119	529.68	2,425	434.04	3,042	370.42	3,670
24,000	624.08	2,211	552.71	2,530	452.91	3,175	386.52	3,829
25,000	650.08	2,303	575.74	2,636	471.79	3,307	402.63	3,989
26,000	676.08	2,395	598.77	2,741	490.66	3,440	418.73	4,149
27,000	702.09	2,488	621.80	2,846	509.53	3,572	434.84	4,308
28,000	728.09	2,580	644.83	2,952	528.40	3,704	450.94	4,468
29,000	754.09	2,672	667.85	3,057	547.27	3,836	467.05	4,628
30,000	780.10	2,764	690.88	3,162	566.14	3,968	483.15	4,787
31,000	806.10	2,856	713.91	3,268	585.01	4,101	499.26	4,947
32,000	832.10	2,948	736.94	3,373	603.88	4,233	515.36	5,106
33,000	858.11	3,041	759.97	3,479	622.76	4,366	531.47	5,266
34,000	884.11	3,133	783.00	3,584	641.63	4,498	547.57	5,425
35,000	910.11	3,225	806.03	3,689	660.50	4,630	563.68	5,585
36,000	936.11	3,317	829.06	3,795	679.37	4,762	579.78	5,744
37,000	962.12	3,409	852.09	3,900	698.24	4,894	595.89	5,904
38,000	988.12	3,501	875.12	4,006	717.11	5,027	611.99	6,063
39,000	1,014.12	3,593	898.15	4,111	735.98	5,159	628.10	6,223
40,000	1,040.13	3,685	921.18	4,217	754.85	5,291	644.20	6,382
42,000	1,092.13	3,869	967.24	4,428	792.60	5,556	676.41	6,702
44,000	1,144.14	4,054	1,013.29	4,638	830.34	5,820	708.62	7,021
46,000	1,196.14	4,238	1,059.35	4,849	868.08	6,085	740.83	7,340
48,000	1,248.15	4,422	1,105.41	5,060	905.82	6,349	773.04	7,659
50,000	1,300.16	4,607	1,151.47	5,271	943.57	6,614	805.25	7,978

55

AMOUNT OF LOAN	12 MOS		24 MOS		30 MOS		36 MOS	
	MONTHLY PAYMENT	TOTAL INTRST	MONTHLY PAYMENT	TOTAL INTRST	MONTHLY PAYMENT	TOTAL INTRST	MONTHLY PAYMENT	TOTAL INTRST
$ 1	0.09	0	0.05	0	0.04	0	0.04	0
2	0.18	0	0.09	0	0.08	0	0.07	1
3	0.26	0	0.14	0	0.11	0	0.10	1
4	0.35	0	0.18	0	0.15	1	0.13	1
5	0.43	0	0.22	0	0.18	0	0.16	1
6	0.52	0	0.27	0	0.22	1	0.19	1
7	0.61	0	0.31	0	0.25	1	0.22	1
8	0.69	0	0.36	1	0.29	1	0.25	1
9	0.78	0	0.40	1	0.33	1	0.28	1
10	0.86	0	0.44	1	0.36	1	0.31	1
20	1.72	1	0.88	1	0.72	2	0.61	2
30	2.58	0	1.32	2	1.07	2	0.91	3
40	3.43	1	1.76	2	1.43	3	1.21	4
50	4.29	1	2.20	3	1.79	4	1.51	4
60	5.15	2	2.64	3	2.14	4	1.81	5
70	6.01	2	3.08	4	2.50	5	2.11	6
80	6.86	2	3.52	4	2.86	6	2.41	7
90	7.72	3	3.96	5	3.21	6	2.71	8
100	8.58	3	4.40	6	3.57	7	3.01	8
200	17.15	6	8.80	11	7.13	14	6.02	17
300	25.72	9	13.20	17	10.70	21	9.03	25
400	34.29	11	17.60	22	14.26	28	12.04	33
500	42.87	14	22.00	28	17.83	35	15.05	42
600	51.44	17	26.40	34	21.39	42	18.05	50
700	60.01	20	30.79	39	24.95	49	21.06	58
800	68.58	23	35.19	45	28.52	56	24.07	67
900	77.15	26	39.59	50	32.08	62	27.08	75
1,000	85.73	29	43.99	56	35.65	70	30.09	83
2,000	171.45	57	87.97	111	71.29	139	60.17	166
3,000	257.17	86	131.96	167	106.93	208	90.25	249
4,000	342.89	115	175.94	223	142.57	277	120.34	332
5,000	428.62	143	219.92	278	178.21	346	150.42	415
6,000	514.34	172	263.91	334	213.85	416	180.50	498
7,000	600.06	201	307.89	389	249.50	485	210.59	581
8,000	685.78	229	351.87	445	285.14	554	240.67	664
9,000	771.50	258	395.86	501	320.78	623	270.75	747
10,000	857.23	287	439.84	556	356.42	693	300.84	830
11,000	942.95	315	483.82	612	392.06	762	330.92	913
12,000	1,028.67	344	527.81	667	427.70	831	361.00	996
13,000	1,114.39	373	571.79	723	463.34	900	391.09	1,079
14,000	1,200.11	401	615.77	778	498.99	970	421.17	1,162
15,000	1,285.84	430	659.76	834	534.63	1,039	451.25	1,245
16,000	1,371.56	459	703.74	890	570.27	1,108	481.34	1,328
17,000	1,457.28	487	747.72	945	605.91	1,177	511.42	1,411
18,000	1,543.00	516	791.71	1,001	641.55	1,247	541.50	1,494
19,000	1,628.72	545	835.69	1,057	677.19	1,316	571.59	1,577
20,000	1,714.45	573	879.67	1,112	712.83	1,385	601.67	1,660
21,000	1,800.17	602	923.66	1,168	748.48	1,454	631.75	1,743
22,000	1,885.89	631	967.64	1,223	784.12	1,524	661.84	1,826
23,000	1,971.61	659	1,011.62	1,279	819.76	1,593	691.92	1,909
24,000	2,057.34	688	1,055.61	1,335	855.40	1,662	722.00	1,992
25,000	2,143.06	717	1,099.59	1,390	891.04	1,731	752.09	2,075
26,000	2,228.78	745	1,143.57	1,446	926.68	1,800	782.17	2,158
27,000	2,314.50	774	1,187.56	1,501	962.32	1,870	812.25	2,241
28,000	2,400.22	803	1,231.54	1,557	997.97	1,939	842.34	2,324
29,000	2,485.95	831	1,275.52	1,612	1,033.61	2,008	872.42	2,407
30,000	2,571.67	860	1,319.51	1,668	1,069.25	2,078	902.50	2,490
31,000	2,657.39	889	1,363.49	1,724	1,104.89	2,147	932.59	2,573
32,000	2,743.11	917	1,407.47	1,779	1,140.53	2,216	962.67	2,656
33,000	2,828.83	946	1,451.46	1,835	1,176.17	2,285	992.75	2,739
34,000	2,914.56	975	1,495.44	1,891	1,211.81	2,354	1,022.84	2,822
35,000	3,000.28	1,003	1,539.43	1,946	1,247.46	2,424	1,052.92	2,905
36,000	3,086.00	1,032	1,583.41	2,002	1,283.10	2,493	1,083.00	2,988
37,000	3,171.72	1,061	1,627.39	2,057	1,318.74	2,562	1,113.09	3,071
38,000	3,257.44	1,089	1,671.38	2,113	1,354.38	2,631	1,143.17	3,154
39,000	3,343.17	1,118	1,715.36	2,169	1,390.02	2,701	1,173.25	3,237
40,000	3,428.88	1,147	1,759.34	2,224	1,425.66	2,770	1,203.34	3,320
42,000	3,600.33	1,204	1,847.31	2,335	1,496.95	2,909	1,263.50	3,486
44,000	3,771.78	1,261	1,935.28	2,447	1,568.23	3,047	1,323.67	3,652
46,000	3,943.22	1,319	2,023.24	2,558	1,639.51	3,185	1,383.84	3,818
48,000	4,114.67	1,376	2,111.21	2,669	1,710.79	3,324	1,444.00	3,984
50,000	4,286.11	1,433	2,199.18	2,780	1,782.08	3,462	1,504.17	4,150

AUTO LOAN PAYMENTS 5.25%

AMOUNT OF LOAN	42 MOS		48 MOS		60 MOS		72 MOS	
	MONTHLY PAYMENT	TOTAL INTRST	MONTHLY PAYMENT	TOTAL INTRST	MONTHLY PAYMENT	TOTAL INTRST	MONTHLY PAYMENT	TOTAL INTRST
$ 1	0.03	0	0.03	0	0.02	0	0.02	0
2	0.06	1	0.05	0	0.04	0	0.04	0
3	0.08	0	0.07	1	0.06	1	0.05	1
4	0.11	1	0.10	1	0.08	1	0.07	1
5	0.14	1	0.12	1	0.10	1	0.09	1
6	0.16	1	0.14	1	0.12	1	0.10	1
7	0.18	1	0.17	1	0.14	1	0.12	2
8	0.21	1	0.19	1	0.16	2	0.13	1
9	0.24	1	0.21	1	0.18	2	0.15	2
10	0.27	1	0.24	2	0.19	1	0.17	2
20	0.53	2	0.47	3	0.38	3	0.33	4
30	0.79	3	0.70	4	0.57	4	0.49	5
40	1.05	4	0.93	5	0.76	6	0.65	7
50	1.31	5	1.16	6	0.95	7	0.82	9
60	1.57	6	1.39	7	1.14	8	0.98	11
70	1.83	7	1.62	8	1.33	10	1.14	12
80	2.09	8	1.86	9	1.52	11	1.30	14
90	2.36	9	2.09	10	1.71	13	1.46	15
100	2.62	10	2.32	11	1.90	14	1.63	17
200	5.23	20	4.63	22	3.80	28	3.25	34
300	7.84	29	6.95	34	5.70	42	4.87	51
400	10.45	39	9.26	44	7.60	56	6.49	67
500	13.06	49	11.58	56	9.50	70	8.12	85
600	15.67	58	13.89	67	11.40	84	9.74	101
700	18.29	68	16.20	78	13.30	98	11.36	118
800	20.90	78	18.52	89	15.19	111	12.98	135
900	23.51	87	20.83	100	17.09	125	14.60	151
1,000	26.12	97	23.15	111	18.99	139	16.23	169
2,000	52.24	194	46.29	222	37.98	279	32.45	336
3,000	78.35	291	69.43	333	56.96	418	48.67	504
4,000	104.47	388	92.58	444	75.95	557	64.89	672
5,000	130.58	484	115.72	555	94.93	696	81.11	840
6,000	156.70	581	138.86	665	113.92	835	97.33	1,008
7,000	182.82	678	162.00	776	132.91	975	113.55	1,176
8,000	208.93	775	185.15	887	151.89	1,113	129.77	1,343
9,000	235.05	872	208.29	998	170.88	1,253	146.00	1,512
10,000	261.16	969	231.43	1,109	189.86	1,392	162.22	1,680
11,000	287.28	1,066	254.57	1,219	208.85	1,531	178.44	1,848
12,000	313.40	1,163	277.72	1,331	227.84	1,670	194.66	2,016
13,000	339.51	1,259	300.86	1,441	246.82	1,809	210.88	2,183
14,000	365.63	1,356	324.00	1,552	265.81	1,949	227.10	2,351
15,000	391.74	1,453	347.15	1,663	284.79	2,087	243.32	2,519
16,000	417.86	1,550	370.29	1,774	303.78	2,227	259.54	2,687
17,000	443.97	1,647	393.43	1,885	322.77	2,366	275.76	2,855
18,000	470.09	1,744	416.57	1,995	341.75	2,505	291.99	3,023
19,000	496.21	1,841	439.72	2,107	360.74	2,644	308.21	3,191
20,000	522.32	1,937	462.86	2,217	379.72	2,783	324.43	3,359
21,000	548.44	2,034	486.00	2,328	398.71	2,923	340.65	3,527
22,000	574.55	2,131	509.14	2,439	417.70	3,062	356.87	3,695
23,000	600.67	2,228	532.29	2,550	436.68	3,201	373.09	3,862
24,000	626.79	2,325	555.43	2,661	455.67	3,340	389.31	4,030
25,000	652.90	2,422	578.57	2,771	474.65	3,479	405.53	4,198
26,000	679.02	2,519	601.72	2,883	493.64	3,618	421.75	4,366
27,000	705.13	2,615	624.86	2,993	512.63	3,758	437.98	4,535
28,000	731.25	2,713	648.00	3,104	531.61	3,897	454.20	4,702
29,000	757.37	2,810	671.14	3,215	550.60	4,036	470.42	4,870
30,000	783.48	2,906	694.29	3,326	569.58	4,175	486.64	5,038
31,000	809.60	3,003	717.43	3,437	588.57	4,314	502.86	5,206
32,000	835.71	3,100	740.57	3,547	607.56	4,454	519.08	5,374
33,000	861.83	3,197	763.71	3,658	626.54	4,592	535.30	5,542
34,000	887.94	3,293	786.86	3,769	645.53	4,732	551.52	5,709
35,000	914.06	3,391	810.00	3,880	664.51	4,871	567.75	5,878
36,000	940.18	3,488	833.14	3,991	683.50	5,010	583.97	6,046
37,000	966.29	3,584	856.29	4,102	702.49	5,149	600.19	6,214
38,000	992.41	3,681	879.43	4,213	721.47	5,288	616.41	6,382
39,000	1,018.52	3,778	902.57	4,323	740.46	5,428	632.63	6,549
40,000	1,044.64	3,875	925.71	4,434	759.44	5,566	648.85	6,717
42,000	1,096.87	4,069	972.00	4,656	797.42	5,845	681.29	7,053
44,000	1,149.10	4,262	1,018.28	4,877	835.39	6,123	713.74	7,389
46,000	1,201.34	4,456	1,064.57	5,099	873.36	6,402	746.18	7,725
48,000	1,253.57	4,650	1,110.86	5,321	911.33	6,680	778.62	8,061
50,000	1,305.80	4,844	1,157.14	5,543	949.30	6,958	811.06	8,396

5.50%   **AUTO LOAN PAYMENTS**

AMOUNT OF LOAN	12 MOS		24 MOS		30 MOS		36 MOS	
	MONTHLY PAYMENT	TOTAL INTRST	MONTHLY PAYMENT	TOTAL INTRST	MONTHLY PAYMENT	TOTAL INTRST	MONTHLY PAYMENT	TOTAL INTRST
$ 1	0.09	0	0.05	0	0.04	0	0.04	0
2	0.18	0	0.09	0	0.08	0	0.07	1
3	0.26	0	0.14	0	0.11	0	0.10	1
4	0.35	0	0.18	0	0.15	0	0.13	1
5	0.43	0	0.23	0	0.18	0	0.16	1
6	0.52	0	0.27	0	0.22	0	0.19	1
7	0.61	0	0.31	0	0.26	1	0.22	1
8	0.69	0	0.36	1	0.29	1	0.25	1
9	0.78	0	0.40	1	0.33	1	0.28	1
10	0.86	1	0.45	1	0.36	1	0.31	1
20	1.72	1	0.89	1	0.72	2	0.61	2
30	2.58	1	1.33	2	1.08	2	0.91	3
40	3.44	1	1.77	2	1.44	3	1.21	4
50	4.30	2	2.21	3	1.79	4	1.51	4
60	5.16	2	2.65	4	2.15	5	1.82	6
70	6.01	2	3.09	4	2.51	5	2.12	6
80	6.87	2	3.53	5	2.87	6	2.42	7
90	7.73	3	3.97	5	3.22	7	2.72	8
100	8.59	3	4.41	6	3.58	7	3.02	9
200	17.17	6	8.82	12	7.16	15	6.04	17
300	25.76	9	13.23	18	10.73	22	9.06	26
400	34.34	12	17.64	23	14.31	29	12.08	35
500	42.92	15	22.05	29	17.88	36	15.10	44
600	51.51	18	26.46	35	21.46	44	18.12	52
700	60.09	21	30.87	41	25.03	51	21.14	61
800	68.67	24	35.28	47	28.61	58	24.16	70
900	77.26	27	39.69	53	32.18	65	27.18	78
1,000	85.84	30	44.10	58	35.76	73	30.20	87
2,000	171.68	60	88.20	117	71.51	145	60.40	174
3,000	257.52	90	132.29	175	107.27	218	90.59	261
4,000	343.35	120	176.39	233	143.02	291	120.79	348
5,000	429.19	150	220.48	292	178.77	363	150.98	435
6,000	515.03	180	264.58	350	214.53	436	181.18	522
7,000	600.86	210	308.67	408	250.28	508	211.38	610
8,000	686.70	240	352.77	466	286.03	581	241.57	697
9,000	772.54	270	396.87	525	321.79	654	271.77	784
10,000	858.37	300	440.96	583	357.54	726	301.96	871
11,000	944.21	331	485.06	641	393.30	799	332.16	958
12,000	1,030.05	361	529.15	700	429.05	872	362.36	1,045
13,000	1,115.88	391	573.25	758	464.80	944	392.55	1,132
14,000	1,201.72	421	617.34	816	500.56	1,017	422.75	1,219
15,000	1,287.56	451	661.44	875	536.31	1,089	452.94	1,306
16,000	1,373.39	481	705.54	933	572.06	1,162	483.14	1,393
17,000	1,459.23	511	749.63	991	607.82	1,235	513.34	1,480
18,000	1,545.07	541	793.73	1,050	643.57	1,307	543.53	1,567
19,000	1,630.90	571	837.82	1,108	679.33	1,380	573.73	1,654
20,000	1,716.74	601	881.92	1,166	715.08	1,452	603.92	1,741
21,000	1,802.58	631	926.01	1,224	750.83	1,525	634.12	1,828
22,000	1,888.41	661	970.11	1,283	786.59	1,598	664.31	1,915
23,000	1,974.25	691	1,014.21	1,341	822.34	1,670	694.51	2,002
24,000	2,060.09	721	1,058.30	1,399	858.09	1,743	724.71	2,090
25,000	2,145.92	751	1,102.40	1,458	893.85	1,816	754.90	2,176
26,000	2,231.76	781	1,146.49	1,516	929.60	1,888	785.10	2,264
27,000	2,317.60	811	1,190.59	1,574	965.36	1,961	815.29	2,350
28,000	2,403.43	841	1,234.68	1,632	1,001.11	2,033	845.49	2,438
29,000	2,489.27	871	1,278.78	1,691	1,036.86	2,106	875.69	2,525
30,000	2,575.11	901	1,322.87	1,749	1,072.62	2,179	905.88	2,612
31,000	2,660.95	931	1,366.97	1,807	1,108.37	2,251	936.08	2,699
32,000	2,746.78	961	1,411.07	1,866	1,144.12	2,324	966.27	2,786
33,000	2,832.62	991	1,455.16	1,924	1,179.88	2,396	996.47	2,873
34,000	2,918.46	1,022	1,499.26	1,982	1,215.63	2,469	1,026.67	2,960
35,000	3,004.29	1,051	1,543.35	2,040	1,251.38	2,541	1,056.86	3,047
36,000	3,090.13	1,082	1,587.45	2,099	1,287.14	2,614	1,087.06	3,134
37,000	3,175.97	1,112	1,631.54	2,157	1,322.89	2,687	1,117.25	3,221
38,000	3,261.80	1,142	1,675.64	2,215	1,358.65	2,760	1,147.45	3,308
39,000	3,347.64	1,172	1,719.74	2,274	1,394.40	2,832	1,177.65	3,395
40,000	3,433.48	1,202	1,763.83	2,332	1,430.15	2,905	1,207.84	3,482
42,000	3,605.15	1,262	1,852.02	2,448	1,501.66	3,050	1,268.23	3,656
44,000	3,776.82	1,322	1,940.21	2,565	1,573.17	3,195	1,328.62	3,830
46,000	3,948.50	1,382	2,028.41	2,682	1,644.68	3,340	1,389.02	4,005
48,000	4,120.17	1,442	2,116.60	2,798	1,716.18	3,485	1,449.41	4,179
50,000	4,291.84	1,502	2,204.79	2,915	1,787.69	3,631	1,509.80	4,353

AUTO LOAN PAYMENTS 5.50%

AMOUNT OF LOAN	42 MOS MONTHLY PAYMENT	42 MOS TOTAL INTRST	48 MOS MONTHLY PAYMENT	48 MOS TOTAL INTRST	60 MOS MONTHLY PAYMENT	60 MOS TOTAL INTRST	72 MOS MONTHLY PAYMENT	72 MOS TOTAL INTRST
$ 1	0.03	0	0.03	0	0.02	0	0.02	0
2	0.06	0	0.05	0	0.04	0	0.04	1
3	0.08	0	0.07	0	0.06	1	0.05	1
4	0.11	1	0.10	1	0.08	1	0.07	1
5	0.14	1	0.12	1	0.10	1	0.09	1
6	0.16	1	0.14	1	0.12	1	0.10	1
7	0.19	1	0.17	1	0.14	1	0.12	2
8	0.21	1	0.19	1	0.16	2	0.14	2
9	0.24	1	0.21	1	0.18	2	0.15	2
10	0.27	1	0.24	2	0.20	2	0.17	2
20	0.53	2	0.47	3	0.39	3	0.33	4
30	0.79	3	0.70	4	0.58	5	0.50	6
40	1.05	4	0.94	5	0.77	6	0.66	8
50	1.32	5	1.17	6	0.96	8	0.82	9
60	1.58	6	1.40	7	1.15	9	0.99	11
70	1.84	7	1.63	8	1.34	10	1.15	13
80	2.10	8	1.87	10	1.53	12	1.31	14
90	2.37	10	2.10	11	1.72	13	1.48	17
100	2.63	10	2.33	12	1.92	15	1.64	18
200	5.25	21	4.66	24	3.83	30	3.27	35
300	7.87	31	6.98	35	5.74	44	4.91	54
400	10.50	41	9.31	47	7.65	59	6.54	71
500	13.12	51	11.63	58	9.56	74	8.17	88
600	15.74	61	13.96	70	11.47	88	9.81	106
700	18.37	72	16.28	81	13.38	103	11.44	124
800	20.99	82	18.61	93	15.29	117	13.08	142
900	23.61	92	20.94	105	17.20	132	14.71	159
1,000	26.23	102	23.26	116	19.11	147	16.34	176
2,000	52.46	203	46.52	233	38.21	293	32.68	353
3,000	78.69	305	69.77	349	57.31	439	49.02	529
4,000	104.92	407	93.03	465	76.41	585	65.36	706
5,000	131.15	508	116.29	582	95.51	731	81.69	882
6,000	157.38	610	139.54	698	114.61	877	98.03	1,058
7,000	183.61	712	162.80	814	133.71	1,023	114.37	1,235
8,000	209.84	813	186.06	931	152.81	1,169	130.71	1,411
9,000	236.07	915	209.31	1,047	171.92	1,315	147.05	1,588
10,000	262.30	1,017	232.57	1,163	191.02	1,461	163.38	1,763
11,000	288.52	1,118	255.83	1,280	210.12	1,607	179.72	1,940
12,000	314.75	1,220	279.08	1,396	229.22	1,753	196.06	2,116
13,000	340.98	1,321	302.34	1,512	248.32	1,899	212.40	2,293
14,000	367.21	1,423	325.60	1,629	267.42	2,045	228.74	2,469
15,000	393.44	1,524	348.85	1,745	286.52	2,191	245.07	2,645
16,000	419.67	1,626	372.11	1,861	305.62	2,337	261.41	2,822
17,000	445.90	1,728	395.37	1,978	324.72	2,483	277.75	2,998
18,000	472.13	1,829	418.62	2,094	343.83	2,630	294.09	3,174
19,000	498.36	1,931	441.88	2,210	362.93	2,776	310.42	3,350
20,000	524.59	2,033	465.13	2,326	382.03	2,922	326.76	3,527
21,000	550.81	2,134	488.39	2,443	401.13	3,068	343.10	3,703
22,000	577.04	2,236	511.65	2,559	420.23	3,214	359.44	3,880
23,000	603.27	2,337	534.90	2,675	439.33	3,360	375.78	4,056
24,000	629.50	2,439	558.16	2,792	458.43	3,506	392.11	4,232
25,000	655.73	2,541	581.42	2,908	477.53	3,652	408.45	4,408
26,000	681.96	2,642	604.67	3,024	496.64	3,798	424.79	4,585
27,000	708.19	2,744	627.93	3,141	515.74	3,944	441.13	4,761
28,000	734.42	2,846	651.19	3,257	534.84	4,090	457.47	4,938
29,000	760.65	2,947	674.44	3,373	553.94	4,236	473.80	5,114
30,000	786.88	3,049	697.70	3,490	573.04	4,382	490.14	5,290
31,000	813.10	3,150	720.96	3,606	592.14	4,528	506.48	5,467
32,000	839.33	3,252	744.21	3,722	611.24	4,674	522.82	5,643
33,000	865.56	3,354	767.47	3,839	630.34	4,820	539.16	5,820
34,000	891.79	3,455	790.73	3,955	649.44	4,966	555.49	5,995
35,000	918.02	3,557	813.98	4,071	668.55	5,113	571.83	6,172
36,000	944.25	3,659	837.24	4,188	687.65	5,259	588.17	6,348
37,000	970.48	3,760	860.49	4,304	706.75	5,405	604.51	6,525
38,000	996.71	3,862	883.75	4,420	725.85	5,551	620.84	6,700
39,000	1,022.94	3,963	907.01	4,536	744.95	5,697	637.18	6,877
40,000	1,049.17	4,065	930.26	4,652	764.05	5,843	653.52	7,053
42,000	1,101.62	4,268	976.78	4,885	802.25	6,135	686.20	7,406
44,000	1,154.08	4,471	1,023.29	5,118	840.46	6,428	718.87	7,759
46,000	1,206.54	4,675	1,069.80	5,350	878.66	6,720	751.55	8,112
48,000	1,259.00	4,878	1,116.32	5,583	916.86	7,012	784.22	8,464
50,000	1,311.46	5,081	1,162.83	5,816	955.06	7,304	816.90	8,817

5.75% AUTO LOAN PAYMENTS

AMOUNT OF LOAN	12 MOS		24 MOS		30 MOS		36 MOS	
	MONTHLY PAYMENT	TOTAL INTRST	MONTHLY PAYMENT	TOTAL INTRST	MONTHLY PAYMENT	TOTAL INTRST	MONTHLY PAYMENT	TOTAL INTRST
$ 1	0.09	0	0.05	0	0.04	0	0.04	0
2	0.18	0	0.09	0	0.08	0	0.07	1
3	0.26	0	0.14	0	0.11	0	0.10	1
4	0.35	0	0.18	0	0.15	0	0.13	1
5	0.43	0	0.23	1	0.18	1	0.16	1
6	0.52	0	0.27	0	0.22	1	0.19	1
7	0.61	0	0.31	0	0.26	1	0.22	1
8	0.69	0	0.36	1	0.29	1	0.25	1
9	0.78	0	0.40	1	0.33	1	0.28	1
10	0.86	0	0.45	1	0.36	1	0.31	1
20	1.72	1	0.89	1	0.72	2	0.61	2
30	2.58	1	1.33	2	1.08	2	0.91	3
40	3.44	1	1.77	2	1.44	3	1.22	4
50	4.30	2	2.22	3	1.80	4	1.52	5
60	5.16	2	2.66	4	2.16	5	1.82	6
70	6.02	2	3.10	4	2.52	6	2.13	7
80	6.88	3	3.54	5	2.87	6	2.43	7
90	7.74	3	3.98	6	3.23	7	2.73	8
100	8.60	3	4.43	6	3.59	8	3.04	9
200	17.20	6	8.85	12	7.18	15	6.07	19
300	25.79	9	13.27	18	10.76	23	9.10	28
400	34.39	13	17.69	25	14.35	31	12.13	37
500	42.98	16	22.11	31	17.94	38	15.16	46
600	51.58	19	26.53	37	21.52	46	18.19	55
700	60.17	22	30.95	43	25.11	53	21.22	64
800	68.77	25	35.37	49	28.70	61	24.25	73
900	77.36	28	39.79	55	32.28	68	27.28	82
1,000	85.96	32	44.21	61	35.87	76	30.31	91
2,000	171.91	63	88.42	122	71.74	152	60.62	182
3,000	257.86	94	132.63	183	107.60	228	90.93	273
4,000	343.81	126	176.84	244	143.47	304	121.24	365
5,000	429.76	157	221.05	305	179.34	380	151.55	456
6,000	515.71	189	265.25	366	215.20	456	181.86	547
7,000	601.67	220	309.46	427	251.07	532	212.17	638
8,000	687.62	251	353.67	488	286.93	608	242.48	729
9,000	773.57	283	397.88	549	322.80	684	272.78	820
10,000	859.52	314	442.09	610	358.67	760	303.09	911
11,000	945.47	346	486.29	671	394.53	836	333.40	1,002
12,000	1,031.42	377	530.50	732	430.40	912	363.71	1,094
13,000	1,117.38	409	574.71	793	466.27	988	394.02	1,185
14,000	1,203.33	440	618.92	854	502.13	1,064	424.33	1,276
15,000	1,289.28	471	663.13	915	538.00	1,140	454.64	1,367
16,000	1,375.23	503	707.33	976	573.86	1,216	484.95	1,458
17,000	1,461.18	534	751.54	1,037	609.73	1,292	515.25	1,549
18,000	1,547.13	566	795.75	1,098	645.60	1,368	545.56	1,640
19,000	1,633.08	597	839.96	1,159	681.46	1,444	575.87	1,731
20,000	1,719.04	628	884.17	1,220	717.33	1,520	606.18	1,822
21,000	1,804.99	660	928.37	1,281	753.20	1,596	636.49	1,914
22,000	1,890.94	691	972.58	1,342	789.06	1,672	666.80	2,005
23,000	1,976.89	723	1,016.79	1,403	824.93	1,748	697.11	2,096
24,000	2,062.84	754	1,061.00	1,464	860.79	1,824	727.42	2,187
25,000	2,148.79	785	1,105.21	1,525	896.66	1,900	757.72	2,278
26,000	2,234.75	817	1,149.41	1,586	932.53	1,976	788.03	2,369
27,000	2,320.70	848	1,193.62	1,647	968.39	2,052	818.34	2,460
28,000	2,406.65	880	1,237.83	1,708	1,004.26	2,128	848.65	2,551
29,000	2,492.60	911	1,282.04	1,769	1,040.13	2,204	878.96	2,643
30,000	2,578.55	943	1,326.25	1,830	1,075.99	2,280	909.27	2,734
31,000	2,664.50	974	1,370.45	1,891	1,111.86	2,356	939.58	2,825
32,000	2,750.46	1,006	1,414.66	1,952	1,147.72	2,432	969.89	2,916
33,000	2,836.41	1,037	1,458.87	2,013	1,183.59	2,508	1,000.20	3,007
34,000	2,922.36	1,068	1,503.08	2,074	1,219.46	2,584	1,030.50	3,098
35,000	3,008.31	1,100	1,547.29	2,135	1,255.32	2,660	1,060.81	3,189
36,000	3,094.26	1,131	1,591.49	2,196	1,291.19	2,736	1,091.12	3,280
37,000	3,180.21	1,163	1,635.70	2,257	1,327.05	2,812	1,121.43	3,371
38,000	3,266.16	1,194	1,679.91	2,318	1,362.92	2,888	1,151.74	3,463
39,000	3,352.12	1,225	1,724.12	2,379	1,398.79	2,964	1,182.05	3,554
40,000	3,438.07	1,257	1,768.33	2,440	1,434.65	3,040	1,212.36	3,645
42,000	3,609.97	1,320	1,856.74	2,562	1,506.39	3,192	1,272.97	3,827
44,000	3,781.87	1,382	1,945.16	2,684	1,578.12	3,344	1,333.59	4,009
46,000	3,953.78	1,445	2,033.58	2,806	1,649.85	3,496	1,394.21	4,192
48,000	4,125.68	1,508	2,121.99	2,928	1,721.58	3,647	1,454.83	4,374
50,000	4,297.58	1,571	2,210.41	3,050	1,793.32	3,800	1,515.44	4,556

60

AUTO LOAN PAYMENTS 5.75%

AMOUNT OF LOAN	42 MOS MONTHLY PAYMENT	42 MOS TOTAL INTRST	48 MOS MONTHLY PAYMENT	48 MOS TOTAL INTRST	60 MOS MONTHLY PAYMENT	60 MOS TOTAL INTRST	72 MOS MONTHLY PAYMENT	72 MOS TOTAL INTRST
$ 1	0.03	0	0.03	0	0.02	0	0.02	0
2	0.06	1	0.05	0	0.04	0	0.04	1
3	0.08	0	0.08	1	0.06	1	0.05	1
4	0.11	1	0.10	1	0.08	1	0.07	1
5	0.14	1	0.12	1	0.10	1	0.09	1
6	0.16	1	0.15	1	0.12	1	0.10	1
7	0.19	1	0.17	1	0.14	1	0.12	2
8	0.22	1	0.19	1	0.16	2	0.14	2
9	0.24	1	0.22	2	0.18	2	0.15	2
10	0.27	1	0.24	2	0.20	2	0.17	2
20	0.53	2	0.47	3	0.39	3	0.33	4
30	0.80	4	0.71	4	0.58	5	0.50	6
40	1.06	5	0.94	5	0.77	6	0.66	8
50	1.32	5	1.17	6	0.97	8	0.83	10
60	1.59	7	1.41	8	1.16	10	0.99	11
70	1.85	8	1.64	9	1.35	11	1.16	14
80	2.11	9	1.87	10	1.54	12	1.32	15
90	2.38	10	2.11	11	1.73	14	1.49	17
100	2.64	11	2.34	12	1.93	16	1.65	19
200	5.27	21	4.68	25	3.85	31	3.30	38
300	7.91	32	7.02	37	5.77	46	4.94	56
400	10.54	43	9.35	49	7.69	61	6.59	74
500	13.18	54	11.69	61	9.61	77	8.23	93
600	15.81	64	14.03	73	11.54	92	9.88	111
700	18.44	74	16.36	85	13.46	108	11.52	129
800	21.08	85	18.70	98	15.38	123	13.17	148
900	23.71	96	21.04	110	17.30	138	14.81	166
1,000	26.35	107	23.38	122	19.22	153	16.46	185
2,000	52.69	213	46.75	244	38.44	306	32.92	370
3,000	79.03	319	70.12	366	57.66	460	49.37	555
4,000	105.37	426	93.49	488	76.87	612	65.83	740
5,000	131.72	532	116.86	609	96.09	765	82.28	924
6,000	158.06	639	140.23	731	115.31	919	98.74	1,109
7,000	184.40	745	163.60	853	134.52	1,071	115.19	1,294
8,000	210.74	851	186.97	975	153.74	1,224	131.65	1,479
9,000	237.09	958	210.34	1,096	172.96	1,378	148.10	1,663
10,000	263.43	1,064	233.71	1,218	192.17	1,530	164.56	1,848
11,000	289.77	1,170	257.08	1,340	211.39	1,683	181.01	2,033
12,000	316.11	1,277	280.45	1,462	230.61	1,837	197.47	2,218
13,000	342.46	1,383	303.82	1,583	249.82	1,989	213.92	2,402
14,000	368.80	1,490	327.19	1,705	269.04	2,142	230.38	2,587
15,000	395.14	1,596	350.56	1,827	288.26	2,296	246.83	2,772
16,000	421.48	1,702	373.93	1,949	307.47	2,448	263.29	2,957
17,000	447.83	1,809	397.30	2,070	326.69	2,601	279.74	3,141
18,000	474.17	1,915	420.68	2,193	345.91	2,755	296.20	3,326
19,000	500.51	2,021	444.05	2,314	365.12	2,907	312.65	3,511
20,000	526.85	2,128	467.42	2,436	384.34	3,060	329.11	3,696
21,000	553.20	2,234	490.79	2,558	403.56	3,214	345.56	3,880
22,000	579.54	2,341	514.16	2,680	422.77	3,366	362.02	4,065
23,000	605.88	2,447	537.53	2,801	441.99	3,519	378.47	4,250
24,000	632.22	2,553	560.90	2,923	461.21	3,673	394.93	4,435
25,000	658.57	2,660	584.27	3,045	480.42	3,825	411.38	4,619
26,000	684.91	2,766	607.64	3,167	499.64	3,978	427.84	4,804
27,000	711.25	2,873	631.01	3,288	518.86	4,132	444.29	4,989
28,000	737.59	2,979	654.38	3,410	538.07	4,284	460.75	5,174
29,000	763.94	3,085	677.75	3,532	557.29	4,437	477.20	5,358
30,000	790.28	3,192	701.12	3,654	576.51	4,591	493.66	5,544
31,000	816.62	3,298	724.49	3,776	595.72	4,743	510.11	5,728
32,000	842.96	3,404	747.86	3,897	614.94	4,896	526.57	5,913
33,000	869.31	3,511	771.23	4,019	634.16	5,050	543.02	6,097
34,000	895.65	3,617	794.60	4,141	653.38	5,203	559.48	6,283
35,000	921.99	3,724	817.98	4,263	672.59	5,355	575.93	6,467
36,000	948.33	3,830	841.35	4,385	691.81	5,509	592.39	6,652
37,000	974.68	3,937	864.72	4,507	711.03	5,662	608.84	6,836
38,000	1,001.02	4,043	888.09	4,628	730.24	5,814	625.30	7,022
39,000	1,027.36	4,149	911.46	4,750	749.46	5,968	641.76	7,207
40,000	1,053.70	4,255	934.83	4,872	768.68	6,121	658.21	7,391
42,000	1,106.39	4,468	981.57	5,115	807.11	6,427	691.12	7,761
44,000	1,159.07	4,681	1,028.31	5,359	845.54	6,732	724.03	8,130
46,000	1,211.76	4,894	1,075.05	5,602	883.98	7,039	756.94	8,500
48,000	1,264.44	5,106	1,121.79	5,846	922.41	7,345	789.85	8,869
50,000	1,317.13	5,319	1,168.53	6,089	960.84	7,650	822.76	9,239

AUTO LOAN PAYMENTS

AMOUNT OF LOAN	12 MOS MONTHLY PAYMENT	12 MOS TOTAL INTRST	24 MOS MONTHLY PAYMENT	24 MOS TOTAL INTRST	30 MOS MONTHLY PAYMENT	30 MOS TOTAL INTRST	36 MOS MONTHLY PAYMENT	36 MOS TOTAL INTRST
$ 1	0.09	0	0.05	0	0.04	0	0.04	0
2	0.18	0	0.09	0	0.08	0	0.07	0
3	0.26	0	0.14	0	0.11	0	0.10	1
4	0.35	0	0.18	0	0.15	0	0.13	1
5	0.44	0	0.23	1	0.18	0	0.16	1
6	0.52	0	0.27	0	0.22	0	0.19	1
7	0.61	0	0.31	0	0.26	1	0.22	1
8	0.69	0	0.36	1	0.29	1	0.25	1
9	0.78	0	0.40	1	0.33	1	0.28	1
10	0.87	0	0.45	1	0.36	1	0.31	1
20	1.73	1	0.89	1	0.72	2	0.61	2
30	2.59	1	1.33	2	1.08	2	0.92	3
40	3.45	1	1.78	3	1.44	3	1.22	4
50	4.31	1	2.22	3	1.80	4	1.52	5
60	5.17	2	2.66	4	2.16	5	1.83	6
70	6.03	2	3.10	4	2.52	6	2.13	7
80	6.89	3	3.55	5	2.88	6	2.44	8
90	7.75	3	3.99	6	3.24	7	2.74	9
100	8.61	3	4.43	6	3.60	8	3.04	9
200	17.21	7	8.86	13	7.19	16	6.08	19
300	25.81	10	13.29	19	10.79	24	9.12	28
400	34.41	13	17.72	25	14.38	31	12.16	38
500	43.02	16	22.14	31	17.97	39	15.19	47
600	51.62	19	26.57	38	21.57	47	18.23	56
700	60.22	23	31.00	44	25.16	55	21.27	66
800	68.82	26	35.43	50	28.75	63	24.31	75
900	77.42	29	39.85	56	32.35	71	27.34	84
1,000	86.03	32	44.28	63	35.94	78	30.38	94
2,000	172.05	65	88.56	125	71.87	156	60.76	187
3,000	258.07	97	132.83	188	107.81	234	91.13	281
4,000	344.09	129	177.11	251	143.74	312	121.51	374
5,000	430.11	161	221.38	313	179.67	390	151.89	468
6,000	516.13	194	265.66	376	215.61	468	182.26	561
7,000	602.15	226	309.93	438	251.54	546	212.64	655
8,000	688.17	258	354.21	501	287.48	624	243.02	749
9,000	774.19	290	398.49	564	323.41	702	273.39	842
10,000	860.21	323	442.76	626	359.34	780	303.77	936
11,000	946.23	355	487.04	689	395.28	858	334.15	1,029
12,000	1,032.25	387	531.31	751	431.21	936	364.52	1,123
13,000	1,118.27	419	575.59	814	467.14	1,014	394.90	1,216
14,000	1,204.29	451	619.86	877	503.08	1,092	425.28	1,310
15,000	1,290.31	484	664.14	939	539.01	1,170	455.65	1,403
16,000	1,376.33	516	708.41	1,002	574.95	1,249	486.03	1,497
17,000	1,462.35	548	752.69	1,065	610.88	1,326	516.41	1,591
18,000	1,548.37	580	796.97	1,127	646.81	1,404	546.78	1,684
19,000	1,634.39	613	841.24	1,190	682.75	1,483	577.16	1,778
20,000	1,720.41	645	885.52	1,252	718.68	1,560	607.54	1,871
21,000	1,806.43	677	929.79	1,315	754.61	1,638	637.91	1,965
22,000	1,892.46	710	974.07	1,378	790.55	1,717	668.29	2,058
23,000	1,978.48	742	1,018.34	1,440	826.48	1,794	698.67	2,152
24,000	2,064.50	774	1,062.62	1,503	862.42	1,873	729.04	2,245
25,000	2,150.52	806	1,106.89	1,565	898.35	1,951	759.42	2,339
26,000	2,236.54	838	1,151.17	1,628	934.28	2,028	789.80	2,433
27,000	2,322.56	871	1,195.45	1,691	970.22	2,107	820.17	2,526
28,000	2,408.58	903	1,239.72	1,753	1,006.15	2,185	850.55	2,620
29,000	2,494.60	935	1,284.00	1,816	1,042.09	2,263	880.93	2,713
30,000	2,580.62	967	1,328.27	1,878	1,078.02	2,341	911.30	2,807
31,000	2,666.64	1,000	1,372.55	1,941	1,113.95	2,419	941.68	2,900
32,000	2,752.66	1,032	1,416.82	2,004	1,149.89	2,497	972.06	2,994
33,000	2,838.68	1,064	1,461.10	2,066	1,185.82	2,575	1,002.43	3,087
34,000	2,924.70	1,096	1,505.37	2,129	1,221.75	2,653	1,032.81	3,181
35,000	3,010.72	1,129	1,549.65	2,192	1,257.69	2,731	1,063.19	3,275
36,000	3,096.74	1,161	1,593.93	2,254	1,293.62	2,809	1,093.56	3,368
37,000	3,182.76	1,193	1,638.20	2,317	1,329.56	2,887	1,123.94	3,462
38,000	3,268.78	1,225	1,682.48	2,380	1,365.49	2,965	1,154.32	3,556
39,000	3,354.80	1,258	1,726.75	2,442	1,401.42	3,043	1,184.69	3,649
40,000	3,440.82	1,290	1,771.03	2,505	1,437.36	3,121	1,215.07	3,743
42,000	3,612.86	1,354	1,859.58	2,630	1,509.22	3,277	1,275.82	3,930
44,000	3,784.91	1,419	1,948.13	2,755	1,581.09	3,433	1,336.58	4,117
46,000	3,956.95	1,483	2,036.68	2,880	1,652.96	3,589	1,397.33	4,304
48,000	4,128.99	1,548	2,125.23	3,006	1,724.83	3,745	1,458.08	4,491
50,000	4,301.03	1,612	2,213.78	3,131	1,796.70	3,901	1,518.84	4,678

AUTO LOAN PAYMENTS   5.90%

AMOUNT OF LOAN	42 MOS MONTHLY PAYMENT	42 MOS TOTAL INTRST	48 MOS MONTHLY PAYMENT	48 MOS TOTAL INTRST	60 MOS MONTHLY PAYMENT	60 MOS TOTAL INTRST	72 MOS MONTHLY PAYMENT	72 MOS TOTAL INTRST
$ 1	0.03	0	0.03	0	0.02	0	0.02	0
2	0.06	1	0.05	0	0.04	0	0.04	1
3	0.08	0	0.08	1	0.06	1	0.05	1
4	0.11	1	0.10	1	0.08	1	0.07	1
5	0.14	1	0.12	1	0.10	1	0.09	1
6	0.16	1	0.15	1	0.12	1	0.10	1
7	0.19	1	0.17	1	0.14	1	0.12	2
8	0.22	1	0.19	1	0.16	2	0.14	2
9	0.24	1	0.22	2	0.18	2	0.15	2
10	0.27	1	0.24	2	0.20	2	0.17	2
20	0.53	2	0.47	3	0.39	3	0.34	4
30	0.80	4	0.71	4	0.58	5	0.50	6
40	1.06	5	0.94	5	0.78	7	0.67	8
50	1.33	6	1.18	7	0.97	8	0.83	10
60	1.59	7	1.41	8	1.16	10	1.00	12
70	1.85	8	1.65	9	1.36	12	1.16	14
80	2.12	9	1.88	10	1.55	13	1.33	16
90	2.38	10	2.11	11	1.74	14	1.49	17
100	2.65	11	2.35	13	1.93	16	1.66	20
200	5.29	22	4.69	25	3.86	32	3.31	38
300	7.93	33	7.04	38	5.79	47	4.96	57
400	10.57	44	9.38	50	7.72	63	6.62	77
500	13.21	55	11.72	63	9.65	79	8.27	95
600	15.85	66	14.07	75	11.58	95	9.92	114
700	18.49	77	16.41	88	13.51	111	11.57	133
800	21.13	87	18.76	100	15.43	126	13.23	153
900	23.77	98	21.10	113	17.36	142	14.88	171
1,000	26.42	110	23.44	125	19.29	157	16.53	190
2,000	52.83	219	46.88	250	38.58	315	33.06	380
3,000	79.24	328	70.32	375	57.86	472	49.58	570
4,000	105.65	437	93.76	500	77.15	629	66.11	760
5,000	132.06	547	117.20	626	96.44	786	82.63	949
6,000	158.47	656	140.64	751	115.72	943	99.16	1,140
7,000	184.88	765	164.08	876	135.01	1,101	115.69	1,330
8,000	211.29	874	187.52	1,001	154.30	1,258	132.21	1,519
9,000	237.70	983	210.96	1,126	173.58	1,415	148.74	1,709
10,000	264.11	1,093	234.40	1,251	192.87	1,572	165.26	1,899
11,000	290.52	1,202	257.84	1,376	212.15	1,729	181.79	2,089
12,000	316.93	1,311	281.28	1,501	231.44	1,886	198.31	2,278
13,000	343.34	1,420	304.71	1,626	250.73	2,044	214.84	2,468
14,000	369.75	1,530	328.15	1,751	270.01	2,201	231.37	2,659
15,000	396.17	1,639	351.59	1,876	289.30	2,358	247.89	2,848
16,000	422.58	1,748	375.03	2,001	308.59	2,515	264.42	3,038
17,000	448.99	1,858	398.47	2,127	327.87	2,672	280.94	3,228
18,000	475.40	1,967	421.91	2,252	347.16	2,830	297.47	3,418
19,000	501.81	2,076	445.35	2,377	366.45	2,987	313.99	3,607
20,000	528.22	2,185	468.79	2,502	385.73	3,144	330.52	3,797
21,000	554.63	2,294	492.23	2,627	405.02	3,301	347.05	3,988
22,000	581.04	2,404	515.67	2,752	424.30	3,458	363.57	4,177
23,000	607.45	2,513	539.11	2,877	443.59	3,615	380.10	4,367
24,000	633.86	2,622	562.55	3,002	462.88	3,773	396.62	4,557
25,000	660.27	2,731	585.99	3,128	482.16	3,930	413.15	4,747
26,000	686.68	2,841	609.42	3,252	501.45	4,087	429.67	4,936
27,000	713.09	2,950	632.86	3,377	520.74	4,244	446.20	5,126
28,000	739.50	3,059	656.30	3,502	540.02	4,401	462.73	5,317
29,000	765.91	3,168	679.74	3,628	559.31	4,559	479.25	5,506
30,000	792.33	3,278	703.18	3,753	578.60	4,716	495.78	5,696
31,000	818.74	3,387	726.62	3,878	597.88	4,873	512.30	5,886
32,000	845.15	3,496	750.06	4,003	617.17	5,030	528.83	6,076
33,000	871.56	3,606	773.50	4,128	636.45	5,187	545.35	6,265
34,000	897.97	3,715	796.94	4,253	655.74	5,344	561.88	6,455
35,000	924.38	3,824	820.38	4,378	675.03	5,502	578.41	6,646
36,000	950.79	3,933	843.82	4,503	694.31	5,659	594.93	6,835
37,000	977.20	4,042	867.26	4,628	713.60	5,816	611.46	7,025
38,000	1,003.61	4,152	890.69	4,753	732.89	5,973	627.98	7,215
39,000	1,030.02	4,261	914.13	4,878	752.17	6,130	644.51	7,405
40,000	1,056.43	4,370	937.57	5,003	771.46	6,288	661.03	7,594
42,000	1,109.25	4,589	984.45	5,254	810.03	6,602	694.09	7,974
44,000	1,162.07	4,807	1,031.33	5,504	848.60	6,916	727.14	8,354
46,000	1,214.90	5,026	1,078.21	5,754	887.18	7,231	760.19	8,734
48,000	1,267.72	5,244	1,125.09	6,004	925.75	7,545	793.24	9,113
50,000	1,320.54	5,463	1,171.97	6,255	964.32	7,859	826.29	9,493

6.00%   AUTO LOAN PAYMENTS

AMOUNT OF LOAN	12 MOS		24 MOS		30 MOS		36 MOS	
	MONTHLY PAYMENT	TOTAL INTRST	MONTHLY PAYMENT	TOTAL INTRST	MONTHLY PAYMENT	TOTAL INTRST	MONTHLY PAYMENT	TOTAL INTRST
$ 1	0.09	0	0.05	0	0.04	0	0.04	0
2	0.18	0	0.09	0	0.08	0	0.07	1
3	0.26	0	0.14	0	0.11	0	0.10	1
4	0.35	0	0.18	0	0.15	1	0.13	1
5	0.44	0	0.23	1	0.18	0	0.16	1
6	0.52	0	0.27	0	0.22	1	0.19	1
7	0.61	0	0.32	1	0.26	1	0.22	1
8	0.69	0	0.36	1	0.29	1	0.25	1
9	0.78	0	0.40	1	0.33	1	0.28	1
10	0.87	0	0.45	1	0.36	1	0.31	1
20	1.73	1	0.89	1	0.72	2	0.61	2
30	2.59	1	1.33	2	1.08	2	0.92	3
40	3.45	1	1.78	3	1.44	3	1.22	4
50	4.31	2	2.22	3	1.80	4	1.53	5
60	5.17	2	2.66	4	2.16	5	1.83	6
70	6.03	2	3.11	5	2.52	6	2.13	7
80	6.89	3	3.55	5	2.88	6	2.44	8
90	7.75	3	3.99	6	3.24	7	2.74	9
100	8.61	3	4.44	7	3.60	8	3.05	10
200	17.22	7	8.87	13	7.20	16	6.09	19
300	25.82	10	13.30	19	10.80	24	9.13	29
400	34.43	13	17.73	26	14.40	32	12.17	38
500	43.04	16	22.17	32	17.99	40	15.22	48
600	51.64	20	26.60	38	21.59	48	18.26	57
700	60.25	23	31.03	45	25.19	56	21.30	67
800	68.86	26	35.46	51	28.79	64	24.34	76
900	77.46	30	39.89	57	32.39	72	27.38	86
1,000	86.07	33	44.33	64	35.98	79	30.43	95
2,000	172.14	66	88.65	128	71.96	159	60.85	191
3,000	258.20	98	132.97	191	107.94	238	91.27	286
4,000	344.27	131	177.29	255	143.92	318	121.69	381
5,000	430.34	164	221.61	319	179.90	397	152.11	476
6,000	516.40	197	265.93	382	215.88	476	182.54	571
7,000	602.47	230	310.25	446	251.86	556	212.96	667
8,000	688.54	262	354.57	510	287.84	635	243.38	762
9,000	774.60	295	398.89	573	323.82	715	273.80	857
10,000	860.67	328	443.21	637	359.79	794	304.22	952
11,000	946.74	361	487.53	701	395.77	873	334.65	1,047
12,000	1,032.80	394	531.85	764	431.75	953	365.07	1,143
13,000	1,118.87	426	576.17	828	467.73	1,032	395.49	1,238
14,000	1,204.94	459	620.49	892	503.71	1,111	425.91	1,333
15,000	1,291.00	492	664.81	955	539.69	1,191	456.33	1,428
16,000	1,377.07	525	709.13	1,019	575.67	1,270	486.76	1,523
17,000	1,463.14	558	753.46	1,083	611.65	1,350	517.18	1,618
18,000	1,549.20	590	797.78	1,147	647.63	1,429	547.60	1,714
19,000	1,635.27	623	842.10	1,210	683.60	1,508	578.02	1,809
20,000	1,721.33	656	886.42	1,274	719.58	1,587	608.44	1,904
21,000	1,807.40	689	930.74	1,338	755.56	1,667	638.87	1,999
22,000	1,893.47	722	975.06	1,401	791.54	1,746	669.29	2,094
23,000	1,979.53	754	1,019.38	1,465	827.52	1,826	699.71	2,190
24,000	2,065.60	787	1,063.70	1,529	863.50	1,905	730.13	2,285
25,000	2,151.67	820	1,108.02	1,592	899.48	1,984	760.55	2,380
26,000	2,237.73	853	1,152.34	1,656	935.46	2,064	790.98	2,475
27,000	2,323.80	886	1,196.66	1,720	971.44	2,143	821.40	2,570
28,000	2,409.87	918	1,240.98	1,784	1,007.41	2,222	851.82	2,666
29,000	2,495.93	951	1,285.30	1,847	1,043.39	2,302	882.24	2,761
30,000	2,582.00	984	1,329.62	1,911	1,079.37	2,381	912.66	2,856
31,000	2,668.06	1,017	1,373.94	1,975	1,115.35	2,461	943.09	2,951
32,000	2,754.13	1,050	1,418.26	2,038	1,151.33	2,540	973.51	3,046
33,000	2,840.20	1,082	1,462.59	2,102	1,187.31	2,619	1,003.93	3,141
34,000	2,926.26	1,115	1,506.91	2,166	1,223.29	2,699	1,034.35	3,237
35,000	3,012.33	1,148	1,551.23	2,230	1,259.27	2,778	1,064.77	3,332
36,000	3,098.40	1,181	1,595.55	2,293	1,295.25	2,858	1,095.19	3,427
37,000	3,184.46	1,214	1,639.87	2,357	1,331.22	2,937	1,125.62	3,522
38,000	3,270.53	1,246	1,684.19	2,421	1,367.20	3,016	1,156.04	3,617
39,000	3,356.60	1,279	1,728.51	2,484	1,403.18	3,095	1,186.46	3,713
40,000	3,442.66	1,312	1,772.83	2,548	1,439.16	3,175	1,216.88	3,808
42,000	3,614.80	1,378	1,861.47	2,675	1,511.12	3,334	1,277.73	3,998
44,000	3,786.93	1,443	1,950.11	2,803	1,583.08	3,492	1,338.57	4,189
46,000	3,959.06	1,509	2,038.75	2,930	1,655.04	3,651	1,399.41	4,379
48,000	4,131.19	1,574	2,127.39	3,057	1,726.99	3,810	1,460.26	4,569
50,000	4,303.33	1,640	2,216.04	3,185	1,798.95	3,969	1,521.10	4,760

AMOUNT OF LOAN	42 MOS		48 MOS		60 MOS		72 MOS	
	MONTHLY PAYMENT	TOTAL INTRST	MONTHLY PAYMENT	TOTAL INTRST	MONTHLY PAYMENT	TOTAL INTRST	MONTHLY PAYMENT	TOTAL INTRST
$ 1	0.03	0	0.03	0	0.02	0	0.02	0
2	0.06	0	0.05	0	0.04	0	0.04	1
3	0.08	0	0.08	1	0.06	1	0.05	1
4	0.11	1	0.10	1	0.08	1	0.07	1
5	0.14	1	0.12	1	0.10	1	0.09	1
6	0.16	1	0.15	1	0.12	1	0.10	1
7	0.19	1	0.17	1	0.14	1	0.12	2
8	0.22	1	0.19	1	0.16	2	0.14	2
9	0.24	1	0.22	2	0.18	2	0.15	2
10	0.27	1	0.24	2	0.20	2	0.17	2
20	0.53	2	0.47	3	0.39	3	0.34	4
30	0.80	4	0.71	4	0.58	5	0.50	6
40	1.06	5	0.94	5	0.78	7	0.67	8
50	1.33	6	1.18	7	0.97	8	0.83	10
60	1.59	7	1.41	8	1.16	10	1.00	12
70	1.86	8	1.65	9	1.36	12	1.17	14
80	2.12	9	1.88	10	1.55	13	1.33	16
90	2.39	10	2.12	12	1.74	14	1.50	18
100	2.65	11	2.35	13	1.94	16	1.66	20
200	5.30	23	4.70	26	3.87	32	3.32	39
300	7.94	33	7.05	38	5.80	48	4.98	59
400	10.59	45	9.40	51	7.74	64	6.63	77
500	13.23	56	11.75	64	9.67	80	8.29	97
600	15.88	67	14.10	77	11.60	96	9.95	116
700	18.52	78	16.44	89	13.54	112	11.61	136
800	21.17	89	18.79	102	15.47	128	13.26	155
900	23.82	100	21.14	115	17.40	144	14.92	174
1,000	26.46	111	23.49	128	19.34	160	16.58	194
2,000	52.92	223	46.98	255	38.67	320	33.15	387
3,000	79.37	334	70.46	382	58.00	480	49.72	580
4,000	105.83	445	93.95	510	77.34	640	66.30	774
5,000	132.29	556	117.43	637	96.67	800	82.87	967
6,000	158.74	667	140.92	764	116.00	960	99.44	1,160
7,000	185.20	778	164.40	891	135.33	1,120	116.02	1,353
8,000	211.65	889	187.89	1,019	154.67	1,280	132.59	1,546
9,000	238.11	1,001	211.37	1,146	174.00	1,440	149.16	1,740
10,000	264.57	1,112	234.86	1,273	193.33	1,600	165.73	1,933
11,000	291.02	1,223	258.34	1,400	212.67	1,760	182.31	2,126
12,000	317.48	1,334	281.83	1,528	232.00	1,920	198.88	2,319
13,000	343.94	1,445	305.31	1,655	251.33	2,080	215.45	2,512
14,000	370.39	1,556	328.80	1,782	270.66	2,240	232.03	2,706
15,000	396.85	1,668	352.28	1,909	290.00	2,400	248.60	2,899
16,000	423.30	1,779	375.77	2,037	309.33	2,560	265.17	3,092
17,000	449.76	1,890	399.25	2,164	328.66	2,720	281.74	3,285
18,000	476.22	2,001	422.74	2,292	348.00	2,880	298.32	3,479
19,000	502.67	2,112	446.22	2,419	367.33	3,040	314.89	3,672
20,000	529.13	2,223	469.71	2,546	386.66	3,200	331.46	3,865
21,000	555.59	2,335	493.19	2,673	405.99	3,359	348.04	4,059
22,000	582.04	2,446	516.68	2,801	425.33	3,520	364.61	4,252
23,000	608.50	2,557	540.16	2,928	444.66	3,680	381.18	4,445
24,000	634.95	2,668	563.65	3,055	463.99	3,839	397.75	4,638
25,000	661.41	2,779	587.13	3,182	483.33	4,000	414.33	4,832
26,000	687.87	2,891	610.62	3,310	502.66	4,160	430.90	5,025
27,000	714.32	3,001	634.10	3,437	521.99	4,319	447.47	5,218
28,000	740.78	3,113	657.59	3,564	541.32	4,479	464.05	5,412
29,000	767.24	3,224	681.07	3,691	560.66	4,640	480.62	5,605
30,000	793.69	3,335	704.56	3,819	579.99	4,799	497.19	5,798
31,000	820.15	3,446	728.04	3,946	599.32	4,959	513.76	5,991
32,000	846.60	3,557	751.53	4,073	618.65	5,119	530.34	6,184
33,000	873.06	3,669	775.01	4,200	637.99	5,279	546.91	6,378
34,000	899.52	3,780	798.50	4,328	657.32	5,439	563.48	6,571
35,000	925.97	3,891	821.98	4,455	676.65	5,599	580.06	6,764
36,000	952.43	4,002	845.47	4,583	695.99	5,759	596.63	6,957
37,000	978.89	4,113	868.95	4,710	715.32	5,919	613.20	7,150
38,000	1,005.34	4,224	892.44	4,837	734.65	6,079	629.77	7,343
39,000	1,031.80	4,336	915.92	4,964	753.98	6,239	646.35	7,537
40,000	1,058.25	4,447	939.41	5,092	773.32	6,399	662.92	7,730
42,000	1,111.17	4,669	986.38	5,346	811.98	6,719	696.07	8,117
44,000	1,164.08	4,891	1,033.35	5,601	850.65	7,039	729.21	8,503
46,000	1,216.99	5,114	1,080.32	5,855	889.31	7,359	762.36	8,890
48,000	1,269.90	5,336	1,127.29	6,110	927.98	7,679	795.50	9,276
50,000	1,322.82	5,558	1,174.26	6,364	966.65	7,999	828.65	9,663

6.25% AUTO LOAN PAYMENTS

AMOUNT OF LOAN	12 MOS MONTHLY PAYMENT	12 MOS TOTAL INTRST	24 MOS MONTHLY PAYMENT	24 MOS TOTAL INTRST	30 MOS MONTHLY PAYMENT	30 MOS TOTAL INTRST	36 MOS MONTHLY PAYMENT	36 MOS TOTAL INTRST
$ 1	0.09	0	0.05	0	0.04	0	0.04	0
2	0.18	0	0.09	0	0.08	0	0.07	1
3	0.26	0	0.14	0	0.11	0	0.10	1
4	0.35	0	0.18	0	0.15	0	0.13	1
5	0.44	0	0.23	0	0.19	1	0.16	1
6	0.52	0	0.27	1	0.22	0	0.19	1
7	0.61	0	0.32	1	0.26	1	0.22	1
8	0.69	0	0.36	1	0.29	1	0.25	1
9	0.78	0	0.40	1	0.33	1	0.28	1
10	0.87	0	0.45	1	0.37	1	0.31	1
20	1.73	1	0.89	1	0.73	2	0.62	2
30	2.59	1	1.34	2	1.09	3	0.92	3
40	3.45	1	1.78	3	1.45	4	1.23	4
50	4.31	2	2.23	4	1.81	4	1.53	5
60	5.18	2	2.67	4	2.17	5	1.84	6
70	6.04	2	3.12	5	2.53	6	2.14	7
80	6.90	3	3.56	5	2.89	7	2.45	8
90	7.76	3	4.00	6	3.25	8	2.75	9
100	8.62	3	4.45	7	3.61	8	3.06	10
200	17.24	7	8.89	13	7.22	17	6.11	20
300	25.86	10	13.34	20	10.83	25	9.17	30
400	34.48	14	17.78	27	14.44	33	12.22	40
500	43.10	17	22.22	33	18.05	42	15.27	50
600	51.71	21	26.67	40	21.66	50	18.33	60
700	60.33	24	31.11	47	25.27	58	21.38	70
800	68.95	27	35.55	53	28.88	66	24.43	79
900	77.57	31	40.00	60	32.49	75	27.49	89
1,000	86.19	34	44.44	67	36.10	83	30.54	99
2,000	172.37	68	88.87	133	72.19	166	61.08	199
3,000	258.55	103	133.31	199	108.28	248	91.61	298
4,000	344.73	137	177.74	266	144.37	331	122.15	397
5,000	430.91	171	222.17	332	180.46	414	152.68	496
6,000	517.09	205	266.61	399	216.56	497	183.22	596
7,000	603.27	239	311.04	465	252.65	580	213.75	695
8,000	689.46	274	355.47	531	288.74	662	244.29	794
9,000	775.64	308	399.91	598	324.83	745	274.82	894
10,000	861.82	342	444.34	664	360.92	828	305.36	993
11,000	948.00	376	488.77	730	397.02	911	335.89	1,092
12,000	1,034.18	410	533.21	797	433.11	993	366.43	1,191
13,000	1,120.36	444	577.64	863	469.20	1,076	396.96	1,291
14,000	1,206.54	478	622.07	930	505.29	1,159	427.50	1,390
15,000	1,292.73	513	666.51	996	541.38	1,241	458.04	1,489
16,000	1,378.91	547	710.94	1,063	577.47	1,324	488.57	1,589
17,000	1,465.09	581	755.37	1,129	613.57	1,407	519.11	1,688
18,000	1,551.27	615	799.81	1,195	649.66	1,490	549.64	1,787
19,000	1,637.45	649	844.24	1,262	685.75	1,573	580.18	1,886
20,000	1,723.63	684	888.67	1,328	721.84	1,655	610.71	1,986
21,000	1,809.81	718	933.11	1,395	757.93	1,738	641.25	2,085
22,000	1,896.00	752	977.54	1,461	794.03	1,821	671.78	2,184
23,000	1,982.18	786	1,021.97	1,527	830.12	1,904	702.32	2,284
24,000	2,068.36	820	1,066.41	1,594	866.21	1,986	732.85	2,383
25,000	2,154.55	854	1,110.84	1,660	902.30	2,069	763.39	2,482
26,000	2,240.72	889	1,155.27	1,726	938.39	2,152	793.92	2,581
27,000	2,326.90	923	1,199.71	1,793	974.48	2,234	824.46	2,681
28,000	2,413.08	957	1,244.14	1,859	1,010.58	2,317	854.99	2,780
29,000	2,499.27	991	1,288.57	1,926	1,046.67	2,400	885.53	2,879
30,000	2,585.45	1,025	1,333.01	1,992	1,082.76	2,483	916.07	2,979
31,000	2,671.63	1,060	1,377.44	2,059	1,118.85	2,566	946.60	3,078
32,000	2,757.81	1,094	1,421.87	2,125	1,154.94	2,648	977.14	3,177
33,000	2,843.99	1,128	1,466.31	2,191	1,191.04	2,731	1,007.67	3,276
34,000	2,930.17	1,162	1,510.74	2,258	1,227.13	2,814	1,038.21	3,376
35,000	3,016.35	1,196	1,555.17	2,324	1,263.22	2,897	1,068.74	3,475
36,000	3,102.53	1,230	1,599.61	2,391	1,299.31	2,979	1,099.28	3,574
37,000	3,188.72	1,265	1,644.04	2,457	1,335.40	3,062	1,129.81	3,673
38,000	3,274.90	1,299	1,688.47	2,523	1,371.50	3,145	1,160.35	3,773
39,000	3,361.08	1,333	1,732.91	2,590	1,407.59	3,228	1,190.88	3,872
40,000	3,447.26	1,367	1,777.34	2,656	1,443.68	3,310	1,221.42	3,971
42,000	3,619.62	1,435	1,866.21	2,789	1,515.86	3,476	1,282.49	4,170
44,000	3,791.99	1,504	1,955.07	2,922	1,588.05	3,642	1,343.56	4,368
46,000	3,964.35	1,572	2,043.94	3,055	1,660.23	3,807	1,404.63	4,567
48,000	4,136.71	1,641	2,132.81	3,187	1,732.41	3,972	1,465.70	4,765
50,000	4,309.07	1,709	2,221.67	3,320	1,804.60	4,138	1,526.77	4,964

AUTO LOAN PAYMENTS
6.25%

AMOUNT OF LOAN	42 MOS		48 MOS		60 MOS		72 MOS	
	MONTHLY PAYMENT	TOTAL INTRST	MONTHLY PAYMENT	TOTAL INTRST	MONTHLY PAYMENT	TOTAL INTRST	MONTHLY PAYMENT	TOTAL INTRST
$ 1	0.03	0	0.03	0	0.02	0	0.02	0
2	0.06	1	0.05	0	0.04	0	0.04	1
3	0.08	0	0.08	1	0.06	1	0.06	1
4	0.11	1	0.10	1	0.08	1	0.07	1
5	0.14	1	0.12	1	0.10	1	0.09	1
6	0.16	1	0.15	1	0.12	1	0.11	2
7	0.19	1	0.17	1	0.14	1	0.12	2
8	0.22	1	0.19	1	0.16	2	0.14	2
9	0.24	1	0.22	2	0.18	2	0.16	3
10	0.27	1	0.24	2	0.20	2	0.17	2
20	0.54	3	0.48	3	0.39	3	0.34	4
30	0.80	4	0.71	4	0.59	5	0.51	7
40	1.07	5	0.95	6	0.78	7	0.67	8
50	1.33	6	1.18	7	0.98	9	0.84	10
60	1.60	7	1.42	8	1.17	10	1.01	13
70	1.86	8	1.66	10	1.37	12	1.17	14
80	2.13	9	1.89	11	1.56	14	1.34	16
90	2.40	11	2.13	12	1.76	16	1.51	19
100	2.66	12	2.36	13	1.95	17	1.67	20
200	5.32	23	4.72	27	3.89	33	3.34	40
300	7.98	35	7.08	40	5.84	50	5.01	61
400	10.63	46	9.44	53	7.78	67	6.68	81
500	13.29	58	11.80	66	9.73	84	8.35	101
600	15.95	70	14.16	80	11.67	100	10.02	121
700	18.60	81	16.52	93	13.62	117	11.69	142
800	21.26	93	18.88	106	15.56	134	13.36	162
900	23.92	105	21.24	120	17.51	151	15.03	182
1,000	26.58	116	23.60	133	19.45	167	16.70	202
2,000	53.15	232	47.20	266	38.90	334	33.39	404
3,000	79.72	348	70.80	398	58.35	501	50.08	606
4,000	106.29	464	94.40	531	77.80	668	66.77	807
5,000	132.86	580	118.00	664	97.25	835	83.46	1,009
6,000	159.43	696	141.60	797	116.70	1,002	100.15	1,211
7,000	186.00	812	165.20	930	136.15	1,169	116.84	1,412
8,000	212.57	928	188.80	1,062	155.60	1,336	133.53	1,614
9,000	239.14	1,044	212.40	1,195	175.05	1,503	150.23	1,817
10,000	265.71	1,160	236.00	1,328	194.50	1,670	166.92	2,018
11,000	292.28	1,276	259.60	1,461	213.95	1,837	183.61	2,220
12,000	318.85	1,392	283.20	1,594	233.40	2,004	200.30	2,422
13,000	345.42	1,508	306.80	1,726	252.85	2,171	216.99	2,623
14,000	371.99	1,624	330.40	1,859	272.29	2,337	233.68	2,825
15,000	398.56	1,740	354.00	1,992	291.74	2,504	250.37	3,027
16,000	425.13	1,855	377.60	2,125	311.19	2,671	267.06	3,228
17,000	451.70	1,971	401.20	2,258	330.64	2,838	283.75	3,430
18,000	478.27	2,087	424.80	2,390	350.09	3,005	300.45	3,632
19,000	504.84	2,203	448.40	2,523	369.54	3,172	317.14	3,834
20,000	531.41	2,319	472.00	2,656	388.99	3,339	333.83	4,036
21,000	557.98	2,435	495.60	2,789	408.44	3,506	350.52	4,237
22,000	584.55	2,551	519.20	2,922	427.89	3,673	367.21	4,439
23,000	611.12	2,667	542.80	3,054	447.34	3,840	383.90	4,641
24,000	637.69	2,783	566.40	3,187	466.79	4,007	400.59	4,842
25,000	664.26	2,899	590.00	3,320	486.24	4,174	417.28	5,044
26,000	690.83	3,015	613.60	3,453	505.69	4,341	433.98	5,247
27,000	717.40	3,131	637.20	3,586	525.14	4,508	450.67	5,448
28,000	743.97	3,247	660.80	3,718	544.58	4,675	467.36	5,650
29,000	770.54	3,363	684.40	3,851	564.03	4,842	484.05	5,852
30,000	797.11	3,479	708.00	3,984	583.48	5,009	500.74	6,053
31,000	823.68	3,595	731.60	4,117	602.93	5,176	517.43	6,255
32,000	850.25	3,711	755.20	4,250	622.38	5,343	534.12	6,457
33,000	876.82	3,826	778.80	4,382	641.83	5,510	550.81	6,658
34,000	903.39	3,942	802.40	4,515	661.28	5,677	567.50	6,860
35,000	929.96	4,058	826.00	4,648	680.73	5,844	584.20	7,062
36,000	956.53	4,174	849.60	4,781	700.18	6,011	600.89	7,264
37,000	983.10	4,290	873.20	4,914	719.63	6,178	617.58	7,466
38,000	1,009.67	4,406	896.80	5,046	739.08	6,345	634.27	7,667
39,000	1,036.25	4,523	920.40	5,179	758.53	6,512	650.96	7,869
40,000	1,062.82	4,638	944.00	5,312	777.98	6,679	667.65	8,071
42,000	1,115.96	4,870	991.20	5,578	816.87	7,012	701.03	8,474
44,000	1,169.10	5,102	1,038.40	5,843	855.77	7,346	734.42	8,878
46,000	1,222.24	5,334	1,085.60	6,109	894.67	7,680	767.80	9,282
48,000	1,275.38	5,566	1,132.80	6,374	933.57	8,014	801.18	9,685
50,000	1,328.52	5,798	1,180.00	6,640	972.47	8,348	834.56	10,088

AUTO LOAN PAYMENTS

AMOUNT OF LOAN	12 MOS		24 MOS		30 MOS		36 MOS	
	MONTHLY PAYMENT	TOTAL INTRST	MONTHLY PAYMENT	TOTAL INTRST	MONTHLY PAYMENT	TOTAL INTRST	MONTHLY PAYMENT	TOTAL INTRST
$ 1	0.09	0	0.05	0	0.04	0	0.04	0
2	0.18	0	0.09	0	0.08	0	0.07	1
3	0.26	0	0.14	0	0.11	0	0.10	1
4	0.35	0	0.18	0	0.15	1	0.13	1
5	0.44	0	0.23	1	0.19	1	0.16	1
6	0.52	0	0.27	0	0.22	1	0.19	1
7	0.61	0	0.32	1	0.26	1	0.22	1
8	0.70	0	0.36	1	0.29	1	0.25	1
9	0.78	0	0.41	1	0.33	1	0.28	1
10	0.87	0	0.45	1	0.37	1	0.31	1
20	1.73	1	0.90	2	0.73	2	0.62	2
30	2.59	1	1.34	2	1.09	3	0.92	3
40	3.46	2	1.79	3	1.45	4	1.23	4
50	4.32	2	2.23	4	1.82	5	1.54	5
60	5.18	2	2.68	4	2.18	5	1.84	6
70	6.05	3	3.12	5	2.54	6	2.15	7
80	6.91	3	3.57	6	2.90	7	2.46	9
90	7.77	3	4.01	6	3.26	8	2.76	9
100	8.63	4	4.46	7	3.63	9	3.07	11
200	17.26	7	8.91	14	7.25	18	6.13	21
300	25.89	11	13.37	21	10.87	26	9.20	31
400	34.52	14	17.82	28	14.49	35	12.26	41
500	43.15	18	22.28	35	18.11	43	15.33	52
600	51.78	21	26.73	42	21.73	52	18.39	62
700	60.41	25	31.19	49	25.35	61	21.46	73
800	69.04	28	35.64	55	28.97	69	24.52	83
900	77.67	32	40.10	62	32.59	78	27.59	93
1,000	86.30	36	44.55	69	36.21	86	30.65	103
2,000	172.60	71	89.10	138	72.41	172	61.30	207
3,000	258.89	107	133.64	207	108.62	259	91.95	310
4,000	345.19	142	178.19	277	144.82	345	122.60	414
5,000	431.49	178	222.74	346	181.03	431	153.25	517
6,000	517.78	213	267.28	415	217.23	517	183.90	620
7,000	604.08	249	311.83	484	253.44	603	214.55	724
8,000	690.38	285	356.38	553	289.64	689	245.20	827
9,000	776.67	320	400.92	622	325.85	776	275.85	931
10,000	862.97	356	445.47	691	362.05	862	306.50	1,034
11,000	949.27	391	490.01	760	398.26	948	337.14	1,137
12,000	1,035.56	427	534.56	829	434.46	1,034	367.79	1,240
13,000	1,121.86	462	579.11	899	470.67	1,120	398.44	1,344
14,000	1,208.15	498	623.65	968	506.87	1,206	429.09	1,447
15,000	1,294.45	533	668.20	1,037	543.08	1,292	459.74	1,551
16,000	1,380.75	569	712.75	1,106	579.28	1,378	490.39	1,654
17,000	1,467.04	604	757.29	1,175	615.49	1,465	521.04	1,757
18,000	1,553.34	640	801.84	1,244	651.69	1,551	551.69	1,861
19,000	1,639.64	676	846.38	1,313	687.90	1,637	582.34	1,964
20,000	1,725.93	711	890.93	1,382	724.10	1,723	612.99	2,068
21,000	1,812.23	747	935.48	1,452	760.31	1,809	643.63	2,171
22,000	1,898.53	782	980.02	1,520	796.51	1,895	674.28	2,274
23,000	1,984.82	818	1,024.57	1,590	832.72	1,982	704.93	2,377
24,000	2,071.12	853	1,069.12	1,659	868.92	2,068	735.58	2,481
25,000	2,157.42	889	1,113.66	1,728	905.13	2,154	766.23	2,584
26,000	2,243.71	925	1,158.21	1,797	941.33	2,240	796.88	2,688
27,000	2,330.01	960	1,202.75	1,866	977.54	2,326	827.53	2,791
28,000	2,416.30	996	1,247.30	1,935	1,013.74	2,412	858.18	2,894
29,000	2,502.60	1,031	1,291.85	2,004	1,049.95	2,499	888.83	2,998
30,000	2,588.90	1,067	1,336.39	2,073	1,086.15	2,585	919.48	3,101
31,000	2,675.19	1,102	1,380.94	2,143	1,122.36	2,671	950.12	3,204
32,000	2,761.49	1,138	1,425.49	2,212	1,158.56	2,757	980.77	3,308
33,000	2,847.79	1,173	1,470.03	2,281	1,194.77	2,843	1,011.42	3,411
34,000	2,934.08	1,209	1,514.58	2,350	1,230.97	2,929	1,042.07	3,515
35,000	3,020.38	1,245	1,559.12	2,419	1,267.18	3,015	1,072.72	3,618
36,000	3,106.68	1,280	1,603.67	2,488	1,303.38	3,101	1,103.37	3,721
37,000	3,192.97	1,316	1,648.22	2,557	1,339.59	3,188	1,134.02	3,825
38,000	3,279.27	1,351	1,692.76	2,626	1,375.79	3,274	1,164.67	3,928
39,000	3,365.57	1,387	1,737.31	2,695	1,412.00	3,360	1,195.32	4,032
40,000	3,451.86	1,422	1,781.86	2,765	1,448.20	3,446	1,225.97	4,135
42,000	3,624.45	1,493	1,870.95	2,903	1,520.61	3,618	1,287.26	4,341
44,000	3,797.05	1,565	1,960.04	3,041	1,593.02	3,791	1,348.56	4,548
46,000	3,969.64	1,636	2,049.13	3,179	1,665.43	3,963	1,409.86	4,755
48,000	4,142.23	1,707	2,138.23	3,318	1,737.84	4,135	1,471.16	4,962
50,000	4,314.83	1,778	2,227.32	3,456	1,810.25	4,308	1,532.46	5,169

AUTO LOAN PAYMENTS 6.50%

AMOUNT OF LOAN	42 MOS MONTHLY PAYMENT	42 MOS TOTAL INTRST	48 MOS MONTHLY PAYMENT	48 MOS TOTAL INTRST	60 MOS MONTHLY PAYMENT	60 MOS TOTAL INTRST	72 MOS MONTHLY PAYMENT	72 MOS TOTAL INTRST
$ 1	0.03	0	0.03	0	0.02	0	0.02	0
2	0.06	1	0.05	0	0.04	0	0.04	0
3	0.09	1	0.08	1	0.06	1	0.06	1
4	0.11	1	0.10	1	0.08	1	0.07	1
5	0.14	1	0.12	1	0.10	1	0.09	1
6	0.17	1	0.15	1	0.12	1	0.11	2
7	0.19	1	0.17	1	0.14	1	0.12	2
8	0.22	1	0.19	1	0.16	2	0.14	2
9	0.25	2	0.22	2	0.18	2	0.16	3
10	0.27	1	0.24	2	0.20	2	0.17	2
20	0.54	3	0.48	3	0.40	4	0.34	4
30	0.81	4	0.72	5	0.59	5	0.51	7
40	1.07	5	0.95	6	0.79	7	0.68	9
50	1.34	6	1.19	7	0.98	9	0.85	11
60	1.61	8	1.43	9	1.18	11	1.01	13
70	1.87	9	1.67	10	1.37	12	1.18	15
80	2.14	10	1.90	11	1.57	14	1.35	17
90	2.41	11	2.14	13	1.77	16	1.52	19
100	2.67	12	2.38	14	1.96	18	1.69	22
200	5.34	24	4.75	28	3.92	35	3.37	43
300	8.01	36	7.12	42	5.87	52	5.05	64
400	10.68	49	9.49	56	7.83	70	6.73	85
500	13.35	61	11.86	69	9.79	87	8.41	106
600	16.02	73	14.23	83	11.74	104	10.09	126
700	18.68	85	16.61	97	13.70	122	11.77	147
800	21.35	97	18.98	111	15.66	140	13.45	168
900	24.02	109	21.35	125	17.61	157	15.13	189
1,000	26.69	121	23.72	139	19.57	174	16.81	210
2,000	53.37	242	47.43	277	39.14	348	33.62	421
3,000	80.06	363	71.15	415	58.70	522	50.43	631
4,000	106.74	483	94.86	553	78.27	696	67.24	841
5,000	133.43	604	118.58	692	97.84	870	84.05	1,052
6,000	160.11	725	142.29	830	117.40	1,044	100.86	1,262
7,000	186.80	846	166.01	968	136.97	1,218	117.67	1,472
8,000	213.48	966	189.72	1,107	156.53	1,392	134.48	1,683
9,000	240.17	1,087	213.44	1,245	176.10	1,566	151.29	1,893
10,000	266.85	1,208	237.15	1,383	195.67	1,740	168.10	2,103
11,000	293.54	1,329	260.87	1,522	215.23	1,914	184.91	2,314
12,000	320.22	1,449	284.58	1,660	234.80	2,088	201.72	2,524
13,000	346.90	1,570	308.30	1,798	254.36	2,262	218.53	2,734
14,000	373.59	1,691	332.01	1,936	273.93	2,436	235.34	2,944
15,000	400.27	1,811	355.73	2,075	293.50	2,610	252.15	3,155
16,000	426.96	1,932	379.44	2,213	313.06	2,784	268.96	3,365
17,000	453.64	2,053	403.16	2,352	332.63	2,958	285.77	3,575
18,000	480.33	2,174	426.87	2,490	352.20	3,132	302.58	3,786
19,000	507.01	2,294	450.59	2,628	371.76	3,306	319.39	3,996
20,000	533.70	2,415	474.30	2,766	391.33	3,480	336.20	4,206
21,000	560.38	2,536	498.02	2,905	410.89	3,653	353.01	4,417
22,000	587.07	2,657	521.73	3,043	430.46	3,828	369.82	4,627
23,000	613.75	2,778	545.45	3,182	450.03	4,002	386.63	4,837
24,000	640.44	2,898	569.16	3,320	469.59	4,175	403.44	5,048
25,000	667.12	3,019	592.88	3,458	489.16	4,350	420.25	5,258
26,000	693.80	3,140	616.59	3,596	508.72	4,523	437.06	5,468
27,000	720.49	3,261	640.31	3,735	528.29	4,697	453.87	5,679
28,000	747.17	3,381	664.02	3,873	547.86	4,872	470.68	5,889
29,000	773.86	3,502	687.74	4,012	567.42	5,045	487.49	6,099
30,000	800.54	3,623	711.45	4,150	586.99	5,219	504.30	6,310
31,000	827.23	3,744	735.17	4,288	606.56	5,394	521.11	6,520
32,000	853.91	3,864	758.88	4,426	626.12	5,567	537.92	6,730
33,000	880.60	3,985	782.60	4,565	645.69	5,741	554.73	6,941
34,000	907.28	4,106	806.31	4,703	665.25	5,915	571.54	7,151
35,000	933.97	4,227	830.03	4,841	684.82	6,089	588.35	7,361
36,000	960.65	4,347	853.74	4,980	704.39	6,263	605.16	7,572
37,000	987.34	4,468	877.46	5,118	723.95	6,437	621.97	7,782
38,000	1,014.02	4,589	901.17	5,256	743.52	6,611	638.78	7,992
39,000	1,040.70	4,709	924.89	5,395	763.08	6,785	655.59	8,202
40,000	1,067.39	4,830	948.60	5,533	782.65	6,959	672.40	8,413
42,000	1,120.76	5,072	996.03	5,809	821.78	7,307	706.02	8,833
44,000	1,174.13	5,313	1,043.46	6,086	860.92	7,655	739.64	9,254
46,000	1,227.50	5,555	1,090.89	6,363	900.05	8,003	773.26	9,675
48,000	1,280.87	5,797	1,138.32	6,639	939.18	8,351	806.88	10,095
50,000	1,334.24	6,038	1,185.75	6,916	978.31	8,699	840.50	10,516

AUTO LOAN PAYMENTS

AMOUNT OF LOAN	12 MOS		24 MOS		30 MOS		36 MOS	
	MONTHLY PAYMENT	TOTAL INTRST	MONTHLY PAYMENT	TOTAL INTRST	MONTHLY PAYMENT	TOTAL INTRST	MONTHLY PAYMENT	TOTAL INTRST
$ 1	0.09	0	0.05	0	0.04	0	0.04	0
2	0.18	0	0.09	0	0.08	0	0.07	0
3	0.26	0	0.14	0	0.11	0	0.10	0
4	0.35	0	0.18	0	0.15	1	0.13	1
5	0.44	0	0.23	1	0.19	1	0.16	1
6	0.52	0	0.27	1	0.22	1	0.19	1
7	0.61	0	0.32	1	0.26	1	0.22	1
8	0.70	0	0.36	1	0.30	1	0.25	1
9	0.78	0	0.41	1	0.33	1	0.28	1
10	0.87	0	0.45	1	0.37	1	0.31	1
20	1.73	1	0.90	2	0.73	2	0.62	2
30	2.60	1	1.34	2	1.09	3	0.93	3
40	3.46	2	1.79	3	1.46	4	1.24	5
50	4.33	2	2.24	4	1.82	5	1.54	5
60	5.19	2	2.68	4	2.18	5	1.85	7
70	6.05	2	3.13	5	2.55	7	2.16	8
80	6.92	3	3.58	6	2.91	7	2.47	9
90	7.78	3	4.02	6	3.27	8	2.77	10
100	8.65	4	4.47	7	3.64	9	3.08	11
200	17.29	7	8.94	15	7.27	18	6.16	22
300	25.93	11	13.40	22	10.90	27	9.23	32
400	34.57	15	17.87	29	14.53	36	12.31	43
500	43.21	19	22.33	36	18.16	45	15.39	54
600	51.85	22	26.80	43	21.80	54	18.46	65
700	60.49	26	31.27	50	25.43	63	21.54	75
800	69.13	30	35.73	58	29.06	72	24.62	86
900	77.78	33	40.20	65	32.69	81	27.69	97
1,000	86.42	37	44.66	72	36.32	90	30.77	108
2,000	172.83	74	89.32	144	72.64	179	61.53	215
3,000	259.24	111	133.98	216	108.96	269	92.29	322
4,000	345.65	148	178.64	287	145.28	358	123.06	430
5,000	432.06	185	223.30	359	181.60	448	153.82	538
6,000	518.47	222	267.96	431	217.92	538	184.58	645
7,000	604.89	259	312.62	503	254.23	627	215.35	753
8,000	691.30	296	357.28	575	290.55	717	246.11	860
9,000	777.71	333	401.94	647	326.87	806	276.87	967
10,000	864.12	369	446.60	718	363.19	896	307.63	1,075
11,000	950.53	406	491.26	790	399.51	985	338.40	1,182
12,000	1,036.94	443	535.92	862	435.83	1,075	369.16	1,290
13,000	1,123.36	480	580.58	934	472.14	1,164	399.92	1,397
14,000	1,209.77	517	625.24	1,006	508.46	1,254	430.69	1,505
15,000	1,296.18	554	669.89	1,077	544.78	1,343	461.45	1,612
16,000	1,382.59	591	714.55	1,149	581.10	1,433	492.21	1,720
17,000	1,469.00	628	759.21	1,221	617.42	1,523	522.97	1,827
18,000	1,555.41	665	803.87	1,293	653.74	1,612	553.74	1,935
19,000	1,641.82	702	848.53	1,365	690.05	1,702	584.50	2,042
20,000	1,728.24	739	893.19	1,437	726.37	1,791	615.26	2,149
21,000	1,814.65	776	937.85	1,508	762.69	1,881	646.03	2,257
22,000	1,901.06	813	982.51	1,580	799.01	1,970	676.79	2,364
23,000	1,987.47	850	1,027.17	1,652	835.33	2,060	707.55	2,472
24,000	2,073.88	887	1,071.83	1,724	871.65	2,150	738.32	2,580
25,000	2,160.29	923	1,116.49	1,796	907.96	2,239	769.08	2,687
26,000	2,246.71	961	1,161.15	1,868	944.28	2,328	799.84	2,794
27,000	2,333.12	997	1,205.81	1,939	980.60	2,418	830.60	2,902
28,000	2,419.53	1,034	1,250.47	2,011	1,016.92	2,508	861.37	3,009
29,000	2,505.94	1,071	1,295.13	2,083	1,053.24	2,597	892.13	3,117
30,000	2,592.35	1,108	1,339.78	2,155	1,089.56	2,687	922.89	3,224
31,000	2,678.76	1,145	1,384.44	2,227	1,125.87	2,776	953.66	3,332
32,000	2,765.17	1,182	1,429.10	2,298	1,162.19	2,866	984.42	3,439
33,000	2,851.59	1,219	1,473.76	2,370	1,198.51	2,955	1,015.18	3,546
34,000	2,938.00	1,256	1,518.42	2,442	1,234.83	3,045	1,045.94	3,654
35,000	3,024.41	1,293	1,563.08	2,514	1,271.15	3,135	1,076.71	3,762
36,000	3,110.82	1,330	1,607.74	2,586	1,307.47	3,224	1,107.47	3,869
37,000	3,197.23	1,367	1,652.40	2,658	1,343.78	3,313	1,138.23	3,976
38,000	3,283.64	1,404	1,697.06	2,729	1,380.10	3,403	1,169.00	4,084
39,000	3,370.06	1,441	1,741.72	2,801	1,416.42	3,493	1,199.76	4,191
40,000	3,456.47	1,478	1,786.38	2,873	1,452.74	3,582	1,230.52	4,299
42,000	3,629.29	1,551	1,875.70	3,017	1,525.38	3,761	1,292.05	4,514
44,000	3,802.11	1,625	1,965.02	3,160	1,598.01	3,940	1,353.57	4,729
46,000	3,974.94	1,699	2,054.33	3,304	1,670.65	4,120	1,415.10	4,944
48,000	4,147.76	1,773	2,143.65	3,448	1,743.29	4,299	1,476.63	5,159
50,000	4,320.58	1,847	2,232.97	3,591	1,815.92	4,478	1,538.15	5,373

AUTO LOAN PAYMENTS 6.75%

AMOUNT OF LOAN	42 MOS		48 MOS		60 MOS		72 MOS	
	MONTHLY PAYMENT	TOTAL INTRST	MONTHLY PAYMENT	TOTAL INTRST	MONTHLY PAYMENT	TOTAL INTRST	MONTHLY PAYMENT	TOTAL INTRST
$ 1	0.03	0	0.03	0	0.02	0	0.02	0
2	0.06	1	0.05	0	0.04	0	0.04	1
3	0.09	1	0.08	1	0.06	1	0.06	1
4	0.11	1	0.10	1	0.08	1	0.07	1
5	0.14	1	0.12	1	0.10	1	0.09	1
6	0.17	1	0.15	1	0.12	1	0.11	2
7	0.19	1	0.17	1	0.14	1	0.12	2
8	0.22	1	0.20	1	0.16	2	0.14	2
9	0.25	2	0.22	2	0.18	2	0.16	3
10	0.27	1	0.24	2	0.20	2	0.17	2
20	0.54	3	0.48	3	0.40	4	0.34	4
30	0.81	4	0.72	5	0.60	6	0.51	7
40	1.08	5	0.96	6	0.79	7	0.68	9
50	1.34	6	1.20	8	0.99	9	0.85	11
60	1.61	8	1.43	9	1.19	11	1.02	13
70	1.88	9	1.67	10	1.38	13	1.19	16
80	2.15	10	1.91	12	1.58	15	1.36	18
90	2.42	12	2.15	13	1.78	17	1.53	20
100	2.68	13	2.39	15	1.97	18	1.70	22
200	5.36	25	4.77	29	3.94	36	3.39	44
300	8.04	38	7.15	43	5.91	55	5.08	66
400	10.72	50	9.54	58	7.88	73	6.78	88
500	13.40	63	11.92	72	9.85	91	8.47	110
600	16.08	75	14.30	86	11.82	109	10.16	132
700	18.76	88	16.69	101	13.78	127	11.86	154
800	21.44	100	19.07	115	15.75	145	13.55	176
900	24.12	113	21.45	130	17.72	163	15.24	197
1,000	26.80	126	23.84	144	19.69	181	16.93	219
2,000	53.60	251	47.67	288	39.37	362	33.86	438
3,000	80.40	377	71.50	432	59.06	544	50.79	657
4,000	107.20	502	95.33	576	78.74	724	67.72	876
5,000	134.00	628	119.16	720	98.42	905	84.65	1,095
6,000	160.80	754	142.99	864	118.11	1,087	101.58	1,314
7,000	187.60	879	166.82	1,007	137.79	1,267	118.51	1,533
8,000	214.40	1,005	190.65	1,151	157.47	1,448	135.44	1,752
9,000	241.20	1,130	214.48	1,295	177.16	1,630	152.37	1,971
10,000	268.00	1,256	238.31	1,439	196.84	1,810	169.30	2,190
11,000	294.80	1,382	262.14	1,583	216.52	1,991	186.23	2,409
12,000	321.60	1,507	285.97	1,727	236.21	2,173	203.16	2,628
13,000	348.40	1,633	309.80	1,870	255.89	2,353	220.08	2,846
14,000	375.19	1,758	333.63	2,014	275.57	2,534	237.01	3,065
15,000	401.99	1,884	357.46	2,158	295.26	2,716	253.94	3,284
16,000	428.79	2,009	381.29	2,302	314.94	2,896	270.87	3,503
17,000	455.59	2,135	405.12	2,446	334.62	3,077	287.80	3,722
18,000	482.39	2,260	428.95	2,590	354.31	3,259	304.73	3,941
19,000	509.19	2,386	452.78	2,733	373.99	3,439	321.66	4,160
20,000	535.99	2,512	476.61	2,877	393.67	3,620	338.59	4,378
21,000	562.79	2,637	500.44	3,021	413.36	3,802	355.52	4,597
22,000	589.59	2,763	524.27	3,165	433.04	3,982	372.45	4,816
23,000	616.39	2,888	548.10	3,309	452.72	4,163	389.38	5,035
24,000	643.19	3,014	571.94	3,453	472.41	4,345	406.31	5,254
25,000	669.99	3,140	595.77	3,597	492.09	4,525	423.24	5,473
26,000	696.79	3,265	619.60	3,741	511.77	4,706	440.16	5,692
27,000	723.58	3,390	643.43	3,885	531.46	4,888	457.09	5,910
28,000	750.38	3,516	667.26	4,028	551.14	5,068	474.02	6,129
29,000	777.18	3,642	691.09	4,172	570.83	5,250	490.95	6,348
30,000	803.98	3,767	714.92	4,316	590.51	5,431	507.88	6,567
31,000	830.78	3,893	738.75	4,460	610.19	5,611	524.81	6,786
32,000	857.58	4,018	762.58	4,604	629.88	5,793	541.74	7,005
33,000	884.38	4,144	786.41	4,748	649.56	5,974	558.67	7,224
34,000	911.18	4,270	810.24	4,892	669.24	6,154	575.60	7,443
35,000	937.98	4,395	834.07	5,035	688.93	6,336	592.53	7,662
36,000	964.78	4,521	857.90	5,179	708.61	6,517	609.46	7,881
37,000	991.58	4,646	881.73	5,323	728.29	6,697	626.39	8,100
38,000	1,018.38	4,772	905.56	5,467	747.98	6,879	643.32	8,319
39,000	1,045.18	4,898	929.39	5,611	767.66	7,060	660.24	8,537
40,000	1,071.98	5,023	953.22	5,755	787.34	7,240	677.17	8,756
42,000	1,125.57	5,274	1,000.88	6,042	826.71	7,603	711.03	9,194
44,000	1,179.17	5,525	1,048.54	6,330	866.08	7,965	744.89	9,632
46,000	1,232.77	5,776	1,096.20	6,618	905.44	8,326	778.75	10,070
48,000	1,286.37	6,028	1,143.87	6,906	944.81	8,689	812.61	10,508
50,000	1,339.97	6,279	1,191.53	7,193	984.18	9,051	846.47	10,946

71

6.90% AUTO LOAN PAYMENTS

AMOUNT OF LOAN	12 MOS MONTHLY PAYMENT	12 MOS TOTAL INTRST	24 MOS MONTHLY PAYMENT	24 MOS TOTAL INTRST	30 MOS MONTHLY PAYMENT	30 MOS TOTAL INTRST	36 MOS MONTHLY PAYMENT	36 MOS TOTAL INTRST
$ 1	0.09	0	0.05	0	0.04	0	0.04	0
2	0.18	0	0.09	0	0.08	0	0.07	1
3	0.26	0	0.14	0	0.11	0	0.10	1
4	0.35	0	0.18	0	0.15	1	0.13	1
5	0.44	0	0.23	1	0.19	1	0.16	1
6	0.52	0	0.27	1	0.22	1	0.19	1
7	0.61	0	0.32	1	0.26	1	0.22	1
8	0.70	0	0.36	1	0.30	1	0.25	1
9	0.78	0	0.41	1	0.33	1	0.28	1
10	0.87	0	0.45	1	0.37	1	0.31	1
20	1.73	1	0.90	2	0.73	2	0.62	2
30	2.60	1	1.35	2	1.10	3	0.93	3
40	3.46	2	1.79	3	1.46	4	1.24	5
50	4.33	2	2.24	4	1.82	5	1.55	6
60	5.19	2	2.69	5	2.19	6	1.85	7
70	6.06	3	3.14	5	2.55	7	2.16	8
80	6.92	3	3.58	6	2.92	8	2.47	9
90	7.79	3	4.03	7	3.28	8	2.78	10
100	8.65	4	4.48	8	3.64	9	3.09	11
200	17.30	8	8.95	15	7.28	18	6.17	22
300	25.95	11	13.42	22	10.92	28	9.25	33
400	34.60	15	17.90	30	14.56	37	12.34	44
500	43.25	19	22.37	37	18.20	46	15.42	55
600	51.89	23	26.84	44	21.84	55	18.50	66
700	60.54	26	31.31	51	25.48	64	21.59	77
800	69.19	30	35.79	59	29.11	73	24.67	88
900	77.84	34	40.26	66	32.75	83	27.75	99
1,000	86.49	38	44.73	74	36.39	92	30.84	110
2,000	172.97	76	89.46	147	72.78	183	61.67	220
3,000	259.45	113	134.19	221	109.16	275	92.50	330
4,000	345.93	151	178.91	294	145.55	367	123.33	440
5,000	432.41	189	223.64	367	181.94	458	154.16	550
6,000	518.89	227	268.37	441	218.32	550	184.99	660
7,000	605.37	264	313.10	514	254.71	641	215.82	770
8,000	691.85	302	357.82	588	291.10	733	246.66	880
9,000	778.33	340	402.55	661	327.48	824	277.49	990
10,000	864.81	378	447.28	735	363.87	916	308.32	1,100
11,000	951.29	415	492.00	808	400.26	1,008	339.15	1,209
12,000	1,037.77	453	536.73	882	436.64	1,099	369.98	1,319
13,000	1,124.25	491	581.46	955	473.03	1,191	400.81	1,429
14,000	1,210.73	529	626.19	1,029	509.42	1,283	431.64	1,539
15,000	1,297.21	567	670.91	1,102	545.80	1,374	462.48	1,649
16,000	1,383.70	604	715.64	1,175	582.19	1,466	493.31	1,759
17,000	1,470.18	642	760.37	1,249	618.57	1,557	524.14	1,869
18,000	1,556.66	680	805.10	1,322	654.96	1,649	554.97	1,979
19,000	1,643.14	718	849.82	1,396	691.35	1,741	585.80	2,089
20,000	1,729.62	755	894.55	1,469	727.73	1,832	616.63	2,199
21,000	1,816.10	793	939.28	1,543	764.12	1,924	647.46	2,309
22,000	1,902.58	831	984.00	1,616	800.51	2,015	678.30	2,419
23,000	1,989.06	869	1,028.73	1,690	836.89	2,107	709.13	2,529
24,000	2,075.54	906	1,073.46	1,763	873.28	2,198	739.96	2,639
25,000	2,162.02	944	1,118.19	1,837	909.67	2,290	770.79	2,748
26,000	2,248.50	982	1,162.91	1,910	946.05	2,382	801.62	2,858
27,000	2,334.98	1,020	1,207.64	1,983	982.44	2,473	832.45	2,968
28,000	2,421.46	1,058	1,252.37	2,057	1,018.83	2,565	863.28	3,078
29,000	2,507.94	1,095	1,297.10	2,130	1,055.21	2,656	894.12	3,188
30,000	2,594.42	1,133	1,341.82	2,204	1,091.60	2,748	924.95	3,298
31,000	2,680.91	1,171	1,386.55	2,277	1,127.99	2,840	955.78	3,408
32,000	2,767.39	1,209	1,431.28	2,351	1,164.37	2,931	986.61	3,518
33,000	2,853.87	1,246	1,476.00	2,424	1,200.76	3,023	1,017.44	3,628
34,000	2,940.35	1,284	1,520.73	2,498	1,237.14	3,114	1,048.27	3,738
35,000	3,026.83	1,322	1,565.46	2,571	1,273.53	3,206	1,079.10	3,848
36,000	3,113.31	1,360	1,610.19	2,645	1,309.92	3,298	1,109.94	3,958
37,000	3,199.79	1,397	1,654.91	2,718	1,346.30	3,389	1,140.77	4,068
38,000	3,286.27	1,435	1,699.64	2,791	1,382.69	3,481	1,171.60	4,178
39,000	3,372.75	1,473	1,744.37	2,865	1,419.08	3,572	1,202.43	4,287
40,000	3,459.23	1,511	1,789.10	2,938	1,455.46	3,664	1,233.26	4,397
42,000	3,632.19	1,586	1,878.55	3,085	1,528.24	3,847	1,294.92	4,617
44,000	3,805.15	1,662	1,968.00	3,232	1,601.01	4,030	1,356.59	4,837
46,000	3,978.12	1,737	2,057.46	3,379	1,673.78	4,213	1,418.25	5,057
48,000	4,151.08	1,813	2,146.91	3,526	1,746.55	4,397	1,479.91	5,277
50,000	4,324.04	1,888	2,236.37	3,673	1,819.33	4,580	1,541.57	5,497

AUTO LOAN PAYMENTS 6.90%

AMOUNT OF LOAN	42 MOS		48 MOS		60 MOS		72 MOS	
	MONTHLY PAYMENT	TOTAL INTRST	MONTHLY PAYMENT	TOTAL INTRST	MONTHLY PAYMENT	TOTAL INTRST	MONTHLY PAYMENT	TOTAL INTRST
$ 1	0.03	0	0.03	0	0.02	0	0.02	0
2	0.06	1	0.05	0	0.04	0	0.04	1
3	0.09	1	0.08	1	0.06	1	0.06	1
4	0.11	1	0.10	1	0.08	1	0.07	1
5	0.14	1	0.12	1	0.10	1	0.09	1
6	0.17	1	0.15	1	0.12	1	0.11	2
7	0.19	1	0.17	1	0.14	1	0.12	2
8	0.22	1	0.20	2	0.16	2	0.14	2
9	0.25	2	0.22	2	0.18	2	0.16	3
10	0.27	1	0.24	2	0.20	2	0.18	3
20	0.54	3	0.48	3	0.40	4	0.35	5
30	0.81	4	0.72	5	0.60	6	0.52	7
40	1.08	5	0.96	6	0.80	8	0.69	10
50	1.35	7	1.20	8	0.99	9	0.86	12
60	1.62	8	1.44	9	1.19	11	1.03	14
70	1.89	9	1.68	11	1.39	13	1.20	16
80	2.15	10	1.92	12	1.59	15	1.37	19
90	2.42	12	2.16	14	1.78	17	1.54	21
100	2.69	13	2.39	15	1.98	19	1.71	23
200	5.38	26	4.78	29	3.96	38	3.41	46
300	8.07	39	7.17	44	5.93	56	5.11	68
400	10.75	52	9.56	59	7.91	75	6.81	90
500	13.44	64	11.95	74	9.88	93	8.51	113
600	16.13	77	14.34	88	11.86	112	10.21	135
700	18.81	90	16.73	103	13.83	130	11.91	158
800	21.50	103	19.12	118	15.81	149	13.61	180
900	24.19	116	21.51	132	17.78	167	15.31	202
1,000	26.87	129	23.90	147	19.76	186	17.01	225
2,000	53.74	257	47.80	294	39.51	371	34.01	449
3,000	80.61	386	71.70	442	59.27	556	51.01	673
4,000	107.48	514	95.60	589	79.02	741	68.01	897
5,000	134.35	643	119.50	736	98.78	927	85.01	1,121
6,000	161.21	771	143.40	883	118.53	1,112	102.01	1,345
7,000	188.08	899	167.30	1,030	138.28	1,297	119.01	1,569
8,000	214.95	1,028	191.20	1,178	158.04	1,482	136.01	1,793
9,000	241.82	1,156	215.10	1,325	177.79	1,667	153.02	2,017
10,000	268.69	1,285	239.00	1,472	197.55	1,853	170.02	2,241
11,000	295.56	1,414	262.90	1,619	217.30	2,038	187.02	2,465
12,000	322.42	1,542	286.80	1,766	237.05	2,223	204.02	2,689
13,000	349.29	1,670	310.70	1,914	256.81	2,409	221.02	2,913
14,000	376.16	1,799	334.60	2,061	276.56	2,594	238.02	3,137
15,000	403.03	1,927	358.50	2,208	296.32	2,779	255.02	3,361
16,000	429.90	2,056	382.40	2,355	316.07	2,964	272.02	3,585
17,000	456.76	2,184	406.30	2,502	335.82	3,149	289.02	3,809
18,000	483.63	2,312	430.20	2,650	355.58	3,335	306.02	4,033
19,000	510.50	2,441	454.10	2,797	375.33	3,520	323.02	4,257
20,000	537.37	2,570	478.00	2,944	395.09	3,705	340.03	4,482
21,000	564.24	2,698	501.90	3,091	414.84	3,890	357.03	4,706
22,000	591.11	2,827	525.80	3,238	434.59	4,075	374.03	4,930
23,000	617.97	2,955	549.70	3,386	454.35	4,261	391.03	5,154
24,000	644.84	3,083	573.60	3,533	474.10	4,446	408.03	5,378
25,000	671.71	3,212	597.50	3,680	493.86	4,632	425.03	5,602
26,000	698.58	3,340	621.40	3,827	513.61	4,817	442.03	5,826
27,000	725.45	3,469	645.30	3,974	533.36	5,002	459.03	6,050
28,000	752.31	3,597	669.20	4,122	553.12	5,187	476.03	6,274
29,000	779.18	3,726	693.10	4,269	572.87	5,372	493.03	6,498
30,000	806.05	3,854	717.00	4,416	592.63	5,558	510.04	6,723
31,000	832.92	3,983	740.90	4,563	612.38	5,743	527.04	6,947
32,000	859.79	4,111	764.80	4,710	632.13	5,928	544.04	7,171
33,000	886.66	4,240	788.70	4,858	651.89	6,113	561.04	7,395
34,000	913.52	4,368	812.60	5,005	671.64	6,298	578.04	7,619
35,000	940.39	4,496	836.50	5,152	691.40	6,484	595.04	7,843
36,000	967.26	4,625	860.40	5,299	711.15	6,669	612.04	8,067
37,000	994.13	4,753	884.30	5,446	730.90	6,854	629.04	8,291
38,000	1,021.00	4,882	908.20	5,594	750.66	7,040	646.04	8,515
39,000	1,047.86	5,010	932.10	5,741	770.41	7,225	663.05	8,740
40,000	1,074.73	5,139	956.00	5,888	790.17	7,410	680.05	8,964
42,000	1,128.47	5,396	1,003.80	6,182	829.68	7,781	714.05	9,412
44,000	1,182.21	5,653	1,051.60	6,477	869.18	8,151	748.05	9,860
46,000	1,235.94	5,909	1,099.40	6,771	908.69	8,521	782.05	10,308
48,000	1,289.68	6,167	1,147.20	7,066	948.20	8,892	816.05	10,756
50,000	1,343.41	6,423	1,195.00	7,360	987.71	9,263	850.06	11,204

AUTO LOAN PAYMENTS

AMOUNT OF LOAN	12 MOS		24 MOS		30 MOS		36 MOS	
	MONTHLY PAYMENT	TOTAL INTRST	MONTHLY PAYMENT	TOTAL INTRST	MONTHLY PAYMENT	TOTAL INTRST	MONTHLY PAYMENT	TOTAL INTRST
$ 1	0.09	0	0.05	0	0.04	0	0.04	0
2	0.18	0	0.09	0	0.08	0	0.07	1
3	0.26	0	0.14	0	0.11	0	0.10	1
4	0.35	0	0.18	0	0.15	1	0.13	1
5	0.44	0	0.23	0	0.19	1	0.16	1
6	0.52	0	0.27	1	0.22	1	0.19	1
7	0.61	0	0.32	1	0.26	1	0.22	1
8	0.70	0	0.36	1	0.30	1	0.25	1
9	0.78	0	0.41	1	0.33	1	0.28	1
10	0.87	0	0.45	1	0.37	1	0.31	1
20	1.74	1	0.90	2	0.73	2	0.62	2
30	2.60	1	1.35	2	1.10	3	0.93	3
40	3.47	2	1.80	3	1.46	4	1.24	5
50	4.33	2	2.24	4	1.83	5	1.55	7
60	5.20	2	2.69	5	2.19	6	1.86	7
70	6.06	3	3.14	5	2.56	7	2.17	8
80	6.93	3	3.59	6	2.92	8	2.48	9
90	7.79	3	4.03	7	3.28	8	2.78	10
100	8.66	4	4.48	8	3.65	10	3.09	11
200	17.31	8	8.96	15	7.29	19	6.18	22
300	25.96	12	13.44	23	10.93	28	9.27	34
400	34.62	15	17.91	30	14.58	37	12.36	45
500	43.27	19	22.39	37	18.22	47	15.44	56
600	51.92	23	26.87	45	21.86	56	18.53	67
700	60.57	27	31.35	52	25.51	65	21.62	78
800	69.23	31	35.82	60	29.15	75	24.71	90
900	77.88	35	40.30	67	32.79	84	27.79	100
1,000	86.53	38	44.78	75	36.44	93	30.88	112
2,000	173.06	77	89.55	149	72.87	186	61.76	223
3,000	259.59	115	134.32	224	109.30	279	92.64	335
4,000	346.11	153	179.10	298	145.73	372	123.51	446
5,000	432.64	192	223.87	373	182.16	465	154.39	558
6,000	519.17	230	268.64	447	218.60	558	185.27	670
7,000	605.69	268	313.41	522	255.03	651	216.14	781
8,000	692.22	307	358.19	597	291.46	744	247.02	893
9,000	778.75	345	402.96	671	327.89	837	277.90	1,004
10,000	865.27	383	447.73	746	364.32	930	308.78	1,116
11,000	951.80	422	492.50	820	400.76	1,023	339.65	1,227
12,000	1,038.33	460	537.28	895	437.19	1,116	370.53	1,339
13,000	1,124.85	498	582.05	969	473.62	1,209	401.41	1,451
14,000	1,211.38	537	626.82	1,044	510.05	1,302	432.28	1,562
15,000	1,297.91	575	671.59	1,118	546.48	1,394	463.16	1,674
16,000	1,384.43	613	716.37	1,193	582.92	1,488	494.04	1,785
17,000	1,470.96	652	761.14	1,267	619.35	1,581	524.92	1,897
18,000	1,557.49	690	805.91	1,342	655.78	1,673	555.79	2,008
19,000	1,644.01	728	850.68	1,416	692.21	1,766	586.67	2,120
20,000	1,730.54	766	895.46	1,491	728.64	1,859	617.55	2,232
21,000	1,817.07	805	940.23	1,566	765.08	1,952	648.42	2,343
22,000	1,903.59	843	985.00	1,640	801.51	2,045	679.30	2,455
23,000	1,990.12	881	1,029.77	1,714	837.94	2,138	710.18	2,566
24,000	2,076.65	920	1,074.55	1,789	874.37	2,231	741.06	2,678
25,000	2,163.17	958	1,119.32	1,864	910.80	2,324	771.93	2,789
26,000	2,249.70	996	1,164.09	1,938	947.23	2,417	802.81	2,901
27,000	2,336.23	1,035	1,208.86	2,013	983.67	2,510	833.69	3,013
28,000	2,422.75	1,073	1,253.64	2,087	1,020.10	2,603	864.56	3,124
29,000	2,509.28	1,111	1,298.41	2,162	1,056.53	2,696	895.44	3,236
30,000	2,595.81	1,150	1,343.18	2,236	1,092.96	2,789	926.32	3,348
31,000	2,682.33	1,188	1,387.95	2,311	1,129.39	2,882	957.20	3,459
32,000	2,768.86	1,226	1,432.73	2,386	1,165.83	2,975	988.07	3,571
33,000	2,855.39	1,265	1,477.50	2,460	1,202.26	3,068	1,018.95	3,682
34,000	2,941.91	1,303	1,522.27	2,534	1,238.69	3,161	1,049.83	3,794
35,000	3,028.44	1,341	1,567.05	2,609	1,275.12	3,254	1,080.70	3,905
36,000	3,114.97	1,380	1,611.82	2,684	1,311.55	3,347	1,111.58	4,017
37,000	3,201.49	1,418	1,656.59	2,758	1,347.99	3,440	1,142.46	4,129
38,000	3,288.02	1,456	1,701.36	2,833	1,384.42	3,533	1,173.33	4,240
39,000	3,374.55	1,495	1,746.14	2,907	1,420.85	3,626	1,204.21	4,352
40,000	3,461.07	1,533	1,790.91	2,982	1,457.28	3,718	1,235.09	4,463
42,000	3,634.13	1,610	1,880.45	3,131	1,530.15	3,905	1,296.84	4,686
44,000	3,807.18	1,686	1,970.00	3,280	1,603.01	4,090	1,358.60	4,910
46,000	3,980.24	1,763	2,059.54	3,429	1,675.87	4,276	1,420.35	5,133
48,000	4,153.29	1,839	2,149.09	3,578	1,748.74	4,462	1,482.11	5,356
50,000	4,326.34	1,916	2,238.63	3,727	1,821.60	4,648	1,543.86	5,579

AUTO LOAN PAYMENTS 7.00%

AMOUNT OF LOAN	42 MOS		48 MOS		60 MOS		72 MOS	
	MONTHLY PAYMENT	TOTAL INTRST	MONTHLY PAYMENT	TOTAL INTRST	MONTHLY PAYMENT	TOTAL INTRST	MONTHLY PAYMENT	TOTAL INTRST
$ 1	0.03	0	0.03	0	0.02	0	0.02	0
2	0.06	1	0.05	0	0.04	0	0.04	1
3	0.09	1	0.08	1	0.06	1	0.06	1
4	0.11	1	0.10	1	0.08	1	0.07	1
5	0.14	1	0.12	1	0.10	1	0.09	1
6	0.17	1	0.15	1	0.12	1	0.11	2
7	0.19	1	0.17	1	0.14	1	0.12	2
8	0.22	1	0.20	2	0.16	2	0.14	2
9	0.25	2	0.22	2	0.18	2	0.16	3
10	0.27	1	0.24	2	0.20	2	0.18	3
20	0.54	3	0.48	3	0.40	4	0.35	5
30	0.81	4	0.72	5	0.60	6	0.52	7
40	1.08	5	0.96	6	0.80	8	0.69	10
50	1.35	7	1.20	8	1.00	10	0.86	12
60	1.62	8	1.44	9	1.19	11	1.03	14
70	1.89	9	1.68	11	1.39	13	1.20	16
80	2.16	11	1.92	12	1.59	15	1.37	19
90	2.43	12	2.16	14	1.79	17	1.54	21
100	2.70	13	2.40	15	1.99	19	1.71	23
200	5.39	26	4.79	30	3.97	38	3.41	46
300	8.08	39	7.19	45	5.95	57	5.12	69
400	10.77	52	9.58	60	7.93	76	6.82	91
500	13.46	65	11.98	75	9.91	95	8.53	114
600	16.15	78	14.37	90	11.89	113	10.23	137
700	18.84	91	16.77	105	13.87	132	11.94	160
800	21.54	105	19.16	120	15.85	151	13.64	182
900	24.23	118	21.56	135	17.83	170	15.35	205
1,000	26.92	131	23.95	150	19.81	189	17.05	228
2,000	53.83	261	47.90	299	39.61	377	34.10	455
3,000	80.75	392	71.84	448	59.41	565	51.15	683
4,000	107.66	522	95.79	598	79.21	753	68.20	910
5,000	134.58	652	119.74	748	99.01	941	85.25	1,138
6,000	161.49	783	143.68	897	118.81	1,129	102.30	1,366
7,000	188.40	913	167.63	1,046	138.61	1,317	119.35	1,593
8,000	215.32	1,043	191.57	1,195	158.41	1,505	136.40	1,821
9,000	242.23	1,174	215.52	1,345	178.22	1,693	153.45	2,048
10,000	269.15	1,304	239.47	1,495	198.02	1,881	170.50	2,276
11,000	296.06	1,435	263.41	1,644	217.82	2,069	187.54	2,503
12,000	322.98	1,565	287.36	1,793	237.62	2,257	204.59	2,730
13,000	349.89	1,695	311.31	1,943	257.42	2,445	221.64	2,958
14,000	376.80	1,826	335.25	2,092	277.22	2,633	238.69	3,186
15,000	403.72	1,956	359.20	2,242	297.02	2,821	255.74	3,413
16,000	430.63	2,086	383.14	2,391	316.82	3,009	272.79	3,641
17,000	457.55	2,217	407.09	2,540	336.63	3,198	289.84	3,868
18,000	484.46	2,347	431.04	2,690	356.43	3,386	306.89	4,096
19,000	511.37	2,478	454.98	2,839	376.23	3,574	323.94	4,324
20,000	538.29	2,608	478.93	2,989	396.03	3,762	340.99	4,551
21,000	565.20	2,738	502.88	3,138	415.83	3,950	358.03	4,778
22,000	592.12	2,869	526.82	3,287	435.63	4,138	375.08	5,006
23,000	619.03	2,999	550.77	3,437	455.43	4,326	392.13	5,233
24,000	645.95	3,130	574.71	3,586	475.23	4,514	409.18	5,461
25,000	672.86	3,260	598.66	3,736	495.04	4,702	426.23	5,689
26,000	699.77	3,390	622.61	3,885	514.84	4,890	443.28	5,916
27,000	726.69	3,521	646.55	4,034	534.64	5,078	460.33	6,144
28,000	753.60	3,651	670.50	4,184	554.44	5,266	477.38	6,371
29,000	780.52	3,782	694.45	4,334	574.24	5,454	494.43	6,599
30,000	807.43	3,912	718.39	4,483	594.04	5,642	511.48	6,827
31,000	834.35	4,043	742.34	4,632	613.84	5,830	528.52	7,053
32,000	861.26	4,173	766.28	4,781	633.64	6,018	545.57	7,281
33,000	888.17	4,303	790.23	4,931	653.44	6,206	562.62	7,509
34,000	915.09	4,434	814.18	5,081	673.25	6,395	579.67	7,736
35,000	942.00	4,564	838.12	5,230	693.05	6,583	596.72	7,964
36,000	968.92	4,695	862.07	5,379	712.85	6,771	613.77	8,191
37,000	995.83	4,825	886.02	5,529	732.65	6,959	630.82	8,419
38,000	1,022.74	4,955	909.96	5,678	752.45	7,147	647.87	8,647
39,000	1,049.66	5,086	933.91	5,828	772.25	7,335	664.92	8,874
40,000	1,076.57	5,216	957.85	5,977	792.05	7,523	681.97	9,102
42,000	1,130.40	5,477	1,005.75	6,276	831.66	7,900	716.06	9,556
44,000	1,184.23	5,738	1,053.64	6,575	871.26	8,276	750.16	10,012
46,000	1,238.06	5,999	1,101.53	6,873	910.86	8,652	784.26	10,467
48,000	1,291.89	6,259	1,149.42	7,172	950.46	9,028	818.36	10,922
50,000	1,345.72	6,520	1,197.32	7,471	990.06	9,404	852.46	11,377

75

7.25%   AUTO LOAN PAYMENTS

AMOUNT OF LOAN	12 MOS		24 MOS		30 MOS		36 MOS	
	MONTHLY PAYMENT	TOTAL INTRST	MONTHLY PAYMENT	TOTAL INTRST	MONTHLY PAYMENT	TOTAL INTRST	MONTHLY PAYMENT	TOTAL INTRST
$ 1	0.09	0	0.05	0	0.04	0	0.04	0
2	0.18	0	0.09	0	0.08	0	0.07	1
3	0.26	0	0.14	0	0.11	0	0.10	1
4	0.35	0	0.18	0	0.15	1	0.13	1
5	0.44	0	0.23	1	0.19	0	0.16	1
6	0.52	0	0.27	0	0.22	1	0.19	1
7	0.61	0	0.32	1	0.26	1	0.22	1
8	0.70	0	0.36	1	0.30	1	0.25	1
9	0.78	0	0.41	1	0.33	1	0.28	1
10	0.87	0	0.45	1	0.37	1	0.31	1
20	1.74	1	0.90	2	0.74	2	0.62	2
30	2.60	1	1.35	2	1.10	3	0.93	3
40	3.47	2	1.80	3	1.47	4	1.24	5
50	4.34	2	2.25	4	1.83	5	1.55	6
60	5.20	2	2.70	5	2.20	6	1.86	7
70	6.07	3	3.15	6	2.56	7	2.17	8
80	6.94	3	3.60	6	2.93	8	2.48	9
90	7.80	4	4.04	7	3.29	9	2.79	10
100	8.67	4	4.49	8	3.66	10	3.10	12
200	17.33	8	8.98	16	7.31	19	6.20	23
300	26.00	12	13.47	23	10.97	29	9.30	35
400	34.66	16	17.96	31	14.62	39	12.40	46
500	43.33	20	22.45	39	18.28	48	15.50	58
600	51.99	24	26.94	47	21.93	58	18.60	70
700	60.65	28	31.43	54	25.59	68	21.70	81
800	69.32	32	35.91	62	29.24	77	24.80	93
900	77.98	36	40.40	70	32.90	87	27.90	104
1,000	86.65	40	44.89	77	36.55	97	31.00	116
2,000	173.29	79	89.78	155	73.10	193	61.99	232
3,000	259.93	119	134.66	232	109.64	289	92.98	347
4,000	346.57	159	179.55	309	146.19	386	123.97	463
5,000	433.22	199	224.44	387	182.73	482	154.96	579
6,000	519.86	238	269.32	464	219.28	578	185.95	694
7,000	606.50	278	314.21	541	255.82	675	216.95	810
8,000	693.14	318	359.09	618	292.37	771	247.94	926
9,000	779.78	357	403.98	696	328.92	868	278.93	1,041
10,000	866.43	397	448.87	773	365.46	964	309.92	1,157
11,000	953.07	437	493.75	850	402.01	1,060	340.91	1,273
12,000	1,039.71	477	538.64	927	438.55	1,157	371.90	1,388
13,000	1,126.35	516	583.52	1,004	475.10	1,253	402.89	1,504
14,000	1,212.99	556	628.41	1,082	511.64	1,349	433.89	1,620
15,000	1,299.64	596	673.30	1,159	548.19	1,446	464.88	1,736
16,000	1,386.28	635	718.18	1,236	584.74	1,542	495.87	1,851
17,000	1,472.92	675	763.07	1,314	621.28	1,638	526.86	1,967
18,000	1,559.56	715	807.95	1,391	657.83	1,735	557.85	2,083
19,000	1,646.20	754	852.84	1,468	694.37	1,831	588.84	2,198
20,000	1,732.85	794	897.73	1,546	730.92	1,928	619.84	2,314
21,000	1,819.49	834	942.61	1,623	767.46	2,024	650.83	2,430
22,000	1,906.13	874	987.50	1,700	804.01	2,120	681.82	2,546
23,000	1,992.77	913	1,032.38	1,777	840.56	2,217	712.81	2,661
24,000	2,079.41	953	1,077.27	1,854	877.10	2,313	743.80	2,777
25,000	2,166.06	993	1,122.16	1,932	913.65	2,410	774.79	2,892
26,000	2,252.70	1,032	1,167.04	2,009	950.19	2,506	805.78	3,008
27,000	2,339.34	1,072	1,211.93	2,086	986.74	2,602	836.78	3,124
28,000	2,425.98	1,112	1,256.81	2,163	1,023.28	2,698	867.77	3,240
29,000	2,512.62	1,151	1,301.70	2,241	1,059.83	2,795	898.76	3,355
30,000	2,599.27	1,191	1,346.59	2,318	1,096.38	2,891	929.75	3,471
31,000	2,685.91	1,231	1,391.47	2,395	1,132.92	2,988	960.74	3,587
32,000	2,772.55	1,271	1,436.36	2,473	1,169.47	3,084	991.73	3,702
33,000	2,859.19	1,310	1,481.24	2,550	1,206.01	3,180	1,022.73	3,818
34,000	2,945.83	1,350	1,526.13	2,627	1,242.56	3,277	1,053.72	3,934
35,000	3,032.48	1,390	1,571.02	2,704	1,279.10	3,373	1,084.71	4,050
36,000	3,119.12	1,429	1,615.90	2,782	1,315.65	3,470	1,115.70	4,165
37,000	3,205.76	1,469	1,660.79	2,859	1,352.20	3,566	1,146.69	4,281
38,000	3,292.40	1,509	1,705.67	2,936	1,388.74	3,662	1,177.68	4,396
39,000	3,379.04	1,548	1,750.56	3,013	1,425.29	3,759	1,208.67	4,512
40,000	3,465.69	1,588	1,795.45	3,091	1,461.83	3,855	1,239.67	4,628
42,000	3,638.97	1,668	1,885.22	3,245	1,534.92	4,048	1,301.65	4,859
44,000	3,812.25	1,747	1,974.99	3,400	1,608.02	4,241	1,363.63	5,091
46,000	3,985.54	1,826	2,064.76	3,554	1,681.11	4,433	1,425.62	5,322
48,000	4,158.82	1,906	2,154.53	3,709	1,754.20	4,626	1,487.60	5,554
50,000	4,332.11	1,985	2,244.31	3,863	1,827.29	4,819	1,549.58	5,785

AMOUNT OF LOAN	42 MOS		48 MOS		60 MOS		72 MOS	
	MONTHLY PAYMENT	TOTAL INTRST	MONTHLY PAYMENT	TOTAL INTRST	MONTHLY PAYMENT	TOTAL INTRST	MONTHLY PAYMENT	TOTAL INTRST
$ 1	0.03	0	0.03	0	0.02	0	0.02	0
2	0.06	0	0.05	0	0.04	0	0.04	0
3	0.09	1	0.08	0	0.06	0	0.06	1
4	0.11	1	0.10	1	0.08	1	0.07	1
5	0.14	1	0.13	1	0.10	1	0.09	1
6	0.17	1	0.15	1	0.12	1	0.11	2
7	0.19	1	0.17	1	0.14	1	0.13	2
8	0.22	1	0.20	2	0.16	2	0.14	2
9	0.25	2	0.22	2	0.18	2	0.16	3
10	0.28	2	0.25	2	0.20	2	0.18	3
20	0.55	3	0.49	4	0.40	4	0.35	5
30	0.82	4	0.73	5	0.60	6	0.52	7
40	1.09	6	0.97	7	0.80	8	0.69	10
50	1.36	7	1.21	8	1.00	10	0.86	12
60	1.63	8	1.45	10	1.20	12	1.04	15
70	1.90	10	1.69	11	1.40	14	1.21	17
80	2.17	11	1.93	13	1.60	16	1.38	19
90	2.44	12	2.17	14	1.80	18	1.55	22
100	2.71	14	2.41	16	2.00	20	1.72	24
200	5.41	27	4.82	31	3.99	39	3.44	48
300	8.11	41	7.22	47	5.98	59	5.16	72
400	10.82	54	9.63	62	7.97	78	6.87	95
500	13.52	68	12.04	78	9.96	98	8.59	118
600	16.22	81	14.44	93	11.96	118	10.31	142
700	18.93	95	16.85	109	13.95	137	12.02	165
800	21.63	108	19.25	124	15.94	156	13.74	189
900	24.33	122	21.66	140	17.93	176	15.46	213
1,000	27.03	135	24.07	155	19.92	195	17.17	236
2,000	54.06	271	48.13	310	39.84	390	34.34	472
3,000	81.09	406	72.19	465	59.76	586	51.51	709
4,000	108.12	541	96.25	620	79.68	781	68.68	945
5,000	135.15	676	120.32	775	99.60	976	85.85	1,181
6,000	162.18	812	144.38	930	119.52	1,171	103.02	1,417
7,000	189.21	947	168.44	1,085	139.44	1,366	120.19	1,654
8,000	216.24	1,082	192.50	1,240	159.36	1,562	137.36	1,890
9,000	243.27	1,217	216.57	1,395	179.28	1,757	154.53	2,126
10,000	270.30	1,353	240.63	1,550	199.20	1,952	171.70	2,362
11,000	297.33	1,488	264.69	1,705	219.12	2,147	188.87	2,599
12,000	324.36	1,623	288.75	1,860	239.04	2,342	206.04	2,835
13,000	351.39	1,758	312.82	2,015	258.96	2,538	223.21	3,071
14,000	378.42	1,894	336.88	2,170	278.88	2,733	240.38	3,307
15,000	405.45	2,029	360.94	2,325	298.80	2,928	257.54	3,543
16,000	432.48	2,164	385.00	2,480	318.71	3,123	274.71	3,779
17,000	459.51	2,299	409.07	2,635	338.63	3,318	291.88	4,015
18,000	486.54	2,435	433.13	2,790	358.55	3,513	309.05	4,252
19,000	513.56	2,570	457.19	2,945	378.47	3,708	326.22	4,488
20,000	540.59	2,705	481.25	3,100	398.39	3,903	343.39	4,724
21,000	567.62	2,840	505.32	3,255	418.31	4,099	360.56	4,960
22,000	594.65	2,975	529.38	3,410	438.23	4,294	377.73	5,197
23,000	621.68	3,111	553.44	3,565	458.15	4,489	394.90	5,433
24,000	648.71	3,246	577.50	3,720	478.07	4,684	412.07	5,669
25,000	675.74	3,381	601.57	3,875	497.99	4,879	429.24	5,905
26,000	702.77	3,516	625.63	4,030	517.91	5,075	446.41	6,142
27,000	729.80	3,652	649.69	4,185	537.83	5,270	463.58	6,378
28,000	756.83	3,787	673.75	4,340	557.75	5,465	480.75	6,614
29,000	783.86	3,922	697.81	4,495	577.67	5,660	497.91	6,850
30,000	810.89	4,057	721.88	4,650	597.59	5,855	515.08	7,086
31,000	837.92	4,193	745.94	4,805	617.51	6,051	532.25	7,322
32,000	864.95	4,328	770.00	4,960	637.42	6,245	549.42	7,558
33,000	891.98	4,463	794.06	5,115	657.34	6,440	566.59	7,794
34,000	919.01	4,598	818.13	5,270	677.26	6,636	583.76	8,031
35,000	946.04	4,734	842.19	5,425	697.18	6,831	600.93	8,267
36,000	973.07	4,869	866.25	5,580	717.10	7,026	618.10	8,503
37,000	1,000.09	5,004	890.31	5,735	737.02	7,221	635.27	8,739
38,000	1,027.12	5,139	914.38	5,890	756.94	7,416	652.44	8,976
39,000	1,054.15	5,274	938.44	6,045	776.86	7,612	669.61	9,212
40,000	1,081.18	5,410	962.50	6,200	796.78	7,807	686.78	9,448
42,000	1,135.24	5,680	1,010.63	6,510	836.62	8,197	721.12	9,921
44,000	1,189.30	5,951	1,058.75	6,820	876.46	8,588	755.45	10,392
46,000	1,243.36	6,221	1,106.88	7,130	916.30	8,978	789.79	10,865
48,000	1,297.42	6,492	1,155.00	7,440	956.13	9,368	824.13	11,337
50,000	1,351.48	6,762	1,203.13	7,750	995.97	9,758	858.47	11,810

AUTO LOAN PAYMENTS

AMOUNT OF LOAN	12 MOS MONTHLY PAYMENT	12 MOS TOTAL INTRST	24 MOS MONTHLY PAYMENT	24 MOS TOTAL INTRST	30 MOS MONTHLY PAYMENT	30 MOS TOTAL INTRST	36 MOS MONTHLY PAYMENT	36 MOS TOTAL INTRST
$ 1	0.09	0	0.05	0	0.04	0	0.04	0
2	0.18	0	0.09	0	0.08	0	0.07	0
3	0.27	0	0.14	0	0.11	0	0.10	1
4	0.35	0	0.18	0	0.15	1	0.13	1
5	0.44	0	0.23	0	0.19	1	0.16	1
6	0.53	0	0.27	1	0.22	1	0.19	1
7	0.61	0	0.32	0	0.26	1	0.22	1
8	0.70	0	0.36	1	0.30	1	0.25	1
9	0.79	0	0.41	1	0.33	1	0.28	1
10	0.87	0	0.45	1	0.37	1	0.32	2
20	1.74	1	0.90	2	0.74	2	0.63	3
30	2.61	1	1.35	2	1.10	3	0.94	4
40	3.48	2	1.80	3	1.47	4	1.25	5
50	4.34	2	2.25	4	1.84	5	1.56	6
60	5.21	3	2.70	5	2.20	6	1.87	7
70	6.08	3	3.15	6	2.57	7	2.18	8
80	6.95	3	3.60	6	2.94	8	2.49	10
90	7.81	4	4.05	7	3.30	9	2.80	11
100	8.68	4	4.50	8	3.67	10	3.12	12
200	17.36	8	9.00	16	7.34	20	6.23	24
300	26.03	12	13.50	24	11.00	30	9.34	36
400	34.71	17	18.00	32	14.67	40	12.45	48
500	43.38	21	22.50	40	18.33	50	15.56	60
600	52.06	25	27.00	48	22.00	60	18.67	72
700	60.74	29	31.50	56	25.67	70	21.78	84
800	69.41	33	36.00	64	29.33	80	24.89	96
900	78.09	37	40.50	72	33.00	90	28.00	108
1,000	86.76	41	45.00	80	36.66	100	31.11	120
2,000	173.52	82	90.00	160	73.32	200	62.22	240
3,000	260.28	123	135.00	240	109.98	299	93.32	360
4,000	347.03	164	180.00	320	146.64	399	124.43	479
5,000	433.79	205	225.00	400	183.30	499	155.54	599
6,000	520.55	247	270.00	480	219.96	599	186.64	719
7,000	607.31	288	315.00	560	256.62	699	217.75	839
8,000	694.06	329	360.00	640	293.28	798	248.85	959
9,000	780.82	370	405.00	720	329.94	898	279.96	1,079
10,000	867.58	411	450.00	800	366.60	998	311.07	1,199
11,000	954.34	452	495.00	880	403.26	1,098	342.17	1,318
12,000	1,041.09	493	540.00	960	439.92	1,198	373.28	1,438
13,000	1,127.85	534	585.00	1,040	476.58	1,297	404.39	1,558
14,000	1,214.61	575	630.00	1,120	513.24	1,397	435.49	1,678
15,000	1,301.37	616	675.00	1,200	549.90	1,497	466.60	1,798
16,000	1,388.12	657	720.00	1,280	586.56	1,597	497.70	1,917
17,000	1,474.88	699	765.00	1,360	623.22	1,697	528.81	2,037
18,000	1,561.64	740	810.00	1,440	659.88	1,796	559.92	2,157
19,000	1,648.40	781	855.00	1,520	696.54	1,896	591.02	2,277
20,000	1,735.15	822	900.00	1,600	733.20	1,996	622.13	2,397
21,000	1,821.91	863	945.00	1,680	769.86	2,096	653.24	2,517
22,000	1,908.67	904	990.00	1,760	806.52	2,196	684.34	2,636
23,000	1,995.43	945	1,035.00	1,840	843.18	2,295	715.45	2,756
24,000	2,082.18	986	1,080.00	1,920	879.84	2,395	746.55	2,876
25,000	2,168.94	1,027	1,124.99	2,000	916.50	2,495	777.66	2,996
26,000	2,255.70	1,068	1,169.99	2,080	953.16	2,595	808.77	3,116
27,000	2,342.46	1,110	1,214.99	2,160	989.82	2,695	839.87	3,235
28,000	2,429.21	1,151	1,259.99	2,240	1,026.48	2,794	870.98	3,355
29,000	2,515.97	1,192	1,304.99	2,320	1,063.14	2,894	902.09	3,475
30,000	2,602.73	1,233	1,349.99	2,400	1,099.80	2,994	933.19	3,595
31,000	2,689.48	1,274	1,394.99	2,480	1,136.46	3,094	964.30	3,715
32,000	2,776.24	1,315	1,439.99	2,560	1,173.12	3,194	995.40	3,834
33,000	2,863.00	1,356	1,484.99	2,640	1,209.77	3,293	1,026.51	3,954
34,000	2,949.76	1,397	1,529.99	2,720	1,246.43	3,393	1,057.62	4,074
35,000	3,036.51	1,438	1,574.99	2,800	1,283.09	3,493	1,088.72	4,194
36,000	3,123.27	1,479	1,619.99	2,880	1,319.75	3,593	1,119.83	4,314
37,000	3,210.03	1,520	1,664.99	2,960	1,356.41	3,692	1,150.94	4,434
38,000	3,296.79	1,561	1,709.99	3,040	1,393.07	3,792	1,182.04	4,553
39,000	3,383.54	1,602	1,754.99	3,120	1,429.73	3,892	1,213.15	4,673
40,000	3,470.30	1,644	1,799.99	3,200	1,466.39	3,992	1,244.25	4,793
42,000	3,643.82	1,726	1,889.99	3,360	1,539.71	4,191	1,306.47	5,033
44,000	3,817.33	1,808	1,979.99	3,520	1,613.03	4,391	1,368.68	5,272
46,000	3,990.85	1,890	2,069.99	3,680	1,686.35	4,591	1,430.89	5,512
48,000	4,164.36	1,972	2,159.99	3,840	1,759.67	4,790	1,493.10	5,752
50,000	4,337.88	2,055	2,249.98	4,000	1,832.99	4,990	1,555.32	5,992

AUTO LOAN PAYMENTS 7.50%

AMOUNT OF LOAN	42 MOS		48 MOS		60 MOS		72 MOS	
	MONTHLY PAYMENT	TOTAL INTRST	MONTHLY PAYMENT	TOTAL INTRST	MONTHLY PAYMENT	TOTAL INTRST	MONTHLY PAYMENT	TOTAL INTRST
$ 1	0.03	0	0.03	0	0.03	0	0.02	0
2	0.06	1	0.05	0	0.05	1	0.04	1
3	0.09	1	0.08	1	0.07	1	0.06	1
4	0.11	1	0.10	1	0.09	1	0.07	1
5	0.14	1	0.13	1	0.11	2	0.09	1
6	0.17	1	0.15	1	0.13	2	0.11	2
7	0.20	1	0.17	1	0.15	2	0.13	2
8	0.22	1	0.20	2	0.17	2	0.14	2
9	0.25	2	0.22	2	0.19	2	0.16	3
10	0.28	2	0.25	2	0.21	3	0.18	3
20	0.55	3	0.49	4	0.41	5	0.35	5
30	0.82	4	0.73	5	0.61	7	0.52	7
40	1.09	6	0.97	7	0.81	9	0.70	10
50	1.36	7	1.21	8	1.01	11	0.87	13
60	1.63	8	1.46	10	1.21	13	1.04	15
70	1.91	10	1.70	12	1.41	15	1.22	18
80	2.18	12	1.94	13	1.61	17	1.39	20
90	2.45	13	2.18	15	1.81	19	1.56	22
100	2.72	14	2.42	16	2.01	21	1.73	25
200	5.43	28	4.84	32	4.01	41	3.46	49
300	8.15	42	7.26	48	6.02	61	5.19	74
400	10.86	56	9.68	65	8.02	81	6.92	98
500	13.58	70	12.09	80	10.02	101	8.65	123
600	16.29	84	14.51	96	12.03	122	10.38	147
700	19.01	98	16.93	113	14.03	142	12.11	172
800	21.72	112	19.35	129	16.04	162	13.84	196
900	24.44	126	21.77	145	18.04	182	15.57	221
1,000	27.15	140	24.18	161	20.04	202	17.30	246
2,000	54.29	280	48.36	321	40.08	405	34.59	490
3,000	81.44	420	72.54	482	60.12	607	51.88	735
4,000	108.58	560	96.72	643	80.16	810	69.17	980
5,000	135.73	701	120.90	803	100.19	1,011	86.46	1,225
6,000	162.87	841	145.08	964	120.23	1,214	103.75	1,470
7,000	190.02	981	169.26	1,124	140.27	1,416	121.04	1,715
8,000	217.16	1,121	193.44	1,285	160.31	1,619	138.33	1,960
9,000	244.31	1,261	217.62	1,446	180.35	1,821	155.62	2,205
10,000	271.45	1,401	241.79	1,606	200.38	2,023	172.91	2,450
11,000	298.60	1,541	265.97	1,767	220.42	2,225	190.20	2,694
12,000	325.74	1,681	290.15	1,927	240.46	2,428	207.49	2,939
13,000	352.89	1,821	314.33	2,088	260.50	2,630	224.78	3,184
14,000	380.03	1,961	338.51	2,248	280.54	2,832	242.07	3,429
15,000	407.18	2,102	362.69	2,409	300.57	3,034	259.36	3,674
16,000	434.32	2,241	386.87	2,570	320.61	3,237	276.65	3,919
17,000	461.47	2,382	411.05	2,730	340.65	3,439	293.94	4,164
18,000	488.61	2,522	435.23	2,891	360.69	3,641	311.23	4,409
19,000	515.76	2,662	459.40	3,051	380.73	3,844	328.52	4,653
20,000	542.90	2,802	483.58	3,212	400.76	4,046	345.81	4,898
21,000	570.05	2,942	507.76	3,372	420.80	4,248	363.10	5,143
22,000	597.19	3,082	531.94	3,533	440.84	4,450	380.39	5,388
23,000	624.34	3,222	556.12	3,694	460.88	4,653	397.68	5,633
24,000	651.48	3,362	580.30	3,854	480.92	4,855	414.97	5,878
25,000	678.63	3,502	604.48	4,015	500.95	5,057	432.26	6,123
26,000	705.77	3,642	628.66	4,176	520.99	5,259	449.55	6,368
27,000	732.92	3,783	652.84	4,336	541.03	5,462	466.84	6,612
28,000	760.06	3,923	677.01	4,496	561.07	5,664	484.13	6,857
29,000	787.21	4,063	701.19	4,657	581.11	5,867	501.42	7,102
30,000	814.35	4,203	725.37	4,818	601.14	6,068	518.71	7,347
31,000	841.50	4,343	749.55	4,978	621.18	6,271	536.00	7,592
32,000	868.64	4,483	773.73	5,139	641.22	6,473	553.29	7,837
33,000	895.79	4,623	797.91	5,300	661.26	6,676	570.58	8,082
34,000	922.93	4,763	822.09	5,460	681.30	6,878	587.87	8,327
35,000	950.08	4,903	846.27	5,621	701.33	7,080	605.16	8,572
36,000	977.22	5,043	870.45	5,782	721.37	7,282	622.45	8,816
37,000	1,004.37	5,184	894.62	5,942	741.41	7,485	639.74	9,061
38,000	1,031.51	5,323	918.80	6,102	761.45	7,687	657.03	9,306
39,000	1,058.66	5,464	942.98	6,263	781.48	7,889	674.32	9,551
40,000	1,085.80	5,604	967.16	6,424	801.52	8,091	691.61	9,796
42,000	1,140.09	5,884	1,015.52	6,745	841.60	8,496	726.19	10,286
44,000	1,194.38	6,164	1,063.88	7,066	881.67	8,900	760.77	10,775
46,000	1,248.67	6,444	1,112.23	7,387	921.75	9,305	795.35	11,265
48,000	1,302.96	6,724	1,160.59	7,708	961.83	9,710	829.93	11,755
50,000	1,357.25	7,005	1,208.95	8,030	1,001.90	10,114	864.51	12,245

AUTO LOAN PAYMENTS

AMOUNT OF LOAN	12 MOS		24 MOS		30 MOS		36 MOS	
	MONTHLY PAYMENT	TOTAL INTRST	MONTHLY PAYMENT	TOTAL INTRST	MONTHLY PAYMENT	TOTAL INTRST	MONTHLY PAYMENT	TOTAL INTRST
$ 1	0.09	0	0.05	0	0.04	0	0.04	0
2	0.18	0	0.10	0	0.08	0	0.07	1
3	0.27	0	0.14	0	0.12	1	0.10	1
4	0.35	0	0.19	1	0.15	1	0.13	1
5	0.44	0	0.23	1	0.19	1	0.16	1
6	0.53	0	0.28	1	0.23	1	0.19	1
7	0.61	0	0.32	1	0.26	1	0.22	1
8	0.70	0	0.37	1	0.30	1	0.25	1
9	0.79	0	0.41	1	0.34	1	0.29	1
10	0.87	0	0.46	1	0.37	1	0.32	2
20	1.74	1	0.91	2	0.74	2	0.63	3
30	2.61	1	1.36	3	1.11	3	0.94	4
40	3.48	2	1.81	3	1.48	4	1.25	5
50	4.35	2	2.26	4	1.84	5	1.57	7
60	5.22	3	2.71	5	2.21	6	1.88	8
70	6.09	3	3.16	6	2.58	7	2.19	9
80	6.95	3	3.61	7	2.95	9	2.50	10
90	7.82	4	4.07	8	3.31	9	2.81	11
100	8.69	4	4.52	8	3.68	10	3.13	13
200	17.38	9	9.03	17	7.36	21	6.25	25
300	26.07	13	13.54	25	11.04	31	9.37	37
400	34.75	17	18.05	33	14.71	41	12.49	50
500	43.44	21	22.55	41	18.39	52	15.62	62
600	52.13	26	27.07	50	22.07	62	18.74	75
700	60.82	30	31.58	58	25.75	73	21.86	87
800	69.50	34	36.10	66	29.42	83	24.98	99
900	78.19	38	40.61	75	33.10	93	28.10	112
1,000	86.88	43	45.12	83	36.78	103	31.23	124
2,000	173.75	85	90.23	166	73.55	207	62.45	248
3,000	260.62	127	135.35	248	110.33	310	93.67	372
4,000	347.50	170	180.46	331	147.10	413	124.89	496
5,000	434.37	212	225.57	414	183.87	516	156.11	620
6,000	521.24	255	270.69	497	220.65	620	187.33	744
7,000	608.12	297	315.80	579	257.42	723	218.55	868
8,000	694.99	340	360.91	662	294.20	826	249.77	992
9,000	781.86	383	406.03	745	330.97	929	281.00	1,116
10,000	868.73	425	451.14	827	367.74	1,032	312.22	1,240
11,000	955.61	467	496.25	910	404.52	1,136	343.44	1,364
12,000	1,042.48	510	541.37	993	441.29	1,239	374.66	1,488
13,000	1,129.35	552	586.48	1,076	478.07	1,342	405.88	1,612
14,000	1,216.23	595	631.59	1,158	514.84	1,445	437.10	1,736
15,000	1,303.10	637	676.71	1,241	551.61	1,548	468.32	1,860
16,000	1,389.97	680	721.82	1,324	588.39	1,652	499.54	1,983
17,000	1,476.84	722	766.93	1,406	625.16	1,755	530.76	2,107
18,000	1,563.72	765	812.05	1,489	661.94	1,858	561.99	2,232
19,000	1,650.59	807	857.16	1,572	698.71	1,961	593.21	2,356
20,000	1,737.46	850	902.27	1,654	735.48	2,064	624.43	2,479
21,000	1,824.34	892	947.39	1,737	772.26	2,168	655.65	2,603
22,000	1,911.21	935	992.50	1,820	809.03	2,271	686.87	2,727
23,000	1,998.08	977	1,037.61	1,903	845.80	2,374	718.09	2,851
24,000	2,084.95	1,019	1,082.73	1,986	882.58	2,477	749.31	2,975
25,000	2,171.83	1,062	1,127.84	2,068	919.35	2,581	780.53	3,099
26,000	2,258.70	1,104	1,172.95	2,151	956.13	2,684	811.76	3,223
27,000	2,345.57	1,147	1,218.07	2,234	992.90	2,787	842.98	3,347
28,000	2,432.45	1,189	1,263.18	2,316	1,029.67	2,890	874.20	3,471
29,000	2,519.32	1,232	1,308.29	2,399	1,066.45	2,994	905.42	3,595
30,000	2,606.19	1,274	1,353.41	2,482	1,103.22	3,097	936.64	3,719
31,000	2,693.06	1,317	1,398.52	2,564	1,140.00	3,200	967.86	3,843
32,000	2,779.94	1,359	1,443.63	2,647	1,176.77	3,303	999.08	3,967
33,000	2,866.81	1,402	1,488.75	2,730	1,213.54	3,406	1,030.30	4,091
34,000	2,953.68	1,444	1,533.86	2,813	1,250.32	3,510	1,061.52	4,215
35,000	3,040.56	1,487	1,578.97	2,895	1,287.09	3,613	1,092.75	4,339
36,000	3,127.43	1,529	1,624.09	2,978	1,323.87	3,716	1,123.97	4,463
37,000	3,214.30	1,572	1,669.20	3,061	1,360.64	3,819	1,155.19	4,587
38,000	3,301.17	1,614	1,714.31	3,143	1,397.41	3,922	1,186.41	4,711
39,000	3,388.05	1,657	1,759.43	3,226	1,434.19	4,026	1,217.63	4,835
40,000	3,474.92	1,699	1,804.54	3,309	1,470.96	4,129	1,248.85	4,959
42,000	3,648.67	1,784	1,894.77	3,474	1,544.51	4,335	1,311.29	5,206
44,000	3,822.41	1,869	1,984.99	3,640	1,618.06	4,542	1,373.74	5,455
46,000	3,996.16	1,954	2,075.22	3,805	1,691.60	4,748	1,436.18	5,702
48,000	4,169.90	2,039	2,165.45	3,971	1,765.15	4,955	1,498.62	5,950
50,000	4,343.65	2,124	2,255.67	4,136	1,838.70	5,161	1,561.06	6,198

AUTO LOAN PAYMENTS 7.75%

AMOUNT OF LOAN	42 MOS		48 MOS		60 MOS		72 MOS	
	MONTHLY PAYMENT	TOTAL INTRST	MONTHLY PAYMENT	TOTAL INTRST	MONTHLY PAYMENT	TOTAL INTRST	MONTHLY PAYMENT	TOTAL INTRST
$ 1	0.03	0	0.03	0	0.03	1	0.02	0
2	0.06	1	0.05	0	0.05	1	0.04	1
3	0.09	1	0.08	1	0.07	1	0.06	1
4	0.11	1	0.10	1	0.09	1	0.07	1
5	0.14	1	0.13	1	0.11	2	0.09	1
6	0.17	1	0.15	1	0.13	2	0.11	2
7	0.20	1	0.18	2	0.15	2	0.13	2
8	0.22	1	0.20	2	0.17	2	0.14	2
9	0.25	2	0.22	2	0.19	2	0.16	3
10	0.28	2	0.25	2	0.21	3	0.18	3
20	0.55	3	0.49	4	0.41	5	0.35	5
30	0.82	4	0.73	5	0.61	7	0.53	8
40	1.10	6	0.98	7	0.81	9	0.70	10
50	1.37	8	1.22	9	1.01	11	0.88	13
60	1.64	9	1.46	10	1.21	13	1.05	16
70	1.91	10	1.71	12	1.42	15	1.22	18
80	2.19	12	1.95	14	1.62	17	1.40	21
90	2.46	13	2.19	15	1.82	19	1.57	23
100	2.73	15	2.43	17	2.02	21	1.75	26
200	5.46	29	4.86	33	4.04	42	3.49	51
300	8.18	44	7.29	50	6.05	63	5.23	77
400	10.91	58	9.72	67	8.07	84	6.97	102
500	13.64	73	12.15	83	10.08	105	8.71	127
600	16.36	87	14.58	100	12.10	126	10.45	152
700	19.09	102	17.01	116	14.11	147	12.19	178
800	21.81	116	19.44	133	16.13	168	13.93	203
900	24.54	131	21.87	150	18.15	189	15.68	229
1,000	27.27	145	24.30	166	20.16	210	17.42	254
2,000	54.53	290	48.60	333	40.32	419	34.83	508
3,000	81.79	435	72.89	499	60.48	629	52.24	761
4,000	109.05	580	97.19	665	80.63	838	69.65	1,015
5,000	136.31	725	121.48	831	100.79	1,047	87.06	1,268
6,000	163.57	870	145.78	997	120.95	1,257	104.47	1,522
7,000	190.83	1,015	170.08	1,164	141.10	1,466	121.88	1,775
8,000	218.09	1,160	194.37	1,330	161.26	1,676	139.30	2,030
9,000	245.35	1,305	218.67	1,496	181.42	1,885	156.71	2,283
10,000	272.61	1,450	242.96	1,662	201.57	2,094	174.12	2,537
11,000	299.87	1,595	267.26	1,828	221.73	2,304	191.53	2,790
12,000	327.13	1,739	291.55	1,994	241.89	2,513	208.94	3,044
13,000	354.40	1,885	315.85	2,161	262.05	2,723	226.35	3,297
14,000	381.66	2,030	340.15	2,327	282.20	2,932	243.76	3,551
15,000	408.92	2,175	364.44	2,493	302.36	3,142	261.18	3,805
16,000	436.18	2,320	388.74	2,660	322.52	3,351	278.59	4,058
17,000	463.44	2,464	413.03	2,825	342.67	3,560	296.00	4,312
18,000	490.70	2,609	437.33	2,992	362.83	3,770	313.41	4,566
19,000	517.96	2,754	461.62	3,158	382.99	3,979	330.82	4,819
20,000	545.22	2,899	485.92	3,324	403.14	4,188	348.23	5,073
21,000	572.48	3,044	510.22	3,491	423.30	4,398	365.64	5,326
22,000	599.74	3,189	534.51	3,656	443.46	4,608	383.06	5,580
23,000	627.00	3,334	558.81	3,823	463.62	4,817	400.47	5,834
24,000	654.26	3,479	583.10	3,989	483.77	5,026	417.88	6,087
25,000	681.53	3,624	607.40	4,155	503.93	5,236	435.29	6,341
26,000	708.79	3,769	631.69	4,321	524.09	5,445	452.70	6,594
27,000	736.05	3,914	655.99	4,488	544.24	5,654	470.11	6,848
28,000	763.31	4,059	680.29	4,654	564.40	5,864	487.52	7,101
29,000	790.57	4,204	704.58	4,820	584.56	6,074	504.94	7,356
30,000	817.83	4,349	728.88	4,986	604.71	6,283	522.35	7,609
31,000	845.09	4,494	753.17	5,152	624.87	6,492	539.76	7,863
32,000	872.35	4,639	777.47	5,319	645.03	6,702	557.17	8,116
33,000	899.61	4,784	801.76	5,484	665.18	6,911	574.58	8,370
34,000	926.87	4,929	826.06	5,651	685.34	7,120	591.99	8,623
35,000	954.13	5,073	850.36	5,817	705.50	7,330	609.40	8,877
36,000	981.39	5,218	874.65	5,983	725.66	7,540	626.82	9,131
37,000	1,008.66	5,364	898.95	6,150	745.81	7,749	644.23	9,385
38,000	1,035.92	5,509	923.24	6,316	765.97	7,958	661.64	9,638
39,000	1,063.18	5,654	947.54	6,482	786.13	8,168	679.05	9,892
40,000	1,090.44	5,798	971.83	6,648	806.28	8,377	696.46	10,145
42,000	1,144.96	6,088	1,020.43	6,981	846.60	8,796	731.28	10,652
44,000	1,199.48	6,378	1,069.02	7,313	886.91	9,215	766.11	11,160
46,000	1,254.00	6,668	1,117.61	7,645	927.23	9,634	800.93	11,667
48,000	1,308.52	6,958	1,166.20	7,978	967.54	10,052	835.75	12,174
50,000	1,363.05	7,248	1,214.79	8,310	1,007.85	10,471	870.58	12,682

81

7.90%   AUTO LOAN PAYMENTS

AMOUNT OF LOAN	12 MOS		24 MOS		30 MOS		36 MOS	
	MONTHLY PAYMENT	TOTAL INTRST	MONTHLY PAYMENT	TOTAL INTRST	MONTHLY PAYMENT	TOTAL INTRST	MONTHLY PAYMENT	TOTAL INTRST
$ 1	0.09	0	0.05	0	0.04	0	0.04	0
2	0.18	0	0.10	0	0.08	0	0.07	1
3	0.27	0	0.14	0	0.12	1	0.10	1
4	0.35	0	0.19	1	0.15	1	0.13	1
5	0.44	0	0.23	1	0.19	1	0.16	1
6	0.53	0	0.28	1	0.23	1	0.19	1
7	0.61	0	0.32	1	0.26	1	0.22	1
8	0.70	0	0.37	1	0.30	1	0.26	1
9	0.79	0	0.41	1	0.34	1	0.29	1
10	0.87	0	0.46	1	0.37	1	0.32	2
20	1.74	1	0.91	2	0.74	2	0.63	3
30	2.61	1	1.36	3	1.11	3	0.94	4
40	3.48	2	1.81	3	1.48	4	1.26	5
50	4.35	2	2.26	4	1.85	6	1.57	7
60	5.22	3	2.72	5	2.22	7	1.88	8
70	6.09	3	3.17	6	2.58	7	2.20	9
80	6.96	4	3.62	7	2.95	9	2.51	10
90	7.83	4	4.07	8	3.32	10	2.82	12
100	8.70	4	4.52	8	3.69	11	3.13	13
200	17.39	9	9.04	17	7.37	21	6.26	25
300	26.09	13	13.56	25	11.06	32	9.39	38
400	34.78	17	18.08	34	14.74	42	12.52	51
500	43.48	22	22.60	42	18.43	53	15.65	63
600	52.17	26	27.11	51	22.11	63	18.78	76
700	60.86	30	31.63	59	25.79	74	21.91	89
800	69.56	35	36.15	68	29.48	84	25.04	101
900	78.25	39	40.67	76	33.16	95	28.17	114
1,000	86.95	43	45.19	85	36.85	106	31.30	127
2,000	173.89	87	90.37	169	73.69	211	62.59	253
3,000	260.83	130	135.55	253	110.53	316	93.88	380
4,000	347.77	173	180.73	338	147.38	421	125.17	506
5,000	434.72	217	225.91	422	184.22	527	156.46	633
6,000	521.66	260	271.10	506	221.06	632	187.75	759
7,000	608.60	303	316.28	591	257.90	737	219.04	885
8,000	695.54	346	361.46	675	294.75	843	250.33	1,012
9,000	782.48	390	406.64	759	331.59	948	281.62	1,138
10,000	869.43	433	451.82	844	368.43	1,053	312.91	1,265
11,000	956.37	476	497.00	928	405.27	1,158	344.20	1,391
12,000	1,043.31	520	542.19	1,013	442.12	1,264	375.49	1,518
13,000	1,130.25	563	587.37	1,097	478.96	1,369	406.78	1,644
14,000	1,217.20	606	632.55	1,181	515.80	1,474	438.07	1,771
15,000	1,304.14	650	677.73	1,266	552.64	1,579	469.36	1,897
16,000	1,391.08	693	722.91	1,350	589.49	1,685	500.65	2,023
17,000	1,478.02	736	768.09	1,434	626.33	1,790	531.94	2,150
18,000	1,564.96	780	813.28	1,519	663.17	1,895	563.23	2,276
19,000	1,651.91	823	858.46	1,603	700.01	2,000	594.52	2,403
20,000	1,738.85	866	903.64	1,687	736.86	2,106	625.81	2,529
21,000	1,825.79	909	948.82	1,772	773.70	2,211	657.10	2,656
22,000	1,912.73	953	994.00	1,856	810.54	2,316	688.39	2,782
23,000	1,999.68	996	1,039.18	1,940	847.38	2,421	719.68	2,908
24,000	2,086.62	1,039	1,084.37	2,025	884.23	2,527	750.97	3,035
25,000	2,173.56	1,083	1,129.55	2,109	921.07	2,632	782.26	3,161
26,000	2,260.50	1,126	1,174.73	2,194	957.91	2,737	813.55	3,288
27,000	2,347.44	1,169	1,219.91	2,278	994.75	2,843	844.84	3,414
28,000	2,434.39	1,213	1,265.09	2,362	1,031.60	2,948	876.13	3,541
29,000	2,521.33	1,256	1,310.27	2,446	1,068.44	3,053	907.42	3,667
30,000	2,608.27	1,299	1,355.46	2,531	1,105.28	3,158	938.71	3,794
31,000	2,695.21	1,343	1,400.64	2,615	1,142.12	3,264	970.00	3,920
32,000	2,782.16	1,386	1,445.82	2,700	1,178.97	3,369	1,001.29	4,046
33,000	2,869.10	1,429	1,491.00	2,784	1,215.81	3,474	1,032.58	4,173
34,000	2,956.04	1,472	1,536.18	2,868	1,252.65	3,580	1,063.87	4,299
35,000	3,042.98	1,516	1,581.36	2,953	1,289.49	3,685	1,095.16	4,426
36,000	3,129.92	1,559	1,626.55	3,037	1,326.34	3,790	1,126.45	4,552
37,000	3,216.87	1,602	1,671.73	3,122	1,363.18	3,895	1,157.74	4,679
38,000	3,303.81	1,646	1,716.91	3,206	1,400.02	4,001	1,189.03	4,805
39,000	3,390.75	1,689	1,762.09	3,290	1,436.86	4,106	1,220.32	4,932
40,000	3,477.69	1,732	1,807.27	3,374	1,473.71	4,211	1,251.62	5,058
42,000	3,651.58	1,819	1,897.64	3,543	1,547.39	4,422	1,314.20	5,311
44,000	3,825.46	1,906	1,988.00	3,712	1,621.08	4,632	1,376.78	5,564
46,000	3,999.35	1,992	2,078.36	3,881	1,694.76	4,843	1,439.36	5,817
48,000	4,173.23	2,079	2,168.73	4,050	1,768.45	5,054	1,501.94	6,070
50,000	4,347.11	2,165	2,259.09	4,218	1,842.13	5,264	1,564.52	6,323

AMOUNT OF LOAN	42 MOS		48 MOS		60 MOS		72 MOS	
	MONTHLY PAYMENT	TOTAL INTRST	MONTHLY PAYMENT	TOTAL INTRST	MONTHLY PAYMENT	TOTAL INTRST	MONTHLY PAYMENT	TOTAL INTRST
$ 1	0.03	0	0.03	0	0.03	1	0.02	0
2	0.06	1	0.05	0	0.05	1	0.04	1
3	0.09	1	0.08	1	0.07	1	0.06	1
4	0.11	1	0.10	1	0.09	1	0.07	1
5	0.14	1	0.13	1	0.11	2	0.09	1
6	0.17	1	0.15	1	0.13	2	0.11	2
7	0.20	1	0.18	2	0.15	2	0.13	2
8	0.22	1	0.20	2	0.17	2	0.14	2
9	0.25	2	0.22	2	0.19	2	0.16	3
10	0.28	2	0.25	2	0.21	3	0.18	3
20	0.55	3	0.49	4	0.41	5	0.35	5
30	0.82	4	0.74	6	0.61	7	0.53	8
40	1.10	6	0.98	7	0.81	9	0.70	10
50	1.37	8	1.22	9	1.02	11	0.88	13
60	1.64	9	1.47	11	1.22	13	1.05	16
70	1.92	11	1.71	12	1.42	15	1.23	19
80	2.19	12	1.95	14	1.62	17	1.40	21
90	2.46	13	2.20	16	1.83	20	1.58	24
100	2.74	15	2.44	17	2.03	22	1.75	26
200	5.47	30	4.88	34	4.05	43	3.50	52
300	8.20	44	7.31	51	6.07	64	5.25	78
400	10.94	59	9.75	68	8.10	86	7.00	104
500	13.67	74	12.19	85	10.12	107	8.75	130
600	16.40	89	14.62	102	12.14	128	10.50	156
700	19.14	104	17.06	119	14.16	150	12.24	181
800	21.87	119	19.50	136	16.19	171	13.99	207
900	24.60	133	21.93	153	18.21	193	15.74	233
1,000	27.34	148	24.37	170	20.23	214	17.49	259
2,000	54.67	296	48.74	340	40.46	428	34.97	518
3,000	82.00	444	73.10	509	60.69	641	52.46	777
4,000	109.33	592	97.47	679	80.92	855	69.94	1,036
5,000	136.66	740	121.84	848	101.15	1,069	87.43	1,295
6,000	163.99	888	146.20	1,018	121.38	1,283	104.91	1,554
7,000	191.32	1,035	170.57	1,187	141.60	1,496	122.40	1,813
8,000	218.65	1,183	194.93	1,357	161.83	1,710	139.88	2,071
9,000	245.98	1,331	219.30	1,526	182.06	1,924	157.37	2,331
10,000	273.31	1,479	243.67	1,696	202.29	2,137	174.85	2,589
11,000	300.64	1,627	268.03	1,865	222.52	2,351	192.33	2,848
12,000	327.97	1,775	292.40	2,035	242.75	2,565	209.82	3,107
13,000	355.30	1,923	316.76	2,204	262.98	2,779	227.30	3,366
14,000	382.63	2,070	341.13	2,374	283.20	2,992	244.79	3,625
15,000	409.96	2,218	365.50	2,544	303.43	3,206	262.27	3,883
16,000	437.29	2,366	389.86	2,713	323.66	3,420	279.76	4,143
17,000	464.62	2,514	414.23	2,883	343.89	3,633	297.24	4,401
18,000	491.95	2,662	438.59	3,052	364.12	3,847	314.73	4,661
19,000	519.28	2,810	462.96	3,222	384.35	4,061	332.21	4,919
20,000	546.61	2,958	487.33	3,392	404.58	4,275	349.69	5,178
21,000	573.95	3,106	511.69	3,561	424.80	4,488	367.18	5,437
22,000	601.28	3,254	536.06	3,731	445.03	4,702	384.66	5,696
23,000	628.61	3,402	560.42	3,900	465.26	4,916	402.15	5,955
24,000	655.94	3,549	584.79	4,070	485.49	5,129	419.63	6,213
25,000	683.27	3,697	609.16	4,240	505.72	5,343	437.12	6,473
26,000	710.60	3,845	633.52	4,409	525.95	5,557	454.60	6,731
27,000	737.93	3,993	657.89	4,579	546.18	5,771	472.09	6,990
28,000	765.26	4,141	682.25	4,748	566.40	5,984	489.57	7,249
29,000	792.59	4,289	706.62	4,918	586.63	6,198	507.05	7,508
30,000	819.92	4,437	730.99	5,088	606.86	6,412	524.54	7,767
31,000	847.25	4,585	755.35	5,257	627.09	6,625	542.02	8,025
32,000	874.58	4,732	779.72	5,427	647.32	6,839	559.51	8,285
33,000	901.91	4,880	804.08	5,596	667.55	7,053	576.99	8,543
34,000	929.24	5,028	828.45	5,766	687.78	7,267	594.48	8,803
35,000	956.57	5,176	852.82	5,935	708.00	7,480	611.96	9,061
36,000	983.90	5,324	877.18	6,105	728.23	7,694	629.45	9,320
37,000	1,011.23	5,472	901.55	6,274	748.46	7,908	646.93	9,579
38,000	1,038.56	5,620	925.91	6,444	768.69	8,121	664.41	9,838
39,000	1,065.89	5,767	950.28	6,613	788.92	8,335	681.90	10,097
40,000	1,093.22	5,915	974.65	6,783	809.15	8,549	699.38	10,355
42,000	1,147.89	6,211	1,023.38	7,122	849.60	8,976	734.35	10,873
44,000	1,202.55	6,507	1,072.11	7,461	890.06	9,404	769.32	11,391
46,000	1,257.21	6,803	1,120.84	7,800	930.52	9,831	804.29	11,909
48,000	1,311.87	7,099	1,169.57	8,139	970.98	10,259	839.26	12,427
50,000	1,366.53	7,394	1,218.31	8,479	1,011.43	10,686	874.23	12,945

AMOUNT OF LOAN	12 MOS		24 MOS		30 MOS		36 MOS	
	MONTHLY PAYMENT	TOTAL INTRST	MONTHLY PAYMENT	TOTAL INTRST	MONTHLY PAYMENT	TOTAL INTRST	MONTHLY PAYMENT	TOTAL INTRST
$ 1	0.09	0	0.05	0	0.04	0	0.04	0
2	0.18	0	0.10	0	0.08	0	0.07	1
3	0.27	0	0.14	0	0.12	0	0.10	1
4	0.35	0	0.19	1	0.15	1	0.13	1
5	0.44	0	0.23	1	0.19	1	0.16	1
6	0.53	0	0.28	1	0.23	1	0.19	1
7	0.61	0	0.32	1	0.26	1	0.22	1
8	0.70	0	0.37	1	0.30	1	0.26	1
9	0.79	0	0.41	1	0.34	1	0.29	1
10	0.87	0	0.46	1	0.37	1	0.32	2
20	1.74	1	0.91	2	0.74	2	0.63	3
30	2.61	1	1.36	3	1.11	3	0.95	4
40	3.48	2	1.81	3	1.48	4	1.26	5
50	4.35	2	2.27	4	1.85	6	1.57	7
60	5.22	3	2.72	5	2.22	6	1.89	8
70	6.09	3	3.17	6	2.59	7	2.20	9
80	6.96	4	3.62	7	2.96	8	2.51	10
90	7.83	4	4.08	8	3.32	10	2.83	12
100	8.70	4	4.53	9	3.69	11	3.14	13
200	17.40	9	9.05	17	7.38	21	6.27	26
300	26.10	13	13.57	26	11.07	32	9.41	39
400	34.80	18	18.10	34	14.76	43	12.54	51
500	43.50	22	22.62	43	18.45	54	15.67	64
600	52.20	26	27.14	51	22.14	64	18.81	77
700	60.90	31	31.66	60	25.83	75	21.94	90
800	69.60	35	36.19	69	29.52	86	25.07	103
900	78.29	39	40.71	77	33.20	96	28.21	116
1,000	86.99	44	45.23	86	36.89	107	31.34	128
2,000	173.98	88	90.46	171	73.78	213	62.68	256
3,000	260.97	132	135.69	257	110.67	320	94.01	384
4,000	347.96	176	180.91	342	147.56	427	125.35	513
5,000	434.95	219	226.14	427	184.45	534	156.69	641
6,000	521.94	263	271.37	513	221.33	640	188.02	769
7,000	608.92	307	316.60	598	258.22	747	219.36	897
8,000	695.91	351	361.82	684	295.11	853	250.70	1,025
9,000	782.90	395	407.05	769	332.00	960	282.03	1,153
10,000	869.89	439	452.28	855	368.89	1,067	313.37	1,281
11,000	956.88	483	497.51	940	405.78	1,173	344.71	1,410
12,000	1,043.87	526	542.73	1,026	442.66	1,280	376.04	1,537
13,000	1,130.85	570	587.96	1,111	479.55	1,387	407.38	1,666
14,000	1,217.84	614	633.19	1,197	516.44	1,493	438.71	1,794
15,000	1,304.83	658	678.41	1,282	553.33	1,600	470.05	1,922
16,000	1,391.82	702	723.64	1,367	590.22	1,707	501.39	2,050
17,000	1,478.81	746	768.87	1,453	627.11	1,813	532.72	2,178
18,000	1,565.80	790	814.10	1,538	663.99	1,920	564.06	2,306
19,000	1,652.79	833	859.32	1,624	700.88	2,026	595.40	2,434
20,000	1,739.77	877	904.55	1,709	737.77	2,133	626.73	2,562
21,000	1,826.76	921	949.78	1,795	774.66	2,240	658.07	2,691
22,000	1,913.75	965	995.01	1,880	811.55	2,347	689.41	2,819
23,000	2,000.74	1,009	1,040.23	1,966	848.44	2,453	720.74	2,947
24,000	2,087.73	1,053	1,085.46	2,051	885.32	2,560	752.08	3,075
25,000	2,174.72	1,097	1,130.69	2,137	922.21	2,666	783.41	3,203
26,000	2,261.70	1,140	1,175.91	2,222	959.10	2,773	814.75	3,331
27,000	2,348.69	1,184	1,221.14	2,307	995.99	2,880	846.09	3,459
28,000	2,435.68	1,228	1,266.37	2,393	1,032.88	2,986	877.42	3,587
29,000	2,522.67	1,272	1,311.60	2,478	1,069.77	3,093	908.76	3,715
30,000	2,609.66	1,316	1,356.82	2,564	1,106.65	3,200	940.10	3,844
31,000	2,696.65	1,360	1,402.05	2,649	1,143.54	3,306	971.43	3,971
32,000	2,783.63	1,404	1,447.28	2,735	1,180.43	3,413	1,002.77	4,100
33,000	2,870.62	1,447	1,492.51	2,820	1,217.32	3,520	1,034.11	4,228
34,000	2,957.61	1,491	1,537.73	2,906	1,254.21	3,626	1,065.44	4,356
35,000	3,044.60	1,535	1,582.96	2,991	1,291.10	3,733	1,096.78	4,484
36,000	3,131.59	1,579	1,628.19	3,077	1,327.98	3,839	1,128.11	4,612
37,000	3,218.58	1,623	1,673.41	3,162	1,364.87	3,946	1,159.45	4,740
38,000	3,305.57	1,667	1,718.64	3,247	1,401.76	4,053	1,190.79	4,868
39,000	3,392.55	1,711	1,763.87	3,333	1,438.65	4,160	1,222.12	4,996
40,000	3,479.54	1,754	1,809.10	3,418	1,475.54	4,266	1,253.46	5,125
42,000	3,653.52	1,842	1,899.55	3,589	1,549.31	4,479	1,316.13	5,381
44,000	3,827.50	1,930	1,990.01	3,760	1,623.09	4,693	1,378.81	5,637
46,000	4,001.47	2,018	2,080.46	3,931	1,696.87	4,906	1,441.48	5,893
48,000	4,175.45	2,105	2,170.91	4,102	1,770.64	5,119	1,504.15	6,149
50,000	4,349.43	2,193	2,261.37	4,273	1,844.42	5,333	1,566.82	6,406

AMOUNT OF LOAN	42 MOS		48 MOS		60 MOS		72 MOS	
	MONTHLY PAYMENT	TOTAL INTRST	MONTHLY PAYMENT	TOTAL INTRST	MONTHLY PAYMENT	TOTAL INTRST	MONTHLY PAYMENT	TOTAL INTRST
$ 1	0.03	0	0.03	0	0.03	1	0.02	0
2	0.06	1	0.05	0	0.05	1	0.04	1
3	0.09	1	0.08	1	0.07	1	0.06	1
4	0.11	1	0.10	1	0.09	1	0.08	2
5	0.14	1	0.13	1	0.11	2	0.09	1
6	0.17	1	0.15	1	0.13	2	0.11	2
7	0.20	1	0.18	1	0.15	2	0.13	2
8	0.22	1	0.20	2	0.17	2	0.15	3
9	0.25	2	0.22	2	0.19	2	0.16	3
10	0.28	2	0.25	2	0.21	3	0.18	3
20	0.55	3	0.49	4	0.41	5	0.36	6
30	0.83	5	0.74	6	0.61	7	0.53	8
40	1.10	6	0.98	7	0.82	9	0.71	11
50	1.37	8	1.23	9	1.02	11	0.88	13
60	1.65	9	1.47	11	1.22	13	1.06	16
70	1.92	11	1.71	12	1.42	15	1.23	19
80	2.20	12	1.96	14	1.63	18	1.41	22
90	2.47	14	2.20	16	1.83	20	1.58	24
100	2.74	15	2.45	18	2.03	22	1.76	27
200	5.48	30	4.89	35	4.06	44	3.51	53
300	8.22	45	7.33	52	6.09	65	5.26	79
400	10.96	60	9.77	69	8.12	87	7.02	105
500	13.69	75	12.21	66	10.14	108	8.77	131
600	16.43	90	14.65	103	12.17	130	10.52	157
700	19.17	105	17.09	120	14.20	152	12.28	184
800	21.91	120	19.54	138	16.23	174	14.03	210
900	24.64	135	21.98	155	18.25	195	15.78	236
1,000	27.38	150	24.42	172	20.28	217	17.54	263
2,000	54.76	300	48.83	344	40.56	434	35.07	525
3,000	82.14	450	73.24	516	60.83	650	52.60	787
4,000	109.51	599	97.66	688	81.11	867	70.14	1,050
5,000	136.89	749	122.07	859	101.39	1,083	87.67	1,312
6,000	164.27	899	146.48	1,031	121.66	1,300	105.20	1,574
7,000	191.64	1,049	170.90	1,203	141.94	1,516	122.74	1,837
8,000	219.02	1,199	195.31	1,375	162.22	1,733	140.27	2,099
9,000	246.40	1,349	219.72	1,547	182.49	1,949	157.80	2,362
10,000	273.77	1,498	244.13	1,718	202.77	2,166	175.34	2,624
11,000	301.15	1,648	268.55	1,890	223.05	2,383	192.87	2,887
12,000	328.53	1,798	292.96	2,062	243.32	2,599	210.40	3,149
13,000	355.91	1,948	317.37	2,234	263.60	2,816	227.94	3,412
14,000	383.28	2,098	341.79	2,406	283.87	3,032	245.47	3,674
15,000	410.66	2,248	366.20	2,578	304.15	3,249	263.00	3,936
16,000	438.04	2,398	390.61	2,749	324.43	3,466	280.54	4,199
17,000	465.41	2,547	415.02	2,921	344.70	3,682	298.07	4,461
18,000	492.79	2,697	439.44	3,093	364.98	3,899	315.60	4,723
19,000	520.17	2,847	463.85	3,265	385.26	4,116	333.14	4,986
20,000	547.54	2,997	488.26	3,436	405.53	4,332	350.67	5,248
21,000	574.92	3,147	512.68	3,609	425.81	4,549	368.20	5,510
22,000	602.30	3,297	537.09	3,780	446.09	4,765	385.74	5,773
23,000	629.68	3,447	561.50	3,952	466.36	4,982	403.27	6,035
24,000	657.05	3,596	585.92	4,124	486.64	5,198	420.80	6,298
25,000	684.43	3,746	610.33	4,296	506.91	5,415	438.34	6,560
26,000	711.81	3,896	634.74	4,468	527.19	5,631	455.87	6,823
27,000	739.18	4,046	659.16	4,639	547.47	5,848	473.40	7,085
28,000	766.56	4,196	683.57	4,811	567.74	6,064	490.94	7,348
29,000	793.94	4,345	707.98	4,983	588.02	6,281	508.47	7,610
30,000	821.31	4,495	732.39	5,155	608.30	6,498	526.00	7,872
31,000	848.69	4,645	756.81	5,327	628.57	6,714	543.54	8,135
32,000	876.07	4,795	781.22	5,499	648.85	6,931	561.07	8,397
33,000	903.45	4,945	805.63	5,670	669.13	7,148	578.60	8,659
34,000	930.82	5,094	830.04	5,842	689.40	7,364	596.14	8,922
35,000	958.20	5,244	854.46	6,014	709.68	7,581	613.67	9,184
36,000	985.58	5,394	878.87	6,186	729.96	7,798	631.20	9,446
37,000	1,012.95	5,544	903.28	6,357	750.23	8,014	648.73	9,709
38,000	1,040.33	5,694	927.70	6,530	770.51	8,231	666.27	9,971
39,000	1,067.71	5,844	952.11	6,701	790.78	8,447	683.80	10,234
40,000	1,095.08	5,993	976.52	6,873	811.06	8,664	701.33	10,496
42,000	1,149.84	6,293	1,025.35	7,217	851.61	9,097	736.40	11,021
44,000	1,204.59	6,593	1,074.17	7,560	892.17	9,530	771.47	11,546
46,000	1,259.35	6,893	1,123.00	7,904	932.72	9,963	806.53	12,070
48,000	1,314.10	7,192	1,171.83	8,248	973.27	10,396	841.60	12,595
50,000	1,368.85	7,492	1,220.65	8,591	1,013.82	10,829	876.67	13,120

AUTO LOAN PAYMENTS

AMOUNT OF LOAN	12 MOS		24 MOS		30 MOS		36 MOS	
	MONTHLY PAYMENT	TOTAL INTRST	MONTHLY PAYMENT	TOTAL INTRST	MONTHLY PAYMENT	TOTAL INTRST	MONTHLY PAYMENT	TOTAL INTRST
$ 1	0.09	0	0.05	0	0.04	0	0.04	0
2	0.18	0	0.10	0	0.08	0	0.07	1
3	0.27	0	0.14	0	0.12	1	0.10	1
4	0.35	0	0.19	1	0.15	1	0.13	1
5	0.44	0	0.23	1	0.19	1	0.16	1
6	0.53	0	0.28	1	0.23	1	0.19	1
7	0.61	0	0.32	1	0.26	1	0.23	1
8	0.70	0	0.37	1	0.30	1	0.26	1
9	0.79	0	0.41	1	0.34	1	0.29	1
10	0.88	1	0.46	1	0.38	1	0.32	2
20	1.75	1	0.91	2	0.75	3	0.63	3
30	2.62	1	1.37	3	1.12	4	0.95	4
40	3.49	2	1.82	4	1.49	5	1.26	5
50	4.36	2	2.27	4	1.86	6	1.58	7
60	5.23	3	2.73	6	2.23	7	1.89	8
70	6.10	3	3.18	6	2.60	8	2.21	10
80	6.97	4	3.63	7	2.97	9	2.52	11
90	7.84	4	4.09	8	3.34	10	2.84	12
100	8.72	5	4.54	9	3.71	11	3.15	13
200	17.43	9	9.07	18	7.41	22	6.30	27
300	26.14	14	13.61	27	11.11	33	9.44	40
400	34.85	18	18.14	35	14.81	44	12.59	53
500	43.56	23	22.68	44	18.51	55	15.73	66
600	52.27	27	27.21	53	22.21	66	18.88	80
700	60.98	32	31.74	62	25.91	77	22.02	93
800	69.69	36	36.28	71	29.61	88	25.17	106
900	78.40	41	40.81	79	33.31	99	28.31	119
1,000	87.11	45	45.35	88	37.01	110	31.46	133
2,000	174.21	91	90.69	177	74.01	220	62.91	265
3,000	261.32	136	136.03	265	111.01	330	94.36	397
4,000	348.42	181	181.37	353	148.02	441	125.81	529
5,000	435.53	226	226.71	441	185.02	551	157.26	661
6,000	522.63	272	272.05	529	222.02	661	188.72	794
7,000	609.73	317	317.39	617	259.03	771	220.17	926
8,000	696.84	362	362.74	706	296.03	881	251.62	1,058
9,000	783.94	407	408.08	794	333.03	991	283.07	1,191
10,000	871.05	453	453.42	882	370.03	1,101	314.52	1,323
11,000	958.15	498	498.76	970	407.04	1,211	345.98	1,455
12,000	1,045.25	543	544.10	1,058	444.04	1,321	377.43	1,587
13,000	1,132.36	588	589.44	1,147	481.04	1,431	408.88	1,720
14,000	1,219.46	634	634.78	1,235	518.05	1,542	440.33	1,852
15,000	1,306.57	679	680.13	1,323	555.05	1,652	471.78	1,984
16,000	1,393.67	724	725.47	1,411	592.05	1,762	503.23	2,116
17,000	1,480.77	769	770.81	1,499	629.06	1,872	534.69	2,249
18,000	1,567.88	815	816.15	1,588	666.06	1,982	566.14	2,381
19,000	1,654.98	860	861.49	1,676	703.06	2,092	597.59	2,513
20,000	1,742.09	905	906.83	1,764	740.06	2,202	629.04	2,645
21,000	1,829.19	950	952.17	1,852	777.07	2,312	660.49	2,778
22,000	1,916.29	995	997.52	1,940	814.07	2,422	691.95	2,910
23,000	2,003.40	1,041	1,042.86	2,029	851.07	2,532	723.40	3,042
24,000	2,090.50	1,086	1,088.20	2,117	888.08	2,642	754.85	3,175
25,000	2,177.61	1,131	1,133.54	2,205	925.08	2,752	786.30	3,307
26,000	2,264.71	1,177	1,178.88	2,293	962.08	2,862	817.75	3,439
27,000	2,351.81	1,222	1,224.22	2,381	999.08	2,972	849.20	3,571
28,000	2,438.92	1,267	1,269.56	2,469	1,036.09	3,083	880.66	3,704
29,000	2,526.02	1,312	1,314.91	2,558	1,073.09	3,193	912.11	3,836
30,000	2,613.13	1,358	1,360.25	2,646	1,110.09	3,303	943.56	3,968
31,000	2,700.23	1,403	1,405.59	2,734	1,147.10	3,413	975.01	4,100
32,000	2,787.34	1,448	1,450.93	2,822	1,184.10	3,523	1,006.46	4,233
33,000	2,874.44	1,493	1,496.27	2,910	1,221.10	3,633	1,037.92	4,365
34,000	2,961.54	1,538	1,541.61	2,999	1,258.11	3,743	1,069.37	4,497
35,000	3,048.65	1,584	1,586.95	3,087	1,295.11	3,853	1,100.82	4,630
36,000	3,135.75	1,629	1,632.30	3,175	1,332.11	3,963	1,132.27	4,762
37,000	3,222.86	1,674	1,677.64	3,263	1,369.11	4,073	1,163.72	4,894
38,000	3,309.96	1,720	1,722.98	3,352	1,406.12	4,184	1,195.17	5,026
39,000	3,397.06	1,765	1,768.32	3,440	1,443.12	4,294	1,226.63	5,159
40,000	3,484.17	1,810	1,813.66	3,528	1,480.12	4,404	1,258.08	5,291
42,000	3,658.38	1,901	1,904.34	3,704	1,554.13	4,624	1,320.98	5,555
44,000	3,832.58	1,991	1,995.03	3,881	1,628.14	4,844	1,383.89	5,820
46,000	4,006.79	2,081	2,085.71	4,057	1,702.14	5,064	1,446.79	6,084
48,000	4,181.00	2,172	2,176.39	4,233	1,776.15	5,285	1,509.69	6,349
50,000	4,355.21	2,263	2,267.07	4,410	1,850.15	5,505	1,572.60	6,614

AMOUNT OF LOAN	42 MOS		48 MOS		60 MOS		72 MOS	
	MONTHLY PAYMENT	TOTAL INTRST	MONTHLY PAYMENT	TOTAL INTRST	MONTHLY PAYMENT	TOTAL INTRST	MONTHLY PAYMENT	TOTAL INTRST
$ 1	0.03	0	0.03	0	0.03	1	0.02	0
2	0.06	1	0.05	0	0.05	1	0.04	1
3	0.09	1	0.08	1	0.07	1	0.06	1
4	0.11	1	0.10	1	0.09	1	0.08	2
5	0.14	1	0.13	1	0.11	2	0.09	1
6	0.17	1	0.15	1	0.13	2	0.11	2
7	0.20	1	0.18	2	0.15	2	0.13	2
8	0.22	1	0.20	2	0.17	2	0.15	3
9	0.25	2	0.23	2	0.19	2	0.16	3
10	0.28	2	0.25	2	0.21	3	0.18	3
20	0.55	3	0.50	4	0.41	5	0.36	6
30	0.83	5	0.74	6	0.62	7	0.53	8
40	1.10	6	0.99	8	0.82	9	0.71	11
50	1.38	8	1.23	9	1.02	11	0.89	14
60	1.65	9	1.48	11	1.23	14	1.06	16
70	1.93	11	1.72	13	1.43	16	1.24	19
80	2.20	12	1.97	15	1.64	18	1.42	22
90	2.48	14	2.21	16	1.84	20	1.59	24
100	2.75	16	2.46	18	2.04	22	1.77	27
200	5.50	31	4.91	36	4.08	45	3.54	55
300	8.25	47	7.36	53	6.12	67	5.30	82
400	11.00	62	9.82	71	8.16	90	7.07	109
500	13.75	78	12.27	89	10.20	112	8.83	136
600	16.50	93	14.72	107	12.24	134	10.60	163
700	19.25	109	17.18	125	14.28	157	12.36	190
800	22.00	124	19.63	142	16.32	179	14.13	217
900	24.75	140	22.08	160	18.36	202	15.90	245
1,000	27.50	155	24.54	178	20.40	224	17.66	272
2,000	54.99	310	49.07	355	40.80	448	35.32	543
3,000	82.49	465	73.60	533	61.19	671	52.97	814
4,000	109.98	619	98.13	710	81.59	895	70.63	1,085
5,000	137.47	774	122.66	888	101.99	1,119	88.28	1,356
6,000	164.97	929	147.19	1,065	122.38	1,343	105.94	1,628
7,000	192.46	1,083	171.72	1,243	142.78	1,567	123.59	1,898
8,000	219.95	1,238	196.25	1,420	163.18	1,791	141.25	2,170
9,000	247.45	1,393	220.78	1,597	183.57	2,014	158.91	2,442
10,000	274.94	1,547	245.31	1,775	203.97	2,238	176.56	2,712
11,000	302.43	1,702	269.84	1,952	224.36	2,462	194.22	2,984
12,000	329.93	1,857	294.37	2,130	244.76	2,686	211.87	3,255
13,000	357.42	2,012	318.90	2,307	265.16	2,910	229.53	3,526
14,000	384.91	2,166	343.43	2,485	285.55	3,133	247.18	3,797
15,000	412.41	2,321	367.96	2,662	305.95	3,357	264.84	4,068
16,000	439.90	2,476	392.49	2,840	326.35	3,581	282.49	4,339
17,000	467.39	2,630	417.02	3,017	346.74	3,804	300.15	4,611
18,000	494.89	2,785	441.55	3,194	367.14	4,028	317.81	4,882
19,000	522.38	2,940	466.08	3,372	387.53	4,252	335.46	5,153
20,000	549.87	3,095	490.61	3,549	407.93	4,476	353.12	5,425
21,000	577.37	3,250	515.14	3,727	428.33	4,700	370.77	5,695
22,000	604.86	3,404	539.67	3,904	448.72	4,923	388.43	5,967
23,000	632.35	3,559	564.21	4,082	469.12	5,147	406.08	6,238
24,000	659.85	3,714	588.74	4,260	489.52	5,371	423.74	6,509
25,000	687.34	3,868	613.27	4,437	509.91	5,595	441.39	6,780
26,000	714.83	4,023	637.80	4,614	530.31	5,819	459.05	7,052
27,000	742.33	4,178	662.33	4,792	550.70	6,042	476.71	7,323
28,000	769.82	4,332	686.86	4,969	571.10	6,266	494.36	7,594
29,000	797.31	4,487	711.39	5,147	591.50	6,490	512.02	7,865
30,000	824.81	4,642	735.92	5,324	611.89	6,713	529.67	8,136
31,000	852.30	4,797	760.45	5,502	632.29	6,937	547.33	8,408
32,000	879.79	4,951	784.98	5,679	652.69	7,161	564.98	8,679
33,000	907.29	5,106	809.51	5,856	673.08	7,385	582.64	8,950
34,000	934.78	5,261	834.04	6,034	693.48	7,609	600.29	9,221
35,000	962.27	5,415	858.57	6,211	713.87	7,832	617.95	9,492
36,000	989.77	5,570	883.10	6,389	734.27	8,056	635.61	9,764
37,000	1,017.26	5,725	907.63	6,566	754.67	8,280	653.26	10,035
38,000	1,044.75	5,880	932.16	6,744	775.06	8,504	670.92	10,306
39,000	1,072.25	6,035	956.69	6,921	795.46	8,728	688.57	10,577
40,000	1,099.74	6,189	981.22	7,099	815.86	8,952	706.23	10,849
42,000	1,154.73	6,499	1,030.28	7,453	856.65	9,399	741.54	11,391
44,000	1,209.72	6,808	1,079.34	7,808	897.44	9,846	776.85	11,933
46,000	1,264.70	7,117	1,128.41	8,164	938.23	10,294	812.16	12,476
48,000	1,319.69	7,427	1,177.47	8,519	979.03	10,742	847.47	13,018
50,000	1,374.68	7,737	1,226.53	8,873	1,019.82	11,189	882.78	13,560

8.50%   AUTO LOAN PAYMENTS

AMOUNT OF LOAN	12 MOS MONTHLY PAYMENT	12 MOS TOTAL INTRST	24 MOS MONTHLY PAYMENT	24 MOS TOTAL INTRST	30 MOS MONTHLY PAYMENT	30 MOS TOTAL INTRST	36 MOS MONTHLY PAYMENT	36 MOS TOTAL INTRST
$ 1	0.09	0	0.05	0	0.04	0	0.04	
2	0.18	0	0.10	0	0.08	0	0.07	
3	0.27	0	0.14	0	0.12	1	0.10	
4	0.35	0	0.19	1	0.15	1	0.13	
5	0.44	0	0.23	1	0.19	1	0.16	
6	0.53	0	0.28	1	0.23	1	0.19	
7	0.62	0	0.32	1	0.26	1	0.23	
8	0.70	0	0.37	1	0.30	1	0.26	
9	0.79	0	0.41	1	0.34	1	0.29	
10	0.88	1	0.46	1	0.38	1	0.32	
20	1.75	1	0.91	2	0.75	3	0.64	
30	2.62	1	1.37	3	1.12	4	0.95	
40	3.49	2	1.82	4	1.49	5	1.27	
50	4.37	2	2.28	5	1.86	6	1.58	
60	5.24	3	2.73	6	2.23	7	1.90	
70	6.11	3	3.19	7	2.60	8	2.21	
80	6.98	4	3.64	7	2.97		2.53	
90	7.85	4	4.10	8	3.35	11	2.85	
100	8.73	5	4.55	9	3.72	12	3.16	
200	17.45	9	9.10	18	7.43	23	6.32	
300	26.17	14	13.64	27	11.14	34	9.48	
400	34.89	19	18.19	37	14.85	46	12.63	
500	43.61	23	22.73	46	18.56	57	15.79	
600	52.34	28	27.28	55	22.28	68	18.95	
700	61.06	33	31.82	64	25.99	80	22.10	10
800	69.78	37	36.37	73	29.70	91	25.26	10
900	78.50	42	40.92	82	33.41	102	28.42	12
1,000	87.22	47	45.46	91	37.12	114	31.57	13
2,000	174.44	93	90.92	182	74.24	227	63.14	27
3,000	261.66	140	136.37	273	111.36	341	94.71	41
4,000	348.88	187	181.83	364	148.48	454	126.28	54
5,000	436.10	233	227.28	455	185.59	568	157.84	68
6,000	523.32	280	272.74	546	222.71	681	189.41	81
7,000	610.54	326	318.19	637	259.83	795	220.98	95
8,000	697.76	373	363.65	728	296.95	909	252.55	1,09
9,000	784.98	420	409.11	819	334.07	1,022	284.11	1,22
10,000	872.20	466	454.56	909	371.18	1,135	315.68	1,36
11,000	959.42	513	500.02	1,000	408.30	1,249	347.25	1,50
12,000	1,046.64	560	545.47	1,091	445.42	1,363	378.82	1,63
13,000	1,133.86	606	590.93	1,182	482.54	1,476	410.38	1,77
14,000	1,221.08	653	636.38	1,273	519.65	1,590	441.95	1,91
15,000	1,308.30	700	681.84	1,364	556.77	1,703	473.52	2,04
16,000	1,395.52	746	727.30	1,455	593.89	1,817	505.09	2,18
17,000	1,482.74	793	772.75	1,546	631.01	1,930	536.65	2,31
18,000	1,569.96	840	818.21	1,637	668.13	2,044	568.22	2,45
19,000	1,657.18	886	863.66	1,728	705.24	2,157	599.79	2,59
20,000	1,744.40	933	909.12	1,819	742.36	2,271	631.36	2,72
21,000	1,831.62	979	954.57	1,910	779.48	2,384	662.92	2,86
22,000	1,918.84	1,026	1,000.03	2,001	816.60	2,498	694.49	3,00
23,000	2,006.06	1,073	1,045.49	2,092	853.71	2,611	726.06	3,13
24,000	2,093.28	1,119	1,090.94	2,183	890.83	2,725	757.63	3,27
25,000	2,180.50	1,166	1,136.40	2,274	927.95	2,839	789.19	3,41
26,000	2,267.72	1,213	1,181.85	2,364	965.07	2,952	820.76	3,54
27,000	2,354.94	1,259	1,227.31	2,455	1,002.19	3,066	852.33	3,68
28,000	2,442.16	1,306	1,272.76	2,546	1,039.30	3,179	883.90	3,82
29,000	2,529.38	1,353	1,318.22	2,637	1,076.42	3,293	915.46	3,95
30,000	2,616.60	1,399	1,363.68	2,728	1,113.54	3,406	947.03	4,09
31,000	2,703.82	1,446	1,409.13	2,819	1,150.66	3,520	978.60	4,23
32,000	2,791.04	1,492	1,454.59	2,910	1,187.78	3,633	1,010.17	4,36
33,000	2,878.26	1,539	1,500.04	3,001	1,224.89	3,747	1,041.73	4,50
34,000	2,965.48	1,586	1,545.50	3,092	1,262.01	3,860	1,073.30	4,63
35,000	3,052.70	1,632	1,590.95	3,183	1,299.13	3,974	1,104.87	4,71
36,000	3,139.92	1,679	1,636.41	3,274	1,336.25	4,088	1,136.44	4,91
37,000	3,227.14	1,726	1,681.86	3,365	1,373.36	4,201	1,168.00	5,04
38,000	3,314.36	1,772	1,727.32	3,456	1,410.48	4,314	1,199.57	5,18
39,000	3,401.58	1,819	1,772.78	3,547	1,447.60	4,428	1,231.14	5,32
40,000	3,488.80	1,866	1,818.23	3,638	1,484.72	4,542	1,262.71	5,45
42,000	3,663.24	1,959	1,909.14	3,819	1,558.95	4,769	1,325.84	5,73
44,000	3,837.68	2,052	2,000.05	4,001	1,633.19	4,996	1,388.98	6,00
46,000	4,012.11	2,145	2,090.97	4,183	1,707.42	5,223	1,452.11	6,27
48,000	4,186.55	2,239	2,181.88	4,365	1,781.66	5,450	1,515.25	6,54
50,000	4,360.99	2,332	2,272.79	4,547	1,855.90	5,677	1,578.38	6,82

AUTO LOAN PAYMENTS 8.50%

AMOUNT OF LOAN	42 MOS		48 MOS		60 MOS		72 MOS	
	MONTHLY PAYMENT	TOTAL INTRST	MONTHLY PAYMENT	TOTAL INTRST	MONTHLY PAYMENT	TOTAL INTRST	MONTHLY PAYMENT	TOTAL INTRST
$ 1	0.03	0	0.03	0	0.03	1	0.02	0
2	0.06	1	0.05	0	0.05	1	0.04	1
3	0.09	1	0.08	1	0.07	1	0.06	1
4	0.12	1	0.10	1	0.09	1	0.08	2
5	0.14	1	0.13	1	0.11	1	0.09	1
6	0.17	1	0.15	1	0.13	2	0.11	2
7	0.20	1	0.18	1	0.15	2	0.13	2
8	0.23	2	0.20	2	0.17	2	0.15	3
9	0.25	2	0.23	2	0.19	2	0.17	3
10	0.28	2	0.25	2	0.21	3	0.18	3
20	0.56	4	0.50	4	0.42	5	0.36	6
30	0.83	5	0.74	6	0.62	7	0.54	9
40	1.11	7	0.99	8	0.83	10	0.72	12
50	1.39	8	1.24	10	1.03	12	0.89	14
60	1.66	10	1.48	11	1.24	14	1.07	17
70	1.94	11	1.73	13	1.44	16	1.25	20
80	2.21	13	1.98	15	1.65	19	1.43	23
90	2.49	15	2.22	17	1.85	21	1.61	26
100	2.77	16	2.47	19	2.06	24	1.78	28
200	5.53	32	4.93	37	4.11	47	3.56	56
300	8.29	48	7.40	55	6.16	70	5.34	84
400	11.05	64	9.86	73	8.21	93	7.12	113
500	13.81	80	12.33	92	10.26	116	8.89	140
600	16.57	96	14.79	110	12.31	139	10.67	168
700	19.33	112	17.26	128	14.37	162	12.45	196
800	22.09	128	19.72	147	16.42	185	14.23	225
900	24.85	144	22.19	165	18.47	208	16.01	253
1,000	27.62	160	24.65	183	20.52	231	17.78	280
2,000	55.23	320	49.30	366	41.04	462	35.56	560
3,000	82.84	479	73.95	550	61.55	693	53.34	840
4,000	110.45	639	98.60	733	82.07	924	71.12	1,121
5,000	138.06	799	123.25	916	102.59	1,155	88.90	1,401
6,000	165.67	958	147.89	1,099	123.10	1,386	106.68	1,681
7,000	193.28	1,118	172.54	1,282	143.62	1,617	124.45	1,960
8,000	220.89	1,277	197.19	1,465	164.14	1,848	142.23	2,241
9,000	248.50	1,437	221.84	1,648	184.65	2,079	160.01	2,521
10,000	276.11	1,597	246.49	1,832	205.17	2,310	177.79	2,801
11,000	303.72	1,756	271.14	2,015	225.69	2,541	195.57	3,081
12,000	331.33	1,916	295.78	2,197	246.20	2,772	213.35	3,361
13,000	358.94	2,075	320.43	2,381	266.72	3,003	231.12	3,641
14,000	386.55	2,235	345.08	2,564	287.24	3,234	248.90	3,921
15,000	414.16	2,395	369.73	2,747	307.75	3,465	266.68	4,201
16,000	441.77	2,554	394.38	2,930	328.27	3,696	284.46	4,481
17,000	469.38	2,714	419.03	3,113	348.79	3,927	302.24	4,761
18,000	496.99	2,874	443.67	3,296	369.30	4,158	320.02	5,041
19,000	524.60	3,033	468.32	3,479	389.82	4,389	337.79	5,321
20,000	552.21	3,193	492.97	3,663	410.34	4,620	355.57	5,601
21,000	579.82	3,352	517.62	3,846	430.85	4,851	373.35	5,881
22,000	607.43	3,512	542.27	4,029	451.37	5,082	391.13	6,161
23,000	635.04	3,672	566.92	4,212	471.89	5,313	408.91	6,442
24,000	662.65	3,831	591.56	4,395	492.40	5,544	426.69	6,722
25,000	690.26	3,991	616.21	4,578	512.92	5,775	444.46	7,001
26,000	717.87	4,151	640.86	4,761	533.43	6,006	462.24	7,281
27,000	745.48	4,310	665.51	4,944	553.95	6,237	480.02	7,561
28,000	773.09	4,470	690.16	5,128	574.47	6,468	497.80	7,842
29,000	800.70	4,629	714.81	5,311	594.98	6,699	515.58	8,122
30,000	828.31	4,789	739.45	5,494	615.50	6,930	533.36	8,402
31,000	855.92	4,949	764.10	5,677	636.02	7,161	551.13	8,681
32,000	883.53	5,108	788.75	5,860	656.53	7,392	568.91	8,962
33,000	911.14	5,268	813.40	6,043	677.05	7,623	586.69	9,242
34,000	938.75	5,428	838.05	6,226	697.57	7,854	604.47	9,522
35,000	966.36	5,587	862.70	6,410	718.08	8,085	622.25	9,802
36,000	993.97	5,747	887.34	6,592	738.60	8,316	640.03	10,082
37,000	1,021.58	5,906	911.99	6,776	759.12	8,547	657.81	10,362
38,000	1,049.19	6,066	936.64	6,959	779.63	8,778	675.58	10,642
39,000	1,076.80	6,226	961.29	7,142	800.15	9,009	693.36	10,922
40,000	1,104.41	6,385	985.94	7,325	820.67	9,240	711.14	11,202
42,000	1,159.63	6,704	1,035.23	7,691	861.70	9,702	746.70	11,762
44,000	1,214.85	7,024	1,084.53	8,057	902.73	10,164	782.25	12,322
46,000	1,270.07	7,343	1,133.83	8,424	943.77	10,626	817.81	12,882
48,000	1,325.29	7,662	1,183.12	8,790	984.80	11,088	853.37	13,443
50,000	1,380.51	7,981	1,232.42	9,156	1,025.83	11,550	888.92	14,002

AUTO LOAN PAYMENTS

AMOUNT OF LOAN	12 MOS		24 MOS		30 MOS		36 MOS	
	MONTHLY PAYMENT	TOTAL INTRST	MONTHLY PAYMENT	TOTAL INTRST	MONTHLY PAYMENT	TOTAL INTRST	MONTHLY PAYMENT	TOTAL INTRST
$ 1	0.09	0	0.05	0	0.04	0	0.04	0
2	0.18	0	0.10	0	0.08	0	0.07	1
3	0.27	0	0.14	0	0.12	1	0.10	1
4	0.35	0	0.19	1	0.15	1	0.13	1
5	0.44	0	0.23	1	0.19	1	0.16	1
6	0.53	0	0.28	1	0.23	1	0.20	1
7	0.62	0	0.32	1	0.27	1	0.23	1
8	0.70	0	0.37	1	0.30	1	0.26	1
9	0.79	0	0.42	1	0.34	1	0.29	1
10	0.88	1	0.46	1	0.38	1	0.32	2
20	1.75	1	0.92	2	0.75	3	0.64	3
30	2.63	2	1.37	3	1.12	4	0.96	5
40	3.50	2	1.83	4	1.49	5	1.27	6
50	4.37	2	2.28	5	1.87	6	1.59	7
60	5.25	3	2.74	6	2.24	7	1.91	9
70	6.12	3	3.19	7	2.61	8	2.22	10
80	6.99	4	3.65	8	2.98	9	2.54	11
90	7.87	4	4.11	9	3.36	11	2.86	13
100	8.74	4	4.56	9	3.73	12	3.17	14
200	17.47	10	9.12	19	7.45	24	6.34	28
300	26.21	15	13.68	28	11.17	35	9.51	42
400	34.94	19	18.23	38	14.90	47	12.68	56
500	43.67	24	22.79	47	18.62	59	15.85	71
600	52.41	29	27.35	56	22.34	70	19.02	85
700	61.14	34	31.90	66	26.07	82	22.18	98
800	69.87	38	36.46	75	29.79	94	25.35	113
900	78.61	43	41.02	84	33.51	105	28.52	127
1,000	87.34	48	45.58	94	37.24	117	31.69	141
2,000	174.68	96	91.15	188	74.47	234	63.37	281
3,000	262.01	144	136.72	281	111.70	351	95.06	422
4,000	349.35	192	182.29	375	148.94	468	126.74	563
5,000	436.68	240	227.86	469	186.17	585	158.42	703
6,000	524.02	288	273.43	562	223.40	702	190.11	844
7,000	611.35	336	319.00	656	260.64	819	221.79	984
8,000	698.69	384	364.57	750	297.87	936	253.47	1,125
9,000	786.03	432	410.14	843	335.10	1,053	285.16	1,266
10,000	873.36	480	455.71	937	372.33	1,170	316.84	1,406
11,000	960.70	528	501.28	1,031	409.57	1,287	348.52	1,547
12,000	1,048.03	576	546.85	1,124	446.80	1,404	380.21	1,688
13,000	1,135.37	624	592.42	1,218	484.03	1,521	411.89	1,828
14,000	1,222.70	672	637.99	1,312	521.27	1,638	443.57	1,969
15,000	1,310.04	720	683.56	1,405	558.50	1,755	475.26	2,109
16,000	1,397.37	768	729.13	1,499	595.73	1,872	506.94	2,250
17,000	1,484.71	817	774.70	1,593	632.96	1,989	538.62	2,390
18,000	1,572.05	865	820.27	1,686	670.20	2,106	570.31	2,531
19,000	1,659.38	913	865.84	1,780	707.43	2,223	601.99	2,672
20,000	1,746.72	961	911.41	1,874	744.66	2,340	633.68	2,812
21,000	1,834.05	1,009	956.98	1,968	781.90	2,457	665.36	2,953
22,000	1,921.39	1,057	1,002.55	2,061	819.13	2,574	697.04	3,093
23,000	2,008.72	1,105	1,048.12	2,155	856.36	2,691	728.73	3,234
24,000	2,096.06	1,153	1,093.69	2,249	893.59	2,808	760.41	3,375
25,000	2,183.39	1,201	1,139.26	2,342	930.83	2,925	792.09	3,515
26,000	2,270.73	1,249	1,184.83	2,436	968.06	3,042	823.78	3,656
27,000	2,358.07	1,297	1,230.40	2,530	1,005.29	3,159	855.46	3,797
28,000	2,445.40	1,345	1,275.97	2,623	1,042.53	3,276	887.14	3,937
29,000	2,532.74	1,393	1,321.54	2,717	1,079.76	3,393	918.83	4,078
30,000	2,620.07	1,441	1,367.11	2,811	1,116.99	3,510	950.51	4,218
31,000	2,707.41	1,489	1,412.68	2,904	1,154.22	3,627	982.19	4,359
32,000	2,794.74	1,537	1,458.25	2,998	1,191.46	3,744	1,013.88	4,500
33,000	2,882.08	1,585	1,503.82	3,092	1,228.69	3,861	1,045.56	4,640
34,000	2,969.41	1,633	1,549.39	3,185	1,265.92	3,978	1,077.24	4,781
35,000	3,056.75	1,681	1,594.96	3,279	1,303.16	4,095	1,108.93	4,921
36,000	3,144.09	1,729	1,640.53	3,373	1,340.39	4,212	1,140.61	5,062
37,000	3,231.42	1,777	1,686.10	3,466	1,377.62	4,329	1,172.29	5,202
38,000	3,318.76	1,825	1,731.67	3,560	1,414.85	4,446	1,203.98	5,343
39,000	3,406.09	1,873	1,777.24	3,654	1,452.09	4,563	1,235.66	5,484
40,000	3,493.43	1,921	1,822.81	3,747	1,489.32	4,680	1,267.35	5,625
42,000	3,668.10	2,017	1,913.95	3,935	1,563.79	4,914	1,330.71	5,906
44,000	3,842.77	2,113	2,005.09	4,122	1,638.25	5,148	1,394.08	6,187
46,000	4,017.44	2,209	2,096.23	4,310	1,712.72	5,382	1,457.45	6,468
48,000	4,192.11	2,305	2,187.37	4,497	1,787.18	5,615	1,520.81	6,749
50,000	4,366.78	2,401	2,278.51	4,684	1,861.65	5,850	1,584.18	7,030

AUTO LOAN PAYMENTS 8.75%

AMOUNT OF LOAN	42 MOS MONTHLY PAYMENT	42 MOS TOTAL INTRST	48 MOS MONTHLY PAYMENT	48 MOS TOTAL INTRST	60 MOS MONTHLY PAYMENT	60 MOS TOTAL INTRST	72 MOS MONTHLY PAYMENT	72 MOS TOTAL INTRST
$ 1	0.03	0	0.03	0	0.03	1	0.02	0
2	0.06	1	0.05	1	0.05	1	0.04	1
3	0.09	1	0.08	1	0.07	1	0.06	1
4	0.12	1	0.10	1	0.09	1	0.08	2
5	0.14	1	0.13	1	0.11	2	0.09	1
6	0.17	1	0.15	1	0.13	2	0.11	2
7	0.20	1	0.18	1	0.15	2	0.13	2
8	0.23	2	0.20	2	0.17	2	0.15	3
9	0.25	2	0.23	2	0.19	2	0.17	3
10	0.28	2	0.25	2	0.21	3	0.18	3
20	0.56	4	0.50	4	0.42	5	0.36	6
30	0.84	5	0.75	6	0.62	7	0.54	9
40	1.11	7	1.00	8	0.83	10	0.72	12
50	1.39	8	1.24	10	1.04	12	0.90	15
60	1.67	10	1.49	12	1.24	14	1.08	18
70	1.95	12	1.74	14	1.45	17	1.26	21
80	2.22	13	1.99	16	1.66	20	1.44	24
90	2.50	15	2.23	17	1.86	22	1.62	27
100	2.78	17	2.48	19	2.07	24	1.80	30
200	5.55	33	4.96	38	4.13	48	3.59	58
300	8.32	49	7.43	57	6.20	72	5.38	87
400	11.10	66	9.91	76	8.26	96	7.17	116
500	13.87	83	12.39	95	10.32	119	8.96	145
600	16.64	99	14.86	113	12.39	143	10.75	174
700	19.41	115	17.34	132	14.45	167	12.54	203
800	22.19	132	19.82	151	16.51	191	14.33	232
900	24.96	148	22.29	170	18.58	215	16.12	261
1,000	27.73	165	24.77	189	20.64	238	17.91	290
2,000	55.46	329	49.54	378	41.28	477	35.81	578
3,000	83.19	494	74.30	566	61.92	715	53.71	867
4,000	110.91	658	99.07	755	82.55	953	71.61	1,156
5,000	138.64	823	123.84	944	103.19	1,191	89.51	1,445
6,000	166.37	988	148.60	1,133	123.83	1,430	107.42	1,734
7,000	194.10	1,152	173.37	1,322	144.47	1,668	125.32	2,023
8,000	221.82	1,316	198.14	1,511	165.10	1,906	143.22	2,312
9,000	249.55	1,481	222.90	1,699	185.74	2,144	161.12	2,601
10,000	277.28	1,646	247.67	1,888	206.38	2,383	179.02	2,889
11,000	305.00	1,810	272.44	2,077	227.01	2,621	196.92	3,178
12,000	332.73	1,975	297.20	2,266	247.65	2,859	214.83	3,468
13,000	360.46	2,139	321.97	2,455	268.29	3,097	232.73	3,757
14,000	388.19	2,304	346.74	2,644	288.93	3,336	250.63	4,045
15,000	415.91	2,468	371.50	2,832	309.56	3,574	268.53	4,334
16,000	443.64	2,633	396.27	3,021	330.20	3,812	286.43	4,623
17,000	471.37	2,798	421.04	3,210	350.84	4,050	304.33	4,912
18,000	499.09	2,962	445.80	3,398	371.48	4,289	322.24	5,201
19,000	526.82	3,126	470.57	3,587	392.11	4,527	340.14	5,490
20,000	554.55	3,291	495.34	3,776	412.75	4,765	358.04	5,779
21,000	582.28	3,456	520.10	3,965	433.39	5,003	375.94	6,068
22,000	610.00	3,620	544.87	4,154	454.02	5,241	393.84	6,356
23,000	637.73	3,785	569.63	4,342	474.66	5,480	411.74	6,645
24,000	665.46	3,949	594.40	4,531	495.30	5,718	429.65	6,935
25,000	693.18	4,114	619.17	4,720	515.94	5,956	447.55	7,224
26,000	720.91	4,278	643.93	4,909	536.57	6,194	465.45	7,512
27,000	748.64	4,443	668.70	5,098	557.21	6,433	483.35	7,801
28,000	776.37	4,608	693.47	5,287	577.85	6,671	501.25	8,090
29,000	804.09	4,772	718.23	5,475	598.48	6,909	519.15	8,379
30,000	831.82	4,936	743.00	5,664	619.12	7,147	537.06	8,668
31,000	859.55	5,101	767.77	5,853	639.76	7,386	554.96	8,957
32,000	887.27	5,265	792.53	6,041	660.40	7,624	572.86	9,246
33,000	915.00	5,430	817.30	6,230	681.03	7,862	590.76	9,535
34,000	942.73	5,595	842.07	6,419	701.67	8,100	608.66	9,824
35,000	970.46	5,759	866.83	6,608	722.31	8,339	626.56	10,112
36,000	998.18	5,924	891.60	6,797	742.95	8,577	644.47	10,402
37,000	1,025.91	6,088	916.37	6,986	763.58	8,815	662.37	10,691
38,000	1,053.64	6,253	941.13	7,174	784.22	9,053	680.27	10,979
39,000	1,081.37	6,418	965.90	7,363	804.86	9,292	698.17	11,268
40,000	1,109.09	6,582	990.67	7,552	825.49	9,529	716.07	11,557
42,000	1,164.55	6,911	1,040.20	7,930	866.77	10,006	751.88	12,135
44,000	1,220.00	7,240	1,089.73	8,307	908.04	10,482	787.68	12,713
46,000	1,275.46	7,569	1,139.26	8,684	949.32	10,959	823.48	13,291
48,000	1,330.91	7,898	1,188.80	9,062	990.59	11,435	859.29	13,869
50,000	1,386.36	8,227	1,238.33	9,440	1,031.87	11,912	895.09	14,446

8.90%　　　AUTO LOAN PAYMENTS

AMOUNT OF LOAN	12 MOS		24 MOS		30 MOS		36 MOS	
	MONTHLY PAYMENT	TOTAL INTRST	MONTHLY PAYMENT	TOTAL INTRST	MONTHLY PAYMENT	TOTAL INTRST	MONTHLY PAYMENT	TOTAL INTRST
$ 1	0.09	0	0.05	0	0.04	0	0.04	0
2	0.18	0	0.10	0	0.08	0	0.07	1
3	0.27	0	0.14	0	0.12	1	0.10	1
4	0.35	0	0.19	1	0.15	1	0.13	1
5	0.44	0	0.23	1	0.19	1	0.16	1
6	0.53	0	0.28	1	0.23	1	0.20	1
7	0.62	0	0.32	1	0.27	1	0.23	1
8	0.70	0	0.37	1	0.30	1	0.26	1
9	0.79	0	0.42	1	0.34	1	0.29	1
10	0.88	1	0.46	1	0.38	1	0.32	2
20	1.75	1	0.92	2	0.75	3	0.64	3
30	2.63	2	1.37	3	1.12	4	0.96	5
40	3.50	2	1.83	4	1.50	5	1.28	6
50	4.38	3	2.29	5	1.87	6	1.59	7
60	5.25	3	2.74	6	2.24	7	1.91	9
70	6.12	3	3.20	7	2.62	9	2.23	10
80	7.00	4	3.66	8	2.99	10	2.55	12
90	7.87	4	4.11	9	3.36	11	2.86	13
100	8.75	5	4.57	10	3.74	12	3.18	14
200	17.49	10	9.13	19	7.47	24	6.36	29
300	26.23	15	13.70	29	11.20	36	9.53	43
400	34.97	20	18.26	38	14.93	48	12.71	58
500	43.71	25	22.82	48	18.66	60	15.88	72
600	52.45	29	27.39	57	22.39	72	19.06	86
700	61.19	34	31.95	67	26.12	84	22.23	100
800	69.93	39	36.52	76	29.85	96	25.41	115
900	78.67	44	41.08	86	33.58	107	28.58	129
1,000	87.41	49	45.64	95	37.31	119	31.76	143
2,000	174.82	98	91.28	191	74.61	238	63.51	286
3,000	262.22	147	136.92	286	111.91	357	95.26	429
4,000	349.63	196	182.56	381	149.21	476	127.02	573
5,000	437.03	244	228.20	477	186.52	596	158.77	716
6,000	524.44	293	273.84	572	223.82	715	190.52	859
7,000	611.84	342	319.48	668	261.12	834	222.28	1,002
8,000	699.25	391	365.12	763	298.42	953	254.03	1,145
9,000	786.65	440	410.75	858	335.72	1,072	285.78	1,288
10,000	874.06	489	456.39	953	373.03	1,191	317.54	1,431
11,000	961.46	538	502.03	1,049	410.33	1,310	349.29	1,574
12,000	1,048.87	586	547.67	1,144	447.63	1,429	381.04	1,717
13,000	1,136.27	635	593.31	1,239	484.93	1,548	412.80	1,861
14,000	1,223.68	684	638.95	1,335	522.23	1,667	444.55	2,004
15,000	1,311.08	733	684.59	1,430	559.54	1,786	476.30	2,147
16,000	1,398.49	782	730.23	1,526	596.84	1,905	508.06	2,290
17,000	1,485.89	831	775.87	1,621	634.14	2,024	539.81	2,433
18,000	1,573.30	880	821.50	1,716	671.44	2,143	571.56	2,576
19,000	1,660.70	928	867.14	1,811	708.74	2,262	603.32	2,720
20,000	1,748.11	977	912.78	1,907	746.05	2,382	635.07	2,863
21,000	1,835.51	1,026	958.42	2,002	783.35	2,501	666.82	3,006
22,000	1,922.92	1,075	1,004.06	2,097	820.65	2,620	698.58	3,149
23,000	2,010.32	1,124	1,049.70	2,193	857.95	2,739	730.33	3,292
24,000	2,097.73	1,173	1,095.34	2,288	895.25	2,858	762.08	3,435
25,000	2,185.13	1,222	1,140.98	2,384	932.56	2,977	793.84	3,578
26,000	2,272.54	1,270	1,186.62	2,479	969.86	3,096	825.59	3,721
27,000	2,359.94	1,319	1,232.25	2,574	1,007.16	3,215	857.34	3,864
28,000	2,447.35	1,368	1,277.89	2,669	1,044.46	3,334	889.09	4,007
29,000	2,534.75	1,417	1,323.53	2,765	1,081.76	3,453	920.85	4,151
30,000	2,622.16	1,466	1,369.17	2,860	1,119.07	3,572	952.60	4,294
31,000	2,709.56	1,515	1,414.81	2,955	1,156.37	3,691	984.35	4,437
32,000	2,796.97	1,564	1,460.45	3,051	1,193.67	3,810	1,016.11	4,580
33,000	2,884.37	1,612	1,506.09	3,146	1,230.97	3,929	1,047.86	4,723
34,000	2,971.78	1,661	1,551.73	3,242	1,268.27	4,048	1,079.61	4,866
35,000	3,059.18	1,710	1,597.37	3,337	1,305.58	4,167	1,111.37	5,009
36,000	3,146.59	1,759	1,643.00	3,432	1,342.88	4,286	1,143.12	5,152
37,000	3,233.99	1,808	1,688.64	3,527	1,380.18	4,405	1,174.87	5,295
38,000	3,321.40	1,857	1,734.28	3,623	1,417.48	4,524	1,206.63	5,439
39,000	3,408.80	1,906	1,779.92	3,718	1,454.78	4,643	1,238.38	5,582
40,000	3,496.21	1,955	1,825.56	3,813	1,492.09	4,763	1,270.13	5,725
42,000	3,671.02	2,052	1,916.84	4,004	1,566.69	5,001	1,333.64	6,011
44,000	3,845.83	2,150	2,008.12	4,195	1,641.29	5,239	1,397.15	6,297
46,000	4,020.64	2,248	2,099.39	4,385	1,715.90	5,477	1,460.65	6,583
48,000	4,195.45	2,345	2,190.67	4,576	1,790.50	5,715	1,524.16	6,870
50,000	4,370.26	2,443	2,281.95	4,767	1,865.11	5,953	1,587.67	7,156

AMOUNT OF LOAN	42 MOS		48 MOS		60 MOS		72 MOS	
	MONTHLY PAYMENT	TOTAL INTRST	MONTHLY PAYMENT	TOTAL INTRST	MONTHLY PAYMENT	TOTAL INTRST	MONTHLY PAYMENT	TOTAL INTRST
$ 1	0.03	0	0.03	0	0.03	1	0.02	0
2	0.06	1	0.05	0	0.05	1	0.04	1
3	0.09	1	0.08	1	0.07	1	0.06	1
4	0.12	1	0.10	1	0.09	1	0.08	2
5	0.14	1	0.13	1	0.11	1	0.09	2
6	0.17	1	0.15	1	0.13	2	0.11	2
7	0.20	1	0.18	2	0.15	2	0.13	2
8	0.23	2	0.20	2	0.17	2	0.15	3
9	0.26	2	0.23	2	0.19	2	0.17	3
10	0.28	2	0.25	2	0.21	3	0.18	3
20	0.56	4	0.50	4	0.42	5	0.36	6
30	0.84	5	0.75	6	0.63	8	0.54	9
40	1.12	7	1.00	8	0.83	10	0.72	12
50	1.39	8	1.25	10	1.04	12	0.90	15
60	1.67	10	1.50	12	1.25	15	1.08	18
70	1.95	12	1.74	14	1.45	17	1.26	21
80	2.23	14	1.99	16	1.66	20	1.44	24
90	2.51	15	2.24	18	1.87	22	1.62	27
100	2.78	17	2.49	20	2.08	25	1.80	30
200	5.56	34	4.97	39	4.15	49	3.60	59
300	8.34	50	7.46	58	6.22	73	5.40	89
400	11.12	67	9.94	77	8.29	97	7.20	118
500	13.90	84	12.42	96	10.36	122	8.99	147
600	16.68	101	14.91	116	12.43	146	10.79	177
700	19.46	117	17.39	135	14.50	170	12.59	206
800	22.24	134	19.88	154	16.57	194	14.39	236
900	25.02	151	22.36	173	18.64	218	16.18	265
1,000	27.80	168	24.84	192	20.71	243	17.98	295
2,000	55.60	335	49.68	385	41.42	485	35.96	589
3,000	83.40	503	74.52	577	62.13	728	53.93	883
4,000	111.20	670	99.36	769	82.84	970	71.91	1,178
5,000	138.99	838	124.19	961	103.55	1,213	89.88	1,471
6,000	166.79	1,005	149.03	1,153	124.26	1,456	107.86	1,766
7,000	194.59	1,173	173.87	1,346	144.97	1,698	125.84	2,060
8,000	222.39	1,340	198.71	1,538	165.68	1,941	143.81	2,354
9,000	250.18	1,508	223.54	1,730	186.39	2,183	161.79	2,649
10,000	277.98	1,675	248.38	1,922	207.10	2,426	179.76	2,943
11,000	305.78	1,843	273.22	2,115	227.81	2,669	197.74	3,237
12,000	333.58	2,010	298.06	2,307	248.52	2,911	215.72	3,532
13,000	361.37	2,178	322.89	2,499	269.23	3,154	233.69	3,826
14,000	389.17	2,345	347.73	2,691	289.94	3,396	251.67	4,120
15,000	416.97	2,513	372.57	2,883	310.65	3,639	269.64	4,414
16,000	444.77	2,680	397.41	3,076	331.36	3,882	287.62	4,709
17,000	472.56	2,848	422.24	3,268	352.07	4,124	305.60	5,003
18,000	500.36	3,015	447.08	3,460	372.78	4,367	323.57	5,297
19,000	528.16	3,183	471.92	3,652	393.49	4,609	341.55	5,592
20,000	555.96	3,350	496.76	3,844	414.20	4,852	359.52	5,885
21,000	583.75	3,518	521.59	4,036	434.91	5,095	377.50	6,180
22,000	611.55	3,685	546.43	4,229	455.62	5,337	395.48	6,475
23,000	639.35	3,853	571.27	4,421	476.33	5,580	413.45	6,768
24,000	667.15	4,020	596.11	4,613	497.04	5,822	431.43	7,063
25,000	694.94	4,187	620.94	4,805	517.75	6,065	449.40	7,357
26,000	722.74	4,355	645.78	4,997	538.46	6,308	467.38	7,651
27,000	750.54	4,523	670.62	5,190	559.17	6,550	485.36	7,946
28,000	778.34	4,690	695.46	5,382	579.88	6,793	503.33	8,240
29,000	806.13	4,857	720.29	5,574	600.59	7,035	521.31	8,534
30,000	833.93	5,025	745.13	5,766	621.30	7,278	539.28	8,828
31,000	861.73	5,193	769.97	5,959	642.01	7,521	557.26	9,123
32,000	889.53	5,360	794.81	6,151	662.72	7,763	575.24	9,417
33,000	917.32	5,527	819.65	6,343	683.43	8,006	593.21	9,711
34,000	945.12	5,695	844.48	6,535	704.14	8,248	611.19	10,006
35,000	972.92	5,863	869.32	6,727	724.85	8,491	629.16	10,300
36,000	1,000.72	6,030	894.16	6,920	745.56	8,734	647.14	10,594
37,000	1,028.51	6,197	919.00	7,112	766.27	8,976	665.12	10,889
38,000	1,056.31	6,365	943.83	7,304	786.98	9,219	683.09	11,182
39,000	1,084.11	6,533	968.67	7,496	807.69	9,461	701.07	11,477
40,000	1,111.91	6,700	993.51	7,688	828.40	9,704	719.04	11,771
42,000	1,167.50	7,035	1,043.18	8,073	869.82	10,189	754.99	12,359
44,000	1,223.10	7,370	1,092.86	8,457	911.24	10,674	790.95	12,948
46,000	1,278.69	7,705	1,142.53	8,841	952.66	11,160	826.90	13,537
48,000	1,334.29	8,040	1,192.21	9,226	994.08	11,645	862.85	14,125
50,000	1,389.88	8,375	1,241.88	9,610	1,035.50	12,130	898.80	14,714

AUTO LOAN PAYMENTS

AMOUNT OF LOAN	12 MOS		24 MOS		30 MOS		36 MOS	
	MONTHLY PAYMENT	TOTAL INTRST	MONTHLY PAYMENT	TOTAL INTRST	MONTHLY PAYMENT	TOTAL INTRST	MONTHLY PAYMENT	TOTAL INTRST
$ 1	0.09	0	0.05	0	0.04	0	0.04	0
2	0.18	0	0.10	0	0.08	0	0.07	1
3	0.27	0	0.14	0	0.12	1	0.10	1
4	0.35	0	0.19	1	0.15	1	0.13	1
5	0.44	0	0.23	1	0.19	1	0.16	1
6	0.53	0	0.28	1	0.23	1	0.20	1
7	0.62	0	0.32	1	0.27	1	0.23	1
8	0.70	0	0.37	1	0.30	1	0.26	1
9	0.79	0	0.42	1	0.34	1	0.29	1
10	0.88	1	0.46	1	0.38	1	0.32	2
20	1.75	1	0.92	2	0.75	3	0.64	3
30	2.63	2	1.38	3	1.13	4	0.96	5
40	3.50	2	1.83	4	1.50	5	1.28	6
50	4.38	3	2.29	5	1.87	6	1.59	7
60	5.25	3	2.75	6	2.25	8	1.91	9
70	6.13	4	3.20	7	2.62	9	2.23	10
80	7.00	4	3.66	8	2.99	10	2.55	12
90	7.88	5	4.12	9	3.37	11	2.87	13
100	8.75	5	4.57	10	3.74	12	3.18	14
200	17.50	10	9.14	19	7.47	24	6.36	29
300	26.24	15	13.71	29	11.21	36	9.54	43
400	34.99	20	18.28	39	14.94	48	12.72	58
500	43.73	25	22.85	48	18.68	60	15.90	72
600	52.48	30	27.42	58	22.41	72	19.08	87
700	61.22	35	31.98	68	26.15	85	22.26	101
800	69.97	40	36.55	77	29.88	96	25.44	116
900	78.71	45	41.12	87	33.62	109	28.62	130
1,000	87.46	50	45.69	97	37.35	121	31.80	145
2,000	174.91	99	91.37	193	74.70	241	63.60	290
3,000	262.36	148	137.06	289	112.05	362	95.40	434
4,000	349.81	198	182.74	386	149.40	482	127.20	579
5,000	437.26	247	228.43	482	186.75	603	159.00	724
6,000	524.71	297	274.11	579	224.09	723	190.80	869
7,000	612.17	346	319.80	675	261.44	843	222.60	1,014
8,000	699.62	395	365.48	772	298.79	964	254.40	1,158
9,000	787.07	445	411.17	868	336.14	1,084	286.20	1,303
10,000	874.52	494	456.85	964	373.49	1,205	318.00	1,448
11,000	961.97	544	502.54	1,061	410.83	1,325	349.80	1,593
12,000	1,049.42	593	548.22	1,157	448.18	1,445	381.60	1,738
13,000	1,136.87	642	593.91	1,254	485.53	1,566	413.40	1,882
14,000	1,224.33	692	639.59	1,350	522.88	1,686	445.20	2,027
15,000	1,311.78	741	685.28	1,447	560.23	1,807	477.00	2,172
16,000	1,399.23	791	730.96	1,543	597.58	1,927	508.80	2,317
17,000	1,486.68	840	776.65	1,640	634.92	2,048	540.60	2,462
18,000	1,574.13	890	822.33	1,736	672.27	2,168	572.40	2,606
19,000	1,661.58	939	868.02	1,832	709.62	2,289	604.20	2,751
20,000	1,749.03	988	913.70	1,929	746.97	2,409	636.00	2,896
21,000	1,836.49	1,038	959.38	2,025	784.32	2,530	667.80	3,041
22,000	1,923.94	1,087	1,005.07	2,122	821.66	2,650	699.60	3,186
23,000	2,011.39	1,137	1,050.75	2,218	859.01	2,770	731.40	3,330
24,000	2,098.84	1,186	1,096.44	2,315	896.36	2,891	763.20	3,475
25,000	2,186.29	1,235	1,142.12	2,411	933.71	3,011	795.00	3,620
26,000	2,273.74	1,285	1,187.81	2,507	971.06	3,132	826.80	3,765
27,000	2,361.19	1,334	1,233.49	2,604	1,008.41	3,252	858.60	3,910
28,000	2,448.65	1,384	1,279.18	2,700	1,045.75	3,373	890.40	4,054
29,000	2,536.10	1,433	1,324.86	2,797	1,083.10	3,493	922.20	4,199
30,000	2,623.55	1,483	1,370.55	2,893	1,120.45	3,614	954.00	4,344
31,000	2,711.00	1,532	1,416.23	2,990	1,157.80	3,734	985.80	4,489
32,000	2,798.45	1,581	1,461.92	3,086	1,195.15	3,855	1,017.60	4,634
33,000	2,885.90	1,631	1,507.60	3,182	1,232.49	3,975	1,049.40	4,778
34,000	2,973.36	1,680	1,553.29	3,279	1,269.84	4,095	1,081.20	4,923
35,000	3,060.81	1,730	1,598.97	3,375	1,307.19	4,216	1,113.00	5,068
36,000	3,148.26	1,779	1,644.66	3,472	1,344.54	4,336	1,144.80	5,213
37,000	3,235.71	1,829	1,690.34	3,568	1,381.89	4,457	1,176.60	5,358
38,000	3,323.16	1,878	1,736.03	3,665	1,419.24	4,577	1,208.39	5,502
39,000	3,410.61	1,927	1,781.71	3,761	1,456.58	4,697	1,240.19	5,647
40,000	3,498.06	1,977	1,827.39	3,857	1,493.93	4,818	1,271.99	5,792
42,000	3,672.97	2,076	1,918.76	4,050	1,568.63	5,059	1,335.59	6,081
44,000	3,847.87	2,174	2,010.13	4,243	1,643.32	5,300	1,399.19	6,371
46,000	4,022.77	2,273	2,101.50	4,436	1,718.02	5,541	1,462.79	6,660
48,000	4,197.68	2,372	2,192.87	4,629	1,792.72	5,782	1,526.39	6,950
50,000	4,372.58	2,471	2,284.24	4,822	1,867.41	6,022	1,589.99	7,240

AMOUNT OF LOAN	42 MOS		48 MOS		60 MOS		72 MOS	
	MONTHLY PAYMENT	TOTAL INTRST	MONTHLY PAYMENT	TOTAL INTRST	MONTHLY PAYMENT	TOTAL INTRST	MONTHLY PAYMENT	TOTAL INTRST
$ 1	0.03	0	0.03	0	0.03	1	0.02	0
2	0.06	1	0.05	0	0.05	1	0.04	1
3	0.09	1	0.08	1	0.07	1	0.06	1
4	0.12	1	0.10	1	0.09	1	0.08	2
5	0.14	1	0.13	1	0.11	2	0.10	2
6	0.17	1	0.15	1	0.13	2	0.11	2
7	0.20	1	0.18	2	0.15	2	0.13	2
8	0.23	2	0.20	2	0.17	2	0.15	3
9	0.26	2	0.23	2	0.19	2	0.17	3
10	0.28	2	0.25	2	0.21	3	0.19	4
20	0.56	4	0.50	4	0.42	5	0.37	7
30	0.84	5	0.75	6	0.63	8	0.55	10
40	1.12	7	1.00	8	0.84	10	0.73	13
50	1.40	9	1.25	10	1.04	12	0.91	16
60	1.68	11	1.50	12	1.25	15	1.09	18
70	1.95	12	1.75	14	1.46	18	1.27	21
80	2.23	14	2.00	16	1.67	20	1.45	24
90	2.51	15	2.24	18	1.87	22	1.63	27
100	2.79	17	2.49	20	2.08	25	1.81	30
200	5.57	34	4.98	39	4.16	50	3.61	60
300	8.36	51	7.47	59	6.23	74	5.41	90
400	11.14	68	9.96	78	8.31	99	7.22	120
500	13.93	85	12.45	98	10.38	123	9.02	149
600	16.71	102	14.94	117	12.46	148	10.82	179
700	19.50	119	17.42	136	14.54	172	12.62	209
800	22.28	136	19.91	156	16.61	197	14.43	239
900	25.07	153	22.40	175	18.69	221	16.23	269
1,000	27.85	170	24.89	195	20.76	246	18.03	298
2,000	55.69	339	49.78	389	41.52	491	36.06	596
3,000	83.54	509	74.66	584	62.28	737	54.08	894
4,000	111.38	678	99.55	778	83.04	982	72.11	1,192
5,000	139.23	848	124.43	973	103.80	1,228	90.13	1,489
6,000	167.07	1,017	149.32	1,167	124.56	1,474	108.16	1,788
7,000	194.92	1,187	174.20	1,362	145.31	1,719	126.18	2,085
8,000	222.76	1,356	199.09	1,556	166.07	1,964	144.21	2,383
9,000	250.61	1,526	223.97	1,751	186.83	2,210	162.23	2,681
10,000	278.45	1,695	248.86	1,945	207.59	2,455	180.26	2,979
11,000	306.29	1,864	273.74	2,140	228.35	2,701	198.29	3,277
12,000	334.14	2,034	298.63	2,334	249.11	2,947	216.31	3,574
13,000	361.98	2,203	323.51	2,528	269.86	3,192	234.34	3,872
14,000	389.83	2,373	348.40	2,723	290.62	3,437	252.36	4,170
15,000	417.67	2,542	373.28	2,917	311.38	3,683	270.39	4,468
16,000	445.52	2,712	398.17	3,112	332.14	3,928	288.41	4,766
17,000	473.36	2,881	423.05	3,306	352.90	4,174	306.44	5,064
18,000	501.21	3,051	447.94	3,501	373.66	4,420	324.46	5,361
19,000	529.05	3,220	472.82	3,695	394.41	4,665	342.49	5,659
20,000	556.90	3,390	497.71	3,890	415.17	4,910	360.52	5,957
21,000	584.74	3,559	522.59	4,084	435.93	5,156	378.54	6,255
22,000	612.58	3,728	547.48	4,279	456.69	5,401	396.57	6,553
23,000	640.43	3,898	572.36	4,473	477.45	5,647	414.59	6,850
24,000	668.27	4,067	597.25	4,668	498.21	5,893	432.62	7,149
25,000	696.12	4,237	622.13	4,862	518.96	6,138	450.64	7,446
26,000	723.96	4,406	647.02	5,057	539.72	6,383	468.67	7,744
27,000	751.81	4,576	671.90	5,251	560.48	6,629	486.69	8,042
28,000	779.65	4,745	696.79	5,446	581.24	6,874	504.72	8,340
29,000	807.50	4,915	721.67	5,640	602.00	7,120	522.75	8,638
30,000	835.34	5,084	746.56	5,835	622.76	7,366	540.77	8,935
31,000	863.19	5,254	771.44	6,029	643.51	7,611	558.80	9,234
32,000	891.03	5,423	796.33	6,224	664.27	7,856	576.82	9,531
33,000	918.87	5,593	821.21	6,418	685.03	8,102	594.85	9,829
34,000	946.72	5,762	846.10	6,613	705.79	8,347	612.87	10,127
35,000	974.56	5,932	870.98	6,807	726.55	8,593	630.90	10,425
36,000	1,002.41	6,101	895.87	7,002	747.31	8,839	648.92	10,722
37,000	1,030.25	6,271	920.75	7,196	768.06	9,084	666.95	11,020
38,000	1,058.10	6,440	945.64	7,391	788.82	9,329	684.98	11,319
39,000	1,085.94	6,609	970.52	7,585	809.58	9,575	703.00	11,616
40,000	1,113.79	6,779	995.41	7,780	830.34	9,820	721.03	11,914
42,000	1,169.47	7,118	1,045.18	8,169	871.86	10,312	757.08	12,510
44,000	1,225.16	7,457	1,094.95	8,558	913.37	10,802	793.13	13,105
46,000	1,280.85	7,796	1,144.72	8,947	954.89	11,293	829.18	13,701
48,000	1,336.54	8,135	1,194.49	9,336	996.41	11,785	865.23	14,297
50,000	1,392.23	8,474	1,244.26	9,724	1,037.92	12,275	901.28	14,892

AUTO LOAN PAYMENTS

AMOUNT OF LOAN	12 MOS		24 MOS		30 MOS		36 MOS	
	MONTHLY PAYMENT	TOTAL INTRST	MONTHLY PAYMENT	TOTAL INTRST	MONTHLY PAYMENT	TOTAL INTRST	MONTHLY PAYMENT	TOTAL INTRST
$ 1	0.09	0	0.05	0	0.04	0	0.04	0
2	0.18	0	0.10	0	0.08	0	0.07	1
3	0.27	0	0.14	0	0.12	1	0.10	1
4	0.36	0	0.19	1	0.15	1	0.13	1
5	0.44	0	0.23	1	0.19	1	0.16	1
6	0.53	0	0.28	1	0.23	1	0.20	1
7	0.62	0	0.33	1	0.27	1	0.23	1
8	0.71	1	0.37	1	0.30	1	0.26	1
9	0.79	0	0.42	1	0.34	1	0.29	1
10	0.88	1	0.46	1	0.38	1	0.32	2
20	1.76	1	0.92	2	0.75	3	0.64	3
30	2.63	2	1.38	3	1.13	4	0.96	5
40	3.51	2	1.84	4	1.50	5	1.28	6
50	4.38	3	2.29	5	1.88	6	1.60	8
60	5.26	3	2.75	6	2.25	8	1.92	9
70	6.13	4	3.21	7	2.63	9	2.24	11
80	7.01	4	3.67	8	3.00	10	2.56	12
90	7.89	5	4.13	9	3.38	11	2.88	14
100	8.76	5	4.58	10	3.75	13	3.20	15
200	17.52	10	9.16	20	7.50	25	6.39	30
300	26.28	15	13.74	30	11.24	37	9.58	45
400	35.03	20	18.32	40	14.99	50	12.77	60
500	43.79	25	22.90	50	18.74	62	15.96	75
600	52.55	31	27.48	60	22.48	74	19.15	89
700	61.30	36	32.06	69	26.23	87	22.35	105
800	70.06	41	36.64	79	29.98	99	25.54	119
900	78.82	46	41.22	89	33.72	112	28.73	134
1,000	87.57	51	45.80	99	37.47	124	31.92	149
2,000	175.14	102	91.60	198	74.93	248	63.84	298
3,000	262.71	153	137.40	298	112.40	372	95.75	447
4,000	350.27	203	183.20	397	149.86	496	127.67	596
5,000	437.84	254	229.00	496	187.32	620	159.59	745
6,000	525.41	305	274.80	595	224.79	744	191.50	894
7,000	612.98	356	320.60	694	262.25	868	223.42	1,043
8,000	700.54	406	366.40	794	299.71	991	255.33	1,192
9,000	788.11	457	412.20	893	337.18	1,115	287.25	1,341
10,000	875.68	508	458.00	992	374.64	1,239	319.17	1,490
11,000	963.25	559	503.80	1,091	412.11	1,363	351.08	1,639
12,000	1,050.81	610	549.60	1,190	449.57	1,487	383.00	1,788
13,000	1,138.38	661	595.40	1,290	487.03	1,611	414.92	1,937
14,000	1,225.95	711	641.20	1,389	524.50	1,735	446.83	2,086
15,000	1,313.52	762	687.00	1,488	561.96	1,859	478.75	2,235
16,000	1,401.08	813	732.80	1,587	599.42	1,983	510.66	2,384
17,000	1,488.65	864	778.60	1,686	636.89	2,107	542.58	2,533
18,000	1,576.22	915	824.40	1,786	674.35	2,231	574.50	2,682
19,000	1,663.79	965	870.20	1,885	711.81	2,354	606.41	2,831
20,000	1,751.35	1,016	916.00	1,984	749.28	2,478	638.33	2,980
21,000	1,838.92	1,067	961.80	2,083	786.74	2,602	670.25	3,129
22,000	1,926.49	1,118	1,007.59	2,182	824.21	2,726	702.16	3,278
23,000	2,014.06	1,169	1,053.39	2,281	861.67	2,850	734.08	3,427
24,000	2,101.62	1,219	1,099.19	2,381	899.13	2,974	765.99	3,576
25,000	2,189.19	1,270	1,144.99	2,480	936.60	3,098	797.91	3,725
26,000	2,276.76	1,321	1,190.79	2,579	974.06	3,222	829.83	3,874
27,000	2,364.33	1,372	1,236.59	2,678	1,011.52	3,346	861.74	4,023
28,000	2,451.89	1,423	1,282.39	2,777	1,048.99	3,470	893.66	4,172
29,000	2,539.46	1,474	1,328.19	2,877	1,086.45	3,594	925.58	4,321
30,000	2,627.03	1,524	1,373.99	2,976	1,123.91	3,717	957.49	4,470
31,000	2,714.60	1,575	1,419.79	3,075	1,161.38	3,841	989.41	4,619
32,000	2,802.16	1,626	1,465.59	3,174	1,198.84	3,965	1,021.32	4,768
33,000	2,889.73	1,677	1,511.39	3,273	1,236.31	4,089	1,053.24	4,917
34,000	2,977.30	1,728	1,557.19	3,373	1,273.77	4,213	1,085.16	5,066
35,000	3,064.87	1,778	1,602.99	3,472	1,311.23	4,337	1,117.07	5,215
36,000	3,152.43	1,829	1,648.79	3,571	1,348.70	4,461	1,148.99	5,364
37,000	3,240.00	1,880	1,694.59	3,670	1,386.16	4,585	1,180.90	5,512
38,000	3,327.57	1,931	1,740.39	3,769	1,423.62	4,709	1,212.82	5,662
39,000	3,415.14	1,982	1,786.19	3,869	1,461.09	4,833	1,244.74	5,811
40,000	3,502.70	2,032	1,831.99	3,968	1,498.55	4,957	1,276.65	5,959
42,000	3,677.84	2,134	1,923.59	4,166	1,573.48	5,204	1,340.49	6,258
44,000	3,852.97	2,236	2,015.18	4,364	1,648.41	5,452	1,404.32	6,556
46,000	4,028.11	2,337	2,106.78	4,563	1,723.33	5,700	1,468.15	6,853
48,000	4,203.24	2,439	2,198.38	4,761	1,798.26	5,948	1,531.98	7,151
50,000	4,378.38	2,541	2,289.98	4,960	1,873.19	6,196	1,595.82	7,450

AMOUNT OF LOAN	42 MOS		48 MOS		60 MOS		72 MOS	
	MONTHLY PAYMENT	TOTAL INTRST	MONTHLY PAYMENT	TOTAL INTRST	MONTHLY PAYMENT	TOTAL INTRST	MONTHLY PAYMENT	TOTAL INTRST
$ 1	0.03	0	0.03	0	0.03	1	0.02	0
2	0.06	1	0.06	1	0.05	1	0.04	1
3	0.09	1	0.08	1	0.07	1	0.06	1
4	0.12	1	0.11	1	0.09	1	0.08	2
5	0.14	1	0.13	1	0.11	2	0.10	2
6	0.17	1	0.16	2	0.13	2	0.11	2
7	0.20	1	0.18	2	0.15	2	0.13	2
8	0.23	2	0.21	2	0.17	2	0.15	3
9	0.26	2	0.23	2	0.19	2	0.17	3
10	0.28	2	0.26	2	0.21	3	0.19	4
20	0.56	4	0.51	4	0.42	5	0.37	7
30	0.84	5	0.76	6	0.63	8	0.55	10
40	1.12	7	1.01	8	0.84	10	0.73	13
50	1.40	9	1.26	10	1.05	13	0.91	16
60	1.68	11	1.51	12	1.26	16	1.09	18
70	1.96	12	1.76	14	1.47	18	1.28	22
80	2.24	14	2.01	16	1.68	21	1.46	25
90	2.52	16	2.26	18	1.88	23	1.64	28
100	2.80	18	2.51	20	2.09	25	1.82	31
200	5.60	35	5.01	40	4.18	51	3.63	61
300	8.39	52	7.51	60	6.27	76	5.45	92
400	11.19	70	10.01	80	8.36	102	7.26	123
500	13.99	88	12.51	100	10.44	126	9.08	154
600	16.78	105	15.01	120	12.53	152	10.89	184
700	19.58	122	17.51	140	14.62	177	12.71	215
800	22.37	140	20.01	160	16.71	203	14.52	245
900	25.17	157	22.51	180	18.80	228	16.34	276
1,000	27.97	175	25.01	200	20.88	253	18.15	307
2,000	55.93	349	50.01	400	41.76	506	36.30	614
3,000	83.89	523	75.02	601	62.64	758	54.45	920
4,000	111.85	698	100.02	801	83.52	1,011	72.60	1,227
5,000	139.82	872	125.02	1,001	104.40	1,264	90.75	1,534
6,000	167.78	1,047	150.03	1,201	125.28	1,517	108.90	1,841
7,000	195.74	1,221	175.03	1,401	146.16	1,770	127.05	2,148
8,000	223.70	1,395	200.04	1,602	167.04	2,022	145.20	2,454
9,000	251.66	1,570	225.04	1,802	187.92	2,275	163.35	2,761
10,000	279.63	1,744	250.04	2,002	208.80	2,528	181.50	3,068
11,000	307.59	1,919	275.05	2,202	229.68	2,781	199.65	3,375
12,000	335.55	2,093	300.05	2,402	250.56	3,034	217.80	3,682
13,000	363.51	2,267	325.06	2,603	271.44	3,286	235.95	3,988
14,000	391.48	2,442	350.06	2,803	292.32	3,539	254.10	4,295
15,000	419.44	2,616	375.06	3,003	313.20	3,792	272.25	4,602
16,000	447.40	2,791	400.07	3,203	334.08	4,045	290.40	4,909
17,000	475.36	2,965	425.07	3,403	354.96	4,298	308.55	5,216
18,000	503.32	3,139	450.08	3,604	375.84	4,550	326.70	5,522
19,000	531.29	3,314	475.08	3,804	396.72	4,803	344.85	5,829
20,000	559.25	3,489	500.08	4,004	417.60	5,056	363.00	6,136
21,000	587.21	3,663	525.09	4,204	438.48	5,309	381.15	6,443
22,000	615.17	3,837	550.09	4,404	459.36	5,562	399.30	6,750
23,000	643.13	4,011	575.10	4,605	480.24	5,814	417.45	7,056
24,000	671.10	4,186	600.10	4,805	501.12	6,067	435.60	7,363
25,000	699.06	4,361	625.10	5,005	522.00	6,320	453.75	7,670
26,000	727.02	4,535	650.11	5,205	542.88	6,573	471.90	7,977
27,000	754.98	4,709	675.11	5,405	563.76	6,826	490.05	8,284
28,000	782.95	4,884	700.11	5,605	584.64	7,078	508.20	8,590
29,000	810.91	5,058	725.12	5,806	605.52	7,331	526.35	8,897
30,000	838.87	5,233	750.12	6,006	626.40	7,584	544.50	9,204
31,000	866.83	5,407	775.13	6,206	647.28	7,837	562.65	9,511
32,000	894.79	5,581	800.13	6,406	668.16	8,090	580.80	9,818
33,000	922.76	5,756	825.13	6,606	689.04	8,342	598.95	10,124
34,000	950.72	5,930	850.14	6,807	709.92	8,595	617.10	10,431
35,000	978.68	6,105	875.14	7,007	730.80	8,848	635.25	10,738
36,000	1,006.64	6,279	900.15	7,207	751.68	9,101	653.40	11,045
37,000	1,034.60	6,453	925.15	7,407	772.56	9,354	671.55	11,352
38,000	1,062.57	6,628	950.15	7,607	793.44	9,606	689.70	11,658
39,000	1,090.53	6,802	975.16	7,808	814.32	9,859	707.85	11,965
40,000	1,118.49	6,977	1,000.16	8,008	835.20	10,112	726.00	12,272
42,000	1,174.42	7,326	1,050.17	8,408	876.96	10,618	762.30	12,886
44,000	1,230.34	7,674	1,100.18	8,809	918.72	11,123	798.60	13,499
46,000	1,286.26	8,023	1,150.19	9,209	960.48	11,629	834.90	14,113
48,000	1,342.19	8,372	1,200.19	9,609	1,002.24	12,134	871.20	14,726
50,000	1,398.11	8,721	1,250.20	10,010	1,044.00	12,640	907.50	15,340

AUTO LOAN PAYMENTS

AMOUNT OF LOAN	12 MOS		24 MOS		30 MOS		36 MOS	
	MONTHLY PAYMENT	TOTAL INTRST	MONTHLY PAYMENT	TOTAL INTRST	MONTHLY PAYMENT	TOTAL INTRST	MONTHLY PAYMENT	TOTAL INTRST
$ 1	0.09	0	0.05	0	0.04	0	0.04	0
2	0.18	0	0.10	0	0.08	0	0.07	1
3	0.27	0	0.14	0	0.12	1	0.10	1
4	0.36	0	0.19	1	0.16	1	0.13	1
5	0.44	0	0.23	1	0.19	1	0.17	1
6	0.53	0	0.28	1	0.23	1	0.20	1
7	0.62	0	0.33	1	0.27	1	0.23	1
8	0.71	1	0.37	1	0.31	1	0.26	1
9	0.79	1	0.42	1	0.34	1	0.29	1
10	0.88	1	0.46	1	0.38	1	0.33	2
20	1.76	1	0.92	1	0.76	3	0.65	3
30	2.64	2	1.38	3	1.13	4	0.97	5
40	3.51	2	1.84	4	1.51	5	1.29	6
50	4.39	3	2.30	5	1.88	6	1.61	8
60	5.27	3	2.76	6	2.26	8	1.93	9
70	6.14	4	3.22	7	2.64	9	2.26	11
80	7.02	4	3.68	8	3.01	10	2.57	13
90	7.90	5	4.14	9	3.39	12	2.89	14
100	8.77	5	4.60	10	3.76	13	3.21	16
200	17.54	10	9.19	21	7.52	26	6.41	31
300	26.31	16	13.78	31	11.28	38	9.61	46
400	35.08	21	18.37	41	15.04	51	12.82	62
500	43.85	26	22.96	51	18.79	64	16.02	77
600	52.62	31	27.55	61	22.55	77	19.22	92
700	61.38	37	32.15	72	26.31	89	22.43	107
800	70.15	42	36.74	82	30.07	102	25.63	123
900	78.92	47	41.33	92	33.83	115	28.83	138
1,000	87.69	52	45.92	102	37.58	127	32.04	153
2,000	175.37	104	91.83	204	75.16	255	64.07	307
3,000	263.06	157	137.75	306	112.74	382	96.10	460
4,000	350.74	209	183.66	408	150.32	510	128.14	613
5,000	438.42	261	229.58	510	187.90	637	160.17	766
6,000	526.11	313	275.49	612	225.48	764	192.20	919
7,000	613.79	365	321.41	714	263.06	892	224.24	1,073
8,000	701.47	418	367.32	816	300.64	1,019	256.27	1,226
9,000	789.16	470	413.24	918	338.22	1,147	288.30	1,379
10,000	876.84	522	459.15	1,020	375.80	1,274	320.33	1,532
11,000	964.52	574	505.06	1,121	413.38	1,401	352.37	1,685
12,000	1,052.21	627	550.98	1,224	450.96	1,529	384.40	1,838
13,000	1,139.89	679	596.89	1,325	488.54	1,656	416.43	1,991
14,000	1,227.57	731	642.81	1,427	526.12	1,784	448.47	2,145
15,000	1,315.26	783	688.72	1,529	563.70	1,911	480.50	2,298
16,000	1,402.94	835	734.64	1,631	601.27	2,038	512.53	2,451
17,000	1,490.62	887	780.55	1,733	638.85	2,166	544.57	2,605
18,000	1,578.31	940	826.47	1,835	676.43	2,293	576.60	2,758
19,000	1,665.99	992	872.38	1,937	714.01	2,420	608.63	2,911
20,000	1,753.68	1,044	918.29	2,039	751.59	2,548	640.66	3,064
21,000	1,841.36	1,096	964.21	2,141	789.17	2,675	672.70	3,217
22,000	1,929.04	1,148	1,010.12	2,243	826.75	2,803	704.73	3,370
23,000	2,016.73	1,201	1,056.04	2,345	864.33	2,930	736.76	3,523
24,000	2,104.41	1,253	1,101.95	2,447	901.91	3,057	768.80	3,677
25,000	2,192.09	1,305	1,147.87	2,549	939.49	3,185	800.83	3,830
26,000	2,279.78	1,357	1,193.78	2,651	977.07	3,312	832.86	3,983
27,000	2,367.46	1,410	1,239.70	2,753	1,014.65	3,440	864.89	4,136
28,000	2,455.14	1,462	1,285.61	2,855	1,052.23	3,567	896.93	4,289
29,000	2,542.83	1,514	1,331.53	2,957	1,089.81	3,694	928.96	4,443
30,000	2,630.51	1,566	1,377.44	3,059	1,127.39	3,822	960.99	4,596
31,000	2,718.19	1,618	1,423.35	3,160	1,164.97	3,949	993.03	4,749
32,000	2,805.88	1,671	1,469.27	3,262	1,202.54	4,076	1,025.06	4,902
33,000	2,893.56	1,723	1,515.18	3,364	1,240.12	4,204	1,057.09	5,055
34,000	2,981.24	1,775	1,561.10	3,466	1,277.70	4,331	1,089.13	5,209
35,000	3,068.93	1,827	1,607.01	3,568	1,315.28	4,458	1,121.16	5,362
36,000	3,156.61	1,879	1,652.93	3,670	1,352.86	4,586	1,153.19	5,515
37,000	3,244.29	1,931	1,698.84	3,772	1,390.44	4,713	1,185.22	5,668
38,000	3,331.98	1,984	1,744.76	3,874	1,428.02	4,841	1,217.26	5,821
39,000	3,419.66	2,036	1,790.67	3,976	1,465.60	4,968	1,249.29	5,974
40,000	3,507.35	2,088	1,836.58	4,078	1,503.18	5,095	1,281.32	6,128
42,000	3,682.71	2,193	1,928.41	4,282	1,578.34	5,350	1,345.39	6,434
44,000	3,858.08	2,297	2,020.24	4,486	1,653.50	5,605	1,409.45	6,740
46,000	4,033.45	2,401	2,112.07	4,690	1,728.66	5,860	1,473.52	7,047
48,000	4,208.81	2,506	2,203.90	4,894	1,803.81	6,114	1,537.59	7,353
50,000	4,384.18	2,610	2,295.73	5,098	1,878.97	6,369	1,601.65	7,659

AMOUNT OF LOAN	42 MOS		48 MOS		60 MOS		72 MOS	
	MONTHLY PAYMENT	TOTAL INTRST	MONTHLY PAYMENT	TOTAL INTRST	MONTHLY PAYMENT	TOTAL INTRST	MONTHLY PAYMENT	TOTAL INTRST
$ 1	0.03	0	0.03	0	0.03	1	0.02	0
2	0.06	1	0.05	0	0.05	1	0.04	1
3	0.09	1	0.08	1	0.07	1	0.06	1
4	0.12	1	0.11	1	0.09	1	0.08	2
5	0.15	1	0.13	1	0.11	2	0.10	2
6	0.17	1	0.16	2	0.13	2	0.11	2
7	0.20	1	0.18	2	0.15	2	0.13	2
8	0.23	2	0.21	2	0.17	2	0.15	3
9	0.26	2	0.23	2	0.19	2	0.17	3
10	0.29	2	0.26	2	0.22	3	0.19	4
20	0.57	4	0.51	4	0.43	6	0.37	7
30	0.85	6	0.76	6	0.64	8	0.55	10
40	1.13	7	1.01	8	0.85	11	0.74	13
50	1.41	9	1.26	10	1.06	14	0.92	16
60	1.69	11	1.51	12	1.27	16	1.10	19
70	1.97	13	1.76	14	1.48	19	1.28	22
80	2.25	15	2.01	16	1.69	21	1.47	26
90	2.53	16	2.27	19	1.90	24	1.65	29
100	2.81	18	2.52	21	2.11	27	1.83	32
200	5.62	36	5.03	41	4.21	53	3.66	64
300	8.43	54	7.54	62	6.31	79	5.49	95
400	11.24	72	10.05	82	8.41	105	7.31	126
500	14.05	90	12.57	103	10.51	131	9.14	158
600	16.85	108	15.08	124	12.61	157	10.97	190
700	19.66	126	17.59	144	14.71	183	12.80	222
800	22.47	144	20.10	165	16.81	209	14.62	253
900	25.28	162	22.62	186	18.91	235	16.45	284
1,000	28.09	180	25.13	206	21.01	261	18.28	316
2,000	56.17	359	50.25	412	42.01	521	36.55	632
3,000	84.25	539	75.37	618	63.01	781	54.83	948
4,000	112.33	718	100.50	824	84.01	1,041	73.10	1,263
5,000	140.41	897	125.62	1,030	105.01	1,301	91.38	1,579
6,000	168.49	1,077	150.74	1,236	126.02	1,561	109.65	1,895
7,000	196.57	1,256	175.87	1,442	147.02	1,821	127.93	2,211
8,000	224.65	1,435	200.99	1,648	168.02	2,081	146.20	2,526
9,000	252.73	1,615	226.11	1,853	189.02	2,341	164.48	2,843
10,000	280.81	1,794	251.24	2,060	210.02	2,601	182.75	3,158
11,000	308.89	1,973	276.36	2,265	231.03	2,862	201.03	3,474
12,000	336.97	2,153	301.48	2,471	252.03	3,122	219.30	3,790
13,000	365.05	2,332	326.61	2,677	273.03	3,382	237.58	4,106
14,000	393.13	2,511	351.73	2,883	294.03	3,642	255.85	4,421
15,000	421.21	2,691	376.85	3,089	315.03	3,902	274.13	4,737
16,000	449.29	2,870	401.98	3,295	336.03	4,162	292.40	5,053
17,000	477.37	3,050	427.10	3,501	357.04	4,422	310.67	5,368
18,000	505.45	3,229	452.22	3,707	378.04	4,682	328.95	5,684
19,000	533.53	3,408	477.34	3,912	399.04	4,942	347.22	6,000
20,000	561.61	3,588	502.47	4,119	420.04	5,202	365.50	6,316
21,000	589.69	3,767	527.59	4,324	441.04	5,462	383.77	6,631
22,000	617.77	3,946	552.71	4,530	462.05	5,723	402.05	6,948
23,000	645.85	4,126	577.84	4,736	483.05	5,983	420.32	7,263
24,000	673.93	4,305	602.96	4,942	504.05	6,243	438.60	7,579
25,000	702.01	4,484	628.08	5,148	525.05	6,503	456.87	7,895
26,000	730.09	4,664	653.21	5,354	546.05	6,763	475.15	8,211
27,000	758.17	4,843	678.33	5,560	567.06	7,024	493.42	8,526
28,000	786.25	5,023	703.45	5,766	588.06	7,284	511.70	8,842
29,000	814.33	5,202	728.58	5,972	609.06	7,544	529.97	9,158
30,000	842.41	5,381	753.70	6,178	630.06	7,804	548.25	9,474
31,000	870.49	5,561	778.82	6,383	651.06	8,064	566.52	9,789
32,000	898.57	5,740	803.95	6,590	672.06	8,324	584.80	10,106
33,000	926.65	5,919	829.07	6,795	693.07	8,584	603.07	10,421
34,000	954.73	6,099	854.19	7,001	714.07	8,844	621.34	10,736
35,000	982.81	6,278	879.31	7,207	735.07	9,104	639.62	11,053
36,000	1,010.89	6,457	904.44	7,413	756.07	9,364	657.89	11,368
37,000	1,038.97	6,637	929.56	7,619	777.07	9,624	676.17	11,684
38,000	1,067.05	6,816	954.68	7,825	798.08	9,885	694.44	12,000
39,000	1,095.13	6,995	979.81	8,031	819.08	10,145	712.72	12,316
40,000	1,123.21	7,175	1,004.93	8,237	840.08	10,405	730.99	12,631
42,000	1,179.37	7,534	1,055.18	8,649	882.08	10,925	767.54	13,263
44,000	1,235.53	7,892	1,105.42	9,060	924.09	11,445	804.09	13,894
46,000	1,291.69	8,251	1,155.67	9,472	966.09	11,965	840.64	14,526
48,000	1,347.85	8,610	1,205.92	9,884	1,008.09	12,485	877.19	15,158
50,000	1,404.01	8,968	1,256.16	10,296	1,050.10	13,006	913.74	15,789

AUTO LOAN PAYMENTS

AMOUNT OF LOAN	12 MOS		24 MOS		30 MOS		36 MOS	
	MONTHLY PAYMENT	TOTAL INTRST	MONTHLY PAYMENT	TOTAL INTRST	MONTHLY PAYMENT	TOTAL INTRST	MONTHLY PAYMENT	TOTAL INTRST
$ 1	0.09	0	0.05	0	0.04	0	0.04	0
2	0.18	0	0.10	0	0.08	0	0.07	1
3	0.27	0	0.14	0	0.12	1	0.10	1
4	0.36	0	0.19	1	0.16	1	0.13	1
5	0.44	0	0.24	1	0.19	1	0.17	1
6	0.53	0	0.28	1	0.23	1	0.20	1
7	0.62	0	0.33	1	0.27	1	0.23	1
8	0.71	1	0.37	1	0.31	1	0.26	1
9	0.80	1	0.42	1	0.34	1	0.29	1
10	0.88	1	0.47	1	0.38	1	0.33	2
20	1.76	1	0.93	2	0.76	3	0.65	3
30	2.64	2	1.39	3	1.14	4	0.97	5
40	3.52	2	1.85	4	1.51	5	1.29	6
50	4.39	3	2.31	5	1.89	7	1.61	8
60	5.27	3	2.77	6	2.27	8	1.93	9
70	6.15	4	3.23	8	2.64	9	2.26	11
80	7.03	4	3.69	9	3.02	11	2.58	13
90	7.91	5	4.15	10	3.40	12	2.90	14
100	8.78	5	4.61	11	3.77	13	3.22	16
200	17.56	11	9.21	21	7.54	26	6.43	31
300	26.34	16	13.81	31	11.31	39	9.65	47
400	35.12	21	18.42	42	15.08	52	12.86	63
500	43.90	27	23.02	52	18.85	66	16.08	79
600	52.68	32	27.62	63	22.62	79	19.29	94
700	61.46	38	32.23	74	26.39	92	22.51	110
800	70.24	43	36.83	84	30.16	105	25.72	126
900	79.02	48	41.43	94	33.93	118	28.94	142
1,000	87.80	54	46.03	105	37.70	131	32.15	157
2,000	175.60	107	92.06	209	75.40	262	64.30	315
3,000	263.40	161	138.09	314	113.09	393	96.45	472
4,000	351.20	214	184.12	419	150.79	524	128.60	630
5,000	439.00	268	230.15	524	188.48	654	160.75	787
6,000	526.80	322	276.18	628	226.18	785	192.90	944
7,000	614.60	375	322.21	733	263.87	916	225.05	1,102
8,000	702.40	429	368.24	838	301.57	1,047	257.20	1,259
9,000	790.20	482	414.27	942	339.26	1,178	289.35	1,417
10,000	878.00	536	460.30	1,047	376.96	1,309	321.50	1,574
11,000	965.80	590	506.33	1,152	414.65	1,440	353.65	1,731
12,000	1,053.60	643	552.36	1,257	452.35	1,571	385.80	1,889
13,000	1,141.40	697	598.39	1,361	490.04	1,701	417.95	2,046
14,000	1,229.20	750	644.42	1,466	527.74	1,832	450.10	2,204
15,000	1,317.00	804	690.45	1,571	565.43	1,963	482.25	2,361
16,000	1,404.80	858	736.48	1,676	603.13	2,094	514.40	2,518
17,000	1,492.60	911	782.51	1,780	640.82	2,225	546.55	2,676
18,000	1,580.40	965	828.54	1,885	678.52	2,356	578.70	2,833
19,000	1,668.20	1,018	874.57	1,990	716.22	2,487	610.85	2,991
20,000	1,756.00	1,072	920.60	2,094	753.91	2,617	643.00	3,148
21,000	1,843.80	1,126	966.63	2,199	791.61	2,748	675.15	3,305
22,000	1,931.60	1,179	1,012.66	2,304	829.30	2,879	707.30	3,463
23,000	2,019.40	1,233	1,058.69	2,409	867.00	3,010	739.45	3,620
24,000	2,107.20	1,286	1,104.72	2,513	904.69	3,141	771.60	3,778
25,000	2,195.00	1,340	1,150.75	2,618	942.39	3,272	803.75	3,935
26,000	2,282.80	1,394	1,196.78	2,723	980.08	3,402	835.90	4,092
27,000	2,370.60	1,447	1,242.80	2,827	1,017.78	3,533	868.05	4,250
28,000	2,458.40	1,501	1,288.83	2,932	1,055.47	3,664	900.20	4,407
29,000	2,546.20	1,554	1,334.86	3,037	1,093.17	3,795	932.35	4,565
30,000	2,633.99	1,608	1,380.89	3,141	1,130.86	3,926	964.50	4,722
31,000	2,721.79	1,661	1,426.92	3,246	1,168.56	4,057	996.65	4,879
32,000	2,809.59	1,715	1,472.95	3,351	1,206.25	4,188	1,028.80	5,037
33,000	2,897.39	1,769	1,518.98	3,456	1,243.95	4,319	1,060.95	5,194
34,000	2,985.19	1,822	1,565.01	3,560	1,281.64	4,449	1,093.10	5,352
35,000	3,072.99	1,876	1,611.04	3,665	1,319.34	4,580	1,125.25	5,509
36,000	3,160.79	1,929	1,657.07	3,770	1,357.04	4,711	1,157.40	5,666
37,000	3,248.59	1,983	1,703.10	3,874	1,394.73	4,842	1,189.55	5,824
38,000	3,336.39	2,037	1,749.13	3,979	1,432.43	4,973	1,221.70	5,981
39,000	3,424.19	2,090	1,795.16	4,084	1,470.12	5,104	1,253.85	6,139
40,000	3,511.99	2,144	1,841.19	4,189	1,507.82	5,235	1,286.00	6,296
42,000	3,687.59	2,251	1,933.25	4,398	1,583.21	5,496	1,350.30	6,611
44,000	3,863.19	2,358	2,025.31	4,607	1,658.60	5,758	1,414.60	6,926
46,000	4,038.79	2,465	2,117.37	4,817	1,733.99	6,020	1,478.90	7,240
48,000	4,214.39	2,573	2,209.43	5,026	1,809.38	6,281	1,543.20	7,555
50,000	4,389.99	2,680	2,301.49	5,236	1,884.77	6,543	1,607.50	7,870

AUTO LOAN PAYMENTS 9.75%

AMOUNT OF LOAN	42 MOS		48 MOS		60 MOS		72 MOS	
	MONTHLY PAYMENT	TOTAL INTRST	MONTHLY PAYMENT	TOTAL INTRST	MONTHLY PAYMENT	TOTAL INTRST	MONTHLY PAYMENT	TOTAL INTRST
$ 1	0.03	0	0.03	0	0.03	1	0.02	0
2	0.06	1	0.06	1	0.05	1	0.04	1
3	0.09	1	0.08	1	0.07	1	0.06	1
4	0.12	1	0.11	1	0.09	1	0.08	2
5	0.15	1	0.13	1	0.11	2	0.10	2
6	0.17	1	0.16	2	0.13	2	0.12	3
7	0.20	1	0.18	2	0.15	2	0.13	3
8	0.23	2	0.21	2	0.17	2	0.15	3
9	0.26	2	0.23	2	0.20	3	0.17	3
10	0.29	2	0.26	2	0.22	3	0.19	4
20	0.57	4	0.51	4	0.43	6	0.37	7
30	0.85	6	0.76	6	0.64	8	0.56	10
40	1.13	7	1.01	8	0.85	11	0.74	13
50	1.41	9	1.27	11	1.06	14	0.93	17
60	1.70	11	1.52	13	1.27	16	1.11	20
70	1.98	13	1.77	15	1.48	19	1.29	23
80	2.26	15	2.02	17	1.69	21	1.48	27
90	2.54	17	2.28	19	1.91	25	1.66	30
100	2.82	18	2.53	21	2.12	27	1.85	33
200	5.64	37	5.05	42	4.23	54	3.69	66
300	8.46	55	7.58	64	6.34	80	5.53	98
400	11.28	74	10.10	85	8.45	107	7.37	131
500	14.10	92	12.63	106	10.57	134	9.21	163
600	16.92	111	15.15	127	12.68	161	11.05	196
700	19.74	129	17.67	148	14.79	187	12.89	228
800	22.56	148	20.20	170	16.90	214	14.73	261
900	25.38	166	22.72	191	19.02	241	16.57	293
1,000	28.20	184	25.25	212	21.13	268	18.41	326
2,000	56.40	369	50.49	424	42.25	535	36.81	650
3,000	84.60	553	75.73	635	63.38	803	55.21	975
4,000	112.80	738	100.98	847	84.50	1,070	73.61	1,300
5,000	141.00	922	126.22	1,059	105.63	1,338	92.01	1,625
6,000	169.19	1,106	151.46	1,270	126.75	1,605	110.41	1,950
7,000	197.39	1,290	176.70	1,482	147.87	1,872	128.81	2,274
8,000	225.59	1,475	201.95	1,694	169.00	2,140	147.21	2,599
9,000	253.79	1,659	227.19	1,905	190.12	2,407	165.61	2,924
10,000	281.99	1,844	252.43	2,117	211.25	2,675	184.01	3,249
11,000	310.19	2,028	277.67	2,328	232.37	2,942	202.41	3,574
12,000	338.38	2,212	302.92	2,540	253.50	3,210	220.81	3,898
13,000	366.58	2,396	328.16	2,752	274.62	3,477	239.21	4,223
14,000	394.78	2,581	353.40	2,963	295.74	3,744	257.61	4,548
15,000	422.98	2,765	378.65	3,175	316.87	4,012	276.01	4,873
16,000	451.18	2,950	403.89	3,387	337.99	4,279	294.41	5,198
17,000	479.38	3,134	429.13	3,598	359.12	4,547	312.81	5,522
18,000	507.57	3,318	454.37	3,810	380.24	4,814	331.21	5,847
19,000	535.77	3,502	479.62	4,022	401.37	5,082	349.61	6,172
20,000	563.97	3,687	504.86	4,233	422.49	5,349	368.01	6,497
21,000	592.17	3,871	530.10	4,445	443.61	5,617	386.41	6,822
22,000	620.37	4,056	555.34	4,656	464.74	5,884	404.81	7,146
23,000	648.57	4,240	580.59	4,868	485.86	6,152	423.21	7,471
24,000	676.76	4,424	605.83	5,080	506.99	6,419	441.61	7,796
25,000	704.96	4,608	631.07	5,291	528.11	6,687	460.01	8,121
26,000	733.16	4,793	656.31	5,503	549.24	6,954	478.41	8,446
27,000	761.36	4,977	681.56	5,715	570.36	7,222	496.81	8,770
28,000	789.56	5,162	706.80	5,926	591.48	7,489	515.21	9,095
29,000	817.76	5,346	732.04	6,138	612.61	7,757	533.61	9,420
30,000	845.95	5,530	757.29	6,350	633.73	8,024	552.01	9,745
31,000	874.15	5,714	782.53	6,561	654.86	8,292	570.41	10,070
32,000	902.35	5,899	807.77	6,773	675.98	8,559	588.81	10,394
33,000	930.55	6,083	833.01	6,984	697.11	8,827	607.21	10,719
34,000	958.75	6,268	858.26	7,196	718.23	9,094	625.61	11,044
35,000	986.95	6,452	883.50	7,408	739.35	9,361	644.01	11,369
36,000	1,015.14	6,636	908.74	7,620	760.48	9,629	662.41	11,694
37,000	1,043.34	6,820	933.98	7,831	781.60	9,896	680.81	12,018
38,000	1,071.54	7,005	959.23	8,043	802.73	10,164	699.21	12,343
39,000	1,099.74	7,189	984.47	8,255	823.85	10,431	717.61	12,668
40,000	1,127.94	7,373	1,009.71	8,466	844.97	10,698	736.01	12,993
42,000	1,184.33	7,742	1,060.20	8,890	887.22	11,233	772.81	13,642
44,000	1,240.73	8,111	1,110.68	9,313	929.47	11,768	809.61	14,292
46,000	1,297.13	8,479	1,161.17	9,736	971.72	12,303	846.41	14,942
48,000	1,353.52	8,848	1,211.65	10,159	1,013.97	12,838	883.21	15,591
50,000	1,409.92	9,217	1,262.14	10,583	1,056.22	13,373	920.01	16,241

101

AUTO LOAN PAYMENTS

AMOUNT OF LOAN	12 MOS		24 MOS		30 MOS		36 MOS	
	MONTHLY PAYMENT	TOTAL INTRST	MONTHLY PAYMENT	TOTAL INTRST	MONTHLY PAYMENT	TOTAL INTRST	MONTHLY PAYMENT	TOTAL INTRST
$ 1	0.09	0	0.05	0	0.04	0	0.04	0
2	0.18	0	0.10	0	0.08	0	0.07	1
3	0.27	0	0.14	0	0.12	1	0.10	1
4	0.36	0	0.19	1	0.16	1	0.13	1
5	0.44	0	0.24	1	0.19	1	0.17	1
6	0.53	0	0.28	1	0.23	1	0.20	1
7	0.62	0	0.33	1	0.27	1	0.23	1
8	0.71	1	0.37	1	0.31	1	0.26	1
9	0.80	1	0.42	1	0.34	1	0.29	1
10	0.88	1	0.47	1	0.38	1	0.33	2
20	1.76	1	0.93	2	0.76	3	0.65	3
30	2.64	2	1.39	3	1.14	4	0.97	5
40	3.52	2	1.85	4	1.52	6	1.29	6
50	4.40	3	2.31	5	1.89	7	1.62	8
60	5.28	3	2.77	6	2.27	8	1.94	10
70	6.16	4	3.23	8	2.65	10	2.26	11
80	7.03	4	3.69	9	3.03	11	2.58	13
90	7.91	5	4.15	10	3.40	12	2.90	14
100	8.79	5	4.61	11	3.78	13	3.23	16
200	17.58	11	9.22	21	7.56	27	6.45	32
300	26.37	16	13.83	32	11.33	40	9.67	48
400	35.15	22	18.44	43	15.11	53	12.89	64
500	43.94	27	23.05	53	18.89	67	16.12	80
600	52.73	33	27.66	64	22.66	80	19.34	96
700	61.51	38	32.27	74	26.44	93	22.56	112
800	70.30	44	36.88	85	30.22	107	25.78	128
900	79.09	49	41.49	96	33.99	120	29.00	144
1,000	87.87	54	46.10	106	37.77	133	32.23	160
2,000	175.74	109	92.20	213	75.53	266	64.45	320
3,000	263.61	163	138.30	319	113.30	399	96.67	480
4,000	351.48	218	184.40	426	151.06	532	128.89	640
5,000	439.35	272	230.50	532	188.83	665	161.11	800
6,000	527.22	327	276.60	638	226.59	798	193.33	960
7,000	615.09	381	322.70	745	264.36	931	225.55	1,120
8,000	702.96	436	368.80	851	302.12	1,064	257.77	1,280
9,000	790.83	490	414.89	957	339.89	1,197	289.99	1,440
10,000	878.70	544	460.99	1,064	377.65	1,330	322.21	1,600
11,000	966.57	599	507.09	1,170	415.42	1,463	354.43	1,759
12,000	1,054.44	653	553.19	1,277	453.18	1,595	386.65	1,919
13,000	1,142.31	708	599.29	1,383	490.95	1,729	418.87	2,079
14,000	1,230.18	762	645.39	1,489	528.71	1,861	451.09	2,239
15,000	1,318.05	817	691.49	1,596	566.48	1,994	483.31	2,399
16,000	1,405.92	871	737.59	1,702	604.24	2,127	515.53	2,559
17,000	1,493.78	925	783.68	1,808	642.01	2,260	547.75	2,719
18,000	1,581.65	980	829.78	1,915	679.77	2,393	579.97	2,879
19,000	1,669.52	1,034	875.88	2,021	717.54	2,526	612.19	3,039
20,000	1,757.39	1,089	921.98	2,128	755.30	2,659	644.41	3,199
21,000	1,845.26	1,143	968.08	2,234	793.07	2,792	676.63	3,359
22,000	1,933.13	1,198	1,014.18	2,340	830.83	2,925	708.85	3,519
23,000	2,021.00	1,252	1,060.28	2,447	868.60	3,058	741.07	3,679
24,000	2,108.87	1,306	1,106.38	2,553	906.36	3,191	773.29	3,838
25,000	2,196.74	1,361	1,152.47	2,659	944.13	3,324	805.51	3,998
26,000	2,284.61	1,415	1,198.57	2,766	981.89	3,457	837.73	4,158
27,000	2,372.48	1,470	1,244.67	2,872	1,019.66	3,590	869.95	4,318
28,000	2,460.35	1,524	1,290.77	2,978	1,057.42	3,723	902.17	4,478
29,000	2,548.22	1,579	1,336.87	3,085	1,095.19	3,856	934.39	4,638
30,000	2,636.09	1,633	1,382.97	3,191	1,132.95	3,989	966.61	4,798
31,000	2,723.96	1,688	1,429.07	3,298	1,170.72	4,122	998.83	4,958
32,000	2,811.83	1,742	1,475.17	3,404	1,208.48	4,254	1,031.05	5,118
33,000	2,899.69	1,796	1,521.26	3,510	1,246.25	4,388	1,063.27	5,278
34,000	2,987.56	1,851	1,567.36	3,617	1,284.01	4,520	1,095.49	5,438
35,000	3,075.43	1,905	1,613.46	3,723	1,321.78	4,653	1,127.71	5,598
36,000	3,163.30	1,960	1,659.56	3,829	1,359.54	4,786	1,159.93	5,757
37,000	3,251.17	2,014	1,705.66	3,936	1,397.31	4,919	1,192.15	5,917
38,000	3,339.04	2,068	1,751.76	4,042	1,435.07	5,052	1,224.37	6,077
39,000	3,426.91	2,123	1,797.86	4,149	1,472.84	5,185	1,256.60	6,238
40,000	3,514.78	2,177	1,843.96	4,255	1,510.60	5,318	1,288.82	6,398
42,000	3,690.52	2,286	1,936.15	4,468	1,586.13	5,584	1,353.26	6,717
44,000	3,866.26	2,395	2,028.35	4,680	1,661.66	5,850	1,417.70	7,037
46,000	4,042.00	2,504	2,120.55	4,893	1,737.19	6,116	1,482.14	7,357
48,000	4,217.74	2,613	2,212.75	5,106	1,812.72	6,382	1,546.58	7,677
50,000	4,393.47	2,722	2,304.94	5,319	1,888.25	6,648	1,611.02	7,997

AUTO LOAN PAYMENTS 9.90%

AMOUNT OF LOAN	42 MOS MONTHLY PAYMENT	42 MOS TOTAL INTRST	48 MOS MONTHLY PAYMENT	48 MOS TOTAL INTRST	60 MOS MONTHLY PAYMENT	60 MOS TOTAL INTRST	72 MOS MONTHLY PAYMENT	72 MOS TOTAL INTRST
$ 1	0.03	0	0.03	0	0.03	1	0.02	0
2	0.06	1	0.06	1	0.05	1	0.04	1
3	0.09	1	0.08	1	0.07	1	0.06	1
4	0.12	1	0.11	1	0.09	1	0.08	2
5	0.15	1	0.13	1	0.11	2	0.10	2
6	0.17	1	0.16	2	0.13	2	0.12	3
7	0.20	1	0.18	2	0.15	2	0.13	2
8	0.23	2	0.21	2	0.17	2	0.15	3
9	0.26	2	0.23	2	0.20	3	0.17	3
10	0.29	2	0.26	2	0.22	3	0.19	4
20	0.57	4	0.51	4	0.43	6	0.37	7
30	0.85	6	0.76	6	0.64	8	0.56	10
40	1.14	8	1.02	9	0.85	11	0.74	13
50	1.42	10	1.27	11	1.06	14	0.93	17
60	1.70	11	1.52	13	1.28	17	1.11	20
70	1.98	13	1.78	15	1.49	19	1.30	24
80	2.27	15	2.03	17	1.70	22	1.48	27
90	2.55	17	2.28	19	1.91	25	1.67	30
100	2.83	19	2.54	22	2.12	27	1.85	33
200	5.66	38	5.07	43	4.24	54	3.70	66
300	8.49	57	7.60	65	6.36	82	5.55	100
400	11.31	75	10.13	86	8.48	109	7.40	133
500	14.14	94	12.66	108	10.60	136	9.24	165
600	16.97	113	15.19	129	12.72	163	11.09	198
700	19.79	131	17.73	151	14.84	190	12.94	232
800	22.62	150	20.26	172	16.96	218	14.79	265
900	25.45	169	22.79	194	19.08	245	16.63	297
1,000	28.27	187	25.32	215	21.20	272	18.48	331
2,000	56.54	375	50.63	430	42.40	544	36.96	661
3,000	84.81	562	75.95	646	63.60	816	55.43	991
4,000	113.08	749	101.26	860	84.80	1,088	73.91	1,322
5,000	141.35	937	126.58	1,076	105.99	1,359	92.38	1,651
6,000	169.62	1,124	151.89	1,291	127.19	1,631	110.86	1,982
7,000	197.89	1,311	177.21	1,506	148.39	1,903	129.33	2,312
8,000	226.16	1,499	202.52	1,721	169.59	2,175	147.81	2,642
9,000	254.43	1,686	227.84	1,936	190.79	2,447	166.28	2,972
10,000	282.70	1,873	253.15	2,151	211.98	2,719	184.76	3,303
11,000	310.97	2,061	278.47	2,367	233.18	2,991	203.23	3,633
12,000	339.24	2,248	303.78	2,581	254.38	3,263	221.71	3,963
13,000	367.51	2,435	329.09	2,796	275.58	3,535	240.19	4,294
14,000	395.78	2,623	354.41	3,012	296.78	3,807	258.66	4,624
15,000	424.05	2,810	379.72	3,227	317.97	4,078	277.14	4,954
16,000	452.32	2,997	405.04	3,442	339.17	4,350	295.61	5,284
17,000	480.58	3,184	430.35	3,657	360.37	4,622	314.09	5,614
18,000	508.85	3,372	455.67	3,872	381.57	4,894	332.56	5,944
19,000	537.12	3,559	480.98	4,087	402.76	5,166	351.04	6,275
20,000	565.39	3,746	506.30	4,302	423.96	5,438	369.51	6,605
21,000	593.66	3,934	531.61	4,517	445.16	5,710	387.99	6,935
22,000	621.93	4,121	556.93	4,733	466.36	5,982	406.46	7,265
23,000	650.20	4,308	582.24	4,948	487.56	6,254	424.94	7,596
24,000	678.47	4,496	607.56	5,163	508.75	6,525	443.42	7,926
25,000	706.74	4,683	632.87	5,378	529.95	6,797	461.89	8,256
26,000	735.01	4,870	658.18	5,593	551.15	7,069	480.37	8,587
27,000	763.28	5,058	683.50	5,808	572.35	7,341	498.84	8,916
28,000	791.55	5,245	708.81	6,023	593.55	7,613	517.32	9,247
29,000	819.82	5,432	734.13	6,238	614.74	7,884	535.79	9,577
30,000	848.09	5,620	759.44	6,453	635.94	8,156	554.27	9,907
31,000	876.36	5,807	784.76	6,668	657.14	8,428	572.74	10,237
32,000	904.63	5,994	810.07	6,883	678.34	8,700	591.22	10,568
33,000	932.89	6,181	835.39	7,099	699.53	8,972	609.69	10,898
34,000	961.16	6,369	860.70	7,314	720.73	9,244	628.17	11,228
35,000	989.43	6,556	886.02	7,529	741.93	9,516	646.65	11,559
36,000	1,017.70	6,743	911.33	7,744	763.13	9,788	665.12	11,889
37,000	1,045.97	6,931	936.64	7,959	784.33	10,060	683.60	12,219
38,000	1,074.24	7,118	961.96	8,174	805.52	10,331	702.07	12,549
39,000	1,102.51	7,305	987.27	8,389	826.72	10,603	720.55	12,880
40,000	1,130.78	7,493	1,012.59	8,604	847.92	10,875	739.02	13,209
42,000	1,187.32	7,867	1,063.22	9,035	890.32	11,419	775.97	13,870
44,000	1,243.86	8,242	1,113.85	9,465	932.71	11,963	812.92	14,530
46,000	1,300.40	8,617	1,164.48	9,895	975.11	12,507	849.88	15,191
48,000	1,356.94	8,991	1,215.11	10,325	1,017.50	13,050	886.83	15,852
50,000	1,413.47	9,366	1,265.73	10,755	1,059.90	13,594	923.78	16,512

10.00% AUTO LOAN PAYMENTS

AMOUNT OF LOAN	12 MOS MONTHLY PAYMENT	12 MOS TOTAL INTRST	24 MOS MONTHLY PAYMENT	24 MOS TOTAL INTRST	30 MOS MONTHLY PAYMENT	30 MOS TOTAL INTRST	36 MOS MONTHLY PAYMENT	36 MOS TOTAL INTRST
$ 1	0.09	0	0.05	0	0.04	0	0.04	0
2	0.18	0	0.10	0	0.08	0	0.07	1
3	0.27	0	0.14	0	0.12	1	0.10	1
4	0.36	0	0.19	1	0.16	1	0.13	1
5	0.44	1	0.24	1	0.19	1	0.17	1
6	0.53	0	0.28	1	0.23	1	0.20	1
7	0.62	0	0.33	1	0.27	1	0.23	1
8	0.71	1	0.37	1	0.31	1	0.26	1
9	0.80	1	0.42	1	0.35	2	0.30	2
10	0.88	1	0.47	1	0.38	1	0.33	2
20	1.76	1	0.93	2	0.76	3	0.65	3
30	2.64	2	1.39	3	1.14	4	0.97	5
40	3.52	2	1.85	4	1.52	6	1.30	7
50	4.40	3	2.31	5	1.90	7	1.62	8
60	5.28	3	2.77	6	2.27	8	1.94	10
70	6.16	4	3.24	8	2.65	10	2.26	11
80	7.04	4	3.70	9	3.03	11	2.59	13
90	7.92	5	4.16	10	3.41	12	2.91	15
100	8.80	6	4.62	11	3.79	14	3.23	16
200	17.59	11	9.23	22	7.57	27	6.46	33
300	26.38	17	13.85	32	11.35	41	9.69	49
400	35.17	22	18.46	43	15.13	54	12.91	65
500	43.96	28	23.08	54	18.91	67	16.14	81
600	52.75	33	27.69	65	22.69	81	19.37	97
700	61.55	39	32.31	75	26.47	94	22.59	113
800	70.34	44	36.92	86	30.25	108	25.82	130
900	79.13	50	41.54	97	34.04	121	29.05	146
1,000	87.92	55	46.15	108	37.82	135	32.27	162
2,000	175.84	110	92.29	215	75.63	269	64.54	323
3,000	263.75	165	138.44	323	113.44	403	96.81	485
4,000	351.67	220	184.58	430	151.25	538	129.07	647
5,000	439.58	275	230.73	538	189.06	672	161.34	808
6,000	527.50	330	276.87	645	226.87	806	193.61	970
7,000	615.42	385	323.02	752	264.68	940	225.88	1,132
8,000	703.33	440	369.16	860	302.50	1,075	258.14	1,293
9,000	791.25	495	415.31	967	340.31	1,209	290.41	1,455
10,000	879.16	550	461.45	1,075	378.12	1,344	322.68	1,616
11,000	967.08	605	507.60	1,182	415.93	1,478	354.94	1,778
12,000	1,055.00	660	553.74	1,290	453.74	1,612	387.21	1,940
13,000	1,142.91	715	599.89	1,397	491.55	1,747	419.48	2,101
14,000	1,230.83	770	646.03	1,505	529.36	1,881	451.75	2,263
15,000	1,318.74	825	692.18	1,612	567.18	2,015	484.01	2,424
16,000	1,406.66	880	738.32	1,720	604.99	2,150	516.28	2,586
17,000	1,494.58	935	784.47	1,827	642.80	2,284	548.55	2,748
18,000	1,582.49	990	830.61	1,935	680.61	2,418	580.81	2,909
19,000	1,670.41	1,045	876.76	2,042	718.42	2,553	613.08	3,071
20,000	1,758.32	1,100	922.90	2,150	756.23	2,687	645.35	3,233
21,000	1,846.24	1,155	969.05	2,257	794.04	2,821	677.62	3,394
22,000	1,934.15	1,210	1,015.19	2,365	831.86	2,956	709.88	3,556
23,000	2,022.07	1,265	1,061.34	2,472	869.67	3,090	742.15	3,717
24,000	2,109.99	1,320	1,107.48	2,580	907.48	3,224	774.42	3,879
25,000	2,197.90	1,375	1,153.63	2,687	945.30	3,359	806.68	4,040
26,000	2,285.82	1,430	1,199.77	2,794	983.10	3,493	838.95	4,202
27,000	2,373.73	1,485	1,245.92	2,902	1,020.91	3,627	871.22	4,364
28,000	2,461.65	1,540	1,292.06	3,009	1,058.72	3,762	903.49	4,526
29,000	2,549.57	1,595	1,338.21	3,117	1,096.54	3,896	935.75	4,687
30,000	2,637.48	1,650	1,384.35	3,224	1,134.35	4,031	968.02	4,849
31,000	2,725.40	1,705	1,430.50	3,332	1,172.16	4,165	1,000.29	5,010
32,000	2,813.31	1,760	1,476.64	3,439	1,209.97	4,299	1,032.55	5,172
33,000	2,901.23	1,815	1,522.79	3,547	1,247.78	4,433	1,064.82	5,334
34,000	2,989.15	1,870	1,568.93	3,654	1,285.59	4,568	1,097.09	5,495
35,000	3,077.06	1,925	1,615.08	3,762	1,323.40	4,702	1,129.36	5,657
36,000	3,164.98	1,980	1,661.22	3,869	1,361.22	4,837	1,161.62	5,818
37,000	3,252.89	2,035	1,707.37	3,977	1,399.03	4,971	1,193.89	5,980
38,000	3,340.81	2,090	1,753.51	4,084	1,436.84	5,105	1,226.16	6,142
39,000	3,428.72	2,145	1,799.66	4,192	1,474.65	5,240	1,258.43	6,303
40,000	3,516.64	2,200	1,845.80	4,299	1,512.46	5,374	1,290.69	6,465
42,000	3,692.47	2,310	1,938.09	4,514	1,588.08	5,642	1,355.23	6,788
44,000	3,868.30	2,420	2,030.38	4,729	1,663.71	5,911	1,419.76	7,111
46,000	4,044.14	2,530	2,122.67	4,944	1,739.33	6,180	1,484.30	7,435
48,000	4,219.97	2,640	2,214.96	5,159	1,814.95	6,449	1,548.83	7,758
50,000	4,395.80	2,750	2,307.25	5,374	1,890.58	6,717	1,613.36	8,081

AUTO LOAN PAYMENTS 10.00%

AMOUNT OF LOAN	42 MOS MONTHLY PAYMENT	42 MOS TOTAL INTRST	48 MOS MONTHLY PAYMENT	48 MOS TOTAL INTRST	60 MOS MONTHLY PAYMENT	60 MOS TOTAL INTRST	72 MOS MONTHLY PAYMENT	72 MOS TOTAL INTRST
$ 1	0.03	0	0.03	0	0.03	1	0.02	0
2	0.06	1	0.06	1	0.05	1	0.04	1
3	0.09	1	0.08	1	0.07	1	0.06	1
4	0.12	1	0.11	1	0.09	1	0.08	2
5	0.15	1	0.13	1	0.11	2	0.10	2
6	0.17	1	0.16	2	0.13	2	0.12	3
7	0.20	1	0.18	2	0.15	2	0.13	2
8	0.23	2	0.21	2	0.17	2	0.15	3
9	0.26	2	0.23	2	0.20	3	0.17	3
10	0.29	2	0.26	2	0.22	3	0.19	4
20	0.57	4	0.51	4	0.43	6	0.38	7
30	0.85	6	0.77	7	0.64	8	0.56	10
40	1.14	8	1.02	9	0.85	11	0.75	14
50	1.42	10	1.27	11	1.07	14	0.93	17
60	1.70	11	1.53	13	1.28	17	1.12	21
70	1.99	14	1.78	15	1.49	19	1.30	24
80	2.27	15	2.03	17	1.70	22	1.49	27
90	2.55	17	2.29	20	1.92	25	1.67	30
100	2.84	19	2.54	22	2.13	28	1.86	34
200	5.67	38	5.08	44	4.25	55	3.71	67
300	8.50	57	7.61	65	6.38	83	5.56	100
400	11.33	76	10.15	87	8.50	110	7.42	134
500	14.16	95	12.69	109	10.63	138	9.27	167
600	17.00	114	15.22	131	12.75	165	11.12	201
700	19.83	133	17.76	152	14.88	193	12.97	234
800	22.66	152	20.30	174	17.00	220	14.83	268
900	25.49	171	22.83	196	19.13	248	16.68	301
1,000	28.32	189	25.37	218	21.25	275	18.53	334
2,000	56.64	379	50.73	435	42.50	550	37.06	668
3,000	84.96	568	76.09	652	63.75	825	55.58	1,002
4,000	113.27	757	101.46	870	84.99	1,099	74.11	1,336
5,000	141.59	947	126.82	1,087	106.24	1,374	92.63	1,669
6,000	169.91	1,136	152.18	1,305	127.49	1,649	111.16	2,004
7,000	198.22	1,325	177.54	1,522	148.73	1,924	129.69	2,338
8,000	226.54	1,515	202.91	1,740	169.98	2,199	148.21	2,671
9,000	254.86	1,704	228.27	1,957	191.23	2,474	166.74	3,005
10,000	283.17	1,893	253.63	2,174	212.48	2,749	185.26	3,339
11,000	311.49	2,083	278.99	2,392	233.72	3,023	203.79	3,673
12,000	339.81	2,272	304.36	2,609	254.97	3,298	222.32	4,007
13,000	368.12	2,461	329.72	2,827	276.22	3,573	240.84	4,340
14,000	396.44	2,650	355.08	3,044	297.46	3,848	259.37	4,675
15,000	424.76	2,840	380.44	3,261	318.71	4,123	277.89	5,008
16,000	453.07	3,029	405.81	3,479	339.96	4,398	296.42	5,342
17,000	481.39	3,218	431.17	3,696	361.20	4,672	314.94	5,676
18,000	509.71	3,408	456.53	3,913	382.45	4,947	333.47	6,010
19,000	538.02	3,597	481.89	4,131	403.70	5,222	352.00	6,344
20,000	566.34	3,786	507.26	4,348	424.95	5,497	370.52	6,677
21,000	594.66	3,976	532.62	4,566	446.19	5,771	389.05	7,012
22,000	622.98	4,165	557.98	4,783	467.44	6,046	407.57	7,345
23,000	651.29	4,354	583.34	5,000	488.69	6,321	426.10	7,679
24,000	679.61	4,544	608.71	5,218	509.93	6,596	444.63	8,013
25,000	707.93	4,733	634.07	5,435	531.18	6,871	463.15	8,347
26,000	736.24	4,922	659.43	5,653	552.43	7,146	481.68	8,681
27,000	764.56	5,112	684.79	5,870	573.68	7,421	500.20	9,014
28,000	792.88	5,301	710.16	6,088	594.92	7,695	518.73	9,349
29,000	821.19	5,490	735.52	6,305	616.17	7,970	537.25	9,682
30,000	849.51	5,679	760.88	6,522	637.42	8,245	555.78	10,016
31,000	877.83	5,869	786.25	6,740	658.66	8,520	574.31	10,350
32,000	906.14	6,058	811.61	6,957	679.91	8,795	592.83	10,684
33,000	934.46	6,247	836.97	7,175	701.16	9,070	611.36	11,018
34,000	962.78	6,437	862.33	7,392	722.40	9,344	629.88	11,351
35,000	991.09	6,626	887.70	7,610	743.65	9,619	648.41	11,686
36,000	1,019.41	6,815	913.06	7,827	764.90	9,894	666.94	12,020
37,000	1,047.73	7,005	938.42	8,044	786.15	10,169	685.46	12,353
38,000	1,076.04	7,194	963.78	8,261	807.39	10,443	703.99	12,687
39,000	1,104.36	7,383	989.15	8,479	828.64	10,718	722.51	13,021
40,000	1,132.68	7,573	1,014.51	8,696	849.89	10,993	741.04	13,355
42,000	1,189.31	7,951	1,065.23	9,131	892.38	11,543	778.09	14,022
44,000	1,245.95	8,330	1,115.96	9,566	934.87	12,092	815.14	14,690
46,000	1,302.58	8,708	1,166.68	10,001	977.37	12,642	852.19	15,358
48,000	1,359.21	9,087	1,217.41	10,436	1,019.86	13,192	889.25	16,026
50,000	1,415.85	9,466	1,268.13	10,870	1,062.36	13,742	926.30	16,694

AUTO LOAN PAYMENTS

AMOUNT OF LOAN	12 MOS		24 MOS		30 MOS		36 MOS	
	MONTHLY PAYMENT	TOTAL INTRST	MONTHLY PAYMENT	TOTAL INTRST	MONTHLY PAYMENT	TOTAL INTRST	MONTHLY PAYMENT	TOTAL INTRST
$ 1	0.09	0	0.05	0	0.04	0	0.04	0
2	0.18	0	0.10	0	0.08	0	0.07	1
3	0.27	0	0.14	0	0.12	1	0.10	1
4	0.36	0	0.19	1	0.16	1	0.13	1
5	0.45	0	0.24	1	0.19	1	0.17	1
6	0.53	0	0.28	1	0.23	1	0.20	1
7	0.62	0	0.33	1	0.27	1	0.23	1
8	0.71	1	0.38	1	0.31	1	0.26	1
9	0.80	1	0.42	1	0.35	2	0.30	2
10	0.89	1	0.47	1	0.38	1	0.33	2
20	1.77	1	0.93	2	0.76	3	0.65	3
30	2.65	2	1.39	3	1.14	4	0.98	5
40	3.53	2	1.86	5	1.52	6	1.30	7
50	4.41	3	2.32	6	1.90	7	1.62	8
60	5.29	3	2.78	7	2.28	8	1.95	10
70	6.17	4	3.24	8	2.66	10	2.27	12
80	7.05	4	3.71	9	3.04	11	2.60	14
90	7.93	5	4.17	10	3.42	13	2.92	15
100	8.81	6	4.63	11	3.80	14	3.24	17
200	17.61	11	9.26	22	7.59	28	6.48	33
300	26.41	17	13.88	33	11.38	41	9.72	50
400	35.22	23	18.51	44	15.18	55	12.96	67
500	44.02	28	23.14	55	18.97	69	16.20	83
600	52.82	34	27.76	66	22.76	83	19.44	100
700	61.63	40	32.39	77	26.55	97	22.67	116
800	70.43	45	37.01	88	30.35	111	25.91	133
900	79.23	51	41.64	99	34.14	124	29.15	149
1,000	88.04	56	46.27	110	37.93	138	32.39	166
2,000	176.07	113	92.53	221	75.86	276	64.77	332
3,000	264.10	169	138.79	331	113.79	414	97.16	498
4,000	352.13	226	185.05	441	151.72	552	129.54	663
5,000	440.17	282	231.31	551	189.64	689	161.93	829
6,000	528.20	338	277.57	662	227.57	827	194.31	995
7,000	616.23	395	323.83	772	265.50	965	226.70	1,161
8,000	704.26	451	370.09	882	303.43	1,103	259.08	1,327
9,000	792.29	507	416.35	992	341.35	1,241	291.47	1,493
10,000	880.33	564	462.61	1,103	379.28	1,378	323.85	1,659
11,000	968.36	620	508.87	1,213	417.21	1,516	356.24	1,825
12,000	1,056.39	677	555.13	1,323	455.14	1,654	388.62	1,990
13,000	1,144.42	733	601.39	1,433	493.07	1,792	421.01	2,156
14,000	1,232.46	790	647.65	1,544	530.99	1,930	453.39	2,322
15,000	1,320.49	846	693.91	1,654	568.92	2,068	485.78	2,488
16,000	1,408.52	902	740.17	1,764	606.85	2,206	518.16	2,654
17,000	1,496.55	959	786.43	1,874	644.78	2,343	550.54	2,819
18,000	1,584.58	1,015	832.69	1,985	682.70	2,481	582.93	2,985
19,000	1,672.62	1,071	878.95	2,095	720.63	2,619	615.31	3,151
20,000	1,760.65	1,128	925.21	2,205	758.56	2,757	647.70	3,317
21,000	1,848.68	1,184	971.47	2,315	796.49	2,895	680.08	3,483
22,000	1,936.71	1,241	1,017.73	2,426	834.42	3,033	712.47	3,649
23,000	2,024.75	1,297	1,063.99	2,536	872.34	3,170	744.85	3,815
24,000	2,112.78	1,353	1,110.25	2,646	910.27	3,308	777.24	3,981
25,000	2,200.81	1,410	1,156.51	2,756	948.20	3,446	809.62	4,146
26,000	2,288.84	1,466	1,202.78	2,867	986.13	3,584	842.01	4,312
27,000	2,376.87	1,522	1,249.04	2,977	1,024.05	3,722	874.39	4,478
28,000	2,464.91	1,579	1,295.30	3,087	1,061.98	3,859	906.78	4,644
29,000	2,552.94	1,635	1,341.56	3,197	1,099.91	3,997	939.16	4,810
30,000	2,640.97	1,692	1,387.82	3,308	1,137.84	4,135	971.55	4,976
31,000	2,729.00	1,748	1,434.08	3,418	1,175.77	4,273	1,003.93	5,141
32,000	2,817.04	1,804	1,480.34	3,528	1,213.69	4,411	1,036.32	5,308
33,000	2,905.07	1,861	1,526.60	3,638	1,251.62	4,549	1,068.70	5,473
34,000	2,993.10	1,917	1,572.86	3,749	1,289.55	4,687	1,101.08	5,639
35,000	3,081.13	1,974	1,619.12	3,859	1,327.48	4,824	1,133.47	5,805
36,000	3,169.16	2,030	1,665.38	3,969	1,365.40	4,962	1,165.85	5,971
37,000	3,257.20	2,086	1,711.64	4,079	1,403.33	5,100	1,198.24	6,137
38,000	3,345.23	2,143	1,757.90	4,190	1,441.26	5,238	1,230.62	6,302
39,000	3,433.26	2,199	1,804.16	4,300	1,479.19	5,376	1,263.01	6,468
40,000	3,521.29	2,255	1,850.42	4,410	1,517.12	5,514	1,295.39	6,634
42,000	3,697.36	2,368	1,942.94	4,631	1,592.97	5,789	1,360.16	6,966
44,000	3,873.42	2,481	2,035.46	4,851	1,668.83	6,065	1,424.93	7,297
46,000	4,049.49	2,594	2,127.98	5,072	1,744.68	6,340	1,489.70	7,629
48,000	4,225.55	2,707	2,220.50	5,292	1,820.54	6,616	1,554.47	7,961
50,000	4,401.62	2,819	2,313.02	5,512	1,896.39	6,892	1,619.24	8,293

AMOUNT OF LOAN	42 MOS		48 MOS		60 MOS		72 MOS	
	MONTHLY PAYMENT	TOTAL INTRST	MONTHLY PAYMENT	TOTAL INTRST	MONTHLY PAYMENT	TOTAL INTRST	MONTHLY PAYMENT	TOTAL INTRST
$ 1	0.03	0	0.03	0	0.03	1	0.02	0
2	0.06	1	0.06	1	0.05	1	0.04	1
3	0.09	1	0.08	1	0.07	1	0.06	1
4	0.12	1	0.11	1	0.09	1	0.08	2
5	0.15	1	0.13	1	0.11	2	0.10	2
6	0.18	2	0.16	2	0.13	2	0.12	3
7	0.20	1	0.18	2	0.15	2	0.14	3
8	0.23	2	0.21	2	0.18	3	0.15	3
9	0.26	2	0.23	2	0.20	3	0.17	3
10	0.29	2	0.26	2	0.22	3	0.19	4
20	0.57	4	0.51	4	0.43	6	0.38	7
30	0.86	6	0.77	7	0.65	9	0.56	10
40	1.14	8	1.02	9	0.86	12	0.75	14
50	1.43	10	1.28	11	1.07	14	0.94	18
60	1.71	12	1.53	13	1.29	17	1.12	21
70	2.00	14	1.79	16	1.50	20	1.31	24
80	2.28	16	2.04	18	1.71	23	1.50	28
90	2.56	18	2.30	20	1.93	26	1.68	31
100	2.85	20	2.55	22	2.14	28	1.87	35
200	5.69	39	5.10	45	4.28	57	3.74	69
300	8.54	59	7.65	67	6.42	85	5.60	103
400	11.38	78	10.20	90	8.55	113	7.47	138
500	14.22	97	12.75	112	10.69	141	9.33	172
600	17.07	117	15.29	134	12.83	170	11.20	206
700	19.91	136	17.84	156	14.96	198	13.06	240
800	22.75	156	20.39	179	17.10	226	14.93	275
900	25.60	175	22.94	201	19.24	254	16.79	309
1,000	28.44	194	25.49	224	21.38	283	18.66	344
2,000	56.88	389	50.97	447	42.75	565	37.31	686
3,000	85.31	583	76.45	670	64.12	847	55.96	1,029
4,000	113.75	778	101.94	893	85.49	1,129	74.61	1,372
5,000	142.18	972	127.42	1,116	106.86	1,412	93.27	1,715
6,000	170.62	1,166	152.90	1,339	128.23	1,694	111.92	2,058
7,000	199.05	1,360	178.38	1,562	149.60	1,976	130.57	2,401
8,000	227.49	1,555	203.87	1,786	170.97	2,258	149.22	2,744
9,000	255.93	1,749	229.35	2,009	192.34	2,540	167.87	3,087
10,000	284.36	1,943	254.83	2,232	213.71	2,823	186.53	3,430
11,000	312.80	2,138	280.32	2,455	235.08	3,105	205.18	3,773
12,000	341.23	2,332	305.80	2,678	256.45	3,387	223.83	4,116
13,000	369.67	2,526	331.28	2,901	277.82	3,669	242.48	4,459
14,000	398.10	2,720	356.76	3,124	299.19	3,951	261.14	4,802
15,000	426.54	2,915	382.25	3,348	320.56	4,234	279.79	5,145
16,000	454.98	3,109	407.73	3,571	341.93	4,516	298.44	5,488
17,000	483.41	3,303	433.21	3,794	363.30	4,798	317.09	5,830
18,000	511.85	3,498	458.70	4,018	384.67	5,080	335.74	6,173
19,000	540.28	3,692	484.18	4,241	406.04	5,362	354.40	6,517
20,000	568.72	3,886	509.66	4,464	427.41	5,645	373.05	6,860
21,000	597.15	4,080	535.14	4,687	448.78	5,927	391.70	7,202
22,000	625.59	4,275	560.63	4,910	470.15	6,209	410.35	7,545
23,000	654.02	4,469	586.11	5,133	491.52	6,491	429.00	7,888
24,000	682.46	4,663	611.59	5,356	512.89	6,773	447.66	8,232
25,000	710.90	4,858	637.08	5,580	534.26	7,056	466.31	8,574
26,000	739.33	5,052	662.56	5,803	555.63	7,338	484.96	8,917
27,000	767.77	5,246	688.04	6,026	577.00	7,620	503.61	9,260
28,000	796.20	5,440	713.52	6,249	598.37	7,902	522.27	9,603
29,000	824.64	5,635	739.01	6,472	619.74	8,184	540.92	9,946
30,000	853.07	5,829	764.49	6,696	641.11	8,467	559.57	10,289
31,000	881.51	6,023	789.97	6,919	662.48	8,749	578.22	10,632
32,000	909.95	6,218	815.46	7,142	683.85	9,031	596.87	10,975
33,000	938.38	6,412	840.94	7,365	705.22	9,313	615.53	11,318
34,000	966.82	6,606	866.42	7,588	726.59	9,595	634.18	11,661
35,000	995.25	6,801	891.90	7,811	747.96	9,878	652.83	12,004
36,000	1,023.69	6,995	917.39	8,035	769.33	10,160	671.48	12,347
37,000	1,052.12	7,189	942.87	8,258	790.70	10,442	690.13	12,689
38,000	1,080.56	7,384	968.35	8,481	812.08	10,725	708.79	13,033
39,000	1,108.99	7,578	993.83	8,704	833.45	11,007	727.44	13,376
40,000	1,137.43	7,772	1,019.32	8,927	854.82	11,289	746.09	13,718
42,000	1,194.30	8,161	1,070.28	9,373	897.56	11,854	783.40	14,405
44,000	1,251.17	8,549	1,121.25	9,820	940.30	12,418	820.70	15,090
46,000	1,308.04	8,938	1,172.21	10,266	983.04	12,983	858.00	15,776
48,000	1,364.92	9,327	1,223.18	10,713	1,025.78	13,547	895.31	16,462
50,000	1,421.79	9,715	1,274.15	11,159	1,068.52	14,111	932.61	17,148

AUTO LOAN PAYMENTS

AMOUNT OF LOAN	12 MOS		24 MOS		30 MOS		36 MOS	
	MONTHLY PAYMENT	TOTAL INTRST	MONTHLY PAYMENT	TOTAL INTRST	MONTHLY PAYMENT	TOTAL INTRST	MONTHLY PAYMENT	TOTAL INTRST
$ 1	0.09	0	0.05	0	0.04	0	0.04	0
2	0.18	0	0.10	0	0.08	0	0.07	1
3	0.27	0	0.14	0	0.12	1	0.10	1
4	0.36	0	0.19	1	0.16	1	0.14	1
5	0.45	1	0.24	1	0.20	1	0.17	1
6	0.53	0	0.28	1	0.23	1	0.20	1
7	0.62	0	0.33	1	0.27	1	0.23	1
8	0.71	1	0.38	1	0.31	1	0.27	2
9	0.80	1	0.42	1	0.35	2	0.30	2
10	0.89	1	0.47	1	0.39	2	0.33	2
20	1.77	1	0.93	2	0.77	3	0.66	4
30	2.65	2	1.40	4	1.15	5	0.98	5
40	3.53	2	1.86	5	1.53	6	1.31	7
50	4.41	3	2.32	6	1.91	7	1.63	9
60	5.29	3	2.79	7	2.29	9	1.96	11
70	6.18	4	3.25	8	2.67	10	2.28	12
80	7.06	5	3.72	9	3.05	12	2.61	14
90	7.94	5	4.18	10	3.43	13	2.93	15
100	8.82	6	4.64	11	3.81	14	3.26	17
200	17.63	12	9.28	23	7.61	28	6.51	34
300	26.45	17	13.92	34	11.42	43	9.76	51
400	35.26	23	18.56	45	15.22	57	13.01	68
500	44.08	29	23.19	57	19.03	71	16.26	85
600	52.89	35	27.83	68	22.83	85	19.51	102
700	61.71	41	32.47	79	26.64	99	22.76	119
800	70.52	46	37.11	91	30.44	113	26.01	136
900	79.34	52	41.74	102	34.24	127	29.26	153
1,000	88.15	58	46.38	113	38.05	142	32.51	170
2,000	176.30	116	92.76	226	76.09	283	65.01	340
3,000	264.45	173	139.13	339	114.14	424	97.51	510
4,000	352.60	231	185.51	452	152.18	565	130.01	680
5,000	440.75	289	231.89	565	190.23	707	162.52	851
6,000	528.90	347	278.26	678	228.27	848	195.02	1,021
7,000	617.05	405	324.64	791	266.32	990	227.52	1,191
8,000	705.19	462	371.01	904	304.36	1,131	260.02	1,361
9,000	793.34	520	417.39	1,017	342.40	1,272	292.53	1,531
10,000	881.49	578	463.77	1,130	380.45	1,414	325.03	1,701
11,000	969.64	636	510.14	1,243	418.49	1,555	357.53	1,871
12,000	1,057.79	693	556.52	1,356	456.54	1,696	390.03	2,041
13,000	1,145.94	751	602.89	1,469	494.58	1,837	422.54	2,211
14,000	1,234.09	809	649.27	1,582	532.63	1,979	455.04	2,381
15,000	1,322.23	867	695.65	1,696	570.67	2,120	487.54	2,551
16,000	1,410.38	925	742.02	1,808	608.71	2,261	520.04	2,721
17,000	1,498.53	982	788.40	1,922	646.76	2,403	552.55	2,892
18,000	1,586.68	1,040	834.77	2,034	684.80	2,544	585.05	3,062
19,000	1,674.83	1,098	881.15	2,148	722.85	2,686	617.55	3,232
20,000	1,762.98	1,156	927.53	2,261	760.89	2,827	650.05	3,402
21,000	1,851.13	1,214	973.90	2,374	798.94	2,968	682.56	3,572
22,000	1,939.27	1,271	1,020.28	2,487	836.98	3,109	715.06	3,742
23,000	2,027.42	1,329	1,066.65	2,600	875.02	3,251	747.56	3,912
24,000	2,115.57	1,387	1,113.03	2,713	913.07	3,392	780.06	4,082
25,000	2,203.72	1,445	1,159.41	2,826	951.11	3,533	812.57	4,253
26,000	2,291.87	1,502	1,205.78	2,939	989.16	3,675	845.07	4,423
27,000	2,380.02	1,560	1,252.16	3,052	1,027.20	3,816	877.57	4,593
28,000	2,468.17	1,618	1,298.53	3,165	1,065.25	3,958	910.07	4,763
29,000	2,556.31	1,676	1,344.91	3,278	1,103.29	4,099	942.58	4,933
30,000	2,644.46	1,734	1,391.29	3,391	1,141.33	4,240	975.08	5,103
31,000	2,732.61	1,791	1,437.66	3,504	1,179.38	4,381	1,007.58	5,273
32,000	2,820.76	1,849	1,484.04	3,617	1,217.42	4,523	1,040.08	5,443
33,000	2,908.91	1,907	1,530.41	3,730	1,255.47	4,664	1,072.59	5,613
34,000	2,997.06	1,965	1,576.79	3,843	1,293.51	4,805	1,105.09	5,783
35,000	3,085.21	2,023	1,623.17	3,956	1,331.56	4,947	1,137.59	5,953
36,000	3,173.35	2,080	1,669.54	4,069	1,369.60	5,088	1,170.09	6,123
37,000	3,261.50	2,138	1,715.92	4,182	1,407.64	5,229	1,202.60	6,294
38,000	3,349.65	2,196	1,762.29	4,295	1,445.69	5,371	1,235.10	6,464
39,000	3,437.80	2,254	1,808.67	4,408	1,483.73	5,512	1,267.60	6,634
40,000	3,525.95	2,311	1,855.05	4,521	1,521.78	5,653	1,300.10	6,804
42,000	3,702.25	2,427	1,947.80	4,747	1,597.87	5,936	1,365.11	7,144
44,000	3,878.54	2,542	2,040.55	4,973	1,673.95	6,219	1,430.11	7,484
46,000	4,054.84	2,658	2,133.30	5,199	1,750.04	6,501	1,495.12	7,824
48,000	4,231.14	2,774	2,226.05	5,425	1,826.13	6,784	1,560.12	8,164
50,000	4,407.44	2,889	2,318.81	5,651	1,902.22	7,067	1,625.13	8,505

AUTO LOAN PAYMENTS 10.50%

AMOUNT OF LOAN	42 MOS MONTHLY PAYMENT	42 MOS TOTAL INTRST	48 MOS MONTHLY PAYMENT	48 MOS TOTAL INTRST	60 MOS MONTHLY PAYMENT	60 MOS TOTAL INTRST	72 MOS MONTHLY PAYMENT	72 MOS TOTAL INTRST
$ 1	0.03	0	0.03	0	0.03	1	0.02	0
2	0.06	1	0.06	1	0.05	1	0.04	1
3	0.09	1	0.08	1	0.07	1	0.06	1
4	0.12	1	0.11	1	0.09	1	0.08	2
5	0.15	1	0.13	1	0.11	2	0.10	2
6	0.18	2	0.16	2	0.13	2	0.12	3
7	0.20	1	0.18	2	0.16	3	0.14	3
8	0.23	2	0.21	2	0.18	3	0.16	4
9	0.26	2	0.24	3	0.20	3	0.17	3
10	0.29	2	0.26	2	0.22	3	0.19	4
20	0.58	4	0.52	5	0.43	6	0.38	7
30	0.86	6	0.77	7	0.65	9	0.57	11
40	1.15	8	1.03	9	0.86	12	0.76	15
50	1.43	10	1.29	12	1.08	15	0.94	18
60	1.72	12	1.54	14	1.29	17	1.13	21
70	2.00	14	1.80	16	1.51	21	1.32	25
80	2.29	16	2.05	18	1.72	23	1.51	29
90	2.57	18	2.31	21	1.94	26	1.70	32
100	2.86	20	2.57	23	2.15	29	1.88	35
200	5.72	40	5.13	46	4.30	58	3.76	71
300	8.57	60	7.69	69	6.45	87	5.64	106
400	11.43	80	10.25	92	8.60	116	7.52	141
500	14.28	100	12.81	115	10.75	145	9.39	176
600	17.14	120	15.37	138	12.90	174	11.27	211
700	19.99	140	17.93	161	15.05	203	13.15	247
800	22.85	160	20.49	184	17.20	232	15.03	282
900	25.70	179	23.05	206	19.35	261	16.91	318
1,000	28.56	200	25.61	229	21.50	290	18.78	352
2,000	57.11	399	51.21	458	42.99	579	37.56	704
3,000	85.67	598	76.82	687	64.49	869	56.34	1,056
4,000	114.22	797	102.42	916	85.98	1,159	75.12	1,409
5,000	142.78	997	128.02	1,145	107.47	1,448	93.90	1,761
6,000	171.33	1,196	153.63	1,374	128.97	1,738	112.68	2,113
7,000	199.89	1,395	179.23	1,603	150.46	2,028	131.46	2,465
8,000	228.44	1,594	204.83	1,832	171.96	2,318	150.24	2,817
9,000	257.00	1,794	230.44	2,061	193.45	2,607	169.02	3,169
10,000	285.55	1,993	256.04	2,290	214.94	2,896	187.79	3,521
11,000	314.11	2,193	281.64	2,519	236.44	3,186	206.57	3,873
12,000	342.66	2,392	307.25	2,748	257.93	3,476	225.35	4,225
13,000	371.22	2,591	332.85	2,977	279.43	3,766	244.13	4,577
14,000	399.77	2,790	358.45	3,206	300.92	4,055	262.91	4,930
15,000	428.33	2,990	384.06	3,435	322.41	4,345	281.69	5,282
16,000	456.88	3,189	409.66	3,664	343.91	4,635	300.47	5,634
17,000	485.44	3,388	435.26	3,892	365.40	4,924	319.25	5,986
18,000	513.99	3,588	460.87	4,122	386.90	5,214	338.03	6,338
19,000	542.55	3,787	486.47	4,351	408.39	5,503	356.81	6,690
20,000	571.10	3,986	512.07	4,579	429.88	5,793	375.58	7,042
21,000	599.65	4,185	537.68	4,809	451.38	6,083	394.36	7,394
22,000	628.21	4,385	563.28	5,037	472.87	6,372	413.14	7,746
23,000	656.76	4,584	588.88	5,266	494.36	6,662	431.92	8,098
24,000	685.32	4,783	614.49	5,496	515.86	6,952	450.70	8,450
25,000	713.87	4,983	640.09	5,724	537.35	7,241	469.48	8,803
26,000	742.43	5,182	665.69	5,953	558.85	7,531	488.26	9,155
27,000	770.98	5,381	691.30	6,182	580.34	7,820	507.04	9,507
28,000	799.54	5,581	716.90	6,411	601.83	8,110	525.82	9,859
29,000	828.09	5,780	742.50	6,640	623.33	8,400	544.60	10,211
30,000	856.65	5,979	768.11	6,869	644.82	8,689	563.37	10,563
31,000	885.20	6,178	793.71	7,098	666.32	8,979	582.15	10,915
32,000	913.76	6,378	819.31	7,327	687.81	9,269	600.93	11,267
33,000	942.31	6,577	844.92	7,556	709.30	9,558	619.71	11,619
34,000	970.87	6,777	870.52	7,785	730.80	9,848	638.49	11,971
35,000	999.42	6,976	896.12	8,014	752.29	10,137	657.27	12,323
36,000	1,027.98	7,175	921.73	8,243	773.79	10,427	676.05	12,676
37,000	1,056.53	7,374	947.33	8,472	795.28	10,717	694.83	13,028
38,000	1,085.09	7,574	972.93	8,701	816.77	11,006	713.61	13,380
39,000	1,113.64	7,773	998.54	8,930	838.27	11,296	732.38	13,731
40,000	1,142.19	7,972	1,024.14	9,159	859.76	11,586	751.16	14,084
42,000	1,199.30	8,371	1,075.35	9,617	902.75	12,165	788.72	14,788
44,000	1,256.41	8,769	1,126.55	10,074	945.74	12,744	826.28	15,492
46,000	1,313.52	9,168	1,177.76	10,532	988.72	13,323	863.84	16,196
48,000	1,370.63	9,566	1,228.97	10,991	1,031.71	13,903	901.40	16,901
50,000	1,427.74	9,965	1,280.17	11,448	1,074.70	14,482	938.95	17,604

109

AUTO LOAN PAYMENTS

AMOUNT OF LOAN	12 MOS		24 MOS		30 MOS		36 MOS	
	MONTHLY PAYMENT	TOTAL INTRST	MONTHLY PAYMENT	TOTAL INTRST	MONTHLY PAYMENT	TOTAL INTRST	MONTHLY PAYMENT	TOTAL INTRST
$ 1	0.09	0	0.05	0	0.04	0	0.04	0
2	0.18	0	0.10	0	0.08	0	0.07	1
3	0.27	0	0.14	0	0.12	1	0.10	1
4	0.36	0	0.19	1	0.16	1	0.14	1
5	0.45	0	0.24	1	0.20	1	0.17	1
6	0.53	1	0.28	1	0.23	1	0.20	1
7	0.62	0	0.33	1	0.27	1	0.23	1
8	0.71	1	0.38	1	0.31	1	0.27	2
9	0.80	1	0.42	1	0.35	2	0.30	2
10	0.89	1	0.47	1	0.39	2	0.33	2
20	1.77	1	0.93	2	0.77	3	0.66	4
30	2.65	2	1.40	2	1.15	5	0.98	5
40	3.54	2	1.86	5	1.53	6	1.31	7
50	4.42	3	2.33	6	1.91	7	1.64	9
60	5.30	4	2.79	7	2.29	9	1.96	11
70	6.18	4	3.26	8	2.68	10	2.29	12
80	7.07	5	3.72	9	3.06	12	2.61	14
90	7.95	5	4.19	11	3.44	13	2.94	16
100	8.83	6	4.65	12	3.82	15	3.27	18
200	17.66	12	9.30	23	7.64	29	6.53	35
300	26.48	18	13.95	35	11.45	44	9.79	52
400	35.31	24	18.60	46	15.27	58	13.05	70
500	44.14	30	23.25	58	19.09	73	16.32	88
600	52.96	36	27.90	70	22.90	87	19.58	105
700	61.79	41	32.55	81	26.72	102	22.84	122
800	70.62	47	37.20	93	30.53	116	26.10	140
900	79.44	53	41.85	104	34.35	131	29.36	157
1,000	88.27	59	46.50	116	38.17	145	32.63	175
2,000	176.54	118	92.99	232	76.33	290	65.25	349
3,000	264.80	178	139.48	348	114.49	435	97.87	523
4,000	353.07	237	185.97	463	152.65	580	130.49	698
5,000	441.33	296	232.46	579	190.81	724	163.11	872
6,000	529.60	355	278.96	695	228.97	869	195.73	1,046
7,000	617.86	414	325.45	811	267.13	1,014	228.35	1,221
8,000	706.13	474	371.94	927	305.29	1,159	260.97	1,395
9,000	794.39	533	418.43	1,042	343.45	1,304	293.59	1,569
10,000	882.66	592	464.92	1,158	381.62	1,449	326.21	1,744
11,000	970.92	651	511.42	1,274	419.78	1,593	358.83	1,918
12,000	1,059.19	710	557.91	1,390	457.94	1,738	391.45	2,092
13,000	1,147.45	769	604.40	1,506	496.10	1,883	424.07	2,267
14,000	1,235.72	829	650.89	1,621	534.26	2,028	456.69	2,441
15,000	1,323.98	888	697.38	1,737	572.42	2,173	489.31	2,615
16,000	1,412.25	947	743.87	1,853	610.58	2,317	521.93	2,789
17,000	1,500.51	1,006	790.37	1,969	648.74	2,462	554.55	2,964
18,000	1,588.78	1,065	836.86	2,085	686.90	2,607	587.17	3,138
19,000	1,677.04	1,124	883.35	2,200	725.07	2,752	619.79	3,312
20,000	1,765.31	1,184	929.84	2,316	763.23	2,897	652.41	3,487
21,000	1,853.57	1,243	976.33	2,432	801.39	3,042	685.03	3,661
22,000	1,941.84	1,302	1,022.83	2,548	839.55	3,187	717.65	3,835
23,000	2,030.10	1,361	1,069.32	2,664	877.71	3,331	750.28	4,010
24,000	2,118.37	1,420	1,115.81	2,779	915.87	3,476	782.90	4,184
25,000	2,206.63	1,480	1,162.30	2,895	954.03	3,621	815.52	4,359
26,000	2,294.90	1,539	1,208.79	3,011	992.19	3,766	848.14	4,533
27,000	2,383.16	1,598	1,255.29	3,127	1,030.35	3,911	880.76	4,707
28,000	2,471.43	1,657	1,301.78	3,243	1,068.52	4,056	913.38	4,882
29,000	2,559.69	1,716	1,348.27	3,358	1,106.68	4,200	946.00	5,056
30,000	2,647.96	1,776	1,394.76	3,474	1,144.84	4,345	978.62	5,230
31,000	2,736.22	1,835	1,441.25	3,590	1,183.00	4,490	1,011.24	5,405
32,000	2,824.49	1,894	1,487.74	3,706	1,221.16	4,635	1,043.86	5,579
33,000	2,912.75	1,953	1,534.24	3,822	1,259.32	4,780	1,076.48	5,753
34,000	3,001.02	2,012	1,580.73	3,938	1,297.48	4,924	1,109.10	5,928
35,000	3,089.28	2,071	1,627.22	4,053	1,335.64	5,069	1,141.72	6,102
36,000	3,177.55	2,131	1,673.71	4,169	1,373.80	5,214	1,174.34	6,276
37,000	3,265.81	2,190	1,720.20	4,285	1,411.97	5,359	1,206.96	6,451
38,000	3,354.08	2,249	1,766.70	4,401	1,450.13	5,504	1,239.58	6,625
39,000	3,442.34	2,308	1,813.19	4,517	1,488.29	5,649	1,272.20	6,799
40,000	3,530.61	2,367	1,859.68	4,632	1,526.45	5,794	1,304.82	6,974
42,000	3,707.14	2,486	1,952.66	4,864	1,602.77	6,083	1,370.06	7,322
44,000	3,883.67	2,604	2,045.65	5,096	1,679.09	6,373	1,435.30	7,671
46,000	4,060.20	2,722	2,138.63	5,327	1,755.41	6,662	1,500.55	8,020
48,000	4,236.73	2,841	2,231.61	5,559	1,831.74	6,952	1,565.79	8,368
50,000	4,413.26	2,959	2,324.60	5,790	1,908.06	7,242	1,631.03	8,717

AMOUNT OF LOAN	42 MOS		48 MOS		60 MOS		72 MOS	
	MONTHLY PAYMENT	TOTAL INTRST	MONTHLY PAYMENT	TOTAL INTRST	MONTHLY PAYMENT	TOTAL INTRST	MONTHLY PAYMENT	TOTAL INTRST
$ 1	0.03	0	0.03	0	0.03	1	0.02	0
2	0.06	1	0.06	1	0.05	1	0.04	1
3	0.09	1	0.08	1	0.07	1	0.06	2
4	0.12	1	0.11	1	0.09	1	0.08	2
5	0.15	1	0.13	1	0.11	2	0.10	2
6	0.18	2	0.16	2	0.13	2	0.12	3
7	0.21	2	0.19	2	0.16	2	0.14	3
8	0.23	2	0.21	2	0.18	3	0.16	4
9	0.26	2	0.24	3	0.20	3	0.18	4
10	0.29	2	0.26	2	0.22	3	0.19	4
20	0.58	4	0.52	5	0.44	6	0.38	7
30	0.87	7	0.78	7	0.65	9	0.57	11
40	1.15	8	1.03	9	0.87	12	0.76	15
50	1.44	10	1.29	12	1.09	15	0.95	18
60	1.73	13	1.55	14	1.30	18	1.14	22
70	2.01	14	1.81	17	1.52	21	1.33	26
80	2.30	17	2.06	19	1.73	24	1.52	29
90	2.59	19	2.32	21	1.95	27	1.71	33
100	2.87	21	2.58	24	2.17	30	1.90	37
200	5.74	41	5.15	47	4.33	60	3.79	73
300	8.61	62	7.72	71	6.49	89	5.68	109
400	11.47	82	10.29	94	8.65	119	7.57	145
500	14.34	102	12.87	118	10.81	149	9.46	181
600	17.21	123	15.44	141	12.98	179	11.35	217
700	20.08	143	18.01	164	15.14	208	13.24	253
800	22.94	163	20.58	188	17.30	238	15.13	289
900	25.81	184	23.16	212	19.46	268	17.02	325
1,000	28.68	205	25.73	235	21.62	297	18.91	362
2,000	57.35	409	51.45	470	43.24	594	37.82	723
3,000	86.03	613	77.18	705	64.86	892	56.72	1,084
4,000	114.70	817	102.90	939	86.48	1,189	75.63	1,445
5,000	143.38	1,022	128.63	1,174	108.09	1,485	94.54	1,807
6,000	172.05	1,226	154.35	1,409	129.71	1,783	113.44	2,168
7,000	200.72	1,430	180.07	1,643	151.33	2,080	132.35	2,529
8,000	229.40	1,635	205.80	1,878	172.95	2,377	151.26	2,891
9,000	258.07	1,839	231.52	2,113	194.57	2,674	170.16	3,252
10,000	286.75	2,044	257.25	2,348	216.18	2,971	189.07	3,613
11,000	315.42	2,248	282.97	2,583	237.80	3,268	207.97	3,974
12,000	344.09	2,452	308.70	2,818	259.42	3,565	226.88	4,335
13,000	372.77	2,656	334.42	3,052	281.04	3,862	245.79	4,697
14,000	401.44	2,860	360.14	3,287	302.66	4,160	264.69	5,058
15,000	430.12	3,065	385.87	3,522	324.27	4,456	283.60	5,419
16,000	458.79	3,269	411.59	3,756	345.89	4,753	302.55	5,781
17,000	487.47	3,474	437.32	3,991	367.51	5,051	321.41	6,142
18,000	516.14	3,678	463.04	4,226	389.13	5,348	340.32	6,503
19,000	544.81	3,882	488.77	4,461	410.75	5,645	359.22	6,864
20,000	573.49	4,087	514.49	4,696	432.36	5,942	378.13	7,225
21,000	602.16	4,291	540.21	4,930	453.98	6,239	397.04	7,587
22,000	630.84	4,495	565.94	5,165	475.60	6,536	415.94	7,948
23,000	659.51	4,699	591.66	5,400	497.22	6,833	434.85	8,309
24,000	688.18	4,904	617.39	5,635	518.84	7,130	453.76	8,671
25,000	716.86	5,108	643.11	5,869	540.45	7,427	472.66	9,032
26,000	745.53	5,312	668.84	6,104	562.07	7,724	491.57	9,393
27,000	774.21	5,517	694.56	6,339	583.69	8,021	510.47	9,754
28,000	802.88	5,721	720.28	6,573	605.31	8,319	529.38	10,115
29,000	831.56	5,926	746.01	6,808	626.93	8,616	548.29	10,477
30,000	860.23	6,130	771.73	7,043	648.54	8,912	567.19	10,838
31,000	888.90	6,334	797.46	7,278	670.16	9,210	586.10	11,199
32,000	917.58	6,538	823.18	7,513	691.78	9,507	605.01	11,561
33,000	946.25	6,743	848.91	7,748	713.40	9,804	623.91	11,922
34,000	974.93	6,947	874.63	7,982	735.02	10,101	642.82	12,283
35,000	1,003.60	7,151	900.35	8,217	756.63	10,398	661.72	12,644
36,000	1,032.27	7,355	926.08	8,452	778.25	10,695	680.63	13,005
37,000	1,060.95	7,560	951.80	8,686	799.87	10,992	699.54	13,367
38,000	1,089.62	7,764	977.53	8,921	821.49	11,289	718.44	13,728
39,000	1,118.30	7,969	1,003.25	9,156	843.11	11,587	737.35	14,089
40,000	1,146.97	8,173	1,028.98	9,391	864.72	11,883	756.26	14,451
42,000	1,204.32	8,581	1,080.42	9,860	907.96	12,478	794.07	15,173
44,000	1,261.67	8,990	1,131.87	10,330	951.19	13,071	831.88	15,895
46,000	1,319.02	9,399	1,183.32	10,799	994.43	13,663	869.69	16,618
48,000	1,376.36	9,807	1,234.71	11,269	1,037.67	14,260	907.51	17,341
50,000	1,433.71	10,216	1,286.22	11,739	1,080.90	14,854	945.32	18,063

AUTO LOAN PAYMENTS

AMOUNT OF LOAN	12 MOS		24 MOS		30 MOS		36 MOS	
	MONTHLY PAYMENT	TOTAL INTRST	MONTHLY PAYMENT	TOTAL INTRST	MONTHLY PAYMENT	TOTAL INTRST	MONTHLY PAYMENT	TOTAL INTRST
$ 1	0.09	0	0.05	0	0.04	0	0.04	0
2	0.18	0	0.10	0	0.08	0	0.07	1
3	0.27	0	0.14	0	0.12	1	0.10	1
4	0.36	0	0.19	1	0.16	1	0.14	1
5	0.45	0	0.24	1	0.20	1	0.17	1
6	0.54	0	0.28	1	0.23	1	0.20	1
7	0.62	0	0.33	1	0.27	1	0.23	1
8	0.71	1	0.38	1	0.31	1	0.27	2
9	0.80	1	0.42	1	0.35	2	0.30	2
10	0.89	1	0.47	1	0.39	2	0.33	2
20	1.77	1	0.94	3	0.77	3	0.66	4
30	2.66	2	1.40	4	1.15	5	0.99	6
40	3.54	2	1.87	5	1.54	6	1.31	7
50	4.42	3	2.34	6	1.92	8	1.64	9
60	5.31	4	2.80	7	2.30	9	1.97	11
70	6.19	4	3.27	10	2.68	10	2.30	13
80	7.08	5	3.73	10	3.07	12	2.62	14
90	7.96	6	4.20	11	3.45	14	2.95	16
100	8.84	6	4.67	12	3.83	15	3.28	18
200	17.68	12	9.33	24	7.66	30	6.55	36
300	26.52	18	13.99	36	11.49	45	9.83	54
400	35.36	24	18.65	48	15.32	60	13.10	72
500	44.20	30	23.31	59	19.14	74	16.37	89
600	53.03	36	27.97	71	22.97	89	19.65	107
700	61.87	42	32.63	83	26.80	104	22.92	125
800	70.71	49	37.29	95	30.63	119	26.20	143
900	79.55	55	41.95	107	34.46	134	29.47	161
1,000	88.39	61	46.61	119	38.28	148	32.74	179
2,000	176.77	121	93.22	237	76.56	297	65.48	357
3,000	265.15	182	139.83	356	114.84	445	98.22	536
4,000	353.53	242	186.44	475	153.12	594	130.96	715
5,000	441.91	303	233.04	593	191.40	742	163.70	893
6,000	530.29	363	279.65	712	229.67	890	196.44	1,072
7,000	618.68	424	326.26	830	267.95	1,039	229.18	1,250
8,000	707.06	485	372.87	949	306.23	1,187	261.91	1,429
9,000	795.44	545	419.48	1,068	344.51	1,335	294.65	1,607
10,000	883.82	606	466.08	1,186	382.79	1,484	327.39	1,786
11,000	972.20	666	512.69	1,305	421.06	1,632	360.13	1,965
12,000	1,060.58	727	559.30	1,423	459.34	1,780	392.87	2,143
13,000	1,148.97	788	605.91	1,542	497.62	1,929	425.61	2,322
14,000	1,237.35	848	652.51	1,660	535.90	2,077	458.35	2,501
15,000	1,325.73	909	699.12	1,779	574.18	2,225	491.09	2,679
16,000	1,414.11	969	745.73	1,898	612.45	2,374	523.82	2,858
17,000	1,502.49	1,030	792.34	2,016	650.73	2,522	556.56	3,036
18,000	1,590.87	1,090	838.95	2,135	689.01	2,670	589.30	3,215
19,000	1,679.26	1,151	885.55	2,253	727.29	2,819	622.04	3,393
20,000	1,767.64	1,212	932.16	2,372	765.57	2,967	654.78	3,572
21,000	1,856.02	1,272	978.77	2,490	803.84	3,115	687.52	3,751
22,000	1,944.40	1,333	1,025.38	2,609	842.12	3,264	720.26	3,929
23,000	2,032.78	1,393	1,071.99	2,728	880.40	3,412	753.00	4,108
24,000	2,121.16	1,454	1,118.59	2,846	918.68	3,560	785.73	4,286
25,000	2,209.55	1,515	1,165.20	2,965	956.96	3,709	818.47	4,465
26,000	2,297.93	1,575	1,211.81	3,083	995.23	3,857	851.21	4,644
27,000	2,386.31	1,636	1,258.42	3,202	1,033.51	4,005	883.95	4,822
28,000	2,474.69	1,696	1,305.02	3,320	1,071.79	4,154	916.69	5,001
29,000	2,563.07	1,757	1,351.63	3,439	1,110.07	4,302	949.43	5,179
30,000	2,651.45	1,817	1,398.24	3,558	1,148.35	4,451	982.17	5,358
31,000	2,739.84	1,878	1,444.85	3,676	1,186.62	4,599	1,014.91	5,537
32,000	2,828.22	1,939	1,491.46	3,795	1,224.90	4,747	1,047.64	5,715
33,000	2,916.60	1,999	1,538.06	3,913	1,263.18	4,895	1,080.38	5,894
34,000	3,004.98	2,060	1,584.67	4,032	1,301.46	5,044	1,113.12	6,072
35,000	3,093.36	2,120	1,631.28	4,151	1,339.74	5,192	1,145.86	6,251
36,000	3,181.74	2,181	1,677.89	4,269	1,378.02	5,341	1,178.60	6,430
37,000	3,270.13	2,242	1,724.50	4,388	1,416.29	5,489	1,211.34	6,608
38,000	3,358.51	2,302	1,771.10	4,506	1,454.57	5,637	1,244.08	6,787
39,000	3,446.89	2,363	1,817.71	4,625	1,492.85	5,786	1,276.81	6,965
40,000	3,535.27	2,423	1,864.32	4,744	1,531.13	5,934	1,309.55	7,144
42,000	3,712.03	2,544	1,957.53	4,981	1,607.68	6,230	1,375.03	7,501
44,000	3,888.80	2,666	2,050.75	5,218	1,684.24	6,527	1,440.51	7,858
46,000	4,065.56	2,787	2,143.97	5,455	1,760.80	6,824	1,505.99	8,216
48,000	4,242.32	2,908	2,237.18	5,692	1,837.35	7,121	1,571.46	8,573
50,000	4,419.09	3,029	2,330.40	5,930	1,913.91	7,417	1,636.94	8,930

AUTO LOAN PAYMENTS 11.00%

AMOUNT OF LOAN	42 MOS MONTHLY PAYMENT	42 MOS TOTAL INTRST	48 MOS MONTHLY PAYMENT	48 MOS TOTAL INTRST	60 MOS MONTHLY PAYMENT	60 MOS TOTAL INTRST	72 MOS MONTHLY PAYMENT	72 MOS TOTAL INTRST
$ 1	0.03	0	0.03	0	0.03	1	0.02	0
2	0.06	1	0.06	1	0.05	1	0.04	1
3	0.09	1	0.08	1	0.07	1	0.06	1
4	0.12	1	0.11	1	0.09	1	0.08	2
5	0.15	1	0.13	1	0.11	2	0.10	2
6	0.18	1	0.16	2	0.14	2	0.12	3
7	0.21	2	0.19	2	0.16	3	0.14	3
8	0.24	2	0.21	2	0.18	3	0.16	4
9	0.26	2	0.24	3	0.20	3	0.18	4
10	0.29	2	0.26	2	0.22	3	0.20	4
20	0.58	4	0.52	5	0.44	6	0.39	8
30	0.87	7	0.78	7	0.66	10	0.58	12
40	1.16	9	1.04	10	0.87	12	0.77	15
50	1.44	10	1.30	12	1.09	15	0.96	19
60	1.73	13	1.56	15	1.31	19	1.15	23
70	2.02	15	1.81	17	1.53	22	1.34	26
80	2.31	17	2.07	19	1.74	24	1.53	30
90	2.60	19	2.33	22	1.96	28	1.72	34
100	2.88	21	2.59	24	2.18	31	1.91	38
200	5.76	42	5.17	48	4.35	61	3.81	74
300	8.64	63	7.76	72	6.53	92	5.72	112
400	11.52	84	10.34	96	8.70	122	7.62	149
500	14.40	105	12.93	121	10.88	153	9.52	185
600	17.28	126	15.51	144	13.05	183	11.43	223
700	20.16	147	18.10	169	15.22	213	13.33	260
800	23.04	168	20.68	193	17.40	244	15.23	297
900	25.92	189	23.27	217	19.57	274	17.14	334
1,000	28.80	210	25.85	241	21.75	305	19.04	371
2,000	57.59	419	51.70	482	43.49	609	38.07	741
3,000	86.39	628	77.54	722	65.23	914	57.11	1,112
4,000	115.18	838	103.39	963	86.97	1,218	76.14	1,482
5,000	143.97	1,047	129.23	1,203	108.72	1,523	95.18	1,853
6,000	172.77	1,256	155.08	1,444	130.46	1,828	114.21	2,223
7,000	201.56	1,466	180.92	1,684	152.20	2,132	133.24	2,593
8,000	230.36	1,675	206.77	1,925	173.94	2,436	152.28	2,964
9,000	259.15	1,884	232.61	2,165	195.69	2,741	171.31	3,334
10,000	287.94	2,093	258.46	2,406	217.43	3,046	190.35	3,705
11,000	316.74	2,303	284.31	2,647	239.17	3,350	209.38	4,075
12,000	345.53	2,512	310.15	2,887	260.91	3,655	228.41	4,446
13,000	374.33	2,722	336.00	3,128	282.66	3,960	247.45	4,816
14,000	403.12	2,931	361.84	3,368	304.40	4,264	266.48	5,187
15,000	431.91	3,140	387.69	3,609	326.14	4,568	285.52	5,557
16,000	460.71	3,350	413.53	3,849	347.88	4,873	304.55	5,928
17,000	489.50	3,559	439.38	4,090	369.63	5,178	323.58	6,298
18,000	518.29	3,768	465.22	4,331	391.37	5,482	342.62	6,669
19,000	547.09	3,978	491.07	4,571	413.11	5,787	361.65	7,039
20,000	575.88	4,187	516.92	4,812	434.85	6,091	380.69	7,410
21,000	604.68	4,397	542.76	5,052	456.60	6,396	399.72	7,780
22,000	633.47	4,606	568.61	5,293	478.34	6,700	418.75	8,150
23,000	662.26	4,815	594.45	5,534	500.08	7,005	437.79	8,521
24,000	691.06	5,025	620.30	5,774	521.82	7,309	456.82	8,891
25,000	719.85	5,234	646.14	6,015	543.57	7,614	475.86	9,262
26,000	748.65	5,443	671.99	6,256	565.31	7,919	494.89	9,632
27,000	777.44	5,652	697.83	6,496	587.05	8,223	513.93	10,003
28,000	806.23	5,862	723.68	6,737	608.79	8,527	532.96	10,373
29,000	835.03	6,071	749.53	6,977	630.54	8,832	551.99	10,743
30,000	863.82	6,280	775.37	7,218	652.28	9,137	571.03	11,114
31,000	892.61	6,490	801.22	7,459	674.02	9,441	590.06	11,484
32,000	921.41	6,699	827.06	7,699	695.76	9,746	609.10	11,855
33,000	950.20	6,908	852.91	7,940	717.50	10,050	628.13	12,225
34,000	979.00	7,118	878.75	8,180	739.25	10,355	647.16	12,596
35,000	1,007.79	7,327	904.60	8,421	760.99	10,659	666.20	12,966
36,000	1,036.58	7,536	930.44	8,661	782.73	10,964	685.23	13,337
37,000	1,065.38	7,746	956.29	8,902	804.47	11,268	704.27	13,707
38,000	1,094.17	7,955	982.13	9,142	826.22	11,573	723.30	14,078
39,000	1,122.97	8,165	1,007.98	9,383	847.96	11,878	742.33	14,448
40,000	1,151.76	8,374	1,033.83	9,624	869.70	12,182	761.37	14,819
42,000	1,209.35	8,793	1,085.52	10,105	913.19	12,791	799.44	15,560
44,000	1,266.93	9,211	1,137.21	10,586	956.67	13,400	837.50	16,300
46,000	1,324.52	9,630	1,188.90	11,067	1,000.16	14,010	875.57	17,041
48,000	1,382.11	10,049	1,240.59	11,548	1,043.64	14,618	913.64	17,782
50,000	1,439.70	10,467	1,292.28	12,029	1,087.13	15,228	951.71	18,523

AMOUNT OF LOAN	12 MOS		24 MOS		30 MOS		36 MOS	
	MONTHLY PAYMENT	TOTAL INTRST	MONTHLY PAYMENT	TOTAL INTRST	MONTHLY PAYMENT	TOTAL INTRST	MONTHLY PAYMENT	TOTAL INTRST
$ 1	0.09	0	0.05	0	0.04	0	0.04	0
2	0.18	0	0.10	0	0.08	0	0.07	0
3	0.27	0	0.15	0	0.12	0	0.10	1
4	0.36	0	0.19	1	0.16	1	0.14	1
5	0.45	0	0.24	1	0.20	1	0.17	1
6	0.54	1	0.29	1	0.24	1	0.20	1
7	0.62	0	0.33	1	0.27	1	0.24	2
8	0.71	1	0.38	1	0.31	1	0.27	2
9	0.80	1	0.43	1	0.35	2	0.30	2
10	0.89	1	0.47	1	0.39	2	0.33	2
20	1.77	1	0.94	3	0.77	3	0.66	4
30	2.66	2	1.41	4	1.16	5	0.99	6
40	3.54	2	1.87	5	1.54	6	1.32	8
50	4.43	3	2.34	6	1.92	8	1.65	9
60	5.31	4	2.81	7	2.31	9	1.98	11
70	6.20	4	3.28	9	2.69	11	2.31	13
80	7.08	5	3.74	10	3.08	12	2.63	15
90	7.97	6	4.21	11	3.46	14	2.96	17
100	8.85	6	4.68	12	3.84	15	3.29	18
200	17.70	12	9.35	24	7.68	30	6.58	37
300	26.55	19	14.02	36	11.52	46	9.86	55
400	35.40	25	18.69	49	15.36	61	13.15	73
500	44.25	31	23.37	61	19.20	76	16.43	91
600	53.10	37	28.04	73	23.04	91	19.72	110
700	61.95	43	32.71	85	26.88	106	23.01	128
800	70.80	50	37.38	97	30.72	122	26.29	146
900	79.65	56	42.06	109	34.56	137	29.58	165
1,000	88.50	62	46.73	122	38.40	152	32.86	183
2,000	177.00	124	93.45	243	76.80	304	65.72	366
3,000	265.50	186	140.18	364	115.19	456	98.58	549
4,000	354.00	248	186.90	486	153.59	608	131.43	731
5,000	442.50	310	233.62	607	191.98	759	164.29	914
6,000	530.99	372	280.35	728	230.38	911	197.15	1,097
7,000	619.49	434	327.07	850	268.77	1,063	230.01	1,280
8,000	707.99	496	373.80	971	307.17	1,215	262.86	1,463
9,000	796.49	558	420.52	1,092	345.56	1,367	295.72	1,646
10,000	884.99	620	467.24	1,214	383.96	1,519	328.58	1,829
11,000	973.49	682	513.97	1,335	422.35	1,671	361.43	2,011
12,000	1,061.98	744	560.69	1,457	460.75	1,823	394.29	2,194
13,000	1,150.48	806	607.42	1,578	499.14	1,974	427.15	2,377
14,000	1,238.98	868	654.14	1,699	537.54	2,126	460.01	2,560
15,000	1,327.48	930	700.86	1,821	575.93	2,278	492.86	2,743
16,000	1,415.98	992	747.59	1,942	614.33	2,430	525.72	2,926
17,000	1,504.48	1,054	794.31	2,063	652.72	2,582	558.58	3,109
18,000	1,592.97	1,116	841.04	2,185	691.12	2,734	591.44	3,292
19,000	1,681.47	1,178	887.76	2,306	729.51	2,885	624.29	3,474
20,000	1,769.97	1,240	934.48	2,428	767.91	3,037	657.15	3,657
21,000	1,858.47	1,302	981.21	2,549	806.31	3,189	690.01	3,840
22,000	1,946.97	1,364	1,027.93	2,670	844.70	3,341	722.86	4,023
23,000	2,035.47	1,426	1,074.66	2,792	883.10	3,493	755.72	4,206
24,000	2,123.96	1,488	1,121.38	2,913	921.49	3,645	788.58	4,389
25,000	2,212.46	1,550	1,168.10	3,034	959.89	3,797	821.44	4,572
26,000	2,300.96	1,612	1,214.83	3,156	998.28	3,948	854.29	4,754
27,000	2,389.46	1,674	1,261.55	3,277	1,036.68	4,100	887.15	4,937
28,000	2,477.96	1,736	1,308.28	3,399	1,075.07	4,252	920.01	5,120
29,000	2,566.46	1,798	1,355.00	3,520	1,113.47	4,404	952.86	5,303
30,000	2,654.95	1,859	1,401.72	3,641	1,151.86	4,556	985.72	5,486
31,000	2,743.45	1,921	1,448.45	3,763	1,190.26	4,708	1,018.58	5,669
32,000	2,831.95	1,983	1,495.17	3,884	1,228.65	4,860	1,051.44	5,852
33,000	2,920.45	2,045	1,541.90	4,006	1,267.05	5,012	1,084.29	6,034
34,000	3,008.95	2,107	1,588.62	4,127	1,305.44	5,163	1,117.15	6,217
35,000	3,097.45	2,169	1,635.34	4,248	1,343.84	5,315	1,150.01	6,400
36,000	3,185.94	2,231	1,682.07	4,370	1,382.23	5,467	1,182.87	6,583
37,000	3,274.44	2,293	1,728.79	4,491	1,420.63	5,619	1,215.72	6,766
38,000	3,362.94	2,355	1,775.52	4,612	1,459.02	5,771	1,248.58	6,949
39,000	3,451.44	2,417	1,822.24	4,734	1,497.42	5,923	1,281.44	7,132
40,000	3,539.94	2,479	1,868.96	4,855	1,535.82	6,075	1,314.29	7,314
42,000	3,716.93	2,603	1,962.41	5,098	1,612.61	6,378	1,380.01	7,680
44,000	3,893.93	2,727	2,055.86	5,341	1,689.40	6,682	1,445.72	8,046
46,000	4,070.93	2,851	2,149.31	5,583	1,766.19	6,986	1,511.44	8,412
48,000	4,247.92	2,975	2,242.76	5,826	1,842.98	7,289	1,577.15	8,777
50,000	4,424.92	3,099	2,336.20	6,069	1,919.77	7,593	1,642.87	9,143

114

AMOUNT OF LOAN	42 MOS		48 MOS		60 MOS		72 MOS	
	MONTHLY PAYMENT	TOTAL INTRST	MONTHLY PAYMENT	TOTAL INTRST	MONTHLY PAYMENT	TOTAL INTRST	MONTHLY PAYMENT	TOTAL INTRST
$ 1	0.03	0	0.03	0	0.03	1	0.02	0
2	0.06	1	0.06	1	0.05	1	0.04	1
3	0.09	1	0.08	1	0.07	1	0.06	1
4	0.12	1	0.11	1	0.09	1	0.08	2
5	0.15	1	0.13	1	0.11	2	0.10	2
6	0.18	2	0.16	2	0.14	2	0.12	3
7	0.21	2	0.19	2	0.16	3	0.14	3
8	0.24	2	0.21	2	0.18	3	0.16	4
9	0.27	2	0.24	3	0.20	3	0.18	4
10	0.29	2	0.26	2	0.22	3	0.20	4
20	0.58	4	0.52	5	0.44	6	0.39	8
30	0.87	7	0.78	7	0.66	10	0.58	12
40	1.16	9	1.04	10	0.88	13	0.77	15
50	1.45	11	1.30	12	1.10	16	0.96	19
60	1.74	13	1.56	15	1.32	19	1.15	23
70	2.03	15	1.82	17	1.54	22	1.35	27
80	2.32	17	2.08	20	1.75	25	1.54	31
90	2.61	20	2.34	22	1.97	28	1.73	35
100	2.90	22	2.60	25	2.19	31	1.92	38
200	5.79	43	5.20	50	4.38	63	3.84	76
300	8.68	65	7.80	74	6.57	94	5.75	114
400	11.57	86	10.39	99	8.75	125	7.67	152
500	14.46	107	12.99	124	10.94	156	9.59	190
600	17.35	129	15.59	148	13.13	188	11.50	228
700	20.24	150	18.18	173	15.31	219	13.42	266
800	23.14	172	20.78	197	17.50	250	15.33	304
900	26.03	193	23.38	222	19.69	281	17.25	342
1,000	28.92	215	25.97	247	21.87	312	19.17	380
2,000	57.83	429	51.94	493	43.74	624	38.33	760
3,000	86.75	644	77.91	740	65.61	937	57.49	1,139
4,000	115.66	858	103.87	986	87.47	1,248	76.65	1,519
5,000	144.57	1,072	129.84	1,232	109.34	1,560	95.82	1,899
6,000	173.49	1,287	155.81	1,479	131.21	1,873	114.98	2,279
7,000	202.40	1,501	181.77	1,725	153.07	2,185	134.14	2,658
8,000	231.32	1,715	207.74	1,972	174.94	2,496	153.30	3,038
9,000	260.23	1,930	233.71	2,218	196.81	2,809	172.47	3,418
10,000	289.14	2,144	259.68	2,465	218.68	3,121	191.63	3,797
11,000	318.06	2,359	285.64	2,711	240.55	3,433	210.79	4,177
12,000	346.97	2,573	311.61	2,957	262.41	3,745	229.95	4,556
13,000	375.89	2,787	337.58	3,204	284.28	4,057	249.12	4,937
14,000	404.80	3,002	363.54	3,450	306.15	4,369	268.28	5,316
15,000	433.71	3,216	389.51	3,696	328.01	4,681	287.44	5,696
16,000	462.63	3,430	415.48	3,943	349.88	4,993	306.60	6,075
17,000	491.54	3,645	441.45	4,190	371.75	5,305	325.77	6,455
18,000	520.45	3,859	467.41	4,436	393.62	5,617	344.93	6,835
19,000	549.37	4,074	493.38	4,682	415.48	5,929	364.09	7,214
20,000	578.28	4,288	519.35	4,929	437.35	6,241	383.25	7,594
21,000	607.20	4,502	545.31	5,175	459.22	6,553	402.41	7,974
22,000	636.11	4,717	571.28	5,421	481.09	6,865	421.58	8,354
23,000	665.02	4,931	597.25	5,668	502.95	7,177	440.74	8,733
24,000	693.94	5,145	623.22	5,915	524.82	7,489	459.90	9,113
25,000	722.85	5,360	649.18	6,161	546.69	7,801	479.06	9,492
26,000	751.77	5,574	675.15	6,407	568.56	8,114	498.23	9,873
27,000	780.68	5,789	701.12	6,654	590.42	8,425	517.39	10,252
28,000	809.59	6,003	727.08	6,900	612.29	8,737	536.55	10,632
29,000	838.51	6,217	753.05	7,146	634.16	9,050	555.71	11,011
30,000	867.42	6,432	779.02	7,393	656.02	9,361	574.88	11,391
31,000	896.33	6,646	804.99	7,640	677.89	9,673	594.04	11,771
32,000	925.25	6,861	830.95	7,886	699.76	9,986	613.20	12,150
33,000	954.16	7,075	856.92	8,132	721.63	10,298	632.36	12,530
34,000	983.08	7,289	882.89	8,379	743.49	10,609	651.53	12,910
35,000	1,011.99	7,504	908.85	8,625	765.36	10,922	670.69	13,290
36,000	1,040.90	7,718	934.82	8,871	787.23	11,234	689.85	13,669
37,000	1,069.82	7,932	960.79	9,118	809.10	11,546	709.01	14,049
38,000	1,098.73	8,147	986.75	9,364	830.96	11,858	728.18	14,429
39,000	1,127.65	8,361	1,012.72	9,611	852.83	12,170	747.34	14,808
40,000	1,156.56	8,576	1,038.69	9,857	874.70	12,482	766.50	15,188
42,000	1,214.39	9,004	1,090.62	10,350	918.43	13,106	804.82	15,947
44,000	1,272.21	9,433	1,142.56	10,843	962.17	13,730	843.15	16,707
46,000	1,330.04	9,862	1,194.49	11,336	1,005.90	14,354	881.47	17,466
48,000	1,387.87	10,291	1,246.43	11,829	1,049.64	14,978	919.80	18,226
50,000	1,445.70	10,719	1,298.36	12,321	1,093.37	15,602	958.12	18,985

AUTO LOAN PAYMENTS

AMOUNT OF LOAN	12 MOS		24 MOS		30 MOS		36 MOS	
	MONTHLY PAYMENT	TOTAL INTRST	MONTHLY PAYMENT	TOTAL INTRST	MONTHLY PAYMENT	TOTAL INTRST	MONTHLY PAYMENT	TOTAL INTRST
$ 1	0.09	0	0.05	0	0.04	0	0.04	0
2	0.18	0	0.10	0	0.08	0	0.07	1
3	0.27	0	0.15	0	0.12	1	0.10	1
4	0.36	0	0.19	1	0.16	1	0.14	1
5	0.45	0	0.24	1	0.20	1	0.17	1
6	0.54	0	0.29	1	0.24	1	0.20	1
7	0.63	1	0.33	1	0.27	1	0.24	2
8	0.71	1	0.38	1	0.31	1	0.27	2
9	0.80	1	0.43	1	0.35	2	0.30	2
10	0.89	1	0.47	1	0.39	2	0.33	2
20	1.78	1	0.94	3	0.78	3	0.66	4
30	2.66	2	1.41	4	1.16	5	0.99	6
40	3.55	3	1.88	5	1.55	7	1.32	8
50	4.44	3	2.35	6	1.93	8	1.65	9
60	5.32	4	2.82	8	2.32	10	1.98	11
70	6.21	5	3.28	9	2.70	11	2.31	13
80	7.09	5	3.75	10	3.09	13	2.64	15
90	7.98	6	4.22	11	3.47	14	2.97	17
100	8.87	6	4.69	13	3.86	16	3.30	19
200	17.73	13	9.37	25	7.71	31	6.60	38
300	26.59	19	14.06	37	11.56	47	9.90	56
400	35.45	25	18.74	50	15.41	62	13.20	75
500	44.31	32	23.43	62	19.26	78	16.49	94
600	53.17	38	28.11	75	23.11	93	19.79	112
700	62.04	44	32.79	87	26.96	109	23.09	131
800	70.90	51	37.48	100	30.82	125	26.39	150
900	79.76	57	42.16	112	34.67	140	29.68	168
1,000	88.62	63	46.85	124	38.52	156	32.98	187
2,000	177.24	127	93.69	249	77.03	311	65.96	375
3,000	265.85	190	140.53	373	115.54	466	98.93	561
4,000	354.47	254	187.37	497	154.06	622	131.91	749
5,000	443.08	317	234.21	621	192.57	777	164.89	936
6,000	531.70	380	281.05	745	231.08	932	197.86	1,123
7,000	620.31	444	327.89	869	269.59	1,088	230.84	1,310
8,000	708.93	507	374.73	994	308.11	1,243	263.81	1,497
9,000	797.54	570	421.57	1,118	346.62	1,399	296.79	1,684
10,000	886.16	634	468.41	1,242	385.13	1,554	329.77	1,872
11,000	974.77	697	515.25	1,366	423.64	1,709	362.74	2,059
12,000	1,063.39	761	562.09	1,490	462.16	1,865	395.72	2,246
13,000	1,152.00	824	608.93	1,614	500.67	2,020	428.69	2,433
14,000	1,240.62	887	655.77	1,738	539.18	2,175	461.67	2,620
15,000	1,329.23	951	702.61	1,863	577.69	2,331	494.65	2,807
16,000	1,417.85	1,014	749.45	1,987	616.21	2,486	527.62	2,994
17,000	1,506.46	1,078	796.29	2,111	654.72	2,642	560.60	3,182
18,000	1,595.08	1,141	843.13	2,235	693.23	2,797	593.57	3,369
19,000	1,683.69	1,204	889.97	2,359	731.75	2,953	626.55	3,556
20,000	1,772.31	1,268	936.81	2,483	770.26	3,108	659.53	3,743
21,000	1,860.92	1,331	983.65	2,608	808.77	3,263	692.50	3,930
22,000	1,949.54	1,394	1,030.49	2,732	847.28	3,418	725.48	4,117
23,000	2,038.15	1,458	1,077.33	2,856	885.80	3,574	758.45	4,304
24,000	2,126.77	1,521	1,124.17	2,980	924.31	3,729	791.43	4,491
25,000	2,215.38	1,585	1,171.01	3,104	962.82	3,885	824.41	4,679
26,000	2,304.00	1,648	1,217.85	3,228	1,001.33	4,040	857.38	4,866
27,000	2,392.61	1,711	1,264.69	3,353	1,039.85	4,196	890.36	5,053
28,000	2,481.23	1,775	1,311.53	3,477	1,078.36	4,351	923.33	5,240
29,000	2,569.84	1,838	1,358.37	3,601	1,116.87	4,506	956.31	5,427
30,000	2,658.46	1,902	1,405.21	3,725	1,155.38	4,661	989.29	5,614
31,000	2,747.07	1,965	1,452.05	3,849	1,193.90	4,817	1,022.26	5,801
32,000	2,835.69	2,028	1,498.90	3,974	1,232.41	4,972	1,055.24	5,989
33,000	2,924.30	2,092	1,545.74	4,098	1,270.92	5,128	1,088.21	6,176
34,000	3,012.92	2,155	1,592.58	4,222	1,309.44	5,283	1,121.19	6,363
35,000	3,101.53	2,218	1,639.42	4,346	1,347.95	5,439	1,154.17	6,550
36,000	3,190.15	2,282	1,686.26	4,470	1,386.46	5,594	1,187.14	6,737
37,000	3,278.76	2,345	1,733.10	4,594	1,424.97	5,749	1,220.12	6,924
38,000	3,367.38	2,409	1,779.94	4,719	1,463.49	5,905	1,253.09	7,111
39,000	3,455.99	2,472	1,826.78	4,843	1,502.00	6,060	1,286.07	7,299
40,000	3,544.61	2,535	1,873.62	4,967	1,540.51	6,215	1,319.05	7,486
42,000	3,721.84	2,662	1,967.30	5,215	1,617.54	6,526	1,385.00	7,860
44,000	3,899.07	2,789	2,060.98	5,464	1,694.56	6,837	1,450.95	8,234
46,000	4,076.30	2,916	2,154.66	5,712	1,771.59	7,148	1,516.90	8,608
48,000	4,253.53	3,042	2,248.34	5,960	1,848.61	7,458	1,582.85	8,983
50,000	4,430.76	3,169	2,342.02	6,208	1,925.64	7,769	1,648.81	9,357

AUTO LOAN PAYMENTS 11.50%

AMOUNT OF LOAN	42 MOS		48 MOS		60 MOS		72 MOS	
	MONTHLY PAYMENT	TOTAL INTRST	MONTHLY PAYMENT	TOTAL INTRST	MONTHLY PAYMENT	TOTAL INTRST	MONTHLY PAYMENT	TOTAL INTRST
$ 1	0.03	0	0.03	0	0.03	1	0.02	0
2	0.06	1	0.06	1	0.05	1	0.04	1
3	0.09	1	0.08	1	0.07	1	0.06	1
4	0.12	1	0.11	1	0.09	1	0.08	2
5	0.15	1	0.14	2	0.11	2	0.10	2
6	0.18	2	0.16	2	0.14	2	0.12	3
7	0.21	2	0.19	2	0.16	3	0.14	3
8	0.24	2	0.21	2	0.18	3	0.16	4
9	0.27	2	0.24	3	0.20	3	0.18	4
10	0.30	3	0.27	3	0.22	3	0.20	4
20	0.59	5	0.53	5	0.44	6	0.39	8
30	0.88	7	0.79	8	0.66	10	0.58	12
40	1.17	9	1.05	10	0.88	13	0.78	16
50	1.46	11	1.31	13	1.10	16	0.97	20
60	1.75	14	1.57	15	1.32	19	1.16	24
70	2.04	16	1.83	18	1.54	22	1.36	28
80	2.33	18	2.09	20	1.76	26	1.55	32
90	2.62	20	2.35	23	1.98	29	1.74	35
100	2.91	22	2.61	25	2.20	32	1.93	39
200	5.81	44	5.22	51	4.40	64	3.86	78
300	8.72	66	7.83	76	6.60	96	5.79	117
400	11.62	88	10.44	101	8.80	128	7.72	156
500	14.52	110	13.05	126	11.00	160	9.65	195
600	17.43	132	15.66	152	13.20	192	11.58	234
700	20.33	154	18.27	177	15.40	224	13.51	273
800	23.23	176	20.88	202	17.60	256	15.44	312
900	26.14	198	23.49	228	19.80	288	17.37	351
1,000	29.04	220	26.09	252	22.00	320	19.30	390
2,000	58.07	439	52.18	505	43.99	639	38.59	778
3,000	87.11	659	78.27	757	65.98	959	57.88	1,167
4,000	116.14	878	104.36	1,009	87.98	1,279	77.17	1,556
5,000	145.18	1,098	130.45	1,262	109.97	1,598	96.46	1,945
6,000	174.21	1,317	156.54	1,514	131.96	1,918	115.75	2,334
7,000	203.24	1,536	182.63	1,766	153.95	2,237	135.04	2,723
8,000	232.28	1,756	208.72	2,019	175.95	2,557	154.33	3,112
9,000	261.31	1,975	234.81	2,271	197.94	2,876	173.63	3,501
10,000	290.35	2,195	260.90	2,523	219.93	3,196	192.92	3,890
11,000	319.38	2,414	286.98	2,775	241.92	3,515	212.21	4,279
12,000	348.41	2,633	313.07	3,027	263.92	3,835	231.50	4,668
13,000	377.45	2,853	339.16	3,280	285.91	4,155	250.79	5,057
14,000	406.48	3,072	365.25	3,532	307.90	4,474	270.08	5,446
15,000	435.52	3,292	391.34	3,784	329.89	4,793	289.37	5,835
16,000	464.55	3,511	417.43	4,037	351.89	5,113	308.66	6,224
17,000	493.59	3,731	443.52	4,289	373.88	5,433	327.95	6,612
18,000	522.62	3,950	469.61	4,541	395.87	5,752	347.25	7,002
19,000	551.65	4,169	495.70	4,794	417.86	6,072	366.54	7,391
20,000	580.69	4,389	521.79	5,046	439.86	6,392	385.83	7,780
21,000	609.72	4,608	547.87	5,298	461.85	6,711	405.12	8,169
22,000	638.76	4,828	573.96	5,550	483.84	7,030	424.41	8,558
23,000	667.79	5,047	600.05	5,802	505.83	7,350	443.70	8,946
24,000	696.82	5,266	626.14	6,055	527.83	7,670	462.99	9,335
25,000	725.86	5,486	652.23	6,307	549.82	7,989	482.28	9,724
26,000	754.89	5,705	678.32	6,559	571.81	8,309	501.58	10,114
27,000	783.93	5,925	704.41	6,812	593.81	8,629	520.87	10,503
28,000	812.96	6,144	730.50	7,064	615.80	8,948	540.16	10,892
29,000	842.00	6,364	756.59	7,316	637.79	9,267	559.45	11,280
30,000	871.03	6,583	782.68	7,569	659.78	9,587	578.74	11,669
31,000	900.06	6,803	808.76	7,820	681.78	9,907	598.03	12,058
32,000	929.10	7,022	834.85	8,073	703.77	10,226	617.32	12,447
33,000	958.13	7,241	860.94	8,325	725.76	10,546	636.61	12,836
34,000	987.17	7,461	887.03	8,577	747.75	10,865	655.90	13,225
35,000	1,016.20	7,680	913.12	8,830	769.75	11,185	675.20	13,614
36,000	1,045.23	7,900	939.21	9,082	791.74	11,504	694.49	14,003
37,000	1,074.27	8,119	965.30	9,334	813.73	11,824	713.78	14,392
38,000	1,103.30	8,339	991.39	9,587	835.72	12,143	733.07	14,781
39,000	1,132.34	8,558	1,017.48	9,839	857.72	12,463	752.36	15,170
40,000	1,161.37	8,778	1,043.57	10,091	879.71	12,783	771.65	15,559
42,000	1,219.44	9,216	1,095.74	10,596	923.69	13,421	810.23	16,337
44,000	1,277.51	9,655	1,147.92	11,100	967.68	14,061	848.82	17,115
46,000	1,335.58	10,094	1,200.10	11,605	1,011.66	14,700	887.40	17,893
48,000	1,393.64	10,533	1,252.28	12,109	1,055.65	15,339	925.98	18,671
50,000	1,451.71	10,972	1,304.46	12,614	1,099.64	15,978	964.56	19,448

AUTO LOAN PAYMENTS

AMOUNT OF LOAN	12 MOS MONTHLY PAYMENT	12 MOS TOTAL INTRST	24 MOS MONTHLY PAYMENT	24 MOS TOTAL INTRST	30 MOS MONTHLY PAYMENT	30 MOS TOTAL INTRST	36 MOS MONTHLY PAYMENT	36 MOS TOTAL INTRST
$ 1	0.09	0	0.05	0	0.04	0	0.04	0
2	0.18	0	0.10	0	0.08	0	0.07	1
3	0.27	0	0.15	1	0.12	1	0.10	1
4	0.36	0	0.19	1	0.16	1	0.14	1
5	0.45	0	0.24	1	0.20	1	0.17	1
6	0.54	0	0.29	1	0.24	1	0.20	1
7	0.63	1	0.33	1	0.28	1	0.24	2
8	0.71	1	0.38	1	0.31	1	0.27	2
9	0.80	1	0.43	1	0.35	2	0.30	2
10	0.89	1	0.47	1	0.39	2	0.34	2
20	1.78	1	0.94	3	0.78	3	0.67	4
30	2.67	2	1.41	4	1.16	5	1.00	6
40	3.55	3	1.88	5	1.55	7	1.33	8
50	4.44	3	2.35	6	1.94	9	1.66	10
60	5.33	4	2.82	8	2.32	10	1.99	12
70	6.22	5	3.29	9	2.71	11	2.32	14
80	7.10	5	3.76	10	3.10	13	2.65	15
90	7.99	6	4.23	12	3.48	14	2.98	17
100	8.88	7	4.70	13	3.87	16	3.31	19
200	17.75	13	9.40	26	7.73	32	6.62	38
300	26.62	19	14.09	38	11.59	48	9.93	57
400	35.50	26	18.79	51	15.46	64	13.24	77
500	44.37	32	23.48	64	19.32	80	16.55	96
600	53.24	39	28.18	76	23.18	95	19.86	115
700	62.12	45	32.87	89	27.05	112	23.17	134
800	70.99	52	37.57	102	30.91	127	26.48	153
900	79.86	58	42.27	114	34.77	143	29.79	172
1,000	88.74	65	46.96	127	38.64	159	33.10	192
2,000	177.47	130	93.92	254	77.27	318	66.20	383
3,000	266.20	194	140.88	381	115.90	477	99.29	574
4,000	354.93	259	187.83	508	154.53	636	132.39	766
5,000	443.66	324	234.79	635	193.16	795	165.48	957
6,000	532.40	389	281.75	762	231.79	954	198.58	1,149
7,000	621.13	454	328.70	889	270.42	1,113	231.67	1,340
8,000	709.86	518	375.66	1,016	309.05	1,272	264.77	1,532
9,000	798.59	583	422.62	1,143	347.68	1,430	297.86	1,723
10,000	887.32	648	469.57	1,270	386.31	1,589	330.96	1,915
11,000	976.06	713	516.53	1,397	424.94	1,748	364.05	2,106
12,000	1,064.79	777	563.49	1,524	463.57	1,907	397.15	2,297
13,000	1,153.52	842	610.44	1,651	502.20	2,066	430.24	2,489
14,000	1,242.25	907	657.40	1,778	540.83	2,225	463.34	2,680
15,000	1,330.98	972	704.36	1,905	579.46	2,384	496.43	2,871
16,000	1,419.72	1,037	751.31	2,031	618.09	2,543	529.53	3,063
17,000	1,508.45	1,101	798.27	2,158	656.72	2,702	562.62	3,254
18,000	1,597.18	1,166	845.23	2,286	695.35	2,861	595.72	3,446
19,000	1,685.91	1,231	892.18	2,412	733.98	3,019	628.81	3,637
20,000	1,774.64	1,296	939.14	2,539	772.61	3,178	661.91	3,829
21,000	1,863.37	1,360	986.10	2,666	811.24	3,337	695.00	4,020
22,000	1,952.11	1,425	1,033.05	2,793	849.87	3,496	728.10	4,212
23,000	2,040.84	1,490	1,080.01	2,920	888.50	3,655	761.19	4,403
24,000	2,129.57	1,555	1,126.97	3,047	927.13	3,814	794.29	4,594
25,000	2,218.30	1,620	1,173.93	3,174	965.76	3,973	827.38	4,786
26,000	2,307.03	1,684	1,220.88	3,301	1,004.39	4,132	860.48	4,977
27,000	2,395.77	1,749	1,267.84	3,428	1,043.02	4,291	893.57	5,169
28,000	2,484.50	1,814	1,314.80	3,555	1,081.65	4,450	926.67	5,360
29,000	2,573.23	1,879	1,361.75	3,682	1,120.28	4,608	959.76	5,551
30,000	2,661.96	1,944	1,408.71	3,809	1,158.91	4,767	992.86	5,743
31,000	2,750.69	2,008	1,455.67	3,936	1,197.54	4,926	1,025.95	5,934
32,000	2,839.43	2,073	1,502.62	4,063	1,236.17	5,085	1,059.05	6,126
33,000	2,928.16	2,138	1,549.58	4,190	1,274.80	5,244	1,092.14	6,317
34,000	3,016.89	2,203	1,596.54	4,317	1,313.43	5,403	1,125.24	6,509
35,000	3,105.62	2,267	1,643.49	4,444	1,352.06	5,562	1,158.33	6,700
36,000	3,194.35	2,332	1,690.45	4,571	1,390.70	5,721	1,191.43	6,891
37,000	3,283.08	2,397	1,737.41	4,698	1,429.33	5,880	1,224.52	7,083
38,000	3,371.82	2,462	1,784.36	4,825	1,467.96	6,039	1,257.62	7,274
39,000	3,460.55	2,527	1,831.32	4,952	1,506.59	6,198	1,290.71	7,466
40,000	3,549.28	2,591	1,878.28	5,079	1,545.22	6,357	1,323.81	7,657
42,000	3,726.74	2,721	1,972.19	5,333	1,622.48	6,674	1,390.00	8,040
44,000	3,904.21	2,851	2,066.10	5,586	1,699.74	6,992	1,456.19	8,423
46,000	4,081.67	2,980	2,160.02	5,840	1,777.00	7,310	1,522.38	8,806
48,000	4,259.14	3,110	2,253.93	6,094	1,854.26	7,628	1,588.57	9,189
50,000	4,436.60	3,239	2,347.85	6,348	1,931.52	7,946	1,654.76	9,571

AUTO LOAN PAYMENTS 11.75%

AMOUNT OF LOAN	42 MOS		48 MOS		60 MOS		72 MOS	
	MONTHLY PAYMENT	TOTAL INTRST	MONTHLY PAYMENT	TOTAL INTRST	MONTHLY PAYMENT	TOTAL INTRST	MONTHLY PAYMENT	TOTAL INTRST
$ 1	0.03	0	0.03	0	0.03	1	0.02	0
2	0.06	1	0.06	1	0.05	1	0.04	1
3	0.09	1	0.08	1	0.07	1	0.06	1
4	0.12	1	0.11	1	0.09	1	0.08	2
5	0.15	1	0.14	2	0.12	2	0.10	2
6	0.18	2	0.16	2	0.14	2	0.12	3
7	0.21	2	0.19	2	0.16	3	0.14	3
8	0.24	2	0.21	2	0.18	3	0.16	4
9	0.27	2	0.24	3	0.20	3	0.18	4
10	0.30	3	0.27	3	0.23	4	0.20	4
20	0.59	5	0.53	5	0.45	7	0.39	8
30	0.88	7	0.79	8	0.67	10	0.59	12
40	1.17	9	1.05	10	0.89	13	0.78	16
50	1.46	11	1.32	13	1.11	17	0.98	21
60	1.75	14	1.58	16	1.33	20	1.17	24
70	2.05	16	1.84	18	1.55	23	1.36	28
80	2.34	18	2.10	21	1.77	26	1.56	32
90	2.63	20	2.36	23	2.00	30	1.75	36
100	2.92	23	2.63	26	2.22	33	1.95	40
200	5.84	45	5.25	52	4.43	66	3.89	80
300	8.75	68	7.87	78	6.64	98	5.83	120
400	11.67	90	10.49	104	8.85	131	7.77	159
500	14.58	112	13.11	129	11.06	164	9.72	200
600	17.50	135	15.73	155	13.28	197	11.66	240
700	20.41	157	18.35	181	15.49	229	13.60	279
800	23.33	180	20.97	207	17.70	262	15.54	319
900	26.24	202	23.60	233	19.91	295	17.48	359
1,000	29.16	225	26.22	259	22.12	327	19.43	399
2,000	58.31	449	52.43	517	44.24	654	38.85	797
3,000	87.47	674	78.64	775	66.36	982	58.27	1,195
4,000	116.62	898	104.85	1,033	88.48	1,309	77.69	1,594
5,000	145.78	1,123	131.06	1,291	110.60	1,636	97.11	1,992
6,000	174.93	1,347	157.27	1,549	132.71	1,963	116.53	2,390
7,000	204.09	1,572	183.48	1,807	154.83	2,290	135.95	2,788
8,000	233.24	1,796	209.70	2,066	176.95	2,617	155.37	3,187
9,000	262.40	2,021	235.91	2,324	199.07	2,944	174.79	3,585
10,000	291.55	2,245	262.12	2,582	221.19	3,271	194.21	3,983
11,000	320.71	2,470	288.33	2,840	243.31	3,599	213.63	4,381
12,000	349.86	2,694	314.54	3,098	265.42	3,925	233.05	4,780
13,000	379.02	2,919	340.75	3,356	287.54	4,252	252.47	5,178
14,000	408.17	3,143	366.96	3,614	309.66	4,580	271.89	5,576
15,000	437.33	3,368	393.17	3,872	331.78	4,907	291.31	5,974
16,000	466.48	3,592	419.39	4,131	353.90	5,234	310.73	6,373
17,000	495.64	3,817	445.60	4,389	376.02	5,561	330.15	6,771
18,000	524.79	4,041	471.81	4,647	398.13	5,888	349.57	7,169
19,000	553.95	4,266	498.02	4,905	420.25	6,215	368.99	7,567
20,000	583.10	4,490	524.23	5,163	442.37	6,542	388.41	7,966
21,000	612.25	4,715	550.44	5,421	464.49	6,869	407.83	8,364
22,000	641.41	4,939	576.65	5,679	486.61	7,197	427.25	8,762
23,000	670.56	5,164	602.86	5,937	508.73	7,524	446.67	9,160
24,000	699.72	5,388	629.08	6,196	530.84	7,850	466.10	9,559
25,000	728.87	5,613	655.29	6,454	552.96	8,178	485.52	9,957
26,000	758.03	5,837	681.50	6,712	575.08	8,505	504.94	10,356
27,000	787.18	6,062	707.71	6,970	597.20	8,832	524.36	10,754
28,000	816.34	6,286	733.92	7,228	619.32	9,159	543.78	11,152
29,000	845.49	6,511	760.13	7,486	641.44	9,486	563.20	11,550
30,000	874.65	6,735	786.34	7,744	663.55	9,813	582.62	11,949
31,000	903.80	6,960	812.55	8,002	685.67	10,140	602.04	12,347
32,000	932.96	7,184	838.77	8,261	707.79	10,467	621.46	12,745
33,000	962.11	7,409	864.98	8,519	729.91	10,795	640.88	13,143
34,000	991.27	7,633	891.19	8,777	752.03	11,122	660.30	13,542
35,000	1,020.42	7,858	917.40	9,035	774.15	11,449	679.72	13,940
36,000	1,049.58	8,082	943.61	9,293	796.26	11,776	699.14	14,338
37,000	1,078.73	8,307	969.82	9,551	818.38	12,103	718.56	14,736
38,000	1,107.89	8,531	996.03	9,809	840.50	12,430	737.98	15,135
39,000	1,137.04	8,756	1,022.24	10,068	862.62	12,757	757.40	15,533
40,000	1,166.19	8,980	1,048.46	10,326	884.74	13,084	776.82	15,931
42,000	1,224.50	9,429	1,100.88	10,842	928.97	13,738	815.66	16,728
44,000	1,282.81	9,878	1,153.30	11,358	973.21	14,393	854.50	17,524
46,000	1,341.12	10,327	1,205.72	11,875	1,017.45	15,047	893.34	18,320
48,000	1,399.43	10,776	1,258.15	12,391	1,061.68	15,701	932.19	19,118
50,000	1,457.74	11,225	1,310.57	12,907	1,105.92	16,355	971.03	19,914

AUTO LOAN PAYMENTS

AMOUNT OF LOAN	12 MOS		24 MOS		30 MOS		36 MOS	
	MONTHLY PAYMENT	TOTAL INTRST	MONTHLY PAYMENT	TOTAL INTRST	MONTHLY PAYMENT	TOTAL INTRST	MONTHLY PAYMENT	TOTAL INTRS
$ 1	0.09	0	0.05	0	0.04	0	0.04	
2	0.18	0	0.10	0	0.08	0	0.07	
3	0.27	0	0.15	1	0.12	1	0.10	
4	0.36	0	0.19	1	0.16	1	0.14	
5	0.45	0	0.24	1	0.20	1	0.17	
6	0.54	0	0.29	1	0.24	1	0.20	
7	0.63	1	0.33	1	0.28	1	0.24	
8	0.72	1	0.38	1	0.31	1	0.27	
9	0.80	1	0.43	1	0.35	2	0.30	
10	0.89	1	0.48	2	0.39	2	0.34	
20	1.78	1	0.95	3	0.78	3	0.67	
30	2.67	2	1.42	4	1.17	5	1.00	
40	3.56	3	1.89	5	1.55	7	1.33	
50	4.45	3	2.36	7	1.94	8	1.67	1
60	5.34	4	2.83	8	2.33	10	2.00	1
70	6.22	5	3.30	9	2.72	12	2.33	1
80	7.11	5	3.77	10	3.10	13	2.66	1
90	8.00	6	4.24	12	3.49	15	2.99	1
100	8.89	7	4.71	13	3.88	16	3.33	2
200	17.77	13	9.42	26	7.75	33	6.65	3
300	26.66	20	14.13	39	11.63	49	9.97	5
400	35.54	26	18.83	52	15.50	65	13.29	7
500	44.43	33	23.54	65	19.38	81	16.61	9
600	53.31	40	28.25	78	23.25	98	19.93	11
700	62.20	46	32.96	91	27.13	114	23.26	13
800	71.08	53	37.66	104	31.00	130	26.58	15
900	79.97	60	42.37	117	34.88	146	29.90	17
1,000	88.85	66	47.08	130	38.75	163	33.22	19
2,000	177.70	132	94.15	260	77.50	325	66.43	39
3,000	266.55	199	141.23	390	116.25	488	99.65	58
4,000	355.40	265	188.30	519	155.00	650	132.86	78
5,000	444.25	331	235.37	649	193.75	813	166.08	97
6,000	533.10	397	282.45	779	232.49	975	199.29	1,17
7,000	621.95	463	329.52	908	271.24	1,137	232.51	1,37
8,000	710.80	530	376.59	1,038	309.99	1,300	265.72	1,56
9,000	799.64	596	423.67	1,168	348.74	1,462	298.93	1,76
10,000	888.49	662	470.74	1,298	387.49	1,625	332.15	1,95
11,000	977.34	728	517.81	1,427	426.23	1,787	365.36	2,15
12,000	1,066.19	794	564.89	1,557	464.98	1,949	398.58	2,34
13,000	1,155.04	860	611.96	1,687	503.73	2,112	431.79	2,54
14,000	1,243.89	927	659.03	1,817	542.48	2,274	465.01	2,74
15,000	1,332.74	993	706.11	1,947	581.23	2,437	498.22	2,93
16,000	1,421.59	1,059	753.18	2,076	619.97	2,599	531.43	3,13
17,000	1,510.43	1,125	800.25	2,206	658.72	2,762	564.65	3,32
18,000	1,599.28	1,191	847.33	2,336	697.47	2,924	597.86	3,52
19,000	1,688.13	1,258	894.40	2,466	736.22	3,087	631.08	3,71
20,000	1,776.98	1,324	941.47	2,595	774.97	3,249	664.29	3,91
21,000	1,865.83	1,390	988.55	2,725	813.72	3,412	697.51	4,11
22,000	1,954.68	1,456	1,035.62	2,855	852.46	3,574	730.72	4,30
23,000	2,043.53	1,522	1,082.69	2,985	891.21	3,736	763.93	4,50
24,000	2,132.38	1,589	1,129.77	3,114	929.96	3,899	797.15	4,69
25,000	2,221.22	1,655	1,176.84	3,244	968.71	4,061	830.36	4,89
26,000	2,310.07	1,721	1,223.92	3,374	1,007.46	4,224	863.58	5,08
27,000	2,398.92	1,787	1,270.99	3,504	1,046.20	4,386	896.79	5,28
28,000	2,487.77	1,853	1,318.06	3,633	1,084.95	4,549	930.01	5,48
29,000	2,576.62	1,919	1,365.14	3,763	1,123.70	4,711	963.22	5,67
30,000	2,665.47	1,986	1,412.21	3,893	1,162.45	4,874	996.43	5,87
31,000	2,754.32	2,052	1,459.28	4,023	1,201.20	5,036	1,029.65	6,06
32,000	2,843.17	2,118	1,506.36	4,153	1,239.94	5,198	1,062.86	6,26
33,000	2,932.02	2,184	1,553.43	4,282	1,278.69	5,361	1,096.08	6,45
34,000	3,020.86	2,250	1,600.50	4,412	1,317.44	5,523	1,129.29	6,65
35,000	3,109.71	2,317	1,647.58	4,542	1,356.19	5,686	1,162.51	6,85
36,000	3,198.56	2,383	1,694.65	4,672	1,394.94	5,848	1,195.72	7,04
37,000	3,287.41	2,449	1,741.72	4,801	1,433.69	6,011	1,228.93	7,24
38,000	3,376.26	2,515	1,788.80	4,931	1,472.43	6,173	1,262.15	7,43
39,000	3,465.11	2,581	1,835.87	5,061	1,511.18	6,335	1,295.36	7,63
40,000	3,553.96	2,648	1,882.94	5,191	1,549.93	6,498	1,328.58	7,82
42,000	3,731.65	2,780	1,977.09	5,450	1,627.43	6,823	1,395.01	8,22
44,000	3,909.35	2,912	2,071.24	5,710	1,704.92	7,148	1,461.43	8,61
46,000	4,087.05	3,045	2,165.38	5,969	1,782.42	7,473	1,527.86	9,00
48,000	4,264.75	3,177	2,259.53	6,229	1,859.91	7,797	1,594.29	9,39
50,000	4,442.44	3,309	2,353.68	6,488	1,937.41	8,122	1,660.72	9,78

AUTO LOAN PAYMENTS 12.00%

AMOUNT OF LOAN	42 MOS		48 MOS		60 MOS		72 MOS	
	MONTHLY PAYMENT	TOTAL INTRST	MONTHLY PAYMENT	TOTAL INTRST	MONTHLY PAYMENT	TOTAL INTRST	MONTHLY PAYMENT	TOTAL INTRST
$ 1	0.03	0	0.03	0	0.03	1	0.02	0
2	0.06	1	0.06	1	0.05	1	0.04	1
3	0.09	1	0.08	1	0.07	1	0.06	1
4	0.12	1	0.11	1	0.09	1	0.08	2
5	0.15	1	0.14	2	0.12	2	0.10	2
6	0.18	2	0.16	2	0.14	2	0.14	3
7	0.21	2	0.19	2	0.16	3	0.14	3
8	0.24	2	0.22	3	0.18	3	0.16	4
9	0.27	2	0.24	3	0.21	4	0.18	4
10	0.30	3	0.27	3	0.23	4	0.20	4
20	0.59	5	0.53	5	0.45	7	0.40	9
30	0.88	7	0.80	8	0.67	10	0.59	12
40	1.18	10	1.06	11	0.89	13	0.79	17
50	1.47	12	1.32	13	1.12	17	0.98	21
60	1.76	14	1.58	16	1.34	20	1.18	25
70	2.05	16	1.85	19	1.56	24	1.37	29
80	2.35	19	2.11	21	1.78	27	1.57	33
90	2.64	21	2.38	24	2.01	31	1.76	37
100	2.93	23	2.64	27	2.23	34	1.96	41
200	5.86	46	5.27	53	4.45	67	3.92	82
300	8.79	69	7.91	80	6.68	101	5.87	123
400	11.72	92	10.54	106	8.90	134	7.83	164
500	14.64	115	13.17	132	11.13	168	9.78	204
600	17.57	138	15.81	159	13.35	201	11.74	245
700	20.50	161	18.44	185	15.58	235	13.69	286
800	23.43	184	21.07	211	17.80	268	15.65	327
900	26.35	207	23.71	238	20.03	302	17.60	367
1,000	29.28	230	26.34	264	22.25	335	19.56	408
2,000	58.56	460	52.67	528	44.49	669	39.11	816
3,000	87.83	689	79.01	792	66.74	1,004	58.66	1,224
4,000	117.11	919	105.34	1,056	88.98	1,339	78.21	1,631
5,000	146.38	1,148	131.67	1,320	111.23	1,674	97.76	2,039
6,000	175.66	1,378	158.01	1,584	133.47	2,008	117.31	2,446
7,000	204.93	1,607	184.34	1,848	155.72	2,343	136.86	2,854
8,000	234.21	1,837	210.68	2,113	177.96	2,678	156.41	3,262
9,000	263.49	2,067	237.01	2,376	200.21	3,013	175.96	3,669
10,000	292.76	2,296	263.34	2,640	222.45	3,347	195.51	4,077
11,000	322.04	2,526	289.68	2,905	244.69	3,681	215.06	4,484
12,000	351.31	2,755	316.01	3,168	266.94	4,016	234.61	4,892
13,000	380.59	2,985	342.34	3,432	289.18	4,351	254.16	5,300
14,000	409.86	3,214	368.68	3,697	311.43	4,686	273.71	5,707
15,000	439.14	3,444	395.01	3,960	333.67	5,020	293.26	6,115
16,000	468.42	3,674	421.35	4,225	355.92	5,355	312.81	6,522
17,000	497.69	3,903	447.68	4,489	378.16	5,690	332.36	6,930
18,000	526.97	4,133	474.01	4,752	400.41	6,025	351.91	7,338
19,000	556.24	4,362	500.35	5,017	422.65	6,359	371.46	7,745
20,000	585.52	4,592	526.68	5,281	444.89	6,693	391.01	8,153
21,000	614.79	4,821	553.02	5,545	467.14	7,028	410.56	8,560
22,000	644.07	5,051	579.35	5,809	489.38	7,363	430.11	8,968
23,000	673.34	5,280	605.68	6,073	511.63	7,698	449.66	9,376
24,000	702.62	5,510	632.02	6,337	533.87	8,032	469.21	9,783
25,000	731.90	5,740	658.35	6,601	556.12	8,367	488.76	10,191
26,000	761.17	5,969	684.68	6,865	578.36	8,702	508.31	10,598
27,000	790.45	6,199	711.02	7,129	600.61	9,037	527.86	11,006
28,000	819.72	6,428	737.35	7,393	622.85	9,371	547.41	11,414
29,000	849.00	6,658	763.69	7,657	645.09	9,705	566.96	11,821
30,000	878.27	6,887	790.02	7,921	667.34	10,040	586.51	12,229
31,000	907.55	7,117	816.35	8,185	689.58	10,375	606.06	12,636
32,000	936.83	7,347	842.69	8,449	711.83	10,710	625.61	13,044
33,000	966.10	7,576	869.02	8,713	734.07	11,044	645.16	13,452
34,000	995.38	7,806	895.36	8,977	756.32	11,379	664.71	13,859
35,000	1,024.65	8,035	921.69	9,241	778.56	11,714	684.26	14,267
36,000	1,053.93	8,265	948.02	9,505	800.81	12,049	703.81	14,674
37,000	1,083.20	8,494	974.36	9,769	823.05	12,383	723.36	15,082
38,000	1,112.48	8,724	1,000.69	10,033	845.29	12,717	742.91	15,490
39,000	1,141.75	8,954	1,027.02	10,297	867.54	13,052	762.46	15,897
40,000	1,171.03	9,183	1,053.36	10,561	889.78	13,387	782.01	16,305
42,000	1,229.58	9,642	1,106.03	11,089	934.27	14,056	821.11	17,120
44,000	1,288.13	10,101	1,158.69	11,617	978.76	14,726	860.21	17,935
46,000	1,346.68	10,561	1,211.36	12,145	1,023.25	15,395	899.31	18,750
48,000	1,405.24	11,020	1,264.03	12,673	1,067.74	16,064	938.41	19,566
50,000	1,463.79	11,479	1,316.70	13,202	1,112.23	16,734	977.51	20,381

AUTO LOAN PAYMENTS

AMOUNT OF LOAN	12 MOS		24 MOS		30 MOS		36 MOS	
	MONTHLY PAYMENT	TOTAL INTRST	MONTHLY PAYMENT	TOTAL INTRST	MONTHLY PAYMENT	TOTAL INTRST	MONTHLY PAYMENT	TOTAL INTRST
$ 1	0.09	0	0.05	0	0.04	0	0.04	0
2	0.18	0	0.10	0	0.08	0	0.07	1
3	0.27	0	0.15	1	0.12	1	0.11	1
4	0.36	0	0.19	1	0.16	1	0.14	1
5	0.45	0	0.24	1	0.20	1	0.17	1
6	0.54	0	0.29	1	0.24	1	0.21	2
7	0.63	0	0.34	1	0.28	1	0.24	2
8	0.72	1	0.38	1	0.32	2	0.27	2
9	0.81	1	0.43	1	0.35	1	0.31	2
10	0.89	1	0.48	1	0.39	2	0.34	2
20	1.78	1	0.95	3	0.78	3	0.67	4
30	2.67	2	1.42	4	1.17	5	1.01	6
40	3.56	2	1.89	5	1.56	7	1.34	8
50	4.45	3	2.36	7	1.95	9	1.67	10
60	5.34	4	2.84	8	2.34	10	2.01	12
70	6.23	5	3.31	9	2.73	12	2.34	14
80	7.12	5	3.78	11	3.11	13	2.67	16
90	8.01	6	4.25	12	3.50	15	3.01	18
100	8.90	7	4.72	13	3.89	17	3.34	20
200	17.80	14	9.44	27	7.78	33	6.67	40
300	26.69	20	14.16	40	11.66	50	10.01	60
400	35.59	27	18.88	53	15.55	67	13.34	80
500	44.49	34	23.60	66	19.44	83	16.67	100
600	53.38	41	28.32	80	23.32	100	20.01	120
700	62.28	47	33.04	93	27.21	116	23.34	140
800	71.18	54	37.76	106	31.10	133	26.67	160
900	80.07	61	42.48	120	34.98	149	30.01	180
1,000	88.97	68	47.20	133	38.87	166	33.34	200
2,000	177.90	135	94.39	265	77.74	332	66.67	400
3,000	266.90	203	141.59	398	116.60	498	100.01	600
4,000	355.87	270	188.77	530	155.47	664	133.34	800
5,000	444.83	338	235.96	663	194.34	830	166.67	1,000
6,000	533.80	406	283.15	796	233.20	996	200.01	1,200
7,000	622.77	473	330.34	928	272.07	1,162	233.34	1,400
8,000	711.73	541	377.53	1,061	310.93	1,328	266.68	1,600
9,000	800.70	608	424.72	1,193	349.80	1,494	300.01	1,800
10,000	889.66	676	471.91	1,326	388.67	1,660	333.34	2,000
11,000	978.63	744	519.10	1,458	427.53	1,826	366.68	2,200
12,000	1,067.59	811	566.29	1,591	466.40	1,992	400.01	2,400
13,000	1,156.56	879	613.48	1,724	505.27	2,158	433.34	2,600
14,000	1,245.53	946	660.67	1,856	544.13	2,324	466.68	2,800
15,000	1,334.49	1,014	707.86	1,989	583.00	2,490	500.01	3,000
16,000	1,423.46	1,082	755.05	2,121	621.86	2,656	533.35	3,201
17,000	1,512.42	1,149	802.24	2,254	660.73	2,822	566.68	3,400
18,000	1,601.39	1,217	849.43	2,386	699.60	2,988	600.01	3,600
19,000	1,690.35	1,284	896.62	2,519	738.46	3,154	633.35	3,801
20,000	1,779.32	1,352	943.81	2,651	777.33	3,320	666.68	4,000
21,000	1,868.29	1,419	991.00	2,784	816.19	3,486	700.02	4,201
22,000	1,957.25	1,487	1,038.19	2,917	855.06	3,652	733.35	4,401
23,000	2,046.22	1,555	1,085.38	3,049	893.93	3,818	766.68	4,600
24,000	2,135.18	1,622	1,132.57	3,182	932.79	3,984	800.02	4,801
25,000	2,224.15	1,690	1,179.76	3,314	971.66	4,150	833.35	5,001
26,000	2,313.12	1,757	1,226.95	3,447	1,010.53	4,316	866.68	5,200
27,000	2,402.08	1,825	1,274.14	3,579	1,049.39	4,482	900.02	5,401
28,000	2,491.05	1,893	1,321.33	3,712	1,088.26	4,648	933.35	5,601
29,000	2,580.01	1,960	1,368.52	3,844	1,127.12	4,814	966.69	5,801
30,000	2,668.98	2,028	1,415.71	3,977	1,165.99	4,980	1,000.02	6,001
31,000	2,757.94	2,095	1,462.90	4,110	1,204.86	5,146	1,033.35	6,201
32,000	2,846.91	2,163	1,510.09	4,242	1,243.72	5,312	1,066.69	6,401
33,000	2,935.88	2,231	1,557.29	4,375	1,282.59	5,478	1,100.02	6,601
34,000	3,024.84	2,298	1,604.48	4,508	1,321.45	5,644	1,133.36	6,801
35,000	3,113.81	2,366	1,651.67	4,640	1,360.32	5,810	1,166.69	7,001
36,000	3,202.77	2,433	1,698.86	4,773	1,399.19	5,976	1,200.02	7,201
37,000	3,291.74	2,501	1,746.05	4,905	1,438.05	6,142	1,233.36	7,401
38,000	3,380.70	2,568	1,793.24	5,038	1,476.92	6,308	1,266.69	7,601
39,000	3,469.67	2,636	1,840.43	5,170	1,515.79	6,474	1,300.02	7,801
40,000	3,558.64	2,704	1,887.62	5,303	1,554.65	6,640	1,333.36	8,001
42,000	3,736.57	2,839	1,982.00	5,568	1,632.38	6,971	1,400.03	8,401
44,000	3,914.50	2,974	2,076.38	5,833	1,710.12	7,304	1,466.69	8,801
46,000	4,092.43	3,109	2,170.76	6,098	1,787.85	7,636	1,533.36	9,201
48,000	4,270.36	3,244	2,265.14	6,363	1,865.58	7,967	1,600.03	9,601
50,000	4,448.29	3,379	2,359.52	6,628	1,943.31	8,299	1,666.70	10,001

AUTO LOAN PAYMENTS 12.25%

AMOUNT OF LOAN	42 MOS		48 MOS		60 MOS		72 MOS	
	MONTHLY PAYMENT	TOTAL INTRST	MONTHLY PAYMENT	TOTAL INTRST	MONTHLY PAYMENT	TOTAL INTRST	MONTHLY PAYMENT	TOTAL INTRST
$ 1	0.03	0	0.03	0	0.03	1	0.02	0
2	0.06	1	0.06	1	0.05	1	0.04	1
3	0.09	1	0.08	1	0.07	1	0.06	1
4	0.12	1	0.11	1	0.09	1	0.08	2
5	0.15	1	0.14	2	0.12	2	0.10	2
6	0.18	2	0.16	2	0.14	2	0.12	3
7	0.21	2	0.19	2	0.16	3	0.14	3
8	0.24	2	0.22	3	0.18	3	0.16	4
9	0.27	2	0.24	3	0.21	4	0.18	4
10	0.30	3	0.27	3	0.23	4	0.20	4
20	0.59	5	0.53	5	0.45	7	0.40	9
30	0.89	7	0.80	8	0.68	11	0.60	13
40	1.18	10	1.06	11	0.90	14	0.79	17
50	1.47	12	1.33	14	1.12	17	0.99	21
60	1.77	14	1.59	16	1.35	21	1.19	26
70	2.06	17	1.86	19	1.57	24	1.38	29
80	2.36	19	2.12	22	1.79	27	1.58	34
90	2.65	21	2.39	25	2.02	31	1.78	38
100	2.94	23	2.65	27	2.24	34	1.97	42
200	5.88	47	5.30	54	4.48	69	3.94	84
300	8.82	70	7.94	81	6.72	103	5.91	126
400	11.76	94	10.59	108	8.95	137	7.88	167
500	14.70	117	13.23	135	11.19	171	9.85	209
600	17.64	141	15.88	162	13.43	206	11.81	250
700	20.58	164	18.52	189	15.66	240	13.78	292
800	23.52	188	21.17	216	17.90	274	15.75	334
900	26.46	211	23.82	243	20.14	308	17.72	376
1,000	29.40	235	26.46	270	22.38	343	19.69	418
2,000	58.80	470	52.92	540	44.75	685	39.37	835
3,000	88.20	704	79.38	810	67.12	1,027	59.05	1,252
4,000	117.59	939	105.83	1,080	89.49	1,369	78.73	1,669
5,000	146.99	1,174	132.29	1,350	111.86	1,712	98.41	2,086
6,000	176.39	1,408	158.75	1,620	134.23	2,054	118.09	2,502
7,000	205.78	1,643	185.20	1,890	156.60	2,396	137.77	2,919
8,000	235.18	1,878	211.66	2,160	178.97	2,738	157.45	3,336
9,000	264.58	2,112	238.12	2,430	201.34	3,080	177.13	3,753
10,000	293.97	2,347	264.57	2,699	223.71	3,423	196.81	4,170
11,000	323.37	2,582	291.03	2,969	246.09	3,765	216.49	4,587
12,000	352.77	2,816	317.49	3,240	268.46	4,108	236.17	5,004
13,000	382.16	3,051	343.94	3,509	290.83	4,450	255.85	5,421
14,000	411.56	3,286	370.40	3,779	313.20	4,792	275.53	5,838
15,000	440.96	3,520	396.86	4,049	335.57	5,134	295.21	6,255
16,000	470.35	3,755	423.31	4,319	357.94	5,476	314.89	6,672
17,000	499.75	3,990	449.77	4,589	380.31	5,819	334.57	7,089
18,000	529.15	4,224	476.23	4,859	402.68	6,161	354.25	7,506
19,000	558.54	4,459	502.68	5,129	425.05	6,503	373.93	7,923
20,000	587.94	4,693	529.14	5,399	447.42	6,845	393.61	8,340
21,000	617.34	4,928	555.60	5,669	469.80	7,188	413.29	8,757
22,000	646.73	5,163	582.05	5,938	492.17	7,530	432.97	9,174
23,000	676.13	5,397	608.51	6,208	514.54	7,872	452.66	9,592
24,000	705.53	5,632	634.97	6,479	536.91	8,215	472.34	10,008
25,000	734.93	5,867	661.42	6,748	559.28	8,557	492.02	10,425
26,000	764.32	6,101	687.88	7,018	581.65	8,899	511.70	10,842
27,000	793.72	6,336	714.34	7,288	604.02	9,241	531.38	11,259
28,000	823.12	6,571	740.79	7,558	626.39	9,583	551.06	11,676
29,000	852.51	6,805	767.25	7,828	648.76	9,926	570.74	12,093
30,000	881.91	7,040	793.71	8,098	671.13	10,268	590.42	12,510
31,000	911.31	7,275	820.16	8,368	693.51	10,611	610.10	12,927
32,000	940.70	7,509	846.62	8,638	715.88	10,953	629.78	13,344
33,000	970.10	7,744	873.08	8,908	738.25	11,295	649.46	13,761
34,000	999.50	7,979	899.53	9,177	760.62	11,637	669.14	14,178
35,000	1,028.89	8,213	925.99	9,448	782.99	11,979	688.82	14,595
36,000	1,058.29	8,448	952.45	9,718	805.36	12,322	708.50	15,012
37,000	1,087.69	8,683	978.90	9,987	827.73	12,664	728.18	15,429
38,000	1,117.08	8,917	1,005.36	10,257	850.10	13,006	747.86	15,846
39,000	1,146.48	9,152	1,031.82	10,527	872.47	13,348	767.54	16,263
40,000	1,175.88	9,387	1,058.28	10,797	894.84	13,690	787.22	16,680
42,000	1,234.67	9,856	1,111.19	11,337	939.59	14,375	826.58	17,514
44,000	1,293.46	10,325	1,164.10	11,877	984.33	15,060	865.94	18,348
46,000	1,352.26	10,795	1,217.02	12,417	1,029.07	15,744	905.31	19,182
48,000	1,411.05	11,264	1,269.93	12,957	1,073.81	16,429	944.67	20,016
50,000	1,469.85	11,734	1,322.84	13,496	1,118.55	17,113	984.03	20,850

123

AUTO LOAN PAYMENTS

AMOUNT OF LOAN	12 MOS		24 MOS		30 MOS		36 MOS	
	MONTHLY PAYMENT	TOTAL INTRST	MONTHLY PAYMENT	TOTAL INTRST	MONTHLY PAYMENT	TOTAL INTRST	MONTHLY PAYMENT	TOTAL INTRST
$ 1	0.09	0	0.05	0	0.04	0	0.04	0
2	0.18	0	0.10	0	0.08	0	0.07	1
3	0.27	0	0.15	1	0.12	1	0.11	1
4	0.36	0	0.19	1	0.16	1	0.14	1
5	0.45	0	0.24	1	0.20	1	0.17	1
6	0.54	0	0.29	1	0.24	1	0.21	2
7	0.63	1	0.34	1	0.28	1	0.24	2
8	0.72	1	0.38	1	0.32	2	0.27	2
9	0.81	1	0.43	1	0.36	2	0.31	2
10	0.90	1	0.48	2	0.39	2	0.34	2
20	1.79	1	0.95	3	0.78	3	0.67	4
30	2.68	2	1.42	4	1.17	5	1.01	6
40	3.57	3	1.90	6	1.56	7	1.34	8
50	4.46	4	2.37	7	1.95	9	1.68	10
60	5.35	4	2.84	8	2.34	10	2.01	12
70	6.24	5	3.32	10	2.73	12	2.35	15
80	7.13	6	3.79	11	3.12	14	2.68	16
90	8.02	6	4.26	12	3.51	15	3.02	19
100	8.91	7	4.74	14	3.90	17	3.35	21
200	17.82	14	9.47	27	7.80	34	6.70	41
300	26.73	21	14.20	41	11.70	51	10.04	61
400	35.64	28	18.93	54	15.60	68	13.39	82
500	44.55	35	23.66	68	19.50	85	16.73	102
600	53.45	41	28.39	81	23.40	102	20.08	123
700	62.36	48	33.12	95	27.29	119	23.42	143
800	71.27	55	37.85	108	31.19	136	26.77	164
900	80.18	62	42.58	122	35.09	153	30.11	184
1,000	89.09	69	47.31	135	38.99	170	33.46	205
2,000	178.17	138	94.62	271	77.97	339	66.91	409
3,000	267.25	207	141.93	406	116.96	509	100.37	613
4,000	356.34	276	189.23	542	155.94	678	133.82	818
5,000	445.42	345	236.54	677	194.93	848	167.27	1,022
6,000	534.50	414	283.85	812	233.91	1,017	200.73	1,226
7,000	623.59	483	331.16	948	272.90	1,187	234.18	1,430
8,000	712.67	552	378.46	1,083	311.88	1,356	267.63	1,635
9,000	801.75	621	425.77	1,218	350.86	1,526	301.09	1,839
10,000	890.83	690	473.08	1,354	389.85	1,696	334.54	2,043
11,000	979.92	759	520.39	1,489	428.83	1,865	367.99	2,248
12,000	1,069.00	828	567.69	1,625	467.82	2,035	401.45	2,452
13,000	1,158.08	897	615.00	1,760	506.80	2,204	434.90	2,656
14,000	1,247.17	966	662.31	1,895	545.79	2,374	468.36	2,861
15,000	1,336.25	1,035	709.61	2,031	584.77	2,543	501.81	3,065
16,000	1,425.33	1,104	756.92	2,166	623.76	2,713	535.26	3,269
17,000	1,514.41	1,173	804.23	2,302	662.74	2,882	568.72	3,474
18,000	1,603.50	1,242	851.54	2,437	701.72	3,052	602.17	3,678
19,000	1,692.58	1,311	898.84	2,572	740.71	3,221	635.62	3,882
20,000	1,781.66	1,380	946.15	2,708	779.69	3,391	669.08	4,087
21,000	1,870.75	1,449	993.46	2,843	818.68	3,560	702.53	4,291
22,000	1,959.83	1,518	1,040.77	2,978	857.66	3,730	735.98	4,495
23,000	2,048.91	1,587	1,088.07	3,114	896.65	3,900	769.44	4,700
24,000	2,137.99	1,656	1,135.38	3,249	935.63	4,069	802.89	4,904
25,000	2,227.08	1,725	1,182.69	3,385	974.62	4,239	836.35	5,109
26,000	2,316.16	1,794	1,230.00	3,520	1,013.60	4,408	869.80	5,313
27,000	2,405.24	1,863	1,277.30	3,655	1,052.58	4,577	903.25	5,517
28,000	2,494.33	1,932	1,324.61	3,791	1,091.57	4,747	936.71	5,722
29,000	2,583.41	2,001	1,371.92	3,926	1,130.55	4,917	970.16	5,926
30,000	2,672.49	2,070	1,419.22	4,061	1,169.54	5,086	1,003.61	6,130
31,000	2,761.57	2,139	1,466.53	4,197	1,208.52	5,256	1,037.07	6,335
32,000	2,850.66	2,208	1,513.84	4,332	1,247.51	5,425	1,070.52	6,539
33,000	2,939.74	2,277	1,561.15	4,468	1,286.49	5,595	1,103.97	6,743
34,000	3,028.82	2,346	1,608.45	4,603	1,325.47	5,764	1,137.43	6,947
35,000	3,117.91	2,415	1,655.76	4,738	1,364.46	5,934	1,170.88	7,152
36,000	3,206.99	2,484	1,703.07	4,874	1,403.44	6,103	1,204.34	7,356
37,000	3,296.07	2,553	1,750.38	5,009	1,442.43	6,273	1,237.79	7,560
38,000	3,385.15	2,622	1,797.68	5,144	1,481.41	6,442	1,271.24	7,765
39,000	3,474.24	2,691	1,844.99	5,280	1,520.40	6,612	1,304.70	7,969
40,000	3,563.32	2,760	1,892.30	5,415	1,559.38	6,781	1,338.15	8,173
42,000	3,741.49	2,898	1,986.91	5,686	1,637.35	7,121	1,405.06	8,582
44,000	3,919.65	3,036	2,081.53	5,957	1,715.32	7,460	1,471.96	8,991
46,000	4,097.82	3,174	2,176.14	6,227	1,793.29	7,799	1,538.87	9,399
48,000	4,275.98	3,312	2,270.76	6,498	1,871.26	8,138	1,605.78	9,808
50,000	4,454.15	3,450	2,365.37	6,769	1,949.23	8,477	1,672.69	10,217

AUTO LOAN PAYMENTS   12.50%

AMOUNT OF LOAN	42 MOS MONTHLY PAYMENT	42 MOS TOTAL INTRST	48 MOS MONTHLY PAYMENT	48 MOS TOTAL INTRST	60 MOS MONTHLY PAYMENT	60 MOS TOTAL INTRST	72 MOS MONTHLY PAYMENT	72 MOS TOTAL INTRST
$ 1	0.03	0	0.03	0	0.03	1	0.02	0
2	0.06	1	0.06	1	0.05	1	0.04	1
3	0.09	1	0.08	1	0.07	1	0.06	1
4	0.12	1	0.11	1	0.09	1	0.08	2
5	0.15	1	0.14	2	0.12	2	0.10	2
6	0.18	2	0.16	2	0.14	2	0.12	3
7	0.21	2	0.19	2	0.16	3	0.14	3
8	0.24	2	0.22	3	0.18	3	0.16	4
9	0.27	2	0.24	3	0.21	4	0.18	4
10	0.30	3	0.27	3	0.23	4	0.20	4
20	0.60	5	0.54	6	0.45	7	0.40	9
30	0.89	7	0.80	8	0.68	11	0.60	13
40	1.19	10	1.07	11	0.90	14	0.80	18
50	1.48	12	1.33	14	1.13	18	1.00	22
60	1.78	15	1.60	17	1.35	21	1.19	26
70	2.07	17	1.87	20	1.58	25	1.39	30
80	2.37	20	2.13	22	1.80	28	1.59	34
90	2.66	22	2.40	25	2.03	32	1.79	39
100	2.96	24	2.66	28	2.25	35	1.99	43
200	5.91	48	5.32	55	4.50	70	3.97	86
300	8.86	72	7.98	83	6.75	105	5.95	128
400	11.81	96	10.64	111	9.00	140	7.93	171
500	14.76	120	13.29	138	11.25	175	9.91	214
600	17.72	144	15.95	166	13.50	210	11.89	256
700	20.67	168	18.61	193	15.75	245	13.87	299
800	23.62	192	21.27	221	18.00	280	15.85	341
900	26.57	216	23.93	249	20.25	315	17.84	384
1,000	29.52	240	26.58	276	22.50	350	19.82	427
2,000	59.04	480	53.16	552	45.00	700	39.63	853
3,000	88.56	720	79.74	828	67.50	1,050	59.44	1,280
4,000	118.08	959	106.32	1,103	90.00	1,400	79.25	1,706
5,000	147.60	1,199	132.90	1,379	112.49	1,749	99.06	2,132
6,000	177.11	1,439	159.48	1,655	134.99	2,099	118.87	2,559
7,000	206.63	1,678	186.06	1,931	157.49	2,449	138.68	2,985
8,000	236.15	1,918	212.64	2,207	179.99	2,799	158.49	3,411
9,000	265.67	2,158	239.22	2,483	202.49	3,149	178.31	3,838
10,000	295.19	2,398	265.80	2,758	224.98	3,499	198.12	4,265
11,000	324.71	2,638	292.38	3,034	247.48	3,849	217.93	4,691
12,000	354.22	2,877	318.96	3,310	269.98	4,199	237.74	5,117
13,000	383.74	3,117	345.54	3,586	292.48	4,549	257.55	5,544
14,000	413.26	3,357	372.12	3,862	314.98	4,899	277.36	5,970
15,000	442.78	3,597	398.70	4,138	337.47	5,248	297.17	6,396
16,000	472.30	3,837	425.28	4,413	359.97	5,598	316.98	6,823
17,000	501.82	4,076	451.86	4,689	382.47	5,948	336.80	7,250
18,000	531.33	4,316	478.44	4,965	404.97	6,298	356.61	7,676
19,000	560.85	4,556	505.02	5,241	427.47	6,648	376.42	8,102
20,000	590.37	4,796	531.60	5,517	449.96	6,998	396.23	8,529
21,000	619.89	5,035	558.18	5,793	472.46	7,348	416.04	8,955
22,000	649.41	5,275	584.76	6,068	494.96	7,698	435.85	9,381
23,000	678.93	5,515	611.34	6,344	517.46	8,048	455.66	9,808
24,000	708.44	5,754	637.92	6,620	539.96	8,398	475.47	10,234
25,000	737.96	5,994	664.50	6,896	562.45	8,747	495.28	10,660
26,000	767.48	6,234	691.08	7,172	584.95	9,097	515.10	11,087
27,000	797.00	6,474	717.66	7,448	607.45	9,447	534.91	11,514
28,000	826.52	6,714	744.24	7,724	629.95	9,797	554.72	11,940
29,000	856.03	6,953	770.82	7,999	652.45	10,147	574.53	12,366
30,000	885.55	7,193	797.40	8,275	674.94	10,496	594.34	12,792
31,000	915.07	7,433	823.98	8,551	697.44	10,846	614.15	13,219
32,000	944.59	7,673	850.56	8,827	719.94	11,196	633.96	13,645
33,000	974.11	7,913	877.14	9,103	742.44	11,546	653.77	14,071
34,000	1,003.63	8,152	903.72	9,379	764.93	11,896	673.59	14,498
35,000	1,033.14	8,392	930.30	9,654	787.43	12,246	693.40	14,925
36,000	1,062.66	8,632	956.88	9,930	809.93	12,596	713.21	15,351
37,000	1,092.18	8,872	983.46	10,206	832.43	12,946	733.02	15,777
38,000	1,121.70	9,111	1,010.04	10,482	854.93	13,296	752.83	16,204
39,000	1,151.22	9,351	1,036.62	10,758	877.42	13,645	772.64	16,630
40,000	1,180.74	9,591	1,063.20	11,034	899.92	13,995	792.45	17,056
42,000	1,239.77	10,070	1,116.36	11,585	944.92	14,695	832.07	17,909
44,000	1,298.81	10,550	1,169.52	12,137	989.91	15,395	871.70	18,762
46,000	1,357.85	11,030	1,222.68	12,689	1,034.91	16,095	911.32	19,615
48,000	1,416.88	11,509	1,275.84	13,240	1,079.91	16,795	950.94	20,468
50,000	1,475.92	11,989	1,329.00	13,792	1,124.90	17,494	990.56	21,320

AUTO LOAN PAYMENTS

AMOUNT OF LOAN	12 MOS		24 MOS		30 MOS		36 MOS	
	MONTHLY PAYMENT	TOTAL INTRST	MONTHLY PAYMENT	TOTAL INTRST	MONTHLY PAYMENT	TOTAL INTRST	MONTHLY PAYMENT	TOTAL INTRST
$ 1	0.09	0	0.05	0	0.04	0	0.04	0
2	0.18	0	0.10	1	0.08	0	0.07	1
3	0.27	0	0.15	1	0.12	1	0.11	1
4	0.36	0	0.19	1	0.16	1	0.14	1
5	0.45	0	0.24	1	0.20	1	0.17	1
6	0.54	0	0.29	1	0.24	1	0.21	2
7	0.63	0	0.34	1	0.28	1	0.24	2
8	0.72	1	0.38	1	0.32	2	0.27	2
9	0.81	1	0.43	1	0.36	1	0.31	2
10	0.90	1	0.48	2	0.40	2	0.34	2
20	1.79	1	0.95	3	0.79	4	0.68	4
30	2.68	2	1.43	4	1.18	5	1.01	6
40	3.57	3	1.90	6	1.57	7	1.35	9
50	4.47	4	2.38	7	1.96	9	1.68	10
60	5.36	4	2.85	8	2.35	11	2.02	13
70	6.25	5	3.32	10	2.74	12	2.36	15
80	7.14	6	3.80	11	3.13	14	2.69	17
90	8.03	3	4.27	12	3.52	16	3.03	19
100	8.93	7	4.75	14	3.92	18	3.36	21
200	17.85	14	9.49	28	7.83	35	6.72	42
300	26.77	21	14.23	42	11.74	52	10.08	63
400	35.69	28	18.97	55	15.65	70	13.43	83
500	44.61	35	23.72	69	19.56	87	16.79	104
600	53.53	42	28.46	83	23.47	104	20.15	125
700	62.45	49	33.20	97	27.38	121	23.51	146
800	71.37	56	37.94	111	31.29	139	26.86	167
900	80.29	63	42.69	125	35.20	156	30.22	188
1,000	89.21	71	47.43	138	39.11	173	33.58	209
2,000	178.41	141	94.85	276	78.21	346	67.15	417
3,000	267.61	211	142.28	415	117.31	519	100.73	626
4,000	356.81	282	189.70	553	156.42	693	134.30	835
5,000	446.01	352	237.13	691	195.52	866	167.87	1,043
6,000	535.21	423	284.55	829	234.62	1,039	201.45	1,252
7,000	624.41	493	331.98	968	273.73	1,212	235.02	1,461
8,000	713.61	563	379.40	1,106	312.83	1,385	268.59	1,669
9,000	802.81	634	426.83	1,244	351.93	1,558	302.17	1,878
10,000	892.01	704	474.25	1,382	391.03	1,731	335.74	2,087
11,000	981.21	775	521.67	1,520	430.14	1,904	369.32	2,296
12,000	1,070.41	845	569.10	1,658	469.24	2,077	402.89	2,504
13,000	1,159.61	915	616.52	1,796	508.34	2,250	436.46	2,713
14,000	1,248.81	986	663.95	1,935	547.45	2,424	470.04	2,921
15,000	1,338.01	1,056	711.37	2,073	586.55	2,597	503.61	3,130
16,000	1,427.21	1,127	758.80	2,211	625.65	2,770	537.18	3,338
17,000	1,516.41	1,197	806.22	2,349	664.75	2,943	570.76	3,547
18,000	1,605.61	1,267	853.65	2,488	703.86	3,116	604.33	3,756
19,000	1,694.81	1,338	901.07	2,626	742.96	3,289	637.90	3,964
20,000	1,784.01	1,408	948.49	2,764	782.06	3,462	671.48	4,173
21,000	1,873.21	1,479	995.92	2,902	821.17	3,635	705.05	4,382
22,000	1,962.41	1,549	1,043.34	3,040	860.27	3,808	738.63	4,591
23,000	2,051.61	1,619	1,090.77	3,178	899.37	3,981	772.20	4,799
24,000	2,140.81	1,690	1,138.19	3,317	938.47	4,154	805.77	5,008
25,000	2,230.01	1,760	1,185.62	3,455	977.58	4,327	839.35	5,217
26,000	2,319.21	1,831	1,233.04	3,593	1,016.68	4,500	872.92	5,425
27,000	2,408.41	1,901	1,280.47	3,731	1,055.78	4,673	906.49	5,634
28,000	2,497.61	1,971	1,327.89	3,869	1,094.89	4,847	940.07	5,843
29,000	2,586.81	2,042	1,375.31	4,007	1,133.99	5,020	973.64	6,051
30,000	2,676.01	2,112	1,422.74	4,146	1,173.09	5,193	1,007.21	6,260
31,000	2,765.21	2,183	1,470.16	4,284	1,212.19	5,366	1,040.79	6,468
32,000	2,854.41	2,253	1,517.59	4,422	1,251.30	5,539	1,074.36	6,677
33,000	2,943.61	2,323	1,565.01	4,560	1,290.40	5,712	1,107.94	6,886
34,000	3,032.81	2,394	1,612.44	4,699	1,329.50	5,885	1,141.51	7,094
35,000	3,122.01	2,464	1,659.86	4,837	1,368.61	6,058	1,175.08	7,303
36,000	3,211.21	2,535	1,707.29	4,975	1,407.71	6,231	1,208.66	7,512
37,000	3,300.41	2,605	1,754.71	5,113	1,446.81	6,404	1,242.23	7,720
38,000	3,389.61	2,675	1,802.14	5,251	1,485.91	6,577	1,275.80	7,929
39,000	3,478.81	2,746	1,849.56	5,389	1,525.02	6,751	1,309.38	8,138
40,000	3,568.01	2,816	1,896.98	5,528	1,564.12	6,924	1,342.95	8,346
42,000	3,746.41	2,957	1,991.83	5,804	1,642.33	7,270	1,410.10	8,764
44,000	3,924.81	3,098	2,086.68	6,080	1,720.53	7,616	1,477.25	9,181
46,000	4,103.21	3,239	2,181.53	6,357	1,798.74	7,962	1,544.39	9,598
48,000	4,281.61	3,379	2,276.38	6,633	1,876.94	8,308	1,611.54	10,015
50,000	4,460.01	3,520	2,371.23	6,910	1,955.15	8,655	1,678.69	10,433

126

AUTO LOAN PAYMENTS   12.75%

AMOUNT OF LOAN	42 MOS MONTHLY PAYMENT	42 MOS TOTAL INTRST	48 MOS MONTHLY PAYMENT	48 MOS TOTAL INTRST	60 MOS MONTHLY PAYMENT	60 MOS TOTAL INTRST	72 MOS MONTHLY PAYMENT	72 MOS TOTAL INTRST
$ 1	0.03	0	0.03	0	0.03	1	0.02	0
2	0.06	1	0.06	1	0.05	1	0.04	1
3	0.09	1	0.09	1	0.07	1	0.06	1
4	0.12	1	0.11	1	0.10	2	0.08	2
5	0.15	1	0.14	2	0.12	2	0.10	2
6	0.18	2	0.17	2	0.14	2	0.12	3
7	0.21	2	0.19	2	0.16	3	0.14	3
8	0.24	2	0.22	3	0.19	3	0.16	4
9	0.27	2	0.25	3	0.21	4	0.18	4
10	0.30	3	0.27	3	0.23	4	0.20	4
20	0.60	5	0.54	6	0.46	8	0.40	9
30	0.89	7	0.81	9	0.68	11	0.60	13
40	1.19	10	1.07	11	0.91	15	0.80	18
50	1.49	13	1.34	14	1.14	18	1.00	22
60	1.78	15	1.61	17	1.36	22	1.20	26
70	2.08	17	1.87	20	1.59	25	1.40	31
80	2.38	20	2.14	23	1.82	29	1.60	35
90	2.67	22	2.41	26	2.04	32	1.80	40
100	2.97	25	2.68	29	2.27	36	2.00	44
200	5.93	49	5.35	57	4.53	72	3.99	87
300	8.90	74	8.02	85	6.79	107	5.99	131
400	11.86	98	10.69	113	9.06	144	7.98	175
500	14.83	123	13.36	141	11.32	179	9.98	219
600	17.79	147	16.03	169	13.58	215	11.97	262
700	20.75	172	18.70	198	15.84	250	13.96	305
800	23.72	196	21.37	226	18.11	287	15.96	349
900	26.68	221	24.04	254	20.37	322	17.95	392
1,000	29.65	245	26.71	282	22.63	358	19.95	436
2,000	59.29	490	53.41	564	45.26	716	39.89	872
3,000	88.93	735	80.12	846	67.88	1,073	59.83	1,308
4,000	118.57	980	106.82	1,127	90.51	1,431	79.77	1,743
5,000	148.21	1,225	133.52	1,409	113.13	1,788	99.72	2,180
6,000	177.85	1,470	160.23	1,691	135.76	2,146	119.66	2,616
7,000	207.49	1,715	186.93	1,973	158.38	2,503	139.60	3,051
8,000	237.13	1,959	213.63	2,254	181.01	2,861	159.54	3,487
9,000	266.77	2,204	240.34	2,536	203.63	3,218	179.49	3,923
10,000	296.41	2,449	267.04	2,818	226.26	3,576	199.43	4,359
11,000	326.05	2,694	293.74	3,100	248.88	3,933	219.37	4,795
12,000	355.69	2,939	320.45	3,382	271.51	4,291	239.31	5,230
13,000	385.33	3,184	347.15	3,663	294.13	4,648	259.26	5,667
14,000	414.97	3,429	373.86	3,945	316.76	5,006	279.20	6,102
15,000	444.61	3,674	400.56	4,227	339.38	5,363	299.14	6,538
16,000	474.25	3,919	427.26	4,508	362.01	5,721	319.08	6,974
17,000	503.89	4,163	453.97	4,791	384.64	6,078	339.03	7,410
18,000	533.53	4,408	480.67	5,072	407.26	6,436	358.97	7,846
19,000	563.17	4,653	507.37	5,354	429.89	6,793	378.91	8,282
20,000	592.81	4,898	534.08	5,636	452.51	7,151	398.85	8,717
21,000	622.45	5,143	560.78	5,917	475.14	7,508	418.80	9,154
22,000	652.09	5,388	587.48	6,199	497.76	7,866	438.74	9,589
23,000	681.73	5,633	614.19	6,481	520.39	8,223	458.68	10,025
24,000	711.37	5,878	640.89	6,763	543.01	8,581	478.62	10,461
25,000	741.01	6,122	667.59	7,044	565.64	8,938	498.57	10,897
26,000	770.65	6,367	694.30	7,326	588.26	9,296	518.51	11,333
27,000	800.29	6,612	721.00	7,608	610.89	9,653	538.45	11,768
28,000	829.93	6,857	747.71	7,890	633.51	10,011	558.39	12,204
29,000	859.57	7,102	774.41	8,172	656.14	10,368	578.33	12,640
30,000	889.21	7,347	801.11	8,453	678.76	10,726	598.28	13,076
31,000	918.85	7,592	827.82	8,735	701.39	11,083	618.22	13,512
32,000	948.49	7,837	854.52	9,017	724.01	11,441	638.16	13,948
33,000	978.13	8,081	881.22	9,299	746.64	11,798	658.10	14,383
34,000	1,007.77	8,326	907.93	9,581	769.27	12,156	678.05	14,820
35,000	1,037.41	8,571	934.63	9,862	791.89	12,513	697.99	15,255
36,000	1,067.05	8,816	961.33	10,144	814.52	12,871	717.93	15,691
37,000	1,096.69	9,061	988.04	10,426	837.14	13,228	737.87	16,127
38,000	1,126.33	9,306	1,014.74	10,708	859.77	13,586	757.82	16,563
39,000	1,155.97	9,551	1,041.44	10,989	882.39	13,943	777.76	16,999
40,000	1,185.61	9,796	1,068.15	11,271	905.02	14,301	797.70	17,434
42,000	1,244.89	10,285	1,121.56	11,835	950.27	15,016	837.59	18,306
44,000	1,304.17	10,775	1,174.96	12,398	995.52	15,731	877.47	19,178
46,000	1,363.45	11,265	1,228.37	12,962	1,040.77	16,446	917.36	20,050
48,000	1,422.73	11,755	1,281.78	13,525	1,086.02	17,161	957.24	20,921
50,000	1,482.01	12,244	1,335.18	14,089	1,131.27	17,876	997.13	21,793

AUTO LOAN PAYMENTS

AMOUNT OF LOAN	12 MOS		24 MOS		30 MOS		36 MOS	
	MONTHLY PAYMENT	TOTAL INTRST	MONTHLY PAYMENT	TOTAL INTRST	MONTHLY PAYMENT	TOTAL INTRST	MONTHLY PAYMENT	TOTAL INTRST
$ 1	0.09	0	0.05	0	0.04	0	0.04	0
2	0.18	0	0.10	0	0.08	0	0.07	1
3	0.27	0	0.15	1	0.12	1	0.11	1
4	0.36	0	0.20	1	0.16	1	0.14	1
5	0.45	0	0.24	1	0.20	1	0.17	1
6	0.54	0	0.29	1	0.24	1	0.21	2
7	0.63	1	0.34	1	0.28	1	0.24	2
8	0.72	1	0.39	1	0.32	2	0.27	2
9	0.81	1	0.43	1	0.36	2	0.31	2
10	0.90	1	0.48	2	0.40	2	0.34	2
20	1.79	1	0.96	3	0.79	4	0.68	4
30	2.68	2	1.43	4	1.18	5	1.02	7
40	3.58	3	1.91	6	1.57	7	1.35	9
50	4.47	4	2.38	7	1.97	9	1.69	11
60	5.36	4	2.86	9	2.36	11	2.03	13
70	6.26	5	3.33	10	2.75	13	2.36	15
80	7.15	6	3.81	11	3.14	14	2.70	17
90	8.04	6	4.28	13	3.53	16	3.04	19
100	8.94	7	4.76	14	3.93	18	3.37	21
200	17.87	14	9.51	28	7.85	36	6.74	43
300	26.80	22	14.27	42	11.77	53	10.11	64
400	35.73	29	19.02	56	15.69	71	13.48	85
500	44.66	36	23.78	71	19.62	89	16.85	107
600	53.60	43	28.53	85	23.54	106	20.22	128
700	62.53	50	33.28	99	27.46	124	23.59	149
800	71.46	58	38.04	113	31.38	141	26.96	171
900	80.39	65	42.79	127	35.30	159	30.33	192
1,000	89.32	72	47.55	141	39.23	177	33.70	213
2,000	178.64	144	95.09	282	78.45	354	67.39	426
3,000	267.96	216	142.63	423	117.67	530	101.09	639
4,000	357.27	287	190.17	564	156.89	707	134.78	852
5,000	446.59	359	237.71	705	196.11	883	168.47	1,065
6,000	535.91	431	285.26	846	235.33	1,060	202.17	1,278
7,000	625.23	503	332.80	987	274.56	1,237	235.86	1,491
8,000	714.54	574	380.34	1,128	313.78	1,413	269.56	1,704
9,000	803.86	646	427.88	1,269	353.00	1,590	303.25	1,917
10,000	893.18	718	475.42	1,410	392.22	1,767	336.94	2,130
11,000	982.50	790	522.97	1,551	431.44	1,943	370.64	2,343
12,000	1,071.81	862	570.51	1,692	470.66	2,120	404.33	2,556
13,000	1,161.13	934	618.05	1,833	509.89	2,297	438.03	2,769
14,000	1,250.45	1,005	665.59	1,974	549.11	2,473	471.72	2,982
15,000	1,339.76	1,077	713.13	2,115	588.33	2,650	505.41	3,195
16,000	1,429.08	1,149	760.67	2,256	627.55	2,827	539.11	3,408
17,000	1,518.40	1,221	808.22	2,397	666.77	3,003	572.80	3,621
18,000	1,607.72	1,293	855.76	2,538	705.99	3,180	606.50	3,834
19,000	1,697.03	1,364	903.30	2,679	745.21	3,356	640.19	4,047
20,000	1,786.35	1,436	950.84	2,820	784.44	3,533	673.88	4,260
21,000	1,875.67	1,508	998.38	2,961	823.66	3,710	707.58	4,473
22,000	1,964.99	1,580	1,045.93	3,102	862.88	3,886	741.27	4,686
23,000	2,054.30	1,652	1,093.47	3,243	902.10	4,063	774.97	4,899
24,000	2,143.62	1,723	1,141.01	3,384	941.32	4,240	808.66	5,112
25,000	2,232.94	1,795	1,188.55	3,525	980.54	4,416	842.35	5,325
26,000	2,322.25	1,867	1,236.09	3,666	1,019.77	4,593	876.05	5,538
27,000	2,411.57	1,939	1,283.63	3,807	1,058.99	4,770	909.74	5,751
28,000	2,500.89	2,011	1,331.18	3,948	1,098.21	4,946	943.44	5,964
29,000	2,590.21	2,083	1,378.72	4,089	1,137.43	5,123	977.13	6,177
30,000	2,679.52	2,154	1,426.26	4,230	1,176.65	5,300	1,010.82	6,390
31,000	2,768.84	2,226	1,473.80	4,371	1,215.87	5,476	1,044.52	6,603
32,000	2,858.16	2,298	1,521.34	4,512	1,255.09	5,653	1,078.21	6,816
33,000	2,947.48	2,370	1,568.89	4,653	1,294.32	5,830	1,111.91	7,029
34,000	3,036.79	2,441	1,616.43	4,794	1,333.54	6,006	1,145.60	7,242
35,000	3,126.11	2,513	1,663.97	4,935	1,372.76	6,183	1,179.29	7,454
36,000	3,215.43	2,585	1,711.51	5,076	1,411.98	6,359	1,212.99	7,668
37,000	3,304.74	2,657	1,759.05	5,217	1,451.20	6,536	1,246.68	7,880
38,000	3,394.06	2,729	1,806.59	5,358	1,490.42	6,713	1,280.38	8,094
39,000	3,483.38	2,801	1,854.14	5,499	1,529.65	6,890	1,314.07	8,307
40,000	3,572.70	2,872	1,901.68	5,640	1,568.87	7,066	1,347.76	8,519
42,000	3,751.33	3,016	1,996.76	5,922	1,647.31	7,419	1,415.15	8,945
44,000	3,929.97	3,160	2,091.85	6,204	1,725.75	7,773	1,482.54	9,371
46,000	4,108.60	3,303	2,186.93	6,486	1,804.20	8,126	1,549.93	9,797
48,000	4,287.23	3,447	2,282.01	6,768	1,882.64	8,479	1,617.31	10,223
50,000	4,465.87	3,590	2,377.10	7,050	1,961.08	8,832	1,684.70	10,649

AUTO LOAN PAYMENTS 13.00%

AMOUNT OF LOAN	42 MOS MONTHLY PAYMENT	42 MOS TOTAL INTRST	48 MOS MONTHLY PAYMENT	48 MOS TOTAL INTRST	60 MOS MONTHLY PAYMENT	60 MOS TOTAL INTRST	72 MOS MONTHLY PAYMENT	72 MOS TOTAL INTRST
$ 1	0.03	0	0.03	0	0.03	1	0.03	1
2	0.06	1	0.06	1	0.05	1	0.05	2
3	0.09	1	0.09	1	0.07	1	0.07	2
4	0.12	1	0.11	1	0.10	2	0.09	3
5	0.15	1	0.14	2	0.12	2	0.11	3
6	0.18	2	0.17	2	0.14	2	0.13	3
7	0.21	2	0.19	2	0.16	3	0.15	4
8	0.24	2	0.22	3	0.19	3	0.17	4
9	0.27	2	0.25	3	0.21	4	0.19	5
10	0.30	3	0.27	3	0.23	4	0.21	5
20	0.60	5	0.54	6	0.46	8	0.41	10
30	0.90	8	0.81	9	0.69	11	0.61	14
40	1.20	10	1.08	12	0.92	15	0.81	18
50	1.49	13	1.35	15	1.14	18	1.01	23
60	1.79	15	1.61	17	1.37	22	1.21	27
70	2.09	18	1.88	20	1.60	26	1.41	32
80	2.39	20	2.15	23	1.83	30	1.61	36
90	2.68	23	2.42	26	2.05	33	1.81	40
100	2.98	25	2.69	29	2.28	37	2.01	45
200	5.96	50	5.37	58	4.56	74	4.02	89
300	8.93	75	8.05	86	6.83	110	6.03	134
400	11.91	100	10.74	116	9.11	147	8.03	178
500	14.89	125	13.42	144	11.38	183	10.04	223
600	17.86	150	16.10	173	13.66	220	12.05	268
700	20.84	175	18.78	201	15.93	256	14.06	312
800	23.81	200	21.47	231	18.21	293	16.06	356
900	26.79	225	24.15	259	20.48	329	18.07	401
1,000	29.77	250	26.83	288	22.76	366	20.08	446
2,000	59.53	500	53.66	576	45.51	731	40.15	891
3,000	89.29	750	80.49	864	68.26	1,096	60.23	1,337
4,000	119.05	1,000	107.31	1,151	91.02	1,461	80.30	1,782
5,000	148.82	1,250	134.14	1,439	113.77	1,826	100.38	2,227
6,000	178.58	1,500	160.97	1,727	136.52	2,191	120.45	2,672
7,000	208.34	1,750	187.80	2,014	159.28	2,557	140.52	3,117
8,000	238.10	2,000	214.62	2,302	182.03	2,922	160.60	3,563
9,000	267.86	2,250	241.45	2,590	204.78	3,287	180.67	4,008
10,000	297.63	2,500	268.28	2,877	227.54	3,652	200.75	4,454
11,000	327.39	2,750	295.11	3,165	250.29	4,017	220.82	4,899
12,000	357.15	3,000	321.93	3,453	273.04	4,382	240.89	5,344
13,000	386.91	3,250	348.76	3,740	295.79	4,747	260.97	5,790
14,000	416.67	3,500	375.59	4,028	318.55	5,113	281.04	6,235
15,000	446.44	3,750	402.42	4,316	341.30	5,478	301.12	6,681
16,000	476.20	4,000	429.24	4,604	364.05	5,843	321.19	7,126
17,000	505.96	4,250	456.07	4,891	386.81	6,209	341.26	7,571
18,000	535.72	4,500	482.90	5,179	409.56	6,574	361.34	8,016
19,000	565.48	4,750	509.73	5,467	432.31	6,939	381.41	8,462
20,000	595.25	5,001	536.55	5,754	455.07	7,304	401.49	8,907
21,000	625.01	5,250	563.38	6,042	477.82	7,669	421.56	9,352
22,000	654.77	5,500	590.21	6,330	500.57	8,034	441.64	9,798
23,000	684.53	5,750	617.04	6,618	523.33	8,400	461.71	10,243
24,000	714.30	6,001	643.86	6,905	546.08	8,765	481.78	10,688
25,000	744.06	6,251	670.69	7,193	568.83	9,130	501.86	11,134
26,000	773.82	6,500	697.52	7,481	591.58	9,495	521.93	11,579
27,000	803.58	6,750	724.35	7,769	614.34	9,860	542.01	12,025
28,000	833.34	7,000	751.17	8,056	637.09	10,225	562.08	12,470
29,000	863.11	7,251	778.00	8,344	659.84	10,590	582.15	12,915
30,000	892.87	7,501	804.83	8,632	682.60	10,956	602.23	13,361
31,000	922.63	7,750	831.66	8,920	705.35	11,321	622.30	13,806
32,000	952.39	8,000	858.48	9,207	728.10	11,686	642.38	14,251
33,000	982.15	8,250	885.31	9,495	750.86	12,052	662.45	14,696
34,000	1,011.92	8,501	912.14	9,783	773.61	12,417	682.52	15,141
35,000	1,041.68	8,751	938.97	10,071	796.36	12,782	702.60	15,587
36,000	1,071.44	9,000	965.79	10,358	819.12	13,147	722.67	16,032
37,000	1,101.20	9,250	992.62	10,646	841.87	13,512	742.75	16,478
38,000	1,130.96	9,500	1,019.45	10,934	864.62	13,877	762.82	16,923
39,000	1,160.73	9,751	1,046.28	11,221	887.37	14,242	782.90	17,369
40,000	1,190.49	10,001	1,073.10	11,509	910.13	14,608	802.97	17,814
42,000	1,250.01	10,500	1,126.76	12,084	955.63	15,338	843.12	18,705
44,000	1,309.54	11,001	1,180.41	12,660	1,001.14	16,068	883.27	19,595
46,000	1,369.06	11,501	1,234.07	13,235	1,046.65	16,799	923.41	20,486
48,000	1,428.59	12,001	1,287.72	13,811	1,092.15	17,529	963.56	21,376
50,000	1,488.11	12,501	1,341.38	14,386	1,137.66	18,260	1,003.71	22,267

129

13.25%   AUTO LOAN PAYMENTS

AMOUNT OF LOAN	12 MOS		24 MOS		30 MOS		36 MOS	
	MONTHLY PAYMENT	TOTAL INTRST	MONTHLY PAYMENT	TOTAL INTRST	MONTHLY PAYMENT	TOTAL INTRST	MONTHLY PAYMENT	TOTAL INTRST
$ 1	0.09	0	0.05	0	0.04	0	0.04	0
2	0.18	0	0.10	0	0.08	0	0.07	1
3	0.27	0	0.15	0	0.12	1	0.11	1
4	0.36	0	0.20	1	0.16	1	0.14	1
5	0.45	0	0.24	1	0.20	1	0.17	1
6	0.54	0	0.29	1	0.24	1	0.21	1
7	0.63	1	0.34	1	0.28	1	0.24	2
8	0.72	1	0.39	1	0.32	2	0.28	2
9	0.81	1	0.43	1	0.36	2	0.31	2
10	0.90	1	0.48	2	0.40	2	0.34	2
20	1.79	1	0.96	3	0.79	4	0.68	4
30	2.69	2	1.43	4	1.19	6	1.02	7
40	3.58	3	1.91	6	1.58	7	1.36	9
50	4.48	4	2.39	7	1.97	9	1.70	11
60	5.37	4	2.86	9	2.37	11	2.03	13
70	6.27	5	3.34	10	2.76	13	2.37	15
80	7.16	6	3.82	12	3.15	15	2.71	18
90	8.05	7	4.29	13	3.55	17	3.05	20
100	8.95	7	4.77	14	3.94	18	3.39	22
200	17.89	15	9.54	29	7.87	36	6.77	44
300	26.84	22	14.30	43	11.81	54	10.15	65
400	35.78	29	19.07	58	15.74	72	13.53	87
500	44.72	37	23.83	72	19.68	90	16.91	109
600	53.67	44	28.60	86	23.61	108	20.29	130
700	62.61	51	33.37	101	27.54	126	23.68	152
800	71.55	59	38.13	115	31.48	144	27.06	174
900	80.50	66	42.90	130	35.41	162	30.44	196
1,000	89.44	73	47.66	144	39.35	181	33.82	218
2,000	178.87	146	95.32	288	78.69	361	67.63	435
3,000	268.31	220	142.98	432	118.03	541	101.45	652
4,000	357.74	293	190.64	575	157.37	721	135.26	869
5,000	447.18	366	238.30	719	196.71	901	169.08	1,087
6,000	536.61	439	285.96	863	236.05	1,082	202.89	1,304
7,000	626.05	513	333.62	1,007	275.39	1,262	236.71	1,522
8,000	715.48	586	381.28	1,151	314.73	1,442	270.52	1,739
9,000	804.92	659	428.94	1,295	354.07	1,622	304.34	1,956
10,000	894.35	732	476.60	1,438	393.41	1,802	338.15	2,173
11,000	983.79	805	524.26	1,582	432.75	1,983	371.96	2,391
12,000	1,073.22	879	571.92	1,726	472.09	2,163	405.78	2,608
13,000	1,162.65	952	619.58	1,870	511.43	2,343	439.59	2,825
14,000	1,252.09	1,025	667.24	2,014	550.77	2,523	473.41	3,043
15,000	1,341.52	1,098	714.90	2,158	590.11	2,703	507.22	3,260
16,000	1,430.96	1,172	762.55	2,301	629.45	2,884	541.04	3,477
17,000	1,520.39	1,245	810.21	2,445	668.79	3,064	574.85	3,695
18,000	1,609.83	1,318	857.87	2,589	708.13	3,244	608.67	3,912
19,000	1,699.26	1,391	905.53	2,733	747.47	3,424	642.48	4,129
20,000	1,788.70	1,464	953.19	2,877	786.81	3,604	676.29	4,346
21,000	1,878.13	1,538	1,000.85	3,020	826.15	3,785	710.11	4,564
22,000	1,967.57	1,611	1,048.51	3,164	865.49	3,965	743.92	4,781
23,000	2,057.00	1,684	1,096.17	3,308	904.84	4,145	777.74	4,999
24,000	2,146.44	1,757	1,143.83	3,452	944.18	4,325	811.55	5,216
25,000	2,235.87	1,830	1,191.49	3,596	983.52	4,506	845.37	5,433
26,000	2,325.30	1,904	1,239.15	3,740	1,022.86	4,686	879.18	5,650
27,000	2,414.74	1,977	1,286.81	3,883	1,062.20	4,866	913.00	5,868
28,000	2,504.17	2,050	1,334.47	4,027	1,101.54	5,046	946.81	6,085
29,000	2,593.61	2,123	1,382.13	4,171	1,140.88	5,226	980.63	6,303
30,000	2,683.04	2,196	1,429.79	4,315	1,180.22	5,407	1,014.44	6,520
31,000	2,772.48	2,270	1,477.44	4,459	1,219.56	5,587	1,048.25	6,737
32,000	2,861.91	2,343	1,525.10	4,602	1,258.90	5,767	1,082.07	6,955
33,000	2,951.35	2,416	1,572.76	4,746	1,298.24	5,947	1,115.88	7,172
34,000	3,040.78	2,489	1,620.42	4,890	1,337.58	6,127	1,149.70	7,389
35,000	3,130.22	2,563	1,668.08	5,034	1,376.92	6,308	1,183.51	7,606
36,000	3,219.65	2,636	1,715.74	5,178	1,416.26	6,488	1,217.33	7,824
37,000	3,309.09	2,709	1,763.40	5,322	1,455.60	6,668	1,251.14	8,041
38,000	3,398.52	2,782	1,811.06	5,465	1,494.94	6,848	1,284.96	8,259
39,000	3,487.95	2,855	1,858.72	5,609	1,534.28	7,028	1,318.77	8,476
40,000	3,577.39	2,929	1,906.38	5,753	1,573.62	7,209	1,352.58	8,693
42,000	3,756.26	3,075	2,001.70	6,041	1,652.30	7,569	1,420.21	9,128
44,000	3,935.13	3,222	2,097.02	6,328	1,730.98	7,929	1,487.84	9,562
46,000	4,114.00	3,368	2,192.33	6,616	1,809.67	8,290	1,555.47	9,997
48,000	4,292.87	3,514	2,287.65	6,904	1,888.35	8,651	1,623.10	10,432
50,000	4,471.74	3,661	2,382.97	7,191	1,967.03	9,011	1,690.73	10,866

AUTO LOAN PAYMENTS 13.25%

AMOUNT OF LOAN	42 MOS		48 MOS		60 MOS		72 MOS	
	MONTHLY PAYMENT	TOTAL INTRST	MONTHLY PAYMENT	TOTAL INTRST	MONTHLY PAYMENT	TOTAL INTRST	MONTHLY PAYMENT	TOTAL INTRST
$ 1	0.03	0	0.03	0	0.03	1	0.03	1
2	0.06	1	0.06	1	0.05	1	0.05	2
3	0.09	1	0.09	1	0.07	1	0.07	2
4	0.12	1	0.11	1	0.10	2	0.09	3
5	0.15	1	0.14	2	0.12	2	0.11	3
6	0.18	2	0.17	2	0.14	2	0.13	3
7	0.21	2	0.19	2	0.17	3	0.15	4
8	0.24	2	0.22	3	0.19	3	0.17	4
9	0.27	2	0.25	3	0.21	4	0.19	5
10	0.30	3	0.27	3	0.23	4	0.21	5
20	0.60	5	0.54	6	0.46	8	0.41	10
30	0.90	8	0.81	9	0.69	11	0.61	14
40	1.20	10	1.08	12	0.92	15	0.81	18
50	1.50	13	1.35	15	1.15	19	1.02	23
60	1.80	16	1.62	18	1.38	23	1.22	28
70	2.10	18	1.89	21	1.61	27	1.42	32
80	2.40	21	2.16	24	1.84	30	1.62	37
90	2.69	23	2.43	27	2.06	34	1.82	41
100	2.99	26	2.70	30	2.29	37	2.03	46
200	5.98	51	5.40	59	4.58	75	4.05	92
300	8.97	77	8.09	88	6.87	112	6.07	137
400	11.96	102	10.79	118	9.16	150	8.09	182
500	14.95	128	13.48	147	11.45	187	10.11	228
600	17.94	153	16.18	177	13.73	224	12.13	273
700	20.92	179	18.87	206	16.02	261	14.15	319
800	23.91	204	21.57	235	18.31	299	16.17	364
900	26.90	230	24.26	264	20.60	336	18.19	410
1,000	29.89	255	26.96	294	22.89	373	20.21	455
2,000	59.77	510	53.91	588	45.77	746	40.42	910
3,000	89.66	766	80.86	881	68.65	1,119	60.62	1,365
4,000	119.54	1,021	107.81	1,175	91.53	1,492	80.83	1,820
5,000	149.43	1,276	134.76	1,468	114.41	1,865	101.04	2,275
6,000	179.31	1,531	161.72	1,763	137.29	2,237	121.24	2,729
7,000	209.20	1,786	188.67	2,056	160.17	2,610	141.45	3,184
8,000	239.08	2,041	215.62	2,350	183.06	2,984	161.66	3,640
9,000	268.96	2,296	242.57	2,643	205.94	3,356	181.86	4,094
10,000	298.85	2,552	269.52	2,937	228.82	3,729	202.07	4,549
11,000	328.73	2,807	296.47	3,231	251.70	4,102	222.27	5,003
12,000	358.62	3,062	323.43	3,525	274.58	4,475	242.48	5,459
13,000	388.50	3,317	350.38	3,818	297.46	4,848	262.69	5,914
14,000	418.39	3,572	377.33	4,112	320.34	5,220	282.89	6,368
15,000	448.27	3,827	404.28	4,405	343.22	5,593	303.10	6,823
16,000	478.16	4,083	431.23	4,699	366.11	5,967	323.31	7,278
17,000	508.04	4,338	458.18	4,993	388.99	6,339	343.51	7,733
18,000	537.92	4,593	485.14	5,287	411.87	6,712	363.72	8,188
19,000	567.81	4,848	512.09	5,580	434.75	7,085	383.92	8,642
20,000	597.69	5,103	539.04	5,874	457.63	7,458	404.13	9,097
21,000	627.58	5,358	565.99	6,168	480.51	7,831	424.34	9,552
22,000	657.46	5,613	592.94	6,461	503.39	8,203	444.54	10,007
23,000	687.35	5,869	619.90	6,755	526.27	8,576	464.75	10,462
24,000	717.23	6,124	646.85	7,049	549.16	8,950	484.96	10,917
25,000	747.12	6,379	673.80	7,342	572.04	9,322	505.16	11,372
26,000	777.00	6,634	700.75	7,636	594.92	9,695	525.37	11,827
27,000	806.88	6,889	727.70	7,930	617.80	10,068	545.57	12,281
28,000	836.77	7,144	754.65	8,223	640.68	10,441	565.78	12,736
29,000	866.65	7,399	781.61	8,517	663.56	10,814	585.99	13,191
30,000	896.54	7,655	808.56	8,811	686.44	11,186	606.19	13,646
31,000	926.42	7,910	835.51	9,104	709.32	11,559	626.40	14,101
32,000	956.31	8,165	862.46	9,398	732.21	11,933	646.61	14,556
33,000	986.19	8,420	889.41	9,692	755.09	12,305	666.81	15,010
34,000	1,016.08	8,675	916.36	9,985	777.97	12,678	687.02	15,465
35,000	1,045.96	8,930	943.32	10,279	800.85	13,051	707.23	15,921
36,000	1,075.84	9,185	970.27	10,573	823.73	13,424	727.43	16,375
37,000	1,105.73	9,441	997.22	10,867	846.61	13,797	747.64	16,830
38,000	1,135.61	9,696	1,024.17	11,160	869.49	14,169	767.84	17,284
39,000	1,165.50	9,951	1,051.12	11,454	892.37	14,542	788.05	17,740
40,000	1,195.38	10,206	1,078.07	11,747	915.26	14,916	808.26	18,195
42,000	1,255.15	10,716	1,131.98	12,335	961.02	15,661	848.67	19,104
44,000	1,314.92	11,227	1,185.88	12,922	1,006.78	16,407	889.08	20,014
46,000	1,374.69	11,737	1,239.79	13,510	1,052.54	17,152	929.49	20,923
48,000	1,434.46	12,247	1,293.69	14,097	1,098.31	17,899	969.91	21,834
50,000	1,494.23	12,758	1,347.59	14,684	1,144.07	18,644	1,010.32	22,743

13.50%   **AUTO LOAN PAYMENTS**

AMOUNT OF LOAN	12 MOS		24 MOS		30 MOS		36 MOS	
	MONTHLY PAYMENT	TOTAL INTRST	MONTHLY PAYMENT	TOTAL INTRST	MONTHLY PAYMENT	TOTAL INTRST	MONTHLY PAYMENT	TOTAL INTRST
$ 1	0.09	0	0.05	0	0.04	0	0.04	0
2	0.18	0	0.10	0	0.08	0	0.07	1
3	0.27	0	0.15	1	0.12	1	0.11	1
4	0.36	0	0.20	1	0.16	1	0.14	1
5	0.45	0	0.24	1	0.20	1	0.17	1
6	0.54	0	0.29	1	0.24	1	0.21	2
7	0.63	1	0.34	1	0.28	1	0.24	2
8	0.72	1	0.39	1	0.32	2	0.28	2
9	0.81	1	0.43	1	0.36	2	0.31	2
10	0.90	1	0.48	2	0.40	2	0.34	2
20	1.80	2	0.96	3	0.79	4	0.68	4
30	2.69	2	1.44	5	1.19	6	1.02	7
40	3.59	3	1.92	6	1.58	7	1.36	9
50	4.48	4	2.39	7	1.98	9	1.70	11
60	5.38	4	2.87	9	2.37	11	2.04	13
70	6.27	5	3.35	10	2.77	13	2.38	16
80	7.17	6	3.83	12	3.16	15	2.72	18
90	8.06	7	4.30	13	3.56	17	3.06	20
100	8.96	8	4.78	15	3.95	19	3.40	22
200	17.92	15	9.56	29	7.90	37	6.79	44
300	26.87	22	14.34	44	11.84	55	10.19	67
400	35.83	30	19.12	59	15.79	74	13.58	89
500	44.78	37	23.89	73	19.73	92	16.97	111
600	53.74	45	28.67	88	23.68	110	20.37	133
700	62.69	52	33.45	103	27.63	129	23.76	155
800	71.65	60	38.23	118	31.57	147	27.15	177
900	80.60	67	43.00	132	35.52	166	30.55	200
1,000	89.56	75	47.78	147	39.46	184	33.94	222
2,000	179.11	149	95.56	293	78.92	368	67.88	444
3,000	268.66	224	143.34	440	118.38	551	101.81	665
4,000	358.21	299	191.11	587	157.84	735	135.75	887
5,000	447.77	373	238.89	733	197.30	919	169.68	1,108
6,000	537.32	448	286.67	880	236.76	1,103	203.62	1,330
7,000	626.87	522	334.44	1,027	276.22	1,287	237.55	1,552
8,000	716.42	597	382.22	1,173	315.68	1,470	271.49	1,774
9,000	805.97	672	430.00	1,320	355.14	1,654	305.42	1,995
10,000	895.53	746	477.78	1,467	394.60	1,838	339.36	2,217
11,000	985.08	821	525.55	1,613	434.06	2,022	373.29	2,438
12,000	1,074.63	896	573.33	1,760	473.52	2,206	407.23	2,660
13,000	1,164.18	970	621.11	1,907	512.98	2,389	441.16	2,882
14,000	1,253.73	1,045	668.88	2,053	552.44	2,573	475.10	3,104
15,000	1,343.29	1,119	716.66	2,200	591.90	2,757	509.03	3,325
16,000	1,432.84	1,194	764.44	2,347	631.36	2,941	542.97	3,547
17,000	1,522.39	1,269	812.21	2,493	670.82	3,125	576.90	3,768
18,000	1,611.94	1,343	859.99	2,640	710.28	3,308	610.84	3,990
19,000	1,701.49	1,418	907.77	2,786	749.74	3,492	644.78	4,212
20,000	1,791.05	1,493	955.55	2,933	789.20	3,676	678.71	4,434
21,000	1,880.60	1,567	1,003.32	3,080	828.66	3,860	712.65	4,655
22,000	1,970.15	1,642	1,051.10	3,226	868.11	4,043	746.58	4,877
23,000	2,059.70	1,716	1,098.88	3,373	907.57	4,227	780.52	5,099
24,000	2,149.25	1,791	1,146.65	3,520	947.03	4,411	814.45	5,320
25,000	2,238.81	1,866	1,194.43	3,666	986.49	4,595	848.39	5,542
26,000	2,328.36	1,940	1,242.21	3,813	1,025.95	4,779	882.32	5,764
27,000	2,417.91	2,015	1,289.98	3,960	1,065.41	4,962	916.26	5,985
28,000	2,507.46	2,090	1,337.76	4,106	1,104.87	5,146	950.19	6,207
29,000	2,597.01	2,164	1,385.54	4,253	1,144.33	5,330	984.13	6,429
30,000	2,686.57	2,239	1,433.32	4,400	1,183.79	5,514	1,018.06	6,650
31,000	2,776.12	2,313	1,481.09	4,546	1,223.25	5,698	1,052.00	6,872
32,000	2,865.67	2,388	1,528.87	4,693	1,262.71	5,881	1,085.93	7,093
33,000	2,955.22	2,463	1,576.65	4,840	1,302.17	6,065	1,119.87	7,315
34,000	3,044.77	2,537	1,624.42	4,986	1,341.63	6,249	1,153.80	7,537
35,000	3,134.33	2,612	1,672.20	5,133	1,381.09	6,433	1,187.74	7,759
36,000	3,223.88	2,687	1,719.98	5,280	1,420.55	6,617	1,221.68	7,980
37,000	3,313.43	2,761	1,767.75	5,426	1,460.01	6,800	1,255.61	8,202
38,000	3,402.98	2,836	1,815.53	5,573	1,499.47	6,984	1,289.55	8,424
39,000	3,492.53	2,910	1,863.31	5,719	1,538.93	7,168	1,323.48	8,645
40,000	3,582.09	2,985	1,911.09	5,866	1,578.39	7,352	1,357.42	8,867
42,000	3,761.19	3,134	2,006.64	6,159	1,657.31	7,719	1,425.29	9,310
44,000	3,940.29	3,283	2,102.19	6,453	1,736.22	8,087	1,493.16	9,754
46,000	4,119.40	3,433	2,197.75	6,746	1,815.14	8,454	1,561.03	10,197
48,000	4,298.50	3,582	2,293.30	7,039	1,894.06	8,822	1,628.90	10,640
50,000	4,477.61	3,731	2,388.86	7,333	1,972.98	9,189	1,696.77	11,084

AMOUNT OF LOAN	42 MOS		48 MOS		60 MOS		72 MOS	
	MONTHLY PAYMENT	TOTAL INTRST	MONTHLY PAYMENT	TOTAL INTRST	MONTHLY PAYMENT	TOTAL INTRST	MONTHLY PAYMENT	TOTAL INTRST
$ 1	0.04	1	0.03	0	0.03	1	0.03	1
2	0.07	1	0.06	1	0.05	1	0.05	2
3	0.10	1	0.09	1	0.07	1	0.07	2
4	0.13	1	0.11	1	0.10	2	0.09	3
5	0.16	2	0.14	2	0.12	2	0.11	3
6	0.19	2	0.17	2	0.14	2	0.13	3
7	0.22	2	0.19	2	0.17	3	0.15	4
8	0.25	3	0.22	3	0.19	3	0.17	4
9	0.28	3	0.25	3	0.21	4	0.19	5
10	0.31	3	0.28	3	0.24	4	0.21	5
20	0.61	6	0.55	6	0.47	8	0.41	10
30	0.91	8	0.82	9	0.70	12	0.62	15
40	1.21	11	1.09	12	0.93	16	0.82	19
50	1.51	13	1.36	15	1.16	20	1.02	23
60	1.81	16	1.63	18	1.39	23	1.23	29
70	2.11	19	1.90	21	1.62	27	1.43	33
80	2.41	21	2.17	24	1.85	31	1.63	37
90	2.71	24	2.44	27	2.08	35	1.84	42
100	3.01	26	2.71	30	2.31	39	2.04	47
200	6.01	52	5.42	60	4.61	77	4.07	93
300	9.01	78	8.13	90	6.91	115	6.11	140
400	12.01	104	10.84	120	9.21	153	8.14	186
500	15.01	130	13.54	150	11.51	191	10.17	232
600	18.01	156	16.25	180	13.81	229	12.21	279
700	21.01	182	18.96	210	16.11	267	14.24	325
800	24.01	208	21.67	240	18.41	305	16.28	372
900	27.01	234	24.37	270	20.71	343	18.31	418
1,000	30.01	260	27.08	300	23.01	381	20.34	464
2,000	60.02	521	54.16	600	46.02	761	40.68	929
3,000	90.03	781	81.23	899	69.03	1,142	61.02	1,393
4,000	120.03	1,041	108.31	1,199	92.04	1,522	81.36	1,858
5,000	150.04	1,302	135.39	1,499	115.05	1,903	101.70	2,322
6,000	180.05	1,562	162.46	1,798	138.06	2,284	122.04	2,787
7,000	210.05	1,822	189.54	2,098	161.07	2,664	142.38	3,251
8,000	240.06	2,083	216.62	2,398	184.08	3,045	162.72	3,716
9,000	270.07	2,343	243.69	2,697	207.09	3,425	183.06	4,180
10,000	300.08	2,603	270.77	2,997	230.10	3,806	203.39	4,644
11,000	330.08	2,863	297.84	3,296	253.11	4,187	223.73	5,109
12,000	360.09	3,124	324.92	3,596	276.12	4,567	244.07	5,573
13,000	390.10	3,384	352.00	3,896	299.13	4,948	264.41	6,038
14,000	420.10	3,644	379.07	4,195	322.14	5,328	284.75	6,502
15,000	450.11	3,905	406.15	4,495	345.15	5,709	305.09	6,966
16,000	480.12	4,165	433.23	4,795	368.16	6,090	325.43	7,431
17,000	510.13	4,425	460.30	5,094	391.17	6,470	345.77	7,895
18,000	540.13	4,685	487.38	5,394	414.18	6,851	366.11	8,360
19,000	570.14	4,946	514.46	5,694	437.19	7,231	386.45	8,824
20,000	600.15	5,206	541.53	5,993	460.20	7,612	406.78	9,288
21,000	630.15	5,466	568.61	6,293	483.21	7,993	427.12	9,753
22,000	660.16	5,727	595.68	6,593	506.22	8,373	447.46	10,217
23,000	690.17	5,987	622.76	6,892	529.23	8,754	467.80	10,682
24,000	720.18	6,248	649.84	7,192	552.24	9,134	488.14	11,146
25,000	750.18	6,508	676.91	7,492	575.25	9,515	508.48	11,611
26,000	780.19	6,768	703.99	7,792	598.26	9,896	528.82	12,075
27,000	810.20	7,028	731.07	8,091	621.27	10,276	549.16	12,540
28,000	840.20	7,288	758.14	8,391	644.28	10,657	569.50	13,004
29,000	870.21	7,549	785.22	8,691	667.29	11,037	589.83	13,468
30,000	900.22	7,809	812.29	8,990	690.30	11,418	610.17	13,932
31,000	930.22	8,069	839.37	9,290	713.31	11,799	630.51	14,397
32,000	960.23	8,330	866.45	9,590	736.32	12,179	650.85	14,861
33,000	990.24	8,590	893.52	9,889	759.33	12,560	671.19	15,326
34,000	1,020.25	8,851	920.60	10,189	782.34	12,940	691.53	15,790
35,000	1,050.25	9,111	947.68	10,489	805.35	13,321	711.87	16,255
36,000	1,080.26	9,371	974.75	10,788	828.36	13,702	732.21	16,719
37,000	1,110.27	9,631	1,001.83	11,088	851.37	14,082	752.55	17,184
38,000	1,140.27	9,891	1,028.91	11,388	874.38	14,463	772.89	17,648
39,000	1,170.28	10,152	1,055.98	11,687	897.39	14,843	793.22	18,112
40,000	1,200.29	10,412	1,083.06	11,987	920.40	15,224	813.56	18,576
42,000	1,260.30	10,933	1,137.21	12,586	966.42	15,985	854.24	19,505
44,000	1,320.32	11,453	1,191.36	13,185	1,012.44	16,746	894.92	20,434
46,000	1,380.33	11,974	1,245.52	13,785	1,058.46	17,508	935.60	21,363
48,000	1,440.35	12,495	1,299.67	14,384	1,104.48	18,269	976.28	22,292
50,000	1,500.36	13,015	1,353.82	14,983	1,150.50	19,030	1,016.95	23,220

AUTO LOAN PAYMENTS

AMOUNT OF LOAN	12 MOS		24 MOS		30 MOS		36 MOS	
	MONTHLY PAYMENT	TOTAL INTRST	MONTHLY PAYMENT	TOTAL INTRST	MONTHLY PAYMENT	TOTAL INTRST	MONTHLY PAYMENT	TOTAL INTRST
$ 1	0.09	0	0.05	0	0.04	0	0.04	0
2	0.18	0	0.10	0	0.08	0	0.07	1
3	0.27	0	0.15	1	0.12	1	0.11	1
4	0.36	0	0.20	1	0.16	1	0.14	1
5	0.45	0	0.24	1	0.20	1	0.18	1
6	0.54	0	0.29	1	0.24	1	0.21	2
7	0.63	1	0.34	1	0.28	1	0.24	2
8	0.72	1	0.39	1	0.32	2	0.28	2
9	0.81	1	0.44	2	0.36	2	0.31	2
10	0.90	1	0.48	2	0.40	2	0.35	3
20	1.80	2	0.96	3	0.80	4	0.69	5
30	2.70	2	1.44	5	1.19	6	1.03	7
40	3.59	3	1.92	6	1.59	8	1.37	9
50	4.49	4	2.40	8	1.98	9	1.71	12
60	5.39	4	2.88	9	2.38	11	2.05	14
70	6.28	5	3.36	11	2.78	13	2.39	16
80	7.18	6	3.84	12	3.17	15	2.73	18
90	8.08	7	4.32	14	3.57	17	3.07	21
100	8.97	8	4.79	15	3.96	19	3.41	23
200	17.94	15	9.58	30	7.92	38	6.82	46
300	26.91	23	14.37	45	11.88	56	10.22	68
400	35.87	30	19.16	60	15.84	75	13.63	91
500	44.84	38	23.95	75	19.79	94	17.03	113
600	53.81	46	28.74	90	23.75	113	20.44	136
700	62.77	53	33.53	105	27.71	131	23.84	158
800	71.74	61	38.32	120	31.67	150	27.25	181
900	80.71	69	43.11	135	35.63	169	30.66	204
1,000	89.67	76	47.90	150	39.58	187	34.06	226
2,000	179.34	152	95.79	299	79.16	375	68.12	452
3,000	269.01	228	143.69	449	118.74	562	102.17	678
4,000	358.68	304	191.58	598	158.32	750	136.23	904
5,000	448.35	380	239.48	748	197.90	937	170.29	1,130
6,000	538.02	456	287.37	897	237.48	1,124	204.34	1,356
7,000	627.69	532	335.27	1,046	277.06	1,312	238.40	1,582
8,000	717.36	608	383.16	1,196	316.64	1,499	272.46	1,809
9,000	807.03	684	431.06	1,345	356.21	1,686	306.51	2,034
10,000	896.70	760	478.95	1,495	395.79	1,874	340.57	2,261
11,000	986.37	836	526.85	1,644	435.37	2,061	374.62	2,486
12,000	1,076.04	912	574.74	1,794	474.95	2,249	408.68	2,712
13,000	1,165.71	989	622.64	1,943	514.53	2,436	442.74	2,939
14,000	1,255.38	1,065	670.53	2,093	554.11	2,623	476.79	3,164
15,000	1,345.05	1,141	718.43	2,242	593.69	2,811	510.85	3,391
16,000	1,434.72	1,217	766.32	2,392	633.27	2,998	544.91	3,617
17,000	1,524.39	1,293	814.22	2,541	672.85	3,186	578.96	3,843
18,000	1,614.06	1,369	862.11	2,691	712.42	3,373	613.02	4,069
19,000	1,703.73	1,445	910.01	2,840	752.00	3,560	647.08	4,295
20,000	1,793.40	1,521	957.90	2,990	791.58	3,747	681.13	4,521
21,000	1,883.07	1,597	1,005.80	3,139	831.16	3,935	715.19	4,747
22,000	1,972.73	1,673	1,053.69	3,289	870.74	4,122	749.24	4,973
23,000	2,062.40	1,749	1,101.59	3,438	910.32	4,310	783.30	5,199
24,000	2,152.07	1,825	1,149.48	3,588	949.90	4,497	817.36	5,425
25,000	2,241.74	1,901	1,197.38	3,737	989.48	4,684	851.41	5,651
26,000	2,331.41	1,977	1,245.27	3,886	1,029.05	4,872	885.47	5,877
27,000	2,421.08	2,053	1,293.17	4,036	1,068.63	5,059	919.53	6,103
28,000	2,510.75	2,129	1,341.06	4,185	1,108.21	5,246	953.58	6,329
29,000	2,600.42	2,205	1,388.96	4,335	1,147.79	5,434	987.64	6,555
30,000	2,690.09	2,281	1,436.85	4,484	1,187.37	5,621	1,021.69	6,781
31,000	2,779.76	2,357	1,484.75	4,634	1,226.95	5,809	1,055.75	7,007
32,000	2,869.43	2,433	1,532.64	4,783	1,266.53	5,996	1,089.81	7,233
33,000	2,959.10	2,509	1,580.54	4,933	1,306.11	6,183	1,123.86	7,459
34,000	3,048.77	2,585	1,628.43	5,082	1,345.69	6,371	1,157.92	7,685
35,000	3,138.44	2,661	1,676.33	5,232	1,385.26	6,558	1,191.98	7,911
36,000	3,228.11	2,737	1,724.22	5,381	1,424.84	6,745	1,226.03	8,137
37,000	3,317.78	2,813	1,772.11	5,531	1,464.42	6,933	1,260.09	8,363
38,000	3,407.45	2,889	1,820.01	5,680	1,504.00	7,120	1,294.15	8,589
39,000	3,497.12	2,965	1,867.90	5,830	1,543.58	7,307	1,328.20	8,815
40,000	3,586.79	3,041	1,915.80	5,979	1,583.16	7,495	1,362.26	9,041
42,000	3,766.13	3,194	2,011.59	6,278	1,662.32	7,870	1,430.37	9,493
44,000	3,945.46	3,346	2,107.38	6,577	1,741.47	8,244	1,498.48	9,945
46,000	4,124.80	3,498	2,203.17	6,876	1,820.63	8,619	1,566.60	10,398
48,000	4,304.14	3,650	2,298.96	7,175	1,899.79	8,994	1,634.71	10,850
50,000	4,483.48	3,802	2,394.75	7,474	1,978.95	9,369	1,702.82	11,302

AMOUNT OF LOAN	42 MOS		48 MOS		60 MOS		72 MOS	
	MONTHLY PAYMENT	TOTAL INTRST	MONTHLY PAYMENT	TOTAL INTRST	MONTHLY PAYMENT	TOTAL INTRST	MONTHLY PAYMENT	TOTAL INTRST
$ 1	0.04	1	0.03	0	0.03	1	0.03	1
2	0.07	1	0.06	1	0.05	1	0.05	2
3	0.10	1	0.09	1	0.07	1	0.07	2
4	0.13	1	0.11	1	0.10	2	0.09	2
5	0.16	2	0.14	2	0.12	2	0.11	3
6	0.19	2	0.17	2	0.14	2	0.13	3
7	0.22	2	0.20	3	0.17	3	0.15	4
8	0.25	3	0.22	3	0.19	3	0.17	4
9	0.28	3	0.25	3	0.21	4	0.19	5
10	0.31	3	0.28	3	0.24	4	0.21	5
20	0.61	6	0.55	6	0.47	8	0.41	10
30	0.91	8	0.82	9	0.70	12	0.62	15
40	1.21	11	1.09	12	0.93	16	0.82	19
50	1.51	13	1.37	16	1.16	20	1.03	24
60	1.81	16	1.64	19	1.39	23	1.23	29
70	2.11	19	1.91	22	1.62	27	1.44	34
80	2.42	22	2.18	25	1.86	32	1.64	38
90	2.72	24	2.45	28	2.09	35	1.85	43
100	3.02	27	2.73	31	2.32	39	2.05	48
200	6.03	53	5.45	62	4.63	78	4.10	95
300	9.04	80	8.17	92	6.95	117	6.15	143
400	12.06	107	10.89	123	9.26	156	8.19	190
500	15.07	133	13.61	153	11.57	194	10.24	237
600	18.08	159	16.33	184	13.89	233	12.29	285
700	21.10	186	19.05	214	16.20	272	14.34	332
800	24.11	213	21.77	245	18.52	311	16.38	379
900	27.12	239	24.49	276	20.83	350	18.43	427
1,000	30.14	266	27.21	306	23.14	388	20.48	475
2,000	60.27	531	54.41	612	46.28	777	40.95	948
3,000	90.40	797	81.61	917	69.42	1,165	61.42	1,422
4,000	120.53	1,062	108.81	1,223	92.56	1,554	81.89	1,896
5,000	150.66	1,328	136.01	1,528	115.70	1,942	102.37	2,371
6,000	180.79	1,593	163.21	1,834	138.84	2,330	122.84	2,844
7,000	210.92	1,859	190.41	2,140	161.98	2,719	143.31	3,318
8,000	241.05	2,124	217.61	2,445	185.12	3,107	163.78	3,792
9,000	271.18	2,390	244.82	2,751	208.25	3,495	184.25	4,266
10,000	301.31	2,655	272.02	3,057	231.39	3,883	204.73	4,741
11,000	331.44	2,920	299.22	3,363	254.53	4,272	225.20	5,214
12,000	361.57	3,186	326.42	3,668	277.67	4,660	245.67	5,688
13,000	391.70	3,451	353.62	3,974	300.81	5,049	266.14	6,162
14,000	421.83	3,717	380.82	4,279	323.95	5,437	286.61	6,636
15,000	451.96	3,982	408.02	4,585	347.09	5,825	307.09	7,110
16,000	482.09	4,248	435.22	4,891	370.23	6,214	327.56	7,584
17,000	512.22	4,513	462.43	5,197	393.37	6,602	348.03	8,058
18,000	542.35	4,779	489.63	5,502	416.50	6,990	368.50	8,532
19,000	572.48	5,044	516.83	5,808	439.64	7,378	388.98	9,007
20,000	602.61	5,310	544.03	6,113	462.78	7,767	409.45	9,480
21,000	632.74	5,575	571.23	6,419	485.92	8,155	429.92	9,954
22,000	662.87	5,841	598.43	6,725	509.06	8,544	450.39	10,428
23,000	693.00	6,106	625.63	7,030	532.20	8,932	470.86	10,902
24,000	723.13	6,371	652.83	7,336	555.34	9,320	491.34	11,376
25,000	753.26	6,637	680.04	7,642	578.48	9,709	511.81	11,850
26,000	783.39	6,902	707.24	7,948	601.61	10,097	532.28	12,324
27,000	813.52	7,168	734.44	8,253	624.75	10,485	552.75	12,798
28,000	843.65	7,433	761.64	8,559	647.89	10,873	573.22	13,272
29,000	873.78	7,699	788.84	8,864	671.03	11,262	593.70	13,746
30,000	903.91	7,964	816.04	9,170	694.17	11,650	614.17	14,220
31,000	934.04	8,230	843.24	9,476	717.31	12,039	634.64	14,694
32,000	964.17	8,495	870.44	9,781	740.45	12,427	655.11	15,168
33,000	994.30	8,761	897.65	10,087	763.59	12,815	675.58	15,642
34,000	1,024.43	9,026	924.85	10,393	786.73	13,204	696.06	16,116
35,000	1,054.56	9,292	952.05	10,698	809.86	13,592	716.53	16,590
36,000	1,084.69	9,557	979.25	11,004	833.00	13,980	737.00	17,064
37,000	1,114.82	9,822	1,006.45	11,310	856.14	14,368	757.47	17,538
38,000	1,144.95	10,088	1,033.65	11,615	879.28	14,757	777.95	18,012
39,000	1,175.08	10,353	1,060.85	11,921	902.42	15,145	798.42	18,486
40,000	1,205.21	10,619	1,088.05	12,226	925.56	15,534	818.89	18,960
42,000	1,265.47	11,150	1,142.46	12,838	971.84	16,310	859.83	19,908
44,000	1,325.73	11,681	1,196.86	13,449	1,018.11	17,087	900.78	20,856
46,000	1,385.99	12,212	1,251.26	14,060	1,064.39	17,863	941.72	21,804
48,000	1,446.25	12,743	1,305.66	14,672	1,110.67	18,640	982.67	22,752
50,000	1,506.51	13,273	1,360.07	15,283	1,156.95	19,417	1,023.61	23,700

14.00% AUTO LOAN PAYMENTS

AMOUNT OF LOAN	12 MOS		24 MOS		30 MOS		36 MOS	
	MONTHLY PAYMENT	TOTAL INTRST	MONTHLY PAYMENT	TOTAL INTRST	MONTHLY PAYMENT	TOTAL INTRST	MONTHLY PAYMENT	TOTAL INTRST
$ 1	0.09	0	0.05	0	0.04	0	0.04	0
2	0.18	0	0.10	0	0.08	0	0.07	1
3	0.27	0	0.15	1	0.12	1	0.11	1
4	0.36	0	0.20	1	0.16	1	0.14	1
5	0.45	0	0.25	1	0.20	1	0.18	1
6	0.54	0	0.29	1	0.24	1	0.21	1
7	0.63	1	0.34	1	0.28	1	0.24	1
8	0.72	1	0.39	1	0.32	2	0.28	1
9	0.81	1	0.44	2	0.36	2	0.31	2
10	0.90	1	0.49	2	0.40	2	0.35	2
20	1.80	2	0.97	3	0.80	4	0.69	5
30	2.70	2	1.45	5	1.20	6	1.03	7
40	3.60	3	1.93	6	1.59	8	1.37	9
50	4.49	4	2.41	8	1.99	10	1.71	12
60	5.39	5	2.89	9	2.39	12	2.06	14
70	6.29	5	3.37	11	2.78	13	2.40	16
80	7.19	6	3.85	12	3.18	15	2.74	19
90	8.09	7	4.33	14	3.58	17	3.08	21
100	8.98	8	4.81	15	3.97	19	3.42	23
200	17.96	16	9.61	31	7.94	38	6.84	46
300	26.94	23	14.41	46	11.91	57	10.26	69
400	35.92	31	19.21	61	15.88	76	13.68	92
500	44.90	39	24.01	76	19.85	96	17.09	115
600	53.88	47	28.81	91	23.82	115	20.51	138
700	62.86	54	33.61	107	27.79	134	23.93	161
800	71.83	62	38.42	122	31.76	153	27.35	185
900	80.81	70	43.22	137	35.73	172	30.76	207
1,000	89.79	77	48.02	152	39.70	191	34.18	230
2,000	179.58	155	96.03	305	79.40	382	68.36	460
3,000	269.37	232	144.04	457	119.10	573	102.54	691
4,000	359.15	310	192.06	609	158.80	764	136.72	922
5,000	448.94	387	240.07	762	198.50	955	170.89	1,152
6,000	538.73	465	288.08	914	238.20	1,146	205.07	1,383
7,000	628.51	542	336.10	1,066	277.89	1,337	239.25	1,613
8,000	718.30	620	384.11	1,219	317.59	1,528	273.43	1,843
9,000	808.09	697	432.12	1,371	357.29	1,719	307.60	2,074
10,000	897.88	775	480.13	1,523	396.99	1,910	341.78	2,304
11,000	987.66	852	528.15	1,676	436.69	2,101	375.96	2,535
12,000	1,077.45	929	576.16	1,828	476.39	2,292	410.14	2,765
13,000	1,167.24	1,007	624.17	1,980	516.08	2,482	444.31	2,995
14,000	1,257.02	1,084	672.19	2,133	555.78	2,673	478.49	3,226
15,000	1,346.81	1,162	720.20	2,285	595.48	2,864	512.67	3,456
16,000	1,436.60	1,239	768.21	2,437	635.18	3,055	546.85	3,687
17,000	1,526.39	1,317	816.22	2,589	674.88	3,246	581.02	3,917
18,000	1,616.17	1,394	864.24	2,742	714.58	3,437	615.20	4,147
19,000	1,705.96	1,472	912.25	2,894	754.27	3,628	649.38	4,378
20,000	1,795.75	1,549	960.26	3,046	793.97	3,819	683.56	4,608
21,000	1,885.53	1,626	1,008.28	3,199	833.67	4,010	717.74	4,839
22,000	1,975.32	1,704	1,056.29	3,351	873.37	4,201	751.91	5,069
23,000	2,065.11	1,781	1,104.30	3,503	913.07	4,392	786.09	5,299
24,000	2,154.90	1,859	1,152.31	3,655	952.77	4,583	820.27	5,530
25,000	2,244.68	1,936	1,200.33	3,808	992.46	4,774	854.45	5,760
26,000	2,334.47	2,014	1,248.34	3,960	1,032.16	4,965	888.62	5,990
27,000	2,424.26	2,091	1,296.35	4,112	1,071.86	5,156	922.80	6,221
28,000	2,514.04	2,168	1,344.37	4,265	1,111.56	5,347	956.98	6,451
29,000	2,603.83	2,246	1,392.38	4,417	1,151.26	5,538	991.16	6,682
30,000	2,693.62	2,323	1,440.39	4,569	1,190.96	5,729	1,025.33	6,912
31,000	2,783.41	2,401	1,488.40	4,722	1,230.65	5,920	1,059.51	7,142
32,000	2,873.19	2,478	1,536.42	4,874	1,270.35	6,111	1,093.69	7,373
33,000	2,962.98	2,556	1,584.43	5,026	1,310.05	6,302	1,127.87	7,603
34,000	3,052.77	2,633	1,632.44	5,179	1,349.75	6,493	1,162.04	7,833
35,000	3,142.55	2,711	1,680.46	5,331	1,389.45	6,684	1,196.22	8,064
36,000	3,232.34	2,788	1,728.47	5,483	1,429.15	6,875	1,230.40	8,294
37,000	3,322.13	2,866	1,776.48	5,636	1,468.84	7,065	1,264.58	8,524
38,000	3,411.92	2,943	1,824.49	5,788	1,508.54	7,256	1,298.75	8,755
39,000	3,501.70	3,020	1,872.51	5,940	1,548.24	7,447	1,332.93	8,985
40,000	3,591.49	3,098	1,920.52	6,092	1,587.94	7,638	1,367.11	9,216
42,000	3,771.06	3,253	2,016.55	6,397	1,667.34	8,020	1,435.47	9,677
44,000	3,950.64	3,408	2,112.57	6,702	1,746.73	8,402	1,503.82	10,138
46,000	4,130.21	3,563	2,208.60	7,006	1,826.13	8,784	1,572.18	10,599
48,000	4,309.79	3,717	2,304.62	7,311	1,905.53	9,166	1,640.53	11,059
50,000	4,489.36	3,872	2,400.65	7,616	1,984.92	9,548	1,708.89	11,520

136

AUTO LOAN PAYMENTS 14.00%

AMOUNT OF LOAN	42 MOS		48 MOS		60 MOS		72 MOS	
	MONTHLY PAYMENT	TOTAL INTRST	MONTHLY PAYMENT	TOTAL INTRST	MONTHLY PAYMENT	TOTAL INTRST	MONTHLY PAYMENT	TOTAL INTRST
$ 1	0.04	1	0.03	0	0.03	1	0.03	1
2	0.07	1	0.06	1	0.05	1	0.05	2
3	0.10	1	0.09	1	0.07	1	0.07	2
4	0.13	1	0.11	1	0.10	2	0.09	2
5	0.16	2	0.14	2	0.12	2	0.11	3
6	0.19	2	0.17	2	0.14	2	0.13	3
7	0.22	2	0.20	3	0.17	3	0.15	4
8	0.25	3	0.22	3	0.19	3	0.17	4
9	0.28	3	0.25	3	0.21	4	0.19	5
10	0.31	3	0.28	3	0.24	4	0.21	5
20	0.61	6	0.55	6	0.47	8	0.42	10
30	0.91	8	0.82	9	0.70	12	0.62	15
40	1.22	11	1.10	13	0.94	16	0.83	20
50	1.52	14	1.37	16	1.17	20	1.04	25
60	1.82	16	1.64	19	1.40	24	1.24	29
70	2.12	19	1.92	22	1.63	28	1.45	34
80	2.43	22	2.19	25	1.87	32	1.65	39
90	2.73	25	2.46	28	2.10	36	1.86	44
100	3.03	27	2.74	32	2.33	40	2.07	49
200	6.06	55	5.47	63	4.66	80	4.13	97
300	9.08	81	8.20	94	6.99	119	6.19	146
400	12.11	109	10.94	125	9.31	159	8.25	194
500	15.13	135	13.67	156	11.64	198	10.31	242
600	18.16	163	16.40	187	13.97	238	12.37	291
700	21.18	190	19.13	218	16.29	277	14.43	339
800	24.21	217	21.87	250	18.62	317	16.49	387
900	27.23	244	24.60	281	20.95	357	18.55	436
1,000	30.26	271	27.33	312	23.27	396	20.61	484
2,000	60.51	541	54.66	624	46.54	792	41.22	968
3,000	90.76	812	81.98	935	69.81	1,189	61.82	1,451
4,000	121.02	1,083	109.31	1,247	93.08	1,585	82.43	1,935
5,000	151.27	1,353	136.64	1,559	116.35	1,981	103.03	2,418
6,000	181.52	1,624	163.96	1,870	139.61	2,377	123.64	2,902
7,000	211.78	1,895	191.29	2,182	162.88	2,773	144.25	3,386
8,000	242.03	2,165	218.62	2,494	186.15	3,169	164.85	3,869
9,000	272.28	2,436	245.94	2,805	209.42	3,565	185.46	4,353
10,000	302.54	2,707	273.27	3,117	232.69	3,961	206.06	4,836
11,000	332.79	2,977	300.60	3,429	255.96	4,358	226.67	5,320
12,000	363.04	3,248	327.92	3,740	279.22	4,753	247.27	5,803
13,000	393.30	3,519	355.25	4,052	302.49	5,149	267.88	6,287
14,000	423.55	3,789	382.58	4,364	325.76	5,546	288.49	6,771
15,000	453.80	4,060	409.90	4,675	349.03	5,942	309.09	7,254
16,000	484.06	4,331	437.23	4,987	372.30	6,338	329.70	7,738
17,000	514.31	4,601	464.56	5,299	395.57	6,734	350.30	8,222
18,000	544.56	4,872	491.88	5,610	418.83	7,130	370.91	8,706
19,000	574.81	5,142	519.21	5,922	442.10	7,526	391.51	9,189
20,000	605.07	5,413	546.53	6,233	465.37	7,922	412.12	9,673
21,000	635.32	5,683	573.86	6,545	488.64	8,318	432.73	10,157
22,000	665.58	5,954	601.19	6,857	511.91	8,715	453.33	10,640
23,000	695.83	6,225	628.51	7,168	535.17	9,110	473.94	11,124
24,000	726.08	6,495	655.84	7,480	558.44	9,506	494.54	11,607
25,000	756.34	6,766	683.17	7,792	581.71	9,903	515.15	12,091
26,000	786.59	7,037	710.49	8,104	604.98	10,299	535.75	12,574
27,000	816.84	7,307	737.82	8,415	628.25	10,695	556.36	13,058
28,000	847.10	7,578	765.15	8,727	651.52	11,091	576.97	13,542
29,000	877.35	7,849	792.47	9,039	674.78	11,487	597.57	14,025
30,000	907.60	8,119	819.80	9,350	698.05	11,883	618.18	14,509
31,000	937.86	8,390	847.13	9,662	721.32	12,279	638.78	14,992
32,000	968.11	8,661	874.45	9,974	744.59	12,675	659.39	15,476
33,000	998.36	8,931	901.78	10,285	767.86	13,072	679.99	15,959
34,000	1,028.62	9,202	929.11	10,597	791.13	13,468	700.60	16,443
35,000	1,058.87	9,473	956.43	10,909	814.39	13,863	721.21	16,927
36,000	1,089.12	9,743	983.76	11,220	837.66	14,260	741.81	17,410
37,000	1,119.38	10,014	1,011.08	11,532	860.93	14,656	762.42	17,894
38,000	1,149.63	10,284	1,038.41	11,844	884.20	15,052	783.02	18,377
39,000	1,179.88	10,555	1,065.74	12,156	907.47	15,448	803.63	18,861
40,000	1,210.13	10,825	1,093.06	12,467	930.74	15,844	824.23	19,345
42,000	1,270.64	11,367	1,147.72	13,091	977.27	16,636	865.45	20,312
44,000	1,331.15	11,908	1,202.37	13,714	1,023.81	17,429	906.66	21,280
46,000	1,391.65	12,449	1,257.02	14,337	1,070.34	18,220	947.87	22,247
48,000	1,452.16	12,991	1,311.68	14,961	1,116.88	19,013	989.08	23,214
50,000	1,512.67	13,532	1,366.33	15,584	1,163.42	19,805	1,030.29	24,181

AUTO LOAN PAYMENTS

AMOUNT OF LOAN	12 MOS		24 MOS		30 MOS		36 MOS	
	MONTHLY PAYMENT	TOTAL INTRST	MONTHLY PAYMENT	TOTAL INTRST	MONTHLY PAYMENT	TOTAL INTRST	MONTHLY PAYMENT	TOTAL INTRST
$ 1	0.09	0	0.05	0	0.04	0	0.04	0
2	0.18	0	0.10	0	0.08	0	0.07	1
3	0.27	0	0.15	1	0.12	1	0.11	1
4	0.36	0	0.20	1	0.16	1	0.14	1
5	0.45	0	0.25	1	0.20	1	0.18	1
6	0.54	0	0.29	1	0.24	1	0.21	2
7	0.63	1	0.34	1	0.28	1	0.25	2
8	0.72	1	0.39	1	0.32	2	0.28	2
9	0.81	1	0.44	2	0.36	2	0.31	2
10	0.90	1	0.49	2	0.40	2	0.35	3
20	1.80	2	0.97	3	0.80	4	0.69	5
30	2.70	2	1.45	5	1.20	6	1.03	7
40	3.60	3	1.93	6	1.60	8	1.38	10
50	4.50	4	2.41	8	2.00	10	1.72	12
60	5.40	4	2.89	9	2.39	12	2.06	14
70	6.30	5	3.37	11	2.79	14	2.41	17
80	7.20	6	3.86	13	3.19	16	2.75	19
90	8.10	7	4.34	14	3.59	18	3.09	21
100	9.00	8	4.82	16	3.99	20	3.43	23
200	17.99	16	9.63	31	7.97	39	6.86	47
300	26.98	24	14.44	47	11.95	59	10.29	70
400	35.97	32	19.26	62	15.93	78	13.72	94
500	44.96	40	24.07	78	19.91	97	17.15	117
600	53.95	47	28.88	93	23.90	117	20.58	141
700	62.94	55	33.70	109	27.88	136	24.01	164
800	71.93	63	38.51	124	31.86	156	27.44	188
900	80.92	71	43.32	140	35.84	175	30.87	211
1,000	89.91	79	48.14	155	39.82	195	34.30	235
2,000	179.81	158	96.27	310	79.64	389	68.60	470
3,000	269.72	237	144.40	466	119.46	584	102.90	704
4,000	359.62	315	192.53	621	159.28	778	137.20	939
5,000	449.53	394	240.66	776	199.10	973	171.50	1,174
6,000	539.43	473	288.79	931	238.91	1,167	205.80	1,409
7,000	629.34	552	336.92	1,086	278.73	1,362	240.10	1,644
8,000	719.24	631	385.05	1,241	318.55	1,557	274.40	1,878
9,000	809.15	710	433.18	1,396	358.37	1,751	308.70	2,113
10,000	899.05	789	481.32	1,552	398.19	1,946	343.00	2,348
11,000	988.96	868	529.45	1,707	438.00	2,140	377.30	2,583
12,000	1,078.86	946	577.58	1,862	477.82	2,335	411.60	2,818
13,000	1,168.77	1,025	625.71	2,017	517.64	2,529	445.89	3,052
14,000	1,258.67	1,104	673.84	2,172	557.46	2,724	480.19	3,287
15,000	1,348.58	1,183	721.97	2,327	597.28	2,918	514.49	3,522
16,000	1,438.48	1,262	770.10	2,482	637.09	3,113	548.79	3,756
17,000	1,528.39	1,341	818.23	2,638	676.91	3,307	583.09	3,991
18,000	1,618.29	1,419	866.36	2,793	716.73	3,502	617.39	4,226
19,000	1,708.20	1,498	914.50	2,948	756.55	3,697	651.69	4,461
20,000	1,798.10	1,577	962.63	3,103	796.37	3,891	685.99	4,696
21,000	1,888.01	1,656	1,010.76	3,258	836.18	4,085	720.29	4,930
22,000	1,977.91	1,735	1,058.89	3,413	876.00	4,280	754.59	5,165
23,000	2,067.82	1,814	1,107.02	3,568	915.82	4,475	788.89	5,400
24,000	2,157.72	1,893	1,155.15	3,724	955.64	4,669	823.19	5,635
25,000	2,247.62	1,971	1,203.28	3,879	995.46	4,864	857.48	5,869
26,000	2,337.53	2,050	1,251.41	4,034	1,035.28	5,058	891.78	6,104
27,000	2,427.43	2,129	1,299.54	4,189	1,075.09	5,253	926.08	6,339
28,000	2,517.34	2,208	1,347.67	4,344	1,114.91	5,447	960.38	6,574
29,000	2,607.24	2,287	1,395.81	4,499	1,154.73	5,642	994.68	6,808
30,000	2,697.15	2,366	1,443.94	4,655	1,194.55	5,837	1,028.98	7,043
31,000	2,787.05	2,445	1,492.07	4,810	1,234.37	6,031	1,063.28	7,278
32,000	2,876.96	2,524	1,540.20	4,965	1,274.18	6,225	1,097.58	7,513
33,000	2,966.86	2,602	1,588.33	5,120	1,314.00	6,420	1,131.88	7,748
34,000	3,056.77	2,681	1,636.46	5,275	1,353.82	6,615	1,166.18	7,982
35,000	3,146.67	2,760	1,684.59	5,430	1,393.64	6,809	1,200.48	8,217
36,000	3,236.58	2,839	1,732.72	5,585	1,433.46	7,004	1,234.78	8,452
37,000	3,326.48	2,918	1,780.85	5,740	1,473.27	7,198	1,269.07	8,687
38,000	3,416.39	2,997	1,828.99	5,896	1,513.09	7,393	1,303.37	8,921
39,000	3,506.29	3,075	1,877.12	6,051	1,552.91	7,587	1,337.67	9,156
40,000	3,596.20	3,154	1,925.25	6,206	1,592.73	7,782	1,371.97	9,391
42,000	3,776.01	3,312	2,021.51	6,516	1,672.36	8,171	1,440.57	9,861
44,000	3,955.82	3,470	2,117.77	6,826	1,752.00	8,560	1,509.17	10,330
46,000	4,135.63	3,628	2,214.03	7,137	1,831.64	8,949	1,577.77	10,800
48,000	4,315.43	3,785	2,310.30	7,447	1,911.27	9,338	1,646.37	11,269
50,000	4,495.24	3,943	2,406.56	7,757	1,990.91	9,727	1,714.96	11,739

AUTO LOAN PAYMENTS   14.25%

AMOUNT OF LOAN	42 MOS MONTHLY PAYMENT	42 MOS TOTAL INTRST	48 MOS MONTHLY PAYMENT	48 MOS TOTAL INTRST	60 MOS MONTHLY PAYMENT	60 MOS TOTAL INTRST	72 MOS MONTHLY PAYMENT	72 MOS TOTAL INTRST
$ 1	0.04	1	0.03	0	0.03	1	0.03	1
2	0.07	1	0.06	1	0.05	1	0.05	2
3	0.10	1	0.09	1	0.08	2	0.07	2
4	0.13	1	0.11	1	0.10	2	0.09	2
5	0.16	2	0.14	2	0.12	2	0.11	3
6	0.19	2	0.17	2	0.15	3	0.13	3
7	0.22	2	0.20	3	0.17	3	0.15	4
8	0.25	3	0.22	3	0.19	3	0.17	4
9	0.28	3	0.25	3	0.22	4	0.19	5
10	0.31	3	0.28	3	0.24	4	0.21	5
20	0.61	6	0.55	6	0.47	8	0.42	10
30	0.92	9	0.83	10	0.71	13	0.63	15
40	1.22	11	1.10	13	0.94	16	0.83	20
50	1.52	14	1.38	16	1.17	20	1.04	25
60	1.83	17	1.65	19	1.41	25	1.25	30
70	2.13	19	1.93	23	1.64	28	1.46	35
80	2.44	22	2.20	26	1.88	33	1.66	40
90	2.74	25	2.48	29	2.11	37	1.87	45
100	3.04	28	2.75	32	2.34	40	2.08	50
200	6.08	55	5.50	64	4.68	81	4.15	99
300	9.12	83	8.24	96	7.02	121	6.23	149
400	12.16	111	10.99	128	9.36	162	8.30	198
500	15.19	138	13.73	159	11.70	202	10.37	247
600	18.23	166	16.48	191	14.04	242	12.45	296
700	21.27	193	19.22	223	16.38	283	14.52	345
800	24.31	221	21.97	255	18.72	323	16.60	395
900	27.34	248	24.71	286	21.06	364	18.67	444
1,000	30.38	276	27.46	318	23.40	404	20.74	493
2,000	60.76	552	54.91	636	46.80	808	41.48	987
3,000	91.14	828	82.36	953	70.20	1,212	62.22	1,480
4,000	121.51	1,103	109.81	1,271	93.60	1,616	82.96	1,973
5,000	151.89	1,379	137.27	1,589	117.00	2,020	103.70	2,466
6,000	182.27	1,655	164.72	1,907	140.39	2,423	124.44	2,960
7,000	212.64	1,931	192.17	2,224	163.79	2,827	145.18	3,453
8,000	243.02	2,207	219.62	2,542	187.19	3,231	165.92	3,946
9,000	273.40	2,483	247.07	2,859	210.59	3,635	186.66	4,440
10,000	303.77	2,758	274.53	3,177	233.99	4,039	207.40	4,933
11,000	334.15	3,034	301.98	3,495	257.38	4,443	228.14	5,426
12,000	364.53	3,310	329.43	3,813	280.78	4,847	248.88	5,919
13,000	394.90	3,586	356.88	4,130	304.18	5,251	269.62	6,413
14,000	425.28	3,862	384.33	4,448	327.58	5,655	290.36	6,906
15,000	455.66	4,138	411.79	4,766	350.98	6,059	311.10	7,399
16,000	486.03	4,413	439.24	5,084	374.37	6,462	331.84	7,892
17,000	516.41	4,689	466.69	5,401	397.77	6,866	352.58	8,386
18,000	546.79	4,965	494.14	5,719	421.17	7,270	373.32	8,879
19,000	577.16	5,241	521.59	6,036	444.57	7,674	394.06	9,372
20,000	607.54	5,517	549.05	6,354	467.97	8,078	414.80	9,866
21,000	637.92	5,793	576.50	6,672	491.36	8,482	435.54	10,359
22,000	668.29	6,068	603.95	6,990	514.76	8,886	456.28	10,852
23,000	698.67	6,344	631.40	7,307	538.16	9,290	477.02	11,345
24,000	729.05	6,620	658.85	7,625	561.56	9,694	497.76	11,839
25,000	759.42	6,896	686.31	7,943	584.96	10,098	518.50	12,332
26,000	789.80	7,172	713.76	8,260	608.35	10,501	539.24	12,825
27,000	820.18	7,448	741.21	8,578	631.75	10,905	559.98	13,319
28,000	850.55	7,723	768.66	8,896	655.15	11,309	580.72	13,812
29,000	880.93	7,999	796.11	9,213	678.55	11,713	601.46	14,305
30,000	911.31	8,275	823.57	9,531	701.95	12,117	622.20	14,798
31,000	941.68	8,551	851.02	9,849	725.34	12,520	642.94	15,292
32,000	972.06	8,827	878.47	10,167	748.74	12,924	663.68	15,785
33,000	1,002.44	9,102	905.92	10,484	772.14	13,328	684.42	16,278
34,000	1,032.81	9,378	933.37	10,802	795.54	13,732	705.16	16,772
35,000	1,063.19	9,654	960.83	11,120	818.94	14,136	725.90	17,265
36,000	1,093.57	9,930	988.28	11,437	842.34	14,540	746.64	17,758
37,000	1,123.95	10,206	1,015.73	11,755	865.73	14,944	767.38	18,251
38,000	1,154.32	10,481	1,043.18	12,073	889.13	15,348	788.12	18,745
39,000	1,184.70	10,757	1,070.63	12,390	912.53	15,752	808.86	19,238
40,000	1,215.08	11,033	1,098.09	12,708	935.93	16,156	829.60	19,731
42,000	1,275.83	11,585	1,152.99	13,344	982.72	16,963	871.08	20,718
44,000	1,336.58	12,136	1,207.90	13,979	1,029.52	17,771	912.56	21,704
46,000	1,397.34	12,688	1,262.80	14,614	1,076.32	18,579	954.04	22,691
48,000	1,458.09	13,240	1,317.70	15,250	1,123.11	19,387	995.52	23,677
50,000	1,518.84	13,791	1,372.61	15,885	1,169.91	20,195	1,037.00	24,664

14.50% AUTO LOAN PAYMENTS

AMOUNT OF LOAN	12 MOS		24 MOS		30 MOS		36 MOS	
	MONTHLY PAYMENT	TOTAL INTRST	MONTHLY PAYMENT	TOTAL INTRST	MONTHLY PAYMENT	TOTAL INTRST	MONTHLY PAYMENT	TOTAL INTRST
$ 1	0.10	0	0.05	0	0.04	0	0.04	0
2	0.19	0	0.10	0	0.08	0	0.07	1
3	0.28	0	0.15	1	0.12	1	0.11	1
4	0.37	0	0.20	1	0.16	1	0.14	1
5	0.46	1	0.25	1	0.20	1	0.18	1
6	0.55	1	0.29	1	0.24	1	0.21	2
7	0.64	1	0.34	1	0.28	1	0.25	2
8	0.73	1	0.39	1	0.32	2	0.28	2
9	0.82	1	0.44	2	0.36	2	0.31	2
10	0.91	1	0.49	2	0.40	2	0.35	3
20	1.81	2	0.97	3	0.80	4	0.69	5
30	2.71	3	1.45	5	1.20	6	1.04	7
40	3.61	3	1.93	6	1.60	8	1.38	10
50	4.51	4	2.42	8	2.00	10	1.73	12
60	5.41	5	2.90	10	2.40	12	2.07	15
70	6.31	6	3.38	11	2.80	14	2.41	17
80	7.21	7	3.86	13	3.20	16	2.76	19
90	8.11	7	4.35	14	3.60	18	3.10	22
100	9.01	8	4.83	16	4.00	20	3.45	24
200	18.01	16	9.65	32	7.99	40	6.89	48
300	27.01	24	14.48	48	11.99	60	10.33	72
400	36.01	32	19.30	63	15.98	79	13.77	96
500	45.02	40	24.13	79	19.97	99	17.22	120
600	54.02	48	28.95	95	23.97	119	20.66	144
700	63.02	56	33.78	111	27.96	139	24.10	168
800	72.02	64	38.60	126	31.96	159	27.54	191
900	81.03	72	43.43	142	35.95	179	30.98	215
1,000	90.03	80	48.25	158	39.94	198	34.43	239
2,000	180.05	161	96.50	316	79.88	396	68.85	479
3,000	270.07	241	144.75	474	119.82	595	103.27	718
4,000	360.10	321	193.00	632	159.76	793	137.69	957
5,000	450.12	401	241.25	790	199.70	991	172.11	1,196
6,000	540.14	482	289.50	948	239.63	1,189	206.53	1,435
7,000	630.16	562	337.75	1,106	279.57	1,387	240.95	1,674
8,000	720.19	642	386.00	1,264	319.51	1,585	275.37	1,913
9,000	810.21	723	434.25	1,422	359.45	1,784	309.79	2,152
10,000	900.23	803	482.50	1,580	399.39	1,982	344.21	2,392
11,000	990.25	883	530.75	1,738	439.32	2,180	378.64	2,631
12,000	1,080.28	963	579.00	1,896	479.26	2,378	413.06	2,870
13,000	1,170.30	1,044	627.25	2,054	519.20	2,576	447.48	3,109
14,000	1,260.32	1,124	675.50	2,212	559.14	2,774	481.90	3,348
15,000	1,350.34	1,204	723.75	2,370	599.08	2,972	516.32	3,588
16,000	1,440.37	1,284	772.00	2,528	639.01	3,170	550.74	3,827
17,000	1,530.39	1,365	820.25	2,686	678.95	3,369	585.16	4,066
18,000	1,620.41	1,445	868.49	2,844	718.89	3,567	619.58	4,305
19,000	1,710.43	1,525	916.74	3,002	758.83	3,765	654.00	4,544
20,000	1,800.46	1,606	964.99	3,160	798.77	3,963	688.42	4,783
21,000	1,890.48	1,686	1,013.24	3,318	838.70	4,161	722.85	5,023
22,000	1,980.50	1,766	1,061.49	3,476	878.64	4,359	757.27	5,262
23,000	2,070.52	1,846	1,109.74	3,634	918.58	4,557	791.69	5,501
24,000	2,160.55	1,927	1,157.99	3,792	958.52	4,756	826.11	5,740
25,000	2,250.57	2,007	1,206.24	3,950	998.46	4,954	860.53	5,979
26,000	2,340.59	2,087	1,254.49	4,108	1,038.39	5,152	894.95	6,218
27,000	2,430.61	2,167	1,302.74	4,266	1,078.33	5,350	929.37	6,457
28,000	2,520.64	2,248	1,350.99	4,424	1,118.27	5,548	963.79	6,696
29,000	2,610.66	2,328	1,399.24	4,582	1,158.21	5,746	998.21	6,936
30,000	2,700.68	2,408	1,447.49	4,740	1,198.15	5,945	1,032.63	7,175
31,000	2,790.70	2,488	1,495.74	4,898	1,238.08	6,142	1,067.06	7,414
32,000	2,880.73	2,569	1,543.99	5,056	1,278.02	6,341	1,101.48	7,653
33,000	2,970.75	2,649	1,592.24	5,214	1,317.96	6,539	1,135.90	7,892
34,000	3,060.77	2,729	1,640.49	5,372	1,357.90	6,737	1,170.32	8,132
35,000	3,150.79	2,809	1,688.73	5,530	1,397.84	6,935	1,204.74	8,371
36,000	3,240.82	2,890	1,736.98	5,688	1,437.77	7,133	1,239.16	8,610
37,000	3,330.84	2,970	1,785.23	5,846	1,477.71	7,331	1,273.58	8,849
38,000	3,420.86	3,050	1,833.48	6,004	1,517.65	7,530	1,308.00	9,088
39,000	3,510.88	3,131	1,881.73	6,162	1,557.59	7,728	1,342.42	9,327
40,000	3,600.91	3,211	1,929.98	6,320	1,597.53	7,926	1,376.84	9,566
42,000	3,780.95	3,371	2,026.48	6,636	1,677.40	8,322	1,445.69	10,045
44,000	3,961.00	3,532	2,122.98	6,952	1,757.28	8,718	1,514.53	10,523
46,000	4,141.04	3,692	2,219.48	7,268	1,837.15	9,115	1,583.37	11,001
48,000	4,321.09	3,853	2,315.98	7,584	1,917.03	9,511	1,652.21	11,480
50,000	4,501.13	4,014	2,412.48	7,900	1,996.91	9,907	1,721.05	11,958

AUTO LOAN PAYMENTS

14.50%

AMOUNT OF LOAN	42 MOS MONTHLY PAYMENT	42 MOS TOTAL INTRST	48 MOS MONTHLY PAYMENT	48 MOS TOTAL INTRST	60 MOS MONTHLY PAYMENT	60 MOS TOTAL INTRST	72 MOS MONTHLY PAYMENT	72 MOS TOTAL INTRST
$ 1	0.04	1	0.03	0	0.03	1	0.03	1
2	0.07	1	0.06	1	0.05	1	0.05	2
3	0.10	1	0.09	1	0.08	2	0.07	2
4	0.13	1	0.12	2	0.10	2	0.09	2
5	0.16	2	0.14	2	0.12	2	0.11	3
6	0.19	2	0.17	2	0.15	3	0.13	3
7	0.22	2	0.20	3	0.17	3	0.15	4
8	0.25	3	0.23	3	0.19	3	0.17	4
9	0.28	3	0.25	3	0.22	4	0.19	5
10	0.31	3	0.28	3	0.24	4	0.21	5
20	0.62	6	0.56	7	0.48	9	0.42	10
30	0.92	9	0.83	10	0.71	13	0.63	15
40	1.23	12	1.11	13	0.95	17	0.84	20
50	1.53	14	1.38	16	1.18	21	1.05	26
60	1.84	17	1.66	20	1.42	25	1.26	31
70	2.14	20	1.94	23	1.65	29	1.47	36
80	2.45	23	2.21	26	1.89	33	1.67	40
90	2.75	26	2.49	30	2.12	37	1.88	45
100	3.06	29	2.76	32	2.36	42	2.09	50
200	6.11	57	5.52	65	4.71	83	4.18	101
300	9.16	85	8.28	97	7.06	124	6.27	151
400	12.21	113	11.04	130	9.42	165	8.35	201
500	15.26	141	13.79	162	11.77	206	10.44	252
600	18.31	169	16.55	194	14.12	247	12.53	302
700	21.36	197	19.31	227	16.47	288	14.62	353
800	24.41	225	22.07	259	18.83	330	16.70	402
900	27.46	253	24.83	292	21.18	371	18.79	453
1,000	30.51	281	27.58	324	23.53	412	20.88	503
2,000	61.01	562	55.16	648	47.06	824	41.75	1,006
3,000	91.51	843	82.74	972	70.59	1,235	62.63	1,509
4,000	122.01	1,124	110.32	1,295	94.12	1,647	83.50	2,012
5,000	152.51	1,405	137.89	1,619	117.65	2,059	104.38	2,515
6,000	183.01	1,686	165.47	1,943	141.17	2,470	125.25	3,018
7,000	213.51	1,967	193.05	2,266	164.70	2,882	146.13	3,521
8,000	244.01	2,248	220.63	2,590	188.23	3,294	167.00	4,024
9,000	274.51	2,529	248.21	2,914	211.76	3,706	187.87	4,527
10,000	305.01	2,810	275.78	3,237	235.29	4,117	208.75	5,030
11,000	335.51	3,091	303.36	3,561	258.82	4,529	229.62	5,533
12,000	366.01	3,372	330.94	3,885	282.34	4,940	250.50	6,036
13,000	396.51	3,653	358.52	4,209	305.87	5,352	271.37	6,539
14,000	427.01	3,934	386.10	4,533	329.40	5,764	292.25	7,042
15,000	457.51	4,215	413.67	4,856	352.93	6,176	313.12	7,545
16,000	488.01	4,496	441.25	5,180	376.46	6,588	334.00	8,048
17,000	518.51	4,777	468.83	5,504	399.99	6,999	354.87	8,551
18,000	549.02	5,059	496.41	5,828	423.51	7,411	375.74	9,053
19,000	579.52	5,340	523.99	6,152	447.04	7,822	396.62	9,557
20,000	610.02	5,621	551.56	6,445	470.57	8,234	417.49	10,059
21,000	640.52	5,902	579.14	6,799	494.10	8,646	438.37	10,563
22,000	671.02	6,183	606.72	7,123	517.63	9,058	459.24	11,065
23,000	701.52	6,464	634.30	7,446	541.16	9,470	480.12	11,569
24,000	732.02	6,745	661.88	7,770	564.68	9,881	500.99	12,071
25,000	762.52	7,026	689.45	8,094	588.21	10,293	521.87	12,575
26,000	793.02	7,307	717.03	8,417	611.74	10,704	542.74	13,077
27,000	823.52	7,588	744.61	8,741	635.27	11,116	563.61	13,580
28,000	854.02	7,869	772.19	9,065	658.80	11,528	584.49	14,083
29,000	884.52	8,150	799.77	9,389	682.33	11,940	605.36	14,586
30,000	915.02	8,431	827.34	9,712	705.85	12,351	626.24	15,089
31,000	945.52	8,712	854.92	10,036	729.38	12,763	647.11	15,592
32,000	976.02	8,993	882.50	10,360	752.91	13,175	667.99	16,095
33,000	1,006.52	9,274	910.08	10,684	776.44	13,586	688.86	16,598
34,000	1,037.02	9,555	937.66	11,008	799.97	13,998	709.74	17,101
35,000	1,067.53	9,836	965.23	11,331	823.49	14,409	730.61	17,604
36,000	1,098.03	10,117	992.81	11,655	847.02	14,821	751.48	18,107
37,000	1,128.53	10,398	1,020.39	11,979	870.55	15,233	772.36	18,610
38,000	1,159.03	10,679	1,047.97	12,303	894.08	15,645	793.23	19,113
39,000	1,189.53	10,960	1,075.55	12,626	917.61	16,057	814.11	19,616
40,000	1,220.03	11,241	1,103.12	12,950	941.14	16,468	834.98	20,119
42,000	1,281.03	11,803	1,158.28	13,597	988.19	17,291	876.73	21,125
44,000	1,342.03	12,365	1,213.43	14,245	1,035.25	18,115	918.48	22,131
46,000	1,403.03	12,927	1,268.59	14,892	1,082.31	18,939	960.23	23,137
48,000	1,464.03	13,489	1,323.75	15,540	1,129.36	19,762	1,001.98	24,143
50,000	1,525.03	14,051	1,378.90	16,187	1,176.42	20,585	1,043.73	25,149

14.75% AUTO LOAN PAYMENTS

AMOUNT OF LOAN	12 MOS MONTHLY PAYMENT	12 MOS TOTAL INTRST	24 MOS MONTHLY PAYMENT	24 MOS TOTAL INTRST	30 MOS MONTHLY PAYMENT	30 MOS TOTAL INTRST	36 MOS MONTHLY PAYMENT	36 MOS TOTAL INTRST
$ 1	0.10	0	0.05	0	0.05	1	0.04	0
2	0.19	0	0.10	0	0.09	1	0.07	1
3	0.28	0	0.15	1	0.13	1	0.11	1
4	0.37	0	0.20	1	0.17	1	0.14	1
5	0.46	1	0.25	1	0.21	1	0.18	1
6	0.55	1	0.30	1	0.25	1	0.21	2
7	0.64	1	0.34	1	0.29	2	0.25	2
8	0.73	1	0.39	1	0.33	2	0.28	2
9	0.82	1	0.44	2	0.37	2	0.32	3
10	0.91	1	0.49	2	0.41	2	0.35	3
20	1.81	2	0.97	3	0.81	4	0.70	5
30	2.71	3	1.46	5	1.21	6	1.04	7
40	3.61	3	1.94	7	1.61	8	1.39	10
50	4.51	4	2.42	8	2.01	10	1.73	12
60	5.41	5	2.91	10	2.41	12	2.08	15
70	6.31	6	3.39	11	2.81	14	2.42	17
80	7.22	6	3.87	13	3.21	16	2.77	20
90	8.12	7	4.36	15	3.61	18	3.11	22
100	9.02	8	4.84	16	4.01	20	3.46	25
200	18.03	16	9.68	32	8.02	41	6.91	49
300	27.05	25	14.52	48	12.02	61	10.37	73
400	36.06	33	19.35	64	16.03	81	13.82	98
500	45.08	41	24.19	81	20.03	101	17.28	122
600	54.09	49	29.03	97	24.04	121	20.73	146
700	63.10	57	33.86	113	28.05	142	24.19	171
800	72.12	65	38.70	129	32.05	162	27.64	195
900	81.13	74	43.54	145	36.06	182	31.09	219
1,000	90.15	82	48.37	161	40.06	202	34.55	244
2,000	180.29	163	96.74	322	80.12	404	69.09	487
3,000	270.43	245	145.11	483	120.18	605	103.63	731
4,000	360.57	327	193.48	644	160.24	807	138.18	974
5,000	450.71	409	241.84	804	200.30	1,009	172.72	1,218
6,000	540.85	490	290.21	965	240.35	1,211	207.26	1,461
7,000	630.99	572	338.58	1,126	280.41	1,412	241.81	1,705
8,000	721.13	654	386.95	1,287	320.47	1,614	276.35	1,949
9,000	811.27	735	435.32	1,448	360.53	1,816	310.89	2,192
10,000	901.41	817	483.68	1,608	400.59	2,018	345.44	2,436
11,000	991.55	899	532.05	1,769	440.65	2,220	379.98	2,679
12,000	1,081.69	980	580.42	1,930	480.70	2,421	414.52	2,923
13,000	1,171.83	1,062	628.79	2,091	520.76	2,623	449.06	3,166
14,000	1,261.97	1,144	677.16	2,252	560.82	2,825	483.61	3,410
15,000	1,352.11	1,225	725.52	2,412	600.88	3,026	518.15	3,653
16,000	1,442.25	1,307	773.89	2,573	640.94	3,228	552.69	3,897
17,000	1,532.39	1,389	822.26	2,734	680.99	3,430	587.24	4,141
18,000	1,622.53	1,470	870.63	2,895	721.05	3,632	621.78	4,384
19,000	1,712.67	1,552	919.00	3,056	761.11	3,833	656.32	4,628
20,000	1,802.81	1,634	967.36	3,217	801.17	4,035	690.87	4,871
21,000	1,892.95	1,715	1,015.73	3,378	841.23	4,237	725.41	5,115
22,000	1,983.09	1,797	1,064.10	3,538	881.29	4,439	759.95	5,358
23,000	2,073.23	1,879	1,112.47	3,699	921.34	4,640	794.49	5,602
24,000	2,163.37	1,960	1,160.84	3,860	961.40	4,842	829.04	5,845
25,000	2,253.51	2,042	1,209.20	4,021	1,001.46	5,044	863.58	6,089
26,000	2,343.66	2,124	1,257.57	4,182	1,041.52	5,246	898.12	6,332
27,000	2,433.80	2,206	1,305.94	4,343	1,081.58	5,447	932.67	6,576
28,000	2,523.94	2,287	1,354.31	4,503	1,121.63	5,649	967.21	6,820
29,000	2,614.08	2,369	1,402.68	4,664	1,161.69	5,851	1,001.75	7,063
30,000	2,704.22	2,451	1,451.04	4,825	1,201.75	6,053	1,036.30	7,307
31,000	2,794.36	2,532	1,499.41	4,986	1,241.81	6,254	1,070.84	7,550
32,000	2,884.50	2,614	1,547.78	5,147	1,281.87	6,456	1,105.38	7,794
33,000	2,974.64	2,696	1,596.15	5,308	1,321.93	6,658	1,139.92	8,037
34,000	3,064.78	2,777	1,644.52	5,468	1,361.98	6,859	1,174.47	8,281
35,000	3,154.92	2,859	1,692.88	5,629	1,402.04	7,061	1,209.01	8,524
36,000	3,245.06	2,941	1,741.25	5,790	1,442.10	7,263	1,243.55	8,768
37,000	3,335.20	3,022	1,789.62	5,951	1,482.16	7,465	1,278.10	9,012
38,000	3,425.34	3,104	1,837.99	6,112	1,522.22	7,667	1,312.64	9,255
39,000	3,515.48	3,186	1,886.36	6,273	1,562.27	7,868	1,347.18	9,498
40,000	3,605.62	3,267	1,934.72	6,433	1,602.33	8,070	1,381.73	9,742
42,000	3,785.90	3,431	2,031.46	6,755	1,682.45	8,474	1,450.81	10,229
44,000	3,966.18	3,594	2,128.19	7,077	1,762.57	8,877	1,519.90	10,716
46,000	4,146.46	3,758	2,224.93	7,398	1,842.68	9,280	1,588.98	11,203
48,000	4,326.74	3,921	2,321.67	7,720	1,922.80	9,684	1,658.07	11,691
50,000	4,507.02	4,084	2,418.40	8,042	2,002.91	10,087	1,727.16	12,178

AUTO LOAN PAYMENTS 14.75%

AMOUNT OF LOAN	42 MOS MONTHLY PAYMENT	42 MOS TOTAL INTRST	48 MOS MONTHLY PAYMENT	48 MOS TOTAL INTRST	60 MOS MONTHLY PAYMENT	60 MOS TOTAL INTRST	72 MOS MONTHLY PAYMENT	72 MOS TOTAL INTRST
$ 1	0.04	1	0.03	0	0.03	1	0.03	1
2	0.07	1	0.06	1	0.05	1	0.05	2
3	0.10	1	0.09	1	0.08	2	0.07	2
4	0.13	1	0.12	2	0.10	2	0.09	2
5	0.16	2	0.14	2	0.12	2	0.11	3
6	0.19	2	0.17	2	0.15	3	0.13	3
7	0.22	2	0.20	3	0.17	3	0.15	4
8	0.25	3	0.23	3	0.19	3	0.17	4
9	0.28	3	0.25	3	0.22	4	0.19	5
10	0.31	3	0.28	3	0.24	4	0.22	6
20	0.62	6	0.56	7	0.48	9	0.43	11
30	0.92	9	0.84	10	0.71	13	0.64	16
40	1.23	12	1.11	13	0.95	17	0.85	21
50	1.54	15	1.39	17	1.19	21	1.06	26
60	1.84	17	1.67	20	1.42	25	1.27	31
70	2.15	20	1.94	23	1.66	30	1.48	37
80	2.45	23	2.22	27	1.90	34	1.69	42
90	2.76	26	2.50	30	2.13	38	1.90	47
100	3.07	29	2.78	33	2.37	42	2.11	52
200	6.13	57	5.55	66	4.74	84	4.21	103
300	9.19	86	8.32	99	7.10	126	6.31	154
400	12.25	115	11.09	132	9.47	168	8.41	206
500	15.32	143	13.86	165	11.83	210	10.51	257
600	18.38	172	16.63	198	14.20	252	12.61	308
700	21.44	200	19.40	231	16.57	294	14.71	359
800	24.50	229	22.17	264	18.93	336	16.81	410
900	27.57	258	24.94	297	21.30	378	18.91	462
1,000	30.63	286	27.71	330	23.66	420	21.01	513
2,000	61.25	573	55.41	660	47.32	839	42.02	1,025
3,000	91.88	859	83.12	990	70.98	1,259	63.03	1,538
4,000	122.50	1,145	110.82	1,319	94.64	1,678	84.04	2,051
5,000	153.13	1,431	138.53	1,649	118.30	2,098	105.05	2,564
6,000	183.75	1,718	166.23	1,979	141.96	2,518	126.06	3,076
7,000	214.38	2,004	193.93	2,309	165.62	2,937	147.07	3,589
8,000	245.00	2,290	221.64	2,639	189.28	3,357	168.08	4,102
9,000	275.63	2,576	249.34	2,968	212.94	3,776	189.09	4,614
10,000	306.25	2,863	277.05	3,298	236.59	4,195	210.10	5,127
11,000	336.88	3,149	304.75	3,628	260.25	4,615	231.11	5,640
12,000	367.50	3,435	332.46	3,958	283.91	5,035	252.12	6,153
13,000	398.13	3,721	360.16	4,288	307.57	5,454	273.13	6,665
14,000	428.75	4,008	387.86	4,617	331.23	5,874	294.14	7,178
15,000	459.38	4,294	415.57	4,947	354.89	6,293	315.15	7,691
16,000	490.00	4,580	443.27	5,277	378.55	6,713	336.16	8,204
17,000	520.62	4,866	470.98	5,607	402.21	7,133	357.17	8,716
18,000	551.25	5,153	498.68	5,937	425.87	7,552	378.18	9,229
19,000	581.87	5,439	526.38	6,266	449.52	7,971	399.19	9,742
20,000	612.50	5,725	554.09	6,596	473.18	8,391	420.19	10,254
21,000	643.12	6,011	581.79	6,926	496.84	8,810	441.20	10,766
22,000	673.75	6,298	609.50	7,256	520.50	9,230	462.21	11,279
23,000	704.37	6,584	637.20	7,586	544.16	9,650	483.22	11,792
24,000	735.00	6,870	664.91	7,916	567.82	10,069	504.23	12,305
25,000	765.62	7,156	692.61	8,245	591.48	10,489	525.24	12,817
26,000	796.25	7,443	720.31	8,575	615.14	10,908	546.25	13,330
27,000	826.87	7,729	748.02	8,905	638.80	11,328	567.26	13,843
28,000	857.50	8,015	775.72	9,235	662.45	11,747	588.27	14,355
29,000	888.12	8,301	803.43	9,565	686.11	12,167	609.28	14,868
30,000	918.75	8,588	831.13	9,894	709.77	12,586	630.29	15,381
31,000	949.37	8,874	858.83	10,224	733.43	13,006	651.30	15,894
32,000	979.99	9,160	886.54	10,554	757.09	13,425	672.31	16,406
33,000	1,010.62	9,446	914.24	10,884	780.75	13,845	693.32	16,919
34,000	1,041.24	9,732	941.95	11,214	804.41	14,265	714.33	17,432
35,000	1,071.87	10,019	969.65	11,543	828.07	14,684	735.34	17,944
36,000	1,102.49	10,305	997.36	11,873	851.73	15,104	756.35	18,457
37,000	1,133.12	10,591	1,025.06	12,203	875.38	15,523	777.36	18,970
38,000	1,163.74	10,877	1,052.76	12,532	899.04	15,942	798.37	19,483
39,000	1,194.37	11,164	1,080.47	12,863	922.70	16,362	819.37	19,995
40,000	1,224.99	11,450	1,108.17	13,192	946.36	16,782	840.38	20,507
42,000	1,286.24	12,022	1,163.58	13,852	993.68	17,621	882.40	21,533
44,000	1,347.49	12,595	1,218.99	14,512	1,041.00	18,460	924.42	22,558
46,000	1,408.74	13,167	1,274.40	15,171	1,088.31	19,299	966.44	23,584
48,000	1,469.99	13,740	1,329.81	15,831	1,135.63	20,138	1,008.46	24,609
50,000	1,531.24	14,312	1,385.21	16,490	1,182.95	20,977	1,050.48	25,635

15.00% AUTO LOAN PAYMENTS

AMOUNT OF LOAN	12 MOS		24 MOS		30 MOS		36 MOS	
	MONTHLY PAYMENT	TOTAL INTRST	MONTHLY PAYMENT	TOTAL INTRST	MONTHLY PAYMENT	TOTAL INTRST	MONTHLY PAYMENT	TOTAL INTRST
$ 1	0.10	0	0.05	0	0.05	1	0.04	0
2	0.19	0	0.10	0	0.09	1	0.07	1
3	0.28	0	0.15	1	0.13	1	0.11	1
4	0.37	0	0.20	1	0.17	1	0.14	1
5	0.46	1	0.25	1	0.21	1	0.18	1
6	0.55	1	0.30	1	0.25	2	0.21	2
7	0.64	1	0.34	1	0.29	2	0.25	2
8	0.73	1	0.39	1	0.33	2	0.28	2
9	0.82	1	0.44	2	0.37	2	0.32	3
10	0.91	1	0.49	2	0.41	2	0.35	3
20	1.81	2	0.97	3	0.81	4	0.70	5
30	2.71	3	1.46	5	1.21	6	1.04	7
40	3.62	3	1.94	7	1.61	8	1.39	10
50	4.52	4	2.43	8	2.01	10	1.74	13
60	5.42	5	2.91	10	2.42	13	2.08	15
70	6.32	6	3.40	12	2.82	15	2.43	17
80	7.23	7	3.88	13	3.22	17	2.78	20
90	8.13	8	4.37	15	3.62	19	3.12	22
100	9.03	8	4.85	16	4.02	21	3.47	25
200	18.06	17	9.70	33	8.04	41	6.94	50
300	27.08	25	14.55	49	12.06	62	10.40	74
400	36.11	33	19.40	66	16.08	82	13.87	99
500	45.13	42	24.25	82	20.09	103	17.34	124
600	54.16	50	29.10	98	24.11	123	20.80	149
700	63.19	58	33.95	115	28.13	144	24.27	174
800	72.21	67	38.79	131	32.15	165	27.74	193
900	81.24	75	43.64	147	36.17	185	31.20	223
1,000	90.26	83	48.49	164	40.18	205	34.67	248
2,000	180.52	166	96.98	328	80.36	411	69.34	496
3,000	270.78	249	145.46	491	120.54	616	104.00	744
4,000	361.04	332	193.95	655	160.72	822	138.67	992
5,000	451.30	416	242.44	819	200.90	1,027	173.33	1,240
6,000	541.55	499	290.92	982	241.08	1,232	208.00	1,488
7,000	631.81	582	339.41	1,146	281.25	1,438	242.66	1,736
8,000	722.07	665	387.90	1,310	321.43	1,643	277.33	1,984
9,000	812.33	748	436.38	1,473	361.61	1,848	311.99	2,232
10,000	902.59	831	484.87	1,637	401.79	2,054	346.66	2,480
11,000	992.85	914	533.36	1,801	441.97	2,259	381.32	2,728
12,000	1,083.10	997	581.84	1,964	482.15	2,465	415.99	2,976
13,000	1,173.36	1,080	630.33	2,128	522.33	2,670	450.65	3,223
14,000	1,263.62	1,163	678.82	2,292	562.50	2,875	485.32	3,472
15,000	1,353.88	1,247	727.30	2,455	602.68	3,080	519.98	3,719
16,000	1,444.14	1,330	775.79	2,619	642.86	3,286	554.65	3,967
17,000	1,534.40	1,413	824.28	2,783	683.04	3,491	589.32	4,216
18,000	1,624.65	1,496	872.76	2,946	723.22	3,697	623.98	4,463
19,000	1,714.91	1,579	921.25	3,110	763.40	3,902	658.65	4,711
20,000	1,805.17	1,662	969.74	3,274	803.58	4,107	693.31	4,959
21,000	1,895.43	1,745	1,018.22	3,437	843.75	4,313	727.98	5,207
22,000	1,985.69	1,828	1,066.71	3,601	883.93	4,518	762.64	5,455
23,000	2,075.95	1,911	1,115.20	3,765	924.11	4,723	797.31	5,703
24,000	2,166.20	1,994	1,163.68	3,928	964.29	4,929	831.97	5,951
25,000	2,256.46	2,078	1,212.17	4,092	1,004.47	5,134	866.64	6,199
26,000	2,346.72	2,161	1,260.66	4,256	1,044.65	5,340	901.30	6,447
27,000	2,436.98	2,244	1,309.14	4,419	1,084.83	5,545	935.97	6,695
28,000	2,527.24	2,327	1,357.63	4,583	1,125.00	5,750	970.63	6,943
29,000	2,617.50	2,410	1,406.12	4,747	1,165.18	5,955	1,005.30	7,191
30,000	2,707.75	2,493	1,454.60	4,910	1,205.36	6,161	1,039.96	7,439
31,000	2,798.01	2,576	1,503.09	5,074	1,245.54	6,366	1,074.63	7,687
32,000	2,888.27	2,659	1,551.58	5,238	1,285.72	6,572	1,109.29	7,935
33,000	2,978.53	2,742	1,600.06	5,401	1,325.90	6,777	1,143.96	8,183
34,000	3,068.79	2,825	1,648.55	5,565	1,366.08	6,982	1,178.63	8,431
35,000	3,159.05	2,909	1,697.04	5,729	1,406.25	7,188	1,213.29	8,678
36,000	3,249.30	2,992	1,745.52	5,892	1,446.43	7,393	1,247.96	8,927
37,000	3,339.56	3,075	1,794.01	6,056	1,486.61	7,598	1,282.62	9,174
38,000	3,429.82	3,158	1,842.50	6,220	1,526.79	7,804	1,317.29	9,422
39,000	3,520.08	3,241	1,890.98	6,384	1,566.97	8,009	1,351.95	9,670
40,000	3,610.34	3,324	1,939.47	6,547	1,607.15	8,215	1,386.62	9,918
42,000	3,790.85	3,490	2,036.44	6,875	1,687.50	8,625	1,455.95	10,414
44,000	3,971.37	3,656	2,133.42	7,202	1,767.86	9,036	1,525.28	10,910
46,000	4,151.89	3,823	2,230.39	7,529	1,848.22	9,447	1,594.61	11,406
48,000	4,332.40	3,989	2,327.36	7,857	1,928.58	9,857	1,663.94	11,902
50,000	4,512.92	4,155	2,424.34	8,184	2,008.93	10,268	1,733.27	12,398

AMOUNT OF LOAN	42 MOS		48 MOS		60 MOS		72 MOS	
	MONTHLY PAYMENT	TOTAL INTRST	MONTHLY PAYMENT	TOTAL INTRST	MONTHLY PAYMENT	TOTAL INTRST	MONTHLY PAYMENT	TOTAL INTRST
$ 1	0.04	1	0.03	0	0.03	1	0.03	1
2	0.07	1	0.06	1	0.05	1	0.05	2
3	0.10	1	0.09	1	0.08	2	0.07	2
4	0.13	1	0.12	2	0.10	2	0.09	2
5	0.16	2	0.14	2	0.12	2	0.11	3
6	0.19	2	0.17	2	0.15	3	0.13	3
7	0.22	2	0.20	3	0.17	3	0.15	4
8	0.25	3	0.23	3	0.20	4	0.17	4
9	0.28	3	0.26	3	0.22	4	0.20	5
10	0.31	3	0.28	3	0.24	4	0.22	6
20	0.62	6	0.56	7	0.48	9	0.43	11
30	0.93	9	0.84	10	0.72	13	0.64	16
40	1.23	12	1.12	14	0.96	18	0.85	21
50	1.54	15	1.40	17	1.19	21	1.06	26
60	1.85	18	1.67	20	1.43	26	1.27	31
70	2.16	21	1.95	24	1.67	30	1.49	37
80	2.46	23	2.23	27	1.91	35	1.70	42
90	2.77	26	2.51	30	2.15	39	1.91	48
100	3.08	29	2.79	34	2.38	43	2.12	53
200	6.15	58	5.57	67	4.76	86	4.23	105
300	9.23	88	8.35	101	7.14	128	6.35	157
400	12.30	117	11.14	135	9.52	171	8.46	209
500	15.38	146	13.92	168	11.90	214	10.58	262
600	18.45	175	16.70	202	14.28	257	12.69	314
700	21.53	204	19.49	236	16.66	300	14.81	366
800	24.60	233	22.27	269	19.04	342	16.92	418
900	27.68	263	25.05	302	21.42	385	19.04	471
1,000	30.75	292	27.84	336	23.79	427	21.15	523
2,000	61.50	583	55.67	672	47.58	855	42.30	1,046
3,000	92.25	875	83.50	1,008	71.37	1,282	63.44	1,568
4,000	123.00	1,166	111.33	1,344	95.16	1,710	84.59	2,090
5,000	153.75	1,458	139.16	1,680	118.95	2,137	105.73	2,613
6,000	184.50	1,749	166.99	2,016	142.74	2,564	126.88	3,135
7,000	215.25	2,041	194.82	2,351	166.53	2,992	148.02	3,657
8,000	246.00	2,332	222.65	2,687	190.32	3,419	169.17	4,180
9,000	276.75	2,624	250.48	3,023	214.11	3,847	190.31	4,702
10,000	307.50	2,915	278.31	3,359	237.90	4,274	211.46	5,225
11,000	338.24	3,206	306.14	3,695	261.69	4,701	232.60	5,747
12,000	368.99	3,498	333.97	4,031	285.48	5,129	253.75	6,270
13,000	399.74	3,789	361.80	4,366	309.27	5,556	274.89	6,792
14,000	430.49	4,081	389.64	4,703	333.06	5,984	296.04	7,315
15,000	461.24	4,372	417.47	5,039	356.85	6,411	317.18	7,837
16,000	491.99	4,664	445.30	5,374	380.64	6,838	338.33	8,360
17,000	522.74	4,955	473.13	5,710	404.43	7,266	359.47	8,882
18,000	553.49	5,247	500.96	6,046	428.22	7,693	380.62	9,405
19,000	584.24	5,538	528.79	6,382	452.01	8,121	401.76	9,927
20,000	614.99	5,830	556.62	6,718	475.80	8,548	422.91	10,450
21,000	645.74	6,121	584.45	7,054	499.59	8,975	444.05	10,972
22,000	676.48	6,412	612.28	7,389	523.38	9,403	465.20	11,494
23,000	707.23	6,704	640.11	7,725	547.17	9,830	486.34	12,016
24,000	737.98	6,995	667.94	8,061	570.96	10,258	507.49	12,539
25,000	768.73	7,287	695.77	8,397	594.75	10,685	528.63	13,061
26,000	799.48	7,578	723.60	8,733	618.54	11,112	549.78	13,584
27,000	830.23	7,870	751.44	9,069	642.33	11,540	570.92	14,106
28,000	860.98	8,161	779.27	9,405	666.12	11,967	592.07	14,629
29,000	891.73	8,453	807.10	9,741	689.91	12,395	613.21	15,151
30,000	922.48	8,744	834.93	10,077	713.70	12,822	634.36	15,674
31,000	953.23	9,036	862.76	10,412	737.49	13,249	655.50	16,196
32,000	983.97	9,327	890.59	10,748	761.28	13,677	676.65	16,719
33,000	1,014.72	9,618	918.42	11,084	785.07	14,104	697.79	17,241
34,000	1,045.47	9,910	946.25	11,420	808.86	14,532	718.94	17,764
35,000	1,076.22	10,201	974.08	11,756	832.65	14,959	740.08	18,286
36,000	1,106.97	10,493	1,001.91	12,092	856.44	15,386	761.23	18,809
37,000	1,137.72	10,784	1,029.74	12,428	880.23	15,814	782.37	19,331
38,000	1,168.47	11,076	1,057.57	12,763	904.02	16,241	803.52	19,853
39,000	1,199.22	11,367	1,085.40	13,099	927.81	16,669	824.66	20,376
40,000	1,229.97	11,659	1,113.23	13,435	951.60	17,096	845.81	20,898
42,000	1,291.47	12,242	1,168.90	14,107	999.18	17,951	888.10	21,943
44,000	1,352.96	12,824	1,224.56	14,779	1,046.76	18,806	930.39	22,988
46,000	1,414.46	13,407	1,280.22	15,451	1,094.34	19,660	972.68	24,033
48,000	1,475.96	13,990	1,335.88	16,122	1,141.92	20,515	1,014.97	25,078
50,000	1,537.46	14,573	1,391.54	16,794	1,189.50	21,370	1,057.26	26,123

15.25% AUTO LOAN PAYMENTS

AMOUNT OF LOAN	12 MOS MONTHLY PAYMENT	12 MOS TOTAL INTRST	24 MOS MONTHLY PAYMENT	24 MOS TOTAL INTRST	30 MOS MONTHLY PAYMENT	30 MOS TOTAL INTRST	36 MOS MONTHLY PAYMENT	36 MOS TOTAL INTRST
$ 1	0.10	0	0.05	0	0.05	1	0.04	0
2	0.19	0	0.10	0	0.09	1	0.07	1
3	0.28	0	0.15	1	0.13	1	0.11	1
4	0.37	0	0.20	1	0.17	1	0.14	1
5	0.46	1	0.25	1	0.21	1	0.18	1
6	0.55	1	0.30	1	0.25	2	0.21	2
7	0.64	1	0.35	1	0.29	2	0.25	2
8	0.73	1	0.39	1	0.33	2	0.28	2
9	0.82	1	0.44	2	0.37	2	0.32	3
10	0.91	1	0.49	2	0.41	2	0.35	3
20	1.81	2	0.98	4	0.81	4	0.70	5
30	2.72	3	1.46	5	1.21	6	1.05	8
40	3.62	3	1.95	7	1.62	9	1.40	10
50	4.52	4	2.44	9	2.02	11	1.74	13
60	5.43	5	2.92	10	2.42	13	2.09	15
70	6.33	6	3.41	12	2.83	15	2.44	18
80	7.24	7	3.89	13	3.23	17	2.79	20
90	8.14	8	4.38	15	3.63	19	3.14	23
100	9.04	8	4.87	17	4.03	21	3.48	25
200	18.08	17	9.73	34	8.06	42	6.96	51
300	27.12	25	14.59	50	12.09	63	10.44	76
400	36.16	34	19.45	67	16.12	84	13.92	101
500	45.19	42	24.31	83	20.15	105	17.40	126
600	54.23	51	29.17	100	24.18	125	20.88	152
700	63.27	59	34.03	117	28.21	146	24.36	177
800	72.31	68	38.89	133	32.24	167	27.84	202
900	81.34	76	43.75	150	36.27	188	31.31	227
1,000	90.38	85	48.61	167	40.30	209	34.79	252
2,000	180.76	169	97.22	333	80.60	418	69.58	505
3,000	271.13	254	145.82	500	120.90	627	104.37	757
4,000	361.51	338	194.43	666	161.20	836	139.16	1,010
5,000	451.89	423	243.03	833	201.50	1,045	173.94	1,262
6,000	542.26	507	291.64	999	241.80	1,254	208.73	1,514
7,000	632.64	592	340.24	1,166	282.10	1,463	243.52	1,767
8,000	723.02	676	388.85	1,332	322.40	1,672	278.31	2,019
9,000	813.39	761	437.45	1,499	362.70	1,881	313.10	2,272
10,000	903.77	845	486.06	1,665	403.00	2,090	347.88	2,524
11,000	994.14	930	534.67	1,832	443.30	2,299	382.67	2,776
12,000	1,084.52	1,014	583.27	1,998	483.59	2,508	417.46	3,029
13,000	1,174.90	1,099	631.88	2,165	523.89	2,717	452.25	3,281
14,000	1,265.27	1,183	680.48	2,332	564.19	2,926	487.04	3,533
15,000	1,355.65	1,268	729.09	2,498	604.49	3,135	521.82	3,786
16,000	1,446.03	1,352	777.69	2,665	644.79	3,344	556.61	4,038
17,000	1,536.40	1,437	826.30	2,831	685.09	3,553	591.40	4,290
18,000	1,626.78	1,521	874.90	2,998	725.39	3,762	626.19	4,543
19,000	1,717.16	1,606	923.51	3,164	765.69	3,971	660.97	4,795
20,000	1,807.53	1,690	972.12	3,331	805.99	4,180	695.76	5,047
21,000	1,897.91	1,775	1,020.72	3,497	846.29	4,389	730.55	5,300
22,000	1,988.28	1,859	1,069.33	3,664	886.59	4,598	765.34	5,552
23,000	2,078.66	1,944	1,117.93	3,830	926.88	4,806	800.13	5,805
24,000	2,169.04	2,028	1,166.54	3,997	967.18	5,015	834.91	6,057
25,000	2,259.41	2,113	1,215.14	4,163	1,007.48	5,224	869.70	6,309
26,000	2,349.79	2,197	1,263.75	4,330	1,047.78	5,433	904.49	6,562
27,000	2,440.17	2,282	1,312.35	4,496	1,088.08	5,642	939.28	6,814
28,000	2,530.54	2,366	1,360.96	4,663	1,128.38	5,851	974.07	7,067
29,000	2,620.92	2,451	1,409.56	4,829	1,168.67	6,060	1,008.85	7,319
30,000	2,711.29	2,535	1,458.17	4,996	1,208.98	6,269	1,043.64	7,571
31,000	2,801.67	2,620	1,506.78	5,163	1,249.28	6,478	1,078.43	7,823
32,000	2,892.05	2,705	1,555.38	5,329	1,289.58	6,687	1,113.22	8,076
33,000	2,982.42	2,789	1,603.99	5,496	1,329.88	6,896	1,148.01	8,328
34,000	3,072.80	2,874	1,652.59	5,662	1,370.17	7,105	1,182.79	8,580
35,000	3,163.18	2,958	1,701.20	5,829	1,410.47	7,314	1,217.58	8,833
36,000	3,253.55	3,043	1,749.80	5,995	1,450.77	7,523	1,252.37	9,085
37,000	3,343.93	3,127	1,798.41	6,162	1,491.07	7,732	1,287.16	9,338
38,000	3,434.31	3,212	1,847.01	6,328	1,531.37	7,941	1,321.94	9,590
39,000	3,524.68	3,296	1,895.62	6,495	1,571.67	8,150	1,356.73	9,842
40,000	3,615.06	3,381	1,944.23	6,662	1,611.97	8,359	1,391.52	10,095
42,000	3,795.81	3,550	2,041.44	6,995	1,692.57	8,777	1,461.10	10,600
44,000	3,976.56	3,719	2,138.65	7,328	1,773.17	9,195	1,530.67	11,104
46,000	4,157.32	3,888	2,235.86	7,661	1,853.76	9,613	1,600.25	11,609
48,000	4,338.07	4,057	2,333.07	7,994	1,934.36	10,031	1,669.82	12,114
50,000	4,518.82	4,226	2,430.28	8,327	2,014.96	10,449	1,739.40	12,618

AUTO LOAN PAYMENTS 15.25%

AMOUNT OF LOAN	42 MOS		48 MOS		60 MOS		72 MOS	
	MONTHLY PAYMENT	TOTAL INTRST	MONTHLY PAYMENT	TOTAL INTRST	MONTHLY PAYMENT	TOTAL INTRST	MONTHLY PAYMENT	TOTAL INTRST
$ 1	0.04	1	0.03	0	0.03	1	0.03	1
2	0.07	1	0.06	1	0.05	1	0.05	2
3	0.10	1	0.09	1	0.08	2	0.07	2
4	0.13	1	0.12	2	0.10	2	0.09	2
5	0.16	2	0.14	2	0.12	2	0.11	3
6	0.19	2	0.17	2	0.15	3	0.13	3
7	0.22	2	0.20	3	0.17	3	0.15	4
8	0.25	3	0.23	3	0.20	4	0.18	5
9	0.28	3	0.26	3	0.22	4	0.20	5
10	0.31	3	0.28	3	0.24	4	0.22	6
20	0.62	6	0.56	7	0.48	9	0.43	11
30	0.93	9	0.84	10	0.72	13	0.64	16
40	1.24	12	1.12	14	0.96	18	0.86	22
50	1.55	15	1.40	17	1.20	22	1.07	27
60	1.86	18	1.68	21	1.44	26	1.28	32
70	2.17	21	1.96	24	1.68	31	1.49	37
80	2.47	24	2.24	28	1.92	35	1.71	43
90	2.78	27	2.52	31	2.16	40	1.92	48
100	3.09	30	2.80	34	2.40	44	2.13	53
200	6.18	60	5.60	69	4.79	87	4.26	107
300	9.27	89	8.39	103	7.18	131	6.39	160
400	12.35	119	11.19	137	9.57	174	8.52	213
500	15.44	148	13.98	171	11.97	218	10.65	267
600	18.53	178	16.78	205	14.36	262	12.77	319
700	21.62	208	19.58	240	16.75	305	14.90	373
800	24.70	237	22.37	274	19.14	348	17.03	426
900	27.79	267	25.17	308	21.53	392	19.16	480
1,000	30.88	297	27.96	342	23.93	436	21.29	533
2,000	61.75	594	55.92	684	47.85	871	42.57	1,065
3,000	92.63	890	83.88	1,026	71.77	1,306	63.85	1,597
4,000	123.50	1,187	111.84	1,368	95.69	1,741	85.13	2,129
5,000	154.37	1,484	139.79	1,710	119.61	2,177	106.41	2,662
6,000	185.25	1,781	167.75	2,052	143.53	2,612	127.69	3,194
7,000	216.12	2,077	195.71	2,394	167.45	3,047	148.97	3,726
8,000	246.99	2,374	223.67	2,736	191.38	3,483	170.25	4,258
9,000	277.87	2,671	251.62	3,078	215.30	3,918	191.53	4,790
10,000	308.74	2,967	279.58	3,420	239.22	4,353	212.82	5,323
11,000	339.62	3,264	307.54	3,762	263.14	4,788	234.10	5,855
12,000	370.49	3,561	335.50	4,104	287.06	5,224	255.38	6,387
13,000	401.36	3,857	363.45	4,446	310.98	5,659	276.66	6,920
14,000	432.24	4,154	391.41	4,788	334.90	6,094	297.94	7,452
15,000	463.11	4,451	419.37	5,130	358.83	6,530	319.22	7,984
16,000	493.98	4,747	447.33	5,472	382.75	6,965	340.50	8,516
17,000	524.86	5,044	475.28	5,813	406.67	7,400	361.78	9,048
18,000	555.73	5,341	503.24	6,156	430.59	7,835	383.06	9,580
19,000	586.61	5,638	531.20	6,498	454.51	8,271	404.34	10,112
20,000	617.48	5,934	559.16	6,840	478.43	8,706	425.63	10,645
21,000	648.35	6,231	587.12	7,182	502.35	9,141	446.91	11,178
22,000	679.23	6,528	615.07	7,523	526.27	9,576	468.19	11,710
23,000	710.10	6,824	643.03	7,865	550.20	10,012	489.47	12,242
24,000	740.97	7,121	670.99	8,208	574.12	10,447	510.75	12,774
25,000	771.85	7,418	698.95	8,550	598.04	10,882	532.03	13,306
26,000	802.72	7,714	726.90	8,891	621.96	11,318	553.31	13,838
27,000	833.60	8,011	754.86	9,233	645.88	11,753	574.59	14,370
28,000	864.47	8,308	782.82	9,575	669.80	12,188	595.87	14,903
29,000	895.34	8,604	810.78	9,917	693.72	12,623	617.15	15,435
30,000	926.22	8,901	838.73	10,259	717.65	13,059	638.44	15,968
31,000	957.09	9,198	866.69	10,601	741.57	13,494	659.72	16,500
32,000	987.96	9,494	894.65	10,943	765.49	13,929	681.00	17,032
33,000	1,018.84	9,791	922.61	11,285	789.41	14,365	702.28	17,564
34,000	1,049.71	10,088	950.56	11,627	813.33	14,800	723.56	18,096
35,000	1,080.59	10,385	978.52	11,969	837.25	15,235	744.84	18,628
36,000	1,111.46	10,681	1,006.48	12,311	861.17	15,670	766.12	19,161
37,000	1,142.33	10,978	1,034.44	12,653	885.10	16,106	787.40	19,693
38,000	1,173.21	11,275	1,062.40	12,995	909.02	16,541	808.68	20,225
39,000	1,204.08	11,571	1,090.35	13,337	932.94	16,976	829.96	20,757
40,000	1,234.95	11,868	1,118.31	13,679	956.86	17,412	851.25	21,290
42,000	1,296.70	12,461	1,174.23	14,363	1,004.70	18,282	893.81	22,354
44,000	1,358.45	13,055	1,230.14	15,047	1,052.54	19,152	936.37	23,419
46,000	1,420.20	13,648	1,286.06	15,731	1,100.39	20,023	978.93	24,483
48,000	1,481.94	14,241	1,341.97	16,415	1,148.23	20,894	1,021.49	25,547
50,000	1,543.69	14,835	1,397.89	17,099	1,196.07	21,764	1,064.06	26,612

147

15.50% **AUTO LOAN PAYMENTS**

AMOUNT OF LOAN	12 MOS MONTHLY PAYMENT	12 MOS TOTAL INTRST	24 MOS MONTHLY PAYMENT	24 MOS TOTAL INTRST	30 MOS MONTHLY PAYMENT	30 MOS TOTAL INTRST	36 MOS MONTHLY PAYMENT	36 MOS TOTAL INTRST
$ 1	0.10	0	0.05	0	0.05	1	0.04	0
2	0.19	0	0.10	0	0.09	1	0.07	1
3	0.28	0	0.15	1	0.13	1	0.11	1
4	0.37	0	0.20	1	0.17	1	0.14	1
5	0.46	1	0.25	1	0.21	1	0.18	1
6	0.55	1	0.30	1	0.25	2	0.21	2
7	0.64	1	0.35	1	0.29	2	0.25	2
8	0.73	1	0.39	1	0.33	2	0.28	2
9	0.82	1	0.44	2	0.37	2	0.32	3
10	0.91	1	0.49	2	0.41	2	0.35	3
20	1.81	2	0.98	4	0.81	4	0.70	5
30	2.72	3	1.47	5	1.22	7	1.05	8
40	3.62	3	1.95	7	1.62	9	1.40	10
50	4.53	4	2.44	9	2.03	11	1.75	13
60	5.43	5	2.93	10	2.43	13	2.10	16
70	6.34	6	3.42	12	2.83	15	2.45	18
80	7.24	7	3.90	14	3.24	17	2.80	21
90	8.15	8	4.39	15	3.64	19	3.15	23
100	9.05	9	4.88	17	4.05	22	3.50	26
200	18.10	17	9.75	34	8.09	43	6.99	52
300	27.15	26	14.62	51	12.13	64	10.48	77
400	36.20	34	19.49	68	16.17	85	13.97	103
500	45.25	43	24.37	85	20.21	106	17.46	129
600	54.30	52	29.24	102	24.26	128	20.95	154
700	63.35	60	34.11	119	28.30	149	24.44	180
800	72.40	69	38.98	136	32.34	170	27.93	205
900	81.45	77	43.86	153	36.38	191	31.42	231
1,000	90.50	86	48.73	170	40.42	213	34.92	257
2,000	180.99	172	97.45	339	80.84	425	69.83	514
3,000	271.49	258	146.18	508	121.26	638	104.74	771
4,000	361.98	344	194.90	678	161.68	850	139.65	1,027
5,000	452.48	430	243.63	847	202.10	1,063	174.56	1,284
6,000	542.97	516	292.35	1,016	242.52	1,276	209.47	1,541
7,000	633.47	602	341.08	1,186	282.94	1,488	244.38	1,798
8,000	723.96	688	389.80	1,355	323.36	1,701	279.29	2,054
9,000	814.45	773	438.53	1,525	363.78	1,913	314.20	2,311
10,000	904.95	859	487.25	1,694	404.20	2,126	349.11	2,568
11,000	995.44	945	535.97	1,863	444.62	2,339	384.02	2,825
12,000	1,085.94	1,031	584.70	2,033	485.04	2,551	418.93	3,081
13,000	1,176.43	1,117	633.42	2,202	525.46	2,764	453.84	3,338
14,000	1,266.93	1,203	682.15	2,372	565.88	2,976	488.75	3,595
15,000	1,357.42	1,289	730.87	2,541	606.30	3,189	523.67	3,852
16,000	1,447.92	1,375	779.60	2,710	646.72	3,402	558.58	4,109
17,000	1,538.41	1,461	828.32	2,880	687.14	3,614	593.49	4,366
18,000	1,628.90	1,547	877.05	3,049	727.56	3,827	628.40	4,622
19,000	1,719.40	1,633	925.77	3,218	767.98	4,039	663.31	4,879
20,000	1,809.89	1,719	974.50	3,388	808.40	4,252	698.22	5,136
21,000	1,900.39	1,805	1,023.22	3,557	848.82	4,465	733.13	5,393
22,000	1,990.88	1,891	1,071.94	3,727	889.24	4,677	768.04	5,649
23,000	2,081.38	1,977	1,120.67	3,896	929.66	4,890	802.95	5,906
24,000	2,171.87	2,062	1,169.39	4,065	970.08	5,102	837.86	6,163
25,000	2,262.37	2,148	1,218.12	4,235	1,010.50	5,315	872.77	6,420
26,000	2,352.86	2,234	1,266.84	4,404	1,050.92	5,528	907.68	6,676
27,000	2,443.35	2,320	1,315.57	4,574	1,091.34	5,740	942.59	6,933
28,000	2,533.85	2,406	1,364.29	4,743	1,131.76	5,953	977.50	7,190
29,000	2,624.34	2,492	1,413.02	4,912	1,172.18	6,165	1,012.41	7,447
30,000	2,714.84	2,578	1,461.74	5,082	1,212.60	6,378	1,047.33	7,704
31,000	2,805.33	2,664	1,510.47	5,251	1,253.02	6,591	1,082.24	7,961
32,000	2,895.83	2,750	1,559.19	5,421	1,293.44	6,803	1,117.15	8,217
33,000	2,986.32	2,836	1,607.91	5,590	1,333.86	7,016	1,152.06	8,474
34,000	3,076.82	2,922	1,656.64	5,759	1,374.28	7,228	1,186.97	8,731
35,000	3,167.31	3,008	1,705.36	5,929	1,414.70	7,441	1,221.88	8,988
36,000	3,257.80	3,094	1,754.09	6,098	1,455.12	7,654	1,256.79	9,244
37,000	3,348.30	3,180	1,802.81	6,267	1,495.54	7,866	1,291.70	9,501
38,000	3,438.79	3,265	1,851.54	6,437	1,535.96	8,079	1,326.61	9,758
39,000	3,529.29	3,351	1,900.26	6,606	1,576.38	8,291	1,361.52	10,015
40,000	3,619.78	3,437	1,948.99	6,776	1,616.80	8,504	1,396.43	10,271
42,000	3,800.77	3,609	2,046.44	7,115	1,697.64	8,929	1,466.25	10,785
44,000	3,981.76	3,781	2,143.88	7,453	1,778.48	9,354	1,536.07	11,299
46,000	4,162.75	3,953	2,241.33	7,792	1,859.32	9,780	1,605.90	11,812
48,000	4,343.74	4,125	2,338.78	8,131	1,940.16	10,205	1,675.72	12,326
50,000	4,524.73	4,297	2,436.23	8,470	2,021.00	10,630	1,745.54	12,839

AUTO LOAN PAYMENTS
15.50%

AMOUNT OF LOAN	42 MOS MONTHLY PAYMENT	42 MOS TOTAL INTRST	48 MOS MONTHLY PAYMENT	48 MOS TOTAL INTRST	60 MOS MONTHLY PAYMENT	60 MOS TOTAL INTRST	72 MOS MONTHLY PAYMENT	72 MOS TOTAL INTRST
$ 1	0.04	1	0.03	0	0.03	1	0.03	1
2	0.07	1	0.06	1	0.05	1	0.05	2
3	0.10	1	0.09	1	0.08	2	0.07	2
4	0.13	1	0.12	2	0.10	2	0.09	2
5	0.16	2	0.15	2	0.13	3	0.11	3
6	0.19	2	0.17	2	0.15	3	0.13	3
7	0.22	2	0.20	3	0.17	3	0.15	4
8	0.25	3	0.23	3	0.20	4	0.18	5
9	0.28	3	0.26	3	0.22	4	0.20	5
10	0.31	3	0.29	4	0.25	5	0.22	6
20	0.62	6	0.57	7	0.49	9	0.43	11
30	0.93	9	0.85	11	0.73	14	0.65	17
40	1.24	12	1.13	14	0.97	18	0.86	22
50	1.55	15	1.41	18	1.21	23	1.08	28
60	1.86	18	1.69	21	1.45	27	1.29	33
70	2.17	21	1.97	25	1.69	31	1.50	38
80	2.48	24	2.25	28	1.93	36	1.72	44
90	2.79	27	2.53	31	2.17	40	1.93	49
100	3.10	30	2.81	35	2.41	45	2.15	55
200	6.20	60	5.62	70	4.82	89	4.29	109
300	9.30	91	8.43	105	7.22	133	6.43	163
400	12.40	121	11.24	140	9.63	178	8.57	217
500	15.50	151	14.05	174	12.03	222	10.71	271
600	18.60	181	16.86	209	14.44	266	12.86	326
700	21.70	211	19.66	244	16.84	310	15.00	380
800	24.80	242	22.47	279	19.25	355	17.14	434
900	27.90	272	25.28	313	21.65	399	19.28	488
1,000	31.00	302	28.09	348	24.06	444	21.42	542
2,000	62.00	604	56.17	696	48.11	887	42.84	1,084
3,000	93.00	906	84.26	1,044	72.16	1,330	64.26	1,627
4,000	124.00	1,208	112.34	1,392	96.22	1,773	85.67	2,168
5,000	155.00	1,510	140.43	1,741	120.27	2,216	107.09	2,710
6,000	186.00	1,812	168.51	2,088	144.32	2,659	128.51	3,253
7,000	217.00	2,114	196.60	2,437	168.38	3,103	149.93	3,795
8,000	247.99	2,416	224.68	2,785	192.43	3,546	171.34	4,336
9,000	278.99	2,718	252.77	3,133	216.48	3,989	192.76	4,879
10,000	309.99	3,020	280.85	3,481	240.54	4,432	214.18	5,421
11,000	340.99	3,322	308.94	3,829	264.59	4,875	235.60	5,963
12,000	371.99	3,624	337.02	4,177	288.64	5,318	257.01	6,505
13,000	402.99	3,926	365.11	4,525	312.70	5,762	278.43	7,047
14,000	433.98	4,228	393.19	4,873	336.75	6,205	299.85	7,589
15,000	464.99	4,530	421.28	5,221	360.80	6,648	321.27	8,131
16,000	495.98	4,831	449.36	5,569	384.86	7,092	342.68	8,673
17,000	526.98	5,133	477.45	5,918	408.91	7,535	364.10	9,215
18,000	557.98	5,435	505.53	6,265	432.97	7,978	385.52	9,757
19,000	588.98	5,737	533.62	6,614	457.02	8,421	406.94	10,300
20,000	619.98	6,039	561.70	6,962	481.07	8,864	428.35	10,841
21,000	650.98	6,341	589.79	7,310	505.12	9,307	449.77	11,383
22,000	681.98	6,643	617.87	7,658	529.18	9,751	471.19	11,926
23,000	712.98	6,945	645.96	8,006	553.23	10,194	492.61	12,468
24,000	743.97	7,247	674.04	8,354	577.28	10,637	514.02	13,009
25,000	774.97	7,549	702.13	8,702	601.33	11,080	535.44	13,552
26,000	805.97	7,851	730.21	9,050	625.39	11,523	556.86	14,094
27,000	836.97	8,153	758.30	9,398	649.44	11,966	578.28	14,636
28,000	867.97	8,455	786.38	9,746	673.49	12,409	599.69	15,178
29,000	898.97	8,757	814.47	10,095	697.55	12,853	621.11	15,720
30,000	929.97	9,059	842.55	10,443	721.60	13,296	642.53	16,262
31,000	960.96	9,360	870.64	10,791	745.65	13,739	663.95	16,804
32,000	991.96	9,662	898.72	11,139	769.71	14,183	685.36	17,346
33,000	1,022.96	9,964	926.81	11,487	793.76	14,626	706.78	17,888
34,000	1,053.96	10,266	954.89	11,835	817.81	15,069	728.20	18,430
35,000	1,084.96	10,568	982.98	12,183	841.87	15,512	749.62	18,973
36,000	1,115.96	10,870	1,011.06	12,531	865.92	15,955	771.03	19,514
37,000	1,146.96	11,172	1,039.14	12,879	889.97	16,398	792.45	20,056
38,000	1,177.96	11,474	1,067.23	13,227	914.03	16,842	813.87	20,599
39,000	1,208.95	11,776	1,095.31	13,575	938.08	17,285	835.29	21,141
40,000	1,239.95	12,078	1,123.40	13,923	962.13	17,728	856.70	21,682
42,000	1,301.95	12,682	1,179.57	14,619	1,010.24	18,614	899.54	22,767
44,000	1,363.95	13,286	1,235.74	15,316	1,058.35	19,501	942.37	23,851
46,000	1,425.95	13,890	1,291.91	16,012	1,106.45	20,387	985.21	24,935
48,000	1,487.94	14,493	1,348.08	16,708	1,154.56	21,274	1,028.04	26,019
50,000	1,549.94	15,097	1,404.25	17,404	1,202.66	22,160	1,070.88	27,103

149

AUTO LOAN PAYMENTS

AMOUNT OF LOAN	12 MOS		24 MOS		30 MOS		36 MOS	
	MONTHLY PAYMENT	TOTAL INTRST	MONTHLY PAYMENT	TOTAL INTRST	MONTHLY PAYMENT	TOTAL INTRST	MONTHLY PAYMENT	TOTAL INTRST
$ 1	0.10	0	0.05	0	0.05	1	0.04	0
2	0.19	0	0.10	0	0.09	1	0.08	1
3	0.28	0	0.15	1	0.13	1	0.11	1
4	0.37	0	0.20	1	0.17	1	0.15	1
5	0.46	1	0.25	1	0.21	1	0.18	1
6	0.55	1	0.30	1	0.25	2	0.22	2
7	0.64	1	0.35	1	0.29	2	0.25	2
8	0.73	1	0.40	2	0.33	2	0.29	2
9	0.82	1	0.44	2	0.37	2	0.32	3
10	0.91	1	0.49	2	0.41	2	0.36	3
20	1.82	2	0.98	4	0.82	5	0.71	6
30	2.72	3	1.47	5	1.22	7	1.06	8
40	3.63	4	1.96	7	1.63	9	1.41	11
50	4.54	4	2.45	9	2.03	11	1.76	13
60	5.44	5	2.94	11	2.44	13	2.11	16
70	6.35	6	3.42	12	2.84	15	2.46	19
80	7.25	7	3.91	14	3.25	18	2.81	21
90	8.16	8	4.40	16	3.65	20	3.16	24
100	9.07	9	4.89	17	4.06	22	3.51	26
200	18.13	18	9.77	34	8.11	43	7.01	52
300	27.19	26	14.66	52	12.17	65	10.52	79
400	36.25	35	19.54	69	16.22	87	14.02	105
500	45.31	44	24.43	86	20.28	108	17.52	131
600	54.37	52	29.31	103	24.33	130	21.03	157
700	63.43	61	34.20	121	28.38	151	24.53	183
800	72.50	70	39.08	138	32.44	173	28.03	209
900	81.56	79	43.96	155	36.49	195	31.54	235
1,000	90.62	87	48.85	172	40.55	217	35.04	261
2,000	181.23	175	97.69	345	81.09	433	70.07	523
3,000	271.84	262	146.54	517	121.63	649	105.11	784
4,000	362.46	350	195.38	689	162.17	865	140.14	1,045
5,000	453.07	437	244.22	861	202.71	1,081	175.17	1,306
6,000	543.68	524	293.07	1,034	243.25	1,298	210.21	1,568
7,000	634.29	611	341.91	1,206	283.79	1,514	245.24	1,829
8,000	724.91	699	390.75	1,378	324.33	1,730	280.27	2,090
9,000	815.52	786	439.60	1,550	364.87	1,946	315.31	2,351
10,000	906.13	874	488.44	1,723	405.41	2,162	350.34	2,612
11,000	996.74	961	537.29	1,895	445.95	2,379	385.38	2,874
12,000	1,087.36	1,048	586.13	2,067	486.50	2,595	420.41	3,135
13,000	1,177.97	1,136	634.97	2,239	527.04	2,811	455.44	3,396
14,000	1,268.58	1,223	683.82	2,412	567.58	3,027	490.48	3,657
15,000	1,359.19	1,310	732.66	2,584	608.12	3,244	525.51	3,918
16,000	1,449.81	1,398	781.50	2,756	648.66	3,460	560.54	4,179
17,000	1,540.42	1,485	830.35	2,928	689.20	3,676	595.58	4,441
18,000	1,631.03	1,572	879.19	3,101	729.74	3,892	630.61	4,702
19,000	1,721.64	1,660	928.04	3,273	770.28	4,108	665.65	4,963
20,000	1,812.26	1,747	976.88	3,445	810.82	4,325	700.68	5,224
21,000	1,902.87	1,834	1,025.72	3,617	851.36	4,541	735.71	5,486
22,000	1,993.48	1,922	1,074.57	3,790	891.90	4,757	770.75	5,747
23,000	2,084.09	2,009	1,123.41	3,962	932.45	4,974	805.78	6,008
24,000	2,174.71	2,097	1,172.25	4,134	972.99	5,190	840.81	6,269
25,000	2,265.32	2,184	1,221.10	4,306	1,013.53	5,406	875.85	6,531
26,000	2,355.93	2,271	1,269.94	4,479	1,054.07	5,622	910.88	6,792
27,000	2,446.55	2,359	1,318.79	4,651	1,094.61	5,838	945.92	7,053
28,000	2,537.16	2,446	1,367.63	4,823	1,135.15	6,055	980.95	7,314
29,000	2,627.77	2,533	1,416.47	4,995	1,175.69	6,271	1,015.98	7,575
30,000	2,718.38	2,621	1,465.32	5,168	1,216.23	6,487	1,051.02	7,837
31,000	2,809.00	2,708	1,514.16	5,340	1,256.77	6,703	1,086.05	8,098
32,000	2,899.61	2,795	1,563.00	5,512	1,297.31	6,919	1,121.08	8,359
33,000	2,990.22	2,883	1,611.85	5,684	1,337.85	7,136	1,156.12	8,620
34,000	3,080.83	2,970	1,660.69	5,857	1,378.40	7,352	1,191.15	8,881
35,000	3,171.45	3,057	1,709.54	6,029	1,418.94	7,568	1,226.19	9,143
36,000	3,262.06	3,145	1,758.38	6,201	1,459.48	7,784	1,261.22	9,404
37,000	3,352.67	3,232	1,807.22	6,373	1,500.02	8,001	1,296.25	9,665
38,000	3,443.28	3,319	1,856.07	6,546	1,540.56	8,217	1,331.29	9,926
39,000	3,533.90	3,407	1,904.91	6,718	1,581.10	8,433	1,366.32	10,188
40,000	3,624.51	3,494	1,953.75	6,890	1,621.64	8,649	1,401.35	10,449
42,000	3,805.73	3,669	2,051.44	7,235	1,702.72	9,082	1,471.42	10,971
44,000	3,986.96	3,844	2,149.13	7,579	1,783.80	9,514	1,541.49	11,494
46,000	4,168.18	4,018	2,246.82	7,924	1,864.89	9,947	1,611.56	12,016
48,000	4,349.41	4,193	2,344.50	8,268	1,945.97	10,379	1,681.62	12,538
50,000	4,530.63	4,368	2,442.19	8,613	2,027.05	10,812	1,751.69	13,061

AUTO LOAN PAYMENTS 15.75%

AMOUNT OF LOAN	42 MOS MONTHLY PAYMENT	TOTAL INTRST	48 MOS MONTHLY PAYMENT	TOTAL INTRST	60 MOS MONTHLY PAYMENT	TOTAL INTRST	72 MOS MONTHLY PAYMENT	TOTAL INTRST
$ 1	0.04	1	0.03	0	0.03	1	0.03	1
2	0.07	1	0.06	1	0.05	1	0.05	2
3	0.10	1	0.09	1	0.08	2	0.07	2
4	0.13	1	0.12	2	0.10	2	0.09	3
5	0.16	2	0.15	2	0.13	3	0.11	3
6	0.19	2	0.17	2	0.15	3	0.13	3
7	0.22	2	0.20	3	0.17	3	0.16	5
8	0.25	3	0.23	3	0.20	4	0.18	5
9	0.29	3	0.26	3	0.22	4	0.20	5
10	0.32	3	0.29	4	0.25	5	0.22	6
20	0.63	6	0.57	7	0.49	9	0.44	12
30	0.94	9	0.85	11	0.73	14	0.65	17
40	1.25	13	1.13	14	0.97	18	0.87	23
50	1.56	16	1.42	18	1.21	23	1.08	28
60	1.87	19	1.70	22	1.46	28	1.30	34
70	2.18	22	1.98	25	1.70	32	1.51	39
80	2.49	25	2.26	28	1.94	36	1.73	45
90	2.81	28	2.54	32	2.18	41	1.94	50
100	3.12	31	2.83	36	2.42	45	2.16	56
200	6.23	62	5.65	71	4.84	90	4.32	111
300	9.34	92	8.47	107	7.26	136	6.47	166
400	12.45	123	11.29	142	9.68	181	8.63	221
500	15.57	154	14.11	177	12.10	226	10.78	276
600	18.68	185	16.93	213	14.52	271	12.94	332
700	21.79	215	19.75	248	16.93	316	15.09	386
800	24.90	246	22.57	283	19.35	361	17.25	442
900	28.02	277	25.40	319	21.77	406	19.40	497
1,000	31.13	307	28.22	355	24.19	451	21.56	552
2,000	62.25	615	56.43	709	48.38	903	43.11	1,104
3,000	93.38	922	84.64	1,063	72.56	1,354	64.67	1,656
4,000	124.50	1,229	112.85	1,417	96.75	1,805	86.22	2,208
5,000	155.62	1,536	141.07	1,771	120.93	2,256	107.78	2,760
6,000	186.75	1,844	169.28	2,125	145.12	2,707	129.33	3,312
7,000	217.87	2,151	197.49	2,480	169.30	3,158	150.89	3,864
8,000	249.00	2,458	225.70	2,834	193.49	3,609	172.44	4,416
9,000	280.12	2,765	253.92	3,188	217.67	4,060	193.99	4,967
10,000	311.24	3,072	282.13	3,542	241.86	4,512	215.55	5,520
11,000	342.37	3,380	310.34	3,896	266.04	4,962	237.10	6,071
12,000	373.49	3,687	338.55	4,250	290.23	5,414	258.66	6,624
13,000	404.62	3,994	366.77	4,605	314.42	5,865	280.21	7,175
14,000	435.74	4,301	394.98	4,959	338.60	6,316	301.77	7,727
15,000	466.86	4,608	423.19	5,313	362.79	6,767	323.32	8,279
16,000	497.99	4,916	451.40	5,667	386.97	7,218	344.88	8,831
17,000	529.11	5,223	479.62	6,022	411.16	7,670	366.43	9,383
18,000	560.24	5,530	507.83	6,376	435.34	8,120	387.98	9,935
19,000	591.36	5,837	536.04	6,730	459.53	8,572	409.54	10,487
20,000	622.48	6,144	564.25	7,084	483.71	9,023	431.09	11,038
21,000	653.61	6,452	592.47	7,439	507.90	9,474	452.65	11,591
22,000	684.73	6,759	620.68	7,793	532.08	9,925	474.20	12,142
23,000	715.86	7,066	648.89	8,147	556.27	10,376	495.76	12,695
24,000	746.98	7,373	677.10	8,501	580.46	10,828	517.31	13,246
25,000	778.10	7,680	705.32	8,855	604.64	11,278	538.87	13,799
26,000	809.23	7,988	733.53	9,209	628.83	11,730	560.42	14,350
27,000	840.35	8,295	761.74	9,564	653.01	12,181	581.97	14,902
28,000	871.48	8,602	789.95	9,918	677.20	12,632	603.53	15,454
29,000	902.60	8,909	818.16	10,272	701.38	13,083	625.08	16,006
30,000	933.72	9,216	846.38	10,626	725.57	13,534	646.64	16,558
31,000	964.85	9,524	874.59	10,980	749.75	13,985	668.19	17,110
32,000	995.97	9,831	902.80	11,334	773.94	14,436	689.75	17,662
33,000	1,027.10	10,138	931.01	11,688	798.12	14,887	711.30	18,214
34,000	1,058.22	10,445	959.23	12,043	822.31	15,339	732.86	18,766
35,000	1,089.34	10,752	987.44	12,397	846.49	15,789	754.41	19,318
36,000	1,120.47	11,060	1,015.65	12,751	870.68	16,241	775.96	19,869
37,000	1,151.59	11,367	1,043.86	13,105	894.87	16,692	797.52	20,421
38,000	1,182.72	11,674	1,072.08	13,460	919.05	17,143	819.07	20,973
39,000	1,213.84	11,981	1,100.29	13,814	943.24	17,594	840.63	21,525
40,000	1,244.96	12,288	1,128.50	14,168	967.42	18,045	862.18	22,077
42,000	1,307.21	12,903	1,184.93	14,877	1,015.79	18,947	905.29	23,181
44,000	1,369.46	13,517	1,241.35	15,585	1,064.16	19,850	948.40	24,285
46,000	1,431.71	14,132	1,297.78	16,293	1,112.53	20,752	991.51	25,389
48,000	1,493.96	14,746	1,354.20	17,002	1,160.91	21,655	1,034.62	26,493
50,000	1,556.20	15,360	1,410.63	17,710	1,209.28	22,557	1,077.73	27,597

16.00%	AUTO LOAN PAYMENTS							

16.00% — **AUTO LOAN PAYMENTS**

AMOUNT OF LOAN	12 MOS		24 MOS		30 MOS		36 MOS	
	MONTHLY PAYMENT	TOTAL INTRST	MONTHLY PAYMENT	TOTAL INTRST	MONTHLY PAYMENT	TOTAL INTRST	MONTHLY PAYMENT	TOTAL INTRST
$ 1	0.10	0	0.05	0	0.05	1	0.04	0
2	0.19	0	0.10	0	0.09	1	0.08	1
3	0.28	0	0.15	1	0.13	1	0.11	1
4	0.37	0	0.20	1	0.17	1	0.15	1
5	0.46	1	0.25	1	0.21	1	0.18	1
6	0.55	1	0.30	1	0.25	2	0.22	2
7	0.64	1	0.35	1	0.29	2	0.25	2
8	0.73	1	0.40	2	0.33	2	0.29	2
9	0.82	1	0.45	2	0.37	2	0.32	3
10	0.91	1	0.49	2	0.41	2	0.36	3
20	1.82	2	0.98	4	0.82	5	0.71	6
30	2.73	3	1.47	5	1.22	7	1.06	8
40	3.63	4	1.96	7	1.63	9	1.41	11
50	4.54	4	2.45	9	2.04	11	1.76	13
60	5.45	5	2.94	11	2.44	13	2.11	16
70	6.36	6	3.43	12	2.85	16	2.47	19
80	7.26	7	3.92	14	3.26	18	2.82	22
90	8.17	8	4.41	16	3.66	20	3.17	24
100	9.08	9	4.90	18	4.07	22	3.52	27
200	18.15	18	9.80	35	8.14	44	7.04	53
300	27.22	27	14.69	53	12.20	66	10.55	80
400	36.30	36	19.59	70	16.27	88	14.07	107
500	45.37	44	24.49	88	20.34	110	17.58	133
600	54.44	53	29.38	105	24.40	132	21.10	160
700	63.52	62	34.28	123	28.47	154	24.61	186
800	72.59	71	39.18	140	32.53	176	28.13	213
900	81.66	80	44.07	158	36.60	198	31.65	239
1,000	90.74	89	48.97	175	40.67	220	35.16	266
2,000	181.47	178	97.93	350	81.33	440	70.32	532
3,000	272.20	266	146.89	525	121.99	660	105.48	797
4,000	362.93	355	195.86	701	162.65	880	140.63	1,063
5,000	453.66	444	244.82	876	203.32	1,100	175.79	1,328
6,000	544.39	533	293.78	1,051	243.98	1,319	210.95	1,594
7,000	635.12	621	342.75	1,226	284.64	1,539	246.10	1,860
8,000	725.85	710	391.71	1,401	325.30	1,759	281.26	2,125
9,000	816.58	799	440.67	1,576	365.96	1,979	316.42	2,391
10,000	907.31	888	489.64	1,751	406.63	2,199	351.58	2,657
11,000	998.04	976	538.60	1,926	447.29	2,419	386.73	2,922
12,000	1,088.78	1,065	587.56	2,101	487.95	2,639	421.89	3,188
13,000	1,179.51	1,154	636.53	2,277	528.61	2,858	457.05	3,454
14,000	1,270.24	1,243	685.49	2,452	569.27	3,078	492.20	3,719
15,000	1,360.97	1,332	734.45	2,627	609.94	3,298	527.36	3,985
16,000	1,451.70	1,420	783.41	2,802	650.60	3,518	562.52	4,251
17,000	1,542.43	1,509	832.38	2,977	691.26	3,738	597.67	4,516
18,000	1,633.16	1,598	881.34	3,152	731.92	3,958	632.83	4,782
19,000	1,723.89	1,687	930.30	3,327	772.58	4,177	667.99	5,048
20,000	1,814.62	1,775	979.27	3,502	813.25	4,398	703.15	5,313
21,000	1,905.35	1,864	1,028.23	3,678	853.91	4,617	738.30	5,579
22,000	1,996.08	1,953	1,077.19	3,853	894.57	4,837	773.46	5,845
23,000	2,086.81	2,042	1,126.16	4,028	935.23	5,057	808.62	6,110
24,000	2,177.55	2,131	1,175.12	4,203	975.89	5,277	843.77	6,376
25,000	2,268.28	2,219	1,224.08	4,378	1,016.56	5,497	878.93	6,641
26,000	2,359.01	2,308	1,273.04	4,553	1,057.22	5,717	914.09	6,907
27,000	2,449.74	2,397	1,322.01	4,728	1,097.88	5,936	949.24	7,173
28,000	2,540.47	2,486	1,370.97	4,903	1,138.54	6,156	984.40	7,438
29,000	2,631.20	2,574	1,419.94	5,079	1,179.21	6,376	1,019.56	7,704
30,000	2,721.93	2,663	1,468.90	5,254	1,219.87	6,596	1,054.72	7,970
31,000	2,812.66	2,752	1,517.86	5,429	1,260.53	6,816	1,089.87	8,235
32,000	2,903.39	2,841	1,566.82	5,604	1,301.19	7,036	1,125.03	8,501
33,000	2,994.12	2,929	1,615.79	5,779	1,341.85	7,256	1,160.19	8,767
34,000	3,084.85	3,018	1,664.75	5,954	1,382.52	7,476	1,195.34	9,032
35,000	3,175.59	3,107	1,713.71	6,129	1,423.18	7,695	1,230.50	9,298
36,000	3,266.32	3,196	1,762.68	6,304	1,463.84	7,915	1,265.66	9,564
37,000	3,357.05	3,285	1,811.64	6,479	1,504.50	8,135	1,300.82	9,830
38,000	3,447.78	3,373	1,860.60	6,654	1,545.16	8,355	1,335.97	10,095
39,000	3,538.51	3,462	1,909.57	6,830	1,585.83	8,575	1,371.13	10,361
40,000	3,629.24	3,551	1,958.53	7,005	1,626.49	8,795	1,406.29	10,626
42,000	3,810.70	3,728	2,056.46	7,355	1,707.81	9,234	1,476.60	11,158
44,000	3,992.16	3,906	2,154.38	7,705	1,789.14	9,674	1,546.91	11,689
46,000	4,173.62	4,083	2,252.31	8,055	1,870.46	10,114	1,617.23	12,220
48,000	4,355.09	4,261	2,350.23	8,406	1,951.78	10,553	1,687.54	12,751
50,000	4,536.55	4,439	2,448.16	8,756	2,033.11	10,993	1,757.86	13,283

AUTO LOAN PAYMENTS 16.00%

AMOUNT OF LOAN	42 MOS		48 MOS		60 MOS		72 MOS	
	MONTHLY PAYMENT	TOTAL INTRST	MONTHLY PAYMENT	TOTAL INTRST	MONTHLY PAYMENT	TOTAL INTRST	MONTHLY PAYMENT	TOTAL INTRST
$ 1	0.04	1	0.03	0	0.03	1	0.03	1
2	0.07	1	0.06	1	0.05	1	0.05	2
3	0.10	1	0.09	1	0.08	2	0.07	2
4	0.13	1	0.12	2	0.10	2	0.09	3
5	0.16	2	0.15	2	0.13	3	0.11	3
6	0.19	2	0.18	3	0.15	3	0.14	4
7	0.22	2	0.20	3	0.18	4	0.16	5
8	0.25	3	0.23	3	0.20	4	0.18	5
9	0.29	3	0.26	3	0.22	4	0.20	5
10	0.32	3	0.29	4	0.25	5	0.22	6
20	0.63	6	0.57	7	0.49	9	0.44	12
30	0.94	9	0.86	11	0.73	14	0.66	18
40	1.25	13	1.14	15	0.98	19	0.87	23
50	1.57	16	1.42	18	1.22	23	1.09	28
60	1.88	19	1.71	22	1.46	28	1.31	34
70	2.19	22	1.99	26	1.71	33	1.52	39
80	2.50	25	2.27	29	1.95	37	1.74	45
90	2.82	28	2.56	33	2.19	41	1.96	51
100	3.13	31	2.84	36	2.44	46	2.17	56
200	6.25	63	5.67	72	4.87	92	4.34	112
300	9.38	94	8.51	108	7.30	138	6.51	169
400	12.50	125	11.34	144	9.73	184	8.68	225
500	15.63	156	14.18	181	12.16	230	10.85	281
600	18.75	188	17.01	216	14.60	276	13.02	337
700	21.88	219	19.84	252	17.03	322	15.19	394
800	25.00	250	22.68	289	19.46	368	17.36	450
900	28.13	281	25.51	324	21.89	413	19.53	506
1,000	31.25	313	28.35	361	24.32	459	21.70	562
2,000	62.50	625	56.69	721	48.64	918	43.39	1,124
3,000	93.75	938	85.03	1,081	72.96	1,378	65.08	1,686
4,000	125.00	1,250	113.37	1,442	97.28	1,837	86.77	2,247
5,000	156.25	1,563	141.71	1,802	121.60	2,296	108.46	2,809
6,000	187.50	1,875	170.05	2,162	145.91	2,755	130.16	3,372
7,000	218.75	2,188	198.39	2,523	170.23	3,214	151.85	3,933
8,000	250.00	2,500	226.73	2,883	194.55	3,674	173.54	4,495
9,000	281.25	2,813	255.07	3,243	218.87	4,132	195.23	5,057
10,000	312.50	3,125	283.41	3,604	243.19	4,591	216.92	5,618
11,000	343.75	3,438	311.75	3,964	267.50	5,050	238.62	6,181
12,000	375.00	3,750	340.09	4,324	291.82	5,509	260.31	6,742
13,000	406.25	4,063	368.43	4,685	316.14	5,968	282.00	7,304
14,000	437.50	4,375	396.77	5,045	340.46	6,428	303.69	7,866
15,000	468.75	4,688	425.11	5,405	364.78	6,887	325.38	8,427
16,000	500.00	5,000	453.45	5,766	389.09	7,345	347.07	8,989
17,000	531.25	5,313	481.79	6,126	413.41	7,805	368.77	9,551
18,000	562.50	5,625	510.13	6,486	437.73	8,264	390.46	10,113
19,000	593.75	5,938	538.47	6,847	462.05	8,723	412.15	10,675
20,000	625.00	6,250	566.81	7,207	486.37	9,182	433.84	11,236
21,000	656.24	6,562	595.15	7,567	510.68	9,641	455.53	11,798
22,000	687.49	6,875	623.49	7,928	535.00	10,100	477.23	12,361
23,000	718.74	7,187	651.83	8,288	559.32	10,559	498.92	12,922
24,000	749.99	7,500	680.17	8,648	583.64	11,018	520.61	13,484
25,000	781.24	7,812	708.51	9,008	607.96	11,478	542.30	14,046
26,000	812.49	8,125	736.85	9,369	632.27	11,936	563.99	14,607
27,000	843.74	8,437	765.19	9,729	656.59	12,395	585.68	15,169
28,000	874.99	8,750	793.53	10,089	680.91	12,855	607.38	15,731
29,000	906.24	9,062	821.87	10,450	705.23	13,314	629.07	16,293
30,000	937.49	9,375	850.21	10,810	729.55	13,773	650.76	16,855
31,000	968.74	9,687	878.55	11,170	753.86	14,232	672.45	17,416
32,000	999.99	10,000	906.89	11,531	778.18	14,691	694.14	17,978
33,000	1,031.24	10,312	935.23	11,891	802.50	15,150	715.84	18,540
34,000	1,062.49	10,625	963.57	12,251	826.82	15,609	737.53	19,102
35,000	1,093.74	10,937	991.91	12,612	851.14	16,068	759.22	19,664
36,000	1,124.99	11,250	1,020.26	12,972	875.46	16,528	780.91	20,226
37,000	1,156.24	11,562	1,048.60	13,333	899.77	16,986	802.60	20,787
38,000	1,187.49	11,875	1,076.94	13,693	924.09	17,445	824.29	21,349
39,000	1,218.74	12,187	1,105.28	14,053	948.41	17,905	845.99	21,911
40,000	1,249.99	12,500	1,133.62	14,414	972.73	18,364	867.68	22,473
42,000	1,312.48	13,124	1,190.30	15,134	1,021.36	19,282	911.06	23,596
44,000	1,374.98	13,749	1,246.98	15,855	1,070.00	20,200	954.45	24,720
46,000	1,437.48	14,374	1,303.66	16,575	1,118.64	21,118	997.83	25,844
48,000	1,499.98	14,999	1,360.34	17,296	1,167.27	22,036	1,041.21	26,967
50,000	1,562.48	15,624	1,417.02	18,017	1,215.91	22,955	1,084.60	28,091

153

AUTO LOAN PAYMENTS

AMOUNT OF LOAN	12 MOS		24 MOS		30 MOS		36 MOS	
	MONTHLY PAYMENT	TOTAL INTRST	MONTHLY PAYMENT	TOTAL INTRST	MONTHLY PAYMENT	TOTAL INTRST	MONTHLY PAYMENT	TOTAL INTRST
$ 1	0.10	0	0.05	0	0.05	1	0.04	0
2	0.19	0	0.10	0	0.09	1	0.08	1
3	0.28	0	0.15	1	0.13	1	0.11	1
4	0.37	0	0.20	1	0.17	1	0.15	1
5	0.46	1	0.25	1	0.21	1	0.18	1
6	0.55	1	0.30	1	0.25	2	0.22	2
7	0.64	1	0.35	1	0.29	2	0.25	2
8	0.73	1	0.40	2	0.33	2	0.29	2
9	0.82	1	0.45	2	0.37	2	0.32	3
10	0.91	1	0.50	2	0.41	2	0.36	3
20	1.82	2	0.99	4	0.82	5	0.71	6
30	2.73	3	1.48	6	1.23	7	1.06	8
40	3.64	4	1.97	7	1.64	9	1.42	11
50	4.55	5	2.46	9	2.04	11	1.77	14
60	5.46	6	2.95	11	2.45	14	2.12	16
70	6.36	6	3.44	13	2.86	16	2.47	19
80	7.27	7	3.93	14	3.27	18	2.83	22
90	8.18	8	4.42	16	3.68	20	3.18	24
100	9.09	9	4.91	18	4.08	22	3.53	27
200	18.17	18	9.82	36	8.16	45	7.06	54
300	27.26	27	14.73	54	12.24	67	10.59	81
400	36.34	36	19.64	71	16.32	90	14.12	108
500	45.43	45	24.55	89	20.40	112	17.65	135
600	54.51	54	29.45	107	24.48	134	21.17	162
700	63.60	63	34.36	125	28.55	157	24.70	189
800	72.68	72	39.27	142	32.63	179	28.23	216
900	81.77	81	44.18	160	36.71	201	31.76	243
1,000	90.85	90	49.09	178	40.79	224	35.29	270
2,000	181.70	180	98.17	356	81.57	447	70.57	541
3,000	272.55	271	147.25	534	122.36	671	105.85	811
4,000	363.40	361	196.34	712	163.14	894	141.13	1,081
5,000	454.25	451	245.42	890	203.92	1,118	176.41	1,351
6,000	545.10	541	294.50	1,068	244.71	1,341	211.69	1,621
7,000	635.95	631	343.58	1,246	285.49	1,565	246.97	1,891
8,000	726.80	722	392.67	1,424	326.27	1,788	282.25	2,161
9,000	817.65	812	441.75	1,602	367.06	2,012	317.53	2,431
10,000	908.50	902	490.83	1,780	407.84	2,235	352.81	2,701
11,000	999.35	992	539.91	1,958	448.62	2,459	388.09	2,971
12,000	1,090.20	1,082	589.00	2,136	489.41	2,682	423.37	3,241
13,000	1,181.04	1,172	638.08	2,314	530.19	2,906	458.65	3,511
14,000	1,271.89	1,263	687.16	2,492	570.97	3,129	493.93	3,781
15,000	1,362.74	1,353	736.24	2,670	611.76	3,353	529.21	4,052
16,000	1,453.59	1,443	785.33	2,848	652.54	3,576	564.49	4,322
17,000	1,544.44	1,533	834.41	3,026	693.32	3,800	599.77	4,592
18,000	1,635.29	1,623	883.49	3,204	734.11	4,023	635.06	4,862
19,000	1,726.14	1,714	932.58	3,382	774.89	4,247	670.34	5,132
20,000	1,816.99	1,804	981.66	3,560	815.67	4,470	705.62	5,402
21,000	1,907.84	1,894	1,030.74	3,738	856.46	4,694	740.90	5,672
22,000	1,998.69	1,984	1,079.82	3,916	897.24	4,917	776.18	5,942
23,000	2,089.54	2,074	1,128.91	4,094	938.03	5,141	811.46	6,213
24,000	2,180.39	2,165	1,177.99	4,272	978.81	5,364	846.74	6,483
25,000	2,271.24	2,255	1,227.07	4,450	1,019.59	5,588	882.02	6,753
26,000	2,362.08	2,345	1,276.15	4,628	1,060.38	5,811	917.30	7,023
27,000	2,452.93	2,435	1,325.24	4,806	1,101.16	6,035	952.58	7,293
28,000	2,543.78	2,525	1,374.32	4,984	1,141.94	6,258	987.86	7,563
29,000	2,634.63	2,616	1,423.40	5,162	1,182.73	6,482	1,023.14	7,833
30,000	2,725.48	2,706	1,472.48	5,340	1,223.51	6,705	1,058.42	8,103
31,000	2,816.33	2,796	1,521.57	5,518	1,264.29	6,929	1,093.70	8,373
32,000	2,907.18	2,886	1,570.65	5,696	1,305.08	7,152	1,128.98	8,643
33,000	2,998.03	2,976	1,619.73	5,874	1,345.86	7,376	1,164.26	8,913
34,000	3,088.88	3,067	1,668.81	6,051	1,386.64	7,599	1,199.54	9,183
35,000	3,179.73	3,157	1,717.90	6,230	1,427.43	7,823	1,234.83	9,454
36,000	3,270.58	3,247	1,766.98	6,408	1,468.21	8,046	1,270.11	9,724
37,000	3,361.43	3,337	1,816.06	6,585	1,508.99	8,270	1,305.39	9,994
38,000	3,452.27	3,427	1,865.15	6,764	1,549.78	8,493	1,340.67	10,264
39,000	3,543.12	3,517	1,914.23	6,942	1,590.56	8,717	1,375.95	10,534
40,000	3,633.97	3,608	1,963.31	7,119	1,631.34	8,940	1,411.23	10,804
42,000	3,815.67	3,788	2,061.48	7,476	1,712.91	9,387	1,481.79	11,344
44,000	3,997.37	3,968	2,159.64	7,831	1,794.48	9,834	1,552.35	11,885
46,000	4,179.07	4,149	2,257.81	8,187	1,876.05	10,282	1,622.91	12,425
48,000	4,360.77	4,329	2,355.97	8,543	1,957.61	10,728	1,693.47	12,965
50,000	4,542.47	4,510	2,454.14	8,899	2,039.18	11,175	1,764.03	13,505

AMOUNT OF LOAN	42 MOS		48 MOS		60 MOS		72 MOS	
	MONTHLY PAYMENT	TOTAL INTRST	MONTHLY PAYMENT	TOTAL INTRST	MONTHLY PAYMENT	TOTAL INTRST	MONTHLY PAYMENT	TOTAL INTRST
$ 1	0.04	1	0.03	0	0.03	1	0.03	1
2	0.07	1	0.06	1	0.05	1	0.05	2
3	0.10	1	0.09	1	0.08	2	0.07	2
4	0.13	1	0.12	2	0.10	2	0.09	3
5	0.16	2	0.15	2	0.13	3	0.11	4
6	0.19	2	0.18	3	0.15	3	0.14	4
7	0.22	2	0.20	3	0.18	4	0.16	5
8	0.26	3	0.23	3	0.20	4	0.18	5
9	0.29	3	0.26	3	0.23	5	0.20	5
10	0.32	3	0.29	4	0.25	5	0.22	6
20	0.63	6	0.57	7	0.49	9	0.44	12
30	0.95	10	0.86	11	0.74	14	0.66	18
40	1.26	13	1.14	15	0.98	19	0.88	23
50	1.57	16	1.43	19	1.23	24	1.10	29
60	1.89	19	1.71	22	1.47	28	1.31	34
70	2.20	22	2.00	26	1.72	33	1.53	40
80	2.52	26	2.28	29	1.96	38	1.75	46
90	2.83	29	2.57	33	2.21	43	1.97	52
100	3.14	32	2.85	37	2.45	47	2.19	58
200	6.28	64	5.70	74	4.90	94	4.37	115
300	9.42	96	8.55	110	7.34	140	6.55	172
400	12.56	128	11.39	147	9.79	187	8.74	229
500	15.69	159	14.24	184	12.23	234	10.92	286
600	18.83	191	17.09	220	14.68	281	13.10	343
700	21.97	223	19.93	257	17.12	327	15.29	401
800	25.11	255	22.78	293	19.57	374	17.47	458
900	28.24	286	25.63	330	22.01	421	19.65	515
1,000	31.38	318	28.47	367	24.46	468	21.83	572
2,000	62.76	636	56.94	733	48.91	935	43.66	1,144
3,000	94.13	953	85.41	1,100	73.36	1,402	65.49	1,715
4,000	125.51	1,271	113.88	1,466	97.81	1,869	87.32	2,287
5,000	156.88	1,589	142.35	1,833	122.26	2,336	109.15	2,859
6,000	188.26	1,907	170.82	2,199	146.71	2,803	130.98	3,431
7,000	219.63	2,224	199.28	2,565	171.16	3,270	152.81	4,002
8,000	251.01	2,542	227.75	2,932	195.61	3,737	174.64	4,574
9,000	282.38	2,860	256.22	3,299	220.06	4,204	196.47	5,146
10,000	313.76	3,178	284.69	3,665	244.52	4,671	218.30	5,718
11,000	345.13	3,495	313.16	4,032	268.97	5,138	240.13	6,289
12,000	376.51	3,813	341.63	4,398	293.42	5,605	261.96	6,861
13,000	407.88	4,131	370.10	4,765	317.87	6,072	283.79	7,433
14,000	439.26	4,449	398.56	5,131	342.32	6,539	305.62	8,005
15,000	470.64	4,767	427.03	5,497	366.77	7,006	327.45	8,576
16,000	502.01	5,084	455.50	5,864	391.22	7,473	349.28	9,148
17,000	533.39	5,402	483.97	6,231	415.67	7,940	371.11	9,720
18,000	564.76	5,720	512.44	6,597	440.12	8,407	392.94	10,292
19,000	596.14	6,038	540.91	6,964	464.58	8,875	414.77	10,863
20,000	627.51	6,355	569.37	7,330	489.03	9,342	436.60	11,435
21,000	658.89	6,673	597.84	7,696	513.48	9,809	458.43	12,007
22,000	690.26	6,991	626.31	8,063	537.93	10,276	480.26	12,579
23,000	721.64	7,309	654.78	8,429	562.38	10,743	502.09	13,150
24,000	753.01	7,626	683.25	8,796	586.83	11,210	523.92	13,722
25,000	784.39	7,944	711.72	9,163	611.28	11,677	545.75	14,294
26,000	815.76	8,262	740.19	9,529	635.73	12,144	567.58	14,866
27,000	847.14	8,580	768.65	9,895	660.18	12,611	589.41	15,438
28,000	878.51	8,897	797.12	10,262	684.64	13,078	611.24	16,009
29,000	909.89	9,215	825.59	10,628	709.09	13,545	633.07	16,581
30,000	941.27	9,533	854.06	10,995	733.54	14,012	654.90	17,153
31,000	972.64	9,851	882.53	11,361	757.99	14,479	676.73	17,725
32,000	1,004.02	10,169	911.00	11,728	782.44	14,946	698.56	18,296
33,000	1,035.39	10,486	939.46	12,094	806.89	15,413	720.39	18,868
34,000	1,066.77	10,804	967.93	12,461	831.34	15,880	742.22	19,440
35,000	1,098.14	11,122	996.40	12,827	855.79	16,347	764.05	20,012
36,000	1,129.52	11,440	1,024.87	13,194	880.24	16,814	785.87	20,583
37,000	1,160.89	11,757	1,053.34	13,560	904.70	17,282	807.70	21,154
38,000	1,192.27	12,075	1,081.81	13,927	929.15	17,749	829.53	21,726
39,000	1,223.64	12,393	1,110.28	14,293	953.60	18,216	851.36	22,298
40,000	1,255.02	12,711	1,138.74	14,660	978.05	18,683	873.19	22,870
42,000	1,317.77	13,346	1,195.68	15,393	1,026.95	19,617	916.85	24,013
44,000	1,380.52	13,982	1,252.62	16,126	1,075.85	20,551	960.51	25,157
46,000	1,443.27	14,617	1,309.56	16,859	1,124.76	21,486	1,004.17	26,300
48,000	1,506.02	15,253	1,366.49	17,592	1,173.66	22,420	1,047.83	27,444
50,000	1,568.77	15,888	1,423.43	18,325	1,222.56	23,354	1,091.49	28,587

AUTO LOAN PAYMENTS

AMOUNT OF LOAN	12 MOS		24 MOS		30 MOS		36 MOS	
	MONTHLY PAYMENT	TOTAL INTRST	MONTHLY PAYMENT	TOTAL INTRST	MONTHLY PAYMENT	TOTAL INTRST	MONTHLY PAYMENT	TOTAL INTRST
$ 1	0.10	0	0.05	0	0.05	1	0.04	0
2	0.19	0	0.10	0	0.09	1	0.08	1
3	0.28	0	0.15	0	0.13	1	0.11	1
4	0.37	0	0.20	1	0.17	1	0.15	1
5	0.46	1	0.25	1	0.21	1	0.18	1
6	0.55	1	0.30	1	0.25	2	0.22	2
7	0.64	1	0.35	1	0.29	2	0.25	2
8	0.73	1	0.40	2	0.33	2	0.29	2
9	0.82	1	0.45	2	0.37	2	0.32	3
10	0.91	1	0.50	2	0.41	2	0.36	3
20	1.82	2	0.99	4	0.82	5	0.71	6
30	2.73	3	1.48	6	1.23	7	1.07	9
40	3.64	4	1.97	7	1.64	9	1.42	11
50	4.55	5	2.47	9	2.05	12	1.78	14
60	5.46	6	2.96	11	2.46	14	2.13	17
70	6.37	6	3.45	13	2.87	16	2.48	19
80	7.28	7	3.94	15	3.28	18	2.84	22
90	8.19	8	4.43	16	3.69	21	3.19	25
100	9.10	9	4.93	18	4.10	23	3.55	28
200	18.20	18	9.85	36	8.19	46	7.09	55
300	27.30	28	14.77	54	12.28	68	10.63	83
400	36.39	37	19.69	73	16.37	91	14.17	110
500	45.49	46	24.61	91	20.46	114	17.71	138
600	54.59	55	29.53	109	24.55	137	21.25	165
700	63.68	64	34.45	127	28.64	159	24.79	192
800	72.78	73	39.37	145	32.73	182	28.33	220
900	81.88	83	44.29	163	36.82	205	31.87	247
1,000	90.97	92	49.21	181	40.91	227	35.41	275
2,000	181.94	183	98.41	362	81.82	455	70.81	549
3,000	272.91	275	147.61	543	122.72	682	106.22	824
4,000	363.88	367	196.81	723	163.63	909	141.62	1,098
5,000	454.84	458	246.02	904	204.53	1,136	177.03	1,373
6,000	545.81	550	295.22	1,085	245.44	1,363	212.43	1,647
7,000	636.78	641	344.42	1,266	286.34	1,590	247.84	1,922
8,000	727.75	733	393.62	1,447	327.25	1,818	283.24	2,197
9,000	818.71	825	442.83	1,628	368.15	2,045	318.64	2,471
10,000	909.68	916	492.03	1,809	409.06	2,272	354.05	2,746
11,000	1,000.65	1,008	541.23	1,990	449.96	2,499	389.45	3,020
12,000	1,091.62	1,099	590.43	2,170	490.87	2,726	424.86	3,295
13,000	1,182.58	1,191	639.64	2,351	531.77	2,953	460.26	3,569
14,000	1,273.55	1,283	688.84	2,532	572.68	3,180	495.67	3,844
15,000	1,364.52	1,374	738.04	2,713	613.58	3,407	531.07	4,119
16,000	1,455.49	1,466	787.24	2,894	654.49	3,635	566.48	4,393
17,000	1,546.45	1,557	836.44	3,075	695.39	3,862	601.88	4,668
18,000	1,637.42	1,649	885.65	3,256	736.30	4,089	637.28	4,942
19,000	1,728.39	1,741	934.85	3,436	777.20	4,316	672.69	5,217
20,000	1,819.36	1,832	984.05	3,617	818.11	4,543	708.09	5,491
21,000	1,910.33	1,924	1,033.25	3,798	859.01	4,770	743.50	5,766
22,000	2,001.29	2,015	1,082.46	3,979	899.92	4,998	778.90	6,040
23,000	2,092.26	2,107	1,131.66	4,160	940.82	5,225	814.31	6,315
24,000	2,183.23	2,199	1,180.86	4,341	981.73	5,452	849.71	6,590
25,000	2,274.20	2,290	1,230.06	4,521	1,022.63	5,679	885.11	6,864
26,000	2,365.16	2,382	1,279.27	4,702	1,063.54	5,906	920.52	7,139
27,000	2,456.13	2,474	1,328.47	4,883	1,104.44	6,133	955.92	7,413
28,000	2,547.10	2,565	1,377.67	5,064	1,145.35	6,361	991.33	7,688
29,000	2,638.07	2,657	1,426.87	5,245	1,186.25	6,588	1,026.73	7,962
30,000	2,729.03	2,748	1,476.08	5,426	1,227.16	6,815	1,062.14	8,237
31,000	2,820.00	2,840	1,525.28	5,607	1,268.06	7,042	1,097.54	8,511
32,000	2,910.97	2,932	1,574.48	5,788	1,308.97	7,269	1,132.95	8,786
33,000	3,001.94	3,023	1,623.68	5,968	1,349.87	7,496	1,168.35	9,061
34,000	3,092.90	3,115	1,672.88	6,149	1,390.78	7,723	1,203.75	9,335
35,000	3,183.87	3,206	1,722.09	6,330	1,431.68	7,950	1,239.16	9,610
36,000	3,274.84	3,298	1,771.29	6,511	1,472.59	8,178	1,274.56	9,884
37,000	3,365.81	3,390	1,820.49	6,692	1,513.49	8,405	1,309.97	10,159
38,000	3,456.78	3,481	1,869.69	6,873	1,554.40	8,632	1,345.37	10,433
39,000	3,547.74	3,573	1,918.90	7,054	1,595.30	8,859	1,380.78	10,708
40,000	3,638.71	3,665	1,968.10	7,234	1,636.21	9,086	1,416.18	10,982
42,000	3,820.65	3,848	2,066.50	7,596	1,718.02	9,541	1,486.99	11,532
44,000	4,002.58	4,031	2,164.91	7,958	1,799.83	9,995	1,557.80	12,081
46,000	4,184.52	4,214	2,263.31	8,319	1,881.64	10,449	1,628.61	12,630
48,000	4,366.45	4,397	2,361.72	8,681	1,963.45	10,904	1,699.42	13,179
50,000	4,548.39	4,581	2,460.12	9,043	2,045.26	11,358	1,770.22	13,728

AMOUNT OF LOAN	42 MOS		48 MOS		60 MOS		72 MOS	
	MONTHLY PAYMENT	TOTAL INTRST	MONTHLY PAYMENT	TOTAL INTRST	MONTHLY PAYMENT	TOTAL INTRST	MONTHLY PAYMENT	TOTAL INTRST
$ 1	0.04	1	0.03	0	0.03	1	0.03	1
2	0.07	1	0.06	1	0.05	1	0.05	2
3	0.10	1	0.09	1	0.08	2	0.07	2
4	0.13	1	0.12	2	0.10	2	0.09	2
5	0.16	2	0.15	2	0.13	3	0.11	3
6	0.19	2	0.18	3	0.15	3	0.14	4
7	0.23	3	0.21	3	0.18	4	0.16	5
8	0.26	3	0.23	3	0.20	4	0.18	5
9	0.29	3	0.26	3	0.23	5	0.20	5
10	0.32	3	0.29	4	0.25	5	0.22	6
20	0.64	7	0.58	8	0.50	10	0.44	12
30	0.95	10	0.86	11	0.74	14	0.66	18
40	1.27	13	1.15	15	0.99	19	0.88	23
50	1.58	16	1.43	19	1.23	24	1.10	29
60	1.90	20	1.72	23	1.48	29	1.32	35
70	2.21	23	2.01	26	1.73	34	1.54	41
80	2.53	26	2.29	30	1.97	38	1.76	47
90	2.84	29	2.58	34	2.22	43	1.98	53
100	3.16	33	2.86	37	2.46	48	2.20	58
200	6.31	65	5.72	75	4.92	95	4.40	117
300	9.46	97	8.58	112	7.38	143	6.60	175
400	12.61	130	11.44	149	9.84	190	8.79	233
500	15.76	162	14.30	186	12.30	238	10.99	291
600	18.91	194	17.16	224	14.76	286	13.19	350
700	22.06	227	20.02	261	17.21	333	15.38	407
800	25.21	259	22.88	298	19.67	380	17.58	466
900	28.36	291	25.74	336	22.13	428	19.78	524
1,000	31.51	323	28.60	373	24.59	475	21.97	582
2,000	63.01	646	57.20	746	49.17	950	43.94	1,164
3,000	94.51	969	85.80	1,118	73.76	1,426	65.91	1,746
4,000	126.01	1,292	114.39	1,491	98.34	1,900	87.88	2,327
5,000	157.51	1,615	142.99	1,864	122.93	2,376	109.85	2,909
6,000	189.01	1,938	171.59	2,236	147.51	2,851	131.81	3,490
7,000	220.52	2,262	200.18	2,609	172.10	3,326	153.78	4,072
8,000	252.02	2,585	228.78	2,981	196.68	3,801	175.75	4,654
9,000	283.52	2,908	257.38	3,354	221.27	4,276	197.72	5,236
10,000	315.02	3,231	285.98	3,727	245.85	4,751	219.69	5,818
11,000	346.52	3,554	314.57	4,099	270.43	5,226	241.65	6,399
12,000	378.02	3,877	343.17	4,472	295.02	5,701	263.62	6,981
13,000	409.52	4,200	371.77	4,845	319.60	6,176	285.59	7,562
14,000	441.03	4,523	400.36	5,217	344.19	6,651	307.56	8,144
15,000	472.53	4,846	428.96	5,590	368.77	7,126	329.53	8,726
16,000	504.03	5,169	457.56	5,963	393.36	7,602	351.49	9,307
17,000	535.53	5,492	486.15	6,335	417.94	8,076	373.46	9,889
18,000	567.03	5,815	514.75	6,708	442.53	8,552	395.43	10,471
19,000	598.53	6,138	543.35	7,081	467.11	9,027	417.40	11,053
20,000	630.03	6,461	571.95	7,444	491.70	9,502	439.37	11,635
21,000	661.54	6,785	600.54	7,826	516.28	9,977	461.33	12,216
22,000	693.04	7,108	629.14	8,199	540.86	10,452	483.30	12,798
23,000	724.54	7,431	657.74	8,572	565.45	10,927	505.27	13,379
24,000	756.04	7,754	686.33	8,944	590.03	11,402	527.24	13,961
25,000	787.54	8,077	714.93	9,317	614.62	11,877	549.21	14,543
26,000	819.04	8,400	743.53	9,689	639.20	12,352	571.17	15,124
27,000	850.54	8,723	772.12	10,062	663.79	12,827	593.14	15,706
28,000	882.05	9,046	800.72	10,435	688.37	13,302	615.11	16,288
29,000	913.55	9,369	829.32	10,807	712.96	13,778	637.08	16,870
30,000	945.05	9,692	857.92	11,180	737.54	14,252	659.05	17,452
31,000	976.55	10,015	886.51	11,552	762.13	14,728	681.01	18,033
32,000	1,008.05	10,338	915.11	11,925	786.71	15,203	702.98	18,615
33,000	1,039.55	10,661	943.71	12,298	811.29	15,677	724.95	19,196
34,000	1,071.06	10,985	972.30	12,670	835.88	16,153	746.92	19,778
35,000	1,102.56	11,308	1,000.90	13,043	860.46	16,628	768.89	20,360
36,000	1,134.06	11,631	1,029.50	13,416	885.05	17,103	790.86	20,942
37,000	1,165.56	11,954	1,058.09	13,788	909.63	17,578	812.82	21,523
38,000	1,197.06	12,277	1,086.69	14,161	934.22	18,053	834.79	22,105
39,000	1,228.56	12,600	1,115.29	14,534	958.80	18,528	856.76	22,687
40,000	1,260.06	12,923	1,143.89	14,907	983.39	19,003	878.73	23,269
42,000	1,323.07	13,569	1,201.08	15,652	1,032.55	19,953	922.66	24,432
44,000	1,386.07	14,215	1,258.27	16,397	1,081.72	20,903	966.60	25,595
46,000	1,449.07	14,861	1,315.47	17,143	1,130.89	21,853	1,010.54	26,759
48,000	1,512.08	15,507	1,372.66	17,888	1,180.06	22,804	1,054.47	27,922
50,000	1,575.08	16,153	1,429.86	18,633	1,229.23	23,754	1,098.41	29,086

AUTO LOAN PAYMENTS

AMOUNT OF LOAN	12 MOS		24 MOS		30 MOS		36 MOS	
	MONTHLY PAYMENT	TOTAL INTRST	MONTHLY PAYMENT	TOTAL INTRST	MONTHLY PAYMENT	TOTAL INTRST	MONTHLY PAYMENT	TOTAL INTRST
$ 1	0.10	0	0.05	0	0.05	1	0.04	0
2	0.19	0	0.10	0	0.09	1	0.08	1
3	0.28	0	0.15	1	0.13	1	0.11	1
4	0.37	0	0.20	1	0.17	1	0.15	1
5	0.46	1	0.25	1	0.21	1	0.18	1
6	0.55	1	0.30	1	0.25	2	0.22	2
7	0.64	1	0.35	1	0.29	2	0.25	2
8	0.73	1	0.40	2	0.33	2	0.29	2
9	0.82	1	0.45	2	0.37	2	0.32	3
10	0.92	1	0.50	2	0.42	3	0.36	3
20	1.83	2	0.99	4	0.83	5	0.72	6
30	2.74	3	1.48	6	1.24	7	1.07	9
40	3.65	4	1.98	8	1.65	10	1.43	11
50	4.56	5	2.47	9	2.06	12	1.78	14
60	5.47	6	2.96	11	2.47	14	2.14	17
70	6.38	7	3.46	13	2.88	16	2.49	20
80	7.29	7	3.95	15	3.29	19	2.85	23
90	8.20	8	4.44	17	3.70	21	3.20	25
100	9.11	9	4.94	19	4.11	23	3.56	28
200	18.22	19	9.87	37	8.21	46	7.11	56
300	27.33	28	14.80	55	12.31	69	10.66	84
400	36.44	37	19.73	74	16.42	93	14.22	112
500	45.55	47	24.67	92	20.52	116	17.77	140
600	54.66	56	29.60	110	24.62	139	21.32	168
700	63.77	65	34.53	129	28.72	162	24.87	195
800	72.87	74	39.46	147	32.83	185	28.43	223
900	81.98	84	44.40	166	36.93	208	31.98	251
1,000	91.09	93	49.33	184	41.03	231	35.53	279
2,000	182.18	186	98.65	368	82.06	462	71.06	558
3,000	273.26	279	147.97	551	123.09	693	106.59	837
4,000	364.35	372	197.29	735	164.11	923	142.12	1,116
5,000	455.44	465	246.62	919	205.14	1,154	177.65	1,395
6,000	546.52	558	295.94	1,103	246.17	1,385	213.18	1,674
7,000	637.61	651	345.26	1,286	287.19	1,616	248.70	1,953
8,000	728.69	744	394.58	1,470	328.22	1,847	284.23	2,232
9,000	819.78	837	443.91	1,654	369.25	2,078	319.76	2,511
10,000	910.87	930	493.23	1,838	410.27	2,308	355.29	2,790
11,000	1,001.95	1,023	542.55	2,021	451.30	2,539	390.82	3,070
12,000	1,093.04	1,116	591.87	2,205	492.33	2,770	426.35	3,349
13,000	1,184.12	1,209	641.19	2,389	533.36	3,001	461.87	3,627
14,000	1,275.21	1,303	690.52	2,572	574.38	3,231	497.40	3,906
15,000	1,366.30	1,396	739.84	2,756	615.41	3,462	532.93	4,185
16,000	1,457.38	1,489	789.16	2,940	656.44	3,693	568.46	4,465
17,000	1,548.47	1,582	838.48	3,124	697.46	3,924	603.99	4,744
18,000	1,639.56	1,675	887.81	3,307	738.49	4,155	639.52	5,023
19,000	1,730.64	1,768	937.13	3,491	779.52	4,386	675.05	5,302
20,000	1,821.73	1,861	986.45	3,675	820.54	4,616	710.57	5,581
21,000	1,912.81	1,954	1,035.77	3,858	861.57	4,847	746.10	5,860
22,000	2,003.90	2,047	1,085.09	4,042	902.60	5,078	781.63	6,139
23,000	2,094.99	2,140	1,134.42	4,226	943.62	5,309	817.16	6,418
24,000	2,186.07	2,233	1,183.74	4,410	984.65	5,540	852.69	6,697
25,000	2,277.16	2,326	1,233.06	4,593	1,025.68	5,770	888.22	6,976
26,000	2,368.24	2,419	1,282.38	4,777	1,066.71	6,001	923.74	7,255
27,000	2,459.33	2,512	1,331.71	4,961	1,107.73	6,232	959.27	7,534
28,000	2,550.42	2,605	1,381.03	5,145	1,148.76	6,463	994.80	7,813
29,000	2,641.50	2,698	1,430.35	5,328	1,189.79	6,694	1,030.33	8,092
30,000	2,732.59	2,791	1,479.67	5,512	1,230.81	6,924	1,065.86	8,371
31,000	2,823.68	2,884	1,528.99	5,696	1,271.84	7,155	1,101.39	8,650
32,000	2,914.76	2,977	1,578.32	5,880	1,312.87	7,386	1,136.91	8,929
33,000	3,005.85	3,070	1,627.64	6,063	1,353.89	7,617	1,172.44	9,208
34,000	3,096.93	3,163	1,676.96	6,247	1,394.92	7,848	1,207.97	9,487
35,000	3,188.02	3,256	1,726.28	6,431	1,435.95	8,079	1,243.50	9,766
36,000	3,279.11	3,349	1,775.61	6,615	1,476.97	8,309	1,279.03	10,045
37,000	3,370.19	3,442	1,824.93	6,798	1,518.00	8,540	1,314.56	10,324
38,000	3,461.28	3,535	1,874.25	6,982	1,559.03	8,771	1,350.09	10,603
39,000	3,552.36	3,628	1,923.57	7,166	1,600.06	9,002	1,385.61	10,882
40,000	3,643.45	3,721	1,972.89	7,349	1,641.08	9,232	1,421.14	11,161
42,000	3,825.62	3,907	2,071.54	7,717	1,723.14	9,694	1,492.20	11,719
44,000	4,007.80	4,094	2,170.18	8,084	1,805.19	10,156	1,563.26	12,277
46,000	4,189.97	4,280	2,268.83	8,452	1,887.24	10,617	1,634.31	12,835
48,000	4,372.14	4,466	2,367.47	8,819	1,969.30	11,079	1,705.37	13,393
50,000	4,554.31	4,652	2,466.12	9,187	2,051.35	11,541	1,776.43	13,951

AMOUNT OF LOAN	42 MOS		48 MOS		60 MOS		72 MOS	
	MONTHLY PAYMENT	TOTAL INTRST	MONTHLY PAYMENT	TOTAL INTRST	MONTHLY PAYMENT	TOTAL INTRST	MONTHLY PAYMENT	TOTAL INTRST
1	0.04	1	0.03	0	0.03	1	0.03	1
2	0.07	1	0.06	1	0.05	1	0.05	2
3	0.10	1	0.09	1	0.08	2	0.07	2
4	0.13	1	0.12	2	0.10	2	0.09	4
5	0.16	2	0.15	2	0.13	3	0.12	4
6	0.19	2	0.18	3	0.15	3	0.14	4
7	0.23	3	0.21	3	0.18	4	0.16	5
8	0.26	3	0.23	3	0.20	4	0.18	5
9	0.29	3	0.26	3	0.23	5	0.20	5
10	0.32	3	0.29	4	0.25	5	0.23	7
20	0.64	7	0.58	8	0.50	10	0.45	12
30	0.95	10	0.87	12	0.75	15	0.67	18
40	1.27	13	1.15	15	0.99	19	0.89	24
50	1.59	17	1.44	19	1.24	24	1.11	30
60	1.90	20	1.73	23	1.49	29	1.33	36
70	2.22	23	2.02	27	1.74	34	1.55	42
80	2.54	27	2.30	30	1.98	39	1.77	47
90	2.85	30	2.59	34	2.23	44	1.99	53
100	3.17	33	2.88	38	2.48	49	2.22	60
200	6.33	66	5.75	76	4.95	97	4.43	119
300	9.49	99	8.62	114	7.42	145	6.64	178
400	12.66	132	11.50	152	9.89	193	8.85	237
500	15.82	164	14.37	190	12.36	242	11.06	296
600	18.98	197	17.24	228	14.84	290	13.27	355
700	22.14	230	20.11	265	17.31	339	15.48	415
800	25.31	263	22.99	304	19.78	387	17.69	474
900	28.47	296	25.86	341	22.25	435	19.90	533
1,000	31.63	328	28.73	379	24.72	483	22.11	592
2,000	63.26	657	57.46	758	49.44	966	44.22	1,184
3,000	94.89	985	86.18	1,137	74.16	1,450	66.33	1,776
4,000	126.52	1,314	114.91	1,516	98.88	1,933	88.43	2,367
5,000	158.14	1,642	143.63	1,894	123.60	2,416	110.54	2,959
6,000	189.77	1,970	172.36	2,273	148.32	2,899	132.65	3,551
7,000	221.40	2,299	201.09	2,652	173.03	3,382	154.75	4,142
8,000	253.03	2,627	229.81	3,031	197.75	3,865	176.86	4,734
9,000	284.66	2,956	258.54	3,410	222.47	4,348	198.97	5,326
10,000	316.28	3,284	287.26	3,788	247.19	4,831	221.07	5,917
11,000	347.91	3,612	315.99	4,168	271.91	5,315	243.18	6,509
12,000	379.54	3,941	344.72	4,547	296.63	5,798	265.29	7,101
13,000	411.17	4,269	373.44	4,925	321.34	6,280	287.39	7,692
14,000	442.80	4,598	402.17	5,304	346.06	6,764	309.50	8,284
15,000	474.42	4,926	430.89	5,683	370.78	7,247	331.61	8,876
16,000	506.05	5,254	459.62	6,062	395.50	7,730	353.71	9,467
17,000	537.68	5,583	488.34	6,440	420.22	8,213	375.82	10,059
18,000	569.31	5,911	517.07	6,819	444.94	8,696	397.93	10,651
19,000	600.93	6,239	545.80	7,198	469.65	9,179	420.04	11,243
20,000	632.56	6,568	574.52	7,577	494.37	9,662	442.14	11,834
21,000	664.19	6,896	603.25	7,956	519.09	10,145	464.25	12,426
22,000	695.82	7,224	631.97	8,335	543.81	10,629	486.36	13,018
23,000	727.45	7,553	660.70	8,714	568.53	11,112	508.46	13,609
24,000	759.07	7,881	689.43	9,093	593.25	11,595	530.57	14,201
25,000	790.70	8,209	718.15	9,471	617.96	12,078	552.68	14,793
26,000	822.33	8,538	746.88	9,850	642.68	12,561	574.78	15,384
27,000	853.96	8,866	775.60	10,229	667.40	13,044	596.89	15,976
28,000	885.59	9,195	804.33	10,608	692.12	13,527	619.00	16,568
29,000	917.21	9,523	833.06	10,987	716.84	14,010	641.10	17,159
30,000	948.84	9,851	861.78	11,365	741.56	14,494	663.21	17,751
31,000	980.47	10,180	890.51	11,744	766.27	14,976	685.32	18,343
32,000	1,012.10	10,508	919.23	12,123	790.99	15,459	707.42	18,934
33,000	1,043.73	10,837	947.96	12,502	815.71	15,943	729.53	19,526
34,000	1,075.35	11,165	976.68	12,881	840.43	16,426	751.64	20,118
35,000	1,106.98	11,493	1,005.41	13,260	865.15	16,909	773.75	20,710
36,000	1,138.61	11,822	1,034.14	13,639	889.87	17,392	795.85	21,301
37,000	1,170.24	12,150	1,062.86	14,017	914.58	17,875	817.96	21,893
38,000	1,201.86	12,478	1,091.59	14,396	939.30	18,358	840.07	22,485
39,000	1,233.49	12,807	1,120.31	14,775	964.02	18,841	862.17	23,076
40,000	1,265.12	13,135	1,149.04	15,154	988.74	19,324	884.28	23,668
42,000	1,328.38	13,792	1,206.49	15,912	1,038.18	20,291	928.49	24,851
44,000	1,391.63	14,448	1,263.94	16,669	1,087.61	21,257	972.71	26,035
46,000	1,454.89	15,105	1,321.39	17,427	1,137.05	22,223	1,016.92	27,218
48,000	1,518.14	15,762	1,378.85	18,185	1,186.49	23,189	1,061.13	28,401
50,000	1,581.40	16,419	1,436.30	18,942	1,235.92	24,155	1,105.35	29,585